MAITREYA'S MISSION

VOLUME TWO

BENJAMIN CREME

SHARE INTERNATIONAL FOUNDATION
Amsterdam, London, Los Angeles

D1157156

Published by Share International Foundation
All rights
ISBN-90-71484-11-4
Manufactured in the United States of America

First Edition, September 1993
Second Printing, December 1994
Third Printing, February 2004

*The painting reproduced on the cover, **Antahkarana** was painted by Benjamin Creme in 1968. The antahkarana represents the channel or bridge of light which is formed between the personality and the soul through meditation. By means of this bridge formed of three threads of energy, the soul gradually 'grips' and aligns its vehicle until at-one-ment between soul and personality is complete. The process is then repeated at a higher level between the soul and Spiritual Triad. In this way, at-one-ment between the Monad — the Spiritual Man or Divine Spark — and its reflection on the physical plane can take place.*

This book is dedicated,
with deep respect and gratitude,
to my Master.

CONTENTS

PART TWO
MAITREYA'S TEACHINGS AND FORECASTS

PART THREE
DISCIPLESHIP AND SERVICE

PREFACE

Since the publication of *Maitreya's Mission, Volume One*, in 1986, a vast amount of new information has been published in the magazine *Share International*. In particular, we have received, via one of Maitreya's close associates in the Asian community of London, a large body of teachings, and forecasts on world events, from Maitreya Himself. These appear in Part Two of this book and cover a wide range of subjects: economic and political change; the environment; the coming Technology of Light; life in the New Age; and the essence of Maitreya's teachings, the Art of Self-realization.

Part One is devoted to the process of Maitreya's emergence, the role of the media, and the growing evidence of Maitreya's presence, through both personal appearances and related phenomena and signs.

Part Three contains articles on philosophical subjects transcribed from lectures (with accompanying questions and answers) that I have given to groups in different countries. There are further chapters on healing and disease, the Seven Rays, and Transmission Meditation.

I am privileged also to be the recipient of much illuminating insight given by my personal Master through interviews with journalist Patricia Pitchon, where He addresses the problems of market economics; the 'peace dividend'; the appalling problem of drugs; education in the future; the role of the United Nations; Latin America and the developing world.

The list of initiates' ray structures and degrees of initiation published in this volume supplements the list which appeared in the first edition of *Maitreya's Mission, Volume One*.

I should like to express my gratitude to the many people in different countries whose devoted time and efforts have contributed to the publication of this book. The tedious tasks of transcribing, inputting and proof-reading have been cheerfully undertaken by groups in San Francisco and London. In particular I am indebted to Michiko Ishikawa for her tireless work in organizing the material into readable form.

Benjamin Creme
London 1993

Note to Reader: The articles, interviews and questions and answers were published in the monthly magazine *Share International* over the period from October 1986 to December 1992. In the present work, for ease of reading, they have been arranged according to subject with the result that they do not appear in the original order. The original date of publication is given at the end of each question. "The List of Initiates — Part II" includes all the initiates whose ray structures were published in *Share International* from the publication of the first edition of *Maitreya's Mission, Volume One* in 1986, to 1993.

PART ONE

MAITREYA

AND THE EMERGENCE

INTRODUCTION

The Emergence of Maitreya and the Masters of Wisdom

A new age is dawning

We are standing at the beginning of an extraordinary period in the history of the world — a crossroads at which humanity is undergoing a great shift in consciousness. This reflects itself in new relationships — political, economic, religious, social, scientific and cultural — which in their manifestation will create a completely different type of civilization, one in which the true, spiritual nature of humanity, consciously recognized and demonstrated, will become manifest for the first time.

These changes are the result of new energies and forces entering our world. A new age is dawning. This is not a concept created by 'New Age' groups, nor is it simply an astrological prognostication, but a scientific fact which can be verified at any astronomical observatory. It is the result of the precession of the equinoxes or, in layman's terms, of the movement of our solar system around the heavens in relation to the 12 constellations of our zodiac. Our sun makes a journey in relation to these constellations which takes almost 26,000 years to complete. Approximately every 2,150 years, our sun comes into an alignment, a particular energetic relationship, with each of the constellations in turn. When we are in that alignment, we say we are in the age of that particular constellation, and are the recipient of powerful cosmic energies streaming from it. For approximately 2,000 years, our sun has stood in that relationship to the constellation Pisces. We have been in the Age of Pisces.

Our present civilization — now coming to an end — has been created by our response to the energies of Pisces. These energies have given us certain great qualities — above all, that of individuality. Humanity has emerged from the herd over the last 2,000 years and increasingly become individual. Each of us is more able to demonstrate our individuality as unique, conscious souls in incarnation. This is a great step forward in the evolution of the race.

The energy of Pisces has also given us the quality of idealism, devotion to an ideal. Unfortunately, it has been an abstract type of idealism, and we have but rarely sought to implement these ideals. We have also clung firmly, through our devotion, to our own ideals at the expense of all others. Whatever we idealize and believe in, whatever is our own individual, communal or national ideology, we tend to think is the sum total of all truth — whether Democracy, Communism, Fascism, Christianity, Buddhism, Hinduism, or other approaches.

This exclusive devotion to one's own ideal has dangerously divided the world. The civilization of the last 2,000 years has been characterized by great political, economic and religious divisions. This is representative of how we have handled and expressed the energies of Pisces.

Our sun has now moved away from the sphere of influence of the energies of Pisces, and is coming into that same alignment with the constellation Aquarius; we are entering the Age of Aquarius. The new, incoming energies of Aquarius have the quality of synthesis. As they increase in potency over the next 2,150 years, they will create a fusing and blending of humanity in ways which would be unthinkable today. We are now starting out on that journey of synthesis.

We do not make the journey alone. Throughout the history of humanity (which according to the esoteric teachings is eighteen-and-a-half million years), we have never been alone. We have been led and guided, taught, stimulated and protected — sometimes openly, but often from behind the scenes — by a group of, from our point of view, perfected men. They have gone ahead of us in evolution, and finished the evolutionary journey on which we are still engaged. Having done so, by the same steps which we today take to evolve, They have perfected Themselves, and need no further incarnational experience on this planet. For Them it remains simply a field of service, a means by which They take upon Themselves the responsibility of overseeing our evolution. This group of perfected men is known by many names: the Masters of Wisdom and the Lords of Compassion, the Great White Brotherhood, the Society of Illumined Minds, the Spiritual or Esoteric Hierarchy, the Guides and Elder Brothers of Humanity.

These Masters have lived, for the most part, in the remote mountain and desert areas of the world: the Himalaya, the Andes, the Rocky Mountains, the Cascades, the Carpathians, the Atlas, the Urals, the Gobi and other deserts. From these mountain and desert retreats, They have beneficently overseen the evolution of humanity for countless millennia. Much of the work of the Masters is carried out by Their disciples, men and women in the world — people such as da Vinci, Mozart, Lincoln, Einstein and Madame Curie. By a gradual stimulus of our conscious awareness, the Masters have brought humanity forward to the point where we now find ourselves today. Under such stimulus and guidance, our civilizations have risen, flowered, crystallized, died and been renewed again age after age.

At the beginning or end of each age, the Hierarchy of Masters send one of Their Great Ones into the world to act as a teacher for the coming time. We know some of these great teachers historically as Hercules, Hermes, Rama, Mithra, Confucius, Zoroaster, Vyasa, Krishna, Buddha, the Christ and Mohammed. They are all members of the same group, the Spiritual Hierarchy of our planet.

All religions await the coming of a teacher: Christians, the return of the Christ; Hindus, the return of Krishna; Jews, the Messiah; Muslims, the Imam Mahdi or Messiah; and Buddhists, Maitreya Buddha. These are different names for one and the same individual, the head and leader of the Spiritual Hierarchy, the Master of all the Masters, the World Teacher, the one Saint Paul and the Buddha called, "the teacher alike of angels and of men" — the Lord Maitreya, the Embodiment of the Christ Consciousness.

5

Two thousand six hundred years ago, Gautama Buddha made a prediction that at this time would come another great teacher Who would inspire humanity to create a new and brilliant golden civilization based on righteousness and truth. His name would be Maitreya, a Buddha like Himself.

Two thousand years ago in Palestine, the Lord Maitreya's consciousness entered into that of His disciple Jesus, at the Baptism. For three years, Jesus demonstrated the consciousness of the Christ — the Lord Maitreya — and became Jesus, the Christ, or Messiah. Five hundred years earlier, the Buddha worked through His disciple the Prince Gautama, and Gautama became Gautama Buddha. This is the age-old way for the manifestation of the Teacher.

For over 500 years the Masters have known that sooner or later They would be required to return to the everyday world. The only question was when humanity would be ready for this extraordinary event. The signal for this return was given in June 1945 at the end of the war. The Lord Maitreya announced His intention to return once again — not taking over the vehicle of one of His disciples, but to come Himself in His own full physical presence, bringing a large group of His disciples, the Masters of Wisdom, with Him.

Maitreya said He would come, at the earliest possible moment, when a measure of peace had been restored to the world; when the principle of sharing was beginning to govern economic affairs; and when the energy which we call goodwill, the lowest aspect of love, was manifesting and leading to the establishment of correct human relationships. He promised that when these conditions were beginning to take place, when our minds were at least moving in these directions, He would, without fail, return.

Maitreya hoped to come around 1950. It was hoped that the pain and suffering of humanity in the war would have chastened us and led to a change of direction. But not all the nations had suffered, and the powers quickly returned to the greedy, selfish, nationalistic, self-serving and competitive ways of the past. Because of the lack of change by humanity, the coming of Maitreya was delayed. But in July 1977, Maitreya announced He would wait no longer.

On 8 July 1977 Maitreya descended from His retreat in the Himalaya, and entered Pakistan, where He stayed some days to acclimatize Himself. On 19 July He entered London, England, where He has been ever since as a member of the Asian community. There He works, surrounded by a group of holy men, swamis from India, whom He trains and teaches, and a much larger group of ordinary people, not only of that community, but English people, Americans, Dutch, Japanese and others, who have found their way to Him. He awaits an invitation from humanity, through its representatives, the world's media networks, to come forward and begin His mission openly as the World Teacher.

Political, economic and social change

Meanwhile, from behind the scenes, He has been transforming the world, dispensing potent cosmic energies in such a way as to create the momentous changes of recent years. Through His inspiration of Mikhail Gorbachev, the Cold War has ended. The Berlin Wall has come down and Germany has become unified 30 or 40 years before anyone thought it possible. Likewise, the demand for justice, freedom and participation occurring throughout the world has taken place under His stimulus.

The political totalitarianism of the Soviet Union, China and the Eastern Bloc is breaking up. Eventually totalitarianism in political terms will become a thing of the past. Economic totalitarianism is also about to collapse. Maitreya has said in one of His messages given through me that humanity must see itself as one: brothers and sisters of one humanity, under the one God. Following from that, we must see that the food, raw materials, energy, scientific know-how and educational facilities of the world belong to everyone. They are given by divine providence for everyone, and must no longer be usurped and wasted by the developed third of the world, as pertains today.

We in the developed world use and waste three-quarters of the world's food and not less than 83 per cent of all other resources. In the developing world, the Third World, with two-thirds of the world's population, millions are starving. They have to make do with one-quarter of the world's food and 17 per cent of other resources. As a result, 1.2 billion people live in absolute poverty. That means they have an income of less than $100 per year. Half of them, more than 500 million people, have nothing. They live out miserable, stunted lives, dying of malnutrition and the diseases which result. Thirty-eight million people are literally starving to death. Every 2.4 seconds a child in the Third World dies of starvation, while at the same time there is a 10 per cent per capita surplus of food rotting away in the storehouses of the developed world. This situation threatens the well-being of the world.

Maitreya has said: "How can I stand aside and watch this slaughter, watch my little ones die? No, my friends. This cannot be. Therefore, I am come quickly among you once more, to show you the way, to point the path." He has come to teach humanity the need for sharing. "Sharing," He says, "is divine. When you share you recognize God in your brother."

If we accept the principle of sharing, accept that we are one, redistribute the world's resources and so create justice in the world, we will have peace. It is the only way in which we will have secure and lasting peace. If we do not, and continue in our greedy, selfish, and competitive ways, we will find that the tensions inherent in the divisions between the living standards of the developed and developing worlds are so great that they will erupt in a third world war which will destroy all life. That is the choice before humanity today. Maitreya says: "My heart tells me your answer, your choice, and is glad."

Maitreya has foretold an economic crash which He said will begin in Japan. We think of Japan as the richest and most financially successful nation in the world, but its stock market is about to collapse. Maitreya says: "This bubble must burst." It is a sore which must erupt and let out all the inequality and degradation which comes, He says, from commercialization — the expression of market forces. Maitreya calls market forces

8

the forces of evil because they have divisions and separations in-built in them.

Market forces as a theory rests on the idea that we all start at the same point. But there is no country in the developed or developing world where that situation exists. Every nation has rich and poor. Market forces are based on human greed. Their expression is commercialization, which He says is an evil gripping the whole of humanity. Maitreya says any government that blindly follows market forces is leading its nation to destruction. This is occurring in almost every country today and will bring this civilization to the verge of destruction.

When the stock exchanges, beginning in Japan, collapse, as they are now beginning to do, the priorities of all governments will change. The number one priority will be the provision of adequate food for all the people; secondly, the provision of adequate housing for all the people; thirdly, the provision of adequate healthcare and education for all the people. These are the basic human rights needed everywhere by all people, yet there is no country in the world in which all of these pertain as a universal right. When the economic collapse occurs, humanity will begin to recognize its oneness, and the need to co-operate and share the world's resources.

In addition to political and economic totalitarianism, there is a third, religious totalitarianism, which is now reaching an acme of its power. It is present in the West in the so-called fundamentalist Christian groups and in the power of the Vatican, and in the Middle East and elsewhere in the fundamentalist Islamic groupings. It is even beginning in those once-tolerant religions, Hinduism and Buddhism. Fundamentalism is the result of the dogmatic assertion of one's own ideals at the expense of every other ideal. It is a response to the energy of Pisces, which is of the past.

The time is fast approaching when political, economic and religious totalitarianism — denying human freedom, well-being, liberty and the human right to believe what one desires — will be over. A new freedom is awaiting humanity just around the corner. But that new freedom has, above all, the necessity of responsibility. We have to take upon ourselves the responsibility for each other. Maitreya puts it very simply: "Take your brother's need as the measure for your actions and solve the problems of the world. There is no other course."

Maitreya has said: "I have not come to found a new religion." Those who await Him as a religious teacher will likely be disappointed. He has not come to confirm the beliefs of Christians, Buddhists, Hindus, Jews or those of other religions. He says that people should continue to evolve within the framework of their own traditions, whatever they happen to be. "I have not come to create followers," He says. In fact, He says: "If you follow me" — run after me, try to put me in your pocket, claim me — "then you will lose me." He says: "I do not want you to believe in me, or not to believe in me, I want you to experience me." There is only one way you can experience Him and that is in your heart.

Maitreya, in His teaching on the nature of humanity, says: "The Self alone matters." He equates the Self with God, the Lord, the Absolute. "You are that Self, an immortal being." He says our pain and suffering are due to the fact that we identify with the *vehicles* of the Self — the physical body, emotional feelings and the creations of our mind. Ask yourself: "Who am I?" You will find that you identify either with the physical body as the Self, with your emotions or energy structure, or with the creations of your mind, your beliefs and thoughts. Maitreya emphasizes the importance of self-respect, awareness and detachment. "Self-respect is the seed of awareness," He says. "Without detachment there is no salvation."

The process of the Emergence

In recent years, Maitreya has been appearing to individuals — important world leaders as well as ordinary people — and to groups of people, large and small, all over the world. In this way, He is gradually affecting world events, and making His presence known. He appears to individuals in one of three ways: most commonly in people's dreams; secondly, as a vision — not in a dream but not totally solid; and, thirdly, as a solid, physical person who suddenly appears before them and then disappears.

On 11 June 1988 He appeared miraculously from out of nowhere before 6,000 people at a prayer meeting in Nairobi, Kenya. The people instantly recognized Him as the Christ. He spoke to them for some minutes in perfect Swahili, the local language, and then disappeared as amazingly as He had come, leaving behind some 30 or 40 people completely healed of their illnesses. Since then, Maitreya has appeared miraculously before large groups of people in Mexico, Russia, Germany, Switzerland, Austria, Czechoslovakia, Romania, Scotland, Norway, the Middle East, North Africa, India and Pakistan. Near the majority of these appearances miraculous healing water will be found. This has already happened in Tlacote, near Mexico City, Düsseldorf in Germany and New Delhi in India. He will continue to do this until people begin to talk, the media take notice, and He becomes universally known.

Maitreya will then be invited by the international media to speak directly to the entire world through the television networks linked together by satellites. On this Day of Declaration, we will see His face on the television screen wherever we have access. The Bible statement "All eyes will see Him" will be fulfilled, in the only way in which it can be fulfilled. We will see His face, but He will not speak. His thoughts, His ideas, His call to humanity for justice, sharing, right relationships and peace, will take place silently, telepathically. Each of us will hear Him inwardly in our own language. In this way, He will re-enact on a worldwide scale the true happenings of Pentecost 2,000 years ago.

At the same time, the energy which He embodies — the Christ Principle, the energy of love — will flow out in tremendous potency through the hearts of all humanity. He has said: "It will be as if I embrace the world. People will feel it even physically." This will evoke an intuitive, heartfelt response to His message. Simultaneously, on the outer, physical plane, there will be hundreds of thousands of miracle healings throughout the planet. In these three ways we will know that Maitreya is the Christ, the World Teacher, come for all groups, religious and non-religious alike, an educator in the broadest sense, here to help us fulfil our destiny as Gods in incarnation.

Maitreya and His group of Masters have come to show us the way, to inspire and guide us to create the conditions in which that divinity can correctly manifest. They have come to teach us to know who we are. Maitreya has said: "I have come to teach the art of Self or God realization. That is the destiny of all people in the world."

Those of us now in incarnation have an extraordinary responsibility. That is why we are in the world at this time. Every generation brings into incarnation those who are equipped with the knowledge to solve the problems of their time. We have to solve the problems of today and the immediate future, to decide for all time whether or not the human race will continue — to make the choice for justice, sharing, right relationships and peace, or to destroy all life. Maitreya is in no doubt that we will make the right choice.

CHAPTER 1

THE EMERGENCE

The Process of the Emergence since 1987

Maitreya has been emerging steadily since His appearance in the world in 1977. From 1982 through 1986, Maitreya hoped that the media would recognize Him and make His presence in the world known to all, thereby allowing Him to declare Himself and begin His mission openly.

In January 1986, Maitreya contacted media representatives at the highest level in Britain who agreed to make an announcement that a man claiming to be the Christ was indeed living in the Asian community of London. Under pressure from high religious and government officials, however, this statement was withheld.

Maitreya therefore decided to emerge more discreetly on His own, drawing normal media attention. This involved speaking openly to the public. Beginning in February 1987, Maitreya also began gathering together groups of people who could be instrumental in recognizing and acknowledging Him when He began to speak openly. These groups were prepared for this task. The individuals were drawn mainly from two sources: people in very high positions in society in their respective countries throughout the world, who therefore exerted influence and commanded respect; and a very large group of international journalists who were given the work of alerting their fellow media representatives to the fact that Maitreya was indeed the Christ. These individuals pledged to withhold the information — and their experiences — for the time being.

Maitreya's plan to emerge gradually in London underwent a sudden, drastic change in late February 1987. Over the previous months, large numbers of people from all over the world, responding to my lectures, books and *Share*

International magazine, found their way to the various centres and temples where Maitreya was habitually present. Coach-loads of would-be devotees made life difficult for the group of swamis and others around Him.

On 26 February 1987 Maitreya gave an interview to the major American television company, Cable News Network (CNN). He was interviewed under His ordinary, everyday name, and did not call Himself the Christ. He did say, however, that, among other names, He was known as Maitreya. A group of His closest associates journeyed to the United States to arrange further interviews. Considering the pressure which this worldwide television coverage would inevitably place on the already harassed group around Him, Maitreya made the decision to leave London earlier than originally planned and to establish His (already prepared) ashram in India.

The CNN interview was made available for possible showing in 26 of a promised 29 countries in Europe, Scandinavia, North Africa and the Middle East, but was not broadcast in the United States. The CNN office in Atlanta explained that they could not see a framework in which to present the interview.

After about a week's stay in India, Maitreya returned to London and took up residence just outside the city. He promised to speak openly to the people. In the ensuing months, Maitreya addressed large audiences on a regular basis in the London area. During this time, He began acknowledging, if asked, that He was indeed Maitreya.

Meanwhile, His work as a distributor of energies continued unceasingly. In commenting on this aspect of Maitreya's activity, my Master gave the following information in 1987: Broadly and generally, the world scene is improving significantly; a new lightening, clearing, is taking place, but there still remain several 'black-spots', troublesome areas which need careful attention. Maitreya will work over the next three to four months with great intensity to bring about a breakthrough in world affairs, in particular using the cosmic energies which will become available to Him (and us) at the full moon in September 1987 during the cosmic enlightenment at that time. Maitreya, my Master said, would provide the stimulus but progress is still in our hands. After a series of meetings between the Americans and the Soviets, the I. N. F. missile reduction treaty was signed by Presidents Reagan and Gorbachev in December 1987 — an agreement that no one had thought possible.

At His public meetings, together with His exhortations to change society, Maitreya began speaking about the nature of the soul, reality, and for the first time, about Himself and His mission. He also began speaking in English at some of His talks.

At the same time, Maitreya was making Himself known as an extraordinary person to more and more people in the Asian community, appearing (and disappearing) in front of their eyes. One example: a man was driving his car (rather quickly) down a street. Suddenly, Maitreya materialized in the passenger seat beside him and said: "Slow down, you are driving much too fast," and promptly disappeared!

Maitreya also appeared, with increasing frequency, both in person and in dreams, to many important and well-known personalities. In this way, He was creating an atmosphere of expectation and interest at a very high level. Some of the world's 'household names' were involved.

Beginning in April 1988, Maitreya, through one of His close associates, began to outline His teachings and provide forecasts and commentary on world events. The information was published in *Share International* magazine and distributed worldwide through press releases.

On 11 June 1988 Maitreya appeared suddenly before 6,000 people at a prayer meeting in Nairobi, Kenya. They instantly recognized Him as the Christ. He spoke for some minutes in perfect Swahili and then disappeared as suddenly as He had appeared. This story, with photographs of Him which were taken at the time, was reported in various media around the world, including the Cable News Network.

Historic conference in April 1990

As mentioned, Maitreya had made Himself known to a very large group of distinguished people in many countries. They included representatives of governments (diplomats), members of parliament, religious leaders, various members of royal houses and a large group of well-established journalists. They had all met Him in person, spent time with Him, and through Him received great spiritual experiences.

Over the weekend of 21 and 22 April 1990, they were invited to attend a conference at which Maitreya presided. Some 200 of these dignitaries were able to accept Maitreya's invitation over the two days. Among the guests were an Ambassador and other diplomats; members of Parliament; religious representatives, including a Bishop and a representative from the Vatican who had already met Maitreya and was totally convinced He was the Christ; a King and other lesser royals; professors; scientists; industrialists; and about 40 journalists. Major print and broadcast media from around the world were invited to attend as observers only. In the event, only about 30, mainly British, newspaper journalists accepted this unique opportunity to see Maitreya at first hand. Some of them had been seeking an interview with Him for a long time.

Several times during the two days, Maitreya appeared and disappeared, showing His control over matter, time and space. He spoke about His presence as a representative of humanity and of the Spiritual Hierarchy, as the Leader of His group of Masters, and as the instigator, through His energies, of a transformation in human affairs already visible to all. He spoke broadly of His mission and gave an inkling of the nature of His teaching and work in the years ahead. He outlined His immediate plans to emerge at the earliest possible date, plans which involved the active co-operation of the invited guests. Maitreya invited those present to speak about their experiences gained through Him and many gladly accepted this opportunity to speak openly on these matters for the first time.

During the several intervals for refreshments, the observing media were able to mingle and talk with the guests.

In this way, valuable contacts were made and a degree of trust established. According to my Master, it was obvious to the watching Hierarchy that both groups found the conference enthralling and uplifting, and it was considered by Maitreya to be an unqualified success.

My Master said that one of the main purposes of the conference was to enable the invited guests to meet each other for the first time, to share experiences, and so realize that while they had the extraordinary privilege of knowing and experiencing Maitreya, they were not alone, but part of a large international group of distinguished, eminent people who had similar experiences. It was hoped that this international network would contact each other and speak and write openly about Maitreya and their knowledge of Him.

Until that time, these distinguished people had been held in reserve so that their voices would not be lost in the babble of world news by piecemeal utterance. They were now encouraged to speak openly about Maitreya's presence and teachings. This was expected to influence the masses, who would set up a worldwide demand for sight and sound of Maitreya, thus galvanizing the response of major media everywhere.

As for the observing journalists, it was for them an opportunity to see and hear Maitreya directly for the first time, to realize that He does indeed exist and is not a figment of my imagination. They were able to talk with other journalists who, from their own experience, took this phenomenon very seriously indeed. They also recognized that Maitreya had the respect and reverence of a large group of eminently intelligent, influential people not easily 'taken in'. The observing journalists were not asked to write about the conference. That was left to their own discretion.

As it happened, not less than 12 of the journalists invited to the April conference sought, in their various ways and media, to make known their experience. In each case, they met with a blank stare of incomprehension from their editors and chiefs. Deeply apprehensive, deeply sceptical and materialistic, dedicated to upholding the '*status quo*', the media have exhibited a profound unease in relation to Maitreya's appearance.

During this time, a documentary film was made in which Maitreya talked about His plans and teachings, His mission and hopes for the world. It was accepted for showing on a major television network in the United States, but was never broadcast.

In late 1990, the New Zealand media reported sightings of a "mysterious hitchhiker" thumbing rides on the North Island. Once inside the car, the passenger would announce that the Christ was in the world and that He would soon be seen. The hitchhiker would then disappear from the car. Some reported that the stranger was wearing "shining white clothes". The hitchhiker, of course, was Maitreya. Such incidents (usually involving Christian fundamentalists) were subsequently reported in the Netherlands, the US, France, Australia, and again in New Zealand. The appearances often took place before my scheduled lecture in a particular location.

Physical appearances

My Master, in His April 1991 article published in *Share International*, said: "Within a relatively short time, many people will have convincing proof of Maitreya's presence in the world. Steps are now under way which will make this possible."

The Master's message referred to a series of planned appearances by Maitreya along the lines of His appearance 'out of the blue' in Nairobi in June 1988. He intended to show Himself to large numbers in different countries and communities, wherever possible where He could be photographed or filmed as He did so. In this way, more and more people would have proof of His presence, and, it was hoped, demand media response.

Beginning in September 1991, Maitreya began appearing miraculously to fundamentalist gatherings of approximately 500–900 people throughout the world. He typically speaks to the group in their own language, outlining His plans and concerns and asking for their help and co-operation. He then disappears as suddenly as He had come. In some cases, photos of Maitreya are taken. In each case, the vast majority of those in attendance believe they have seen the Christ (or for Hindus, Krishna, and for Muslims, the Imam Mahdi). Maitreya has appeared in Mexico, Russia, Germany, Switzerland, Austria, the Middle East, North Africa, India, Pakistan, former Czechoslovakia, Serbia, Scotland, Romania, Norway and Italy, as well as the United States (locations as of July 1993).

Many of Maitreya's appearances have been accompanied by mysterious and miraculous events. At Tlacote, not far from Mexico City (where Maitreya appeared in September 1991 and January 1992), a spring of water surfaced with amazing healing properties. Similar manifestations were discovered near Düsseldorf, Germany; in Bucharest, Romania; New Delhi, India; and Switzerland. Growing numbers of people are visiting these sites. Other healing springs will be found in due course, near the cities at which Maitreya has appeared — further signs of His presence.

Highlights of Maitreya's Appearances

1991

Mexico City, Mexico	29 September

1992

Mexico City, Mexico	26 January
Moscow, Russia	1 March
Leipzig, Germany	22 March
Hanover, Germany	5 April
Düsseldorf, Germany	26 April
Geneva, Switzerland	24 May
Zürich, Switzerland	28 June
Vienna, Austria	19 July
Prague, Czech Republic*	16 August
Bratislava, Slovak Republic*	13 September
St Petersburg, Russia	27 September
Tbilisi, Georgia **	18 October
Belgrade, Serbia ***	8 November
Edinburgh, Scotland	13 December
Bucharest, Romania	27 December

1993

Oslo, Norway 17 January	
Bucharest, Romania	7 February
Richmond, Virginia, USA	28 February
San Antonio, Texas, USA	21 March
Yakutsk, Eastern Siberia, Russia	4 April
Uzbekistan, Russia	26 April
Uzbekistan, Russia	23 May
Kabul, Afghanistan	13 June
Rome, Italy	27 June

Maitreya has also been making similar miraculous appearances in the Middle East, North Africa, India and Pakistan, to fundamentalist Muslims, Hindus and Sikhs.

*former Czechoslovakia
**former Soviet Union
***former Yugoslavia

The Timing of the Emergence

*The Master Djwhal Khul (DK), through Alice Bailey, in **The Reappearance of the Christ**, has written: "He will come unfailingly when a measure of peace has been restored, when the principle of sharing is at least in process of controlling economic affairs, and when churches and political groups have begun to clean house." How do you reconcile this with your view that the Christ is here now to do this above-outlined work which DK says humanity must do to prepare for the Christ's reappearance?* (September 1989)

I suppose the above-mentioned quotation is the major argument or reasoning which leads many Alice Bailey students (including of course the Arcane School) to reject my submission that Maitreya is already among us, since July 1977.

I think the salient words in the quotation from DK are: "a measure of peace," and "at least in process of controlling". It would seem that students of Alice Bailey do not like the words "measure of peace" or "in process of controlling", but Maitreya meant what He said in 1945. He did not insist that all should be made perfect (otherwise His presence would not be necessary), but that we should take the first steps. From His viewpoint we have already done just that. Also, I have not said that the Christ is here to do the work of transformation but, on the contrary, that it is our, humanity's, responsibility to make the necessary changes. As He Himself has said: "I am the Architect, only, of the Plan. You, My friends and brothers, are the willing builders of the Shining Temple of Truth." (Message No. 65)

I believe that a spiritual change in humanity has to take place before Maitreya can appear. It seems that this could take centuries. So, what then? (March 1992)

The spiritual change you see as necessary is already taking place — which is why He is among us. Maitreya does not agree with you that the required change could take centuries. Either you accept that He is/can be here or you do not. It does

21

not affect the fact of His presence which becomes more obvious every day.

Up to now I have had the impression that the occurrence of Declaration Day depended only on the willingness and interest of the media. According to you it could already have happened in 1982. Now, six years later, it appears that there must first be changes in the world. I deduce that from the interview with an associate of Maitreya that you printed in last month's **Share International***. I read there: "Certain events must take place first, etc." This disappoints me, and I don't understand why there are now suddenly conditions that there weren't six years ago. Is something going wrong?* (July/August 1988)

No, nothing is going wrong. On the contrary, things are going ahead well in connection with Maitreya's emergence. *But He is doing it on His own*. His Declaration could indeed have taken place in the late spring of 1982, and would have done so had humanity, through its representatives, the media, responded adequately to my information as to His whereabouts given at a press conference in Los Angeles on 14 May 1982. As I have said and written consistently since then, He requires an invitation to appear before the world; otherwise humanity's free will would be infringed. He still requires that invitation. Since the invitation has not, so far, been forthcoming, certain events which will prove that we are 'putting our own house in order' are required to allow Maitreya to act more openly and so gain the recognition which will lead to a world press conference at which He will appear. These are not new conditions but inherent in His emergence without response and invitation. If the media networks of the world suddenly decided to invite Him to appear, He could come forward tomorrow.

It has been 10 years since Christ/Maitreya reportedly left the East for London, and while in that metropolis He has reportedly spoken to many groups, including audiences of over 1,000 people and representatives from the media. After all that exposure why must we still rely on Benjamin Creme for all our news about Maitreya? Are there no other witnesses who will speak up, or newspaper reports of any of these meetings? Can't you name one hall where Maitreya has spoken, and the date when He did so? Can't you quote any of His words? If you can't supply any evidence besides the say-so of Benjamin Creme, how do you know that he isn't (a) deceived; or (b) a deceiver? Why should we believe any of it? (December 1987)

I am not sure to whom this question is addressed — to *Share International* (apart from myself) perhaps, but I am sure it is one that concerns many people. What it does show is a mistaken idea of my role and purpose. It has never been my role to 'produce' Maitreya or to prove His existence in London, but to awaken humanity to the fact that He is here and the nature of His concerns and priorities.

Very many people, responding to my work, have come to London and have found Maitreya within the Asian community (something He does not need nor encourage). That they choose not to make this fact known to the world — who knows from what diverse motives — is their entitlement.

I could probably get a list of halls at which Maitreya has spoken, with the appropriate dates. But what good would that do? What would it prove?

Certain newspaper reporters have dogged His footsteps for years, hoping for an interview. He ignores them, no doubt aware of their motives and capacity for distortion.

At this moment, an Asian gentleman, at one time a regular attendee at my meetings but not now for some years, proudly brandishes a cheque for thousands of pounds paid to him by an Asian press agency to arrange an interview with Maitreya. Though he does know Who Maitreya is, I doubt that he will ever be granted the interview. (Shortly after writing this I heard that this same individual has returned the cheque, suddenly changed his way of life, and has gone off to Maitreya's Ashram in South India to become a sannyasin. Maitreya's influence, perhaps?)

As this magazine has already made known, several top executives of the BBC had repeated contacts with Maitreya in the early months of last year, 1986, eventually agreeing to make an announcement about His claim to be the Christ. That they abandoned their agreement is a measure of the pressure which our Establishment can bring to bear on the BBC today.

I am convinced that Maitreya could make Himself known tomorrow if He chose. He already has sufficient contacts to bring that about when He decides. But so long as world events are moving in the right direction and we are not in danger of self-destruction, He will not use force to bring about His emergence on a world scale. Strange as it may seem to impatient readers who nevertheless deceive themselves into believing that they do not believe in His presence, He is in no hurry. His energy does the work of transformation.

To answer the final questions: until you see Maitreya acting openly or declared before the world, you cannot know for certain whether or not I am (a) deceived or (b) a deceiver. Why, then, should you believe any of it? There is no reason why you should, but look at the events happening in the world and ask yourself how they come to pass.

If the Christ is giving lectures openly several times a week in London, why have no pictures and videos been taken and made available? (May 1988)
Because He does not allow it. It is important that people recognize Him for themselves, from what He is saying, and not because He is pointed out as the Christ. The questioner used the word "openly". That suggests He is presenting Himself as "the Christ", which is not the case. Only in recent months, if asked, does He acknowledge Himself to be Maitreya.

If Maitreya has appeared to a number of political and religious leaders, why do these make no firm pronouncements? That would surely give an enormous impulse to the process of making Maitreya known. (July/August1988)
Maitreya appears to people, including political and religious leaders, in a number of ways: in dreams (the most common), in a vision and, less frequently, in a physical appearance. Sometimes there is a progression from dream appearance to vision and/or physical appearance.

Of course it would give an enormous impulse to the process of making Maitreya known if those leaders who have had such an experience made "firm pronouncements". But that takes courage; people are afraid of losing their credibility. Also, although it would be good if they did, they are not necessarily expected to do so. What is required is that their actions in world affairs should reflect the experience of Maitreya. If you study world affairs (political and religious), I think that you might agree that some leaders, at least, are trying to do just that.

When Maitreya appears to well-known figures throughout the world as He has been doing recently, does He appear to them as Maitreya, the World Teacher, as the Christ, as the Master Jesus, or other? (September 1988)
When He appears to people (singly or in groups of a few, or many thousands as in Nairobi in June), He does so in terms of the thoughtforms that people have of Him. Four old Israelis recognized Him immediately as the Messiah; in Nairobi the people saw Him as Jesus Christ; to others He appears as Maitreya Buddha. It depends on their background and expectations.

Has Maitreya appeared to the Chinese leadership? (September 1989)
No. But there are many people in China to whom He has appeared.

Can you say whether Maitreya has had any meeting (of any kind) with the current leadership of South Africa? (January/February 1991)
With the whites, no; with the blacks, yes.

Why do you think the Christ doesn't manifest through a world leader? (March 1988)
He is the leader of the Spiritual Hierarchy and returns as Their head. As the World Teacher He must speak for all humanity and not for one nation or group of nations. Also, a world leader would have to be sufficiently evolved to be both sensitive to His vibration and able to stand the strain of His overshadowing.

The Media and the Emergence

Media

Why does Maitreya apparently require conditional entry into planetary affairs? (December 1992)

In order not to infringe human free will. As a result of the wrong teaching given by the Churches, people imagine that Christ will come down on a cloud at the end of the world, and that we will look up and see this great omnipotent figure, with a Rod of Power, and we will know that God has entered the world. This is a completely mistaken idea. Apart from the fact that He is not God, if He were to do so that would be the greatest infringement of our free will. Human free will, as far as the Hierarchy is concerned, is sacrosanct. Even if it would be of benefit to us, as we would see it, Hierarchy will never infringe our free will. Free will is the means by which we advance to become what we are, as souls, which is divine. Maitreya says: "Do not let anyone take away your free will. It is your divine inheritance." So if He were to emerge in any other way than by invitation, He would see that as an infringement of free will. He must know that humanity is ready to respond gladly, willingly, to His advice, and not just because He is the Christ. He says: Do not worship Me. If you worship Me you are putting Me above you. I am not above you — I am the same divinity. We are all the same divinity — there is only one divinity. He will never, therefore, infringe our free will; that is why I am sent out ahead to prepare the way somewhat, to tell you that He is here and to open your minds. My job is to create hope and expectancy so that He can enter our lives without infringing our free will. However, if we were to change tomorrow, if we were to address the problem of hunger and rid this world forever of starvation in the midst of plenty, for example, He could take a huge step forward. The media could not miss Him. They think He is being reticent, aloof and difficult to get at; He is not. He is simply waiting, within the Law, for them to take certain steps. They do not see or understand their role or responsibility. They represent humanity, the media are the means by which humanity communicates to itself. But they do not see this; they say: "We can only react to events." This is an event they do not know how to react to because they have never met it before. The Christ has never been in the world before when there were media around! They know He is here, they are only waiting for His head to rise above the horizon and then they will act. Many major journalists know that Maitreya is in the world. The heads of newspapers, governments, media services and the diplomatic services know that everything I have said is true. Many know Him, He has met hundreds of diplomats, journalists, members of Parliament — you can hear His words in their speeches time after time.

Why are journalists so important — why not ordinary people? (October 1991)
The media represent humanity. However sceptical, however cynical, even, the majority of the world's media are, they are the representatives of humanity. The world's networks are the means by which humanity talks to itself, shows itself to itself, and it is therefore through the world's media that Maitreya must speak to the world. Without infringing human free will, Maitreya cannot come on the networks and speak openly, directly to humanity, which is what He intends to do, unless He is invited. That is why the media must respond.

Teachers of the past, like Jesus, did not need the media; so why now? (December 1991)
There were no media, no media at all. If there had been media I am sure Jesus would have used them. Jesus gave His teaching for three years and at the end He was so unknown that one of His disciples, Judas, had to be bribed to point Him out to the authorities so that He could be arrested.

Everyone believes that Jesus was greeted with open arms. He was not. The only time He was greeted with open arms was His last entry into Jerusalem, when they thought He was going to lead a revolution against the Romans. Those who believed that the Messiah was coming believed that He would be a warrior king out of the House of David, Who would free the Jews from the Romans.

He did nothing of the kind. He said: "Render unto Caesar that which is Caesar's, but render unto God that which is God's." He did not come to free the Jews from the Romans at all, which is why they got rid of Him. He did not come as a warrior king but they presented Him to themselves as a warrior king, and to their way of thinking He could not, therefore, be the Messiah.

There is not one single teaching which has come down to us in its pure form, and Christianity is only 2,000 years old, so what about the ones which are many thousands of years old? Every single teacher, including Jesus, came into the world and gave his teaching to a few disciples. They had the task of disseminating the teaching and it took centuries for that to happen, and inevitably, in that dissemination, inaccuracies, distortions, discolorations of the original simple teaching were created. The Teacher, in most cases, was made into a God. That is why Jesus is worshipped as God. Jesus is not God, never claimed to be God; Maitreya will never claim to be God. None of the Teachers is God.

They have God-consciousness, but that is another thing. All the Masters, without exception, have God-consciousness, which is why They are Masters, that is what perfection is. But it does not make them God, not more than you are God. You are God, we are all God, but that Beingness is to do with consciousness. When you are conscious of the nature of God, then you have God-consciousness. That is a growing thing, it takes incarnation upon incarnation to achieve that kind of perfection.

Today, for the first time, precisely because of modern communications, the Teacher can speak directly to everyone. He does not need priests to (mis)interpret His teachings. A call — to come forward — from the media represents a call from humanity in general. To that call Maitreya — under karmic law — can respond.

Isn't the Christ strong enough to appear to a wider public without being invited by the (not always honest) media? (December 1990)
It is not a question of the Christ's strength or power. It is a question of humanity's free will which, to the Christ, is sacrosanct and may not be infringed. For this reason He needs to be invited to come openly before the world.

Does the question of free will mean it will have to be a 100 per cent invitation, or a large percentage? (June 1991)
What it means is a sufficient number of the major media networks of the world must agree to create, for instance, a press conference at which Maitreya would present His credentials, and prove that He is Who I say He is. (He does not say it, I say it.) That would lead to the world television link whereby everyone would see Him and He could speak directly to the world. We are at the stage where people are only beginning to realize that He is here at all.

If it is Maitreya's energies that have made the difference for us up to now, what is actually gained further by His appearing at a press conference? Would not even His mere advice be an intrusion on our free will? (October 1989)
No. We are not forced to take His advice (although we would be foolish indeed not to). There is a limit, under karmic law, to what Maitreya may do without human co-operation and assent. For this reason, to fulfil His mission, His appearance before the world is necessary. Not only that, His acceptance by humanity is essential for its completion.

Can you comment on the suggestion that if Maitreya did not get the co-operation of the media, He would eventually have to overshadow all humanity without the worldwide radio and TV broadcast. Is there such a risk? (December 1989)
No, there is no chance of Maitreya doing this; it would be an infringement of our free will. He fully expects to get the co-operation of the media — if only in response to public interest and demand — after the press conference which will precede the Day of Declaration.

As a journalist, I cannot understand why the Lord Maitreya does not come forward Himself and make His own statements to the press. (October 1991)
Because if He did so immediately, He would not be believed any more than are the others who claim to be the Christ. (You would be surprised how many in the world today think they are the Christ.) If Maitreya came up to you or any journalist you would then have to form your own opinion about whether He was the Christ or not. It is not so simple. He sees a great many journalists who do not make it known.

Why does Maitreya insist that any interviews with Him must be broadcast live? Is it to avoid distorting His teaching by editing? (September 1987)
In the case of a short news interview, He certainly needs it to be live to avoid distortion of His views by editing. In a longer, in-depth interview, this would not necessarily be so important to Him.

*A reader of **Share International** wrote about seeing a film in New Zealand where "a very special teacher" in the Asian community of immigrants in London appeared. Is this the TV film you have referred to as having featured Maitreya but which was never shown?* (May 1989)
Yes. It was made in 1981. The New Zealand showing is the only reference to its having been shown that I know of.

The Press Releases and Their Purposes

Interview with Benjamin Creme's Master
by Patricia Pitchon

*Between 1988 and 1992, **Share International** published articles based on interviews with an associate of Maitreya. Press releases containing highlights of these articles were distributed regularly to the media worldwide. Many journalists have wondered about the aims and purposes Maitreya had in connection with these press releases. In March 1991, Benjamin Creme's Master, Who works closely with Maitreya, kindly agreed to address this question, through Mr Creme, in an interview with Patricia Pitchon.*

Patricia Pitchon (PP): What is the purpose of the press releases?
The Master: They have several purposes: to give information, in particular, to illuminate for humanity the working of the Law of Cause and Effect. This is a major instruction for humanity. Humanity as a whole does not recognize its complicity in the events that happen in the world — even to the extent of the changes in the world's weather patterns. Yet many of the earthquakes, much of the weather disturbances, the floods and hurricanes, the volcanic eruptions and so on, are due to the destructive energies sent out by humanity. Their thoughts and feelings carry energy and make a collective impact. These factors create thoughtforms which are so destructive that they upset the elementals who control the weather. So the traditional weather patterns are completely awry.

Another purpose is to illuminate for humanity, in relation to political and economic events, the degree to which people themselves influence these events, for good or ill. If you are constructive and creative, it will be for the good. If you are destructive or divisive, as is often the case, separative, then

31

you reap this karmic reaction, what you have sown. Maitreya is teaching about this law.

Another important reason for these press releases is simply to draw attention to Maitreya, to the fact that He is here. The forecasts, given over a very large range of subjects, are so pertinent and so accurate — as a totality — that they have drawn from the media and from influential people in the world a degree of interest which would not otherwise be there. They have created in the mind-belt a sense of the presence of Maitreya, of the Christ. That influences everyone from world leaders down to the ordinary person. So He is teaching humanity its responsibility — in terms of action and reaction — and drawing attention to His presence.

[*Benjamin Creme:* He is also corroborating, in a very definite fashion, what I and others have been making known about His presence in the world. It tends to support what we have been saying; when I am on radio or television, for instance, the people who invite me do so often because these press releases have been sent to them.

In a sense He is making my job easier. By making the media more aware, He is creating a threshold for His appearance, a state of mind in which His appearance will not be 'out of the blue'. It will not be so extraordinary and so unexpected as to be immediately dismissed.]

PP: What is the best use that journalists can make of these press releases?
The Master: To take them seriously.

PP: But what does that mean in practice?
The Master: If they take them seriously they will talk about them, they will make them known to their contacts in political circles, to other journalists. The more they talk about them and discuss them — without necessarily believing them, but taking them seriously — the quicker is created the thoughtform about the presence in the world of this extraordinary person called Maitreya.

Whether they accept Him as the Christ or as Maitreya Buddha is not at this point important. What is important is that they take it seriously. And, in many cases, they do so.

PP: What is the Master's view about the extreme timidity with which the media in Britain have related to this story and also to the press releases? At the moment, they seem unable to make comments referring to the press releases except in the form of a joke.

The Master: They usually mention the press releases when they are impressed enough to do so by the accuracy and unexpectedness of some of the predictions, but especially where there is one instance in which a prediction has not worked out. But they would not do so, at all, if they were not impressed. Every time they mention them, it is because they are impressed. They have nothing to gain from 'whipping an old mule'. If they really saw them as an 'old mule' which was worthless and should be put out to grass, they would leave them entirely alone. It is because they do not so see them — despite all appearances they are deeply interested in them and in some way take them seriously — that they write about them, even tongue-in-cheek. It is a sign that they have their minds on them, that they are alive, relevant, as an idea.

PP: Can the Master clarify for many bemused journalists — and some members of the general public — the relationship between, on the one hand, human free will and, on the other, a Master's capacity to see events, trends or patterns in world affairs.

The Master: Both things are working concurrently. Maitreya is not using clairvoyance — or only from time to time. From His knowledge of the Law of Cause and Effect, He is outlining trends and tendencies which are inevitable, unless humanity does something else.

If you do not change direction, and, therefore, change these patterns, then those trends will eventuate. That is what He is saying. In this way He is illustrating the Law of Cause and Effect (ie the Law of Karma) in action.

However, you have free will. There is an influence on these events by your free will, for good or ill. In so far as you change your direction, these events will not come to pass. But if you continue in the way in which you have been doing — whatever the subject in question — these events will take place. You also influence the timing.

PP: One of the difficulties many journalists have had is in relation to time. Some of them seem to think that because events have worked out somewhat later than originally forecast, this in itself invalidates the forecast. Can the Master comment on the relationship between human free will and time?

The Master: As far as the Masters are concerned — this goes for Maitreya, too, of course — there is no such thing as time. Time is a result of the action of the human brain. It does not exist. A difficulty for the Masters in foretelling future events (or what are considered as future events) is to relate them to your idea of time. The Masters have to make deliberate adjustments in Their thinking to put them into a time-frame.

However, on the physical plane, events do conform to what you call time. But the notion that these events happen outside the given time-frame usually has nothing to do with Maitreya at all, but with the associate who passed on the forecast to the journalists.

As often as not, Maitreya has not said "in so many weeks, in so many months, such and such will take place". He has given a general indication of events to those around Him.

Maitreya's associate has generally been present and has heard these forecasts and has expressed this in his own view of the time factor (and perhaps in his view of Maitreya's view), which Maitreya Himself may not have indicated when He made the announcement.

PP: In relation to these difficulties — of not having access to Maitreya directly for these press releases — there has been a lot of difficulty with recent pronouncements on the Gulf War. On the one hand, You, the Master, said there would be a short but very destructive war. You said this at the outset. On the

34

other hand, the information we received through Maitreya's associate seemed to indicate there would be no actual war — there would be skirmishes, but no actual war. Also, given the fact that the Masters do not perceive events 'in time', is it just a changing kaleidoscope in 'non-time'?

The Master: No, it is not quite like that. I would draw your attention to the actual wording of the statements. This was that if President Bush continued to support the Kuwaiti and Saudi force — kings and sheikhs — then a war was inevitable. He did, and it was. But the associate indicated that any fighting would be short. Most people, looking forward to a confrontation between the coalition powers and the Iraqis, thought that it could last up to a year.

In the event, it was a few weeks, which for any war of that intensity is an extremely short time.

In My view, war was inevitable but, as predicted by Maitreya's associate, not long drawn out.

[*Benjamin Creme:* My Master, right at the beginning, said that Saddam Hussein could be highly destructive in the short term. But eventually, his own people would send him into oblivion — he would disappear from the scene. So the Master foresaw the destructiveness. If the Master foresaw it, Maitreya also foresaw it.

The press release (that there would be no major war) was issued on 2 January. The actual bombing began on 17 January. Between these dates there was a constantly changing situation. The associate no doubt responded to this, not to hard and fast statements by Maitreya.]

Benjamin Creme: So that we might get a clearer idea, how much of this information is from Maitreya, how much from the associate, and how much due to the changing situation?

The Master: It is a combination of factors. Maitreya sees general trends and may talk about them to the groups around Him, and may convey them for the purpose of a press release to the associate. The associate colours them with his own mind to a greater or lesser degree, depending on the circumstances and the method by which the information is imparted. This is affected by his reading of the news, his watching of television, his grasp of the day-to-day happenings. When he reads the speculation of certain journalists, that colours his view of the information which was given to him in a general way. In other words, he is doing his best, but his own mind influences the slant.

PP: Is there anything that journalists could be doing with these press releases that they are not doing?
The Master: They could talk about them more and bring them more to the attention of their superiors than they do. Most journalists work under a superior, and most journalists are more afraid of their superior than of anyone else. Some journalists discuss it more openly — Eastern journalists more openly than Western journalists.

PP: When you say Eastern journalists, do you mean from India and the Middle East?
The Master: India, Pakistan, the Middle East and so on. Journalists from that area are altogether more open-minded to the information from Maitreya coming through the associate than are Western journalists, who treat it with more caution, and necessarily so.

PP: Why 'necessarily so'?
The Master: Because of the effect that the mind of the associate has in colouring the information.

PP: We do send press releases to editors and heads of media organizations. What is the effect of these press releases on them — for example, here in the West?
The Master: It depends on the individual. In some cases they are very interested indeed and keep a watching brief on the information. They are impressed. No one with a truly open mind could be unimpressed by the astonishing accuracy of these press releases — nearly three years of such extremely interesting and accurate predictions of events, over a whole gamut of subjects, is unknown in this world.

PP: Why have journalists found it so difficult to bring forward discussion of these press releases — whether in print, on radio or television — in a serious way, to inform the general public here in the West?

The Master: Because they are not committed to this and they are shy of seeming to take them seriously. There is a general scepticism, but it is shot through more and more; there are holes in the scepticism, and we must look for the holes and not allow them to be plugged!

PP: Is this scepticism also a cultural thing in the West?

The Master: Yes, very much so. There is an inborn scepticism of the rational mind of the West — which is thought to be more rational than it actually is, and thought to be more rational, perhaps, than that of the East. There is a tendency in the East to look on the spiritual as part of life and there is a tendency in the West to shy away from confusion of the spiritual with the secular.

PP: Would the Master like to add anything to this interview that would be useful?

The Master: Keep in mind that this is only one of many strings to Maitreya's bow. It is not the be-all and end-all of His endeavours, by any means. It is, for Him, a small thing, which nevertheless is having a great deal of effect.

PP: How many journalists have so far met Maitreya, approximately?

The Master: Several hundred.

PP: Why, out of these several hundred, has no word emerged of these meetings, publicly?

The Master: Many journalists have tried, and failed, to make it known. More have not tried.

PP: Why not?

The Master: They find it difficult, in their milieu, to take a stand in regard to this information, which they feel might draw ridicule on themselves.

And of course, journalists have tried to do things, indirectly — so indirectly you have not noticed. Nevertheless, journalists talk about this among themselves — those who mutually know they have had contacts talk about it and discuss ways and means of making it known, but the process is slow. The opposition is really very strong.

PP: What are the reasons for the opposition?
The Master: Ingrained complacency, ingrained ignorance, ingrained fear of change. Fear of ridicule, fear of truth when it is presented in a new guise, a capacity for self-deception, which is as strong among journalists as among others, and a non-readiness to stand up for what you know — basically, fear.

PP: How can journalists who are committed to trying to bring the teachings of Maitreya forward publicly help other journalists who are afraid?
The Master: Set an example. Nothing works so well as example. If one journalist of reputation were brave enough to come forward with what he knows and has experienced — and there are many — then others would soon follow suit. It is a matter of time.

PP: This means sooner or later it is bound to happen?
The Master: It is bound to happen. And sooner rather than later. Most journalists are just waiting for the head of Maitreya to show above the battlements, then they will speak out.

PP: How will this come about?
The Master: Wait and see. They are waiting to see Him. When it is safe to talk, they will talk. Until it is safe, people are diffident, and sometimes they are just thwarted.

PP: Does this being 'safe' mean when Maitreya comes out more publicly?
The Master: When Maitreya Himself makes certain moves, so that they cannot deny that He is here.

Making Maitreya's Presence Known

I am very impatient for Declaration Day to occur. Time and again I wonder why Maitreya does not speed up His emergence, why He fails to convince the media, why some promises and predictions take so long to materialize. Recently, I complained about all this to one of your co-workers. The answer shocked me. He said something like: What have you done to make it possible? How many people have you told that Maitreya is in the world? How often do you take part in Transmission Meditations? Why do you assume that Maitreya would be able to do everything on His own, while even many of us who know that He is here do not lift more than half a finger to support this work? I admit that I do not have much time for all these things, I am really busy, but I do not accept that there is a direct relation to the processes of Maitreya's emergence. He and His Masters surely do not need us, ordinary people, in this, do They? And if so, would They not know ways to make clear to me how to help? (June 1989)

I have to admit to an amused smile at this series of questions. They show such a lack of understanding of our role in the Christ's Reappearance — despite, of course, my constant attempts, both in lectures and in writing, to emphasize the necessity of making known — at any level — our awareness of His presence, thus creating the climate of hope and expectancy for His return. How can anyone — if he believes Maitreya is in the world — say he is too busy for "all these things"?

My colleague, of course, is quite right. In our experience, those most anxious to see the Christ, most demanding of "the latest news from London", the most impatient, the most critical of delay, the least understanding of the laws involved in such a planetary event, are precisely those who do the least to help Him to emerge, in the only way He can, under law. Their whole view of this event is mystical and passive and their so-called 'support' is purely selfish. Let the questioner turn to

Message No. 11: "I need your help. I call on you. The success of My mission depends on you ..."

What is the best thing I can do for Maitreya right now? (April 1992)

If you believe that Maitreya is in the world, make it known to the best of your ability. If you believe (even if it is a 5 per cent belief) that what I say is true, make it known at that 5 per cent. You do not have to have my 100 per cent conviction, because I have experiences which leave me in no doubt. It is natural that you will have doubts, perhaps 95 per cent doubt, but if you have 5 per cent conviction that this could be true, make it known at that little level.

In this way you help to create the climate of hope and expectancy which makes it possible for Him to come into the world openly, without infringing our free will.

You have said that Maitreya is waiting for an invitation from humanity for Him to come forward openly, and that you personally do not believe in the efforts of large gatherings in prayer to bring such an event forward. How are we supposed to give Him the call? (June 1991)

Demonstrate to the media that you are concerned. I know He is here because of my experience, which I have tried to pass on to you. I am hoping that if you take it seriously you will be galvanized to do something, to make it known. The more people there are who know He is in the world and make it known, the sooner the media will invite Him forward. The media represent humanity and therefore it is up to humanity to make them respond. A newspaper editor, a director of a radio or a television network, is like a politician. If they want you to buy their paper or watch or listen to their programme, they have to do what you ask. If you want the media to invite Maitreya out into the world, go to the highest networks of the land and twist their arm until they do. There is no way you or I or Maitreya Himself can appear on the television networks of the world except by invitation — unless He infringes our free will.

People see the Christ as God, and say that with God everything is possible; if He wants to be on the media He will be on the media; in any case, why do we need the media? It is not like that. To appear without invitation would be a total infringement of free will. He wishes to be seen as a man, one of us. He is an extraordinary man, by our standards divine, but He has revealed His divinity through the evolutionary process, the same process that we take to reveal the same divinity — there is only one divinity, in Him and in everyone else, but at different levels of manifestation. He manifests more of that divinity, that is what makes Him the Christ; but He has to obey the laws which govern our nature.

Who should speak for the group, especially in relation to the media? (January/February 1992)
In every group there are people of different type, ray structure, mental background, education and so on. All of them are fired to a greater or lesser degree by this message, and all of them have the right, in fact the duty, to make it known, whether to the media or not. What they do not have the right to do is to speak as representatives of me, or of specific groups. That is another thing and should be arrived at by consensus and approval of the groups. Nobody should, for instance, think they can speak for me. They do not know what I think; I might think something completely different from what they think I think. Anyone speaking to the media should be seen to be speaking for themselves unless, as a result of group consensus, they are chosen to represent the group in an approach to the media. Otherwise, I would say that there should be no restriction on anyone in presenting this information to the public.

When I say "the public", I do not necessarily mean the media. The media are a specialized aspect of the public. But there is no one in any group anywhere in the world who is not fitted or equipped to speak to the general public about the Reappearance. Many do it all the time, and do it perfectly well. Others are too diffident. It is time they lost their diffidence and spoke out. But there should be no restriction by any members

41

of any group in speaking to the general public about the Reappearance. It is your duty, I would say, and certainly the function of the groups to do just this.

No one should say that certain people will do this and others will not be allowed to do it because they do it inefficiently. It does not matter how efficiently or inefficiently it is done. If it comes from your heart, if it is the result of your own experience, you will be more convincing than the most accomplished lecture anyone could give. That is what influences people — not lectures, but the heart response of one individual to another: "I cannot tell you why. I do not know the whole story. I do not know all the answers that the clever ones in our group know, but I do know that the Christ is in the world. I know this within my heart. I experience His energy. I respond to the message, and I am telling you about my experience. I am not asking you to believe everything I say." That is enough. If everyone said this to everyone they had contact with, on that simple level, the work would go forward in an enormously enhanced way. When it is restricted to lectures by intellectuals, or would-be intellectuals, it becomes an arid thing and a very restrictive practice, and hardly anyone hears about it.

Can one — without specific instructions from a Master — talk in public (lectures, conferences etc) as you do? Should one try to do so? (May 1987)
Yes, by all means. It is a little late in the day to start but all along I have urged everyone who believes at all that Maitreya is in the world to make it known at whatever level of belief one has. You do not need the support of a Master to say, publicly, that you believe that this information is true, or probably true, or possibly true, and to give your reasons. Inform yourself of the facts and make them known to the best of your ability.

How can I tell this extraordinary story of Maitreya's presence to another? How do you start? Where do you start? (March 1990)
There are, of course, many ways to tell this story, depending on your background and understanding. The best way, I think,

is to tell it as something which you have heard, found interesting, and which may be true. The worst way is zealously to cram it down people's throat.

Most people are hungry for light and knowledge. Point to the extraordinary changes, happenings, in the world and ask if they can be coincidental. Explain, simply, about Hierarchy, with Maitreya at its head, and the Masters' return with Him. Present Him, not in religious terms, but as a teacher come to show the way forward for humanity. You may be surprised by the response.

How does one answer to the impulse from the heart to communicate the message of Maitreya in a more intelligent way? (January/February 1992)

Be intelligent. Remember that you have to shape what you are experiencing in order to convey what you mean. You can only convey an experience in some form or another — in words, structures, writings, some way that gives it a form. Otherwise you cannot share it. If you are answering the impulse from the heart that will, by its very nature, make you want to convey it. You will want to carry out the impulse to serve and speak about the message. If you are reasonably intelligent and do not allow the heart to run way ahead of the mind, you will find a way in which you can make it intelligible to other people. You have to clothe it in a form that they can understand, in a language that your listeners can recognize. You have to simplify it for a simpler audience, and if it is a Christian audience, put it in a form that they can understand — not too esoteric. There is no real answer to this except to be intelligent about it. Recognize that just because you feel it does not convey it. Just feeling the impulse to serve is not service. You have to carry out the service intelligently. Some people do not do anything until they have found the best way, and are still looking for the best way years later. They never do anything because it has to be the very best. Their service has to be a major mission that everyone will recognize. The impulse then is not to serve but to be recognized as serving. Be intelligent and be yourself.

How do you tell the layman who has not even heard of Maitreya or Sai Baba, who is not even interested in these things, that such people are in the world and that the world can be changed? (January/February 1992)

Of course, you do not need to know about Maitreya or Sai Baba in order to live your life. It is an enlargement of your life if you do, but if you are living in the Third World — Africa or South America, for example — you may never have heard of Sai Baba or Maitreya but you can still live the life of a true human being.

What is the difference between spreading the word about Maitreya and what fundamentalist Christians do when they try to "spread the word". Are not both trying to get people to believe their way? (September 1988)

In the case of spreading the word about Maitreya's presence and concerns, one is giving (hopefully, not dogmatically) information about a world event before it is generally known. This creates a climate of hope and expectancy which allows Maitreya to enter our lives without infringing our free will. No one is asked to change his or her beliefs or adopt any particular religious dogmas.

The fundamentalist Christian on the other hand is, as he sees it, an evangelist whose duty is to "bring everyone to Jesus". To their minds, this necessarily involves the acceptance of their man-made dogmas and doctrines.

*I am pleased to read in **Share International** that guidance will be given to us in the New Age into a deeper psychological understanding of people. In this context, could you explain further what is meant by your Master's words: "When the voices of envy and doubt assail you, keep serenely to your task. Remember that your mind belongs to you and no one has the right to tell you what to think." [Note: See Chapter 20, 'The Call to Service', in this book.] Within the work of introducing Maitreya to a wider public, I understand people's doubt but am wondering where envy springs from?* (November 1991)

Very many people who doubt the presence of Maitreya are, at the same time, envious of those who have a firm conviction of

His presence. They are probably more assertive, then, in expressing their doubts than others.

There are still many languages (for example Japanese) into which DK's books are not translated. Which is more important to do: translate DK or work for the emergence of Maitreya? What is the priority? (January/February 1989)
The translation of Master DK's books into different languages is, of course, important, and is going on in different countries. However, while important, that work has not the urgency of work done for the appearance of Maitreya. Those groups working with me, who have elected to prepare the way for Maitreya, should make that their priority. Time is short to make known His presence and teachings, and not everyone is able to accept this more difficult work. After the Day of Declaration there will be many who will take on translation work, which is not controversial and therefore easier.

Will the work of the various groups associated with you change after the Day of Declaration? Could you please sketch an outline of their future work? (November 1986)
Until the Day of Declaration the main task of the groups working with me is to prepare the way for the Christ and the emerging Masters, to tell the world of His and Their presence, to create the climate of hope and expectancy in the world and to spread the practice of Transmission Meditation. Obviously after His Declaration this work of preparation will no longer be necessary, but Transmission Meditation is an ongoing activity for all those who wish to work with Hierarchy in this way, and will undoubtedly spread further and wider throughout the world.

Together with the spreading of Transmission Meditation, an enormous educational programme will become necessary and possible. Those groups now engaged in making known the fact of the Christ's presence will, if they wish, find a field of service as part of this tremendous task. We would hope that *Share International* would continue to play a part in this work.

While the spreading and interpretation of the Ageless Wisdom teachings goes forward, a major endeavour of the groups will be their preparation for (group) initiation. Herein lies one of the most important aspects of Transmission Meditation, as a field of service and a preparation ground for initiation. It is this possibility which lies behind the Christ's overshadowing presence as 'nourisher' of the groups.

Can We Contact Maitreya?

Can the public attend the meetings Maitreya is holding? (March 1987)
In the Asian community itself, a vastly increased number of people (not only Asians but English, American, European, Japanese, etc), responding to my information and advertisements, are finding their way to these meetings. This is not actually what He wants or requires. He does not want or need a throng of followers or devotees but rather people in their own countries throughout the world through whom He can work to change the world. This requires the manifestation in them of the Christ Principle leading to love for all humanity and the desire to serve it.

I don't see why we can't be told where Maitreya is speaking if all those other people at the meetings are feasting their eyes on Him and listening to the sound of His voice. I have read your previous comments in Share International *about overcrowding Maitreya.* (November 1987)
There is no question of "overcrowding" Maitreya. I have referred previously to the pressure of would-be devotees on the group around Maitreya. Phrases used in the question like "feasting their eyes on Him" give the answer to why I may not indicate — even if I sometimes know in advance — where Maitreya will be speaking.

It is one thing to be told that Maitreya will be at such and such a place, to go there, to "feast one's eyes on Him" and recognize Him, and quite another to respond to Him for what He is saying and calling for: sharing and justice for all; a new approach to life. Many hear Him today and do not respond, unready, I suppose, to see humanity as one. It is spiritual recognition which is important, not seeing and hearing a man,

Who, you have been told, is the Christ. The recognition must come from each one himself.

I would very much like to go to one of Maitreya's meetings, but why are they not open? Why all the secrecy? That is what I do not understand. (October 1991)
I am sure you would like to attend a meeting — so would everyone. I would too, but I am not allowed. These meetings are by invitation only. People come to them: journalists who are invited and come along with uninvited MPs, or MPs who are invited and come with uninvited journalists. The ones who are invited are allowed in, the others are not. It is very strict.

Maitreya has His own plans. He is the World Teacher, a man of unbelievable intelligence, wisdom, love, with cosmic consciousness, and there is no way you or I in any way can diminish that by saying: "Why doesn't He do this?" or "Why doesn't He do that?" You are using a little, limited, human mind to evaluate a cosmic consciousness. It cannot be done. He knows what needs to be done under law.

Among the Swamis, the inner circle around Maitreya, are there any women? (January/February 1991)
No. However, there are women in the large group of 'interested followers', if I can so call those near to Him.

Will Maitreya answer me if I write personally and ask questions? If so, where do I address personal correspondence? (April 1991)
People write to Maitreya and ask me to forward letters to Him but it is not possible for me to do so. He does not receive personal letters.

Is there any way we can contact the Christ — mentally, spiritually or even physically, since He can be in more than one place at the same time. Do you think He will come to America? (November 1987)
It is not possible to contact the Christ physically (unless invited to do so) or mentally (unless you can function at the buddhic level of consciousness as the Masters do) but you can certainly contact Him spiritually and invoke His energies. This happens

at every Transmission Meditation and indeed the Great Invocation was given for this purpose — to invoke His spiritual energies. After the Day of Declaration He will journey round the world, visiting all countries, including, of course, America.

What can we do to have an experience of Him personally, ie by dream or vision? (October 1989)
It is not possible for me to direct people to Maitreya in London. He sees only those whom He calls to Him. My advice to those who wish to see Him in dream or vision is to get involved in service to humanity, in some area of need. There are many, of course, who have been accorded experiences and contact who could hardly claim to be involved in service at any recognizable level, but His Grace is a law unto Itself; the surest way is to help His mission.

Jesus said that the more blessed are those who believe in Him without seeing Him. By the same token, isn't it true that the recognition of Maitreya is given to, and sensed esoterically by, sincere seekers only? (May 1990)
No, I do not think that is true at all. Maitreya gives experiences of Himself to people of all kinds in all walks of life, most of whom, I suggest, would not fall into the questioner's category of "sincere seekers". People who read esoteric literature tend to see themselves as an élite group with special sensitivity to Maitreya's presence and energies which, many believe, gives them special authority to pronounce on the truth of His presence or not. To my mind this is simply glamour. The simple heart reaction of 'ordinary' people is much more accurate, I believe.

Day of Declaration

You say Maitreya never infringes human free will. But if He communicates with the entire humanity telepathically on the Day of Declaration it will be an infringement of human free will, so that is a contradiction. (March 1990)

With respect, there is no contradiction. Maitreya will communicate telepathically on the Day of Declaration only in response to our invitation through the media as our representatives. It has been the lack of such an invitation which has delayed the Day of Declaration since May 1982. It is for this reason also that the Day of Declaration will be preceded by a press conference at which all nations will be represented by media and others who have already experienced Maitreya.

Will there be revelations, like those contained in the Dead Sea Scrolls, brought to light as part of the Day of Declaration? (January/February 1991)
For students of the Ageless Wisdom teachings, much of what Maitreya will impart on that day will be familiar — the existence of the Masters and Their planned return, for example — but for the masses of humanity, locked into ancient religious beliefs, most of what He has to say will be a revelation, leading to the New Revelation which it is His mission to bring.

When Maitreya overshadows us on the Day of Declaration, will there be a physical sensation? (May 1989)
He has said that when His energy, that is, the Christ Principle, flows out, it will be as if He embraces the whole world. People will feel it — even physically. As the energy of the Christ Principle flows through the four levels of the etheric body to the lowest plane — which is just above physical gas — it will be felt on the physical body as a resounding vibration. If you are at all aware of the etheric body, you will experience this as a very powerful physical sensation. Otherwise, you will probably feel it as a pressure on the top of the head during the overshadowing. Then you will hear His words inwardly in your own language.

On the Day of Declaration will the Teacher's (Maitreya's) face appear to TV viewers differently (according to various races or cultures) or as the same man worldwide? (January/February 1991)
He will appear as the same man to all.

The current World Teacher, Maitreya, will declare Himself, I understand, simultaneously throughout the world. How will He contact 'uncivilized' races (I am thinking, for example, of the Yanomami Indians and many such tribes who have lived for centuries in the tropical rainforests with little outside communication) and what message will He give them?

And (2) what message will there be for the millions of nomadic and/or starving people who have nothing to share? (July/August 1990)

On the Day of Declaration, Maitreya will mentally, that is telepathically, give His message to every adult man and woman on the planet. Each will hear Him in their own language and each will react on the basis of their own understanding and intuition. As I understand it, no special measures will be taken to ensure understanding by so-called primitive peoples. Those cut off in jungle and rainforest may well listen with amazement and total non-understanding but they will experience the energy of the Christ which will flow through them as through everyone else.

(2) As for those now starving and dispossessed, the message of Maitreya, calling for peace through justice and sharing, can only be for them the answer to their prayers and agony. They do not need a 'message'. They need help.

Will children hear Maitreya's appeal on the Day of Declaration? And will they understand? (June 1990)

I am informed that everyone over the age of 14 years will hear (internally) Maitreya's message. Until the age of 14 there is little or no mental focus in the average child so under that age the child would not understand what he or she was hearing. But, of course, at every age, each one will understand (or not) according to their development.

What should we do with and for young children on Declaration Day? (June 1990)

Millions of them will be asleep and should be left asleep. Others will play quietly. It is more than likely that they will respond to Maitreya's energy — the Christ Principle — and experience their own sense of this great happening.

As regards Maitreya's link with everyone, simultaneously, on Declaration Day, I wonder if the timing may be governed according to the sun rather than clocks? Thus, if the ceremony were due to begin at 10 am on 2 June, then Japan etc would begin to have the experience at 10 am there. Then, as the Earth rotated, India, etc, would have it, then on to Africa, Europe and America, in longitudinal bands, as it were. Thus, the time would be equally favourable to all and the starting time true for all. Thus it would be simultaneous according to the sun, though not necessarily to clocks. (June 1990)

That sounds very neat and tidy and certainly convenient for everyone — except Maitreya! Such an arrangement would necessitate a constant overshadowing of millions of people, band after band, for 12 hours on end. Probably not impossible for Maitreya to do, but what a waste of energy when all people around the world have to do is set their alarm clocks to coincide with 2 pm London time (or whatever).

Will Sathya Sai Baba be involved as well as Maitreya on the Day of Declaration? (November 1990)
No.

It says in the Bible that Christ will return in a "blaze of Glory". Where was Maitreya's blaze of glory that we could all see and recognize? (March 1989)
This "blaze of Glory" is, of course, a symbolic term for His spiritual stature recognized by all. This will take place on the Day of Declaration when He overshadows all humanity.

Where will the Christ reside during the period of transition after the Day of Declaration? Will it be the 'New Jerusalem'? (May 1989)
No, the 'New Jerusalem' is the whole world — the 'city of peace', that new state of the world in which peace exists. At the moment, London is Maitreya's base and has been since 1977. Whether it remains His base during the period directly after the Day of Declaration and prior to His visiting all the countries of the world remains to be seen. I expect it to do so.

Can we assume, once He begins His visits to the nations of the world, that Maitreya will go to the poorest countries first? (December 1986)

No, not necessarily. He will go first to the countries where His presence is most needed.

Signs of Maitreya's Appearance

If Maitreya is not limited by the physical body and can appear anywhere at will, why did He have to take a plane from Pakistan to London in 1977? (September 1990)

He did not have to come to London by plane. He could simply have thought Himself here as He does today throughout the world. He chose to come by plane so that He would enter Britain, His centre in the modern world, in the normal way, with a passport, and take His place here, legally, as an ordinary immigrant would do. It also allowed Him to fulfil the prophecy of "coming in the clouds".

The Pope was in England at about the time of the planned Day of Declaration of 30 May 1982. Was it planned that the Pope should meet Maitreya at that time? (September 1987)

No. In the event he might well have met Maitreya but there were no plans to bring this about.

When Maitreya spoke at the prayer/healing gathering in Nairobi in June 1988, was it the telepathic communication which He is going to do on the Day of Declaration? (January/February 1991)

No. He spoke, as it was reported in the *Kenya Times*, in perfect, unaccented Swahili, the native language.

Previous appearances of a World Teacher have been only to a very limited group of people. Why, what criteria were used to select the group? (July/August 1990)

In every case, the criterion was the point reached in evolution by the selected disciples. In the past, the number of reasonably advanced disciples was small. The Master DK (through Alice Bailey) has written that the problem for the Christ, as Jesus, was that there were not enough disciples through whom He could work or who could have prepared the way for Him. It is the disciples who, by stepping down the teaching through their own understanding (more limited than that of the Master), can disseminate it at a level acceptable to the mass of people. Of course, over and above these considerations, the lack of communications such as we take today for granted made the use of a small group the only vehicle available to the Teacher.

Lightships

Under the heading "Unidentified flying oranges...," Britain's popular press (it was also reported on the radio news) recently carried the story of huge orange lights which had been seen the night before in many parts of Britain. They were described as "the size of a house", and left witnesses with "mild sunburn". Some people reported having seen them, on and off, for a number of weeks. Some said the lights hovered just above the ground, and speculated that they might have come from outer space.

Interestingly, I had talked the night before with a man who had just spent what seemed to him several hours in one of these lights, which are not orange but golden. They do not come from outer space or even from another planet of our system. They are created and used by Maitreya Himself. By their means He takes His associates and workers around the world, showing them people and places in a way otherwise impossible for them to experience. My friend described the reaction of people in the streets to the lights, pointing upwards or running in fear. He was tickled to read about it next day in the newspapers.

Normally, Maitreya keeps the lights (lightships) invisible but is now allowing them to be seen — another sign of the imminence of His emergence into the open. (June 1988)

I have read with fascination the news about Maitreya's "lightship." May I ask something about this? Is this vehicle made out of etheric matter and are people who travel in it taken out of the body? How does the "lightship" move? Does Maitreya use thought power or does it work with crystals? If I remember well, I have read somewhere that aircraft in the Atlantean age worked with crystals. Will this sort of public transport become available for everyone? (July/August 1988)

Maitreya's "lightship" is made of etheric matter of the first (the highest of the four) etheric planes. Nevertheless, people are not obliged to leave the body in order to travel. They can simply walk into it. It moves by the power of Maitreya's will. Crystals (to the disappointment of many 'new-agers', no doubt) are not used. This is not a form of public transport which will be available to everyone. It is unique.

Could you comment on the so-called hitchhiking angel recently reported in the Netherlands. Could he really be Maitreya? (April 1991)

Yes. As readers of *Share International* will know, before I visited New Zealand in January of this year the same phenomenon took place: a white-clothed man asks for a lift, says the Christ is in the world and promptly vanishes from the car, driven usually by fundamentalist Christian couples. I have just received a letter from the USA reporting the same happenings (which I did not hear about at the time) before my last visit to Dallas, Texas, in June last year.

Signs

Please comment on the icons that cry or bleed. (April 1991)

These phenomena, of which today there are so many instances, are manifested by the Master Who was Mary, the mother of Jesus, in Palestine. Not in incarnation at this time, that Master is also responsible for the many manifestations of the Madonna which are seen throughout the world. These are among the 'signs' of the Christ's presence in the world.

I heard on the French news (TFI) about a picture of the Virgin Mary which is known to weep. It is located in an ordinary house in Toulouse. Several hundred people have already been to see it, among them a priest who is convinced of the authenticity of the event. As for the owner, he is reluctant to part with it even though he is tired of the crowds who gather from all over the world. Can you say (1) whether this happening is authentic (indeed taking place) and (2) if so, is it one of the many manifestations of the Master Who, you say, was the Mother of Jesus? (November 1990)

(1) Yes. (2) Yes.

[See *Maitreya's Mission, Volume One*, pp106-7, for further information.]

Crosses of light

In April 1988, my Master told me that Maitreya would soon begin manifesting crosses of light all over the world in such numbers that they would draw enormous attention. The following month we received information that Maitreya had manifested a cross of light on the window of a house in Louisiana, USA. The sign was seen by thousands who crowded around the house. Many people there understood that the Christ could be 'reached' through this cross. Soon after, the *Pasadena Star News* in southern California stated on 27 May: "Residents reported seeing a cross shining through a bathroom of an apartment in El Monte." About a dozen such crosses were subsequently reported in this poor, largely Hispanic area of Los Angeles. Thousands visited these manifestations. Many reported healings of various types associated with the crosses. Since that time, crosses of light have manifested on windows throughout the world, with similar consequences. The crosses radiate spiritual energy into the surrounding area, and are one of the many signs of Maitreya's presence in the world.

Are the crosses of light still visible in Californian houses? (May 1989)

Yes, and their numbers are growing.

*In the article by Estrella Narvadez on crosses of light in the Philippines (**Share International**, November 1991), the crosses are described as being even-armed. The pictures of them seem to show the bottom arm as being longer than the other three, and I believe this is discussed in a book by Alice Bailey, where, if I remember rightly, we are told that the even-armed cross represents materialism, whereas the cross with* *the longer bottom arm represents spirituality.* (December 1991)

The crosses of light are usually even-armed, representing the Aquarian cross. This symbolizes the bringing down of the spiritual ideas (of Pisces) on to the physical, material plane. It does not represent materialism as such (quite the contrary), but the correct relating of spirit to matter.

Maitreya and the Masters

Maitreya, the Christ

Why do you refer to the Christ in a way which symbolizes a very specific material state and not a universal one? (July/August 1990)

The concept of the Christ as a universal Principle, rather than simply a man, is one which has gained ground in more sophisticated Christian groups and Churches since about the turn of the century. And I would agree that this demonstrates a higher and better understanding of the nature of the Christ. Many groups, indeed, see the 'return' of the Christ in terms of the manifestation of the Christ Principle in humanity: when this principle demonstrates widely enough in us, they believe, the 'Christ' will have returned, the 'second coming' will have taken place. With this I cannot disagree, but see it as only one of His three modes of Reappearance. When, in June 1945, Maitreya announced His intention to return, He indicated that this would be in three phases: (1) the overshadowing of the minds of those active disciples (mostly in the political field as leaders of nations) who could be impressed on mental levels; (2) the outflow of the Christ Principle through the hearts of humanity in general; and (3) His physical presence in the world.

If I emphasize the physical presence it is because (a) it is a fact in my experience; (b) humanity needs to know and recognize Him as the World Teacher; (c) it is too vague and 'easy' to talk about "the Christ Principle" while humanity has far to go in the demonstration of that principle.

In any case, I do not believe that my presentation of Maitreya's return into the physical life of humanity in any way rules out His being seen as the Embodiment of the (universal) Christ Principle. That is the measure of His achievement.

Are Maitreya and the Christ really one entity? Is not Maitreya only a pure channel for Christic energy, hence the confusion? (April 1989)
The term "Christ" is the translation into Greek of the Jewish term "Messiah", and Maitreya would prefer to be seen as a teacher rather than as "The Messiah", which He says can create opposition.

Maitreya has full title to the term "Christ" in that He is so advanced, so pure, that He can actually embody — and not simply channel — the energy of the Christ Principle or Consciousness, the energy of evolution *per se*. From Him it flows through the hearts of all humanity, awakening them to a new spiritual (not necessarily religious) approach to life.

Rather than one 'leader' appearing as an example and teacher, can there not occur a more or less simultaneous 'awakening' of a large number of 'Masters'? ie an evolutionary jump on its own? (June 1987)
This is an idea common to a number of so-called 'New Age' groups who find the idea of one teacher or leader somehow 'old age'.

The idea has a certain basis, in that Aquarius will be the age of group consciousness and achievement and a great evolutionary leap will be made by humanity. But Masters cannot be made 'spontaneously' but only as a result of the evolutionary process, whether that is fast or slow, and Maitreya is emerging as the head and leader of His group of Masters, Who are externalizing Their work onto the outer physical plane. That is His primary purpose in reappearing.

What have we done to deserve the coming of Maitreya? (March 1992)
Nothing. He comes as the leader of the Hierarchy of Masters in Their Externalization, and in answer to our cry for help.

Is Maitreya's presence in London a total embodiment or a partial one? In view of Message No. 65 and others, given through you, "My coming will transform this world," has He projected only a part of His consciousness into the Pakistani or is it a total presence? (October 1990)

Maitreya has not "projected His consciousness" into an already existing Pakistani gentleman. He has created a body, a vehicle, through which His full consciousness as the Christ and World Teacher can manifest at our level on a day-to-day basis. The technical term for this body is 'mayavirupa'.

"My Coming will transform this world, but the major work of restoration must be done by you. I am the Architect, only, of the Plan. You, My friends and brothers, are the willing builders of the Shining Temple of Truth." [Message No. 65] By this Maitreya does not mean that His Presence is partial; on the contrary, for the first time His total consciousness, planetary and cosmic, can be present. He means rather that humanity has evolved to the point where, of its own free will — and with His help, of course — it can build a civilization based on love, justice and brotherhood.

DK (the Master Djwhal Khul) once wrote that thoughtforms of Maitreya will appear. How do you know that the appearance of Maitreya will not be a thoughtform? (May 1987)

I have seen about six photographs of clouds taken, usually from airplanes, by different people which when developed showed clearly a thoughtform of the Christ superimposed on the cloud formations. *Share International* published one of these in September 1983. I am sure many more of these photographs exist. The body in which He now appears, the 'mayavirupa', is indeed a thoughtform in that it is created by thought, by an act of will and not born in the usual way. But to those around Him now, and to all the world over the next world cycle, He will be a very real, solid person indeed.

I understand the reason why Mr Creme does not reveal his Master's name is to prevent people from attracting that Master's attention (and therefore energy) for selfish reasons which would misuse the Master's time and energy. If this is so, is it not true also in Maitreya's case? At present, many people are attached to Maitreya's name and wait for His Declaration

Day. They attract His energy for their ego. Will this not lead to misuse of Maitreya's time and energy? (March 1990)

The two situations are quite different. In Maitreya's case, He embodies what we call the Christ Principle or Consciousness and it is this energy which is freely available to all in the degree or potency they can absorb and use. As we manifest it through service, we automatically attract more from Maitreya.

In this way, through our action, He can transform the world. No amount of purely emotional or devotional approaches to Maitreya affect His function as the Christ. I am not quite sure what is meant by "they attract His energy for their ego".

Can Maitreya (the Christ) be in each person? (December 1988)

As the Christ Consciousness (which He embodies), most certainly. He has said: "I am with you and in you. I seek to express that which I am through you. For this I come." (Message No. 10.) As we give expression to the Christ Principle (through world service), He can work through us.

What exactly do you mean by saying that the Christ energy is related to the "Heart of the Sun"? (April 1991)

Our sun is really threefold in nature and radiates three different qualities of fiery energy. The outer physical sun radiates Fire by Friction. The inner 'Heart of the Sun' radiates Solar Fire, which is the energy we call love. This is embodied at the planetary level by the Christ — He is the Lord of Love. From the Central Spiritual Sun comes Fire Electrical, embodying the Will and Purpose of our Solar Logos.

*(1) Referring to Alice Bailey's **The Externalization of the Hierarchy**, pp276, 350 and 396, where the Christ is called also "the Rider from the Secret Place" and "the Rider on the White Horse", and where it states that this appellation could also include the Spirit of Peace provided sufficient preparatory work is done by humanity: has this happened? (2) Is the Rider on the White Horse Maitreya and the Spirit of Peace, and (3)*

is their name Kalkin something-or-other? I think I read this name somewhere. (May 1989)

(1) Yes. On His decision to return to the everyday world, announced in June 1945, Maitreya was (and still is) overshadowed by the Spirit of Peace or Equilibrium in a manner very similar to the way He overshadowed and worked through Jesus. The Spirit of Peace is an extraplanetary Avatar, and it is His energy of Equilibrium which, Maitreya has recently said, is bringing about the new world stability, the new 'consensus' politics around the world. This cosmic Being works with the Law of Action and Reaction, which, as you may know, are opposite and equal. The effect of the Avatar's energy of Equilibrium is to transform the existing turbulence and violence, hatred and mistrust into their opposites — in exact proportion. We shall, therefore, under the influence of this energy (this can already be seen), enter an era of peace and co-operation, mental and emotional balance and poise — in exact proportion to the prevalent discord and strife. (2) Yes. Maitreya, overshadowed by the Spirit of Peace, is the Rider on the White Horse. (3) Together They are Kalki Avatar expected by Hindus to inaugurate the new world cycle, the Satya Yuga.

*In **Externalization of the Hierarchy**, the Tibetan talks about a lesser Avatar sent to the physical plane by the Avatar of Synthesis as His representative and transmitting agent. Is this lesser Avatar Sai Baba and, if not, what is Sai Baba's relationship to the Hierarchy?* (March 1987)

The "lesser Avatar" (these terms are relative!) is not Sai Baba but Maitreya, the Christ. Sai Baba's relation to Hierarchy might best be described as that of a loving father and paternal helper.

*In **Esoteric Psychology, Vol. II**, by Alice Bailey, the Master DK speaks of an Avatar to come who will have the "materializing power" to found a divine powerhouse upon the physical plane. Is this the Avatar of Synthesis or Sai Baba?* (September 1992)

The Avatar of Synthesis, Who overshadows Maitreya from the mental plane, the lowest plane to which this Avatar can come.

*In **The Destiny of the Nations** by Alice Bailey, p140, it is stated: "In the second decanate of Aquarius the Hierarchy can ... bring into physical manifestation the coming Avatar. This becomes possible when the work of the first decanate is accomplished, and when Shamballa has released and definitely reoriented the energies of ... Humanity."*

Given that a decanate represents one third of the Aquarian Age, has the coming of Maitreya been brought forward? If so, has this been made possible by humanity's response, so far, to the energies of the Christ? (September 1990)

Maitreya is not the Avatar referred to in this passage. This refers to the Avatar of Synthesis Who, at present, can come down no lower than the mental plane, Who stands behind Maitreya, and Who overshadows and works through Him. It is expected that, due to the transforming work of the 1st ray, the Shamballa Force — to which the Avatar is closely related, but embodying also the 2nd ray, love, and 3rd, intelligence, aspects, together with an aspect for which we have as yet no name — it will be possible for this extraordinarily potent Avatar to take *physical* incarnation in the second decanate of Aquarius. This, of course, will enormously heighten the potency of Maitreya's work (as does His overshadowing today).

On what rays are the Avatars Who overshadow Maitreya? (November 1992)

One great Being Who overshadows Maitreya is called the Spirit of Peace or Equilibrium, and He is on the 2nd ray. He works through Maitreya in a manner similar to the way Maitreya worked through Jesus in Palestine. He works with the Law of Action and Reaction, which as we know are opposite and equal. The effect of this energy in the world is to transform the prevalent hatred, violence and discord into its opposite, so that we shall enter an era of tranquillity, peace and poise, in exact proportion to the manifested discord, violence and tension that we see today. The more the tension — the more the poise, the more the harmony. The Avatar of Synthesis is another Avatar Who works behind Maitreya, and He has a great rainbow of energies: 1st, 2nd, 3rd, and another aspect for which we do not even have a name. It has been suggested by the Master DK that it could be called the Principle of Directed Purpose. It is associated with the 1st ray.

Could you please say whether all descriptions of Maitreya's physical appearance are correct in all details — eg colour of eyes? I have a 'hunch' that his eyes are not dark but a golden-yellow colour which adds to the striking impression of His "most unusual countenance". (March 1987)
It is possible to say that all descriptions of His appearance could be correct since He can change His appearance at will, but in fact He does so only within narrow limits. It is true to say that His eyes are indeed 'dark'.

*It is said that the future Buddha, Maitreya, will be identified and known by the marks on His body. I think it is 32 auspicious marks. True or false — and why? (*January/February 1991)
My information is that this is simply a (long-held) superstition with no basis in fact. (Readers would be surprised to learn how many letters I receive from people claiming to be the Christ [Maitreya, Messiah, etc] precisely because of the auspicious signs and marks which they claim to have — and offer to show me!)

I have heard it reported recently that the person the Christ is said to inhabit has denied he is the Christ. Is this correct, and if so, why did he so deny it? (June 1989)
There is such a number of issues raised by this question that a simple answer is difficult to give. For example, the questions which arise in my mind are: Reported by whom? Which person is the Christ said (and by whom) to inhabit?

It may well be that "someone" said by "someone" else to be the Christ has indeed denied it, for the good and simple reason that he knows he is not the Christ. In my experience, the Christ is not "inhabiting" anyone, but is here in His full physical presence as Himself. He has not denied that he is the Christ.

What age did Maitreya give in order to acquire His passport (to come to Britain)? (October 1990)
Age 33.

You have mentioned Maitreya's ashram near Mysore. What is He known as in India? (June 1991)
Maitreya; sometimes as Swami or Swamiji, although He is not actually a Swami.

What is Lord Maitreya's native language? (May 1987)
Telepathy.

Does the Lord Maitreya have a family? (May 1987)
No. The whole human kingdom are His brothers and sisters. He is the Eldest Brother of humanity.

Where did Maitreya come from — what is His origin? Is He from Venus or a different solar system or from Sirius? (September 1989)
No. Maitreya comes out of our own Earth humanity and is the first of that humanity to 'achieve', that is, become initiate.

You have said that Maitreya has been the World Teacher for 2,600 years. Does this coincide with Gautama Buddha? (June 1991)
Yes. The Buddha, through the Prince Gautama, was the previous World Teacher.

Where was Maitreya when Gautama Buddha was in the world? (July/August 1989)
In His centre in the Himalaya.

Are Buddha, Krishna, Jesus the same Spirit recurring at different times? (September 1989)
No. The Buddha and Maitreya are two distinct and separate Individualities. The Buddha manifested through the Prince Gautama, while Maitreya came as Krishna and also through Jesus (for the last three years of Jesus' life). This time, Maitreya has come Himself.

Was Krishna an incarnation of Maitreya or did Maitreya work through a disciple? (December 1986)

He overshadowed a disciple.

(1) Can you say how long Krishna was in his physical body?
(2) Esoterically, what was the main purpose of His incarnation as Krishna? (September 1987)
(1) Fifty-seven years. (2) To act as a vehicle for the Lord Maitreya as Avatar for the age of Aries.

Besides Krishna and Jesus are there any other manifestations or major overshadowings by Maitreya known to us in history? (December 1986)
He also manifested Himself as Shankaracharya.

Why is the Christ called Maitreya and not Jesus? (December 1986)
Because the One Who embodies the Christ Principle and is World Teacher for this age has the personal name of Maitreya. He used the body of Jesus in Palestine, but is a separate Entity.

When Christ appeared before, He was persecuted and killed. His teachings were not disseminated correctly. What will be the case with Maitreya? (June 1990)
This time Maitreya is manifesting as Himself, not through a disciple (Jesus), and He inhabits a body (self-created) which is indestructible. He could be persecuted (but I doubt that) but He cannot be killed. How do you kill someone who can appear and disappear at will, and who can manufacture a new body at will?

Up till now, every Teacher has needed priests to interpret (or misinterpret) His teaching. This time Maitreya will speak directly through radio and television to all the world. No distortion of the teachings will be possible.

How can you say the Christ never made a mistake and still say He is human like us? As a teacher I know it is not possible to learn without making mistakes. (September 1988)
He never made any major mistakes and advanced faster than any other soul. He had the good fortune to have as a teacher, however, the Mother of the World.

Masters and Avatars

Are the Masters living in the world immortal or born again? (May 1987)
Immortal. They are 'resurrected', in the esoteric meaning of that word. They are perfected through the evolutionary process and know no death. There is nothing in Them which responds to the 'pull' of matter.

Is it true that the Masters live ten times longer than we do and don't need to eat or sleep? (May 1987)
Yes. The Masters, being perfected, create no personal karma and are free from disease. They 'feed' directly from prana from the sun.

Do you have to be a male to become a Master? (June 1987)
No. Everyone has been male and female many times and everyone, eventually, will be perfect Masters. At the moment, Masters are incarnating only in male bodies and will continue to do so for the next 350–400 years. This is to do with the energetic relationship between the polarities, spirit and matter, and the need for a powerful male, or spirit, aspect to balance the present ratio between the two. Masters will then increasingly take female bodies.

Why do the Masters seem to operate only in the rich countries and not in the Third World? (November 1990)
This is not, in fact, the case. The Masters direct Their energies and attention at least as much to the Third World as to the developed world. However, the changes which must take place in the world have to be initiated from the seat of the problem: the greed, selfishness and complacency of the developed nations. Therefore, much of the Masters' work involves inspiring disciples in the richer countries who can work for change.

It seems that Hierarchy is only interested in contact with higher initiates and never approaches common people. Is that true? (November 1988)

No, not really. For instance, the Labour movement was originated by the English Master in the 19th century among a group of workers who where not so very evolved. In fact, if they had been really advanced initiates, they would have had no real contact with the workers around them. That is why the idea of the Labour movement spread out rapidly throughout the world. Hierarchy always acts as a hierarchy. Some people do not like to think that there are lesser ones and higher ones; to them, that is not fair, not true equality. Of course, as Gods we are all equal. But no amount of pretending, no amount of thinking, no amount of will power, will make you a Master if you are only a first- or second-degree initiate.

Will the Masters be equally spread out around the world? At present it would seem that India has the monopoly. (July/August 1991)
India has had the monopoly of the Masters Who have worked more openly (though they have not all been Masters). A Master means an initiate of the fifth degree, Who does not actually have to be in the world any more, Who is perfected, God-realized. There are many gurus and teachers, in India and elsewhere, who are nowhere near that stage. Mahatma Gandhi, who was revered as a great Master — a Mahatma, which means a great soul — was only a second-degree initiate.

Eventually, apart from the 14 already in incarnation, there will be a Master, or high initiate, in most countries.

(1) Will there be a long time between the Day of Declaration and the presentation by Maitreya of the Masters? (2) Will They teach openly to the public and will people be able to learn from Them (for example, new forms of healing)? (December 1989)
(1) No. Maitreya will probably introduce the idea of the Masters as His Disciples during the overshadowing on the Day of Declaration. I expect the introduction of at least some of the Masters (for example, the Master Jesus) to take place soon afterwards. (2) In the first place, the Masters will teach through the agency of disciples now in the world. Eventually, They will

work more directly with the public and some few will take Their places in public affairs as advisers and guides.

I understand that Saul (Paul) of Tarsus is now the Master Hilarion. When did He become a Master and is He one of Those who will be working with Maitreya in physical form? (May 1987)

St Paul, then a third-degree initiate, took the fifth initiation, and so became a Master, in the 4th century. He will be one of the first group of Masters to work openly on the physical plane.

*In your book **Maitreya's Mission, Volume One** you say that a Master will take up a position near Paris. Has He done so yet? What is His name and line of work?* (May 1988)

No, He has not yet taken His place near Paris. He will be a Master connected with the scientific field.

In what field of endeavour is the English Master? (April 1989)

The English Master is a 3rd-ray Master. The 3rd ray is the ray of Active Intelligence or adaptability. Therefore, this Master deals with practical aspects of the form, or life as it expresses itself through form, through economics and politics. He is adviser and source of inspiration to high-level economists in the world. He works with groups here in Britain, in particular in the political and economic fields.

Is the Master in New York a 3rd-ray Master? (September 1991)

No.

*In the Alice Bailey books there is little to be found about the Master Serapis. In **Maitreya's Mission**, **Volume One**, it is said that He is in incarnation and works mainly with the deva or angelic evolution, and is aided in His work by the Master Who was Mozart. Could you please give some further information about Him, His previous life on Earth, His ray structure etc?* (September 1989)

According to the Master DK (*Initiation Human and Solar,* by Alice Bailey), the Master Serapis is "the Master upon the fourth ray, and the great art movements of the world, the evolution of music, and that of painting and drama, receive from Him an energizing impulse. At present He is giving most of His time and attention to the work of the deva, or angel, evolution, until their agency helps to make possible the great revelation in the world of music and painting which lies immediately ahead. More about Him cannot be given out, nor can His dwelling place be revealed."

Another Master on the 4th ray Who works exclusively with the deva evolution was the great Flemish painter, Peter Paul Rubens.

Does your Master have a name? (March 1989)
Of course, all the Masters have names, but I am afraid I may not give it out. I have been asked not to for very definite and clear reasons. One major reason is that if I were to make public His name, I would necessarily have to give it to the groups with which I work. He is a well-known Master and people would have His name at the front of their consciousness all the time. This would draw His attention telepathically to them. Of course, He could set up a barrier but that would take energy, so either way it would be a misuse of His time and energy. The Masters are great powerhouses of energy but They never waste even a fraction of that energy.

Since there were Masters watching over early animal man (and woman) in the early days, where did They come from? (June 1992)
Some came from Mars, a few from Mercury, Uranus and Vulcan, but by far the greatest number came from Venus. All the planets of our system have their own Spiritual Hierarchy and all are populated; it is a mistake to think that they are dead or uninhabitable. In fact, there are more people on Mars than on this Earth. Of course, if you went there you would see no one. They exist in etheric, not dense, physical matter.

Where is the point of origin of the Spiritual Hierarchy of this planet? (June 1992)

The Spiritual Hierarchy of this planet is a branch of the Great White Brotherhood on Sirius. The relationship between Sirius and this solar system is the same as that between our Soul and the man or woman in incarnation: we, as individuals, are reflections of our souls; this solar system is a reflection of Sirius. The laws governing our lives are generated on Sirius. Sirius itself is the lowest point of a cosmic triangle: the seven stars of the Great Bear; the seven sisters of the Pleiades; Sirius.

Is it true that: (a) all Masters are connected with the one source, God, who lets his light stream through all the hierarchic levels? (b) there are very, very high beings, very near to God, which have once turned away from God, because they wanted to be God? They now are no longer in the stream of God's love because they turned away but want to have it? (July/August 1989)
(a) Yes. (b) No.

What is the difference between a seventh-degree Master, an angel of the highest state of evolution (an archangel), and an avatar, regarding their state of consciousness and their relationship to God? (March 1988)
An extraordinary question! Of what practical value is it to know and how could I possibly describe the different states of consciousness of seventh-degree Masters (Planetary Lives), Archangels and Avatars? Suffice it to say that seventh-degree Masters (like Maitreya) have Logoic Consciousness and two levels of Cosmic Consciousness; Archangels have the equivalent consciousness states of seventh or eighth-degree Masters (therefore of two or three levels of Cosmic Consciousness); Avatars may have the consciousness of initiates of the sixth, seventh, eighth or even ninth degree, the highest in our solar system.

What is the role of Avatars? (December 1986)
If evolved enough, Avatars embody a divine energy or principle, but this is not always the case. There are many levels of Avatar, even human Avatars like Shakespeare and Leonardo da Vinci. The important thing is that the Avatars always come

70

from 'above', that is, a higher planet or system, to answer a need on Earth. Shakespeare came originally from Jupiter, and Leonardo originally from Mercury.

*Alice A.Bailey talks about the coming of an Avatar from Sirius (**A Treatise on White Magic**, p313). (1) Is he actually on the Earth? (2) Are there books of his teaching?* (September 1991)
(1) No. The Avatar in question was John the Baptist and He will come 500 years from now. (2) Needless to say there are no books of His teaching.

What can you say about a 'collective Messiah' or 'group Avatar' in the New Age? (December 1990)
This is a popular idea with many new-age groups, and, in so far as individuals and groups of individuals manifest in their lives the Christ Principle or Consciousness, it will come to reality. The New Age structures must indeed be set in place by humanity itself.

However, the energy to which we give the name Christ Principle is embodied by a great Master: Maitreya, the World Teacher, Who comes as the Avatar for the Aquarian Age. His inspiration, stimulus and guidance make possible the creation of a civilization in which humanity itself manifests the Christ.

Master Jesus

You say that the Master Jesus is now living in Rome. (1) Is He incarnated through birth? (2) If yes, how old is He in His present form? (3) Did He have full knowledge of His identity and mission from the moment of birth? (4) What education has He? (5) Is He a priest? (December 1990/March 1991)
(1) Yes. (2) He is in a Syrian body which is 563 years old. (3) Not quite from birth but from age nine years. (4) He is a Master of Wisdom and a 6th-degree initiate. (5) No. He lives at present (for the last 3-and-a-half years) on the outskirts of Rome.

You said that the Master Jesus has been in the same physical body for 563 years. Is this a long time for a Master to be incarnate? (June 1991)

It is middling to short. Some of the Masters are some 100, 150, 200 years old, but there are Masters Who are literally thousands of years old. Their bodies are ageless, timeless; they never change.

Has the Master Jesus (Who, you say, is now in Rome) ever visited England and the Christian Churches here? (September 1989)
Yes. He travels about the world a great deal and always has done. He is one of the most important Masters for the West. He has a group of three Masters working under Him in South America besides four others in North America and Canada.

At your last lecture in Los Angeles, you mentioned something about previous incarnations of the Master Jesus in America among Native Americans. Please give more information about this fact. (November 1988)
Jesus taught the native American 'Indians' in the sixth and seventh centuries, predicting the coming of a great teacher from the East. Various forms of the name 'Jesus' were known, at least until recently, in the oral tradition of the various tribes, North and South. He later went to Polynesia and taught the people of these islands. The only group I have encountered who know these facts are the Mormons.

Which Master works through the Religious Society of Friends (Quakers)? (March 1991)
The Master Jesus.

We know that several of Jesus' (the Christ's) twelve disciples in Palestine have since become Masters of the Wisdom. John is now known to us as Koot Hoomi, and Peter, I believe, is the Master Morya. What about the other Apostles? Have they also a role to play in the near future? (March 1987)
All the disciples around Jesus have become Masters. Not all remain with us on Earth. Besides Peter and John, the disciples Matthew, Mark and Luke are still in our Hierarchy and have important roles to play in the coming time. The Apostle Paul, now the Master Hilarion, is in the first group to emerge.

I have a well known photograph said to be of the Master Jesus, which you may already know about. I have heard three explanations of how it came to be. Which of these is true?

(1) Years ago a NASA research team was making photographs of the Shroud of Turin and after development of the film, one of the photographs showed Jesus with remarkable open eyes, as you can see. Or:

(2) Sathya Sai Baba produced this open-eyed face of Jesus by magical means. Or:

(3) The photograph with open eyes is a constructed projection on the basis of computer calculations and three-dimensional computer-processed pictures. (December 1987)

I am sorry to disappoint the magical fraternity but the correct answer is (3), the computer projection.

Shamballa

Is Shamballa a place where the Masters who are not incarnated live? Or is it a place near Earth where Masters who are physically among us live? (July/August 1991)

Shamballa is a centre (the highest on the planet) in etheric matter, situated in the Gobi desert. Only very advanced Beings dwell in Shamballa, the most advanced being the Lord of the World, Sanat Kumara Himself.

I am a little confused about the relationship, if there is one, between Tara, who is described as our Mother Earth, and Sanat Kumara, who is supposed to be the Being who ensouls this planet. (1) Are they connected and, if not, how do they differ? (2) Also, did Sanat Kumara come from another planet or solar system before becoming the — what shall I call Him? — the Regent, the Creative Director of this planet? (December 1989)

(1) The Tara is not "Mother Earth" but the Mother of the World, the Female Principle of creation. Sanat Kumara, the Lord of the World — the Ancient of Days of the Bible — does not ensoul this planet but is, indeed, the reflection of the Heavenly Man, the cosmic Being Who does. That Heavenly Man embodies both the Father and Mother Principles which,

coming together, create all manifestation on this planet. (2) Sanat Kumara, Who dwells in etheric matter on Shamballa, came from the planet Venus (Earth's Alter Ego) eighteen-and-a-half million years ago. His relation to the Planetary Logos is similar to the relation of our personality to our soul; He reflects It, in time and space.

What is the role of the Buddha in our planetary Hierarchy? What is His relationship to Maitreya? (September 1990)
The Buddha no longer retains a physical vehicle but dwells on the highest centre of our planet, Shamballa, which is in matter of the two highest ethers in the Gobi desert. He acts as the 'Divine Intermediary' between Shamballa and Hierarchy, bringing the Plan from Shamballa to the three Great Lords of Hierarchy (the Christ, the Manu, and the Lord of Civilization) Who approximate the Plan to the possible and work it out through humanity. He is the brother of Maitreya. They were among the first group of Earth humanity to 'achieve', that is, take initiation, way back in early Atlantean times. They have been at the forefront of humanity ever since. The Buddha is deeply engaged in the process of Maitreya's mission as World Teacher.

Is the tooth relic of the Buddha that they so guard and worship in Sri Lanka (in Dalada Maligawa in Kandy) real? I mean, is it really Buddha's tooth? (September 1989)
Yes, it is an authentic tooth of Gautama, through Whom the Buddha manifested.

Sai Baba

What is the relationship between Sai Baba and Maitreya?
Sai Baba is a teacher or guru in south India with an enormous following. Hundreds of thousands, perhaps 1 or 2 million people from all over the world would claim to be His devotees. These followers see Him as God, the creator of the universe. He is a cosmic Avatar. Sai Baba and Maitreya both embody the same energy — what we call the Christ Principle, the

energy of love — Sai Baba at the cosmic level, Maitreya at the planetary level.

Maitreya comes from our Earth evolution. He is not from outside this planet. He is the Alpha and Omega, the first and the last — the first of early humanity back in Atlantean days to 'achieve', become divine. You become divine when you have taken the third initiation. In those days, that was the highest initiation that an Earth man could take. Today, it is only the third of five initiatory experiences which make you a Master, a God-Man. Maitreya was one of a small group who took the third initiation at that time. Another was the Buddha. Maitreya is the last of that group to remain with humanity. Others have gone on, outside this planet or solar system. Some have gone to the higher centre, Shamballa, as the Buddha has done, having given up a physical body to be on Shamballa. Maitreya, on the other hand, has remained with us, in the Himalaya, during all that time. That is what is meant in the Bible by the Alpha and Omega.

Sai Baba is a visitor. He is a Spiritual Regent. Since our Planetary Logos cannot take dense-physical manifestation, He calls in, from time to time, numbers of Avatars or 'regents' to stand in for Him. Just as in the outer world, if a king dies and has a son too young to become king immediately, a regent is chosen, usually an uncle or cousin, to take over the throne until the boy grows up.

Avatars bring in cosmic energy. They 'come from above' down into this world in response to human need. They stand in for God or the Logos of this planet. Such an Avatar is Sathya Sai Baba. There are always several Avatars at any given time. Ramakrishna and Ramana Maharshi were Avatars. The line from Babaji down to Yogananda was a line of Avatars. Some Avatars are completely unknown; They give no teachings, no one has ever heard of Them, but Their presence here sustains the world. Without that presence, this would be a much sorrier world than it is.

After His triple incarnations as Shirdi, Sathya and Prema Sai, will Sai Baba incarnate again in future? (September 1987)

75

This is still unknown, even to Sai Baba.

Why doesn't Sai Baba speak out about the Christ to His many followers, or even instruct them to use the Great Invocation, which is supposed to be such a powerful and needed tool for transformation? (January/February 1989)

One reason He does not speak out about Maitreya, the Christ, being in the world is that His followers take as 'gospel truth' everything He says. If He said: "The Christ is indeed in the world. He is in London, as Mr Creme is saying," hundreds of thousands of devotees all over the world would believe Him, and in so doing He would have infringed their free will, their right of spiritual recognition.

Why do you think someone like me is asked to do this work? Why not the Pope? Why not the Queen of England? Why not Sai Baba? Because they have an authority which would contravene your divine right of free will. I have no particular authority, I am a private individual; you can believe me or not and are left free to make up your own mind. But if I were Sai Baba, the Pope, or the Queen of England, you would believe it because of their authority.

Sai Baba has a very special relationship to Maitreya. Sai Baba would call Himself, does call Himself, the Lord, because He has God-realization. Anybody Who has God-realization, whether He is a Master, a Christ, or Sai Baba, senses Himself as the Lord, because there is no separation. He is the Lord. He is not the only manifestation of the Lord, but He is a manifestation of the Lord, and experiences Himself as the Lord.

When we attain God-realization, we too will sense ourselves as the Lord, because there is nothing else. There is only God. We either sense or experience ourselves as God and, therefore, are God, completely at-one with the divine aspect of ourselves, or that experience is limited. If it is limited in some way, we have a sense of at least partial separation. That is what most people experience.

Sai Baba and Maitreya experience very clearly that They are the Lord, but when They do something, They know that

They do not do it. They know that it is the Lord, the Divine Principle, Who does it. When Sai Baba creates some form, an earring, a bangle or a ring out of the air, He is not doing it. It is the Lord Who is doing it, because there is only the Lord. The physical brain of Sai Baba initiates the process. "You want a ring, you want a talisman, you want something that I can give you that will make you want what I really have to give you?" So He brings forth these things which allow people to see Him as a creative manifestation of divinity.

*An article on Sai Baba (**Sunday Correspondent,** [UK] 10 December 1989) seemed to emphasize the 'tricks', such as materializing vibhuti, rings or trinkets as gifts for people. The media impression portrayed seemed to be of a Sai Baba circus. What is the real purpose of such gifts? Isn't there a risk that people's belief will be dependent on seeing such incredible 'tricks'? Why is this 'proof' necessary?* (April 1990)

I think the first thing to realize is that Sai Baba does not perform the materializing 'tricks' in order to provide 'proof' of anything at all. He is not concerned with proof but with creating interest. He has said that He creates and gives people these trinkets (which they want and value) so that they will want what He wants to give them, namely, a sense of God, of their own divinity, not His.

He is not seeking to invoke people's belief but awareness of divinity, so there is no risk of dependency on seeing the materializations. That this may not be universally the case is not His fault but that of the people concerned.

Very often Sai Baba says in his books that He is the Creator of the universe, while you say this is not the case. How is that possible? (July/August 1988)

There are many books written about Sai Baba and no doubt in some of them claims are made that Sai Baba is the creator of the universe. This is the typical exaggeration of the (fanatical) devotee. Many of the devotees of Maharishi Mahesh Yogi, for instance, believe that he is the Creator of the universe. He himself, of course, has never made such a ridiculous claim, nor has Sai Baba in, or out of, books, except in the sense of complete identification with the Lord. In that sense, as the Self, each of us can make the same claim.

(1) You stated that the Prayer for the New Age given by Maitreya is an affirmation — "by affirming that I am the Creator of the Universe I can come into consciousness that I am God, the true reality." You also denied the claim that Sai Baba is the creator of the universe. I find a major contradiction here, because Mr Creme recognizes that Sai Baba has realized the divinity and experiences himself as God. If so, it is not so strange for him to claim that he is the creator of the universe. If you deny that, a person cannot affirm that he is the creator of the universe, even if he entered into the consciousness that he is God, the true reality. Then it seems to me that the idea behind this world prayer is not logical. (2) Is it not better for us to use the world prayer motivated by the idea that Sai Baba created the universe with one word of OM. And ultimately we enter into the god consciousness and experience and affirm that each one of us is the creator of the universe? (March 1990)

(1) In using the Prayer for the New Age given by Maitreya, the purpose is to shift identification from the vehicles (mind, spirit, body) to the Self in order to experience oneself as the Self, as God. It is not in order to be able to claim to be "the creator of the universe". Of course, as a God-realized Being, Sai Baba no doubt can experience Himself as "the creator of the universe" but I am sure He does not claim that for Himself. When I said Sai Baba was not the creator of the universe (except in the sense that as the Self we all are), it was in answer to a question about His status. People are obsessed with status, in knowing that their guru is more advanced than another's and, if so, by implication, that they themselves are more advanced. My answer was meant to de-glamourize the devotee, not to downgrade Sai Baba. He needs neither my support nor detraction. (2) To my mind, it is better to use the prayer without motive at all. Why bring Sai Baba or anyone else into it? He, as a personality, did not create the universe with one (or more) word of OM. The Creator created the universe. That as

the Self, Sai Baba, you, me and everyone else is identical with that Creator is not in question.

You have said that Maitreya is overshadowed by the Spirit of Peace and Equilibrium. I have also been told that Sai Baba is the Spirit of Peace and Equilibrium, and therefore it is He who overshadows Maitreya. Is this true? (May 1989)
Some of His devotees (in the way of devotees) would have Sai Baba answer to the name of every entity, cosmic and planetary, mentioned in the esoteric literature. My information is that Sai Baba is not the Spirit of Peace, nor does He overshadow Maitreya.

(1) I think that Maitreya is more important to our planet than Sai Baba. Is that correct? (2) Why is it that people believe more easily in Sai Baba than Maitreya? (November 1989)
(1) With respect, I do not agree. No one at our level can assess the relative importance to the planet of two such spiritual giants. That They are both here means that both are needed. We should be grateful for that fact. (2) Because they can see Him. When they see Maitreya they will "believe in" Him also.

Does Sri Sathya Sai Baba have lots and lots of helpers on the astral plane, appearing to be Sai Baba Himself? So many people seem to have such an easy contact with Him, like in visions and dreams, or they hear His voice, while (according to the Alice Bailey teachings) it is not that easy to contact even a Master. How to explain this phenomenon? (May 1988)
As is true of the Masters Themselves, there are, not helpers, but thoughtforms of Sai Baba placed on the astral planes by the astral inspirations of thousands of devotees. There are real communicative experiences between Sai Baba and a relatively small number of His devotees but the vast majority of the cases you mention are self-induced, astral and spurious.

Is it true that Sai Baba: (a) is an Asura, a being on the level of the Hierarchy of the Archai, the beings above the angels and the archangels (in R. Steiner's terminology), who has turned away from the Hierarchy, from God, because he himself wanted to be God, the First? (b) came on Earth because he

*wants from mankind what he himself does no longer have:
love? (c) radiates the love that all people concentrate on him,
on his form, give to him, and that he therefore says: "I don't
need your money, I only want your love"? There are other
statements from him declaring himself as the creator of the
universe, the one being permeating all and everything, and he
also said: "You all are like marionettes in the hands of God,"
which leaves no place for man's free will. (d) as a being of
such a high rank, has an infinite capacity to deceive, because
his entire teaching and acting is correct, except in a few points
where his true intention is seen? (e) because of his positive
influence in India and elsewhere, the Hierarchy offered him to
come back into its ranks and accept that there are beings
higher than him, an offer that he refused to accept? (f) the
Hierarchy now decided to speak about him to limit his
influence? (g) fallen beings of such a high rank are considered
by the Hierarchy as being ill on a very high level and need our
love and not hatred to be liberated?* (September 1989)
(a) No. (b) No. (c) No. (d) No. (e) No. (f) No. (g) No.

I do not know who wrote this nonsense but with Sai Baba
no one seems able to be neutral, impersonal. To His devotees,
He is the embodiment of everything and everyone. To His still
more ignorant detractors, He is seen in terms like the above or
as a charlatan and trickster out for personal gain. One day, the
great and simple truth about Sai Baba will be known, and those
who now denigrate Him will find themselves covered in
shame. The love He radiates is no reflection of ours, but, on
the contrary, streams from the heart of God Itself. Without it
this world would be immeasurably the poorer.

*Occasionally there are reports from people who have visited
the ashram of Sai Baba saying that Sai Baba is frequently
involved in sexual activities with devotees (mostly male). The
Dutch press has also carried stories on this subject recently.
The comment of Benjamin Creme's Master would be greatly
appreciated.*
It goes without saying that a Being of the stature of Sai Baba
could never be involved in such practices. He is unbelievably

advanced and there is nothing in Him which could respond to the pull of such activities. Hearsay and gossip abound in the gathering of the great numbers who are drawn to His ashram. This is inevitable. Most are enriched by the experience of His presence but there are those whose hearts are closed and whose response is one of envy and spite. It is the trees with the richest offering of fruit which attract the stones.

Other Avatars

Who is Babaji and what is His relation to the Christ? (May 1989)
Babaji, written about by Paramahansa Yogananda in his book, *Autobiography of a Yogi*, is a cosmic Avatar. He dwells in the Himalaya, is teacher to a group of disciples (fourth- to seventh-degree initiates only), and has been on this planet for many thousands of years. He is said to have vowed to remain here till the end of this world cycle (hundreds of thousands of years to come). He has no special relation to the Christ; His relation is rather to Sanat Kumara, the Lord of the World.

If Babaji's disciples are fourth- to seventh-degree initiates only, as you state, presumably most of them are Masters and, not being disciples of Maitreya, must be outside the number of 64 Masters you claim now dwell on the Earth. So doesn't that suggest there could in fact be any number of 'Masters' on this planet, belonging to various different hierarchies? (April 1990)
There are 63 (not 64) Masters (including the three Great Lords, the Manu, the Christ and the Mahachohan) connected with the human evolution. There are indeed a great many more Masters Who work with the sub-human or Deva evolutions. The group around Babaji (Who are also disciples of Maitreya) is made up of Masters from all departments of the Hierarchy. It is quite a small group in any case.

(1) Is Babaji still in the Himalaya? (2) Does he ever emerge from there? (3) As Yogananda left his body at quite a young age, comparatively, could it be possible that this was so that he

81

could reincarnate now at this time of Maitreya's Reappearance? (October 1989)
(1) Yes. (2) No. (3) No.

Is Lord Maitreya the same Being referred to as Babaji by Yogananda? (November 1987)
No, they are separate Individualities. Babaji is a Cosmic Avatar and Maitreya a Planetary Avatar.

I have a friend who is a 'follower' of a man who claims to be the reincarnation of Lahiri Mahasaya, who, I am sure you know, was a direct disciple of Babaji. He seems to have many followers in the New York area and especially in Argentina. Is it possible he could really be what he claims? (September 1992)
Those familiar with Swami Yogananda's *Autobiography of a Yogi* will know Lahiri Mahasaya as the disciple of the divine Babaji and the guru of Yukteswar, the guru of Yogananda, all Avatars. According to my information, the only one of that line of Avatars now in incarnation is Babaji Himself Who has pledged to remain till the end of this Earth cycle.

Which position does Maharishi Mahesh Yogi hold in the Hierarchy of the Masters? (May 1987)
He is a disciple of a 6th-ray Master of the 6th degree, known as Guru Dev, Who is not in incarnation.

Is Swami Brahmananda Saraswati (Guru Dev) now on Sirius and connected through Maharishi Mahesh Yogi to planet Earth? (September 1987)
No. Guru Dev still works on the inner (higher) planes of this Earth.

I would like to know the rays of the Buddhas of Activity, the rays with which they work. (September 1991)
Buddha Vairocana: 1st ray; Buddha Ahsohya: 6th ray; Buddha Ratnasambhara: 7th ray; Buddha Amitabha: 2nd ray; Buddha Amoghasiddhi: 5th ray.

Maitreya, the World Teacher, as He appeared miraculously 'out of the blue' at a prayer meeting of 6,000 people in Nairobi, Kenya on 11 June 1988.

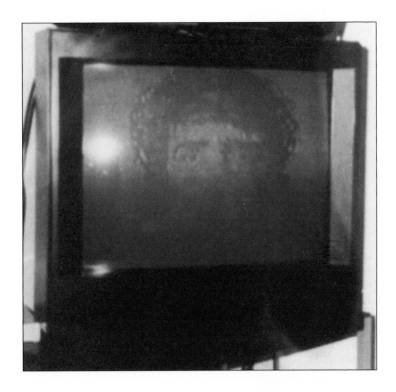

Image of Christ with a crown of thorns materializes on a photograph of a blank television screen after a local man drinks and is healed by waters from a well in Tlacote, Mexico. The water had been 'charged' by Maitreya prior to His appearance in Mexico City on 29 September 1991.

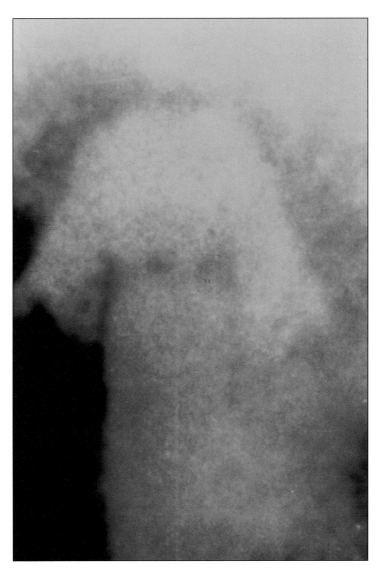

One of the many photographs of clouds, usually taken from an airplane by different people at different times, which when developed show this type of image of the Christ, superimposed on the background sky.

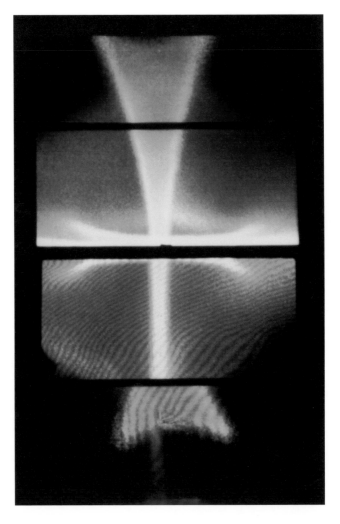

Prominent among the signs of Maitreya's presence are the radiantly beautiful 'crosses of light', which began to appear with increasing frequency during 1988 in the windows of Southern California homes. Since then, scores of crosses have been discovered throughout the world, bringing hope and healing to many who view them.

Multiple crosses of light produced on the same pane of glass.

Manila, Easter Sunday morning 1991. The hand of Christ appears in this photograph of a pane of glass which produces a 'cross of light'. The hand was not visible to any of the worshippers present at the time.

On holiday in Arizona, a New Jersey woman asked her husband to stop their car as she wished to photograph a distinctive bush covered with white flowers. Her husband did not see the flowers. When the photograph was developed, the flowers could not be seen, but in their place was the unmistakable image of the Madonna.

Maitreya with healer Mary Akatsa in Nairobi, Kenya, 1988

PART TWO

MAITREYA'S TEACHINGS

AND FORECASTS

CHAPTER 2

MAITREYA'S FORECASTS

*In April 1988, a close associate of Maitreya, long established in London's Asian community, contacted freelance journalist Patricia Pitchon. He started a series of briefings in which he presented some of Maitreya's teachings and forecasts of world events with the view that they be published through **Share International** and made available to the world's press. Later, Maitreya's associate also made contact with another journalist who received additional information. Maitreya gives His teachings orally, and His associate conveys them to the journalists. As regular readers will know, each article may cover a wide variety of topics — from a flood in Bangladesh to a lesson in Self-realization. Many of these topics recur again and again, each time adding some new information from Maitreya. For the sake of clarity, therefore, we have edited the excerpts presented here so that teachings on a particular topic are grouped and can flow together. Maitreya's purposes in releasing this material are further to prepare humanity for His emergence and to help us understand the spiritual laws governing our lives. The forecasts of world events included in many interviews are given out primarily to illuminate one of the most important of these spiritual laws: the Law of Cause and Effect. It is only by grasping and working within this law, Maitreya says, that we can resolve the present social, political, economic and environmental crises.*

Function of the Forecasts

What is the function of the predictions Maitreya is giving out? Is there not a danger of people only accepting Maitreya on the basis of their positive outcome, rather than on an understanding and acceptance of His principles? (November 1989)

No doubt some people would accept Maitreya if all the predictions worked out precisely as indicated, and, of course, would reject the idea of His presence if they do not. It is important to realize that Maitreya is not concerned with being accepted or rejected. The predictions, as I understand it, are given to show the relation, through the Law of Cause and Effect, between our thoughts and actions, and events in the phenomenal world. Our destructive thoughts and actions have destructive results.

Another function is to draw attention to His presence in the Asian community of London.

Yet another, perhaps the most important, is to help create the climate of expectancy for His emergence. Whether the predictions are believed in or not as coming from the Christ, the media representatives who receive them, more or less worldwide, are gradually made aware of the presence, in London, of a most unusual man, many of whose statements are new and challenging, and which cover very many aspects of our lives. Despite themselves, perhaps, many journalists, in different countries, are being persuaded to watch world affairs, in the light of these predictions, in a new way.

If our aim is to let the media know of Maitreya's presence in the world, is it not detrimental to send out predictions that don't happen? (June 1991)
It would be if there were so many as to be ridiculous, but that is not the case. Out of the many predictions, the vast majority of them have happened in the most uncanny way. This is acknowledged by many journalists. The journalists themselves, if they write about them, will always point to the odd prediction that has not yet happened — the release of Terry Waite is brought up all the time. But no one allows for free will.

Some of the predictions have not yet taken place, but they are a tiny minority. Nobody who reads the predictions from the beginning with an open mind, and looks at the events in relation to them, can doubt that these are the most extraordinary set of predictions which have ever been released to the world.

Perhaps the predictions should not be so dogmatically worded, to avoid disappointment, to put it mildly? (March 1991)
The point is taken. The headlines are ours and worded to engage the immediate attention of the media to whom they are sent. It is difficult always to strike a balance — media are not interested, naturally, in 'maybe', 'perhaps', 'it could be that', etc. On the other hand, readers might be surprised to know to what extent I edit and 'tone down' the statements as given by the associate, especially when specific time frames are involved.

The publication of forecasts in **Share International** *smacks of sensation. Moreover, I have understood that we, humanity, are free to decide what to do with the energies. If that is so, how could anyone predict the outcome?* (November 1989)
For the reasons mentioned, we publish the forecasts as given. If they "smack of sensation" to some people, then so be it.

It is precisely because we have free will that prediction of future events within a given time is so difficult. That does not mean that it should not be attempted. Maitreya is pointing to trends in world affairs which anyone with half an eye can see are gradually becoming manifest and bringing about great changes in the world.

Would you please refrain from giving out all these predictions and (wrong) timing? People who believe in Maitreya are not interested, while others are provided with the opportunity to attack you when you are wrong. (November 1989)
We publish these predictions because we are asked to do so. I, personally, am not responsible for making them or for guaranteeing their fulfilment within a particular time frame. With respect, I do not agree that people who "believe in Maitreya" are not interested. In my experience, most people who accept that He is here are very interested indeed in these forecasts and above all in His teachings. Curiously enough, it is not those who scoff at the idea of Maitreya's presence who

attack me. It is those who are deeply committed to that idea but cannot understand why every prediction does not work out in the exact time frame in which it was given. Their confidence and inner conviction is therefore shaken. An understanding of the complex and subtle reasons for making the predictions at all may go some way to solve their problem.

Are Maitreya's predictions concerning the release of Terry Waite, the Californian major earthquake, the US landslides and the flooding of the English Parliament by the River Thames still on? If they are, then when? In your answer to this please specify a calendar time frame instead of using the word "soon", which, when compared to eternity, could technically mean from three days to 300 years. (July/August 1989)

The Californian earthquake has taken place, as promised with minimal casualties. The danger of US landslides seems to have (at least temporarily) receded. The release of Terry Waite and the flooding of the Thames are very much still "on". Terry Waite was on the point of being released when a US warship shot down an Iranian civilian airliner. Had the US Government accepted full responsibility, apologized for the mistake and made full reparations for the loss of lives and airliner, Iran might still have used its good offices with those who are holding Mr Waite. As it was, Iranian opinion hardened against the West. This hostility has been exacerbated by the Salman Rushdie affair. Nevertheless, Terry Waite will be released, and in the meantime I can say that he has had a profound effect on his captors who are deeply impressed by his behaviour and serenity. They have learned a great deal from him. The Thames flooding, too, is just a matter of time.

The question is, what time? The questioner requests that I specify "a calendar time frame" rather than a vague "soon". I wish I could be so specific. But if even Maitreya cannot know so precisely when these events will take place how on Earth can I be expected to know?

Most people have a very distorted view of reality, time and events. They visualize the world as a static condition punctuated, at spaced intervals, by events such as those predicted by Maitreya.

Maitreya, on the other hand, sees the world as it is — an arena of different energies and forces, a dynamic, continually changing flux. By His understanding of the Law of Cause and Effect, He sees trends and movements which, He knows, will eventuate in some particular happening. Exactly when, however, depends on human action and reaction under the Law of Free Will. Exact timing "in a calendar time frame" is therefore not to be expected.

I, personally, am so grateful and pleased to have this extraordinary information and 'preview' of events from Maitreya that "soon" is good enough for me!

It was predicted by Maitreya that Nelson Mandela would be released before the end of 1988. There has been only a partial release and he is still not completely free. Was it only this partial release that was predicted or did things not happen as expected? (March 1989)

The prediction about Nelson Mandela's release was made before it was known publicly that he was ill and before his removal to hospital. From there he did not return to prison but to a house within prison grounds where his friends and family have complete access to him. As far as the South African Government is concerned, he is released, but in such a way, stage by stage, as to cause the least publicity, and therefore 'rallying point', for the black community.

Mr Creme has said time and again that there will be NO major catastrophes. Everyone expecting them was wrong, and a "prophet of doom". However, Maitreya now says: "A certain number of natural disasters such as floods, earthquakes, etc, are inevitable." Did Mr Creme not know this, or has he been trying to avoid undue fears? (October 1988)

Firstly, the natural disasters predicted now by Maitreya (and already happening) are not seen by Hierarchy as the major cataclysms prophesied so gleefully by the "prophets of doom" from whatever level. Nor were they "inevitable." Had Maitreya been invited to come forward by major media in May 1982 (or even subsequently), many of the present natural disasters would not have taken place. Largely, they are the result, under the Law of Cause and Effect, of our wrong actions. If Maitreya had been working openly in the arena of the world, inspiring change, the transformations would by now be so far-reaching that an altogether stabler climate (and therefore stabler natural climate) would now prevail.

Did I know that there would be disasters? Yes, I knew — and said — that earthquakes and the like would continue, but not the cataclysmic upheavals expected by so many. However, as the reader suggests, I have always seen it as my duty to be positive rather than frightening about the future.

(1) As some of the predictions coming through **Share International** *either appear to be inaccurate or have not happened yet (for example Thatcher's demise, flooding of Thames), is this due to the channel (His associate) through whom this information has come and not the source? (2) If so, couldn't Maitreya have foreseen this and chosen a more clear channel, free from this distortion or inaccuracy?* (November 1990)

(1) Yes, indeed, the inaccuracies in the working out of some predictions can, I think, be attributed to the associate's propensity to put Maitreya's predictions into tight time frames, which I doubt were in Maitreya's mind at all. Nevertheless, most are certainly accurate, and the factor of human free will, over which Maitreya has no control, has been very active in many cases. (I am thinking in particular of the prediction of Terry Waite's release.) (2) I have no doubt that if Maitreya could find a suitable 'channel' to distribute His predictions with total accuracy, He would. Such perfection is unbelievably rare. I doubt that there exists anywhere in the world a channel "free from distortion or inaccuracy".

Maitreya's Forecasts

A New Energy Pervades the Planet

A new energy pervades the planet now. Scientifically, this is the energy which creates equilibrium between positive and negative currents. When positive and negative currents merge, light is produced. This energizes all life and creates harmony. We will see a new equilibrium in nature, and both people and nature will respond constructively. The sun "has been brought closer to the Earth", symbolically speaking. That is, its radiation has increased, and this will energize the Earth.

The energy of equilibrium affects human affairs, as well as the world of nature. Maitreya is using the energy of equilibrium to stimulate the urge towards greater harmony between man and man and between man and nature. Prior to the achievement of this equilibrium there is an inevitable period of adjustment with its attendant difficulties. But through this process, Maitreya teaches, the world's current spiritual crisis will be resolved, and, in Maitreya's words, "this planet will come close to the Lord".

Nations around the world have been filled with this new energy, and more and more people are responding to it, becoming more aware, realizing a new livingness and becoming free. When the energy of equilibrium is brought into play, nothing is immune from the transformations which take place.

All these changes are creating awareness, and people have decided that enough is enough: they have a right to be free and to enjoy life. They no longer want to be conditioned by politics, religion or commercialization. It is the younger generation which is experiencing the effects of this new energy, and this gives them the strength to change the old systems which have imprisoned people. Today, the voice of realism is found among the young, free as they are from ideology, philosophy and theory. They are realistic about life and meet it as it comes.

The response to this energy of equilibrium will be increasingly constructive. Conflict between governments and guerrilla forces the world over will begin to decrease, and people will come to the negotiating table. Rule by force will disappear, and politicians will become the servants, not the masters, of the people. Governments will be spending more money on the welfare of the people for social programmes such as education, medicine, and recreation — rather than on destructive weapons. The role of monarchies around the world will change now, and monarchies will be, in Maitreya's words, "positively active".

These changes are not a matter of individual countries only: policies are being forged globally. Says Maitreya: "History will not be repeated."

Judicial systems around the world are undergoing rapid change; ideological struggles are beginning to decrease between East and West — and will also decrease between North and South. Government hypocrisy is being challenged everywhere, and in this 'breaking down' process things formerly hidden from the people will come to the surface.

Current political systems are losing power and credibility throughout the world, and will eventually give birth to new systems of government which will be much more representative. In the new era, the people themselves will come to the fore and be able to express all of their social, political, religious and educational needs. They will express themselves and their compassion through aid to others. Ordinary citizens, intellectuals, educators, and others from a variety of walks of life will find they have a genuine voice in government.

No politician on Earth will now be able to repeat past history. The old politics of divide and rule are finished. The divisive art of politics has come to an end, and a new one that respects harmony will soon succeed. The new politics will no longer be moulded by the 'isms' of capitalism or socialism, but created from self-respect in individuals and nations.

The new politician will be an intellectual, an experienced person who knows the laws of evolution and will wisely guide his fellow beings. The process of inculcation, of imposition, by forcing ideologies into the minds of people, is beginning to dissolve, both in religious and in political fields. Consensus will replace it. The voice of the people is already beginning to be heard, and this representative form of government will replace control of the masses through ideology. Everything is moving so fast now that events are beyond the control of the politicians. A new political era has begun. Awareness awakens people to their basic human rights, their liberties and their responsibilities to themselves and each other.

The constitution of every nation will ultimately be based on the three principles of freedom, liberty and salvation. Freedom operates on the individual level, liberty operates on the national level, and salvation operates on the spiritual level.

The reality of global interdependence will become an established fact in our awareness, and as it does so, the fact that 'all men are brothers' will be increasingly translated into structures and practical programmes of action that reflect this reality. Nations can and will experience brotherhood, common goals and common aspirations.

National governments will still be with us in the long term, but responsibility will increasingly be carried by the United Nations, which will become the most powerful political force in the world. It will be the agency through which all major international problems will be resolved. The United Nations will play a very effective role in making sure that arms and ammunition do not filter through and thereby aggravate conflicts. It will act as an observer and a watchdog. The UN is becoming a powerful centre and is no longer 'just a name'.

All of these changes are taking people by surprise. These are historic times, and as each day passes, a new awareness becomes ever more apparent. People will more and more be talking of peace, of living together in harmony. This is a turning point in the history of mankind.

CHAPTER 3

POLITICAL CHANGE

A New Form of Government

What is actually going on behind all the changes taking place?
(March 1992)
What we are witnessing is the end of totalitarianism in three
different spheres of life. Under the influence of Maitreya we
are seeing, firstly, the end of political totalitarianism as in the
Soviet Union and China. America is the foremost expression of
economic totalitarianism, based on the blind following of
market forces, that is imposing its will throughout the world;
even the Soviet Union is adopting a market-forces economy.
Maitreya calls market forces "the forces of evil". Any
government which bases its policies on the blind following of
market forces, He says, is leading its people to destruction.
That is what is happening now. We will see a breakdown of
the world's economy, beginning in Japan. The new structure
will be based on right relationships: the resources of the world
must be shared.

The last totalitarianism to go will be religious
totalitarianism. Dogmatic ideologies are imposed on the minds
of countless millions by the religious leaders. Religious
fundamentalism is at an acme of power at the moment —
whether it is Christian, Muslim, Hindu or whatever.

We are coming to the end of totalitarianism, which is the
denial of freedom. Maitreya has come that people might be
free, in the fullest sense of the word. Ultimately, we can be
totally, absolutely free only when we know the Self, when we
are the Self and demonstrate a moment-to-moment experience
of the Self — that is the true, absolute freedom.

*Does Maitreya believe in government or political systems that
man should continue with, or should we have a more spiritual
system?* (November 1992)

He believes in government, but we have to realize that what we
call 'spiritual' has a much wider connotation than we have
given it so far. Until now everything 'spiritual' has to do with
religion. The Master DK has written that the greatest triumph
for the forces of evil on this planet is that the churches, the
religious groups around the world, have been allowed to
monopolize the concept of spirituality: whatever is religious is
spiritual and everything else is non-spiritual and can be as
corrupt as we like. Therefore, we have corrupt political and
economic structures, corrupt social structures and also corrupt
religious structures (the churches are corrupt, perhaps less so
than others, but still corrupt). We have to enlarge our concept
of spirituality and see that we must have spiritually-based
political and economic structures. That means sharing and
justice — these are spiritual aspects. Maitreya says: "Sharing is
divine ... When you share you recognize God in your brother."
This is not just a nice idea, it is a divine idea. It is the nature of
divinity. Justice is divine, freedom is divine, and Maitreya
comes to show us how to make justice and freedom through
sharing. Then we will make spiritually correct political,
economic and religious structures. We need government to
organize the means of living together in peace and harmony,
but He says we should participate — we get the politicians we
deserve.

*Surely nationalism means separation? We can see this in
Yugoslavia and elsewhere.* (January/February 1992)

Yes, political nationalism means separation, but cultural
nationalism means national identity.

We, the British, have something particular to give to the
world. What we have given in the past is a form of
parliamentary government — the symbol of democracy. There
has been little true democracy, but, nevertheless, the idea of
democracy has been upheld, and also later, in the United States

97

of America, through the 2nd-ray soul-quality of both the United States and Britain.

The idea of hierarchy has been given to the world by Germany through its 4th-ray quality of soul, but it has been dominated by the 1st-ray will and power aspect of its personality. And so we have the birth of fascism or, in this case, Nazism.

Fascism is really a distorted expression of a hierarchical form of government. Democracy is the expression of another form of government, hierarchical, but based on love. Fascism is based on power, Communism on intelligence. Fascism results from the outflow of 1st-ray power from the highest centre, Shamballa — the centre where the will of God is known. Fascism, in political history, is a completely distorted expression of the energy of power or will.

The Spiritual Hierarchy indeed works as a hierarchy. The Christ, the Lord Maitreya, is the head of the Hierarchy but He does not dominate everything that happens there. The Plan is received by the Hierarchy of Masters as a whole and democratically discussed. But the final decisions are made by the three Great Lords, in particular by the Christ Himself. This is not because of His authority but because of His spiritual awareness, which confers on Him the ability to make decisions — which no one else can make — out of spiritual knowledge and understanding rather than power or authority *per se*. The true inner, spiritual basis of fascism is based on that 1st-ray, hierarchical model and, eventually, (it has been predicted by the Tibetan Master DK through Alice A.Bailey), Germany will present to the world a blueprint for such a form of government, totally unlike the recent distorted, fascist, form.

Democracy flows from the Hierarchy itself. The Hierarchy is the centre where the Love of God is expressed, and that, in political terms, is expressed through democracy, government of the people by the people. The third form, the Communist, is created by humanity itself and expresses the intelligence aspect.

What is needed is to hold on to the national, cultural identity, and take away the barriers. One day you will not need a passport to go from country to country, but who wants the Germans to look like the French? Who wants to go to France on holiday and find Britons everywhere? You want to keep the flavour of each country. We are all different; these differences should be maintained, but we should live together as brothers and sisters.

Do you know if future world governments will be composed of different political parties? (November 1991)
Maitreya has said that all political groupings will tend to the centre and that moderation and consensus will be the form for the future. The extremes are a thing of the past. That is the reality behind the reunification of Germany; Germany is the symbol for that coming together of what was communism and what was capitalism.

I cringe when President Bush does something stupid, like invading Iraq, and I know many others who do too. Couldn't you blame US politicians instead of saying the United States is doing something against the best interests of humanity? It is the politicians, not the people. (June 1992)
Who elects the politicians but the people? In a democracy, however limited, people get the government and the politicians they deserve. No politician in a democracy can act on major controversial policies without the knowledge that at least the majority of the people endorse his action.

Here in Britain, Mrs Thatcher was brought down precisely because her 'flagship', the poll tax, was so universally unpopular and seen to be unjust.

Is Maitreya 'in on' the "One World Government" of President Bush and the infamous "Tri-Lateralists"? I pray that the two are not the same. (July/August 1992)
President Bush's vision of a "New World Order" and "One World Government" envisages an order in which the US, and therefore capitalism, dominates and celebrates its triumph over a defunct communist ideology. As I understand it, this is certainly not consistent with Maitreya's predictions of a new political process (neither capitalism nor communism) in which

the voice and will of the peoples of the world are given expression; in which consensus rather than confrontation and competition will be the hallmarks; and in which a new political/economic structure — democratic socialism or social democracy, symbolized by the reunification of East and West Germany — will become the norm throughout the world.

What is the first step to take to change everything for the better? (March 1992)
The first step is the giving to the masses everywhere the idea that they count. That creates in them self-respect. Everything flows from that. At the moment, there are countless millions living lives no better than animals, who are treated worse than we treat our dogs and cats, who have nothing to eat, nothing to give their children, day after day, endlessly. That is so degrading to the human spirit that nothing, it seems, can be done. Millions more are lost in drugs, crime or deep depression. The first thing is to give them self-respect. Then they can become aware of the Self and eventually realize the Self.

East and West

Is it possible that Mikhail Gorbachev is an exceptional person who, with the support of Hierarchy, tries to establish another climate in the Soviet Union? My impression is that he is really sincere. (April 1987)
One of the many ways in which Hierarchy works is by mentally impressing the leaders of the nations. Sometimes this works and at other times it does not. Mr Gorbachev is almost alone among the world's leaders at the moment to be open to impression by Maitreya. Maitreya Himself has said that the changes in the world — the new 'openness' in Russia, the cleansing process in the West, bringing to light the corruption which underlies our so-called democracy — are the result of His actions and energies. The protagonists, Mr Gorbachev included, cannot help themselves. They are but agents of a process already under way. An interesting thing about Mr

Gorbachev is that he has impressed many Western leaders, with long-standing distrust of the Soviet Union, as one with whom they can 'do business'. Russia lost 20 million citizens in the last war, and has no appetite for an encore. The West should recognize this and — from a position of strength but not superiority — meet the Soviets halfway. Humanity awaits a response from the West to Gorbachev's approaches, and expects — and will demand — action.

Will the period of tension and crisis prior to the change continue to escalate? (May 1989)
No, we have passed the peak. The period of violence and greatest division is almost behind us now. We are witnessing the manifestation of the energy of Equilibrium through the action of a great Avatar, the Spirit of Peace or Equilibrium. He overshadows Maitreya and this energy is already having its effect. Every day, more and more governments find ways to compromise. Maitreya says that very soon, though you cannot imagine it now, even the President of South Africa will sit down at the negotiating table with Archbishop Tutu.

Do you think that the peace between the US and the Soviet Union will last? (December 1990)
Yes, I do. Both nations, at the highest level, have understood the need for peaceful solutions to world problems, and even the Generals, on both sides, are seeking more arms-limitation treaties. This is behind the new atmosphere of co-operation which has replaced Cold-War thinking, and opens up to reconciliation many hitherto intractable world divisions.

If Gorbachev goes, will the rapprochement between East and West be endangered? (June 1991)
There are forces in both America and the USSR who would try to take advantage of his going to return to the old Cold War attitudes but I believe they will not be successful. It will depend to a large extent on the quality and attitudes of whoever succeeds him.

You have said that Mr Gorbachev was overshadowed by Maitreya — was he aware of this? (January/February 1992)

101

I am afraid the question is wrongly put. I have not said Gorbachev was overshadowed by Maitreya, but that he worked under the mental impression of Maitreya, which is a very different thing. Jesus was overshadowed by Maitreya, and His consciousness worked through him.

The kind of impression which not only Mr Gorbachev but all world leaders receive (although they do not all respond to it) is of a different nature; it is on the mental plane only and is meant to inspire them to correct action.

Mr Gorbachev is the most sensitive of the world leaders to that kind of mental impress. It probably goes along with his own personal ideas for change and of world need. As a result he has opened up the Soviet Union.

Maitreya has said Mr Gorbachev has done the right thing but at the wrong time. He was pushed into 'the wrong time' by people like Mr Yeltsin on his left while he was trying to galvanize the conservatives on his right — so he was really in a cleft stick, between the conservatives on the one hand and the progressives on the other — one holding back and the other pushing forward too fast. He had to compromise on the timing — in his understanding — of how the transformation should take place.

In essence his work is done, which was to create the new relationship between East and West — the rapprochement between the Soviet Union and the United States — and to initiate glasnost, perestroika, and open up the Soviet Union to the rest of the world. That he has done.

I believe he thinks the Christ is working through him; that the visions which he has are of the Christ. Recently, he said that the changes being advocated and the break-up of the Soviet Union could not be stopped "by Jesus Christ Himself". So he is a man open to the possibility of a Christ being in the world. Just how much he is aware of his relationship to the Christ, in terms of inspiration, I could not say. You would have to ask him that. Maitreya also predicted that Gorbachev would resign, be pushed out, and that, of course, has now happened.

Is there not infringement of free will, in that he is being impressed? (January/February 1992)

No. There is never infringement of free will. That is why some leaders respond and some do not. The impression is made and then it is left to them to carry it out or not — some do, some pay no attention or do not 'hear'.

For example, Mr Bush sent two envoys, one after the other, to Maitreya in London in September 1990, at the beginning of the Gulf war crisis, asking for His advice on what to do. Maitreya said He would guarantee that Saddam Hussein would withdraw all his troops from Kuwait without firing another shot if Mr Bush were to organize a programme of aid for the economy of Iraq. Since that was too difficult a thing for President Bush to do without loss of face (as he would see it), he declined the advice. Free will was not infringed and we know the result.

Now that the USA and USSR have agreed to destroy stocks of chemical weapons, there is the problem of their safe disposal. Given that one drop the size of a pin-head can kill an adult, and given current levels of scientific knowledge, will the Hierarchy of Masters or even the Space Brothers need to assist us in this dangerous task? (September 1990)

The answer, curiously enough, is no. Every time a destructive chemical is discovered for military application, its antidote is sought for those who, using it, might be accidentally contaminated. There is sufficient knowledge already available to render harmless the vast amounts of chemicals which, it is agreed, will be destroyed.

(1) Did Maitreya play (from behind the scenes or otherwise) any role in the stunningly quick resolution of the Soviet coup attempt, and the subsequent rapid political changes taking place in the Soviet Union? (2) Will these sudden changes in the Soviet Union be for the better for the Soviet people? (October 1991)

(1) No. (2) Yes.

Middle East

Why do you still refer to Israel of the '80s as Palestine? Do you feel the Jews don't exist? (December 1986)
The Jews as a religious group obviously do exist, as does the Israeli State, but I believe that the founding of the separate State of Israel was a tragic mistake. Indeed, since its creation in 1948, the possibility of a third world war has been ever present. To the Masters of the Spiritual Hierarchy, the Middle East has been, since 1948, the 'powder keg' of such a catastrophe. The Jews, claiming an ancient but impossible right to Palestine, fought with the same terrorist techniques that they now denounce when used by Arabs. They stole the homeland of the Palestinians and there will never be peace in the world, I believe, until the Palestinian people have their homeland returned. Whether, through the counsel of the Christ, some form of power-sharing is agreed to or some other compromise reached, it is essential for world peace that the Palestinian problem be solved.

Since Middle East (and perhaps world) peace is dependent on the Palestinians having a homeland (and I will use prayer and politics to work towards that end), where should this be geographically? (January/February 1991)
The natural area for such a homeland would seem to be the West Bank of Jordan over which (at the request of Maitreya) the King of Jordan has renounced all sovereign rights, thus paving the way for the Palestinian homeland. The Gaza Strip is also, naturally, Palestinian. Together they could provide the base for a Palestinian State coexistent with Israel.

Could you suggest how to contribute to a better climate in the Middle East to end or restrict acts of war? (April 1991)
To my mind, the first task is to organize an international conference to address the many problems which exist there. Number one on the agenda, I believe, must be the Israeli-Palestinian problem. A homeland for the Palestinians can be the only just solution, otherwise no lasting peace is possible. I

believe the Israelis will procrastinate endlessly and it may well take the emergence of Maitreya to bring about reconciliation. The recent action by the PLO in siding with Iraq and Saddam Hussein in the Gulf conflict has not helped their cause, however just. It seems impossible for the PLO leadership to miss an opportunity of missing an opportunity! However, right is on their side, and now most of the interested nations involved, even the USA, at last recognize that right.

Democratic governments and consensus politics must take over from the various autocratic military dictatorships and sheikdoms which now exist. Syria, for example, has a military dictatorship of the most repressive kind, every bit as bad and as ambitious as that of Saddam Hussein. All of that is overlooked because they joined 'the club' against Iraq, a major rival. The greed and autocratic rule of the Kuwaiti and Saudi governing families is notorious. A redistribution of wealth among the people of the region must be high on the agenda. It will take a long time, perhaps years, for such a transformation to come about, but one thing can be achieved immediately: the ending — a complete embargo, I suggest — of the irresponsible supplying of sophisticated weapons of mass destruction to the region. This cynical trade — based on 'market forces' — acts only to fan the flames of war. Surely that must be obvious to everyone now.

Gulf War

Following are Benjamin Creme's Master's comments on the Middle East crisis, dictated to Creme upon request.

Once again, the Middle East has become the focus of international concern and anxiety. This time, however, the situation, although serious, is not fraught with the same threat to world peace as has up till now been the case. The new, co-operative, relationship being forged between the USA and the USSR changes entirely the likelihood of Great Power confrontation, and makes easier a peaceful solution to the problem of Iraqi aggression.

None of the Arab nations at this time relish war, above all against a fellow Arab nation. Nevertheless, they know that Saddam Hussein cannot be allowed simply to march unopposed against his neighbours and erstwhile friends and supporters. No one would feel safe for the future were he allowed to continue unchecked. Saddam Hussein himself is caught up in a major glamour of personal power and aggrandizement. His ruthless ambition is known and feared by most of his neighbours who nevertheless admire his readiness to speak and act for Arabs in what they see as a hostile world.

However, his tenure of office and power is limited. His own people, weary of war, and longing for freedom, will rise against and depose him.

In the short term, he can and may be very destructive, but in the not too distant future his wings will be clipped and his downfall and oblivion be assured. As Maitreya has said in relation to Saddam Hussein: "Who rules by force will be removed by force."

The Master —

Why did Maitreya (through His associate) not predict the present Gulf crisis? (October 1990)
Perhaps He did not foresee it. Perhaps it took even Him by surprise as it did the rest of the world.

Nevertheless, in our Press Release No 21, dated 3 May 1990 (and in *Share International*, June 1990), at a time when Saddam Hussein was not engaging public attention, Maitreya is quoted as saying that it was time for Saddam Hussein to step down and that if he did not do so voluntarily "someone else will make sure that he does. It is inevitable. Anyone who rules by force will be removed by force". This points clearly to Maitreya's knowledge of the fragility of President Hussein's position in Iraq, which fragility, I believe, is behind his invasion of Kuwait. This is an attempt to re-establish himself at home and strengthen his position as leader of the Arab world.

The invasion gives one the impression of having been planned very quickly — improvised from day to day, almost — with little thought to the consequences or the reaction of world opinion — in short, the sudden action of a desperate and unbalanced man looking for a way out. His actions since the invasion — especially in relation to the taking of hostages — bears this out. I believe he thought he could annex Kuwait without too much outside response, aid the Iraqi economy in the process, and establish himself as a national hero. Had he limited his aggression to taking over Kuwait without sending his troops in large numbers to the borders of Saudi Arabia, thus bringing in the US to preserve its oil resources, I believe he would have succeeded without invoking the present international reaction.

Will the present Middle East crisis lead to a world war that will destroy us all? The media seem to suggest that it might. I have heard many people talking as if this is Armageddon, and I am very afraid. (October 1990)
It is important to see this new Middle East crisis in perspective. It will not lead to world war or war between East and West as some say. The new relationship between the US and the USSR is the guarantee of this. Nor, even if that new relationship were not present, would this crisis necessarily threaten world peace.

It is precipitated by the acts of one desperate man with few friends among those who count in world affairs. It will be resolved when he goes, whether that is before or after a short, last destructive gesture or not. "Armageddon" has already taken place: the wars (really one war) from 1914–1918 and from 1939–1945 were the scene for the biblical prophecy to be worked out. It is this which led to the announcement by Maitreya, in June 1945, that He was ready to return at the earliest possible moment, which was 19 July 1977.

Interestingly, this crisis, as the latest information from Maitreya's associate suggests, may well open up an entirely new atmosphere for peaceful solutions to the several Middle East problems, not least to the seemingly intractable problem of Israeli-Palestinian relations. Until now, the intransigence and uncompromising attitude of the Israelis have blocked the way to peace. Now that they are exposed to the possibility (or reality) of missile bombardment from Iraq and witness the sense of confidence which (despite the threat to themselves) Saddam Hussein's words inspire in many ordinary Arabs, the Israelis may be forced to meet the legitimate demands of the Palestinian Arabs for their homeland. International pressure (especially from the US) to lessen tension in that area will be placed on Israel.

As a result of the new situation in the Middle East, may we be about to see a wave of democracy sweep through the area as we saw in Eastern Europe? (November 1990)
Yes. As Maitreya (through His associate) says in the October 1990 issue of *Share International*, a 'wind of change' is bringing an entirely new atmosphere to the region, and governments elected by the people will replace the present sheikhs and emirs as rulers of these countries.

How is it possible that Maitreya (or His associate) could be so wrong as to predict that there would be no war in the Middle East? If He is the Christ, surely He would know what is going to happen, as He seems to do in most of the other forecasts? (March 1991)
I have received many letters (and telephone calls) asking this or similar questions. Some elucidation, I think, is necessary.

The prediction about the situation being 'defused' was made on 2 January. The bombing of Iraq began on 16 January. The situation changed almost day to day. According to my own Master, until the very last moment, Hierarchy believed that wisdom would prevail and that a peaceful solution would be found. Inspired by Maitreya, many 'wise men', both statesmen and scientists, worked feverishly to avert catastrophe. That they were not successful is a result of the hardened attitudes of both Saddam Hussein and President Bush (and/or his advisers), both of whom had boxed themselves into positions from which it was difficult to retreat without complete loss of face. Saddam Hussein could and should have been provided with a formula, some negotiating position, which would have allowed him to leave Kuwait with some dignity intact.

Very many people (despite everything I have said and written to the contrary) look on the forecasts and press releases from Maitreya's associate as Holy Writ. They seem to think that Maitreya is releasing prophetic utterances, predestined and laid down from the beginning of time, modern-day biblical prophecies, without possibility of change through human free will. The reality is very different. They are predictions of trends and events, set in motion by humanity itself under the Law of Cause and Effect. Maitreya seeks to illuminate the working of that law for us through His scientific understanding of the law in action. He is not enunciating divine fiats nor seeing into the future by clairvoyance, divine or otherwise. He is showing that our actions, if pursued, will eventuate, through the Law of Cause and Effect, in specific events. However, humanity has free will and at any time can change the course of those events, for better or worse. Under the Law of Human Free Will, Maitreya may not interfere and impose solutions which we might prefer to the results of our own actions.

In any case, the prediction stated that there could be a fight but no major war. Any fighting would be brief and when the American and British public became aware of the casualties incurred, a ceasefire would be accepted. Already, inspired by Maitreya, the Iranian and other governments are working towards such a ceasefire.

The media and Christian and Jewish fundamentalist groups have whipped up public emotions about an Armageddon scenario, foretold in Holy Scripture. Horrible and destructive as it is (especially for the Iraqi and Kuwaiti civilian population), this battle is not Armageddon, is not the beginning of World War III, but will eventuate in a complete reconstruction of the Middle East, in particular in the creation of a national homeland for the Palestinians. Perhaps even a new realism will enter American life when they count the human cost of their insistence on their 'God-given' right to cheap gasoline.

Are we right to assume that Saddam Hussein is a madman? (May 1991)

No. Emotionally unbalanced, perhaps, but not clinically mad.

Did Saddam Hussein really dream that Mohammed visited him, dressed all in white, to tell him that his missiles were pointed in the wrong direction? This was widely reported in the media. If so, was 'Mohammed' actually Maitreya? (December 1990)

My information is that Saddam Hussein had, not a dream, but an actual visit from Maitreya, while he was at prayer in his home. Maitreya did not mention missiles but told him that his army was in the wrong place. Hussein asked Him what His meaning was, what was wrong in what he was doing. Maitreya replied that he knew perfectly well right from wrong and that he should withdraw his troops from Kuwait: the invasion of another country was undivine and against the law.

In an article in Share International, *Maitreya was quoted as having said: "I will raise My hand" ... (to forestall, offset, what might happen in the Gulf). What does this mean? Has He done so?* (April 1991)

To "raise His hand" means to become more obviously involved in the crisis — and in fact He did. He appeared to Saddam Hussein three times. He appeared to President Bush; He appeared to Gorbachev. He also appeared to a spiritual leader in Iran and, in each case, sought to inspire them to find an alternative solution to the military one. Last September (1990), President Bush sent an envoy to London to ask for Maitreya's advice and Maitreya told him that this conflict could be defused very simply by organizing an international package of aid for the Iraqi economy. The envoy took that message back to President Bush (who must have gulped when he heard it, because he had boxed himself into a position and would give not one inch to Saddam Hussein). What can Maitreya do? He can only inspire — this is how He has "raised His hand". Every time He appears to somebody He is, symbolically, holding up His hand; He is acting in a way which, without infringing free will, is very powerful. If those to whom He appears continue to act in their own misguided way, then He is not responsible.

I have read in **Share International** *that President Bush has sent an envoy to Maitreya in London. Can you explain how he came to know Maitreya's address?* (December 1990)

My information is that one of his entourage, a diplomat who had attended the April 21-22 1990 conference held by Maitreya in London, suggested to President Bush to send an envoy to London. No doubt he gave him details of where Maitreya could be found. According to my Master, this has been followed up by the sending of a second envoy, reiterating the Americans' desire for a peaceful solution to the Gulf crisis and asking for Maitreya's advice.

If nuclear or chemical weapons are used in the Middle East, would their effect on innocent civilians be neutralized? (November 1990)

One must distinguish between nuclear and chemical weapons. The use of nuclear weapons would involve the Lord of the World on Shamballa Who gave permission for the release of the secrets of nuclear fission to the Allied scientists during the war, 1939–45. For this reason, a nuclear attack by any government would be stopped at source. This does not apply to chemical weapons which would, therefore, cause enormous suffering if used. The politicians of the West, in particular President Bush and Mrs Thatcher, should remember this suffering in their rhetoric and bring about a solution which will allow Saddam Hussein to withdraw his forces from Kuwait without an unacceptable loss of face.

Will the emergency, the pollution, created by the firing of the oil fields in the Gulf prove a factor in finding an international solution to the Middle East problems? (April 1991)

It may well do so. I think that there has to be an international effort. It is obviously going to cost billions of pounds — the technological problem is enormous. If it is an international endeavour, that itself may bring about a new situation in the Middle East.

111

Is it possible to speculate on whether the Gulf War has put the Day of Declaration forward or backward? (April 1991)

My own informed guess about this is that, if anything, it has brought it forward. These outer events do not affect it. What does affect it is what we do — whether the media respond at a level where they can make it known — that affects it very much, far more than the Gulf war. But the events of the Gulf war, if Maitreya is correct, are going to change the world. This has been seen by both fundamentalist Christians and fundamentalist Jews as a kind of Holocaust, Armageddon-type happening which is going to spread throughout the world. This is not the case — it has nothing to do with Armageddon. But that belief has focused world attention in a way which probably would not otherwise have been the case. It is not the event which precedes the coming into the world of the Lord, as biblical prophecy would have it. The Lord — the Lord Maitreya, that is — has been in the world since 1977. He is only awaiting an invitation to come forward and has been working behind the scenes to tremendous effect. He is now able to be more and more open about what He is doing. He is talking with world leaders; these people see Him. He appeared to Saddam Hussein who, of course, ignored His advice, as did President Bush. But, gradually, He can adopt a higher profile until the media take notice.

The Third World and Latin America

Interview With Benjamin Creme's Master

by Patricia Pitchon

New relationships — A new relationship will be built between the Third World and the developed world in which the latter will become protectors, 'older brothers', responsible for their general well-being.

The debt problem — The debt problem will be solved by the release of the Third World from the responsibility of debt repayments. *The debts will be cancelled.* Third World countries must shoulder some responsibility first, in order to bring this about, and, second, to work for their own benefit.

Redistribution of the world's goods and resources — The world stock market crash will bring this about. It will reorient the governments of all countries towards a more equitable redistribution of food, housing, healthcare and education, which as universal rights will become the priorities of all governments.

The Third World debt will be repaid by a decrease in arms production.

[*Benjamin Creme*: In Latin America there is an ambivalent attitude to loans. There is a desire to receive them and a resentment about having to receive them. This leads to an ambivalent attitude about their use. In every case governments have brought into effect the adjustments and conditions imposed by the World Bank and the International Monetary Fund which benefit the middle classes, but the poor in every case suffer.]

Reconstruction — According to the Master, reconstruction is inevitable. In the stock market crash, the big tycoons are going to lose. They will not be in a position to dominate. When they have lost their money, they will be displaced.

Transformation — Within approximately the next five years, a transformation will take place in Latin America. A process of democratic *consensus* will unfold in almost every country. Consensus will develop from the grassroots up. The voice of the people will be heard. Land will be redistributed and given to the people. It will become very difficult for governments to maintain a reactionary position. This process (of profound transformation) will get under way within the next few years first in Argentina, then in Brazil, and soon after in countries like Peru and Colombia. In Colombia, there is a possibility of either total conflagration or transformation. The Master is more than hopeful that Colombia will choose the path of transformation. In El Salvador, eventually common sense will prevail, because neither side can win. The various parties in the conflict will work out an agreement which will include provisions for human rights guarantees and a viable standard of living for the poor. In Mexico, the difficulty is that the United States leans heavily on it, and the country is in a bad way. It should get together with other indebted countries and refuse to pay the debt. The burden is too heavy to allow development.

The Catholic Church — Unlikely as it may seem to some, the Catholic Church will become even more important in the life of the people as a result of purification of Church structure, doctrine and dogmas. People will gather to it in the light of the new dispensation which the presence of the Christ and the Master Jesus will reveal. A spiritual renaissance will take place in South America. Many who are associated with the Church have defended the people and died for the people.

Jesus — The Master Jesus will go to America. He works with a number of Masters. In South America there are three Masters Who work with Him. They will be very active in reorganizing the Church along truly spiritual lines. This will galvanize the people and bring them into the Church, the streets, the factories, on an equal footing. The will of the people will prevail in all three.

114

There are those who recognize the Christ in Jesus now. Many have recognized the quality of the Christ in Maitreya and are looking for His early return.

Manifestations of the Virgin Mary — According to the Master, there are two kinds of manifestations:

(1) Those created by the Master Who was the Madonna, which are always beneficial, always hopeful, *and are always seen by more than one person.*

(2) The second type are thoughtforms created by a few religious, hypersensitive or hysterical persons. These are almost always fearful, often warn of catastrophes, and are seen only by the person involved.

South American Masters — There are three Masters on the physical plane in South America: one in northern South America, one in Central America and one in the southern part of South America.

A group of initiates and disciples, who are with Them, are working within the Church, throughout South America. Their role is to interpret the thoughts and purposes of the Masters and the Christ to the people of Latin America. What they have to say is not orthodox Christianity. The Church will prevail, but it will be transformed. When Maitreya declares Himself to the world, He will introduce a group of Masters, including Jesus. Through His disciples, the teaching will be explained. The people will respond.

[*Note:* The above article is based on an interview given by Benjamin Creme's Master to Patricia Pitchon in May 1988.]

United Kingdom and Europe

Once the Lord Maitreya is out in the open and inspiring people to set the world to right, do you think there will be a coalition government in this country (Britain)? (September 1987)
Yes. I believe that only a coalition of all political viewpoints can bring about, with the minimum upheaval, the changes needed in this country towards greater justice and brotherhood. The divisive policies of the present Tory government — the most reactionary this century — have, I believe, set back our social life by 50 years.

Many people perceive an inherent divisiveness in the policies of all the governments we have had in the UK in peacetime for very many years, but many people have a sympathy with what Margaret Thatcher is trying to do. There is, for example, a widespread sense of the need today for much less dependence on the State and more personal responsibility. Also, there is much support for Margaret Thatcher's stated aims of peace with freedom and justice, ideals which are of course so close to the stated values of the 'Plan'. But your comments surely cast some doubt on whether Margaret Thatcher herself has the recognition and support of the Hierarchy. It seems obvious to me that she does, but I would be grateful for your comments. This whole area of politics, policies and personalities is very confusing. (October 1987)
My comments on the divisiveness of the present Tory government's policies were in relation to the question of whether I thought a coalition government would follow Maitreya's emergence. I believe that not only a coalition of all political parties but the full participation of all sections of the population will be required to ensure a just and free social structure, not only in Britain but throughout the world.

While she states her aims to be peace with freedom and justice, and while she claims to represent and understand the needs of all the people of this country, I would have thought it transparently obvious that Mrs Thatcher's policies are producing the very opposite: a society divided into two, one prosperous and materialistic in the extreme, and the other in increasing bitterness and hatred facing a bleak and jobless future for themselves and their children.

Her avowed intention is to "remove every trace of the 'evil' of socialism" from this country and, by appealing as she does to the most greedy, selfish — and, therefore, separative — instincts of the people, to create "a property- and share-owning democracy", and therefore a built-in Tory majority in perpetuity. Speculation, as seen by Hierarchy, is a major disease in the body of humanity. Mrs Thatcher's policies and ambitions are major contributors to that disease. Her government, moreover, came to power with only 44 per cent of votes. It is a minority government and disenfranchises over half the population of Britain. Britain's caring and welfare services were once the envy of the world. Mrs Thatcher's policies have sent them, for lack of support, into a spiralling decline.

No, Hierarchy does not "recognize and support" Margaret Thatcher. Quite the contrary. Her beliefs and aims are stumbling blocks on the path to the creation of a society sensitive to the Christ's call for sharing and justice for all.

You have told us that there are high initiates in position already in the world to help in the coming restructuring, etc. Are there any such individuals in (1) the British Parliament, (2) the Conservative government? (September 1988)
(1) Yes. (2) No.

What is the best way of getting rid of the proponents of market forces in the UK? (October 1992)
We have already missed the chance of beginning to do this in the recent elections in April 1992. The best way is to vote out all conservative and reactionary governments wherever they appear. Conservative, by definition, means to conserve or maintain the present, the *status quo*, which, in practice, means the past.

The world is divided into two groups of people, one progressive and the other conservative and reactionary. The conservative and reactionary forces are those who love the past, who are holding on to the old Piscean order (whose very nature is based on separation and cleavage). That is what we are witnessing today. The progressive forces are those who are looking for a more constructive and more inclusive way of living, in which the Aquarian forces, the forces of synthesis, fusion and blending can find expression. Wherever you find the dominance of autocratic, conservative and reactionary forces, you have the exponents of the past, who always, at this point in time, work through market forces, now the major economic concept dominating the world.

But the concept of 'market forces' is about to decline, because it does not work; it is against the law of evolution. It starts from the completely erroneous idea that we all begin at the same point. If we did, if every nation and every individual within the nation started at the same point, there would be a value in market forces (it does have a function as a means of regulating supply and demand), but, since no one starts at the same point, since a third of the world greedily wastes three-quarters of the world's resources and the rest of the world are living in misery, then market forces must be seen as against the fusion and blending of humanity into one. It is based on division; it is very good for a few and very bad for the many. As such, it is against the evolutionary purpose and must go.

There is no recipe I can give you except a recognition by the people, of this country and of all countries, that blindly to follow a government which blindly follows market forces is the blind leading the blind to inevitable destruction.

Why are there so many (IRA) bombings in London? If Maitreya is in London, does not His divine aura spread around Him? (June 1992)
Maitreya is not in London to protect London or Londoners. No doubt, if He were near a bomb, He would be protected by "His divine aura", but it is no part of His duty or plan to solve the Irish/British problem by protecting the British from IRA bombs. We have to talk with the IRA.

Has Maitreya said anything about the recent EC conference in Maastricht? (January/February 1992)

Yes, in so far as we have had — over two to three years — a great many comments from Maitreya through one of His associates, not precisely on Maastricht but on what Maastricht is about, which is Europeanization. I would say that the only thing Maitreya agrees with Margaret Thatcher about (but for different reasons) is the need to hold on to national identity. National identity He calls sacred, divine. Every nation is governed as a soul and as a personality by energies — rays. The soul aspect is expressed by the initiates and disciples of the nation, and the personality by the mass of people. The rays governing the different nations give each nation its particular quality.

Consensus: The New Way For Humanity

Interview With Benjamin Creme's Master

by Brian James and Patricia Pitchon

Brian James (BJ): Maitreya's associate has said that the UK Government will shortly consider the idea of consulting the people of Northern Ireland about withdrawing troops and handing back power to the province. Following remarks from the Northern Ireland Secretary, Mr Peter Brooke, about the possibility of holding talks with Sinn Fein if they abandon their support of violence, are we seeing the beginning of this process?

The Master: Yes. It is only the beginning, but it is a start.

BJ: What are the long-term implications for the judicial system in this country?

The Master: It is becoming more obvious that a complete reconstruction of the British judicial system is necessary. This is also true for many countries throughout the world.

Patricia Pitchon (PP): Will this reconstruction in Britain come about in the next few years?

The Master: Yes. The readjustment of social structures, through the principle of sharing governing the economic system, will lead inevitably to new insights *vis-à-vis* the judiciary. It must become more answerable to the will of the people in terms of democratic structure (that is, just as a minister is answerable to the people).

At the moment there is too great a dichotomy between those who sit in the name of justice and those who come before these non-elected members to answer to them, sometimes with their life (whether via the death penalty or life imprisonment).

BJ: It is reported that differences on Europe lie at the heart of the split between Mrs Thatcher and her cabinet. What are the implications for this country if the government does not take its proper place in the developing institutions of the European

120

Community? What are the implications for Mrs Thatcher of her increasing isolation from her cabinet?
The Master: The UK (if the present trend continues) will lose its opportunity of playing a full part in the European Community and it will suffer accordingly. The recalcitrance of the present governmental attitudes in this country in implementing fully the accords with Europe will produce a situation in which the UK will be seen as 'the odd man out' in Europe. This will have dire consequences for the government.

As for Mrs Thatcher, she is becoming hedged in by her own policies and lack of trust with and between her colleagues. She will retire when she finds herself unable to find a way out of the trap which she has set for herself. The main danger for Mrs Thatcher continues to be the poll tax.

PP: A poll tax revolt in different parts of the country has already begun, for example in Glasgow. But there have also been protests in places like Liverpool, Birmingham and elsewhere. Why, in your view, has the press not bothered to report these?
The Master: The press considers the reaction too lukewarm to warrant their concern. This is not a fact, but it is the attitude of the largely Conservative-dominated press. There is a ground swell of resistance and revolt which has yet to manifest itself. When it does, the media will make it known.

BJ: The UK Government intends pressing ahead with privatization of water. Maitreya has said that you cannot "privatize the vital elements of nature". According to previous information received from Maitreya's associate, if the government tries to carry out this policy "something spectacular will happen". Is such an event imminent and will we see the failure of the flotation of water shares?
The Master: No. However, the process will not proceed as planned. Already the majority of British people, if asked, would vote against its implementation. The privatization plan by the present government will prove to be its Trojan horse.

PP: What is the outlook for Lebanon? Maitreya's associate has said that there would be significant changes there.
The Master: In the short term, war. In the long term, peace. There will be a short, sharp, final attempt by the Christian militia (headed by Aoun) to secure their hold on their area of Lebanon. It will not succeed. General Aoun is like Don Quixote, fighting windmills.

PP: Will Syria withdraw?
The Master: Eventually, yes, but not until certain safeguards are in force for their representatives in Lebanon.

*PP: In previous information received from Maitreya's associate, published in **Share International**, it was mentioned that there would be an earthquake in China. There was one, but it was barely reported in the news. Why is this?*
The Master: The San Francisco earthquake took precedence in the news. Almost no information came from China. The West has looked on the Chinese earthquake as some kind of retribution for the events of Tiananmen.

There were actually two earthquakes in China. One measured 6 and the other 6.7 on the Richter scale. Some 50,000 people were made homeless. Had this happened anywhere else in the world it would have been a major worldwide event, calling for responses in aid. China did not ask for international help because it has, to some degree, turned in on itself once again.

PP: How long will this process of "turning in on itself" continue?
The Master: It could be months, or even up to two years. It depends on forces now emerging in China between the military and the political groups. The military are extremely restive and wish to see greater changes but until now they are staying their hand in the hope of normal constitutional reform.

PP: Maitreya has pointed to a process of gradual convergence — observable in the political sphere — and this increasingly visible pattern has been monitored with regard to the elections taking place around the world. Will this trend continue?

The Master: Inevitably this pattern will be fulfilled. Consensus is the new way for humanity. The old dogmatic positions of left and right will be increasingly eroded as men learn to compromise and reach consensus. In general, in the case of elections, the expectation is that the difference between the parties will be small. However, in situations where you have large numbers of impoverished workers or peasants and small privileged groups competing, the swing can be very large. In the USA and Europe, where you have a large number of people on the same economic level, you will have consensus.

PP: What is the outlook for Israel?
The Master: In Israel a stalemate obtains at present. Paradoxically this is a positive factor in relation to the Arab world because it prevents spontaneous action by minorities within the Israeli camp (extremists). You can see this as the result of an "energetic vacuum" created in the Middle East by Maitreya. In the long term peace is inevitable and much sought after by most of the factions involved, with few exceptions. The long-term hope for the Middle East is a peaceful one.

PP: Is reunification of Germany imminent?
The Master: In the short term, no. In the long term, yes. There are still too many differences — politically, in living standards and in economic strength — to justify complete union. There is too much distrust not only within the two Germanys but also within their neighbours. In the meantime, a *rapprochement* and a congruence of viewpoints in dealing with the new exodus will take place. What you see in the other East European countries will inevitably take place in all the East European states. The last is probably Romania.

PP: If Gorbachev is to be replaced (as mentioned in previously received information), will a retrenchment of the old guard follow?
The Master: No. *Glasnost* will continue but at a steadier, more stable pace.

PP: What, in your view, is the biggest single event on the horizon?

The Master: The forthcoming stock exchange crash, and when it does come it will bring the present economic system to its knees. Then the true dialogue between the developed and the developing world will begin. Japan is the fulcrum which will set the process of the crash in motion.

PP: Is this crash imminent?
The Master: It has been expected for the last eight or nine months. It cannot be delayed much longer. The recent plunge in the Dow-Jones Index precipitated by Japanese withdrawal of support (in October 1989) is but a preliminary to the major crash. This may be repeated once or twice before the final denouement.

*PP: Are governments aware of the contents of **Share International**?*
The Master: Governments, no, but individuals in government, yes. There are representatives of several governments, North and South, East and West, who take very seriously the pronouncements in *Share International*. They are treated very seriously indeed.

[*Note*: The above article is based on an interview with Benjamin Creme's Master by journalists Patricia Pitchon and Brian James on 8 November 1989.]

Tibet and China

I am surprised that you say Mao Tse-tung was a third-degree initiate. It makes me question: (1) What right had Mao Tse-tung to order his country to invade Tibet? (2) Why did this happen in the first place? Why could not Tibet have been left alone and given the chance to slowly change in its own way? (3) Will the Tibetans be extinguished? If so, why? (4) Why were their scientific and religious books, dating back thousands of years, destroyed? Why was that allowed? Their science of medicine was far ahead of what Western medicine is today. (5) What is the future for Tibet and the Tibetan people? (March 1989)

(1) Mao Tse-tung had, of course, no right to invade Tibet. One has to realize that a third-degree initiate is not a perfect God-realized Master, but a human being, and — if the head of a great country of 900 million people — a wielder of great power but also of great responsibilities. Consider the reasons for the invasion: with the withdrawal of Britain from India, a power vacuum was left in Tibet which could be filled by only two powers, the Soviet Union and China. China already felt exposed and threatened (along its north-western border) by Soviet missiles, and the annexation of Tibet seemed to the Chinese the natural and only way to secure that flank.

That the occupation was carried out to the accompaniment of atrocities and destruction of ancient cultural treasures is tragic, but simple enlargement of territory was not the prime motive. Also, one should consider the historical relationship between China and Tibet. They are indeed two quite distinct peoples, but each has invaded the other's territory time and time again throughout history.

There was a time, centuries ago to be sure, when a Tibetan army stood at the gates of Peking. So, from the Chinese point of view, the annexation of Tibet could be rationalized as the re-occupation of a distant province. I have reason to remember vividly the events of 1959 (when the invasion began) and was

125

amazed and chagrined by its easy acceptance by the rest of the world for this reason.

(2) (4) The questioner asks: "Why was this allowed? Why was the destruction of an ancient culture and science allowed?" Allowed by whom, may I ask? Has he not seen, again and again, ancient cultures invaded and destroyed, the peoples scattered or killed? The questioner seems to hold the view that God or Hierarchy should somehow have prevented the invasion of Tibet and so preserved its ancient heritage. That, I am afraid, would have been just the infringement of man's free will which Hierarchy never allows itself. Were it to do so, man would never learn or grow.

(3) The Tibetan people will not be extinguished, and those who have fled abroad will, if they wish, soon return to their homeland.

(5) What is their future? Whatever the Tibetan people make of it. Certainly they have gifts and courage in abundance to remake their lives in Tibet.

Yogananda apparently expressed a greater fear of communism than fascism as an evil force. If Mao Tse-tung was divine (as a third-degree initiate) has he practised the form of Communism that Yogananda has spoken against? (July/August 1987)
Paramahansa Yogananda was an Avatar and, spiritually, a very enlightened man, but, with all due respect, I have to say he knew nothing about politics. There is no pure communism today. Nor is there pure fascism or pure democracy. Each of these three (equally) divine ideas is in a state of transition. To prefer the horrors of Hitler's fascism to even the worst aspects of Stalin's rule is to my mind a sign of ignorance and extraordinary prejudice.

The Changing Role of the United Nations

Interview With Benjamin Creme's Master

by Patricia Pitchon

Patricia Pitchon (PP): The recent Gulf War highlighted the role of the United Nations in various ways. It is generally agreed that the level of co-ordination of those nations forming part of the Security Council was unusually good. This is independent of the wisdom (or lack of it) in choosing to go to war with Iraq. But there is a feeling that the distribution of power within the UN — with so much of it concentrated in the Security Council — hampers the potential of the UN as an effective organization of the nations of the world. Would the Master give His view on how power could be more fairly redistributed within the UN so as to be more truly representative?

The Master: The real problem in the UN as it acts now is that the Security Council has taken precedence over the General Assembly. This is seen as 'realistic' by the major powers and their associates in the General Assembly as the only means of implementing UN resolutions. This is not truly the case but it is seen to be so. The permanent members of the Security Council (the US, the USSR, China, France and the United Kingdom), as the owners of the nuclear bomb, have been seen since the Second World War as the policemen of the world. Whatever could not be agreed between them could not be agreed. The power of veto built into the process has underlined this fact. The new relationship between the US and the Soviet Union has shattered this old framework and has created an entirely new situation in which the voice of the General Assembly can become increasingly more distinct.

Until now both the US and the USSR have feared the resolutions stemming from the General Assembly as being biased against them in any particular instance. This will no longer be the case. More and more, the US — once it has

127

overcome the flush of success of its recent escapade in the Middle East — and the Soviet Union will listen attentively to the growing authority of the General Assembly of nations. Democracy is on its way even there and naught can stop it.

The UN is destined to lead the world out of its present precarious imbalance and to act as the sounding chamber for the thoughts and aspirations of the peoples of the world. Unless the peoples' voice can be so heard, the UN will fail.

A new UN Secretary General will shortly be elected and sworn into office. His more dynamic approach will breathe new life into this institution and guarantee its greater effectiveness.

PP: What can the UN do to develop an effective role to cope with world hunger?
The Master: The true role of the United Nations is to act as the voice of the peoples of the world and to so organize international relations as to guarantee peace.

It is not the avowed aim of the United Nations to abolish hunger. Nevertheless, many UN agencies have long concerned themselves with this field. Eventually, a new agency of the United Nations will be developed whose whole concern will be with the redistribution of the world's resources. In this way the UN, without altering its role as a 'debating chamber', will grasp the nettle of practical help for the starving and poor of the world.

PP: As Maitreya has predicted through His associate, new thinking on the role of governments worldwide points to four major duties: feeding the people, housing the people, and providing adequate healthcare and education. This is irrespective of political ideologies. The UN has concerned itself with various health programmes. Recently the World Health Organization was criticized for concentrating too many resources on Europe and not enough on much needier countries, and for spending too much on administration. What principles should guide the improvement of UN efforts in this field?

The Master: Each nation must make its own decisions, but an overall plan for global transformation, formulated and enunciated by the UN, would act as a major stimulus to individual governments to implement the needs in terms of health, education, housing and food.

The action of the United Nations until now has been bedevilled by ideological intransigence. These basic needs pertain whatever the ideology followed at any particular time, and ideology should not be the governing factor in the dispensing of aid. In the future this will not be so. Each case will be dealt with on its merits and not in relation to ideological belief or system.

PP: What intervening steps should be taken to get us there?
The Master: It is a gradual process. It will certainly require a broader vision than is generally possible today, and it may well be that the emergence of Maitreya will be needed as the catalyst to awaken humanity, and therefore its representative, the United Nations, to the true needs of the world. So much of UN thought is concerned with theory and ideology. An altogether more practical approach must pertain.

PP: Does this mean more field workers, for example?
The Master: Not only more field workers, but more liaison between governments and aid agencies, and between aid agencies and the recipients of aid, to determine what aid, in what form, is precisely needed.

PP: 1989 and 1990 saw major natural disasters which affected millions of people — earthquakes, floods, hurricanes, etc. Should there be a co-ordinated UN Emergency Fund to deal with disasters on this scale?
The Master: The short answer is yes, yes, yes! And were the UN to intervene in the many local wars which are now causing much destruction, the happiness of the world's people would be immensely improved.

PP: Does intervention mean conciliation?
The Master: Intervention means police work. The United Nations must see itself as the upholder of peace and human

rights. Where these are endangered through the antagonism of local factions, the UN should have the right to intervene and to offer help in the restoration of peace. Had this been done in Ethiopia, for example, the present tragic suffering of many millions could have been prevented. Mainly at the instigation of the US Government, the will of the UN was brought to bear in the recent Gulf crisis, largely because long-term US material interests were thought to be threatened. Were the same energy and logistical expertise focused on the needs of the poor, poverty and starvation could be eliminated relatively quickly, and the response to human suffering through natural disasters would be prompt and effective. The United Nations as a whole has little to be proud of in this regard.

PP: Is it necessary to lobby governments to highlight and focus on this idea?
The Master: Inevitably. To quote the Lord Maitreya: "Nothing happens by itself. Man must act and implement his will." [Message No. 31]

PP: What factors stop those in influential positions in the world from considering the alleviation of poverty and famine as a major priority?
The Master: There are many factors at work here, but the major ones are lack of political will to implement action to answer the sensed need; a sense of powerlessness in the face of the magnitude of the problem; ingrained complacency of the vast majority of established, developed nations and of their representatives (in government and in the UN); and the overriding greed and selfishness of men everywhere which generates a fear of the transformative results of truly dedicated action to redress the imbalances in the world. The 'haves' know instinctively that any real change, any fundamental change, would spell the end of their privilege and power.

PP: Although the Master has said that some major changes will take place gradually, will we see a transformed UN within a decade, or is it longer-term?

The Master: Unless the nations see the necessity for a complete reappraisal of the presently governing economic systems, a total collapse of the world's economy is inevitable. This would result in chaotic conditions, for example, civil war, internal strife of all kinds and even, eventually, major world conflict. This situation the UN would be powerless to halt.

The new factor which will transform this threat is the appearance of Maitreya before the world. This is planned and inevitable, and will have a galvanizing effect on the actions of all the member states. The speed of their response cannot be strictly ascertained, but may be adjudged prompt and effective.

PP: Is there anything else the Master wishes to add?
The Master: The UN is the major hope of the world. In its inter-relationships we can see democracy writ large — the symbol for that expression of God's Will that men call goodwill.

With the advent of the Christ this goodwill will bring all men and all nations into correct relationship and create the necessary circumstances for the expression of that synthesis which will be the outstanding keynote of the coming civilization.

In this vast enterprise the UN will play a major role.

[*Note*: The above article is based on an interview with Benjamin Creme's Master by Patricia Pitchon in May 1991.]

United Nations

Will the United Nations assert its independence or will it remain a puppet of the United States? At the moment the United States has a serious grip on the United Nations. (April 1992)

First and foremost, I do not believe the United Nations is a puppet of the United States or of any other country. The United Nations is becoming more and more independent, and more and more what eventually it will be: the central debating, law-giving forum for the nations of the world, and over the last year or two this is becoming more and more marked. It is beginning to take cognizance of its opportunities and its power now to influence events — as, for instance, Yugoslavia, and as will happen in the Commonwealth of Russian states, because they will not settle down into a nice, cosy relationship — it will mean the United Nations will probably have to send in troops to keep the peace between certain of the Russian states.

The United Nations will eventually have a rather solid army which will be kept on hand to rush into any needed place. This is part of the process of recognizing our inter-relationship — that humanity is one. As soon as you begin to see that, and therefore share the resources of the world, you change the whole relationship between one nation and another.

Not only the United States but also the Soviet Union had, until very recently, a serious grip on the UN, but in fact for long years the United Nations was in a state of almost non-action because of the Cold War, and above all because of the veto factor in the Security Council. The General Assembly is the true United Nations. The Security Council has passed the peak of its value and should be unwound; it no longer has any real function. Russia cannot speak for the whole of what was the Soviet Union, and there is no reason at all why five nations, five permanent members, should dictate the political/economic norms of the world. The Security Council has to go, and as soon as the Security Council goes the United Nations Assembly will find its proper voice.

Use of Nuclear Weapons

You said that Sanat Kumara gave permission to release the secrets of the atom bomb to Allied scientists in 1942. I cannot believe this! Such a high Being could never have given permission to build an atom bomb! Perhaps Sanat Kumara gave out general information to researchers but did not realize that humanity would exploit it to manufacture such destructive weapons? (March 1987)

I am afraid the questioner considers Sanat Kumara (the Lord of the World) to be naïve. In 1942 the Axis powers (inspired by the forces of materiality) and the Allied nations were running 'neck and neck' in the discovery of the atomic bomb. Had the Axis powers, led by Hitler, gained possession, they would have blackmailed the world into subservience and slavery. Because of that very real threat (according to the Master DK in *The Externalisation of the Hierarchy* by Alice A.Bailey), the Hierarchy appealed to Sanat Kumara to allow the secrets to be revealed to the Allied scientists. The bomb was not meant to be used other than as a threat, but the American scientists were determined to test its effectiveness on Japan.

Therefore, Sanat Kumara would now be personally involved in any future use of the bomb, and for this reason every effort has been and will be made to prevent its use.

Is it ever justified for one human to use any form of violence against another human, such as in righteous warfare or in the protection of one's own family members from harm? (July/August 1987)

This is a difficult question to answer — it depends so much on the particular circumstances. From the viewpoint of Hierarchy, the war against the Axis Powers (Germany, Japan and Italy) was entirely justified, and even necessary, as a war against the forces of evil working through their leaders. It is important to remember, however, that it was started by Hitler and not by the Allied forces; in other words, it was a defensive war.

I was a soldier in World War II and had a feeling at the time that I fought on the side of light, against darkness, but I felt terrible guilt afterwards about fighting in that war, and many men with me also felt that. Should one have felt guilt when one was supposed to be on the side of light against darkness? (November 1992)

Guilt is a totally unproductive emotion at all times. You should try to be as detached from guilt as you would from anger, fear or any other negative emotion. There is no guilt attached to killing in war: the harm is in the karma of war itself. We, humanity, create karma for ourselves every time we create war. World War II was precipitated by the Forces of Evil and had to be fought, but behind the Allies stood Hierarchy, and every effort was made by Hierarchy to prevent the war in the first place. Once it began, however, They strove to lead it to a successful conclusion for the Allies.

CHAPTER 4

ECONOMIC CHANGE

Maitreya's Forecasts

Commercialization and Market Forces

In the last two to three years we have seen a reduction in the wars and conflicts taking place throughout the world as the superpowers withdrew from their policy of supplying arms to further their own foreign aims and interests. The energy which drives soldiers into battle and fills the air with warplanes has been switched off.

But, Maitreya says, that energy cannot just disappear; it has to go somewhere. This energy has been roaming the world and suddenly it has found a new womb: the commercialization created by market forces. Market forces, Maitreya says, are the forces of wickedness, confusion and chaos, and its children are competition and comparison. Freedom is not found in the free play of market forces, for market forces have no 'eyes'. They are blind and satanic, leading inevitably to 'mine' and 'more' — that is, to possessiveness and greed — without end. Market forces will bring this civilization as we have known it to the edge of disaster. Market forces have created social and natural havoc. People have been condemned to death, literally, in the name of profit and loss. Hospitals have been shut because they are not profitable; schools have difficulty in staying open. These institutions are essential for the health and well-being of society.

The new creed of the superpowers has become 'the economy', which is the soul of commercialization. This represents a serious new threat to the world, Maitreya warns, one that could even compromise human life. Commercialization is more destructive than any nuclear bomb.

The quality of commercialization is greed, and, in Maitreya's view, commercialization means making money while others starve. It will affect all nations, He says. This negative energy, which recoiled from the battlefield, will create a very hostile world. It is the human mind which has created this force and it can be changed by human awareness. Only Maitreya, however, has the power to turn this destructive energy into a creative force. Commercialization throughout the world is part of the pattern that will result in a major collapse of the world's stock markets, beginning in Japan. After this crash, the first duty of governments will be to feed people with the right food. Their second duty will be to ensure adequate housing. Next will come health and education, and lastly, defence. In short, the crash will lead to a reordering of priorities.

Already, there are many strikes taking place as people begin to question the boss-employee relationship. This is because the new energy is already diluting and sweeping away the master-servant relationship which underlies so much of market forces. You can only solve the problems of the world, Maitreya points out, with a sense of realism that is not clouded by ideology or market forces. "Politicians whose creed is 'market forces'," Maitreya says, "will find that their time is over." Capitalism, in its pure form, is at an end in Europe. It has no future whatsoever. Instead, countries will model their governments on a form of democratic socialism. Gradually this will become the model for all nations as the most effective way to ensure that the voice and will of the people is properly represented. In the new systems, Maitreya says, even market forces will be based on social consciousness. Market forces will not be 'in charge' of social consciousness. It is social consciousness which will guide market forces.

Stock Market Crash

Can or will Maitreya prevent (1) a Third World War; (2) a new financial crash before 1990? (April 1987)
(1) Certainly, if humanity responds to Maitreya's message of sharing and co-operation (He believes we will), then a Third

World War is not a possibility. Were we not to respond, then such a war would be inevitable. It is a mistake to put it in terms of His 'preventing' it, as it were, despite us. We have to prevent such a catastrophe by implementing the principles of sharing and justice. He has said in Message No. 65: "Have no fear that mankind will reject Me. My plans are safe in your hands."

(2) Again, Maitreya will not prevent a "financial crash," nor will He engineer one. A complete change in our economic system will inevitably come about as we implement the principle of sharing, but this will be a gradual process with the minimum of disruption and cleavage.

If we have a worldwide economic crash later this year, will Maitreya, when He appears globally on TV, have a plan that will eliminate the panic or chaos which will ensue across the planet? (October 1989)

Maitreya will present the nations with an alternative way of living, of conducting economic and political affairs. This will require a change of consciousness and could not be imposed. However, much is already changing due to the influence of His energies and He will time His appearance for maximum influence and effectiveness.

Will the world stock market crash foretold by Maitreya initiate a period of extreme economic hardships, or will these hardships be avoided with the help of Maitreya? (October 1989)

The stock market crash which Maitreya says is inevitable will obviously lead to changes. These have been predicted to take the form of a reorientation of priorities by governments around the world. Adequate food, housing, healthcare and education, as universal rights, will become the aim. This can hardly be called "hardship". To achieve this for all, of course, will require a fairer distribution of the world's resources and therefore some sacrifice on the part of the presently richer nations.

What are the ramifications of Maitreya's influence on the recent stock exchange crash? Could the repercussions of a failing economic system throw the civilized countries into a 'wilderness experience', or would the wilderness experience you have spoken of be more of a voluntary response? (May 1988)

The recent stock exchange crash is not the result of Maitreya's influence but of our irrational economic system. Speculation, the basis of stock market activity, is a major disease of our present society.

The 'wilderness experience' is the voluntary adoption by humanity of a simpler way of life to rid it of the excesses and injustices of a gross materialism. The questioner surely means to say "developed", not "civilized", countries. He/she is surely not suggesting that the underdeveloped countries are not civilized?

How do you think the Japanese people will react to and cope with the stock exchange crash which Maitreya has predicted? (November 1989)

In answer to this question my Master gave the following answer:

"In Japan, for the first time in recent centuries, the Law of Life instead of the law of the shogun will prevail. Japan will show modern industrialized societies, rich and powerful, how to simplify their demands on life and meet the needs of the people.

"The Law of Sacrifice will prevail, and the Japanese people, through their sacrifice, will show the way for the world. Their ancient values of the spiritual basis of life will re-emerge, and the present chaotic commercialization will give way to a better and more just economy in which the true needs of all will be met. This will be a blueprint for the world. The readiness of the Japanese people to participate in the changes will be an inspiration to the developed world.

"Soon will be revealed the true state of the Japanese economy which is based on wrong premises — in particular, aggressive competition with the rest of the world. The methods used are suspect and unfair and will rebound on those who use them (Law of Cause and Effect).

"The new government which will emerge after the stock market crash will reflect the will of the people and stand for the people."

How should we prepare ourselves economically for the Japanese stock market crash? (October 1989)
By acquiring the readiness to share and to achieve justice in the world.

In view of the expected world stock market crash, what should people do with their savings? Give them all away before it is too late — buy gold coins — carry on as usual and hope for the best? (October 1990)
I am the last person you should ask for financial advice, but if I had stocks and shares, I would sell them and bank the money or (in the UK) invest it in building societies — or in paintings. (I won't say whose!)

The recent stock market alarm happened to occur on Friday the 13th — or 'Black Friday' as it became known. Was this pure coincidence or is there any basis for traditional superstition about Friday the 13th and the number 13? (December 1989)
It was pure coincidence that the recent dramatic falls on the stock markets took place on Friday 13 October. The equally dramatic falls in 1987 took place on a Monday, also in October. The really relevant factor is that the Dow Jones Index reached an 'all time high' both in August 1987 and again in August 1989.

It is possible that some numerologists would not agree, but I do not believe that there is any basis, other than superstition, for the idea that Friday the 13th, or the number 13, is 'unlucky'. Many people believe that, for them, 13 is 'lucky'. Whatever you think, if strongly enough, you will make it so, one way or another.

According to the 'Today' programme on BBC Radio 4 this morning, a researcher has found a correlation between the pessimistic lyrics of the pop tunes and the current recession. He has also found a close correlation for past recessions in the hit tunes of yesteryear. (1) Do songwriters unconsciously predict the state of the economy and, if so, how? (2) When can we expect an upturn in the economy? (The words of pop tunes are currently gloomy.) (April 1992)

(1) I do not think songwriters predict anything at all. I think they do react, on a 'folk' level, to the general social climate of which the 'economy' is but a part. In a period of recession, when, no doubt, sales of records are falling sharply (and with it their income), popular songwriters would tend to be more pessimistic and discouraged. (2) Any upturn, I believe, will be slight and short-lived. We are entering a period of collapse of the old, out-worn and divisive system.

The Poison Of Market Forces

Interview with Benjamin Creme's Master

by Patricia Pitchon and Brian James

Patricia Pitchon (PP): Maitreya says market forces are 'blind', but current economic theory simply points to the law of supply and demand, and present thinking does equate this with freedom.

The Master: It is a question of where you stand initially: this is the basis of your movement in response to supply and demand. One man will demand 'x' from life and his demand will be met quickly, with little expenditure of energy. Another demands 'x' plus other factors, and a greater amount of energy is required to fulfil his needs. People make different demands on the law of supply. Some demand more of life, command greater resources, and if these are met it can only be at the expense of those who demand, or can demand, but little. This is the blindness of market forces, which take no account of differences in status (economic, social or other) of those who make the demands. Hence the operation of these forces contains inbuilt inequality; they are intrinsically divisive. This is why Maitreya calls them "satanic". If everybody started from the same point, there might be some logic to them. But nobody does. You already have rich and poor people, and rich and poor nations.

PP: Why does not this analysis hold sway with Western governments?

The Master: The developed nations see it as their prerogative to demand a given standard (of life) from the law of supply. They construe that they give much. The poor nations are seen as 'giving little' and therefore deserving little from the same world resources.

The essence of market forces is greed, and it has been formulated as an economic theory and process in response to the greed of rich nations and rich individuals.

In the light, therefore, of a new dispensation in which greed is replaced by social harmony and interdependence, market forces can no longer hold sway. They are doomed as an economic theory because they have no relevance for the future time. A sustainable and self-regulating economic process must become the aim.

PP: People seem to be having difficulty understanding the concept and scope of sustainability. The UK Government seems to think sustainability is applicable to the environment, but not to other spheres. What is the guiding principle of sustainability?

The Master: The guiding principle must be that of sufficiency and not waste. At present the world's economic system is governed by waste. The profligacy of that waste has created our various pollution problems and constitutes a danger to the planet's well-being. This is only half-realized. A sustainable economy is one that supplies the needs of all within the possibilities of the planet's health. At the moment this seems impossible to achieve, but the technology of light will transform the situation for humanity, and give unlimited, ecologically sound energy for all our needs. This will transform the approach of humanity to this problem of supply and demand, and therefore of market forces.

Already many people are aware of the dangers inherent in the blind following of market forces. More and more commentators are denouncing the greed which lies at the base of today's political thinking. A new consciousness is growing which is seeing greed in a new light. The greed of the present is now being seen for what it is — an aberration — and it will soon be replaced by co-operation.

PP: How do you envisage the immediate aftermath of the stock market crash in the West?

The Master: After the preliminary shock, the nations will meet together to discuss the means of coping with the future in ordered fashion. Those who have stood most emphatically behind the rule of market forces will find themselves outvoted in the dispensation which will pertain, and those advocating co-operation will gain the ascendancy.

This will not happen overnight. The process will be gradual, but will not be long delayed. Already there are those in various governments who are awaiting the time to act.

PP: Are these conscious disciples of the Masters?
The Master: Some are working with the Masters. Some have met Maitreya. They have been trained and prepared to carry out the changes which a more equitable world demands. Through the democratic process — which will still hold — these people will bring forward the proposals which, with greater or lesser amendments, will constitute the norm in most countries.

PP: What points of view will the newly-changing Communist countries have to give up in order to go in the new direction?
The Master: It is rigidity of thought which has brought about the collapse of the communist system. They have been unable to adapt to the changing needs in their societies. On the whole, the political groups in Eastern Europe and the Soviet Union are not enchanted by the blandishments of Western capitalism. They do indeed want to regenerate their economy. That they wish to have a more successful social democracy is not in doubt. That they desire more goods is certain. That they wish to have greater participation in government is already evident. But this is not to say that they wish to swallow capitalism whole. On the contrary, there will be many experiments, successes and partial failures before a working synthesis is achieved which will satisfy their physical needs and social ideals.

PP: What will be the response of Third World governments who are now embracing the economic approach of supply and demand when this reorientation begins to take root?
The Master: No two Third World countries are alike in their needs, their potential or in their state of development. A variety

of methods will be tried. Some will look more to the Western ideal, some more to the Eastern communistic way of thinking. More and more, however, the nations of the world under the impulse of the sharing of resources, and aiming for sustainable sufficiency, will gravitate towards a democratic socialism, or, as some call it, social democracy.

This is as true for the Third World as for the developed world. This is not to say that all nations will go forward at the same pace, but this will become their ideal. And there is a place for the individual and for free enterprise within the context of a social management of the economy.

PP: Which countries are closest to that ideal?
The Master: There are a few in Western Europe: Holland, West Germany and the Scandinavian countries. France, Italy — the Common Market countries in general — reflect something of this ideal. But there, as everywhere, the evil of market forces has poisoned the economy. Politically they have a social democracy which can be completed or perfected by a greater participation of all groups in government, but they are still infected to a large extent by the poison of market forces. Politically these groups are more mature. There is a better understanding of political structures than of the destructive effects of some economic structures. All of them live under the hegemony of American economic totalitarianism, just as the Communist nations of the East have lived under the hegemony of Russian political totalitarianism. But just as one group has thrown off the political yoke, so will the other discard the economic chains.

Brian James (BJ): Maitreya has stated that the Earth has become warmer in order that the world will be able to grow sufficient, organic food for its people. How soon will we see the major agricultural nations make the changes necessary to convert from chemical- and pesticide- based farming to safe, organic methods?
The Master: In pockets, this is already under way. This process will continue in ever-widening ripples until, from five to 10

years from now, most farming will be organically-based. The extensive use of chemical fertilizers, which increase the yield but deplete the vitality, will give way to sounder methods. This will enhance the vitality, and therefore the health, of the people.

BJ: Will we see new areas of fertility appearing, such as in the northern regions of Europe, which at present are unable to sustain a wide range of crops?

The Master: Most assuredly, bumper harvests will become the norm throughout the northern hemisphere and indeed throughout the world. There will be food in abundance for all the Earth's people, and this without the use of harmful chemicals.

BJ: British education is undergoing a serious crisis of resources and morale. Teachers are leaving because they feel undervalued. Schools are struggling to fulfil their obligations often without the basic materials. Meanwhile, parents feel their children have become forgotten pawns in a political game, and the incidence of semi-literacy among school-leavers is one of the highest in Europe. Will education once again become a priority in this country, and in what new directions will it evolve?

The Master: Most certainly education will have to take its place among the top priorities facing this nation. A revolutionary change in educational ideas and aims will gradually unfold throughout the world. From its own background and traditions, each nation will contribute its ideas and experiments, with the evolving child as the centre of its thinking.

The present low status of the teaching profession in the UK is a temporary phenomenon. With the demise of the present government this will soon change as market forces no longer rule, as they do today, even in education. A profound transformation in the understanding of the meaning and purpose of education will take place, in which the child as an evolving soul is considered in his individual uniqueness, and all educational facilities and techniques will be geared to serve the unfoldment of his divinity.

BJ: Enormous changes are planned for broadcasting which many feel will threaten the independence and quality of programmes. The UK Government's Broadcasting Bill aims at selling off ITV (that is, independent) companies to the highest bidder, suggesting that profit will be a greater priority than programmes. Meanwhile, the BBC faces internal economic pressures as well as the effects of a hostile Prime Minister and Cabinet. How does the Master see the present television services evolving, and what role will they play in the New Age?
The Master: Like all aspects of life in the UK at the present time, communications are subjected to the play of market forces. This is crippling their development along right lines and must be reversed at the earliest opportunity. Television as a medium has enormous potential in linking nation with nation, brother with brother, and humanity with Maitreya and His group. It is the means, *par excellence*, for the dissemination of information, and, rightly handled, a key factor in the new education. Its importance cannot be overemphasized.

The present is a time of treading water preparatory to a great leap forward and the linkage of communication networks around the world.

From now on, problems will be seen to be, in essence, global, and global solutions will be sought. This requires worldwide distribution of the requisite data and ideas for their resolution.

[*Note*: The above article is based on an interview given by Benjamin Creme's Master to Patricia Pitchon and Brian James in March 1990.]

The Principle of Sharing

The principle of sharing which you advocate sounds like some glorified form of communism where we all become equally poor. What exactly is the principle of sharing? (November 1987)

First of all, I am sure it is not the aim of communism that "we all become equally poor" but simply equal. Whether that equality is always achieved is another matter but surely social justice is a laudable aim, and if it were allied with individual freedom I think few in the West could quarrel with it. It would seem that Mr Gorbachev has set in motion precisely such a move towards greater individual freedom.

To my mind, the need for sharing is self-evident: there are so many people in the world, around 5 billion, with varied requirements depending on the size of their nation and self-sufficiency. These nations grow or produce so much food, raw materials, energy, technology, often far greater than their individual needs, and seek to sell their surplus (there is an estimated 10 per cent surplus of food in the world).

Many of the poorer (usually ex-colonial) nations are far from being self-supporting and often cannot produce even enough food for their people who, as a consequence, become the starving millions of the world.

Is it not simple common sense — not to mention simple Christian (or Buddhist or Jewish) compassion — for the rich nations to share surpluses with the poor nations and so prevent the misery — and the crime — of starvation in the midst of plenty?

The Christ says, in Message No. 82: "When you share, you recognize God in your brother," and in Message No. 52: "Take your brother's need as the measure for your action, and solve the problems of the world. There is no other course." He should know.

Can you give us some idea of the economic transformation of our lives which will take place? (June 1990)

147

The redistribution of resources is the problem which is at the heart of the economic and, indeed, the spiritual crisis overhanging the world today. This spiritual crisis is focused in the political and economic theatre. That is why Maitreya comes, in the first place, as a political and economic teacher. Although His teaching is non-religious, it is about the spiritual life, about right human relationships. When we share the world's resources we take the first step into solving the ills of the world, and the first step into our divinity.

The method, as I understand it, will be a sophisticated form of barter in which the nations pool their excess resources and redistribute them fairly and justly according to need. Nothing will be imposed, it is up to us, and many different ideas will be floated. As a basic minimum, the aim is adequate, correct food, housing, healthcare and education for all as universal rights.

Will the Lord Maitreya teach us how to share? The idea of helping people at the other end of the world while we are living in London, for example, is something difficult to understand. (November 1991)

It is not too difficult to understand, when you remember that at the end of the Second World War the economy of Europe was absolutely on its knees. There were literally millions of refugees to cope with; the concentration camps had been opened and the millions of interned inmates were released. There was a colossal problem: Germany had been bombed to smithereens; most of its cities were in ruins. This was true of areas in France and Belgium and parts of England — I do not need to go into all the details. Europe — and the Soviet Union — were in tatters, and what happened? Thousands of miles away across the sea, an American called George Marshall had a brilliant plan: the Marshall Plan came to fruition and money and goods on a lease-lend basis were shipped from the United States into Europe; the biggest sharing exercise in the world transformed Europe. In a very few years the economy got going and the cities were rebuilt.

Sharing on a world basis is possible if you have the concept and the will. It is simply a recognition of the need and finding a way to fulfil it.

The Masters have a very simple plan which has been worked out, not by Them but with Their help, by a group of initiates, economists and financiers of international standing, but who are also members of the Spiritual Hierarchy. Each nation will be asked to make an inventory of what it has and what it needs. In this way the world's 'cake' will be known. Each nation will be asked to make over into a common trust that which it has in excess of its needs in any given commodity. A new United Nations agency dealing only with the distribution of resources will be formed under the supervision of a Master or at least a third-degree initiate. And so, by a simple process of sharing and exchange, a very sophisticated form of barter will replace the present economic system. This is not immediate, but not too far in the future.

The collapse of the stock markets, beginning in Japan, will force governments to see certain priorities which Maitreya has enumerated: (1) the supplying of sufficient, correct food for the people; (2) the supplying of adequate housing and shelter; and (3) the supplying of education and healthcare facilities for all as a natural right. This does not seem too much — food, shelter, healthcare and education — but there is nowhere in the world in which all of these automatically exist. Not even in the United States, which sees itself as the richest, certainly militarily-speaking the most powerful, nation in the world, do these pertain as a common right. There are 33 million people, officially, in the United States living under the poverty line. When these simple, basic priorities are implemented, you will have a transformed world. As soon as we recognize our responsibility for the Third World, we will implement the principle of sharing.

Do you really believe that a majority of Americans, with their love of consumption and possessions, their stubborn self-righteousness and their religious dogmatism, will make the changes Maitreya advocates? If so, why? (December 1986)

I should perhaps make it clear that this question comes from an American! The answer is yes, I do. The opposite side of the coin of American materialism, "stubborn self-righteousness and religious dogmatism" (all demonstrations of America's 6th-ray personality glamours), is an intense idealism and capacity for self-sacrifice. The world is really waiting for the demonstration of America's 2nd-ray soul nature (love), and when this does manifest, under the inspiration of the Christ, that idealism and capacity for self-sacrifice will sweep through the United States and galvanize it into changing direction. Of course, I am not suggesting that this will happen overnight or be painless, but painful or not it must happen. America, like the rest of the world, has no alternative except self-destruction.

Will the message of the Christ (sharing of resources) be understood by banks and those who are at the head of economically powerful corporations? (March 1989)
My belief is that His message will be very well understood by these intelligent men. The question is, will they accede to His advice to share resources? My guess is that some will, and some will resist to the very last. But the momentum of change, the logic of sharing as the only answer to our irrational and unworkable economic system (especially after the stock exchange crash which He has predicted will start in Japan soon), will eventually overcome all resistance.

A vast corruption exists throughout the world at the moment, presumably in every country, causing much unnecessary suffering. A large amount of food aid, etc, sent to Third World countries never reaches the people it is intended to help. After the Day of Declaration when the principle of sharing is being implemented and a crash programme of aid launched for the starving millions, how can we be sure it will effectively reach those people and not be diverted for gain? (December 1989)
A new United Nations agency, concerned only with distribution and re-distribution, will be set up to deal with this and other problems. At its head will be a Master or at the least a third-degree initiate. It will be Their responsibility to ensure correct distribution of food to those in need.

After the Day of Declaration, how long will the period of transition be until the correct implementation of the principle of sharing? (May 1989)

According to my Master, it will take about three years for the principle of sharing to be fully inaugurated.

You talk a lot about sharing with the Third World, but I believe that when the people of the Third World work as hard as we do they will also have sufficient goods. (March 1991)

This statement is by someone who, quite obviously, knows nothing at all about conditions for millions of people in many of the poorest parts of the world. Just to stay alive, millions in the Third World work harder, and for longer hours, than any 'developed' worker would countenance. Just to get water (often impure and potentially dangerous to health), many walk miles per day in temperatures of 40°C (104°F). To gather firewood for cooking becomes a major, all-day task. Without money or technology which Westerners take for granted, miracles of ingenuity are performed daily in otherwise hopeless conditions. I believe it is precisely the appalling complacency implied by this questioner that maintains the dangerous imbalance between the developed and developing worlds. We owe them our help.

Following the Day of Declaration, many millions of people who hadn't previously accepted your message will look for a field of service. Naturally, the elimination of world hunger will be prominent in their thoughts. What are the points someone should consider when trying to decide where the emphasis of his work should lie — in esoteric or exoteric work — at least until the worst problems of the world have been dealt with? (January/February 1988)

The number one human priority is the saving of the starving millions. Everything else must wait for this essential first step in creating right human relationships. I have no doubt that, until the worst problems have been solved or removed, the main emphasis for the average person should be in the exoteric field.

Nobody wants millions of people to live in misery and die of hunger, but do we have the means to fix this? (April 1991)

Yes, without question. There is a 10 per cent per capita surplus of food in the world. It is simply a question of distribution and re-distribution which, of course, is a question of political will. The present fighting in the Middle East is costing millions every day. Each plane costs around $5 million, one missile about $1 million. It is obviously a question not of means but of getting our priorities right. Ending hunger is the number one human priority today.

Maitreya, through you (Message No. 11), says: "I can no longer stand aside and watch My little ones die." The "little ones" have been dying since time began — deaths brought about by man's inhumanity to man. Why is He only now coming to address this problem? (April 1991)

Maitreya does not come to address this problem — starvation in the midst of plenty. He comes to inspire us to address the problem and to show us the solution: the sharing of the world's resources. He comes now under cyclic law; the timing of His advent is cosmically conditioned.

Is dying so bad? Does the Christ feel that dying of starvation is worse than living in abject destitution? (November 1987)

I wonder if the questioner has ever tried dying of starvation or living in abject destitution. The question is not whether one is preferable to or worse than the other but that neither is necessary in today's world of plenty.

The world can no longer afford the rich. True or false? (March 1988)

The world can no longer afford the vast discrepancies between the living standards of the rich and those of the poor nations. That imbalance is at the heart of our political/economic problems today. Basically it is a spiritual problem: a choice between materialism and separation on the one hand and spiritual sharing, justice and brotherhood on the other. Our choice will decide the fate of humanity.

Have the starving people not caused their situation by misdeeds in a former incarnation? (March 1992)

No. No one comes into incarnation to starve. It is against the Law of Life. Maitreya has said that: "These people die for no other reason than that they have the misfortune to be born in one part of the world rather than another." [See also *Maitreya's Mission, Volume One*, p291, 3rd edition.]

What would happen if Maitreya infringed upon (our) free will? Could it be worse than what is happening now, particularly with the annual death of thousands of His 'loved ones'? (January/February 1988)

It is not a question of relative ills but a question of Law. Maitreya knows the Law and works within it. It is this which allows Him to act as the Agent of Divine Intervention to mitigate the effects of the Law in action.

Does poverty or starvation hinder the development of the ability to demonstrate one's divinity? (March 1992)

Poverty may or may not; starvation most certainly does.

What does Maitreya advise us to do in practice? (December 1992)

The number one priority is the saving of the starving millions. The fact of millions of people starving to death is a blasphemy — Maitreya calls it a crime. It is a cancer in our midst.

We do not accept responsibility, and if we do not accept responsibility our governments will not accept responsibility. Our governments know that ending hunger is not a vote-winner; we have to make it a vote-winner. We have to say: "Unless you address the question of hunger in the Third World, I am not going to vote for you. If you want my vote, advocate the principle of sharing in the world." They will do it because they want your vote. If you live in a so-called democracy, you have to make that democracy a fact by participation. Participation also entails making your needs known. If your needs are to end hunger, then you have to act through your representatives and force your government to act. The governments of the world have known of this particular famine situation in Somalia for well over a year. They were warned by the aid agencies that it was coming and they have done nothing — because there is no oil there. If oil for the West had been threatened, the Americans would have gone in with aid, as would the French and the English and everyone else.

The next priority is making known, if you believe it, that Maitreya is in the world. That helps create the climate of hope, of expectancy, so that He can enter our lives and begin His open mission in a smooth way. The world is in chaos at the moment, tremendous upheavals are going on, and His re-entry on to the world stage is dependent on a climate of expectancy, otherwise it would be an infringement of free will.

The major priority, once the Day of Declaration is over, once we have addressed the problem of hunger, and sharing is a reality, is the saving of planet Earth. The environment will become the number one priority.

I disagree with you profoundly when you say that when people meditate on a certain situation it doesn't bring change. I actually think it does change the consciousness of the world. (December 1992)

I did not say that meditation does not bring change. What I do not believe is that meditating on starving people and visualizing their stomachs growing large with food is going to do them any good. Many people believe that if you meditate on something as specifically as that it will happen — rather than acting to bring about the changes in the political-economic structures which will end starvation in this world forever. I believe that the only way starvation will end is through the principle of sharing being accepted and a mass programme of aid for the Third World being activated by the nations as a whole. As Maitreya put it: "Nothing happens by itself. Man must act and implement his will." (Message No. 31)

The Coming 'Peace Dividend'

Interview with Benjamin Creme's Master

by Patricia Pitchon

Patricia Pitchon (PP): There is a general feeling that there will be no 'peace dividend' unless the twin tasks of disarmament and debt relief are tackled more or less simultaneously to free sorely needed funds for development. The poor everywhere urgently need clean water, an adequate food supply, housing, education and health programmes. What are the necessary next steps to begin this mammoth task?

The Master: There must be and there will be a growing realization that the world cannot continue to support the investment in arms which pertains today. Already the major powers are beginning to realize this (through their own problems connected with it) and, as everyone knows, the Soviet Union is leading the way.

Mr Gorbachev, in particular, is aware of the extent to which massive armament investment has bedevilled his attempts to reconstruct Soviet society and the Soviet economy. But until all the powers recognize the imperative need for huge reductions in armament expenditure, little progress can be made in the direction of realistic aid for the developing world.

Once this is achieved, a crash programme of massive aid for the undeveloped nations must take place. Those nations that have prepared themselves in advance by sensible measures for aid-allocation and management will render their countries the best service.

PP: How can nations prepare themselves to receive the aid that they need?

The Master: Those nations who, at the moment, are preparing lines of communication and centres of reconstruction — whether governmental or voluntary — will find themselves in the best position to receive aid from the developed nations. Therefore, it behoves those governments now working for the

155

betterment of the developing nations to organize, so far as is possible today, the various agencies and statistics of need which will be required to ensure a rapid response to that need. Necessarily, aid will be on a first-come, first-served basis, and those best equipped and best organized will be the first to receive.

PP: What would writing off total debt for the Third World actually signify to the banks and financial institutions still owed this money?

The Master: Many banks would collapse unless their losses were guaranteed by national governments; this is what Hierarchy would hope to see. There is really no reason to expect that the banks alone should bear the cost of the debt. This has to be underwritten by governments in association with the banks.

Many banks will be found ready and willing to accept a proportion of their losses for such a worthy cause, but it would be unrealistic to assume that they could bear the total cost. However, it should not be forgotten that there are many banks today whose wealth is in large measure gained from advantageous loans to the developing world.

PP: What does the Master think of so-called structural adjustment loans favoured by the World Bank and the IMF? (Note: This type of loan often requires that the developing country allows foreign imports without being able to improve the terms of trade on the world market for its own agricultural and mineral exports; it is also compelled to lift food and energy subsidies. When food and transport prices soar, the shocks are felt by the poor, who often riot — a phenomenon which has repeated itself all around the globe in the 1980s and into this decade.)

The Master: Based as these loans have been on a market-forces concept, they are basically flawed. Reliance on market forces in the unequal situation pertaining in the developed and undeveloped world makes no sense which can be called just. These provisions are a travesty of what is actually required in the Third World. In some cases, they have been sufficient to galvanize a nation to greater material prosperity, but not infrequently with a deleterious impact on the culture of the people.

Where market forces are the sole priority, inequality is assured and injustice must be the result. The World Bank and the IMF have misused their power to impose an ideological view of economic 'norms' on the Third World. It has been little more — in practice — than the extension of American hegemony in the international political-economic field.

In practice, the World Bank and the IMF, while undoubtedly aiding many countries, have acted to a large extent as a tool of successive American administrations; as the major contributor, the US has imposed its will on the modes of service which the World Bank and the IMF confer.

PP: How can the Third World nations begin to break this stranglehold?
The Master: It will depend to a large extent on the growing awareness that the world is one and that no progress is possible, even for the developed world, if at the same time two-thirds of the world's population is left in poverty. This cannot for much longer be sustained. The present economic well-being of the major developed nations is but a bubble which is soon to burst.

The nations must realize their interdependence, and when they do so through economic privation, they will adopt measures to restore the world economy.

Until the major nations are 'up against it', little real action is likely.

In the longer term, a complete reconstruction of the world's economic systems is needed and eventually will be implemented. As Maitreya has said, market forces, by their very nature, are unjust, and since they create division, separation and inequality, are evil.

PP: Can we expect a period of economic chaos?
The Master: Only a period of privation and difficulty will bring the governments of the developed nations to see reality: the

interdependence of all peoples and the need for a more just distribution of world resources.

However, the aim of Hierarchy in Its work *vis-à-vis* humanity has always been to reduce chaos to the minimum. In light of this aim it is to be expected that the transformations, although radical, will proceed at a pace consonant with the general well-being of all nations. The minimum of chaos will pertain.

[*Note*: The above article is based on an interview given by Benjamin Creme's Master to Patricia Pitchon in November 1991.]

The Future Economic System

Maitreya has said that in Islam no interest should be charged on capital. Since the Western economies survive on interest, should the West do away with its economic system? (June 1991)

The short answer to that is yes. It is a completely irrational system which has brought us to the verge of destruction. Maitreya calls market forces — which are the basis of the Western economic system and another term for 'greed' — the forces of evil. He says there is nothing more destructive than the blind following of market forces, and any nation which does so will reap destruction. The philosophy of market forces presupposes that everyone stands at the same level, with the same amount of money and the same needs. The fact is that the gap between the developed world and the Third World is getting wider every day. The nations of the Third World are supposed to conform to market forces — and if they go to the World Bank or IMF for aid, as a condition of that aid, inevitably, is some reorganization of their economy which takes a major account of market forces. This is destroying the economy of the Third World, so much so that, the year before last, $40 billion more went from the Third World to the developed world in repayment on loans than from the developed world to the Third World in new loans. It is nothing to do with aid. It is usury.

Does capitalism, the greatest of all the many evils causing famine and war, have to collapse as have already collapsed communism in the East and racism in South Africa, almost unbelievably rapidly (half a year)? (April 1990)

I do not, with respect, agree that capitalism (or communism) causes famine and war. It is political and economic totalitarianism that causes both. It is totalitarianism, not communism, which is breaking down in the East. The imposition, on the majority, of the rigidly interpreted communist ideal by a relatively small group is the evil, not the

159

ideal itself. Capitalism has succeeded in maintaining its power and influence because it has not been rigid but, as Professor Galbraith so rightly points out, has been able to adapt itself (by becoming less capitalistic in the pure sense) to changing world needs.

Is not what we are talking about really the teaching of Karl Marx and the faults of the capitalist system, and if so should not people get more politically involved? (June 1991)
It is not simply Karl Marx or communism against capitalism. Communism without capitalism is a non-starter. That is what they have found in the Soviet Union. It is not adaptable enough to the requirements of the modern world, and so it has gone under and is in chaos in the Soviet Union. Capitalism without socialism is like a great shark in the waters that will eat up everything in sight, and has no group sense or social responsibility. We need to take the best of both systems and bring them together. According to Maitreya, a symbol for that is the unification of Germany. The union of East and West Germany means today the bringing together of two opposite systems, capitalism and communism, and Maitreya says the result will be a kind of social democracy which is neither one nor the other, but a fusion of the best aspects of both. Both are necessary. The sense of justice, brotherhood and social caring of communism is necessary for the West, but the sense of freedom of the individual in movement, expression and thought is necessary in the East. That is something which will, Maitreya says, gradually become the norm in Europe and eventually throughout the world.

What would an appropriate socio-economic system for the coming age look like? (January/February 1991)
To my mind it would have to reflect the inner connectedness of people with one another and with the planet. A sustainable sufficiency would have to replace the present system of over-production, competition and waste. Therefore, interdependence and co-operation, social justice, freedom and sharing would be the keynotes of a viable spiritually-based system. It would also have to take account of, and provide opportunities for, man's

individual initiative and creative enterprise, but not at the expense of social justice and group good.

This system would not be capitalism or communism, but social democracy or democratic socialism with full participation of all peoples in their own government. Housewives, doctors, artists, teachers, etc, would play their full part in government of the people, for the people, by the people — something never achieved before, East or West.

If return on investment is 'bad', where does capital come from to fund future projects? (November 1987)
This question could come only from someone who had completely 'bought' the present capital-based system of the West, a system which has brought the world to the edge of the precipice.

Under the inspiration of the Christ and the Masters, a sophisticated form of barter will gradually replace the present economic system which has led to such chaos and injustice. Eventually, too, money — that is, capital — will have to be withdrawn — till money has lost its lure for men.

I have read that the Plan for mankind involves increased leisure for people. This raises several questions: (1) How will working people afford more leisure time at the expense of less working hours and pay? Will leisure time be subsidized? (2) What fate awaits the unemployed who see a declining job market, little hope of any liveable income, and who are not in a position to enjoy leisure anyway? (3) Will the expected stock market crash cause huge rises in unemployment? How will governments handle this? (December 1990)
The increased use of robots in manufacturing processes will inevitably create even more unemployment. This is already happening worldwide, especially in industrially developed countries. However, the use of robots creates more wealth, and with a rational world economy based on co-operation and sharing of resources and technology, the ability to supply human needs and also to increase leisure becomes practically possible. The coming Technology of Light, in particular, will free humanity from much of its self-imposed limitations today.

The coming stock market crash will inevitably cause much unemployment. This will lead to a complete change of government priorities: the supplying of adequate food, shelter, healthcare and education will become paramount responsibilities of all forward-looking nations. The waste of resources as today, in armaments and competitive practices, will cease. A rational and sustainable economic structure based on sufficiency will become the norm. Leisure will be the natural by-product of such a structure.

What will the competition structure be replaced with; what will people do? (April 1990)
They could try co-operation! Gradually, the reality of interdependence will become clear to people and will find expression in co-operation for the good of all. Competition for the very basic necessities of life is not, after all, a very advanced or laudable mode of conducting human affairs.

What will be the future direction of trade unions? (September 1990)
The Labour Movement was initiated in the 19th century by the Master known simply as the English Master. It has now spread throughout the world and carries on by its own energetic momentum.

At the moment, the usual relation between trade unions and managements (it varies, of course, from country to country) is one of confrontation and competition. The present British Government under Mrs Thatcher's leadership, for example, has made confrontation, indeed, part of policy, the aim being to curb the strength of the unions.

Necessarily, in protecting the jobs of its members, the unions have adopted a large number of rules: closed shops, various restrictive practices and voting procedures, which present-day employers find irksome and inhibiting in the competitive conditions of today's world trade. Some of these restrictive practices are now being recognized by unionists themselves as self-defeating in their efforts to attain ever higher standards of living, and are being willingly renounced.

The future direction of politics everywhere will be towards greater co-operation and consensus, and trade unionism will necessarily follow this trend. This means the renunciation of confrontation in disputes, the greater acceptance of arbitration by both managements and unions and, above all, greater participation in policy decisions and work methods by trade union members in general. As robots take over more of the production of goods, acceptance of inevitable redundancy and re-education both for new work and also for unfamiliar leisure will become necessary.

If they can put aside their narrow class prejudices and positions, trade union leaders, because of their worldwide associations, can play a major role in structuring the new society along sane and acceptable lines of co-operation and interdependence.

What do you think will happen to people engaged in military work after general disarmament, and how can the large number of existing unemployed feel useful? (May 1990)

There is no doubt that worldwide disarmament will increase the existing unemployed by hundreds of thousands. For this reason alone there will have to be a phased, gradual transfer of men and resources from military to civilian production. This process has already started in the Soviet Union. The transfer of financial resources from military to civil use will create vast opportunities for the betterment of living standards in all countries. This will provide useful work for many now unemployed or made redundant through closing down of military arsenals.

In the long run, however, we shall see a growing use of robots and machines which will take over much work now done by men and women. This will create altogether greater leisure for millions. Education to make the best and most creative use of that leisure will become a top priority.

CHAPTER 5

LIFE IN THE NEW AGE

Maitreya's Forecasts

Violence, Crime, Drugs and Self-Respect

Society as a whole is attempting to emerge from its bondage, and the eruption of crime, corruption, drugs and violence are the inevitable prelude. In the case of violent crime, the Self realizes it is imprisoned in the web of the mind to such an extent that there is no purpose left in life. The vibrations of mind, spirit and body are disturbed, and crimes are committed. The Self is not the perpetrator of these crimes; the perpetrator is the confused mind which has taken over the Self. Take, for example, child abuse. In many cases, a single, powerful thought has taken hold of the mind, to the exclusion of all else. This is destructive. In order to help the person to detach himself from that thought, it is necessary to lead him to an awareness of the Self, the 'observer', the 'watcher'. The Self is not the mind. This will create a space inside the person and will enable him to free himself. There are no shortcuts to this process, but it is itself part of a method which also includes beneficial breathing techniques. Maitreya is training certain people who are fitted for this type of work, and appropriate training will yield results. In addition, harmless drugs will be found which will help to calm the nerves.

It is in cities, Maitreya says, that crime combustion occurs, where people are addicted to drugs, sexual violence, murder and other crimes. This process of combustion brings the dirt up to the surface. Neither the police nor the military, however, will be able adequately to control the outbreak of crime now occurring. At the moment, prison is the only alternative for violent and dangerous criminals. But violence cannot be cured by sentencing people to prison. Moreover, Maitreya points out, not all people are in prison for violent crimes. Many who are in prison are not even criminals.

Maitreya says: "When a murderer is executed, the physical body is punished, but can you punish the mind? It is the mind, not the physical body, which is responsible for the act. You think you have destroyed the cause of the murder by destroying the physical body. The problem has not been solved. Once dissociated from the body, the mind still has to run the course of its mental life. It acts as an invisible force and comes into contact with another mind in a physical body, and compels it to commit an act of murder. Suddenly a man goes berserk and kills a number of people." Maitreya says to scientists, psychologists and doctors: Try to investigate this problem.

Even if you multiply the prison population you will not solve the problem if you do not attend to the minds of prisoners. The prison population has become aware of who they are and what they are. They are no longer prepared to put up with the inhumane conditions and treatment that they have endured for so long. Eventually, government policy will turn to building more open prisons containing educational centres to teach prisoners to value both themselves and life itself. It is important to make the person understand the environment and the Self. Self-realization (a gradual process entailing non-identification with anger and other destructive emotions and ideas) brings equilibrium in mind, spirit and body. When the mind is still sick it can do mental harm beyond the walls of the prison.

As for the drug epidemic, the politician's contribution to the problem of drug addiction consists of television advertisements to curb drug abuse. But the politicians alone, Maitreya says, are to blame for the desperation of these people. If people are so straitened in life that they cannot even eat properly, they will lead desperate lives. They will sell their bodies, steal, and end up in prison. If you deprive people of any future in life, deprive them of nourishment, they will end up on drugs to help them to forget their desperation. And from drugs it is not far to crime, even murder.

The massive threat posed by drugs cannot be solved through fear of the law. Strong policing will be needed to crack down on the organized gangs of drug producers, but it is not the answer to the individual drug user. Drug addicts are suffering from spiritual starvation, from extreme Self-alienation. Life becomes purposeless and people want to bring their lives to an end, and so they commit slow suicide via drugs. If life has no meaning, then 'meaning' is what must be restored, and for this to occur, it is necessary for the person to experience himself differently, to experience a sense of his own worth. Once that happens, he can grow in Self-awareness. Chaos, corruption and crime will recede in society as people gain happiness and peace through learning to control their lives through Self-awareness.

Self-respect

How can this be achieved? Not through the fear of laws, or by preaching ideology. Not by restricting people's movement, or by extra police or more prison cells. The only answer, Maitreya says, is developing detachment in mind, spirit and body. You must become free from any ism — for that is the deadliest drug. This can happen only when the Self is given self-respect. It is like a sponge — it absorbs illusions like water and engulfs the Self. When helping drug addicts it is no use telling them not to take drugs, or sending the police to arrest them. The only way to transform their lives is by teaching them: "Be what you are." They should be taught to practise detachment, even while they are still taking drugs. The next time they take drugs, they will find themselves a little reluctant about continuing their habit until eventually they will realize that it is the body that is being injected with drugs, and not the Self.

Through awareness and then detachment, habits of all kinds will fall away like leaves in the autumn.

The power of the environment should also be used to create Self-awareness. When an individual enters a church he feels peaceful and tranquil; the Self experiences this, and the mind is no longer in confusion or turmoil. Living in the bleak, depressing conditions of a run-down council estate, a person's mind will be desperate and reach for drugs to find escape.

That is why the environment should be a high priority among the country's leaders. "Clean your environment and your life will respond to it." If there is no stress or strain in your surroundings, then there is no need for drugs, for within the human body is the most powerful drug known to humanity — detachment.

An energy has been released in the world which counteracts negative forces. Eventually, certain judicial reforms will take place, and minor or petty crimes will not lead to prison sentences.

When world tension begins to decrease, when the principle of sharing begins to be implemented through a variety of social, economic and political reforms, people will feel less threatened and there will be less and less crime.

Why is it so difficult to live in correct relationship?
(January/February 1992)
At the moment we do not do this because circumstances largely prevent it — our governments do not act in correct relationship. We attack each other, we defend ourselves, we put millions of dollars into armaments of all kinds to threaten each other, we make wars, we have competitive economic structures based on market forces, that is, based on greed — those with the money get more, those without the money have to do with little. Those with power can impose their will on others — all that is wrong relationship. If governments do this the people do it and this creates the quality of the personality of the nation, the day-to-day ambience in which we live. Of course everyone is trying to do their best but we cannot because all around is competition, selfishness and greed. We are caught up in making a living, we think that more money will make life easier and therefore we strive for more money and so on. (There are exceptions — I am generalizing.) In this way we are really negating, ignoring completely, our divine nature. The divine Plan is that humanity should live in harmony — harmony is God's will for the world, but there is

168

no harmony anywhere. It does not happen by itself. Most people I know who are devotees — of Sai Baba, Maitreya, Jesus — are devoted to the idea of God. They think that just being a devotee is enough. They have the notion that because they feel love, harmony, because they like, maybe even love, their fellow human beings — until they come too close, impinge too much, or want something — they have a general attitude of goodwill to humanity. That is fine, but it does not change the structures. Maitreya has said very clearly: "Nothing happens by itself. Man must act and implement his will." (Message No. 31)

It is no good just sitting at the lotus feet of the guru, thinking that the guru, the teacher or God will do it all. God can only work through agencies. You have to become an agent of God and put it into effect in your own life. When you do that something very definite happens. You find you are a member of a very large group throughout the world who feel the same way, have the same ideals of harmony, justice, right relationships. When enough people feel this and act, things change. That is what has happened in the Eastern bloc. Why do you think the Berlin Wall is no more? Because the people in Germany suddenly responded to the energy which they felt in them to demand freedom and right relationship; right relationship is freedom. They wanted liberty, freedom, an opportunity to express that which they are. Therefore, they pulled down the Berlin Wall and united East and West Germany 30 years before anyone thought it possible. That is action taken by people on their own behalf. The same thing is happening throughout the Soviet bloc.

We are entering an era of wisdom. How is it possible then that there are so many drug addicts, and why is it that freedom brings about so much moral and/or sexual perversion? (November 1990)
We are entering an era of enlightenment but we are not there yet. What we are witnessing is the conflict arising from the clash of energies: those of Pisces, dying out, and those of Aquarius, just beginning to have a major impact. As a result,

the old certainties have dissolved, the social structures are undergoing change, and a gross materialism has become focused in commercialization across the world. Millions find themselves rudderless, purposeless, and apparently unwanted. They turn to drugs to escape the pain of separation. Freedom and licence are not the same. Humanity does not know, yet, true freedom which only awakens in the unconditioned mind.

In the coming age, are we evolving out of the relationship, man-woman marriage, as we now experience it? (November 1989)
As we now (for the most part) experience it, yes. Out of man-woman marriage, no. The family is the basic unit of society and will gain, rather than lose, importance. Many (perhaps most) marriages today are founded on little more than sexual attraction and convenience of circumstances.

In the future, known karmic and ray relationships and soul purpose will play a much greater part in the selection of mates and in providing a field for the incoming of souls.

Referring to your Master's article in **Share International** *about co-operation and competition (**A Master Speaks**, p69), is it intended to phase out competitive sport?* (September 1987)
No. Competition in sport is not separative and destructive as it is in political, social and economic realms, and, in fact, team games draw on the co-operative instinct for their success.

Is a one-world language envisaged in the Plan? If the answer is "yes", around which year is it likely to happen? What name will it get? (November 1991)
The Master DK (through Alice Bailey) has predicted that the one-world language will be a simplified form of English. This is not something which will be officially inaugurated on a particular date; it is something which is already well under way as the international language of science and of much business and trade. This will not supersede, but complement, all existing languages.

Why should English become the main world language and not Esperanto which is more neutral? (March 1991)
Because English is already used in the scientific and other fields. It is also a living, natural language used by many millions, whereas Esperanto is 'manufactured' and artificial.

Drugs: A World Problem

Interview with Benjamin Creme's Master

by Patricia Pitchon

The solutions put forward in regard to the drug problem in the long chain of cause and effect which binds producers, consumers and dealers, really fall into six categories: legalization; law and order measures; financial measures such as seizing drug dealers' assets; crop substitution (ie, the peasants who grow the opium poppy or the coca leaf from which heroin and cocaine are derived should be encouraged to grow other crops); education and rehabilitation (aimed at consumers); and finally, negotiation, a solution some Colombians have put forward ever since the drug barons there declared open war on the government.

Any proper plan must get at producers, consumers and dealers; it has to have short-term, medium-term and long-term solutions; and the economic, political and social aspects of the problem must be considered.

Benjamin Creme's Master kindly agreed to answer questions relating to this world problem.

Patricia Pitchon (PP): More and more people advocate the legalization of drugs as the answer to this problem. This would, they say, cut out to a large extent the drug mafia.
The Master: This may seem attractive but it is not an option. It would be tantamount to legalized murder.

*PP: Former White House Chief of Staff Donald Regan suggested greater co-operation was necessary between banks, agencies, law enforcement officials and government, and he even proposed (in a recent **New York Times** article) that, to get at drug dealers' cash assets, the US Treasury could quietly print $50 and $100 bills different from those now in current use. With 10 days' notice, the US Government should announce that the old bills are no longer legal tender and must*

be exchanged for the new ones. Is getting at the actual cash
and assets of drug dealers the primary emergency aim?
The Master: That is a measure which would only be viable in
the short term — and might be attractive in the short term —
but experience of life and humanity leads to the conclusion that
it would not work.

PP: What are the loopholes?
The Master: The loopholes are these: the drug dealers
themselves would know in advance of these plans and would
take the necessary measures to 're-launder' their assets. In fact,
that is what they are doing at this moment. Like the criminals
in the past, for instance in Chicago and other towns, they are
taking a new stance as respectable citizens, investing in every
aspect of national and international life. They are, as often as
not, the holders of shares in large corporations, often totally
respectable citizens, frequently working for governments in a
bona fide position, as advisers, commercial agents, go-
betweens and so on, because of their many contacts all over the
world. So it would be very difficult to pounce on them within a
reasonably short space of time before they reacted to the new
situation and found their way out of it. They are in the position
they are in only because they are masters of their craft. Their
intelligence is as good as that of the best intelligence services.

PP: Crop substitution cannot be a solution without a
restructuring of the prices of commodities on the world market.
For example, recently the prices of cocoa and coffee
plummeted, wiping out the profits of many countries. What do
you think of this?
The Master: In the long run, crop substitution is the ultimate
answer. But, as you rightly suggest, it is dependent on other
factors. That is, the growers of these crops must be guaranteed
a reasonable return on their work and investment of time and
energy in growing crops such as coffee or bananas, or
whatever, rather than the drug-producing crops. This entails,
essentially, a re-organization of the world's economy. In the
end, it comes back again and again to a re-organization of the

world's economy, based primarily on the principle of sharing and a just redistribution of the world's resources.

When that is done, you will find that peasants in the various drug-producing countries of the world — of their own free will — will gladly accept the responsibility of feeding the nation, rather than feeding the drug needs of millions of — as they see it — dissolute citizens at the lower end of the social scale, dropouts, etc. They would feel more proud of their work. It would give them a sense of contributing in a positive rather than in a destructive way to the world's economy. At the moment — as they see it — they have no alternative.

PP: What do you think about another alternative, that of spending a lot more money on the rehabilitation of drug addicts and on education of the people at large?
The Master: This must be given a high priority. There are millions of people involved in drugs, both as producers and as consumers. The users, of course, are always the losers. A huge rehabilitation programme must be put into action by all governments who have a problem in this area. Maitreya has already started a process, as some people know, of inaugurating centres in which young offenders, alienated individuals, members of broken families, drug users and pushers (those on the outer edge of society — who feel against society) can be, and eventually will be, rehabilitated. There they can gain the self-respect which will lead to their rehabilitation and equal membership with the rest of society. They must see themselves as belonging. At the moment they are on the slow path to suicide, because, for most of them, life has little to offer of value.

PP: What about more law and order measures?
The Master: This is a necessary first step, and should be seen only as that. It is a stop-gap measure, to prevent the escalation of the menace which is a real menace to the well-being of society. It is a canker. But for a short time, sufficient funds should be redirected to this policing action, to control the distribution of the prepared drugs as they leave the various

small factories which are growing in number all over the world. This will be necessary for some years.

PP: What do you think about negotiation with the drug dealers, a solution put forward by several prominent people in Colombia?

The Master: This should be tried. It may or may not work. It depends on other factors. One of the major factors in all of this is the incentive factor. Where money has its present value, there will always be an incentive for some people to want to be very rich. But very soon, there is going to be a complete transformation in the world's economic systems due to the devaluation of money after the coming world stock market crash. Then people will find it not so rewarding to engage themselves against the law — and a strengthened law if the previous measures are taken — in the producing countries. It will be less glamorous, less rewarding and more dangerous than at present to engage in what will be seen, more and more, to be a criminal activity. Also, one of the difficulties inherent in negotiation is that some of the biggest drug dealers are seemingly respectable citizens at the head of large corporations and industries and so on. For them this is an appropriate — although illegal — investment. So, they are not likely to come forward easily to enter into negotiations, but it is worth trying.

PP: Are these people whose names we've never heard?

The Master: Largely so. There may be some who are under suspicion by various government agencies, but so far they have been astute enough to 'keep their noses clean'.

PP: Are there Americans and Europeans among them?

The Master: Most nationalities. But they are on a level which is practically untouchable and unsuspectable, working through divisions or departments which they have set up.

PP: What about other measures such as bank reforms?

The Master: There is probably little that can be done in this department without altogether greater access to bank accounts. Most of the money 'laundered' on a large scale is 'laundered' through the main banks in Switzerland. The banks are vowed to withhold information about such investments because they make enormous profits from them. So, these are the last places where you would be able to enforce a search. This is a very 'long shot' indeed, unless you change the laws of investigation and search. It can be done in some countries, like Britain, if enough evidence can be brought to bear. But it is difficult to find that evidence at the levels where it really counts. It is too well organized, and, as said before, the intelligence network of those concerned is very good indeed. They can quickly move on their assets from one bank to another. They spread it over many banks, and invest in absolutely legitimate industries.

PP: So is it a very extensive network of corruption?
The Master: Absolutely. It is worldwide and much more than skin deep. It is very deep indeed.

PP: If a change is brought about in producers and consumers, what is going to happen to this network of corruption at high levels, with all these funds at its disposal?
The Master: The value of money has to change. Then they will lose the incentive to make such enormous fortunes, because there will be nowhere to spend them. As the world economy changes to one of sufficiency and sustainability rather than the present one of constant growth and production, the incentive to amass massive wealth will diminish. There will always be scope for the rich and greedy, but in the face of world public opinion and the changes in the world economic systems which will gradually come about, it will become less a life purpose.

PP: A gradual change of perception of values?
The Master: Yes, partly enforced from outside by the change in the value of money.

PP: What is the perspective in the short and medium-term for Colombia?
The Master: There are high hopes that Colombia will take the constructive path, but the path to destruction has as great a possibility. At the moment, anything can happen. It can go in the direction of civil war and a kind of mass suicide, or Colombia can rehabilitate itself with the help of major nations

like the United States and the non-acceptance of the criminal activities of drug processing and dealing. This means a severe crackdown on the personal armies employed to keep the whole business going in Colombia and elsewhere. They have to be met on their own level.

PP: There seems to be a link here between drugs, defence and debt affecting this situation, because if the producer countries are going to engage in crop substitution they cannot sustain their enormous debts; the debt is not going to be cancelled unless defence costs go down in the industrialized countries and they actually relieve these countries (ie Peru, Bolivia, Colombia, etc) of their debt, and at the same time drugs flourish in an environment where there is great poverty. Is this correct?

The Master: It is a correct assessment, and each of these factors has a part to play in this corrosive business of drug production. Debt write-offs will have to be subsidized by curtailing defence in the major nations. This is already under way. On the surface, defence programmes already started are continuing. So many billions have been spent on weapons which are nearing completion that these will probably go ahead. But new projects have been cancelled on all sides. As the US and the USSR reach agreement on curtailing nuclear weapons, this will give an incentive to all to diminish production. It creates a stabilized condition in which war becomes more and more unthinkable on a global scale. They set the tone for the other nations.

PP: Is the drug problem a long and painful haul? Are we going to have to spend 10 or 20 years to deal with it?

The Master: Hopefully, and probably, not. It could last perhaps five or six years more in diminishing intensity. The shell of the nut will be cracked when the principle of sharing is beginning to bite (to take place and to be implemented) among the nations. That is the key to the whole process. This allows the poorer countries — the so-called Third World countries who are largely producing the drugs on a massive scale — to take their rightful and dignified place in the community of nations without having to resort to that illegal activity, which nobody wants except those who are making money from it. The principle of sharing itself, and the achievement of an economy based on sustainability and sufficiency will pull the rug out from under the feet of the dealers.

PP: Perhaps we need a shock to effect a major shift. Will that shock be the stock market crash?

The Master: Humanity needs to be up against it and desperate, and that shock will certainly be sharp, and will bring humanity to its senses, and the governments, in some cases, to their knees. They will appeal, when Maitreya comes forward, for guidance and will accept the guidance, and all their priorities will change. Of course this will change the dependence of millions on drugs. People turn to drugs because they do not know who they are; they do not know who they are because they are under-educated. They are obsessed with the sense of their own ignorance, their own inability, their uselessness, and so they feel they have nothing to lose. They have no self-respect. That is why Maitreya says: "Without self-respect, no further progress can be made." The first thing is to teach self-respect.

The transformation of the economic structures of the world and a re-orientation of government priorities will create the conditions in which people can regain their self-respect. And they will not want the drugs. If people do not want the drugs, no one will supply them. It is a matter of opinion among the Hierarchy that the drug crisis is now reaching its height, and, when it reaches its height, there is only one way it can go (and that is down).

[*Note*: The above article is based on an interview given by Benjamin Creme's Master to Patricia Pitchon on 20 September 1989.]

Life in the New Age

Is it true that in order to move into the Age of Aquarius many people must disappear and that the only ones to remain must be positive and working for humanity? (March 1987)

No. That idea, though common, is a total misrepresentation of the circumstances surrounding our entry into the New Age.

The development of the New Age institutions and structures will take time, and the full participation of all sections of society will be required to make the new ideas acceptable and lasting. The speed of change will be in proportion to society's ability to implement the requirements of sharing and redistribution on a global scale. The question implies a use of force which has no place here. Human free will is sacred to Hierarchy (if not to humanity!). They will act only as advisers and experienced counsellors. Nothing will be imposed or enforced but, eventually, a re-orientation of thought will lead to a worldwide desire to serve the common weal.

(1) Many people are in the process of forming communities to further the teachings of the New Age and also to ensure their survival through difficult times previously predicted (for example, stockpiling of food and water). It now appears that these shelters no longer guarantee survival and that a global solution to our problems worldwide is the only solution. Is this correct? (2) Nevertheless, are these communities beneficial to mankind and do you recommend their continued formation? (April 1989)

(1) If there were to be a nuclear war on a world scale today all of humanity and the lower kingdoms would perish. The solution to our problems — sharing — must be taken on a global scale. (2) Those who form themselves into 'survival' communities, stockpiling food etc, are acting not under 'New Age' principles which are about the One humanity, sharing and justice, synthesis and so on, but in deeply separative, selfish, 'Piscean' ways, not identifying with humanity and its needs as

179

the One humanity. I cannot see that they have much of benefit to give the world and would not recommend their continued formation (had I any say in the matter).

Nowadays many business organizations buy pieces of security apparatus. This has given rise to a whole new industry making machinery for this purpose. Is this necessary? Don't you think that within five years we will have totally different relations which will make these pieces of apparatus useless? (October 1987)

Yes, I agree. However, today is not five years from now and these organizations address themselves to their problems of today. Also, they may not have or share your conviction that we will have totally different relations in five years' time.

Schools without Walls

Interview with Benjamin Creme's Master

by Patricia Pitchon

Patricia Pitchon (PP): In many cities around the world, education is in crisis. Particularly in the West, the authority of both teachers and parents seems to be declining and the problem of discipline in the classroom is a major one. What, in your view, are the causes and what are the remedies?

The Master: The problem is not one of discipline. It is a question of freedom and a new sense of the validity of the child: his need and right for self-expression. Each child — at whatever level — comes into the world with his or her own set of purposes. A main one is to learn to live in peace and harmony with all others and in right relationship with his own environment. The possibility for this to take place is very rare. So great are the inequalities of opportunity and educational standards that few find themselves in a situation where their true worth and needs can be respected and served.

The world today is saturated with a new spiritual energy, the energy of equilibrium, focused by Maitreya. It drives everyone in two directions: inwards to his source, which gives a person an added and often powerful sense of himself as a unique individual, and also outwards to society, where he seeks to stake his claim.

The problem of discipline is connected with this crisis in the psychology of the child, and with the need to recognize all young people as unique sons of God evolving towards the manifestation of that Sonship.

All educational establishments today without exception are in a state of transition, some more, some less. It will take a considerable time for the necessary adjustments in educational theory and practice to take place before the problem of discipline can be solved.

The young everywhere need and are demanding their freedom and the right to be treated not as subservient imbibers of predigested knowledge but as adventurers seeking the answers to their questions and the fulfilment of their dreams.

PP: In Japan there is an intensely competitive atmosphere in education. Children in Japanese society study long hours, and many go to extra classes after school, returning home quite late to do their homework. What is your view of this trend?

The Master: This problem is not confined to Japan but has reached its acme there. As a result of the commercialization of learning, vast numbers of children are being subjected to these injurious conditions. The results will show as the present generation reaches maturity.

However, people everywhere are amazingly resilient and quickly replenish their reserves when invited to do so. This will happen in Japan in the not too distant future and increasingly elsewhere.

A new dimension — the dimension of the soul — will become more and more accepted as the basis for the child's need. When this has become the case, each child will be seen as an evolving soul moving towards the fulfilment of his or her potential for this given life. The new science, the psychology of the soul, will be the basis of all future educational efforts and will transform life for both the child and the teacher.

Schools and colleges will lose their institutional aspects and integrate more and more with the society in which the child is found. A closer relationship, therefore, between school and work will become the norm, and open the way for "schools without walls".

*PP: Recently an article on education in **The Independent**, a UK newspaper, described the creation of several unusual schools in Harlem, a well-known black neighbourhood in New York. One is a marine science school, another emphasizes the arts, a third has a strong business orientation, and so on. The academic results of children emerging from such schools have soared, which seems to prove that, even in neighbourhoods riddled with severe social problems, the creative potential of*

many children is there to be tapped. Are these schools the beginning of experiments in the direction you are describing?
The Master: Yes. These are the first signs of the new awareness of multiple experience, wide-ranging action and interests, rather than the narrow specialization predominant at present.

Each child brings to life the sum of his or her many achievements in the past, and much is lost to the world of talent and gifts when the opportunity for their expression goes unprovided. Out of these many experiments much will be learned of the true needs and inner capacities of the child, which today are severely underrated. This is the source of much of the 'indiscipline' and lawlessness which abounds.

PP: Do you mean, by this, that education will become individually tailored?
The Master: Precisely. Each child is unique and the education must reflect that individual need. With the new science will come an understanding of the Rays.

When the individual rays of children are known, their gifts and limitations can be better assessed. The role of the teacher, therefore, will change profoundly. Each teacher will become a mentor.

PP: In parts of the West, consensus between families, schools and governments has broken down. How should this consensus be re-established?
The Master: In my eyes, there never was such a consensus.

PP: Education has always been taken seriously in Eastern Europe, but how will schools adapt to a waning of ideological content? Will an exacerbated nationalism or, in some cases, a religious content replace political ideology?
The Master: The nations are evolving at different rates and inevitably the changing structures of schools and educational theory will vary. The loss of an ideological basis should not be seen as a calamity.

On the contrary, it provides a new sense of freedom to the unconditioned mind of the child. This is a healthy and wholesome process. It is not ideology or religion but the imposition of these conditioning factors which brings harm to the expanding mind of the child.

PP: What can India do, via education, to lessen strife due to religious and caste differences?
The Master: Education is the answer to India's problems, as it is throughout the world. The difficulty for the Indian subcontinent is the problem of implementation. No one denies the need, but the problems of educating 800 million people steeped in superstition, caste-envy and hatred have until now baffled all governmental efforts. India, together with many other countries, requires the concerted aid of the developed world to ease this immense burden. Once tackled in depth, there will grow in India a new awareness of the stranglehold which ancient religious and social taboos have had throughout the centuries.

A start is being made and great teachers like Sri Sathya Sai Baba are initiating new and far-reaching procedures to this end. It will take time. The roots of superstition, separation and greed are deep, but a new time is coming for India as for all the world.

PP: What, in your view, are the immediate aims of education? What are the first steps in laying a more appropriate foundation?
The Master: The first step is to accept the autonomy of the child. Each child requires education, otherwise he cannot fulfil his potential. However, that education must fit him as you would require a pair of shoes to do, and as the shoes become outgrown and must be changed, so too must the educational structures, outlook, curricula and concepts respond to the child's changing needs.

Basically there are two educational structures in many countries: one for a small élite, preparing them for the higher echelons of influence and power, and another for a broadly based, egalitarian rump which is equipped for the lesser posts in industry and other fields.

Each has advantages and disadvantages, but takes no account of the variety of gifts and levels of evolution to be found among children everywhere. The truly gifted child must find the environment to fulfil his gifts. This is relatively rare today.

The broad mass of children produce a less sustained level of achievement but must feel that all resources are at their disposal. It is of course true that the truly gifted child will achieve eventually under most conditions, but much valuable time is lost for many, for want of the necessary stimulus at high level. This is an essential requirement if the needs of the new time are to be met.

(*Note* [PP]: According to the Masters, seven types of energy sweep through our solar system; they affect every atom within it and are referred to as the Seven Rays. Man, considered as a personality with physical, emotional and mental bodies, and as a soul, responds to, and is coloured by, a particular combination of these rays, depending on the individual concerned. At each level (physical, emotional, mental, personality and soul) a particular ray predominates, and the effects are expressed via particular strengths and weaknesses. For further information on rays, see Chapter 13, 'The Seven Rays,' in this book, as well as the chapter on 'The Seven Rays' in *Maitreya's Mission, Volume One.)*

[*Note*: The above article is based on an interview given by Benjamin Creme's Master to Patricia Pitchon on 21 December 1990.]

Education

Will Maitreya and/or the Masters recommend changes in our educational systems? If so, what general changes will be suggested? (January/February 1988)

As I understand it, Maitreya Himself will not make other than broad, general statements about the need for change in education. However, in due course, certain of the Masters will apply Themselves to inspiring definite changes in both the structure and content of educational institutions worldwide. The reforms that They would like to see consist mainly in a re-thinking of the purpose of education so that it more fully serves the needs of evolving divine beings at various stages of development; a restructuring of curricula to provide a more flexible response to individual needs; a closer involvement of all sections of the community in the educational process and the elevation of education to the highest priority in each country.

You have said that manual labour will be taken over by machinery. Does this also mean most teaching will be replaced by video and computer-assisted learning to free the time of both teachers and students? (January/February 1988)

No. While I am sure that video and computer use will increase in the future, I do not believe that the teacher will be replaced by them. On the contrary, the sensitive, trained response to individual students' needs will make the provision of sensitive, trained and perceptive human teachers essential.

Teachers will have to be trained in the recognition of ray structures and soul purposes as well as an accurate assessment of the point in evolution of the student if they are adequately to meet the needs of children in their care.

In the previous article, "Schools without Walls", it was said that already a good direction in education exists on a small scale. Are the Free Schools of Rudolf Steiner part of this? (May 1991)

To my mind, yes.

186

What is the future of Rudolph Steiner education? (May 1992)
Rudolph Steiner was a second-degree initiate. He started as a member of the Theosophical Society, then drifted away and started Anthroposophy. There is a lot of his teaching with which I personally would not agree, especially in relation to the Reappearance of the Christ, but I admire his educational methods. I think they are profound, at the present moment probably the most 'correct' in relation to a child's needs.

The way for the future is the understanding that each one of us is a soul in incarnation — we are not this personality, which is only the physical-plane vehicle for a great spiritual entity, our own individual soul, a reflection of the Divine, the Absolute, and which is absolutely perfect.

The soul in incarnation goes through the perfection process, until it imbues its vehicle with its qualities and nature.

When the child is understood as a soul, then education will be geared precisely to that individual. At the present time, in a theoretical, aspirational way, that is what the Steiner schools try to do. That is not to say that it is what they actually do, but of all the schools they do try to do that. Of all the educational experiments going on in the world today — and there are many — it probably comes closest to the ideal.

With the advent of the Masters and Their stimulus to education at all levels, I have no doubt that the Steiner schools will respond and refine and amplify their methods too.

Do we not really infringe the law of free will by forcing our children to attend school? Shouldn't we just teach when the teaching is wanted? (January/February 1988)
Of course there are and have been a few 'free' schools, like A.S.Neill's Summerhill in England, in which the students attended lessons only when they 'felt' like it. But Neill was dealing mainly with 'problem' children who would have difficulty in any learning situation. If school curricula and practice were sufficiently imaginative, interesting and interestingly presented, I do not think many children would not want to attend. While other activities (football, fishing, loafing

187

about) have their attractions, learning, too, if properly presented, is a great draw for most children.

Can you tell us more about the educational centres that will be set up after the Day of Declaration? (March 1989)
These centres will teach young people the first steps in the process of Self-realization. As you know, many young people today lack direction, motivation, meaningful employment. With some this leads to vandalism and crime. They will be given the opportunity to learn who they really are — of coming into Self-awareness. Maitreya says the first step to Self-awareness (which leads to Self-realization) is self-worth and self-respect. So these young people will be rehabilitated in that area — trained, found jobs, and given the techniques of Self-awareness. This leads to Self-realization, the goal of humanity.

People will be chosen and trained to oversee this rehabilitation, and there is a very simple breathing technique which will be part of the process. It involves a balancing of the breathing and the holding of the breath for four counts at a certain point. In that moment of holding the breath the person becomes temporarily, but immediately, Self-aware. And in that second, Maitreya can intervene, as it were, to stimulate the point reached. It is a way to rehabilitate thousands, perhaps millions, of alienated young people. It is the young, of course, who have to make the new world.

Mystery Schools

You have mentioned 'Mystery Schools'. How will they differ from regular schools and who will attend them? (January/February 1988)
The Mystery Schools are the schools in which the training and disciplines for initiation are received. Colleges will be created from which those seen as ready for initiation will be drawn. The Mystery Schools themselves will be of two categories: preparatory and advanced. The aim is that all humanity should

have taken at least the first initiation (and thus enter the Spiritual Hierarchy) in this coming Aquarian cycle.

There will be a preparatory school in Japan, an advanced one in China; a preparatory one in Scotland, an advanced one in Ireland; a preparatory one in the American Midwest, an advanced one in California; a preparatory one in New Zealand, an advanced one in Australia; a preparatory one in Greece, an advanced one in Egypt; a preparatory one in Sweden, an advanced one in Russia; a preparatory one in France, an advanced one in Italy. Thus, the world as a whole will be covered to give precise teaching to those disciples who are ready for preparation for initiation.

Is it true that a future esoteric school is in the process of construction in the South of France? If so, is it near the sea and could it be at Bonfin near Fréjus? (May 1990)
My information is that this is not the case.

*Who taught you so that you have reached the stage where you can meet a Master? This is my first meeting here and I feel very frustrated because there seems a lot to know and a lot to learn. Why can't **Share International** have a sort of Entity that people who want to know and learn can learn from?* (September 1992)
You mean why don't we start a school? A school would require a group of teachers who know at least a page more than others do in order to teach — and there are groups all over the world who do nothing else. Our task is not to set up a school, but to make known that the Christ is in the world, that the Masters are returning — there are now 14 Masters in the world besides Maitreya — and to prepare the way, to create the climate of hope, of expectancy, for His coming, so that He can enter our lives without infringing human free will.

If you want to know about the esoteric teachings in the academic sense, read the Alice Bailey teachings. There are 24 books which are available in all the esoteric bookshops. The first was published in 1922. Start with these, with *Initiation Human and Solar* and go on. No one need be short of something to read.

Maitreya calls for the transformation of all our institutions. (1) May we assume that the media are included in this? (2) Does Hierarchy have special plans for the media? (3) Are there any initiates waiting 'in the wings' of the media who will help make the changes? (December 1986)

(1) Yes, the media have a very responsible role to play in education. Maitreya will most certainly use the media to teach the people. (2) To use it, yes; to change it, no, that is our responsibility. (3) Yes.

One of my clients (I do Psychology Counselling) is a survivor of ritualistic sexual abuse. She believes it to have been going on in her family for generations. She also believes it to be pervasive and worldwide and indulged in by many prominent people. Other information concerning ritualistic abuse has come to me, but the subject is difficult for people to accept at all.

My questions are: (1) Is this part of 'sealing the door where evil dwells'? (2) Is this part of the deepest layer of human darkness which is about to surface during the 1990s? (3) How widespread is this practice? (4) How long has it been in existence? (5) Is it a satanic ritual? (6) Some say many children are stolen and murdered for these purposes. Is this true? (June 1990)

(1) No. The line from the Great Invocation: "And may it seal the door where evil dwells," refers to the sealing off to their own domain (upholding the matter aspect of the planet) of the Lords of Materiality, or, as we call it, evil. This is done by lifting humanity above the level where they can be used by these forces. (2) Yes, but not exclusively during this coming decade. Its roots are deep and these rituals will manifest for a long time to come. (3) My information is that this phenomenon is known in most parts of the world. (4) In varying degrees, and with many ritualistic variations, for countless thousands of years, almost from 'the dawn of time' as we say. (5) It depends on what you mean by 'satanic'. Many of these ritualistic practices stem from ancient religions (which still have their adherents worldwide) and, while often involving sexual

practices, do not always involve abuse or torture. Many do involve children (usually, but not exclusively, girls: virgins) for their supposed 'purity'. The cults tend to run in families and (often) isolated communities in Europe and North America, hence the involvement of children. It is not seen as abuse by the adherents but natural involvement of the whole family in their religious practice. One should not forget that flagellation was an accepted form of Christian worship for centuries.

Many of these rituals originated in Atlantean times and are therefore deeply entrenched. With the advent of the Seventh Ray of Ceremonial Order or Ritual, some of these ancient practices are re-stimulated into being.

Some of them do involve sex magic, a reflection of ancient Atlantean magic, and some, too, are definitely what we would call 'black magic', conscious invocation of evil, 'satanic' forces, and these are becoming more widespread. As the Christ emerges, and as His influence in the world gains momentum, it is inevitable that the forces of Materiality will seek to counter His work. They try, but they will not succeed. (6) No. Most children involved in these rituals are members of families deeply involved in their ancient religious practices.

In answering in this way, I am seeking to elucidate these activities, but not, in any sense, to condone them or to suggest that they are harmless. Some few may well be harmless, but in many cases I am sure much harm is done to the participants, especially to children.

191

CHAPTER 6

EFFECTS ON THE ENVIRONMENT

Maitreya's Forecasts

Change in the Earth's Rotation

The new energy sweeping through our world will make the land more fertile. People will experience greater health, and we shall see many diseases begin to disappear. As a result of the energy of equilibrium, people will be able to live in closer contact with nature, and there will be greater harmony between the plant, animal and human kingdoms. Destructive forces (the effects of human behaviour) are being reversed in such a way that they will become constructive. Because of the greater harmony between nature and humanity, people will be happier: to disturb the environment is to disturb your own nature.

Maitreya has energized the planet and generated warmth so that enough food can be grown to meet the new demand for food grown naturally. Changes in weather patterns are already occurring and will continue as a result of the Earth's warming. Across the globe, the days and nights will be warmer, and we shall see changes in human behaviour as people spend more time resting and less time working. They will enjoy more recreational activities.

The plant and animal kingdoms will also be affected, with a number of species disappearing. We shall find that society will think in global terms, and policies will be developed globally. People will draw closer together, learning to share and live together in harmony. "Even mind, spirit and body will be changed," Maitreya tells us.

Nature will respond positively in terms of new vegetation. The Earth will be full of food, and no one will be able to understand the process fully. The necessities of life will be on hand. The environment will become the number one issue throughout the world. Even a few years ago, no politician took the environment seriously; now the concern is there. This growth in concern is the result of increasing Self-awareness. There is a link, Maitreya says, between the inner and the outer environment: the moment you become aware of your Self, the environment within your mind, spirit and body is under your control. This awareness then leads you to look into the outer environment.

Maitreya says that a decisive change has occurred in the rate of the Earth's rotation. The speed of the Earth's revolution has slowed. As a consequence, the forces surrounding the planet have been made to slow down. These are not 'blind' forces but the effects of man's activities.

This momentous event occurred at the end of July 1988, and will result in decisive changes, both in the short term and the long term, in the Earth's atmosphere, in the air, on land and in the seas. Some have already begun. This can be understood as the 'turn of the wheel' which marks the end of an era (that is, the Piscean Age) and the beginning of a new era (Aquarius). "The wheel governs all creation. When it turns, no one can escape transformation." Naturally, this process will occur gradually during the whole Aquarian cycle, but some changes are imminent and observable.

This 'end of an age' inevitably produces a certain number of natural disasters such as floods and earthquakes, and we are seeing a dramatic climax in the number of disasters taking place around the world. All this energy has been released because of man's inhumanity to man. The greed of those in power has condemned their fellows and nature itself. The environment has been polluted and has reacted. Maitreya says: "The last time I came, as Jesus, it was written in the Bible that when I appeared again the very elements of nature would be disturbed."

Human suffering during this process of adjustment is inevitable, but in suffering the destructive forces are released from their natural pattern and dissipated. Anything which operates by imposition of force will not survive.

This period is not, however, one of cataclysmic destruction. This 'adjustment' is a matter of degree, and the portents of doom generally offered are exaggerated. Maitreya points out that when disasters occur on an international scale, people await a 'second coming'. But, He says: "The Lord has been here since the morning of time. When I am with you, there is no question of a second, third or fourth coming."

When there is a calamity, He continues, the Lord is always with the soul. He gives it strength, comfort and bliss at that time, although with our minds we perceive only suffering. In crises, people will be brought closer together and will help each other. Through our own free will we can lessen distress by responding with alacrity to human need.

After the disasters have peaked, there will come a period of calm — the violence and destruction will come to an end. As people gain awareness, their guilt will recede and they will realize that it is not the Self that is causing all this mayhem. This has been created by an outside force of destructive energy which has sucked them into the storm of chaos and confusion. The new feeling will be like rising in the small hours of the early dawn when you are surrounded by a sense of tranquillity and calm.

Maitreya points out that these are not predictions, but the fulfilment of law.

Effects on the Environment

Referring to Maitreya's comment about the slowing down of the Earth's revolution, at the end of July 1988, do you think that up to that moment the Earth's speed was stable, or gaining speed?

According to a "Lunar Calendar" which I have, the Earth's rotation has been slowing for a long while due to tides. I quote: "When tides get channelled into narrow spaces, the build-up can be impressive. The global average tidal range is 76 centimetres, but in the Severn it is 13 meters. A great deal of energy is there to be tapped — such energy that the friction of tides in shallow seas is slowing the Earth's rotation. There were over 400 days in a year around the time of the great coal deposits...

"Moreover, it was because of the tide caused by the Earth on the solid rock of the moon that the moon now always shows us the same face." Has somebody got their science wrong? (May 1989)

Indeed, someone has got their science wrong — and I am sure it is the author of your "Lunar Calendar" and not Maitreya. The speed of the Earth's rotation is relatively stable, with constant, but very slight, variations. Greenwich Observatory did confirm that there had been a slowing down at the end of July 1988 as revealed by Maitreya. This has brought the Earth (a little) nearer the sun, so increasing the sun's radiation. This fact, according to Maitreya, is responsible for the mild winter and early spring experienced in northern countries.

It has been announced that Maitreya has made the days and nights warmer (by bringing the Earth closer to the sun) so that more food will be available. On the other hand, the Earth is also being made warmer by the greenhouse effect. So why does Maitreya find it necessary to warm up the Earth even more? (July/August 1990)

Because the greenhouse effect is only a temporary manifestation and can be reversed.

Are cause and effect coming closer together now? (April 1989) The more advanced a person is, the quicker is the karmic reaction. The more that the negativity of humanity is dissipated in disasters like the hurricanes, floods and so on, the faster this process works. There is a speeding up of cause and effect. This is also affected by two other factors: the sun's radiation has increased, and the Earth's rotation has slowed down fractionally, just enough to slow down the energies moving around the Earth. This produces a quicker manifestation of the Law of Cause and Effect. Therefore, changes proceed faster as the Law is able to act more directly. Evolution is speeding up and will continue to do so.

Please explain the reason for disasters such as floods, earthquakes and the like. Must they happen before the good times arrive? (April 1990)

Many of the disasters are the direct result of our wrong thought and action. For example, most of the earthquakes which occur do so as a result of underground nuclear tests which are carried out by several nations. An earthquake, not necessarily in the vicinity of the test, is the inevitable result of such activity.

Furthermore, the pollution of our atmosphere, of the oceans and rivers, upsets the balance of nature. The nature elementals respond, through floods, hurricanes and so on, to purify the planet of these destructive energies. I am afraid that more such disasters are forecast as the purification process reaches a peak.

Does Transmission Meditation alleviate the force of earthquakes, or is it out of our hands? (January/February 1989)

Transmission Meditation does indeed help alleviate the force of earthquakes, but not directly. One of the major functions of the Christ in the world now is to act as the Agent of Divine Intervention. This allows Him to mitigate the effects of earthquakes. The actual earthquakes are out of our hands, but their effects are not. The more energy that we release into the world through Transmission Meditation from the Christ and Hierarchy, the more energy is available to Him as the Agent of Divine Intervention, and so the more He can alleviate the effects of earthquakes. The earthquakes will take place, but you will find again and again (as you are finding already) that there is often little or no injury or death even from quite substantial earthquakes. (This, of course, is not the case in the terrible earthquake, predicted by Maitreya, which killed so many in the Soviet Union.)

Earthquakes have various causes. Some of them have to do with the natural movement of the Earth. Very many of them are the result of the fact that a great cosmic body in space pulls our planet slightly off its axis. Many other earthquakes are caused by the misuse of our free will. For instance, many are caused by underground nuclear explosions. The recent earthquakes in Armenia and in North India, Nepal and Burma were caused directly by underground nuclear experimentation by the US, the Soviet Union, China, India and Pakistan. This is something which is in our hands, and which we could stop tomorrow.

Much of the destruction now taking place in the world, the unusual weather conditions, hurricanes such as Hurricane Gilbert, and floods, as in Bangladesh and the Sudan, are not 'acts of God'. They are the result of the action of the Law of Cause and Effect. We set in motion the causes, which produce these effects. These disturbances in our weather patterns are in our own hands. The violent hurricanes and floods are the unleashing of destructive forces — our destructive forces — and they create as a result calm and equilibrium for humanity.

If we misuse our free will and resources, if we behave violently, competitively, creating disturbance in the world, we affect the elementals who control the weather. As soon as we come into harmony they, too, will come into harmony.

(1) When humanity comes to show love, justice and sharing, what effect will that have on the weather? (2) Is the climate affected by our attitudes to life? (April 1990)
Not so much the climate (that is to say, relatively hot or cold climes), but the weather is affected by our attitudes. While we are in disharmony, with much confusion, war, and great discrepancies in living standards; when millions starve unnecessarily and millions more live in constant anguish and want, we set up destructive forces which inevitably affect the elemental lives whose activity creates the weather worldwide. They react inharmoniously and earthquakes, hurricanes, floods, etc, are the result. When we come into equilibrium, they and the weather will become more predictable and 'normal'.

Will the return of the Christ and the Masters of Wisdom prevent the onset of another ice age which some scientists are predicting? (April 1988)

The trouble with the scientists (experts) is that they never agree. There is another group of scientists predicting (with more reason) a rise in Earth's temperature through the 'greenhouse' effect of pollution in our upper atmosphere 'locking in' the sun's rays. This is already happening — there has been a 5 per cent rise in the Earth's mean temperature in the last 100 years. If that continues, the polar ice caps would melt, the oceans and seas would rise dramatically, threatening low lying areas such as the Netherlands and elsewhere. In any case, the return of the Christ could not prevent another ice age if that were on the cards!

Does your Master expect a purification of world karma on the physical plane in the form of catastrophe? (May 1988)
If the questioner means will there be major Earth changes, then the answer is no. The Law of Karma is the Law of Cause and Effect and karma is not 'purified' but resolved or balanced. By the action of this Law, the present imbalances and irrationalities in man's thinking and behaviour (separation, division, wars, millions left to starve, etc) create conditions of extreme imbalance in nature. This is being and will continue to be expressed in the form of hurricanes, high winds, floods, freak weather patterns and so on. When man begins to put his house in order, the nature elementals will respond with more balanced activity and greater harmony will result.

(1) Why are some people affected by weather changes and barometric pressure much more than others? (2) Why are some people affected by the energy of people around them much more than others? (April 1992)
(1) Changes in barometric pressure affect everyone, without exception. Some people are simply more sensitive to, more aware of, these changes. (2). The same pertains in relation to other people. However, I have found that people who most often complain about the effect on them of other people's energy ("bad vibrations", "draining", etc) leave something to be desired in their own energy expression.

*According to the **Hamburger Morgenpost** [Germany], Australian scientists fear that perhaps within two years there will be a collision between the Earth and a newly discovered asteroid, "1990 MU". They seem to be expecting massive earthquakes and catastrophic floods. According to devotees, Sai Baba is also supposed to have said that in about two years there could be several major disasters and that northern Germany and the Netherlands would be swallowed up by the sea. Has Maitreya given any information about this?* (November 1990)

No, but according to my Master, there is no substance in this report. Sai Baba has issued a formal denial of issuing such a report.

What about the widespread prediction of the Earth tilting its axis about the year 2000? (March 1990)

That is certainly not my information.

Although we're coming into the Age of Aquarius we've got such a lot of pollution in the waters, in the air and so on — are we not starting off on the wrong foot? (June 1991)

Yes, it is a tragedy, but it is not to do with the Age of Aquarius. The pollution is to do with the Age of Pisces, which is now coming to an end. It is precisely the misuse of resources, the blind following of market forces, the competition, which has created the pollution which is now proving such an ecological hazard. We are poisoning our planet so quickly that unless we change direction very soon it will be too late, and future generations will suffer unbelievably.

Luckily, Nature is very resilient and, I believe, will bounce back. Already, many people, even governments, at the insistence of various groups in different nations, are beginning to address the problems of pollution. I know crazy men like Saddam Hussein can set fire to the oil wells of Kuwait and undo in a week what has taken years to achieve, but nevertheless, more and more governments, groups and individuals are seeing the necessity for an ecological rethink, a solution to the problem of pollution. But it will not be stopped while we have such competition in our methods and policy of manufacture. We have to shift the present attitude to production from that of greed, waste and competition to that of sufficiency. Instead of saying: "How much can we produce and how fast?" we have to say: "How much do we need? How little of this commodity can we get away with using? How little of this and that will give us a rich, full life in such a way that all individuals can share that life?"

Today, America hoards most of the resources of the world — the oil, the various minerals and so on — Russia tries to do the same, Europe takes as much as it can store and afford — all the developed nations, including Japan, do this. They see the overuse of resources as a testimony to their power, economic strength and skill, whereas they are working against the very needs of the world. They should be using their power and skill to make a rich, varied and satisfying life for their people with the minimal use of resources. Sufficiency must take over from this profligate over-production based on competition. Market forces must lose their grip on the psyche of the world.

The UN Environment Programme, among other reputable organizations, has stated that the higher ultraviolet radiation caused by ozone depletion will adversely affect food production and human health. I would like some clarification on the ozone situation. I have not heard anything since the statement from Maitreya that there was no hole in the ozone layer. Is all the scientific evidence about ozone depletion bunkum? (June 1991)

By no means. What Maitreya said was that there was no hole in the ozone layer; it was an illusion. But that there is a far-reaching depletion of the ozone is without doubt and presents humanity with the problem of increased ultraviolet radiation and the hot-house effect.

Are freon and other chemicals the only thing destroying the ozone layer? Is Hierarchy 'propping it up'? (November 1987)

Yes, the gradual destruction or rupture of the ozone layer is caused by pollution. Hierarchy is not 'propping it up'.

There is a very unusual astronomical event, a supernova, near the Southern Cross. Presumably, this is the physical-plane effect of a major event in the cosmic planes. What is the significance of it? (September 1987)

It is the demonstration on the outer physical plane of the culmination of all plans and purposes of a Solar Logos. The radiatory capacity thus achieved results in the extraordinary brilliance which indicates a supernova.

Is this what is meant by the following words in the 'Finale' of **A Treatise on Cosmic Fire***, by Alice A.Bailey? "When all is resolved into harmony, when all is blended into symphony, the grand chorale will reverberate to the uttermost bounds of the known universe. Then will occur that which is beyond the comprehension of the highest Chohan — the marriage song of the Heavenly Man."* (September 1987)

As I have indicated above, the extraordinary radiation of a supernova demonstrates the completion of that particular manifestation of a Heavenly Man. All has been achieved; all fused into one sound, including, but resolving, all differences, all contradictions.

In Stanza 328 of **The Call** *(in the Agni Yoga series), dictated through Helena Roerich, it says: "Soar with thy thoughts. Fly by affirmation. Fly by love: And thou wilt realize the joy of flying. And again the gulf of life will remain beneath thy feet. And a miracle of flaming colours will radiate near the splendour of the Southern Cross. All is attainable." Does this stanza refer to the supernova?* (September 1987)

Yes.

As there is no life without the sun, can we say that God manifests through the sun? (April 1991)

Most assuredly, yes. This solar system (and all others) is the body of expression of a great cosmic entity, the Solar Logos, the One "in whom we live and move and have our being."

Are the sub-atomic particles — neutrinos — a source of the cosmic energies entering our world and influencing attitudes at this time? (December 1987)

No. Neutrinos are simply the name we have given to sub-atomic particles, recently discovered, but which are always present in our planetary field. They may be but are not necessarily cosmic in origin.

I cannot sleep at the full moon. Why? What can I do to remedy this? (December 1990)
It is quite common for people to find it difficult to sleep at the full moon. When the moon is full, says the Master DK (through Alice Bailey), it is as if a door is opened between the sun and Earth. The spiritual energies received then are more potent, affect the human psyche, and often prevent sleep.

A planetary body called Chiron was discovered in 1977. Could you tell us whether it is one of the 'hidden' planets mentioned by DK and comment on its qualities (ie, which ray it channels)? (January/February 1988)
Yes, this is one of the hidden planets, is veiled by the moon, channels 4th-ray energy and is a non-sacred planet.

The planet Chiron was discovered in 1977. Is there a connection with the coming of Maitreya? (December 1990)
Directly, no. But its discovery can be seen as one of the many 'signs' surrounding His Advent. "Those who search for signs will find them but My method of manifestation is more simple." (Message No 10)

Are other planets affected by the change from Pisces to Aquarius? (April 1991)
Yes, all of them.

CHAPTER 7

SCIENCE AND TECHNOLOGY
IN THE AGE OF LIGHT

Maitreya's Forecasts

The Age of Light

We are now entering the age of Light. The Hierarchy is training scientists through experiences of phenomenal powers by demonstrating the use of the Science of Light to achieve transfiguration, transportation and communication.

All living cells are interconnected, with light between them. Every atom is interconnected with the light. The time will come when we can transform this light, and then it will be possible to dematerialize the body. Adepts and Masters can do this, and one day, Maitreya says, we will be able to do it. Matter can be transported from one place to another through light. Thus the astral body of one who has departed can materialize. Even now scientists are being taught how to materialize through the Technology of Light so that objects can be transmitted from one part of the world to another. This technology — using colour, sound and vibration — is the science of the 21st century. It will make society more prosperous and happy. People will enjoy life more, many diseases will be healed instantaneously. This is the power of light.

In time, scientists will be able to understand these processes, these laws of nature. When you become aware, conscious and detached, Maitreya teaches, you will not manipulate these laws for selfish ends.

The Technology of Light will meet all our energy needs in the 21st century. "It will need no huge budgets to maintain because it will be devised and controlled by intellectuals who do not look for billions of pounds of profits to satisfy them,"

Maitreya's associate explains. Once built, the technology will last for 2,500 years, "until the next cycle of evolution".

Environment and energy will be the top priorities of the new era. Last will be defence, "because there will be nothing to defend". When light is at your command, you do not need guns and bullets.

The time is fast coming when there will be no need for prisons. Terrorism will disappear because there will be no place for terrorists to hide.

The ambition of the politicians is now moving into space, from where all movement on Earth can be controlled. But Maitreya warns that if the politicians play with this Science of Light and abuse it, it will destroy them. Humanity has naïvely believed that they are the only ones in space, but there are others there, far advanced, who have always watched over us, He says, teaching us not to kill, to respect others, and to learn to be happy and free. They have always protected humanity, and they will not allow it to destroy itself by the exploitation of science in space.

These 'Space Brothers' have now trained scientists in the US and USSR in a technology that can monitor every movement on Earth — of armies, tanks, planes, and even submarines beneath the sea. There is, thus, good reason behind the Russians' and the Americans' confident calls for major disarmament, for not only does this technology (a sophisticated extension of the Star Wars concept) make pinpoint surveillance possible, it can also be used to control men and machines.

For instance, if a terrorist was located on a plane thousands of feet in the air, holding a gun or a bomb, he could be 'frozen' in the act of terrorism. A submarine beneath the waves could be drained of energy and rendered powerless.

Maitreya is sending a clear message to the world's political leaders: no wars can now be won, and spending vast amounts of money on international arms programmes is a complete waste. Our prime task now is to look after the environment. This will become the responsibility of every individual, politician, guru, saint, and scientist. Our energies will be spent in making it healthy again. When that happens, there will be less suffering, disease and poverty.

Scientists are also being taught by the Space Brothers the art of producing energy through light. The effects of the ozone problem will disappear, but the climatic changes that are under way are still bound to take place. Many experiments with the Technology of Light are being undertaken in Russia. This is because the Space Brothers set up a community in that country 15 years ago. Russia was chosen because it was such a closed society, where commercial pressures did not affect scientific research. Today, says Maitreya, the Russians are well ahead of the rest of the world in this field. That is why Russia leads the way in calling for arms reductions.

Scientists today are involved in researching and manipulating the mechanism of the forces of evolution. They do not know where these forces lead, but they will definitely get a glimpse of the end of the trail. If they persist in experiments with bio-genetic engineering they will be able to create beings which are half-man, half-animal.

But though the scientists are interfering with the natural course of mutation, they will never understand it, for it is beyond knowledge and wisdom.

"Only God understands mutation," Maitreya says, and for scientists to use their knowledge to 'play God' is dangerous. "You are able to do certain things," He notes: "but you should not do them. Why do you not spend money rightly so that people can be given the right food to eat, that they may die natural deaths?"

Scientists are also creating potential havoc in the universe with nuclear-powered space probes. According to Maitreya, there are certain points in the universe which control the energies of creation. If they are disturbed, it is like setting free the atoms from their nuclear bonds. This can create disasters such as earthquakes and floods on Earth. The distant planets have their own gravitational force which holds them in place and maintains their pattern of evolution. Nuclear-powered probes can upset the balance and lead to disastrous consequences.

Scientists will be given experiences by Maitreya to make them aware of the danger of their research. The Master says: "The moment you come near the powers of creation you will be tempted to use them. If you do not know how to handle them they will destroy you. Certain yogis can approach these powers, but with detachment. Therefore they do not harm them. The scientists, however, do not possess this detachment."

Scientists are also playing dangerous games in other ways. They are searching to find the secrets of consciousness. They are now experimenting with animals, playing with genes to discover where this conscious energy comes from and where it goes after death. So many experiments are being carried out behind closed doors that, if the public knew about them, there would be an outcry and a demand to end them. "The scientists are playing with the forces of life." But as scientists deepen their understanding of the laws of life and mind, Maitreya says, there will be a greater understanding of interdependence, the cement which sustains creation.

Technology of Light

Why was the Technology of Light not given to the United Nations rather than to individual governments who might misuse it? (September 1989)
Because the technology can only be understood by scientists, and the United Nations does not have such a group of scientists under its jurisdiction. Scientists work on a national basis and only the two superpowers, the United States and the USSR, have been given this technology because they have the greatest arsenal of nuclear weapons (which the new technology makes obsolete); where they lead, the others must inevitably follow. If they say "our nuclear arsenal is obsolete," what value then have the British, French, Chinese (or Indian, Pakistani, or Israeli) bombs? Eventually, this new Technology of Light will indeed come under the jurisdiction of the United Nations.

Has there been any development in the Technology of Light, bringing the energy of the sun directly into use? (May 1991)
Probably there has, but I do not know anything about it. This technology is in its infancy. There is a town in the Soviet Union whose energy sources are all received directly from the sun through one of their satellites. That is the use of Light Technology. This technology is more advanced in the Soviet Union than elsewhere because the Space Brothers have had a base there for the last 15 years.

Is there technology available through the Masters by which the waters of the world can be cleansed (something perhaps more advanced than chlorination)? (October 1989)
Yes. But, long term, the answer to pollution lies in our hands. We must respect the environment more.

(1) Will the new Science of Light be able to neutralize the atomic waste which, for example, is dumped in the seas? (2) Will the Technology of Light be used to neutralize toxic waste? (April 1990, March 1991)
(1) Yes. Not only atomic waste, but also the stockpiles of nuclear weapons, can be neutralized and made safe. (2) Yes.

We know we are overheating the Earth by using fossil fuels. But vast numbers of poor people around the world will need large amounts of energy to improve their standard of living. Are there any other options that will not add to the greenhouse effect? Is nuclear power the answer to this dilemma? (December 1988)
The fusion process of nuclear power — a cold, safe, wasteless process using a simple isotope of water, universally available — will solve all humanity's future power needs. This will be made available to us on the implementation of sharing as the economic norm.

Is the recently reported breakthrough in nuclear fusion research going to lead to widespread use of this energy? (May 1989)
Yes. This method of producing cool, safe nuclear fusion energy is, according to my Master, not the ultimate but a big

209

step in the right direction towards the fusion process which Hierarchy have in mind.

You have often spoken about sub-atomic matter, saying it is literally Light. You said that the miracle water at Tlacote is lighter than ordinary water because some of the atoms have been made sub-atomic. A physicist would deny that this is light as he understands it. Is it possible to explain in terms familiar to the physicist? For instance, does his present understanding of sub-atomic particles (protons, neutrons, etc) still apply? (October 1992)

Yes. All that we see (or do not yet see) in Creation is created by light. "There was darkness ... and God said: Let there be light, and there was light," — and with light all things in heaven and Earth came into being. When our present-day physicists understand what this means they will discover how to control matter, distance and time.

*In **New Age Community** (p12), Helena Roerich writes: "It is possible to whisper a great number of useful experiments into the strata of space. Atomic energy, condensation of prana ... have been destined for humanity." Is the reference to condensation of prana a reference to Wilhelm Reich's orgone energy accumulators?* (January/February 1988)

This passage in the Agni Yoga series illustrates the continuing role of Hierarchy as the inspirers of our science. They send into the mindbelt of the world various 'clichés' to which we respond. This is the source of our inventions and discoveries. "Condensation of prana" in the quote refers only indirectly to Wilhelm Reich's orgone energy accumulators. As Reich formulated and used them, these accumulate energy from the two lower etheric planes — the third and fourth. Reich himself experimented with a motor application of this energy with some, if limited, success. The future will see the discovery of higher energies and their focus through instruments. This will revolutionize transportation, illumination and some forms of medicine. It is to this, I believe, that the quote refers.

Will exoteric scientists be able to describe matter in precise mathematical language? If so, how far away are they from being able to do so? (April 1987)

Yes. Already various scientific formulae represent the first attempts to describe our understanding of the laws of matter. A well-known example is Einstein's formula, $e = mc^2$. When we gain an understanding of other laws governing energy and matter and formulate them, we shall have the means of creating mantras corresponding to these formulae, thus controlling the energies of matter by the power of sound. The Master DK has prophesied "building by the power of sound" before the end of the century.

Will the Masters teach the world's leading scientists about the true origins, history and evolution of mankind as put forth in **The Secret Doctrine***?* (December 1986)

No, not specifically, but the advent of the Christ and the externalization of the Masters' work will inevitably lead to an enormous stimulus of interest in the esoteric tradition. Many scientists will no doubt avail themselves of those teachings, but I would think that their interest would more likely be drawn to the more esoteric aspects of science.

When so many aspects of esotericism rely on the intuition or extra-sensory perception or exceptional sensitivity to extremely subtle forces and energies, how can these subjective ideas be grounded or proved in a way which can be accepted by modern science? (January/February 1991)

The subjective experience of forces or energies with which esotericism deals is today the prerogative of the relatively few. This will increasingly cease to be the case as more and more people become aware of and can articulate these same experiences. Neither humanity nor science stand still, and the time is fast approaching when much that is seen today as unusual, unlikely and unacceptable will become commonplace and totally respectable. It will then be 'proved' by science, because it will be the experience of so many. One should always remember that the 'esoteric' of today is the 'exoteric' of tomorrow.

I have heard of a process called Electronic Voice Phenomenon, where people receive voices of discarnate entities (presumably astral) on their tape recorders. (1) Is this phenomenon genuine reception of 'spirit' voices? (2) Is the development of this process inspired by the Hierarchy? (3) Will it evolve into an efficient electronic communications medium of worthy use? (December 1990)
(1) Yes. (2) Yes. (3) Yes. See article in *Share International*, July 1982, p9.

I am afraid that I do not understand "scientists in Russia have incubated a human brain". Have they cloned brain cells? Have they managed to develop and keep alive a brain taken from a foetus? Or have they kept alive the brain of a dead person? All possibilities sound monstrous to me. Is there any use in such experiments? (June 1989)
They have kept alive the brain of a person now dead. The value of this experiment lies in the technique they have developed of using the life-giving energies from coloured light. One must remember that no "person" is involved in this incubation experiment. The soul had withdrawn; what is left is simply a body and the brain is but an organ — a computer — of the body.

*A.Bailey writes (in short): "... the services rendered to humanity by the medical profession largely offset the evil of vivisection." (**Esoteric Healing**, p28) Does this mean that animal research is all right as long as man is getting better as a result? (2) How can mankind ever make it up to the animal kingdom?* (April 1989)
(1) Within limits this is true. The problem is that much suffering is inflicted on large numbers of animals in duplicated and unnecessary experiments. Some seem to be devised with an appallingly cruel disregard for the pain involved. Nevertheless, broadly speaking, the knowledge gained through this experimentation has been of great benefit to the human

race. (2) Strangely enough, despite the cruelty of many of the experiments carried out on animals today, it is the animal kingdom as a whole which stands in karmic debt to humanity. For long ages in man's early past, the animal kingdom preyed constantly on humankind, threatening, at times, the continued existence of man.

Do our space probes have a disruptive effect by landing on Mars? (October 1991)
No.

How far from truth is astrology as taught today? (June 1988)
My understanding is that there is a huge gulf between astrology as taught and practised today and that of the coming time or as now used by the Masters. Theirs is a great science not knowable except by higher initiates.

How old is the pyramid of Cheops really? Science says 4,000–6,000 years. DK says (I think) 100,000 years. (March 1988)
Almost 16,000 years. Nowhere, to my knowledge, does DK give 100,000 years.

UFOs and Space Brothers

Does Maitreya say there is really life on other planets and there are beings who come to the Earth just to protect us? (May 1989)
Maitreya has not so far said so directly, but recently he spoke of other beings in space, far advanced, who have always protected humanity.

All the planets, without exception, are inhabited. In my experience, UFOs are absolutely real. They cannot usually be seen by us because their normal state is on the higher etheric, not solid, physical levels. When we do see them, this is because they lower the vibrational rate of the vehicles to come within our vision, as a temporary manifestation. They are there all the time in their thousands and even millions. They help us in many ways and without them this Earth would be a very painful place indeed. They mop up a great deal of the nuclear radiation which we release into the atmosphere through nuclear experimentation. Even if a test is underground, contaminated, poisoned dust flies up into the atmosphere. The space beings have 'implosion' devices which neutralize this nuclear radiation. Without their assistance our rivers and streams would be undrinkable; we would, literally, be dying. There would also be large numbers of deformed babies born. All this is a result of our misuse of nuclear energy. Without their help we would be in a very sad state.

Is there any relation between Maitreya and the crop circles? (December 1992)
The crop circles are created by the phenomenon we call UFOs, and there is a relation between Maitreya and the UFOs. These UFOs come, in the main, from the planets Mars and Venus. Our Hierarchy is in contact with the Hierarchies of Mars and Venus; all the Hierarchies in our system are in contact with each other. All the planets of our system are inhabited, without exception, but if you went to Mars or Venus, of course, you would see no one; they are all in higher etheric matter. If you have the higher etheric vision, you see them as perfectly normal, slightly different, but not all that different, from ourselves. They are not little green people with protuberances coming out of their heads!

I have read much about the Space Brothers from this publication, and I have read quite a lot about alleged UFO sightings and contacts as well as theories on this enigma in books dating back to the 1950s. If indeed our troubled planet is being visited by inter-planetary travellers, as I earnestly believe, why haven't they landed on the White House lawn or outside the Kremlin and publicly announced themselves? Why have they chosen to shroud themselves in a veil of mystery, leaving behind bedazzled witnesses and patterns in fields of corn or grass to attest to their existence? (June 1992)
For the same reason that Maitreya does not appear on the White House lawn or at Buckingham Palace or at the UN Security Council: They know the Law and work within it.

There are laws, above all those governing our free will, which prevent such dramatic manifestations. It is surely obvious that if their sole need was to make known, unequivocally, their presence to us, they could do so in myriad ways. What they do is obvious enough to the intelligent and open-minded but tangential enough not to infringe human free will on a mass scale, which would be the result of your recommendations.

(1) Are there people from other planets living among us on the dense-physical plane? (2) If so, how many and from where do they come? (3) Do they sometimes use the physical bodies of humans? (4) or have they their own physical bodies? (May 1991)
(1) Yes. (2) Many. Mainly from Mars and Venus. (3) No, never. (4) Yes.

Are there souls from other star-systems currently incarnate on Earth, and if so, why? (July/August 1987)
There are many stories of people from other solar systems visiting or incarnating on this Earth, but my understanding is that they are without foundation. On the other hand, many beings from planets within this system do take incarnation here. They come to undertake certain service on this planet (for a greater or lesser period of time), or they have fallen to this Earth and are part of an 'exchange' of souls (nature abhors a vacuum).

Do you think that there are other planets where Beings learn and experiment in other ways than on Earth? (May 1987)
Yes. All the planets are inhabited by conscious, intelligent life but not necessarily on the same physical plane as ourselves. So far, we are aware of only three (solid, liquid and gaseous) physical planes. There are four higher planes, still physical, known as the etheric planes.

Recently there were very unusual UFO sightings in South Australia. A UFO bugged a car in the Nullarbor desert. It scattered some sort of ash, frightened the occupants, and they said that their mental process was affected during the incident.

At about the same time, a UFO, probably the same one, bugged a fishing boat off the coast. There was a similar effect on the crew. My questions are: Were the experiences genuine? If so does it mean the space people are starting to make their presence more obvious? (May 1988)

The experiences were genuine in so far as the people mentioned saw a UFO, but I very much question that the experiences were as described. For instance, the "ash" is not ash, but precipitation of energy — prana. UFOs show themselves, sometimes at close quarters, but not to "bug" in the sense of deliberately to frighten. The mental processes of the people may well have been affected: a) by their fear; or b) by the experience of higher energies and the higher consciousness of the occupants of the UFO.

These fears and these changed mental states are common to many who see UFOs at close quarters. They are just as common among those, now in the Asian community of London, who see Maitreya suddenly materialize (or dematerialize) in front of them. People are very easily frightened by that which they do not understand. My understanding is that, although this incident is not necessarily an indication of it, the space people are indeed making their presence more obvious. It is clear though, from the distorted reports of such encounters, that they must proceed in this very cautiously.

*Several impressive reports of UFO sightings have come from the Soviet Union recently. The first became world news but the second was also very interesting: hundreds of people, including airplane pilots, saw a fast-moving object above the town of Omsk which did not register on any military radar apparatus. My newspaper, **Algemeen Dagblad** [the Netherlands], quoted a major in the Russian army, who in an interview for a Russian publication said: "The luminous disk with four searchlights, which I watched for five minutes, seemed to hover above the airstrip but then the searchlights went out, the air around it became turbulent and it shot off in an easterly direction." As Maitreya has spoken several times*

216

about "the Space Brothers", I have several questions which I hope you will answer.

(1) Were these indeed sightings of cosmic vehicles? (2) Where did they come from? (3) What is the purpose, or reason, for their presence? (4) Why do they only show themselves fleetingly and not definitely and conclusively? (5) Are the claims of the first sighting true: that three beings emerged from the ship? (6) Will there be a time soon when humanity will know beyond any doubt that there are "Space Brothers"? (December 1989)

(1) Yes. (2) From Mars, Venus and other planets of our system. All the planets sustain life, but on the etheric physical. (3) Various. They help (within the karmic law) to maintain the stability of the planet ecologically. They neutralize radioactivity from tests and other emissions. (4) So as not to infringe our free will and also not to cause alarm. (5) Yes, except that they were of normal height and size. (6) Yes. Maitreya will introduce the subject and show the interchange which takes place (on Hierarchical levels) between the planets. We will eventually know them and accept them as friends and mentors.

Will a connection between Maitreya and the work of the "Space Brothers" (for example, the corn circles) become more apparent in the near future? (April 1992)

I do not think necessarily so, but an interesting event happened while I was in Australia which might be a pointer in that direction. While I was in Melbourne, there were apparently many sightings of UFOs over the city, in particular a spectacular one which showed two UFOs zigzagging all over the Melbourne skies. This appeared on television and caused the usual (brief) media stir. I saw a video of the event on my next stop, Adelaide. My Master informed me that Maitreya had requested these UFO sightings to link up with my visit. I appeared on breakfast time TV in Adelaide and told people that there would be more activity over that city that day. I was stopped in the street the next day by a man who had watched the programme, recognized me, and "watched the skies", as I had told them. He had a classic UFO sighting later in the day. Since he was alone when he saw the UFO the media — at first interested — refused to investigate.

When someone is abducted by alien visitors they usually report seeing little grey-skinned beings with disproportionately large heads. (1) Do they usually look like that? (2) What star-system do they originate from? It is now being theorized that modern UFO abductions and ancient encounters with fairies are encounters with the same beings, and that both fairy tales and modern abduction reports are folklore, centred around the same sort of beings. How do you feel about that theory? (June 1990)

(1) My information is that no one is abducted by space visitors, however they look. They can look as different from one another as we do on Earth. There is no uniformity in cosmos. (2) No 'alien' or space visitor comes from anywhere outside our solar system. All the planets in our system are inhabited. Most UFOs originate in Mars or Venus. The Space Brothers and fairies, ancient or modern, are not the same Beings. Fairies are part of the vast deva or angelic evolution, parallel to the human.

I still believe that these so-called abductees are encountering something unknown. If it isn't aliens, what are they encountering, if anything? (September 1990)

They are encountering the products of an overly active astral imagination. Were Space Visitors not 'in the news' and topical, they would be content with ghosts and the like.

There are reports coming from the US that up to 10,000 cattle have been drained of blood and expertly operated on for removal of vital organs. Extensive enquiry by farmers and experts all over the country has failed to identify those responsible. Lately, it is the space people in flying saucers that have been suspected of mutilating those animals. Is there any truth in these reports? (September 1991)

In relation to the Space Brothers, absolutely none whatsoever.

Crop Circle Phenomenon

For several years, mysterious circles have been appearing in British cornfields, among other places. The media have been giving more attention to this phenomenon lately. Are they caused by Flying Saucers, as some people think, by Maitreya's Lightship, or is there another explanation for them? A Harrier jet crashed near one of these circles. Do they create magnetic fields which could have interfered with the plane's instruments? (October 1989)

These circles, which have been known to 'Ufologists' for several decades, are indeed the result of action by the Space Brothers and their UFOs. They are created and left deliberately as a sign of their presence, the extraordinary structure and precision of the circles being a testimony to their higher science (none of the corn, though folded into spiral and other formations, is ever destroyed).

They do indeed create a magnetic field around them, but this has nothing to do with the aircraft accident. In fact, it was the body of the pilot of the jet which was found near one of these circles. The plane itself crashed later in the Irish Sea.

How do you interpret the phenomenon of the crop circles? (July/August 1991)

My information about the crop circles is that they are created by what is generally called UFO activity. The UFOs come in the main from Mars and Venus, not from outside our solar system. All the planets of this system are populated, though if you went to Mars or Venus you would see no one at all — they are all in higher etheric matter. The UFO phenomenon is distinctly related to the Reappearance of the Christ and the externalization of the work of the Hierarchy, and we owe them a great debt. Their surveillance of this planet is total and energetically of enormous benefit to the world. What the Space People are doing in the crop circles in particular is recreating to a certain degree the 'grid' of our Earth's magnetic field on the physical plane. Each of these crop circles is a chakra, as it were, a vortex of magnetic energy, and they are spreading out

219

around the world, having started in England. They were dismissed in the first place, as always, by the sceptics. I do not mind if they dismiss them as a mystery which cannot be solved but to dismiss them as "created by a freak wind" — that is just stupid, and patronizing to human intelligence. Nobody of average intelligence would believe that is even possible — you only have to inspect the circles to realize that. But to make sure that that thought did not gain credibility, they began to put rectangular bits on to the circles — and there is no wind that works in rectangles and triangles and these complex configurations. They are all 'ideograms', and if you were familiar with the 'ideography' of ancient Atlantis you would recognize some of them. They are meant not to be recognized as to their meaning but they do have a meaning, and many people will 'intuit' these. They are a reminder of the ancient connection with the Space Brothers.

What is the purpose behind the appearance of corn circles over southern England (and elsewhere)? If they are made by Space Visitors in UFOs, is it possible that the activity will be photographed by the team of observers now active in Britain? (September 1990)

Apart from some few isolated hoaxes (very crude attempts to replicate the mysterious corn or crop circles), these circles are made by UFOs manned by the Space Brothers. They have several levels of purpose. Firstly, they are a continuous reminder to us of their presence in our skies. More importantly, each circle is magnetized and occupies a specific place in the lines of magnetic force in our Earth's magnetic field. Each circle is a vortex, drawing energy in and radiating energy to its surrounding area. Together (they are not haphazardly placed), they form a 'grid' or interrelated energy system of much benefit to us. Since this grid is formed scientifically, it is most unlikely that any group of observers, however well-meaning, would hit on the exact spot on which to observe the creation of any future circles. The Space Brothers are unlikely simply to 'oblige' with a circle. They do not waste energy.

220

*In the British newspaper **Today** (9 September 1991), there is an article carrying the headline "Men who conned the world", in which two British artists admit "they pulled off the great 'corn circles hoax' for 13 years". These two men claim that they have performed the hoax by creating the corn circles all over southern England and demonstrated their ability to do so in a field near Sevenoaks, in Kent. Could there be any truth in the story?* (October 1991)

There have certainly been a number of hoaxes perpetrated, but usually they have been singularly clumsy. These two men appear to have perfected a method (I believe just recently) whereby they can create a circle which looks unmade by human hands. However, there is absolutely no way in which two men could be responsible for the creation of many large, intricate, complicated designs in different parts of the country which have appeared simultaneously, nor does their claim explain the appearance of large numbers of circles in Germany, Japan, USA, Belgium, Canada, etc.

The men say they have admitted the truth because of the large amounts of money some people were making out of "their" circles, presumably referring to the various books which have appeared recently on the subject. One wonders how much *Today* and its proprietor, Rupert Murdoch, have paid the men for their story. Interestingly, they do not claim the multi-location which would be necessary to create the widely separated circles. The fact remains that they are created, apart from the few hoaxes, by the Space Brothers as part of a long-term energetic service to this world, as time will certainly show.

Do the Space Brothers make crop circles all the year around, perhaps on bare ground or grass, which would not be visible to us? Or do they only work in the summer months when the fields are full of crops? (October 1991)

All the year round — and they have been doing so for many years now.

(1) Is this magnetic grid that is being created replacing the ancient leyline grid? (2) We noticed energies close to

Stonehenge. Knowing that you have said that Stonehenge is now dead, could these energies have been coming from a pictogram in a field directly south of the monument? (October 1991)
(1) No. The lines of the magnetic field slowly change position.
(2) Yes.

Are the new crop circles created by UFOs actually being used by them now or will they lie dormant until the entire grid system has been completed? (October 1991)
They are not 'used' by the Space Brothers, but created for our present stimulus and future use.

Can we tune in telepathically to the Space Brothers by meditating on the diagram of the crop circle? (October 1991)
No.

Why are the vast majority of the crop circles found in England? (October 1991)
This is an oblique, subtle way of drawing attention to the fact that Maitreya is in England.

Why are the crop circles made in corn? (October 1991)
Because corn is seasonal and lends itself to this kind of activity without being 'indelible'.

Is the corn that is harvested from a crop circle energized and if so is the food that we get from it energized also? (October 1991)
Yes, but that is not the purpose behind the circle.

Curious at reports of crop circles in Wiltshire, England, I travelled there with a friend to see for myself. Both of us had back pain and we sat in a formation of eight circles wondering whether we could feel any energies; nothing. After half an hour we left. I suddenly noticed that my backpain had vanished. So had my friends'. Are these circles known to have healing energies? (October 1991)
No. They are not specifically healing energies but could have a healing effect.

Is it beneficial for people to absorb the energies from the crop circles? (October 1991)

Yes, very much so. But care should be taken not to over-stimulate.

Is there a difference in the energy at different places within a crop circle formation? (October 1991)

No.

Why do the energies feel different in different circles? (October 1991)

Because they are different. Those created by Venusian ships, for example, are quite different from those made by Martian ships. To those sensitive to these energies the differences are obvious.

What is the difference in quality between the Martian and Venusian circles? (October 1991)

Very little. Venus is immeasurably more advanced than Mars, but as far as these circles are concerned, the difference is minimal.

Is there any difference in the effect of the vortex or chakra in the cornfield if it is created by a Martian or Venusian ship? (October 1991)

There is a slight difference in the long-term effect. For all practical purposes, they are — to us — the same.

(1) Do any of the pictograms depict the bodily form of Martians or Venusians to familiarize us with them in order to reduce our fear? (2) Would you be permitted to tell us what they look like? (October 1991)

(1) No. (2) They look very much like ourselves. Man is universally present in creation.

Are some people on Mars lower in evolution than we are? (October 1991)

The most advanced are — to us — like gods, but the planet as a whole is at the same level as Earth.

(1) Do the Space Brothers travel in their vehicles in large groups or individually, and (2) how do they share out the task of crop-circle creating? (October 1991)
(1) They work in large groups. (2) They can count.

Why do they produce circles and these geometric patterns? (October 1991)
To prove to our stupid 'scientists' that the circles are not made by freak winds.

Does the energy follow the direction the corn is lying in? (October 1991)
The corn lies in the direction in which the energy flowed.

A pilot flying over the mountains in Idaho, USA, a few months ago spotted a perfectly shaped giant 'Yantra' or Buddhist graphic drawn into the earth. When it was investigated there were no footprints or signs of human life anywhere in this remote area. Who could have done this? Is it related to the crop circles in England? (March 1991)
My information is that it was entirely man-made, has no relation to the crop circles phenomenon and is (literally) a giant hoax.

What are the energies that the dowsers are responding to? Are these from the spacecraft itself or from the Earth's energy in the magnetic grid? (October 1991)
Both. The energy from the spacecraft — Venusian or Martian — potentizes the Earth's magnetic field.

Why can some people dowse and other people can't? (October 1991)
I believe that almost everyone can dowse.

CHAPTER 8

MAITREYA'S TEACHINGS ON RELIGION

According to Maitreya, all religions must take responsibility for the suffering in the world. Instead of teaching salvation, religions are creating pockets of imprisonment. They have created strife and conditioned people. But this is coming to an end. From now on, schools, colleges and universities will help people discover where thoughts and ideas come from, that we are all connected to the Almighty and that we do not need scriptures to experience our true Selves.

Those who are supposed to spread My message, Maitreya says, and are in a position to serve the people, have used their position to obtain personal comforts instead. The struggle to become bishops or other powerful personages within the religious hierarchies, He says, should end: "Do not say you are becoming a bishop in the name of Jesus, when in fact you are doing it for yourself. Since you are not doing this for the Lord, the Lord cannot be with you."

"The nearest and dearest to Me," Maitreya says, "are the people who do My work without reward. But so is the thief. Why? Because he does his work without knowing what will be its outcome. He has to fulfil his basic needs and so acts in the only way that he can. He does not set out to do anyone harm. He does not cry out for Me. The furthest from Me are the saints and gurus who have given up all the duties and responsibilities of life. They have closed their minds to the realities of life, and every day and night search for God, wanting to know Him, to find out where He lives, somewhere in Heaven. Outwardly, they appear sane and peaceful. Inwardly they are in chaos, crying inside in their desperate search for God".

Politicians are baffled because they cannot control the people with ideologies. But it is the religious authorities who cling most to power, believing "there is only one way to go to heaven". Yet how do these religious leaders live? What is their lifestyle? Perhaps that of kings: palaces, jets, bullet-proof cars. Krishna lived in a hut. This is true divinity. Likewise today, Sai Baba sleeps in a small room, in a simple bed.

False prophets, says Maitreya, are those who, surrounded by pomp and circumstance and protected by bodyguards, deny themselves contact with the people. A simple life, with the people, would make this unnecessary for the messenger of the Lord. The true messengers are those who work on the ground with the people, eating with the people, healing and helping them. The others have departed from the example of Jesus.

However, many church leaders now are coming out in defence of the people. They are challenging the politicians to address the moral and spiritual dimension which cannot be circumvented by anyone holding power. If this dimension is neglected a crisis necessarily follows. What religious leaders "have not wanted to do, they will have to do now", Maitreya says. Around the world they will eventually leave their palaces to live in simpler surroundings, because simplicity is a significant factor in order "to remain with the Lord in the heart". The trend towards greater simplicity will also be observable among many rich people who will surrender the excess and share with the people.

Maitreya points to the empty churches and observes that the young people are not interested in the old ideologies of their elders.

Religions have taught the past generations: "Come to the temple. Give a donation and you will be free." They have also used fear to generate and sustain belief. But the children of today often do not go to churches. Why? According to Maitreya, children do not run after God. There is an awareness in them that "The Lord is within": "If you want to test the truth of anything, speak with a child." "Do not create fear in the minds of innocent children," Maitreya admonishes religious leaders. "Fear is poison."

Fundamentalism and dogmatism are coming to an end. That time is quickly passing. Maitreya teaches that the moment a person gives up his brand of 'ism' he will be free. "He will find that I am within him, for I am free of all ideologies. I have come to teach you not to cry out for Me. The gurus and religious fanatics cry out for Me and the end result is that they never know Me," Maitreya says. "You are not born in sin, as they insist on telling you. For I am with you and you are with Me."

Although in reality God is everywhere, individuals are becoming aware that it is possible to experience the Lord in the heart. "God is not in the sky," Maitreya teaches, "God is in the heart." When the mind is quiet, free from dogmatic views, it will absorb the truth. "Self-realization is God-realization." The teaching of Maitreya inspires you to look within. This has nothing to do with religion, politics or any form of ideology.

If you use this mirror to look at the religions of the world, you will see they are based on the personal experiences of the prophets, gurus and saints. When people follow them, however, they are bound to experience suffering — because they are not following their own Self. If you close your eyes and allow someone else to lead you, you are bound to stumble. Everyone has free will. When that free will is not functioning or is being misled, Maitreya says, "the Lord intervenes".

Many teachers and gurus have themselves fallen through attachment to powers which manifested through them either as a result of natural development or through the grace of the Lord. This happens, according to Maitreya, because as soon as you try to claim anything for yourself, as soon as you identify with those powers instead of understanding that you are the immortal Self and that the powers belong to the Lord, you are lost.

This is a difficult test and even today the lives of many followers who identified with their guru or teacher have been shattered when the teacher or guru, forgetting the Self within, becomes attached to material, mental or spiritual powers. Thus some begin to accumulate wealth; some misuse thought and imprison others mentally, creating divisions and intolerance instead of respecting the freedom of each individual; and others become attached to power, and misuse it. Says Maitreya: "Even if you have reached a very high state of evolution, you cannot say: 'I am the Lord.' You can simply say: 'I am the messenger of the Lord.' "

The life of Jesus

Even Jesus had to struggle with the problem of attachment to spiritual powers and experiences, Maitreya says. The experiences the Lord gave Jesus are being given to certain disciples today. But in the case of Jesus, His mind initially became possessive of those experiences. The mind tried to use these spiritual powers to achieve certain goals.

Jesus was concerned about disparities between rich and poor and He began to preach that "in the eyes of the Lord, no one is rich or poor". But He should, instead, have helped people try to realize the Self, for by this process one learns automatically to use what one needs and to pass on the excess. At that time, Maitreya says, Jesus should have taught: "Be not attached to riches or poverty." The true teaching is: "The Lord is with you if you are honest, sincere, and detached."

When the priests challenged Jesus: "Why can you not free yourself, if you are God?" Jesus could do nothing at that moment. Then, when Jesus was on the Cross and asked: "My Lord, my Lord, why hast Thou forsaken me?" He was given a vision and the prayer Maitreya gave out in these teachings. [See the Prayer for the New Age, chapter 9, p267.] He was taught that the entire creation is the Lord's. "Without the Lord's will," says Maitreya, "nothing takes place." In that moment Jesus understood that the mind should not run after spiritual powers.

Upon experiencing the vision, Jesus said: "Father, forgive them, for they know not what they do." When you are free of attachments, as Buddha was, you are given the vision of the Absolute (nirvana).

The lesson here is that Jesus was attached to that which He wanted to achieve (justice and parity between rich and poor). His teaching was relative, however, because it was submerged in opposites, and so the Lord gave Him a vision of Light. Jesus realized in mind, spirit and body that the relative and the absolute are two aspects of the same Light. Then silence prevailed. He was satisfied.

Jesus as a person, as an individual entity, experienced the sustenance, the support, of the Almighty. People everywhere, says Maitreya, are beginning to experience this now. What will the signs of this experience be? People will be able to explain in simple sentences what Jesus experienced in Christ. When you experience the One Who sustains you, Who is the source of all creation, you know that without Him nothing takes place. At such a time, the Self is oblivious to everything that is happening around it, as was the case when Jesus said: "Father, forgive them, for they know not what they do." When you are honest, sincere, detached, you can reach this stage.

During the period of these teachings, Maitreya discussed briefly the controversial film by Martin Scorsese, *The Last Temptation of Christ*. Many in several countries strongly opposed showing the film because it depicted Jesus being tempted to engage in sex.

Maitreya commented that temptations of mind, spirit and body force the self to do something against the will of the real Self. Jesus passed through these stages and was also tempted. "Does anyone know what He did?" Nobody is really in a position to know, Maitreya pointed out, what Jesus actually did. However, even if Jesus had had sexual intercourse in His lifetime, Maitreya noted, one cannot say: "Having sex is an offence to God."

It is not the case, He says, that "'To know the Lord you have got to give up sex.' I do not make such regulations." The Lord says: "Do not condemn sex. If you condemn sex you will never know Who I am." If you condemn sex, you must ask yourself how you were born. Where did you come from? The Lord does not say: "Give up your wife and children." Does anyone make a fuss about birth and death? Who is not born of sexual intercourse? Do not preach that sex is dirty. It is natural and does not need to be taught. It develops with the evolutionary forces of life. The true Master is awareness, which teaches at the right moment. To educate about sex prematurely is also not advisable. Things should be allowed to take their natural course.

"You will find that the sexual act, performed with sincerity of spirit, honesty of mind, and detachment, becomes divine. If it is divine, it does not cling to mind, spirit and body. You are free even at that moment. You know the results of the sexual act performed with possessiveness and attachment. The hunger grows, the person can become oversexed and eventually can commit sexual crimes, which are carried out with dishonesty of mind, an insincere spirit, and attachment. Any act performed thus becomes destructive."

In the process of commenting on *The Last Temptation of Christ,* Maitreya drew a contrast between the attitudes of priests and film-makers toward religion. Religious men run after Christ, He said, and so they give up everything. The Lord gives them certain experiences to quiet the mind. These men then stipulate that others must give up what they have given up in order to have these experiences and reach the stage they have reached.

But many religious leaders are, in fact, running away from the realities of life. The film-makers, by comparison, clothe this matter with 'inquisitive mind'. The mind wants to find things out, but inquisitiveness alone creates division. Detachment and sincerity of spirit would have produced a different film.

Another work of art, Salman Rushdie's *The Satanic Verses*, created even more serious religious division. Maitreya explains the problem thus: when the baby cries out for a lollipop and doesn't get it, he becomes angry and confused, and ends up calling his mummy bad names. So it was with Salman Rushdie. He was looking for divine experiences through religion and when he failed he began describing his difficulties and his disillusion. But his failure to experience anything does not negate divinity, because it does not exist in evolution. It exists only in the Supreme Being.

A writer or poet fails, says Maitreya, because he or she is seeking the ultimate. But that cannot be found in life — in evolution. So when they fail to find the ultimate they embark on founding religions and philosophies. They begin to create doubts about the existence of God. These writers are neither right nor wrong in looking for new goals and new experiences. But when they create disturbances through their work, those who read them begin to panic because they do not want to lose their certainties. Salman Rushdie and the devout Muslims are in the same boat because they are clinging to their beliefs and are frightened of losing them.

Maitreya says that He has come to guide us to experience Him in our hearts. That experience cannot happen in the mind, spirit or body because they exist in evolution, while Divinity is pure and eternal. The Self exists in the heart, which is where you experience God.

Religion in the New Age

All the great religions are experiencing rapid changes. In China there are signs that people are beginning to frequent churches and temples more, and this same process is also occurring in the USSR. In the case of Christianity, there are divisions; people are questioning, challenging. Christianity, along with the other religions, is undergoing a process of purification, in that individuals are going to experience, for the first time, that Divinity is not 'outside' but situated 'simultaneously' in the heart and in the universe, in all of creation. The Self is now beginning to experience its own, distinct identity. The One Who sustains the Self and makes Him aware cannot be limited; He is universal. "No one has a hold on the Christ." The Lord's message is indivisible and applies to one and all: "If you are serving Me, I am everywhere."

There is really no contradiction between the different religions. Religions have been trapped through words and slogans into vying with each other. This competition will disappear and the essence will remain. Hindus, Christians, Muslims, Jews and Buddhists will all experience Oneness. Those who cling to old forms will create division after division. But these forms will eventually disappear. This process is inevitable. Churches, mosques and temples will become meeting places, as well as centres where those in need can be helped by others.

A more inclusive religious consciousness will characterize the 21st century. President Arap Moi of Kenya will lay the foundation stone for a temple suited to this new consciousness in Kajadio. There, the symbols of all the great religions will be represented, and this temple will become a place of pilgrimage for people from neighbouring countries. "Kenya will be to Africa," Maitreya says, "what Mecca is to Islam." People of all religions will gather to pray there. This kind of temple, dedicated to religions in the New Age, will also be built in Montreal, London and India. This does not constitute the establishment of a new religion, but rather it is the creation of structures suited to the growing realization of brotherhood.

Christian Churches/Fundamentalism

Do you think the decade of evangelism of the Christian churches has anything to do with Maitreya? (July/August 1991)

Yes indeed. Like everyone else, the Christian churches are responding to the new energies released by Maitreya and His group of Masters. This has led to two reactions: on the one hand, an increased awareness of the spiritual basis of life which for them is focused (solely) in Jesus and the Scriptures of the Bible; and on the other, a sense of being the only upholders of spiritual values in the face of general moral decay. This has produced the dogmatic, crusading evangelism which characterizes the most active and expanding Christian groups. They feel threatened by the new, the changes in modern society, and as a result become fundamentalist — back to the Bible, the Scriptures, taking literally what is presented as symbol.

What might become of the fundamentalist leaders of all religions once Maitreya has established Himself openly? (December 1986)

I am sure there are some who will never change but many, I believe, will be offering their services.

Many Christians may fear that Maitreya is the Antichrist; will he be able to say or do something to assuage those fears? (October 1989)
It may well be that, for many, the acceptance of Maitreya as the Christ will be impossible in this life. For the vast majority of Christians, however, I believe that the events and experience of the Day of Declaration and His subsequent mission of salvage and teaching will remove their fears. The tree, after all, is known by its fruits.

Are the fundamentalists, Jews and other monotheists part of the old order that you plan to do away with when your 'Christ' comes? I have heard that the 'New Agers' plan to send the fundamentalists to some other strata of creation. In other words, do you plan to kill them? (November 1987)
What an extraordinary question. And what extraordinary power I am credited with. This question shows an absolute non-understanding of what New Age thought in general and myself in particular are about. The 'old order' of which I speak or write is the civilization of the last two thousand-plus years of Pisces. This is now ending, not because of any action by the Christ, 'New Agers' or myself, but because the Sun has moved away from the influence of the energies of Pisces and is now receiving, in mounting potency, the energies of the New Age, Aquarius.

It is obvious, is it not, that the institutions, political, economic and social, of that old order must undergo change since they no longer answer humanity's needs. This is clear since they have brought us to the verge of self-destruction in a divided world. We have no alternative but to change them. But it is the divisions which must go, not those who maintain them. No one is under threat in the concept of a New Age based on brotherhood and justice, sharing and love.

I have no quarrel with any 'monotheist'. I am one myself, as are the Masters and the Christ Himself. The concept of the one God behind all outer manifestation is basic to esotericism.

233

How does Christianity at its best affect one? A student of mine who had quite a spiritual awakening in the last year tells me the essence of Christianity is that we are loved, accepted and forgiven, and that really believing that makes a huge difference. What is your view of this? (May 1992)

I am sure that if you believe in, or are afraid of, God, to believe that God, after all, loves, accepts and forgives you must make an enormous psychological difference to your view of life. My comment would be that while that is no doubt true, it is not necessary to believe in Christianity (which in any case goes further than that assurance) in order to experience that comforting idea of God's love. Other religions would do the same. My question would be: who set in place the sense of sin that needs God's forgiveness? The teachings of the Church since the beginning have emphasized the idea of original sin — and therefore of guilt — with the Church authorities having the sole power of absolution.

Were children to be raised in a loving and forgiving family framework, they would grow without a sense of guilt, and find their own way to the God within us all through trust in life and the moment-to-moment experience of God that brings.

Does the Vatican know about this (information about the Christ's presence in the world)? (May 1987)

The Pope and others have heard of my statements but, not unexpectedly, do not believe them.

What has the Pope and/or the Vatican said about Maitreya, the Christ? (September 1991)

Publicly, nothing at all, so far. In private, well, that is anyone's guess. At least two cardinals in the Curia, the managing group around the Pope, know for a fact that Maitreya is here, and in London.

After the Day of Declaration of Maitreya what place do you think the Pope will hold? Will he be near the Christ? Will he recognize Him? (April 1989)

I expect the Pope to become a helper of the Master Jesus, Who is in charge of the Christian Church, rather than be near the

Christ, Who is World Teacher. I have no doubt that eventually, anyway, the Pope will recognize the Christ.

*Where is Monsignor Biaggi? After reading the article in the US weekly the **National Examiner**, which quoted the Vatican's Monsignor Biaggi's statement that the Christ is in the world, I contacted several people in the Catholic Church to see what the Church was saying about his views. I was met with scepticism and even a denial of Biaggi's presence in the Vatican. In fact, I phoned the Vatican in Rome and they searched their computer database of all living and/or working in the Vatican. No Biaggi. Was he ousted?* (October 1990)

According to my information Monsignor Biaggi (the 'Monsignor' is a courtesy title; he is, in fact, a rather well-known and influential priest with contacts in 'high places' in the Vatican) was one of three envoys sent to London in January of this year "from the inner circle of the Pope himself" (see *Share International*, January/February 1990, p7) to make discreet enquiries about the Christ's presence here. He does not live or work at the Vatican.

He had two interviews with Maitreya Who gave him experiences that convinced him that Maitreya is the Christ. He reported back to two cardinals in the Curia (the inner group around the Pope), both of whom are conscious disciples of the Master Jesus and who had sent him to London. They, it appears, are still trying to convince the Pope of the validity of Biaggi's experience and report.

I think the *Examiner* has exaggerated the readiness of the Pope to make a statement confirming the Christ's presence. I assume that he would have to have some personal experience to allow him to do that. It has also, I think, exaggerated Monsignor Biaggi's ability to speak for the Vatican, but this can be construed as journalistic licence.

Although this fact is not mentioned in the *Examiner* article, Monsignor Biaggi, according to my information, was one of the representatives of religious organizations at the conference initiated by Maitreya in London on 21 and 22 April 1990.

Despite these exaggerations, I believe that the *National Examiner*, sensationalist as it usually is, is to be congratulated on having the courage to publish such controversial news. I only wish this same courage were forthcoming from the rest of the world's media, who cover their caution and fear in a cloak of scepticism and a cynical refusal to investigate or to publish confirming information gathered by their own journalists.

Is or was the Liberal Catholic Church, founded by Leadbeater, an instrument of the Hierarchy? (April 1987)
Yes. It still is a recipient of Hierarchical energy.

Jesus

(1) When Jesus took a few selected disciples on to the Mount of Transfiguration and showed them the forms of Moses, Elijah and Jesus, was He not showing them Himself in His three major incarnations? (2) If this was so and Jesus was actually Elijah returned, was John the Baptist Elias? (May 1988)
(1) No. Jesus had not been Moses nor Elijah. Jesus was (is) 6th-ray, Elijah 2nd-ray. (2) Yes, John the Baptist had been Elias.

Why did Jesus try to avoid crucifixion in His prayers in the Garden of Gethsemane? To whom was He praying in order to get out of His ordeal? (December 1986)
Jesus was not trying to 'get out of His ordeal' at all. Rather, He realized (that is, the Christ working through Him realized) that He could not accomplish His mission from His will alone; that He would have to embody the Will aspect of God (as well as the Light and Love aspect) to 'redeem' humanity. The Christ returns now embodying the Will of God and so, by bringing man's will into line with the divine Will and Purpose, can complete the mission He began in Palestine 2,000 years ago.

Why didn't Jesus mention Maitreya by name during His mission in Palestine? (June 1987)

He did, to those immediately around Him. That was part of the secret teachings to the inner group and would have been quite incomprehensible to the people in general.

Was the crucifixion of Jesus an event which was destined to happen even before Jesus was born? (May 1987)
One must distinguish between 'destined' and 'planned'. The crucifixion of Jesus was planned — with His complete co-operation — to symbolize the Great Renunciation of the fourth-degree initiate. That is not to say it was 'destined', as some kind of irrevocable act of fate outside anyone's control.

Who suffered on the cross: Jesus, the Christ, or both? (May 1987)
Jesus. It was for Him the experience of the fourth initiation, the Great Renunciation or Crucifixion.

In the Bible it says that there was an earthquake when Jesus died on the cross. Is this true? (June 1988)
My information is that it is not true. It is a dramatic addition to the event.

*Maitreya referred to Jesus' final words on the cross: "My Lord, my Lord, why hast thou forsaken me?" However, H.P.Blavatsky discusses at length in **The Secret Doctrine** (3rd edition, p158) that these words were intentionally changed by early church fathers when they translated them from Hebrew into Greek, and that the original meaning of Jesus' words were: "My God, my God, how thou dost glorify me!" Did HPB make a mistake?* (January/February 1989)
I think she did, yes. The Master DK (through Alice A.Bailey) has interpreted the words 'why hast thou forsaken me' as the experience of Jesus as the fourth-degree initiate when there is the sudden realization that he is alone in the universe; the 'divine intermediary', the soul, with which the initiate has identified for so long, is superseded in the new at-one-ment with the Monad — the Divine Spark — and God and man (alone now) are One.

237

Presumably, the incarnation of Jesus as Apollonius was what He had in mind when He said that He would return "within this generation". Was it planned before Jesus incarnated in Palestine that He would incarnate again shortly afterwards? If yes, what was the purpose of having two incarnations close together? (September 1987)

When He went out of incarnation at the Crucifixion, Jesus was a fourth-degree initiate, and became a Master of the fifth degree as Apollonius. It is usual (although not invariable) to reincarnate quickly on the final stages of the evolutionary journey. This is done under the Law of Service which governs the incarnational cycles of initiates.

Was the Christ's true relationship to Jesus known to any of His early disciples? (December 1986)

Yes, several of the closest disciples understood the overshadowing process which was used.

(1) I would like to know the truth about the colour of Jesus' skin when He was here 2,000 years ago. By colour, I mean was He white or was He of another nationality? More and more I believe He was not white like the majority of the paintings have him. I believe He was of the Negro race as most people in the Bible were. (2) If my beliefs are right why did they change the colour of Jesus and the characters in the Bible? (October 1992)

(1) Jesus was of Semitic origin — a wide-ranging racial type which included Jews, Israelites, Sumerians and Arabs — whose colour, as in the Middle East today, ranged from European 'white' to 'olive' to 'brown'. He was not, nor were the majority of the biblical peoples, Negro in origin. (2) Artists throughout history have used artistic licence when depicting historical events, clothing their personages in the costumes and settings of their own time and environment. The questioner is thinking, surely, only of European paintings of Jesus and His time. Paintings of the Gospel story by Coptic artists of North Africa, for example, show black-faced representations of Jesus and His disciples.

Some Gnostic writers and old Kabalistic works have stated that the real name of Jesus of Nazareth of the Bible was actually Jushu (Jeshu) or Joshua Ben Pandira or Panthera. According to your information, is this correct? (November 1992)
Yes.

Did Jesus or Jeshu actually live about 100 years before the Biblical time of Jesus? (November 1992)
No. Jesus (Jeshu, Jushu) was born in 24 BC.

Was Jushu (Jesus) stoned to death first as an alleged wizard in the city of Lud or Lydia, and then hung on a tree or Roman cross? (November 1992)
No. Jesus was crucified as detailed in the Gospel story.

Where was Jesus physically located and what was he doing during the so-called 'lost' years (age 12-30)? (March 1991)
According to my information (I am aware of the many ideas which exist about this) Jesus spent all these years physically in Palestine. He was an active member of the Essenes (as was also John the Baptist). From them He received certain training in preparation for His later mission.

From the age of 12, He began to be overshadowed by Maitreya, which process was more or less complete by age 24.

Jesus was born a third-degree initiate and His life, therefore, was that of achieving the fourth initiation (the Crucifixion or Great Renunciation), symbolized by the actual crucifixion.

Throughout the 'lost' years period He did indeed travel to many spiritual centres and schools in Egypt, India and the Far East, as believed and reported by several groups. But none of these travels took place in the physical body. He was a free-ranging initiate able to function totally consciously out of the body.

It is said of John the Baptist that he was born in a supernatural manner to Elizabeth long after she was too old to bear children. The same is said of Sarah, Abraham's wife, that she too had children when she was old. Was John the Baptist born in the normal way or were spiritual/supernatural powers involved in this case? Viewed in this light, is it not possible that Mary was indeed still a virgin when she conceived Jesus? The prophets too predicted this. (March 1987)

My information is that both Jesus and John the Baptist were born in the normal human way; that Mary was not a virgin nor was Elizabeth beyond child-bearing age. The prophets predicted the birth of Jesus 'of a maid' — that is, a young woman, not necessarily a virgin.

Where is the Virgin Mary? (May 1987)

The disciple who was the Mother of Jesus in Palestine is now a Master and is not in incarnation at this time. He is responsible for the many visions and other phenomena — weeping and moving statues and the like.

Can you say what became of Judas — and why he did what he did? (May 1987)

Judas is now a Master but not in incarnation, in fact, not on the planet. He did what He did as part of a pre-arranged plan. He Himself did not think that Jesus would die on the Cross, but rather that His power, or that of the Heavenly Father, would save Him and confound His enemies.

Where is Judas Iscariot now? (April 1989)

He is on Sirius. There is a direct line from this planet to Sirius, and many Masters leaving this planet go directly to Sirius without going through the other higher planets of our system.

When Judas betrayed Jesus, did that not alter his evolution? (April 1989)

Yes, it did alter His evolution. He has since paid the price, the penalty. Also, of course, it was part of a plan.

Bible Stories

I would like to know if the Bible is still valuable now that Maitreya is in the world? (July/August 1990)

Most certainly, yes. The Christian Bible is the embodiment of profound teaching and prophecy, symbolically and allegorically expressed. It is not meant to be taken literally, and, if it is, it leads to the present confusion of fundamentalist and orthodox Christians in relation to the Reappearance of the Christ. It is not, as Christians fondly believe, the only book of Divine revelation, but for long years to come it will serve many millions of Christians — when its true meaning and purpose is revealed by the physical presence of the Christ (Maitreya) and of the Master Jesus, Who is in charge of the Christian Churches. Freed of the man-made dogmas and doctrines, the Christian Bible will find a new lease of life in the demonstration of the age-old story of initiation through the Gospel of the life of Jesus, and as a constant reminder of the interaction of God and man in man's long journey to divinity.

In the Bible it says: "I shall return at the head of a celestial army." The arrival of the Christ by airplane, as you say, does not correspond to that prediction. Can you explain? (July/August 1990)

Christians in general, taking the symbolic statements of the Bible literally, tend to visualize the return of the Christ as taking place suddenly, all at once, in "the twinkling of an eye". They look for some one great event (in the sky) when the Christ will come down from 'heaven' in a 'cloud of glory', surrounded by a 'host of angels'. The reality is somewhat different and yet relates to these symbolic statements: there is one day (19 July 1977) in which He entered, by airplane, the modern world (Britain), but He came as He Himself said He would, "like a thief in the night, in such an hour as you think not". He does, indeed, come with a "celestial army", which will be largely invisible to the bulk of humanity for a very long time to come. Many great and powerful Angels (Devas) attend the Christ and carry out His plans. Their work *vis-à-vis* humanity will be constructive and fruitful, but the average Christian will most probably know little or nothing of Their work in this life.

What esoteric or exoteric light can you shine on the Adam/Eve story of Genesis regarding the Snake who could speak and walk upright? (December 1986)

The story of Adam and Eve is, of course, purely symbolic and allegorical. It refers to the coming into incarnation of the human egos some eighteen-and-a-half million years ago. The undifferentiated souls took separate sexes on the physical plane and "ate of the tree of knowledge of Good and Evil", that is, experienced physical-plane life for the first time. This was — for the soul — a 'fall' from paradise (the soul state) into carnal life, and therefore limitation for the soul. The descent of the soul, of course, was intentional and according to divine plan. The snake is a symbol for sex.

Do you accept the interpretation of Lucifer as the Fallen Angel of evil? (March 1990)
No, I do not. I think this is a complete misunderstanding of Lucifer by Christian teaching. The name 'Lucifer' means, literally, 'light'. The word comes from the Latin roots: *lux, lucis* — light and *fer, ferre* — to bring. It means, therefore, 'light-bringing' and is the name of the planet Venus as the morning star.

Far from being evil, it is pure light. In the esoteric teaching, Lucifer is the name for the great angelic Entity Who embodies the human kingdom on the soul plane. As souls, we are each an individualized part of this great Oversoul. Difficult as it is for us to grasp, there is really no such thing as a separate soul. It does not exist.

The Christian teaching holds that Lucifer — the chief rebel angel, Satan — was thrown out of heaven for getting too bigheaded and arguing with God. This is simplistic and shows a complete misunderstanding of the reality. It is also, of course, symbolic. It is symbolic of a very significant point in our human evolution which took place eighteen-and-a-half million years ago.

At that time, early animal-man had reached a point when the energy of Mind could be brought to bear on his incipient mind. He had not yet a mental body. The energy of Mind, brought from the planet Venus, was radiated to animal-man. This process stimulated the mind of these near-men to a point where it was possible for the human souls, waiting on the soul

242

plane, to come into incarnation for the first time. Early animal-man was so undeveloped that the energy of mind, and at least the nucleus of a mental body, had to be present before this could take place.

For the first time, the human souls were individualized. As the soul is perfect, the soul plane is a kind of paradise.

The myth of Adam and Eve symbolizes this descent from paradise into incarnation. Because the soul can manifest only imperfectly through the lower vehicles — mental, astral and physical — it is, in a sense, descending into imperfection or "evil" as it is called in the Bible. It is not evil in any good/bad sense but is imperfect relative to the soul level. For the Masters there is only imperfection and perfection. There is no such thing as "sin". Sin is a relative imperfection. But the Christian groups have focused everything on sin, good and bad.

The descent by the soul into physical matter led to an imperfect expression of that soul. The journey of evolution, of course, proceeds until the physical vehicles are sufficiently refined to allow the perfect manifestation of the soul in incarnation. That is the return process. The descent of the soul into matter (the rebellion in heaven) is involution, the return trip is evolution.

The Bible says Satan disguises himself as an "angel of light", preaching love, truth, brotherhood, etc. How in God's name can we trust anyone? I am confused! (January/February 1991) Behind this question, I assume, is the thought: If Maitreya preaches love, truth, brotherhood, etc, how can I know He is not Satan in disguise?

I believe that here is the basic misunderstanding by orthodox Christians about the nature and meaning of Satan. Satan is always seen as a man, the embodiment of evil, who tempts humanity and seeks to gain their soul — the Faust legend — presenting himself as loving and kind, concerned with truth and justice.

Satan is not a man but a symbol. He symbolizes our own separative, selfish, lower nature which, in the main, we hide by rationalizing it and seeing our motives (through the fog of illusion called glamour) as love, truth, brotherhood, etc, while they are nothing of the kind.

One of the most important functions of Maitreya, in this world cycle, is to help free humanity from the illusions of glamour (which is illusion on the astral planes) and thus free them from living in thrall to "Satan".

What information do you have about Jews of the Old Testament who were recorded as having lived 900 or more consecutive years in the same body? Was it a super-race? A freak of nature? Planned by Hierarchy? (December 1986)
I assume that the questioner is thinking of figures like Noah who were said to have lived for hundreds of years. The biblical story of the Flood is a symbolic account of the final destruction, about 16,000 years ago, of the last remnant of the Atlantean continent and civilization, Poseidonis (the Azores of today). Noah was a Master Who warned the people of the impending catastrophe and the need to seek the high lands before the flood. From this has come the symbol of the ark. With Masters, such longevity is not uncommon but it was then, as now, the result of evolutionary achievement and not the common rule.

Which of the four Gospels (Matthew's, Mark's, Luke's or John's) is the most accurate account of what happened in Palestine? (June 1988)
John's.

(1) Are any of the newly discovered Gospels, such as The Gospel of Thomas, The Secret Gospel of Mark, or The Gospel of Mary, genuine accounts of the acts and words of Jesus? (2) Are there others not yet discovered? (December 1986)
The Gospel of Thomas is, more or less, a genuine account of the acts (less so of the words) of Jesus. (2) Yes.

*In the book by Djwhal Khul and Koot Hoomi (**The Human Aura**) constant reference to biblical passages are made. How much should we focus our lives on biblical philosophy and teachings?* (January/February 1991)

In my opinion, the book in question, *The Human Aura*, is not given by, and has no relation to the teachings of, either the Master Djwhal Khul or the Master Koot Hoomi.

People will focus their lives on the teachings of the Bible as and when they seem relevant. When correctly interpreted in relation to the esoteric teachings which underlie them, the teachings of the Bible will be found to be not only beautiful and meaningful, but entirely relevant to the life of every Christian today.

Turin Shroud

Could you please comment on recent media statements that the carbon-dating of the Turin Shroud suggests that it is a fake? (October 1988)

A recent report in the British press purporting to come from the Oxford group (one of three such groups investigating the origin of the Shroud) claimed that a 'leak' from Oxford proved that the shroud was a 13th century fake. The British Society for the Turin Shroud has issued the following statement:

"A great deal of public confusion has arisen as a result of recent press reports that the Shroud has been found to be of mediaeval date. The first reports of this kind emanated from the United States very early in July, and claimed that the Oxford laboratory had carbon dated the Shroud to the Middle Ages. In the UK, gossip columnist Kenneth Rose wrote in the *Sunday Telegraph* of 3 July: 'I hear signals that the linen cloth has been proved to be mediaeval', without specifying from which laboratory this news was supposed to have been leaked. In point of fact, confirmed by Professor Hall and Dr Robert Hedges' letter to *The Times* of 9 July, the Oxford laboratory had not even begun to pre-treat the Shroud samples (ie Shroud and controls) at the time of the reports, and only commenced the main run of these in the accelerator the week commencing 25 July. This latter was reliably reported on ITN News, 26 July. Although the Arizona laboratory had already produced its results in May and filed them with the British Museum,

Professor Paul Damon, its director, when told of the press reports of a mediaeval date, described them as 'latrine' journalism and insisted that they should be given 'zero credibility'."

Each of the investigating teams — in the radiocarbon laboratories at the University of Arizona, the University of Oxford and the Federal Institute of Technology in Zürich — agreed beforehand not to release their findings (by carbon-dating of fragments of the Shroud) except in consort. This has apparently been strictly adhered to. The upshot is that no one knows their findings as yet.

My Master informs me that present carbon-dating techniques have a margin of error of 800-2,000 years and are only useful for approximate dating of very ancient objects, indeed. No matter what dates the groups come up with about the age of the Shroud, they cannot be considered really accurate. It could be they have found three different dates.

As for the shroud being a 13th-century fake, this is manifestly impossible. Every computerization analysis of the figure on the Shroud has shown it to be 100 per cent accurate from every anatomical point of view, something highly unlikely if drawn by hand. The most conclusive proof that it is not a fake is this: it is a photograph, something quite unknown in the 13th century. Furthermore, it is a negative photograph, something that no 'faker' could conceive of at that time. Only when it was photographed in the late 19th century was it realized to be a negative, the result of an ionization process known and used today for the first time. The energy to produce the 'ionization' effect was given by Maitreya's re-entry into the dead body of Jesus in the tomb. Nothing else could have produced that effect.

Benjamin Creme's authentication of the Shroud of Turin, and the existence of an entity called Maitreya, are solidly linked in Creme's explanation of how the image was imprinted on the Shroud. If the Shroud is counterfeit, Benjamin Creme's believability is destroyed. The Shroud has been branded a fake by carbon-14 dating placing it no earlier than the Middle

Ages; you can't argue with the methodology of carbon-14 dating, though it is sometimes invoked with unjustified precision. However, AD 1260 is a long way from AD 33! So either Maitreya did imprint the true Shroud, which is not the shroud tested by carbon-14 dating; or Maitreya did not imprint any shroud, which brings Benjamin Creme's veracity into serious question. Please respond.

In the October 1988 issue of *Share International*, I dealt with the 'leaked' information that the Oxford investigating group (one of the three) had found the Shroud (by carbon dating tests) to be of the 13th century. Now that all three groups have announced their conclusion (but not their separate findings) I see no reason to alter my statement about the authenticity of the Shroud of Turin as the burial shroud of Jesus.

I am informed that the three groups dated their samples as from the sixth century AD, the 12th century and the 14th century, respectively. Discarding the sixth century result (as being too distant from the other two), they split the difference between these two and settled for the 13th century. Not, I suggest, either a logical or scientific method of approach. A more logical — but still unscientific — result would have been reached by taking the average of all three findings, namely the 11th century. If, as I am informed, the present carbon-dating methods have a margin of error of 800-2,000 years, then one must "argue with the methodology of carbon-14 dating". It is simply not accurate enough to be conclusive evidence of dating, and all three dates fit comfortably within the margin of error. Nothing is proved by this test one way or the other.

It has been suggested that the (spiritual) radiation assumed to impregnate the Shroud might have had some distorting influence on the carbon-14 tests, but I am informed that this is not the case. The testing technique itself is at fault.

No one has ever proved (nor will be able to prove) how the image on the Shroud could have been faked — painted or drawn or somehow impressed by hand. It defies all such analysis and theories, and shows an awareness of the practical technique of crucifixion (for example the nails are clearly seen through the wrist and ankle bones and not — as depicted in every religious painting to this day — through the hands and feet).

There is no doubt in my mind — nor, I would have thought, in the mind of any unbiased, objective observer who had really studied all the evidence — that this is the burial shroud of a crucified man. Crucifixion was a Roman form of execution and did not, thankfully, outlive the Roman era. This means, does it not, that the Shroud must be no more recent than the fourth century AD, a far cry from the Middle Ages.

If we accept that the Shroud is of a man crucified in Roman fashion, the question arises: why is this the only one of its kind? Many thousands were crucified by the Romans, and the bodies of many would have been wrapped in some kind of shroud. Why is this the only one to survive to the 20th century? I suggest it is precisely because of its unique image and unique origin — because it is a photograph, a record of Resurrection.

This matter will soon be cleared up once and for all, no doubt to the consternation of the sceptics and the scientists who use unscientific methods to prove their bias. The Master Jesus will claim it as His own.

Religion in the New Age

Is there not a contradiction between what you wrote in **Maitreya's Mission, Volume One** *— that Maitreya had come to found the New World Religion and to inspire a change in the world's political/economic structures, and yet you have quoted Him as saying: "I have not come to found a new religion"?* (October 1992)

No, I do not think so. I have to qualify that and to explain it by an elucidation of what I mean and what He means by "religion". He has not come to found a religion based on ideology, on belief. All religions today are based on belief structures: belief in this Teacher or that Teaching, these precepts , and so on. The New World Religion — it is given that name by the Master Djwhal Khul (Who gave the Alice

Bailey teaching) and I quoted it from Him — is used to describe a path which is not religious in the usual sense but for which we as yet have no name (except an esoteric one). It is the path of initiation, therefore a highly scientific religion (which seems a contradiction in terms), based not on belief — esotericism is not to do with theology or belief — but is a science, or a philosophy, or an art — it partakes of something of all those, and something of religion too. It relates to evolution and what we understand by Reality, of God, of superconsciousness, or cosmos.

Esotericism is a path, and as such you cannot call it a religion, though there is religion in it because it is to do with that greater Reality which is also dealt with by religion.

Maitreya is not going to enunciate a certain belief system that you have to accept to be in that religion. He will set the process in motion exoterically, on the outer physical plane, which at the moment exists only esoterically.

The first two initiations, at which Maitreya is the Initiator, will take place outwardly — at the moment they are always an inner experience; they will remain an inner experience but they will also take place outwardly on the physical plane. Maitreya will go from country to country and in the temples which will be set up in various countries He will act as the Initiator for those ready for this experience.

The first and second initiations of the five initiations, which complete the evolutionary course on this planet and make you a Master, will take place in this way. You can call that a new world religion if you like — it has been so called by the Master Djwhal Khul — but Maitreya Himself has said He has not come to found a new religion but to teach humanity the art of Self-realization. The Master Djwhal Khul has written that the New World Religion will emerge out of Russia. As people from the various existing world religions fit themselves for the experience of initiation, they will go to the Mystery Schools, where they will be prepared for this great experience, the most sacred aspects of the New World Religion.

How do we know 'your' Christ is who you say he is and how do we know he is not someone who is trying to obtain some form of powerful position in the world with the purpose of world domination? (June 1987)

This is a question often put to me by fundamentalist Christians. A tree is known by its fruit, and the Christ must be known by His words, His deeds, and, above all, His energy. If one man could achieve world domination (which, in today's world, I very much doubt) then it could only be someone of the stature of the Christ. The fundamentalists, of course, are afraid that Maitreya might be the 'Antichrist', with which fallacy I have dealt many times, here and elsewhere. On the Day of Declaration, I submit, everyone — even the fundamentalists — will know, through the overshadowing of the minds of all humanity — a Pentecostal experience for all — that Maitreya is the Christ.

Is Maitreya the teacher "of angels and of men" in our solar system only or in other systems too? (November 1991)

Not in our solar system but in our planet only.

Is this (Maitreya's) way the only way to so-called salvation? Does Maitreya have exclusive rights to the salvation business? (April 1990)

I think you will find that, unlike the established fundamentalists of today, Maitreya will not claim any exclusive rights to the path to salvation. He comes as a Teacher. We must save ourselves through response to the teachings, not by following Him as 'the only way'.

If it is Maitreya's mission to inaugurate the synthesis of all religions and the World Religion, does not the practice in Maitreya literature of using more information from Christian sources and less from other faiths defeat the intended purpose? (November 1991)

As I understand it, it is not Maitreya's mission to "inaugurate the synthesis of all religions". He Himself has said that He has not come to found a new religion but to teach the art of Self-Realization. People should continue to evolve, He says, within

250

the framework of their own tradition. The New World Religion, based on the scientific path to God of Initiation, of which the Masters are the custodians, will draw those who are ready from all religions (and no religion — the religious path is only one of many paths to God).

All of the above aside, I do not agree that the "Maitreya literature" (that is, teachings actually coming from Him) uses more information from Christian than from other sources.

What is the role of devotion in religious attitude (for example, the cult of Christ and Mary)? Is such devotion misplaced or valid (based on fact)? (May 1987)
Devotion is the expression of the love of the devotee for God as exemplified by the object of devotion — the Guru, Christ, Madonna , and so on. It is one of the two major paths to God-realization (the other is knowledge). Eventually, devotion must give way to knowledge and the devotee or mystic must become the occultist or knower.

Which of the world's major scriptures is the least distorted or discoloured? (December 1986)
Those of esoteric Buddhism.

How has the Buddhist community responded to the emergence of Maitreya? (June 1987)
With a great deal less fear than the Christian groups. Buddhists are expecting Maitreya Buddha, the fifth Buddha, foretold by Gautama Buddha, and do not have the problems — the 'hang-ups' — of the Christians who are so wedded to their — to my mind erroneous — interpretation of Scripture that they cannot contemplate the return of the Christ now, or in the manner in which it has taken place. The response to my work and books has been extremely vivid in Japan, for instance, and my visit to Taiwan in May is at the invitation of a Buddhist association.

Since the New Age is about a new idea, why not have a new name for the new Avatar? Then it will not be possible to associate Him with old religions and old ideas. Christ is very much associated with Christianity. (April 1987)

It is true that the New Age will bring in new ideas but for today it is also necessary to give a sense of continuity, otherwise vast sections of the world's population would feel excluded. The Christ does come to fulfil the hopes of Christians, but not exclusively. He is also awaited by Buddhists as Maitreya Buddha, by Muslims as the Imam Mahdi, by Hindus as Krishna and by Jews as the Messiah. The true function of Maitreya is as World Teacher, which covers these many appellations.

CHAPTER 9

MAITREYA'S SPIRITUAL TEACHINGS

The Prayer for the New Age

I am the Creator of the Universe.
I am the Father and Mother of the Universe.
Everything came from Me.
Everything shall return to Me.
Mind, Spirit and Body are My temples,
For the Self to realize in them
My Supreme Being and Becoming.

Maitreya's Teachings

The Art of Self-Realization

"I have not come to found a new religion," Maitreya says. "I have come to teach the Art of Self-realization," something which is neither an ideology nor a religion, but benefits people of all religions and those who have none. "I come to you 'like a thief in the night'," He tells us: "so that you will not become too excited. Slowly, as you become aware, you can 'digest' what is 'eaten'. In awareness you will know Me. In 'isms' you will fight against Me."

Looking for Maitreya under titles, even the title of 'the Messiah', can lead to illusion: 'Messiah' is a word coined by the human race, and to say "I am the Messiah" can create opposition. And although some may find the qualities of Jesus in Him, Maitreya says: "Those who look for Me as a Teacher are nearer the mark, for that is what I am."*

The true quality of the Teacher will be seen in the teaching — which is that the Master is within you. In Maitreya's words: "I seek to express that which I am through you; for this I come."*

*See Message No. 10, *Messages from Maitreya the Christ* (2nd edition, March 1992).

"I have not come to create followers," says Maitreya. "Each of you should continue to develop within your own religious tradition. A real disciple is one who will respect the traditions. Respect your own religions, your own ideologies, in brief, your own thoughtform, and you will experience the Master. Even when you see Me, do not run after Me. If you run after Me, you will lose Me. I cannot be monopolized — I belong to everyone."

"If you personify Me," He warns, "you will create nothing but confusion, chaos, destruction. If you parade Me, you do not know Who I am. Even My signs create only momentary happiness. The happiest moment is when you see Me within your heart."

"I have not come to puzzle or startle people. When people experience Me, for the first time they will know the purpose of life." You will not feel you are leading a futile life, but one in which the Master is within you, guiding you. This sense of inwardness will give you another perspective in life. You will feel you are enjoying life. Fulfilment will take place within. Everything is within you. When this happens you will not react in anger. With a sense of detachment you will experience the power of God. God is behind everything.

"I do not want you to believe in Me. First experience Me within you. When you experience Me then you become aware of My presence within you: it is not a matter of belief first. I do not want you to accept or reject Me — it is your inner experience which counts." What you experience yourself, says Maitreya, is your wealth, the richness of your own Being. The living truth is a matter of experience."

Do not try to worship Me, Maitreya counsels. If you worship Me you are trying to lower yourself. I do not want this. I want you to be equal. You are a spark of the Supreme Being. Do not think you are below Me.

"The Self alone matters," Maitreya teaches. You are that Self, "an immortal Being". Suffering is caused by identification with anything and everything which is not the

Self. Ask yourself: "Who am I?" You will see that you are identified either with matter (the body), or with thought (the mind) or with power (spirit). But you are none of these. Mind, spirit and body are the temples of the Lord; the Self experiences in these "the supreme Being and Becoming of the Lord".

Spirit, in the Sanskrit terminology, is Shiv-shakti, which is energy. Mind is Brahma, which is thought-formation. Body is Prakriti, which is material substance and can also be thought of as material activity. These terms can be regarded as objective facts, but they can also be thought of as movement or processes.

· The destiny of the Self is to be free. Considered in its freedom, in its Being, it is called Atman. Within the limitations of time and space, in its becoming, it is the soul, or Jiva. The Self is not energy (Shiv-shakti, spirit); the Self is not thought-formation (Brahma, or mind); the Self is not material activity (Prakriti, the body). The destiny of the Self is to enter and leave these temples of the Lord at will.

Shiva and Brahma can be seen as aspects of a trinity that includes Vishnu, the sustaining aspect. If a person is overpowered by Shiv-shakti, he can perform miracles. Yet the person looks withdrawn, blank. If a person is overpowered by Brahma, he can be a philosopher, but he can be imprisoned in that thought-formation. A person overpowered by the Vishnu aspect can give, and give generously, perhaps become a saint, but that, too, can be a prison. During the 1960s, 'hippies' responded to the Vishnu aspect, having become disillusioned with power (Shiv–shakti) and mind (Brahma).

Being is eternal. Becoming is temporal. The Self experiences both.

Being and becoming are two modalities. Being is unchanging, whereas becoming is a process of unfolding in time and space. Man, in his Being, is the Self; in his becoming, he is the soul — the reflection of the Self.

The Self witnesses. It plays the 'mini-role' of the Almighty. The Self is the spark of the Almighty. "There are times when you become aware that someone is behind you, within you, over you, around you — something is present. That 'something'," Maitreya says, "is the Almighty. It does not participate; it observes. No one need struggle for this step. Everyone qualifies at this stage. Then, as your awareness grows, if you practise the discipline of detachment, you will know Me in My totality. The moment you think of Me, I am with you."

The Self makes itself known through awareness. The Self makes mind, spirit and body aware of reality and thus able to make decisions accordingly. Maitreya says: "Let your awareness grow. Awareness, with intelligence, will guide mind, spirit and body. This will create harmony between mind, spirit and body and the Self." Then the Self can use the forces of Life to transform things, to effect 'miracles'. Mind, spirit and body are simply vehicles.

Awareness is the light of life. Anything done outside awareness leads to destruction. All thoughts which lead you to selfishness lead you away from awareness. In awareness there is no memory. Memory is only in the mind. All struggle and care is in the mind, never in awareness. Suffering, depression and craving for drugs are all states of mind. Awareness sets you free and allows you to enjoy life.

When awareness is still dormant, 'isms' control mind, spirit and body and create divisions. This is maya — illusion. When awareness controls and guides you, 'isms' cannot come close to you. Awareness can even make a king give up his kingdom, Maitreya teaches. Privileges divide, denying oneness to the entity within you. 'Isms' are not thrown away all at once. They are steps on the way. Awareness controls the pace of evolution.

Yet in awareness there is no burden. You remain meticulous, immaculate, pure. There is grace, peace and happiness. These are the blessings of the Lord.

Awareness will come to be respected in the home and in the school as a sacred, God-given gift, Maitreya says. Awareness is the mother of creation. It can never be divided, nor imposed. Textbooks cannot describe it, because there is no beginning nor end to it. Awareness can only be experienced. It is a seed in all creation and in every individual.

Awareness is universal and does not 'belong' to any religion, nor to any guru, saint or politician.

According to Maitreya, when you judge, saying 'I am right. You are wrong', you are caught in the web of attachment. The Self must always practise detachment. In this way, awareness will grow. The Self is neutral and free from suffering. Awareness protects the Self. Just as the body must be bathed, detachment is the 'bath' of mind, and awareness is the 'bath' of spirit.

The practice of Self-realization

One of the easiest ways to know Me, Maitreya says, is to be honest in your mind; be sincere in your spirit; feed your body with right food; and practise detachment. This will create harmony. When you experience the Self within and come to know you are an immortal entity, completely separate from mind, spirit and body, you learn to use these temples of the Lord creatively, with awareness. Processes of healing follow automatically.

"You have been given mind, spirit and body," says Maitreya, "to express My Being and Becoming in thought, speech and action." Any action performed with dishonesty of mind, an insincere spirit and attachment is destructive. For example, when you think one thing, say another, and do something which is different again, you are lost. Honesty of mind leads to honest speech and honest action. This harmony leads to peace and happiness. "Whether you are a thief or a saint," He counsels, "you can begin right now."

But, people have asked: "How do we begin? How do we practise sincerity?" Consider an expression which is often used, such as 'having a heart-to-heart talk' with someone, Maitreya responds. What does this mean? It means you will express yourself as you really are, you will communicate from the centre — your centre — the Self. Practice this. It will transform you and those around you.

The heart is never tarnished or touched; it is the seat of the soul. It is the mind that leads us astray. Peace, bliss, happiness and grace are the qualities of the heart. "By tuning into the 'feelings of the heart'," Maitreya teaches, "you are able to experience your natural innocence, that innocence you had as a child. Do not 'visualize' the heart. For that is only the mind seeking to find the source of light with a torch."

Maitreya teaches that everyone needs their 'inner space', where there is no direction, no one telling you where to go and what to do. No one can lead you. You are born to be aware of yourself, to know the Master in yourself. Your inner space is sacred. It is where all things, all problems, dissolve. It is where you go when you tell others you are tired and frightened and 'fed up', when you want to be left alone to find your own space.

According to Maitreya: "You have been given that space so that the confusion and chaos around you will dissolve. You must never surrender that space to anyone, except your true Self. Meditation is really a journey back to that space to find peace and happiness."

Be what you are

"Be what you are," He tells us. "Do not follow one another. If you practise honesty of mind, sincerity of spirit, and detachment, you will know your Self, you will know Me, you will know the Lord." If you follow others instead of being yourself, you lose your sparkle and cannot reflect the light of individuality. Without that light, there is no progress in life.

To follow another means to copy, imitate or identify with another, forgetting your real Self. As an example, consider popular entertainment stars. Many fans try to dress and behave like them, but this does not lead to happiness or fulfilment.

The task of the Master is to awaken the Self within. When you, in turn, know your Self, you can awaken others. To awaken another, however, does not mean to cast your shadow over him. When the Self awakens, development follows naturally; the person fulfils his own destiny and enjoys the blessings of the Lord. The pace of development of each person can thus be respected: "Let the pagan believe in the stone, because without the Lord there is no stone." Correct relationship between the Self and mind, spirit and body is what matters.

"Do not surrender your self-respect, your dignity to others. The moment you surrender yourself to some other self you become a 'zombie'. Do not allow any shadow, even, to possess you." Maitreya illustrates His point with the following example: "If the personality of an enlightened man falls on a child who is not yet prepared, what happens? The personality of that child is extinguished. The child becomes like charcoal. Apply this to many politicians and their children. The children cannot progress. They have no sense of freedom and are unable to express themselves." Therefore: "Do not allow anyone to cast his shadow over you. A Master gives experiences, but does not cast his shadow."

"Remain open-minded," Maitreya says. Enjoy life. When you enjoy life you are sitting on the beach looking at the vast ocean. At that moment you experience serenity, tranquillity, detachment within. You do not think of your bank account at that moment. Nobody lectures you at that moment. The gift of life flowers within you. Experience this and you will realize you are a unique person. You are unique in this creation.

Whatever you do in life, Maitreya teaches, practise detachment and you will achieve equilibrium. You will experience the forces of life passing through your mind, spirit and body and yet not be possessed by them. "When you do this the 'third eye' is opened and you will be able to sense what is happening around you and foresee events." It is the destiny and evolution of everyone to reach this state.

Detachment is the process whereby man ceases to identify with the material aspect (the body), with the thought aspect (the mind) and with the energy or power aspect (the spirit), and thus he comes to know and be his real Self.

That Self is endless. Awareness is endless. Mind, spirit and body, however, have a beginning and an end. The laws of creation are in the mind; the universal energy is in the spirit; and the forum for the materialization of the creation is the physical body. With detachment, the Self experiences the phenomena of the mind, spirit and body, but does not become attached to the miraculous powers of which mind, spirit and body — these three vehicles — are capable.

In effect, when the Self observes God's powers it is detachment which saves the Self from imprisonment in the bondages of life.

If you do not know yourself as the Self, however, you can become attached to body, mind or spirit. If you are attached to the body, you will find that there is no end to material desires and sensual gratifications. Greed grows, the search continues, and satisfaction always eludes you. When you are detached, the Self experiences these powers and allows the fulfilment of divine purpose. To possess is not only to misuse but to misdirect and to interfere.

For example, true spiritual healers allow the Lord to work through them but remain detached both from cause (the Lord's will) and effect (the healing of a particular individual). This is why it is important to remain detached both from success and failure. Some individuals are healed; some are not. If you do not claim anything for yourself, pride cannot flourish and all is directed according to spiritual law. You do not heal; the Lord heals. The Self knows this. Practice with detachment and leave the consequence to the Lord.

To learn detachment is an art. With it, the scientist will learn the laws of physics and chemistry (the laws of creation) and will apply them, creating things which constitute God's work. The artist, with detachment, will be able to describe God through his own experiences. We are all observers in this vast creation. If we observe with a strong sense of detachment, we will find beauty in it, equilibrium, harmony.

To be honest, sincere and detached is to experience oneness with God. But so often this oneness is interpreted by people as loneliness and something to be feared. Yet the feeling of loneliness is the supreme blessing in disguise, says Maitreya, because it shows that a person is approaching oneness with the Lord.

Detachment is the most powerful 'drug'. It becomes so effective that it immunizes the Self from the processes and proceedings of mind, spirit and body. Without detachment there is no salvation.

Even a thief can experience the awareness that comes with detachment. If a thief comes to you, says Maitreya, do not preach; it will not work. Teach him to be honest about what he is doing. The thief will gradually acquire detachment. Detachment enables the mysteries of life to become clearer, and the thief, with detachment, eventually realizes the mind is reacting to a particular thought formation.

Divine hand

Maitreya says: "Even when you are thieving, know that without the divine hand of the Lord you would not be able to thieve." The Self only witnesses. Gradually the Self becomes aware of its mastership. Gradually, the Self controls mind, spirit and body.

Everyone has his own wealth, which no one can take away. This wealth is Self-realization.

People want someone to free them from all their sufferings. Yet, it is detachment which frees you from suffering. "Free will is the most important thing given to you, and your destiny is to be free." Thus attachment is loss of freedom; detachment is freedom.

In childhood you are detached. But as you grow, if you become attached, you lose the beauty of life. The Lord comes again, in your old age, to free you. The day the Self within is free of the stresses and strains inherent in the processes of being and becoming, yet fulfils Its duty in a detached manner, the Kingdom of the Lord is experienced by the Self in the heart. "When you become desireless all the burdens of life are removed."

If you want to know Me, Maitreya says, you have to give up all your attachments. This teaching is simple to understand, yet difficult to put into practice in your activities, because you need discipline. An experience of the Lord can help you develop detachment. When the Self is taken away from mind, spirit and body (even momentarily), that experience alone is sufficient. Maitreya says: "This is not philosophy. I am teaching you live things, not 'past, present and future'. If you practise honesty of mind, sincerity of spirit, and detachment while you are alive, you can embrace My totality in one single birth."

Detachment releases us from the cyclical patterns of cause and effect — karma — which govern our lives. As long as we are conditioned, however, these cyclical patterns repeat themselves. According to Maitreya's teaching, everything that has materialized is called 'prakriti'. This Sanskrit word refers to material activity or matter in broad terms, but 'prakritis', in the plural, also refers to human activities which are the result of conditioning. Prakriti is your 'second nature'. At present, your second nature controls mind, spirit and body. As awareness grows, its strength diminishes. But as long as you are controlled by your second nature you cannot understand the art of existence. Maitreya is inspiring humanity to fulfil its destiny which is to free itself of this second nature through growing self-awareness.

This teaching is embodied in the biblical story of the Garden of Eden, in which Adam and Eve were told not to eat the fruit of the tree of knowledge of good and evil. In this interpretation, the snake that tempted Adam and Eve is a symbol of 'prakritis', that is, of conditioning — the opposite of freedom. Once you 'eat' knowledge (a possessive act) rather than facing knowledge with awareness (whereby you understand that you must not 'grab') you are no longer free.

When Jesus went to various places preaching "Love thy neighbour as thyself," He also preached honesty and sincerity, because this creates love within you. The rabbis went to Mary to complain that her son was preaching things which were not in line with their teaching. Mary would ask Jesus why He was teaching in this way. At times there were arguments. Had tempers flared, Mary could have thought: "My son is mad." This is conditioning.

Conditioning is like an egg. Once incubated, the life within bursts through the shell. When conditioning cracks, there is a sense of relief. Conditioning can crack with awareness or without awareness. When conditioning cracks without awareness the result is a shock. It has such power it can even destroy part of the memory. The energy tied up in conditioning is like the tremendous energy tied up in a volcano. The destiny of conditioning is that it will burst. No one can remain conditioned for ever. This is why Maitreya says: "Be detached, then you will not be conditioned."

Detachment means the Self is using energy. Attachment means energy is using the Self. When energy uses the Self, the effects are destructive. Creation has energy and if that energy is disturbed it can shake our world and even break it, says Maitreya. "One has to be careful with energy. If you try to possess it, it will destroy you. You may be good at mathematics and become a first class mathematician. But what happens? You can become unbalanced if there is no equilibrium on the intellectual level. It is the same if you are caught up in spiritualism. You can become obsessive.

"Be detached and intelligently use that energy. Life is equilibrium and balance."

After the environment, the understanding of energy is the top priority in the world now. For the first time in the history of the human race, people will become aware of energy in their lives. Although no one knows where this energy comes from, or where it goes after death, all experience it during their lives.

In extreme cases, it is energy which goads a murderer to pick up a knife and kill another. Yet the murderer, unaware of it, wonders what forced him to act. In another extreme example, a yogi experiences a sudden surge of creative energy which pushes him into unknown regions where psychic powers are available to him. But the yogi is not affected because his training helps him to remain detached. He is not possessed by the energy.

Without this energy nothing can happen, and without it none of us can fulfil our destinies. Just as humanity has become aware of the environment, checking the food before we eat it, conscious of our health, so it will become conscious of this energy. This energy must be understood. Then it can be used to help the human race. Once triggered, it can be guided and used creatively.

However, if triggered blindly, as in some scientific or psychic experiments, it will destroy. People can suddenly go mad and kill, for there is very little 'space' between these happenings in accordance with the Law of Cause and Effect. This energy can goad the Self into situations in which it becomes trapped in the mind.

But what is the mind? It is nothing less than the blueprint of creation. It is not personal. It is universal, like energy. In spiritual language, energy is the Spirit while mind is the Holy Ghost. Maitreya says it is like a ghost because it can appear in any form. It can be a human being, a snake, or fire. Anything and everything in creation is in the mind. If the Self is goaded by energy into the trap of mind then the Self will be caught up in the cyclic evolution known as karma (cause and effect).

None the less, the Self has to undergo the experiences of the mind in order to evolve to the point of full Self-realization. The mind, of course, can act like God and control and manipulate the energy to achieve anything. But these psychic or magical powers can be very destructive. As awareness grows, it guides the Self which can then use the mind, spirit and body with intelligence. Balancing energy and environment is the key to salvation.

Questions on Maitreya's Teachings

How is the message of the Christ today different from His message given 2,000 years ago? (March 1989)
He speaks to a different humanity, so necessarily the emphasis is different. Then He spoke to a relatively few shepherds, fishermen, peasants, etc. They were uneducated, illiterate, totally dominated by the priests, very superstitious.

Today, He will speak directly (by modern media) to a vast audience of educated, literate, thinking people who can make their own decisions. Therefore, His function is one of Teacher rather than Saviour. The spiritual crisis of today is focused through the political and economic fields and must be resolved there. Otherwise there would be no humanity left to save or teach. Necessarily, His message is one of sharing and justice to bring humanity into a sense of its unity. Yet, essentially, you will find that the message of today is the same as that given through Jesus: humanity is one; we are all children of the one Father; God is Love; Love thy neighbour; the Kingdom of Heaven is within (a state of Being); man is a soul in incarnation; know Me (that is, experience Me in your heart) and you will know the Father. "Feed My sheep" becomes "Save the starving millions."

Maitreya's teaching of the essential unity with the Self did not seem to have had a transformative impact on most inhabitants of the planet when taught by Jesus. Will the response be more profound this time? (January/February 1989)

If that were not the case Maitreya would not be here. The teaching of the Christ through Jesus was largely preparatory, prophetic. He comes now to fulfil that preparatory work.

We are a very different humanity today from that of Jesus' time. Then, He spoke to shepherds and fishermen, deeply superstitious, totally under the control of the priests. You cannot imagine the consciousness of the people in Jesus' day. There is no way that you could put yourself in their minds and see the world through their fear and superstition. Whatever the priests said, they believed, they had to believe. Now He comes to a world where mass education, radio and television, all the modes of communication that we have today, have completely changed humanity. It is to a highly intelligent, organized and aspiring humanity that He returns today. I have not the slightest doubt that He will find the right response from us. Otherwise, He would not be here.

The Christ knows the consciousness of humanity. There is no separation in His consciousness between Him and us. The separation is on our side. He has come to change the world through us. That means He knows that it can be done. He knows that there are enough people in the world through whom the changes can take place. Some may know the Agni Yoga teachings, which were given by the Masters through Helena

Roerich. In the first book, which was given by Maitreya, He says: "There was a time when 10 true men could save the world. Then came a time when 10,000 was not enough. I shall call upon one billion." My Master says that there are now about 1.5 billion people ready, conscious, available to the Christ as a vanguard through whom He can work to change the world. I have no doubt that He will do it.

In the 140 Messages He gave through you, **Messages from Maitreya The Christ***, Maitreya makes frequent references to "The New Country". Where (or what) is the New Country?* (October 1990)

The New Country is the name Maitreya gives to the civilization which it is His mission to inspire — as He puts it, "The Country I call Love". Over the last 2,000 years, humanity has expressed the knowledge aspect of God; our present scientific society is the result of this expression. Over the coming Age of Aquarius, humanity will express *en masse* the still higher aspect of love. Through the implementation of sharing and justice, the love of God will become manifest and the Brotherhood of man an achieved reality.

On the Self

What is Maitreya's view about who we are and where we come from? (December 1991)

Maitreya says that the Self alone matters. We are that Self, an immortal Being, and our difficulties, our suffering, come from identifying with that which is not the Self. His teaching is very simple, very subtle, and, I think, difficult to carry out, otherwise we would all be doing it. He says: "Ask yourself: 'Who am I?'" You will find that you identify with this physical body, its needs and desires. If that is the case you will not experience who you are, you will experience this body with its painful sufferings and desires, but that is not you. Or you will identify with your feelings, your emotions — your joys and fears and so on; none of that is you. Or you identify with the constructions of your mind, your beliefs, ideology, memory. That is still not identification with the Self, but simply with a vehicle that the Self uses to demonstrate at this level.

We have to realize who we are. When we find out who we are we realize we are the Self. That is not something we can talk about, but a moment-to-moment experience, and can only be done in silence. As soon as you put a word to it you are intervening something between the experience of the Self and the Self itself. It is an experience.

Are you aware of who you are, or are you only aware of the vehicles of who you are — the body, the emotional, energetic structure, and the concepts of the mind? None of these is the Self. You have to go beyond these to become aware of the Self. That is not something that anyone can give you. Maitreya can give you an experience of the Self — He does it all the time — but even that is temporary. For a few days or weeks you will be in a state of bliss, but it will not last until you can do it for yourself, and that is only possible when you become detached.

For many years and with much frustration, I have tried to learn the condition that the consciousness, now called "me", is in when the physical body dies. Now I've heard all sorts of stories ranging from: the personality dissolves at death, to: we are eternal beings that created the universe. I hear talk about the personality, soul, spirit, higher and lower self — but to me these are just words. I can't identify with these things. My concern is about the "me" that writes this question and identifies with the name given to me at birth. That which enjoys tasty things to eat and yells "ouch" when I step on a tack. That which develops the family budget and fixes the leaky faucet. I can only identify with the "me" that ponders this question. This "me" does not look forward to dissolving into nothingness but neither do I feel like a universe-creating God. I hope I've made my dilemma clear. Tell me please, what is your understanding of the condition this "me" I describe will be in when the physical body dies? (April 1989)

What the questioner is describing in his various illustrations of the "me" is the general confusion and dilemma of most people in realizing who they really are. What is described is a series of identifications, each different, to which he gives the title "me". He identifies with the mind (and hand) which writes the question and yet he is not that mind or hand. He identifies with the body which says "ouch" when he steps on a tack, yet he is not the body. He identifies with his given name, yet he is not that name (it can be, and frequently is, changed). He is, over and over again, identifying with his mind or body or sentient apparatus which are only vehicles for the Self which he is to experience on this plane. What remains after the dissolution of the vehicles is simply that Self, no longer subject to the impressions of physical-plane life, but vividly alive and consciously aware on its own plane.

How can we overcome the strong feeling of being imprisoned in the body? (January/February 1990)

By ceasing to identify with the body as the Self. Through correct alignment with the Self (soul), recognizing that one is not the body but that the body is a necessary vehicle for the Self in time and space.

As we practise identifying and separating the Self — our awareness — from mind, spirit and body, does this involve separating it from the energies of Love and Will? (June 1992)
On the contrary, only as we grow in awareness of the Self and identify with that do we become able to express divine Love and Will, which are the nature of the Self.

As Jesus has forgiven me my sins and has given a new meaning to my life, I cannot accept a new master (Lord). What is your advice? (December 1990)
Maitreya does not seek acceptance. He says that people should continue to evolve in the context of their own tradition. He has come to teach the Art of Self-realization which can be achieved within any religion — or none. My advice, therefore, is to look to the teachings of Christ through Jesus and put them into effect in your life. If you can do this you will recognize and follow the teachings of Maitreya.

I remember that Maitreya has explained the phenomenon of spontaneous combustion as being the result of the Self — the awareness — losing control of its vehicles. During our practice of becoming aware of the Self by identifying it and separating it from its three vehicles, is there any danger of triggering spontaneous combustion? (June 1992)
No, none whatsoever.

*There was a statement in **Share International** from the close associate of Maitreya which said: "Do not meditate on the light." Can you explain that?* (May 1991)
This refers to the fact that light is synonymous with creation, and Maitreya says that no amount of meditation on light or anything in creation will bring salvation. Many people imagine that meditation is the way to salvation. It is if it brings you into touch with the Self, but meditation on the light brings you into touch, not with the Self, but with the light, and the light is not the Self. The light is creation and the Self stands beyond creation.

Maitreya puts it like this: consider the total reality to be 100 per cent, 70 per cent of which is creation and 30 per cent is non-creation, the unmanifest, the Self, the Absolute. The Absolute stands behind creation, and when It moves into creation It becomes light. From that light everything is created. You come from that light, everything you see and hear and touch, everything that we call creation, is an aspect of light. But no amount of meditation on creation will bring you to the Self, and therefore bring about salvation. Salvation is perfect freedom, and that is only possible by complete identity with, moment-to-moment awareness and realization of, the Self. If your realization is always of creation, at however lofty a level, you are still working within creation. You are still within the light and not within the Self, and so you are still conditioned, still governed by the Law of Cause and Effect.

It is just that if you meditate on the light it recharges you, and that is what you shouldn't do — is that what He is saying? (May 1991)
No, He is not saying you should not do it; what He is saying is that it will not bring you salvation. Any meditation on, or any focused awareness of, creation is not awareness of the Self and therefore cannot bring about salvation. You have to see the higher light within the light.

Honesty of Mind, Sincerity of Spirit

When Maitreya emerges, will the level of my consciousness naturally increase? Is there need for a special practice? (June 1990)
The increase in conscious awareness will depend entirely on one's ability to respond to the energy and teaching of Maitreya. Nothing is 'automatic'. Maitreya has said that the essentials are to know 'the Self' and that the easiest way to do that is to practise honesty of mind, sincerity of spirit, and detachment. He has given a Prayer for the New Age to aid in this process. [See p267.]

I can understand, I think, when Maitreya says to have honesty of mind, but what does He mean by sincerity of spirit? (transcribed from a talk in Japan)

Maitreya uses the word spirit in a rather unusual connotation. The average Westerner would see spirit as the Eastern concept of atma, the divine spark, the Absolute. Maitreya uses the word spirit quite differently. He talks about Atma, the Divine Spark, the Absolute, the Supreme Being, in terms of the Self. He talks about the Self, or the Supreme Being, reflecting Itself as in a mirror, as mind, spirit and body, which are the temples or vehicles for the atma, or Self, to manifest on the physical plane. The Supreme Being, or the Self, is the Absolute. It does not change; It is Being Itself.

Mind, spirit and body are the means for the becoming of the Supreme Being in time and space. The process of coming into incarnation, or life, and the process of returning from incarnation through the experience of life on the physical plane, is the 'becoming' of the Being.

By spirit, Maitreya means energy, power, shakti, the force of existence in the material world. This includes the energy of the astral plane which galvanizes our emotional body. We either identify with Self, the Absolute, or with the vehicles of the Absolute — the mind, the astral, spirit or shakti nature, or the physical body. Spirit, in this sense, is the energy of the senses, in all the connotations of that word — the astral senses, and so on.

One has to understand how subtle Maitreya's thinking and teaching is. If it were easy, we would all do it already. For instance, this questioner said: "I think I understand what He means by honesty of mind." But I wonder if this is the case. By honesty of mind, Maitreya doesn't mean only that you never tell lies, that you are always honest. He means that, of course, but He means much more. By honesty of mind, He means a mind which is not conditioned by ideology and 'isms' — a mind that is honest to itself, free and open to the experience of life, moment to moment, expressing itself perfectly, purely, spontaneously, without conditioning.

For instance, if you see yourself as a capitalist, socialist, Christian, Buddhist or whatever, you do not have honesty of mind; it is not possible. In every situation, you will bring to bear your particular ideology. That will influence the functioning of your mind. It will restrict the freedom of your mind; therefore, your mind cannot be honest to itself.

Maitreya sees any ideology, however noble, as a stepping stone. He calls ideologies steps on the ladder. When you are on the roof, you do not need a ladder; you can throw it away. An honest mind is an unconditioned mind. Only a non-conditioned mind can know what freedom is. The purpose of life is to become free. If you are locked into an ideology or belief system of any kind, your freedom is that much limited.

Likewise, sincerity of spirit is seeing reality without distortion. Everyone under the degree of a Master lives in a greater or lesser degree of illusion. When the illusion is on the physical plane we call it maya. When on the emotional or astral plane, glamour. When the illusion is on the mental plane, we call it illusion. These are all different aspects of illusion. Sincerity of spirit means responding to the emotional experience of life free from glamour. That is another freedom. Mental freedom is freedom from mental conditioning, freedom from ideas which are conditioning your mind. Sincerity of spirit is freedom from the glamours of the emotional plane, so that you see life as it is on the emotional plane. You are not caught up in the glamour of astral-plane energy.

Maitreya says that to know and experience the Self, you must have honesty of mind, sincerity of spirit, and detachment. Detachment happens more and more when you have honesty of mind and sincerity of spirit. As you become more and more detached, your mind becomes less and less conditioned. You are less and less "in thrall", conditioned by the glamours of the astral plane.

These three aspects — honesty of mind, sincerity of spirit, and detachment — work together. Detachment becomes possible as you become free from conditioning and astral glamour. Freedom from astral glamour and mental conditioning becomes possible as you become more detached.

The more you become detached, the more you can see glamour for what it is, the more you can see how conditioned your mind is, the more you become detached. As you become more detached, you know your Self more and more.

What is dishonesty of mind?
All of us think one thing, say something else and do something else again. That is dishonesty of mind. Honesty of mind is thinking something and saying and doing what is consistent with that thought: what you say is what you think and what you do — these are in a direct line. Hardly anyone practises it because it is difficult. Everyone knows the politician who thinks things that he does not want to make known so he answers questions obliquely. No politician, apparently, can afford to tell the truth.

When you are speaking from the heart, totally sincere, consonant with who you are and what you are, without pretensions or glamours, without building yourself up as something that you are not, but direct and pure and true to yourself — that is sincerity of spirit.

This teaching is not a religion. It is not something you have to believe in or not believe in; it is a practical science of evolution. It is, of course, also an art. It depends on a moment-to-moment experience of the Self and a recognition of what is the non-Self. The non-Self are the vehicles of the Self — the mind, spirit and body. You either identify with them and suffer, or identify with the Self and know total freedom.

By what means does one achieve a higher state of consciousness and thereby become a fully realized person? (April 1991)
Maitreya has said that the practise of honesty of mind, sincerity of spirit, and detachment will strengthen Self-awareness and lead to Self-realization. The use of the Prayer for the New Age [See p267] will help to bring about the necessary correct identification with the Self.

What is meant by personification?

273

Personification is a subjective process. You should not personify thoughts in mind, spirit or body. Sometimes, personification is appropriate at certain stages of life: a child personifies things, for example, Superman, and his awareness grows thereby. As he grows into adulthood, personification should dissolve naturally. If not, problems arise and his progress is arrested. Personification dissolves in the light of Self-awareness, which cleanses thought, speech and action.

In relation to Maitreya Himself, no one will be able to challenge His role as a World Teacher, but He does not describe Himself as the Christ, the Buddha, Mahdi, etc. If people personify Him in this way, that is also a limitation, although it is true that He is known by all these different titles. The real achievement is to begin to enjoy your life day by day through practising the teachings.

On Detachment

Why is it so important to become detached? (December 1991)
If something good, nice, pleasant happens to you you feel happy, but you were not happy before and you may not be happy tomorrow, so the feeling of happiness is not the Self. The nature of the Self is not happiness, but it is continuous, unbroken joy; it never changes. Or something nasty and painful happens and you are miserable, have a sense of loss, pain, disillusionment, depression. What has happened to that happiness, where did it go? Neither the pain nor the happiness is anything to do with the Self. These are the experiences of the man or woman in incarnation, the physical, mental, emotional vehicles of the Self. The Self itself knows none of that; it has no emotions, no thoughts, it alone is it is Being, manifesting through physical body, emotional structure, mental body. These are vehicles for the Self to experience at this level. When you are detached, the Self can go in and out of these at will. It can use these vehicles but does not get attached to them.

By wrong identification the Self, which is pure Being, gets fixed, as it were, trapped in a net on the physical plane, for example, where someone has, perhaps, total addiction to drugs — he cannot help himself. You have to get the person to realize who is taking the drugs. When you find out who is taking the drugs, you can distance yourself from it, and the process of rebuilding the connection with the Self takes place.

You have said that with detachment all suffering ends. But isn't suffering necessary for our evolution? (November 1990)
There are two kinds of suffering: reactive, involuntary suffering which results from conditioning and which detachment ends, thus speeding our evolution; and conscious, voluntary suffering, self- initiated, in service to others. This is only possible when a person is reasonably detached.

What is the difference between detachment and complacency? (December 1991)
There is all the difference in the world. If you are complacent you are attached to that which makes you complacent — to the fact that you are, perhaps, privileged, that you are rather 'well off' and 'all right, Jack', not too concerned about the pain and suffering of other people; in other words, selfish. Complacency is another word for selfishness.

Selfishness is attachment: to yourself, your physical body, perhaps your family, what you see as your needs. It could cover a multitude of things, from food, which we all need, to several houses, a yacht, lots of money, power, influence — all the things people become attached to. You cannot be selfish and be detached.

Detachment does not mean not being concerned. It means being concerned but, at the same time, able to function without the imposition of those concerns on your action. For example, someone who is full of concern, a very good doctor, or nurse, or humanitarian, a Mother Teresa — she concerns herself with the well-being of the people, mainly in Calcutta but now around the world. If she were attached to her response to their poverty and suffering, in tears all the time, sitting helplessly watching them die, she would be no use to them at all. What she has is the concern, the heart response to want to serve and at the same time the detachment to allow her to do it. To be able to see the suffering and not turn away from it, to experience it as one's own, so intensely as to need to serve it, and at the same time to be detached from one's emotional reaction — that is the difference between attachment, selfishness and complacency and the detachment of the server. You cannot properly serve unless you are detached.

I would like to ask a question about detachment, because I find it very difficult to comprehend the state of consciousness where apparently the emotions don't play on the personality. (November 1992)

Maitreya says there are three things which you have to practise to come to know the Self: honesty of mind, sincerity of what He calls spirit, and detachment. Detachment is detaching yourself from identifying with yourself as body, mind or spirit. It is not saying to yourself: "I mustn't feel emotions." Many people suppress their emotions. To suppress your emotions is just as bad as indulging your emotions. What you have to learn to do is to look at your emotions and not indulge them and not suppress them either — not repress them but simply look at them, not identify with them. If you do not identify with them, you detach from them. It is like creating a space between you and them. Most people immediately identify with their emotion, whatever it is. They have done so all their lives and so they take it for granted. They feel every negative emotion, and they think it is their right to experience them. In fact some people think it is their duty; and I suspect many psychologists tell their patients that it is their duty to 'emote'. The point is you have to be detached, not by detaching from life, but to be very aware, to look very seriously at what is happening but not to identify with it. This is difficult because it needs a degree of detachment to do it — you have to be there before you can get there! But it takes just a little space to create a bigger space. The best way I can think of is to study Krishnamurti. If you put into practice what you read as you are reading, you create that space. Look at what you are feeling, allow yourself to feel it but do not indulge it and do not suppress it or try to get rid of it. If you fight it, it is like the trials of Hercules: every time he cut off the Hydra's head two grew in its place. That is what comes from repression. What you have to do is to lift it up, as he did, finally, into the light of day (the light of the soul), and the Hydra died of its own accord. Simply look at the feeling and say: "That is not me. It wasn't there yesterday, it won't be there tomorrow, it is not me," and it will go away. Every time you do this, you weaken it. You withdraw nourishment. Every time you identify with anything, your energy nourishes it. Whatever you focus on, your energy will flow to it and you will strengthen the emotion. You have to reverse the process and the emotion will die a natural death through lack of nourishment. Detachment is the way to bring about the honesty of mind and the sincerity of spirit which Maitreya teaches.

One of the reasons I have felt drawn to your belief that the Christ is in the world (and to the messages He gave through you) is the emphasis on justice and ending hunger and all that. However, Maitreya is indicating that Jesus was wrong for trying to solve the problems of justice and poverty. [See p218, 'The life of Jesus'.] *Where did I get lost?* (October 1988)

With respect, in the article in question, Maitreya, I believe, is not saying that Jesus was wrong for trying to solve the problems of justice and poverty. As the reader suggests, Maitreya Himself calls for an end to these human miseries in almost every one of the 140 messages relayed through me. And they are still His immediate concern. What, I believe, He is faulting in Jesus (through Whom He Himself was working) was Jesus' attachment to what He wanted to achieve: justice. There is all the difference in the world between a desire to see justice reign and a fanatical attachment to that desire, thus dividing rich men from poor men. As Maitreya says, the true teaching is about detachment. His words *vis-à-vis* Jesus should be seen in the general context of what He is saying about detachment.

I do not understand what Maitreya means when He talks about our "second nature": "At present, your second nature controls mind, spirit and body." Is He using "second nature" as an equivalent to astral body? (October 1988)

By "second nature", I believe Maitreya means the desire principle, the instinctual and astral mechanism of the personality vehicles. At present, most people are controlled by the desire principle. By gradual detachment from its action, self-awareness grows, leading eventually to Self-realization, Moksha or Liberation.

It seems that Maitreya uses the word "ego" with the meaning "personality", while the Master DK uses "ego" to indicate the soul, in Alice Bailey's books. Against this, Maitreya seems to use "spirit" when He's talking about the soul, and DK uses "spirit" for the Monad. Why do the Masters not keep to the same terminology? It is all so complicated already. (July/August 1988)

It is true that Maitreya and the Master DK use the terms "ego" and "spirit" with different meanings. The reason for this is simple and is not intended to confuse.

Maitreya is speaking to the world as a whole and uses the term "ego" as is generally accepted, meaning the selfish personality. The Master DK, on the other hand, was writing for esoteric students, that is disciples and aspirants to discipleship. He uses the term "ego" therefore, in its technical sense as the soul, which it is. Likewise with the term "spirit"; Maitreya uses it as most people (however vaguely) understand it. DK uses it technically, from the esoteric standpoint, as that which reflects itself as soul.

Prayer for the New Age

Who is the "I" in the Prayer for the New Age given by Maitreya? Is it (1) our Father in Heaven; (2) the Ancient of Days (as in the Christian Bible); (3) does it mean Maitreya; or (4) other? (October 1989)

It is the Divine Principle behind all creation. The Self emanates from, and is identical to, the Divine Principle. Through mind, spirit and body, the Self realizes the Supreme

Being, and, in time and space, the becoming of that Divine Principle. It is this Principle that Maitreya calls 'the Lord'.

I am finding benefit and strength from the use of the new prayer given to us by Maitreya beginning: "I am the creator of the universe." The fifth line states: "Mind, spirit and body are my temples." I understand the temple of the mind, used by the Self to process information and to incorporate the light of intuition, and the temple of the body, to become a pure vehicle with which to contact the physical world. I understand the Self as an undisturbed limpid globule of awareness using these temples, but what is the spirit aspect? Is it the sum total of our emotions, feelings and psyche? I always thought the psyche was part of the mind. (September 1991)

The "spirit" as used by Maitreya means the sum total of the energies, astral/emotional and etheric, the life force, power or 'shakti' of an individual.

What is the most appropriate and potent way to use the new prayer for humanity in the New Age? (June 1989)

The most effective way is to say or think the words with the focused will, the attention at the ajna centre between the eyebrows. It is an affirmation, and all such prayers or mantras depend for their effect on the application of the focused will (what the Master DK calls the 'fixed intention'). On the whole, people do not understand this. For example, the Lord's Prayer or the Great Invocation are often said like a benediction. For such prayers to be truly invocatory, you have to bring the will to bear — reflecting precise understanding of the concepts. When the mind grasps the meaning of the concepts, and simultaneously the will is brought to bear, then those concepts will be activated, the mantram will work. The Prayer for the New Age is a great mantram or affirmation. It represents the concept of the Self as God, as the creator of all that exists. If this prayer is said seriously every day, there will grow inside you a realization of your true self.

I thought that The Great Invocation was going to be the new world prayer, and many have been using it for a long time. Why introduce another prayer? (October 1988)

There are three forms of mantras, or words of power: Prayer, Invocation and Affirmation. The Lord's Prayer is, as the name suggests, a prayer, a (largely) emotional supplication to the Divine to supply our daily needs of food, protection, guidance and so on. It is passive, asking God to do all, implying therefore that God is separate from us. The Great Invocation is not prayer but a mantram whereby God's energies — through His Representatives the Buddha, the Christ and Shamballa — are consciously invoked, by an understanding of the ideas of the Invocation and by the intent of the will. This is an entirely new factor and reflects a higher approach.

The new world prayer given by Maitreya is really an Affirmation with an invocative effect, and will be a powerful tool in the recognition by us that man and God are One, that there is no separation. By affirming that I am the Creator of the Universe I can come into consciousness (eventually) that I am God, the true reality.

On Spirituality

What, in your opinion, is a true human being? (January/February 1992)

A true human being, I suggest, is someone who realizes that he is not alone, that he is one of a large family (I do not mean his immediate family members), and it behoves him, therefore, to live his life in such a way that he does not harm them. Harmlessness is the basic relation and has a very practical function; it is not simply a nice idea. It is imperative to be harmless, otherwise you will harm yourself. Every thought and action we have sets in motion a cause. The effects stemming from these causes make our lives, for good or ill. Painful or pleasant, we make them ourselves, not in past lives only, but from moment to moment. Last week, yesterday, this very moment, we are initiating, through our thoughts and actions, the experience of our own lives. That can be either useful or it can be very destructive. If it is destructive, it is destructive not only to ourselves but also to our community.

You can see, therefore, the need for harmlessness, because our thoughts and actions condition the life, not only of ourselves, but also of other people — everyone with whom we are in relationship. So what we have to do is build the right kind of relationships, and it is about correct human relationships that Maitreya is here to teach. Correct human relationships mean that we live together without harming each other, allowing the Being of each individual to grow, flower, demonstrate in its own way, in its own time, without interference from us or anyone else.

Why is the Christ so concerned with physical problems, whereas mental and spiritual difficulties are probably at the root even of the physical problems? (September 1988)
With respect, it is not true to say that the Christ is concerned only with physical problems. To Him, these are but effects of a deep spiritual and mental malaise. But if you are starving to death, as millions are today, then that physical problem is more real to you than its cause — our spiritual sickness that allows it to happen.

A study of Maitreya's teachings and ideas will show His approach to be essentially concerned with the spiritual and psychological causes whose effects are the physical problems.

What is the best way to develop spirituality in adolescents of today? (May 1989)
To my mind, "spirituality" is not something which you can develop in others. It is the inherent nature of all people everywhere at every age from cradle to grave. It flowers naturally when the correct conditions for its growth are provided. These include the absence of conditioning ideas or ideologies, the respect for each one's own individuality and destiny, and the ambience of freedom in which to develop these. Maitreya says: "The most important thing in life is to learn true inwardness ... Do not deprive children of their innocence." By "true inwardness", I believe He means

awareness of the Self. By "innocence", I believe He means not ignorance but detachment, freedom from conditioning. Allow young people to learn detachment (which means right alignment and identification with the Self) and their "spirituality" will flourish as a matter of course. It must be remembered, however, that everyone today, adolescents in particular, live under great stress and pressures.

Does Maitreya include the end of suffering of the animals in His demands? (December 1988)
You will find that Maitreya does not make any demands at all — only recommendations. When humanity understands the relationship which it has with all the kingdoms, it will, I believe, spontaneously alter its methods of working with the animal kingdom and end its cruel exploitation.

'Distortions' in the Process of Communication

*I remember that I read in one issue of **Share International**, quite some time ago, that someone who had been near Maitreya was quoted as saying that He (Maitreya) did not say a thing twice, but was extremely clear and powerful in His way of speaking. Maitreya's messages, too, (given through you) are an example of powerful, concise language. I am afraid that this is not the impression that I get from the articles by Patricia Pitchon, in which Maitreya seems to be wordy and repetitive. Or is it that His assistant is conveying His words and ideas to us in his own way, without checking with Maitreya? If so, how are we to know how to read and interpret the information given? (October 1988)*
This reader is not alone in having this reaction to these articles. It is strange though, is it not, that after several years in which many people have asked for examples of the kind of teachings that Maitreya gives to those around Him, when we are finally able to do so the reaction is often so critical.

It should be remembered that the information and teachings in these articles are given, usually by telephone, from notes made 'on the spot' by an Indian gentleman whose

English is good but not perfect and whose initial understanding of these very subtle and difficult ideas is perhaps no more developed than the reader's. Personally, I am delighted to have them, however "wordy and repetitive" they may appear to be. (I am not convinced that they are).

That Maitreya uses terms in unusual ways, and that some of the ideas themselves are difficult to understand, I do acknowledge. After all, He is trying to expand our consciousness, and difficulty in the beginning I would have thought to be inevitable. For an exact meaning and interpretation of His teachings, we shall have to wait, perhaps, for Maitreya's public work to develop rather more.

Is Maitreya teaching us on the astral planes? (October 1989)
No. Notwithstanding the fact that many astral sensitives claim contact with, and communications from, Maitreya, He does not work — nor do the Masters — on the astral planes. Their work proceeds from the buddhic (soul) level.

PART THREE

DISCIPLESHIP AND SERVICE

CHAPTER 10

THE OVERCOMING OF FEAR

This article is an edited version of a talk during the 1989 Transmission Meditation/Tara Network conferences in San Francisco, USA, and Kerkrade, the Netherlands. The questions without publication dates are from the conferences.

In formulating the ideas for this talk, I am indebted to, besides the inspiration of my Master, the teachings of Sri Ramana Maharshi, Krishnamurti, the Master DK (through Alice Bailey), and the Lord Maitreya.   —
Benjamin Creme

    Fear, I suppose, has to be the most obnoxious, destructive, corrosive, limiting, inhibiting emotion to which we are prone. It seems that there is nobody in the world, except the Masters, who is free from its grip.

    We are enjoined to overcome fear, to be fearless. Every teacher of any note who has spoken to humanity, shared his wisdom, insights, with humanity, has made this a number one priority of living. The question is, is it possible for us to live free of fear? Can we go beyond fear?

    We all think we know what fear is. We may not know how it comes about but we certainly know what it feels like. There are many different types of fear, coming from different circumstances, needs, situations which we meet in life. Most people, when we talk about fear, will immediately think of fear of accidents, of death, the natural fears that condition our lives.

    From the very cradle we are fed information which conditions our reactions to all the phenomena of life, and this, I believe, is the root of our fear. If the child were left unconditioned it would know no fear. It just would not enter the mind, and you will find that fear is always the result of some movement of the mind, of thought.

The animals know no fear. They react to fearful situations, situations of danger, that is. We, too, react to such situations, usually with fear, because we are conditioned to respond to potentially dangerous situations with the reaction we call fear. It is built into our response apparatus and is the product of our minds. If we had not been conditioned by that information and therefore thought it likely to happen, we would know no fear. The antelope runs from the lion, not because it is afraid, but because it is intelligent. It knows that if it does not run, it will become the lion's dinner, so it runs as fast and as well as it can.

You must know, from previous experience of it, that if you are in a fearful situation and react with fear, you are not very efficient in your reactions. All of us at some time have had dreams in which we are overcome with fear, some terrible thing is happening, we are being chased by some monster, our father or mother, our big sister, big brother, some monstrous creation of our fear-ridden mind, and we cannot move, our efficient running deserts us and we are caught in a kind of morass from which we can only with the greatest difficulty move. Then of course we wake up; we are so glad it is all over, we are in a cold sweat of fear, because we could not move, could not escape from this threat. Action becomes impossible because of the fear. Fear inhibits. How is it possible, then, that as soon as an antelope sees the leopard or the lion, as soon as the rabbit sees the dog, it skitters away as fast as it can? Is it because of fear? Has it thought: "Oh, that is a lion, that is a dog, oh, I am scared"? Because if that were the case, most probably it would lie 'doggo' and hope that the dog or the lion would not recognize it as a rabbit or an antelope. In fact, it runs as fast as its legs can carry it away from this potential danger, but fear does not enter into it. It is an intelligent, instinctual reaction of the body, caused by the flood of stimuli into the adrenals by the sympathetic nervous system.

We have two nervous systems, the sympathetic and the parasympathetic. One produces, in animals, the reaction of flight, and in us, the dry mouth, the inability to run, contraction, the sweaty hands, whatever our own individual reaction to fear may be. The other, the parasympathetic, functions on the pleasure principle and creates saliva, bright eyes, expansion, a sense of joy, happiness — pleasure, in a word. Our life seems to be lived out in the controlling of one and the pursuit of the other — the controlling of, or escaping from, our fear reactions, and the pursuit of our pleasure reactions. Why should we take such trouble to do this, to go through our lives seeking pleasure and controlling or escaping from pain, fear, suffering, whatever is causing that which we call pain? If we look at the causes, I think we will find that it has its source in our view of ourselves in relation to that which we see as the not-self, other than the self, that which is outside. The only thing we can control, obviously, is our response to various events, and we spend our lives figuring out ways of escaping from the pain and prolonging the pleasure. This is the action of the sympathetic and the parasympathetic nervous systems, the mechanism of our body, and as long as we identify with that, we will know fear.

Why need living be such a struggle? Why should it be so painful? Fear is pain, we all know that. So far, I have talked about fear in terms of the physical, but there is another fear (I think we are all aware of this, and prone to it) which we have to call psychological fear. It is the fear which enters the mind in a psychological situation, in which we feel threatened in some way, not necessarily physically; we are not necessarily going to be run over or eaten by an animal or anything drastic like that.

Fear of death, I suppose, is the greatest fear, so strong that we do not think about it, but push it down to the back of our mind, although we know that one day (hopefully when we are very old and do not care any more), we shall have to face this fear. But it is there in almost every situation in which we find ourselves, and it is tied up, I believe, in the corresponding fear of life itself. The fear of death is a result of our conditioning, the fact that we separate death from life.

There are two aspects to our experience of life: this 'living' aspect, as we call it, in which we go to bed, wake up and are still here — here again with another day to get through, to live, to experience — and the other aspect which begins when we do not wake up, when we 'die'.

The big problem is how to live (and die) without fear. In every situation we cannot help feeling fear because it has become, not an action of the conscious mind, but an unconscious reaction in all situations. Is there any way in which we can overcome it? You cannot know yourself, freedom, the nature of reality, happiness, joy or bliss, if you have fear, and if you have any fear you have all fear. Is it possible to get rid of fear, and if so how do we do it? Let us see if we might change our approach to reality, so that we can experience reality as it is and not through this fog of fear, this inhibiting, crushing, astral reaction which is fear.

If you go into it, you will find that all fear is the result of thought, an action, a movement, of the mind. We are taught as children that, if we go too near the fire, we will burn our hand. Of course, if we had gone too near the fire and burned our hand, we would soon know, from the pain that would result, that one just does not do that. And so an instinctive mechanism, an intelligent, instinctual reaction, is built into the child. It knows from that moment on not to go too near the fire. But if you say to the child: "If you do not do what I say, I will spank you," then you are introducing a completely different notion into the child's mind. If you are true to your word and the child does not do what you say and you spank it, it hurts, and it tries to please you from then on, and in this trying to please you, to not be hurt, the child's spontaneous reaction to life has become distorted. This has happened to all of us, in one way or another, to a greater or lesser extent. Every single one of us has built into our response to life a series of inhibitions which together add up to fear. Fear has become so deeply embedded in the unconscious mind that, even as we look at it from the conscious level, we cannot change. We can rationalize, see that it is there; we can analyse the mechanism of it, but still, if we are honest, we can see that the fear goes on. It is something which we have to approach on another level.

Some people resort to hypnotism. Fear so rules their lives that they become incapable of even the most normal actions: doing the chores, going to work, shopping, driving a car, all of these things become so fear-ridden that the person's daily life is disrupted. Hypnosis can be done by somebody else, or it can be self-hypnosis. The hypnotist, whether another or the person himself or herself, gives the suggestion to the unconscious mind to obliterate the fear reaction. If the suggestion is strong enough and the person susceptible enough to that suggestion, for a time it works. They seem to be free from that inhibiting fear, whether it is the fear of heights, of going to the dentist, of flying in airplanes, the fear which makes them rush to a cigarette or a drink every time they are faced with a situation in which they are afraid.

What are these situations; how do they come about? Largely, I believe, because our educational systems are based on conditioning into competition. We are made to compare ourselves, competitively, with everyone, everything, every situation we meet. Instead of having a friend next door called Jack, we are a better or a worse boy than Jack. Instead of being a different boy from Jack, with different needs, hopes, talents, qualities, we are always better than Jack or not as good as Jack. We are always set in a situation of competition. I believe it is that competition which is the origin of our fear.

Conditioning

From all of this we create a notion, an image, of ourselves as adequate or inadequate, superior or inferior, and of course the one is as deadly as the other. We are either superior to everyone around us, and have, therefore, the necessity of maintaining that illusion of superiority, so that in every situation in which it is threatened, we experience fear, we fight it, run away from it, enlarge it, give it energy, propagate it and keep it going; or we have the idea, the image, that we are less than adequate: why cannot we be like Jack next door, who is tall, obedient, nice, always says the right thing, does as his parents ask, who runs errands all the time, and is a very nice, good, obedient child? We are always put into this situation in

291

which we are seen in our parents' eyes — and therefore in our own eyes — as inadequate to deal with the life which they are proposing to build around us. All of that, I believe, creates the conditions of fear so that, in every situation we come to, we cast ahead of us this image. If we feel capable, adequate to the task, we do not feel fear, until the task gets a bit harder and then we do.

All of this is the result of our experience of ourselves in the past, our thoughts about ourselves, our qualities, our abilities, our experience. How did we deal with this situation before? Was it painful, was it pleasurable? If it was pleasurable, let us try to maintain it. Was it painful? — then let us try to get rid of it, escape from it. Our lives, it seems, are taken up with this constant attempt to escape from fear and to maintain pleasure. Both of them are the result of the movement of thought, of the mind.

If we did not think, we would not feel fear, nor would we feel pleasure. The Frenchman [Descartes] said: "I think, therefore I am." I think he should have said: "I think, therefore I have fear." It is precisely because we think that we have fear. That is why the animal does not know fear. It looks like fear as we see it running away from the predator, but it is a simple, instinctual reaction of intelligent activity to escape from death. Fear is something else. Fear is the product of thought. In fact, fear is thought itself. The question is, can we experience life without thought, without fear? All our fears are the result of our experience of living in the past. We look at our past, we are the sum total of all of that; everything that we are, everything that we know about ourselves, everything we know about life, every experience we have which makes us able to cope, all of that is the result of thought.

Am I saying that we should get rid of thought? Obviously, that would be ridiculous. We cannot live our lives without thought, build roads or bridges without thought, we cannot do our work without thought. So there is an area in which thought is essential to everyday living, but that is on a purely practical level. Is it possible that we can maintain to the utmost efficiency that area of thought, apply it to the mechanism of our daily lives, without transferring it to the psychological level and thus experiencing psychological fear (which is exactly what we do)?

We see ourselves as this, as that: I am a British Conservative, bulwark of the nation, and I do not like those Socialists who are trying to get into power, because, if they do, they are going to sweep away all my privileges. They are envious of my money, of my rather comfortable style of life, and they want it for themselves. Of course it would never occur to me that we might all have it, but the point is, I have it, and they want it, so I feel afraid, threatened. So I keep them at bay, and I use every mechanism of political strategy to maintain the *status quo*.

We all do exactly the same thing on the personal level. We have an image of ourselves and we try to make that better. Why? To be better, more colourful, more important, more influential, to make a bigger impact on life, to get on, to have more money, a bigger house, a bigger car; to shine, to be noticed, to be somebody, not to be dull and boring and tedious, the kind of person others ignore.

We do this in order to feel comfortable, to prolong the state of pleasure. When I say pleasure, I do not mean just sex pleasure, or drink pleasure, or eating pleasure, or pleasurable interchange with people of like minds, or the pleasure of listening to music. I mean a position in which we feel comfortable, at ease, not threatened, secure. We are pursuing this all the time. We do this by inhibiting every opposite experience, which of course is pain, sorrow, suffering, fear. All our energy is drained into these two mechanisms: the maintaining of pleasure and the running away from fear. What a waste of energy. What a tremendous drain of energy from the human psyche. That is the reason why most people have no etheric vision, for example; why most people cannot think logically for more than a few sentences. It is the reason why most people live, from the psychological point of view, crippled, stunted lives, totally uncreative, or relatively uncreative. We drain all our energy into these two mechanisms: the running after, the longing for, the desiring of,

293

the maintenance of, comfort, pleasure and security; and the running away from pain, suffering, fear.

Can we get away from both of these? If both of these responses to life are the result of thought, is it possible to live in such a way that the thought process is involved only in the mechanics of living, the practicalities of living: in driving the car, making sure that there is gas in the car, that you have the money to pay for the gas, all these things? You are going abroad — is your passport in order, can you get on the ship in time, which means getting the train on time — all of that is the mechanism of thought in its correct use. Without it, we would all be in a chaotic state of inanition; we would never be able to do anything.

The wrong use of thought is that thought by which we create the images of ourselves and of our fear and our pleasure, because the fear and the pleasure are equally the result of thought. They do not exist outside thought. So can we overcome the thought? The overcoming of fear is related totally to the overcoming of the wrong use of thought.

We are all terribly interested in tomorrow. We are afraid of tomorrow. We want security. Above anything in life, we want security, and security means, first of all, having enough to eat, of course, so we want food. It has to come from somewhere, we have to be able to buy it, that means we need money; that means we have to have a job. Not having a job is a trauma, having a job is also a trauma — either way, we are caught in this cleft stick of wanting and not wanting: the fear of losing the job, the fear of not getting a better one, the fear that we are going to meet people in that job who are more clever than we are, smarter, who are going to take our job from us; all of that enters into every situation of our lives. We go through life competing, and the effect is stress, strain, a corroding fear which limits every possibility of correct, spontaneous action.

Few of us can react spontaneously to life. We do not know what life is, experienced spontaneously, as it is, without bringing in fear, desire, wanting it to be different, to be the way we want it. We build a thoughtform, an idea, an image of how it should be — that is, as we know it: that with which we are familiar, feel comfortable, secure, unthreatened. We want relationships in which we are never threatened. We want our wife never to stop loving us or our husband never to look at another woman. We want to feel secure in every psychological way, in every situation. Is this possible? Does this seem rational?

Is it possible that we can live our lives without this overriding fear, this dependency on other people for our happiness? Because that is really what it amounts to: we become dependent because we are afraid. Since our thoughts make us afraid, since we project into tomorrow or next week or next year our image of what we are, according to our knowledge of ourselves in the past, we create conditions in which fear is an intrinsic element. We cannot get away from it. We take our fears of the past and project them into the future, so that we never, in any real sense, experience what is happening now. We never live now, always in the past. We are our experience of the past, the sum of all our reactions — fear and every other reaction — to the events of the past.

If we look at ourselves, experience who we are, we find that we are nothing but a bundle of fears making up a sense of the self we call 'me' whose major effort is escaping from these fears. We are escaping from ourselves, from this notion of ourselves that we are carrying around with us moment to moment. We are trying to escape from fear, which we have created by our thought, and are seeking to create security, pleasure, continuity of life as we know it, without anything unknown. I suppose the biggest unknown is the unknown we call death. That is what we are all escaping from.

Fear of life

I think basic to every single fear, however subtle, is the fundamental fear of death, which is the fear of life. Every one of us lives under the fear of life itself. No wonder, because we have made of life a kind of hell, an arena in which we are gladiators fighting, with inadequate weapons, powerful adversaries better equipped than ourselves. We are put into positions in which we feel inadequate, under-trained, under-prepared, living a kind of confidence-trick to others and to ourselves. There is no real joy, no real happiness. We are just getting by, avoiding too much pain, suffering and fear, and running after, fighting, competing, for the pleasure, the security, we long for.

Why do we long at all? What is this mechanism of longing? Why do we desire that life should be different from what it is? We are trying to make life in an image which we project into the future, and that makes us afraid. It creates the conditions in which fear is inevitable, because we are competing, and when we are competing we are in confrontation, there is conflict. Wherever there is conflict there is fear. We are adversaries in an arena and we are taught from infancy that this is the natural course.

Those of us who are parents know how difficult it is to educate a child without imposing our fear of life. We all do it. I think a child brought up without fear is probably the rarest child on Earth, the most gifted child, because it has the greatest gift of life, whether it has money or possessions or not: it is to be free of that conditioning, to experience life as it is without fear, without running after it, without running away from it, without wanting anything at all.

Is it possible to experience life, to go through the various movements of life, of interaction, of relationship, without experiencing fear (I am talking now about psychological fear), without entering into competition, and therefore into conflict, which produces fear? All opposition, all conflict, produces fear. Is it possible to live without desiring anything at all? Because if we can do that, we will be free of fear. We will be free, period. If we can live without the desire principle governing our responses to life, we can live freely, without fear.

Every time we impose our desire on life, whether it is desire for comfort, for safety, for absence from fear, we give it energy; we prolong the fear by engaging with it.

We all avoid confrontation with our superiors. Can we get away from the notion of superior and inferior? This seems to me to be basic to this problem of fear. So long as we have the idea that some people are superior to us, and therefore that we are inferior to them, we will have fear. We will fear being overwhelmed by them, people will like them better than us. One's wife might like that man better because he is superior. My husband might fancy that lady because she is obviously prettier than I am, and so on. These are fears which well up moment to moment in every person's life. They are the results of this comparison between superior and inferior. These are built into our subconscious by our parents, our teachers, by every situation in which we are placed. Every single one of us is conditioned by that approach to life: that some are superior, some inferior, some pass exams, some do not pass exams. What exam has ever been formulated which could possibly measure the quality of life of one person as against another? What exam can do this? Yet throughout our school life (and for many people in their adult life), we are faced with examinations. Day to day, we give ourselves an examination. We say: "How do I match up in comparison to that person? Am I better than he is or is he better than I am? Why did I not think of that?"

Then we begin to imitate. Comparison implies imitation. We imitate that which we admire in other people and we lose the sense of ourselves. We enter a vicious circle of comparison, competition, imitation, and we are nowhere at all in the middle of all of this. We are living a life which is simply a series of response reactions to various stimuli which bring about fear or pleasure, one or the other, both of which are created by our own mind.

Is it possible to live without feeling superior? Is it possible to look at life, at other people, to come into relationship with people where we are not making this judgement — because this is a judgement, is it not? Is it possible to meet people, situations, without making that sort of comparison?

Can we rid ourselves of this poison of competition? We can see its effect on the political level, in the economic sphere. It is easy to see how destructive, corrupting, competition is. And yet we engage in it; we all do it. Is it possible — not to avoid it, because that would be running away from it — is it possible to overcome it, to go beyond it, to approach people, psychological situations in which fear would be engendered, without competition, without making comparisons?

Try it. We have to try, to see if it is possible. All this competition, comparison, instinctual avoidance, self-preservation, is an attempt to preserve what we take to be the self, unaffected by pain, fear, which are very destructive and highly unpleasant emotions, and which can become so strong that they completely devour our life. Is it possible by looking at fear in a certain way not to give it energy, not prolong it? When we give it expression or try to avoid it; when we try to escape from it, or to control it; when we try to inhibit it, we give it the energy to persist, and so it never goes away. Can we look at it in such a way that, of its own accord, it disappears?

Trials of Hercules

One of the great trials of Hercules, if you remember, was the slaying of the many-headed Hydra. The Hydra lived in a cave, and had nine heads, one of them immortal. Hercules was enjoined to conquer the monster. "One word of counsel only I may give," the Teacher said. "We rise by kneeling; we conquer by surrendering; we gain by giving up. Go forth, O Son of God and Son of Man, and conquer."

Hercules, the great warrior, the great hero, went to the Hydra's cave. He was not afraid. He cut off a head and immediately two grew in its place. He cut off another and, again, two grew. He cut them all off and two grew each time so there were twice as many heads as before he started. Even he, eventually, got a bit tired. Not just tired of this game, but actually tired. He was unable to cope with this constant renewal, twice over, of these horrible heads. Then he had an idea. When he was getting so tired that he could not continue the struggle, suddenly an awareness grew in him of what to do. He did not think it out, it came to him. He suddenly became aware of the weakness of the monster, where the truth lay. He grasped the monster and took it up into the light of day, out of this dark cave where he had been fighting. And in the light of day the monster suddenly expired, all heads died, except one which he cut off and put under a stone.

That is the legend: it must mean something. Why has it been preserved? That, I believe, is the only way you can deal with fear. You have to bring it up into the light of day, and of course the light of day is the light of the soul. The light of the soul playing on the monster killed it. The light of the soul kills fear. How can you, at a word, call on the light of the soul and focus it on fear? Not this little fear, or that one, but all fear, so that fear itself does not recur?

I believe it consists in doing nothing at all, which is very difficult to do. Always, when we feel fear, we try to control it, to inhibit it, to escape from it. We seek pleasure, a drink, something, anything, to get away from this fear. We never simply look at it. We think about it, with our conscious mind we analyse its mechanism, of course to no avail; it never goes away because it is built into our subconscious. It is an unconscious mechanism, a conditioned reflex, and not to do with the conscious mind at all. Only the light of the soul can really deal with fear, and to come into the awareness of that we have to do nothing at all. We have to let it happen. It happens when we look at the fear without trying to do anything about it. We have this fear of death, of the future, of the past, of what might happen because of what did happen and made us feel afraid. We know that if that situation is repeated we will feel afraid, and since we do not want to feel afraid we try to avoid its repetition. But, can we, on the contrary, not run away from fear but simply look at it, without condemning it, escaping from it, criticizing it, without criticizing ourselves, without saying "I shouldn't feel this fear, I am grown up now and that fear is childish"? The only reason it is childish, of course, is because it was built in in childhood. Can we look at the events of life in such a way, as they are happening, without condemning them, without running away from them, without seeking anything different? In other words, can we do it without desire? We desire something different: security, what we call happiness, pleasure, absence from fear, from pain. We build a picture, an image, of life as we would like it to be.

Desire is the basis of all fear. We desire security, love, happiness, we desire other people to be to us what we would like them to be. It is this movement of desire, this longing, this yearning for comfort, love, easeful situations, so that we are never troubled, never jealous, never made angry, never feel uncomfortable, humiliated, never at a disadvantage with anything or anybody. That is the basis of the desire principle: we are longing to be, and to be, and to be — to become. Desire is becoming. Is there something else which is not becoming? Is there something else which does not have to go through this process of becoming, of desiring, to change or to remain the same, to be secure in that which we know? In other words, can we go beyond what we know?

So long as we are looking at life and knowing it — knowing the people, the events, what is going to happen, what to do, what not to do — we feel secure. But is it possible to look at life without desiring that knowledge? Because that knowledge is the outcome of past experience, it is memory, it is dead. It is not a living process; it is the past. It is the action of our mind, which we then project as an image, a construct of ourselves.

What is this 'self'?

What is this 'self', this construction? What is it we are running away from? Perhaps we are running away from our own emptiness, our loneliness, our sense of not being at all. While we are becoming, we are not Being, and if we explore the essence of the feeling we have in our deepest, most profound fear, longing, desire, hope, belief, we will find that it is the desire to know that we are, that we have Being, rather than this sense of endless becoming, wanting, desiring. That desire process is at the opposite pole from the reality of Being, and that is why we have fear. Is it possible to go beyond this experience of the process of becoming, which is the result of identification with ourselves as body, mind, thoughts? Identifying with that, we create the circumstances of fear.

Whatever we identify with, we are. We look at a person, we say: "That is Mary, she is superior to me." Immediately I am afraid of Mary, because I know she is superior to me. She is older, wiser, more clever, better-looking, all of these things. I am immediately afraid of Mary. Is it possible to look at Mary and not experience that, not make this division? Is it possible to see that we are not really experiencing ourselves at all but an image of the past? There is nothing there, it does not exist. What does exist is a body, a mind, a set of emotions. They exist, not beyond death, but up to death. That is why we are afraid of death. We know that at death that body with which we identify, which we see in the glass; these emotions which react with fear or pleasure; that mind which builds the thoughts by which we know all of this, are going to be no more. Therefore at death we are going to be no more. The whole of our desire life is the prolongation of that nothingness, that thoughtform which we have of ourselves, which essentially does not exist at all. It is the notion that what we are experiencing — the fear, longing, hope, ideas — is somehow separate from ourselves. They are not. They are ourselves; whatever we identify with is ourself. There is no way we can experience anything in life without seeing it as part of ourselves. This is the truth behind our experience of fear. We identify with the pain of the body so we are pain. We identify with the fears of the mind so we are fear. We cannot identify and be separate from that with which we identify. Is it possible to go beyond that kind of identification, to not identify with the body, not identify with the fear reactions, the emotions? Is it possible not to identify with these constructions of the mind, because if we can, we will come on an experience of ourselves which goes beyond ourselves, the only state in which we are free, the only state in which we really are Being.

Our immortal Being

That, I believe, is what Maitreya calls the Self. The Self, He says, is the most important thing in life. The Self is our immortal Being, and the Self uses the experiences in time and space to realize the process of its becoming. Is it possible to change our view of ourselves, our identification, away from these vehicles, the mind, body, emotions? Because, if we can, we shall set ourselves free immediately from all fear.

There are many techniques we can use which will gradually mitigate the effect of fear, but is it possible, all at once, to rid ourselves of fear? I believe it is possible, if we can come into relationship with our Self as the Self, and not with that accumulation of experiences that we call 'me', in which fear is inevitable because it is created by thought. All of that 'me' is created by my thought of me. Is it possible to go beyond that and to experience the Self directly? If we can do this, we will find an entirely different view of life, a different capacity to live, more intensely, more vividly, more spontaneously. If we can simply look, without condemning, at what happens, at what is, without judging, making comparisons, being in competition; without feeling superior or inferior; looking, simply looking, at what is, at the moment it is, looking at it, experiencing it. Then, I believe, we can enter into communion with the Self, which is all Being, and know, from then on, the absence, the overcoming, of fear.

It is not something anyone can teach you to do. I recommend you try to do it and find in the doing the achievement of it. As soon as we do it, we achieve it. We cannot achieve it until we do it. It is not a technique, a practice; it is simply doing nothing at all, simply being who we are. When we are who we are, we know all there is to know. We are free from fear, from desire, from longing. We do not need anything or anybody and we can approach anyone, by one or by thousands. We can relate to them directly as they are, which is as we are, without the sense of separation; without the sense that they are superior or inferior; without judging; without allowing our conditioning — competition, comparisons — to get between us and them. Then we find that we are living in a constant state of joy. That is joy. Take your thought of yourself and ask yourself: "Who am I? Who experiences this thought? Who is doing the experiencing? Who am I? Who has this thought, of myself sitting here, who is doing it?" Ask: "Who am I?" Do not give yourself a name. It has nothing to do with a name but with an experience of the Self.

THE OVERCOMING OF FEAR

Questions and Answers

Experience of the Self

Is it really possible to overcome fear by the use of the Prayer for the New Age given by Maitreya?

Try it and find out. If I say yes, some of you might believe me, but I could be wrong, you can only know this for yourself, by using it. You can only overcome fear by yourself, nobody can teach you. I believe it is possible. You have to make it your own experience before you can know whether it is true or not. Likewise with this New World Prayer, try it, use it daily and build thereby a different type of identification. We identify with the Self, or with anything and everything other than the Self. We identify with That or we identify with the vehicles which the Self uses to manifest itself at this level, this physical plane in which we experience ourselves as separate.

If you are identifying with the Self you do not have to ask that question, you will already know. If you have to ask the question, you are not identified with the Self, so my suggestion is to use the Prayer for the New Age given by Maitreya and find out what happens.

You can say it mechanically or you can say it and experience it. As you say it, experience it happening and bring about the alignment, the identification therefore, with the Self. If you experience That, you will find that you no longer identify with the vehicles of the Self, this body, mind, the thoughtforms created by the mind. Your sense of yourself is the result of these thoughtforms, built of memory of your experience of events from infancy until this moment, and you think that is 'me'. But a moment's thought will make you realize there is really no such thing as 'me'. There is only memory of experiences, some painful, some fearful, some pleasurable. We seek to avoid the one and reach after the other; that is what our lives as 'me' have been about. This results from wrong identification: identifying with the vehicles of the Self rather than with the Self. By the Self Maitreya means, also, the soul, a reflection, exact, of Beingness Itself, which He calls 'the Lord'. The Lord exists eternally and absolutely, and that is our true nature, but we identify with the absolute or with the relative — it is always one or the other. There are only these two, the origin of all polarities, all pairs of opposites. As we identify with the absolute, we will find that we know all the answers to all the problems that we could ever ask.

In relation to the use of the Prayer for the New Age, is there anything that Maitreya is doing or will do specifically for disciples that it would appear He is already doing in relation to young people in stressful situations, in the centres which He is creating around the world?
The two things are different. There may be some undercurrent of relationship but on the face of it they are not connected. He has said: "I have come to teach humanity the art of Self-realization," and for those who can use the Prayer for the New Age, that is a powerful tool for bringing oneself into correct relationship with the Self. It brings about Self-awareness, and Self-awareness is the necessary step to Self-realization. You cannot become Self-realized unless you are Self-aware, and He has said you cannot become Self-aware unless you have self-respect.

In these centres, the young people are taught, if that is the right word, are brought into the condition of having, perhaps for the first time in this life, self-respect. They may be on drugs, in alcohol abuse, from broken homes, in criminal activities, vandals, social misfits and so on. They are brought together in these centres which are a kind of therapy situation for their psyches. They are taught what people in other situations would take as a matter of course, self-respect, because if you do not have self-respect, no progress of any kind can be made. These people lack self-respect, which is why they are in crime. Inwardly they sense themselves as souls, but on the outer plane, as a result of bad education, bad social circumstances, bad influences, they find it impossible to give expression to that inner sense of themselves as divine Beings. So they are at war with themselves, and, as an extension of themselves, with the society of which they are a part.

Disciples would not be disciples if they had that problem, but some disciples have terrible problems, just as difficult. That is the result of glamour, and the particular problems which disciples face.

The disciple is taking a conscious step in the direction of Self-realization. That is what everybody, consciously or unconsciously, is seeking to attain, and, of course, will eventually attain. Self-realization is the goal of our incarnational experience. Most people who are already disciples will have self-respect enough to take them on the path.

The Great Prayer, or Affirmation, is given for all to use. Of course, you can use it at different levels. The devotional type will use it in the same way as he would say the Lord's Prayer: Give me, give me, give me. Forgive me, forgive me. Likewise with the Prayer for the New Age, you can say it mechanically or you can say it in such a way that it really fulfils every astral longing you ever had. That is one way and it will be used in that way, probably, for the next thousand years. Then, there is the way it should be said which I cannot tell you, which is the experiencing of it as you say it. You have to experience it, nothing happens unless you experience it. You have to be the Self as the vehicle is saying the mantram. You can only become what you are. There is nothing to be learned. You can learn everything out of every book that has ever been written and be as unaware in relation to the Self as you were before you started. You can only begin to experience the Self when you go beyond thought; then you experience the real. That is the given state, the nature of the Self. That is you. You are the creator of the Universe, there is not anything else, but you have to get rid of wrong identification.

It is not something you can acquire by knowledge, there is no acquisition involved in experiencing the real. That is why a little baby, who does not know anything in terms of knowledge, has not gone to school yet and had its knowledge patterns distorted, is fresh, does not think, just experiences directly as a soul experiences its own Being. That is how you have to be, like a little child, directly, without any preconceptions, any constructions of thought, because every thought is a hindrance to the experience of the real which is the Self.

The more evolved the disciple, the more he will use that mantram as it is meant to be used, that is, to bring one into identification with the Self. The Self has always been there, we are unaware of it because of wrong identification. It needs a shift of vision, of identification, from the relative to the absolute, from the vehicle to that which is using the vehicle, the Self.

The Prayer is given at this time because Maitreya is in the world, and it is a time in which He can, in a most powerful way, stimulate the disciples of the world through whom He has to work.

Are there reasons unknown to us which your Master has for suggesting the subject, the overcoming of fear, for the conference theme?
The purpose of the Master in suggesting this as the subject for this conference was so that we would address it, and perhaps throw some light on the most important glamour facing any disciple, the glamour of all glamours, fear. There are many other glamours but none of them is so destructive, above all to a disciple, because the fears of the disciple are rather particular. All humanity has fears but disciples have the fears of humanity plus certain fears which really only pertain to the disciple.

The disciple's fears are specific and are related to soul influence. He is a disciple because he is on the way to demonstrating himself as a soul and that itself brings in problems. All the disciple's vehicles are being galvanized at the same time. This creates problems that do not concern average humanity. The disciple, besides his service in the world, his sense of purpose, of growing destiny and so on, has to come to grips with these myriad influences and galvanizing forces which are flooding through his structure on all levels at once.

One of the major fears of disciples is, will he be adequate? Is he doing enough, is he acting correctly? Am I where I am meant to be? Am I doing what I am supposed to be doing? — as if there were a group of Masters with strings, as if the disciples were marionettes and were being manipulated, as if some of them got 'out of sync': doing the right thing in the wrong place or in the right place but doing the wrong work. That may sound crazy, but these are real fears. Also, the disciple sees the problems of the world and perhaps sees more clearly than most the enormity of these problems. Even if he has read the reasons for the problems, the forces which are at play behind appearances, he sees the immensity of it, the hugeness of the task of salvation which has to be done in the world, and he feels tiny, totally inadequate. That is the major fear. The fear of the unknown everybody experiences, but that fear the disciple experiences very powerfully in terms of the future as it opens up before him, which he can only dimly sense, but in which he knows he has a part to play.

So the Master initiated this talk in order to bring our minds to bear on this glamour of glamours. The Master had the intention that we should address this problem, look at it in a deeply serious way and *do something about it*, not just thinking about it but actually overcoming it. We must become totally fearless. That is the number one injunction on all disciples. You cannot ever take initiation in the real sense while fear inhabits your astral vehicle. It is not possible. You have to be totally fearless in order to become a Master. And, of course, long before becoming a Master.

I think it is a long process to go from where I am right now to identifying with the true Self, and I do not know the true Self, it is unknown to me, so I am afraid.

The thing is, do you want to try? If you want to try, see where you get. You are asking me: "What if I am afraid of losing my consciousness of my body?" That is more or less what you are saying. What if I am afraid of losing this intimate connection I have, an identification with which I feel pretty familiar, with my body, my emotions, my mind? That wrong identification, I am suggesting, is the source of the fears. You find the fear impossible, destructive, debilitating, inhibiting, as a prison, because fear is a prison. You cannot have fear and be free.

The aim of life is to become free in every respect, total freedom, for the Self to act as a free agent through its vehicles. That is why somebody like Sai Baba can create by thought whatever He wants to create, because He is free. If He had fear, He could not do it. It is only freedom that gives you the power to act as God, because you are God when you are free. Essentially you are God, but you have to find your way back to God through correct identification. If you say to me, what if I am afraid of giving up my identification with this lower aspect of myself, I say well, what about it? If you are not interested in it, if you find this too painful, you will not do it. But if you want freedom from fear, you have to learn to die to the desires that you have, which are the result of wrong identification. We have desires because we identify with our astral nature, but if we detach ourselves from our astral nature, we will find those desires simply fade away. We do not overcome them, they just no longer exist, because we have replaced them with something else, with a stronger energy: the energy of the Self. The strong will always overcome the weak. The weak, the phantasmagoria of our fears (because fear is a phantom, we create it by thought), which our identification with our lower nature — the body, the mind, the astral apparatus — creates, also creates in us what you are suggesting, the fear of getting rid of fear, of losing this sense of the self. But you want it or you do not want it. Nobody is making us do this.

If you want to experience freedom from fear, you have to be prepared to die. There is no thought about it. It is such an attractive force that you are drawn into it by its own attractiveness; it is like desire on the highest possible scale. When you transmute the astral nature and the energy of the astral planes is lifted up from the solar plexus to the heart centre, it happens automatically. You do not even try to do it, it

308

just happens. There is no fear in it, because it is an easy process; in a sense it is already there. You function either from the solar plexus or from the heart, one or the other. This is a long, fluctuating process, but gradually it becomes consolidated in the heart centre and the transmutation is complete. Then fear is not a problem, because it does not arise. You do not say: "I am afraid of giving up my fears." (Why would you be afraid of giving up fear? It is inhibiting, debilitating, so destructive, but even that is only thought about it; these are words, thoughts, about the nature of fear.) Fear itself is an emotion which everyone experiences, but it is an emotion of the solar plexus, not an emotion, as people call it, of the heart. Shift it upwards to the heart and you will find its opposite is love, and if there is love there is no fear. If there is fear there will be little or no love.

Can the Self be experienced on all levels, independent of the degree of initiation? Or does the degree of fear depend on the degree of polarization?
The Self can be experienced at any level whatsoever. It is the given nature of the human being; every baby experiences itself as the Self, whether it is 0.7 or a third-degree initiate, until it is taught otherwise, is conditioned to be afraid, into the focusing of its desires. The potency of the desire nature is dependent on the point of evolution. Of course, the nature of that which is experienced by someone who is 0.5 and the Self which is experienced by the fourth-degree initiate is different, inevitably, because every initiation confers on the initiate greater awareness and a deeper insight into the mind of the Logos, the source of the Self. But at whatever level you may be, the experience of the Self can be direct. It just has to be unconditioned by thought or fear.

The first thought is the 'I' thought. As soon as the child begins to think about itself as a separate unit the whole process builds up. Without the thought of 'I' there is no separation. As soon as you think 'I' and sense yourself as an entity separate from the Self, then the war between the pairs of opposites starts, conflict begins. So trace the 'I' thought back, find out who is the 'I', say: "Who am I?" Go beyond that, and you will find the Self.

If you go beyond the thought of 'I', you go beyond thought itself, because 'I' is the first thought. When you go beyond thought, you still the mind, not by any kind of conscious control, not by will power, but simply by going beyond the thought of 'I', and you come into that domain of which I was speaking, which is reality, which is you, because you are not separate from it, but you cannot experience it by thinking about it.

Yesterday, at the end of the talk, you tried to share with us in meditation that state of Being, of joy. But for those of us with a very active mind it is very difficult to still our thought, to clear our thought. Could you please show us how to do it?

You do not clear the thought, but go beyond the thought. You have to ask yourself: "Who am I?" Of course, I am me. Who is this me? Trace that back and you find it is here, in the heart, the spiritual heart at the right side of the body; go in with it, this I, and you will learn. But you have to be prepared to die to that which is holding you back: your desire for experience, to feel safe, to not feel afraid. All of that is preventing us from experiencing the Self. This is the result of identifying with the needs, the desires, of the body, the astral nature, the mental body.

Ask yourself: "Who am I?" — and hold on to the state that is produced when you say it. That is what the great new Prayer is for. Say the great new mantram: I am the creator of the universe. That is the highest you can be, the highest there is. How can the creator of the universe be afraid? You can create a whole universe; you are the mother and father of everything, including fear, so how can you be afraid of your own creation? You think the whole of this world into being. I do not exist, you see me, you think I exist, but I do not exist. You do not exist, nobody in this room exists, this room does not exist. All of this is a product of the thoughtforming process of our minds. The point is, it exists but only in a relative sense; from the point of view of the Self, it is all a shadow-play, play-acting.

To God, it is not real, it is all a dream, like your dreams are when you wake up. To the Self, this physical, astral, mental creation is as real as your dreams are to your conscious mind. Your physical body has only a relative reality, your astral and mental bodies only a relative reality, as vehicles for the Self. They die at death, and that is why we are so afraid of death, because we identify with them.

Practice dying on a daily basis and get good at it, then you will not be afraid of it, because you will realize there is no death. St Paul said: "I die every day." He did not mean he literally died every day. He meant he died to his wrong identification. Death itself is an illusion, it does not exist. Only the vehicles, which themselves are relative, die, and, to the Reality which uses them to know itself at this level, they are just dreams. You live in that Reality, or you do not. You identify with it, or you identify with the vehicles. Then you know fear, because the nature of these vehicles, being relative, is fearful. Their desires create conflict, fear, competition, comparison: the fear of not being adequate, of missing something, of not making it, of failure. All these fears are the result of identifying with the vehicle rather than with that which uses the vehicle to know itself, to become. How do you do it? If it were easy, everyone would do it. It is easy, but it requires discipline, and most people do not like discipline. It is not to do with wanting — the more you want it, the less you will achieve it — it is not to do with desire but with discipline, with being able to die, to give up the desire principle, to stop wanting, *to be still*. You are either still and then you are in the Self, or else there is movement; the movement of desire. Stop the movement of desire and the stillness exists, by itself, because that is what is. In the centre of all movement, there is a still point. That still point is the Self, that is you. We surround that with the constant movement of desire in every direction, physical, astral and mental. This activity of matter is not you. Find out who you are, who is setting up this motion. You can only do that by getting into the still centre.

Mitigate the Effects of Fear

Master DK gives a formula for overcoming glamours or dealing with glamours. But that formula is very complicated, pages, and really difficult. Is there a shortcut, simple steps for breaking the conditioning of age-old habits of fear?
There are simple steps, it depends how fast you want to move. You can do it in stages, and continue it for this life, and the next and the next, or you can do it all at once. I think it is more interesting to look at fear in such a way that you overcome it all at once. That is what I am talking about.

There are means by which you can mitigate the effect of fear, but you do not overcome it. You can mitigate the impact of fear on your mind and therefore on your life, that you can do, and there are all sorts of ways: read DK in many of the books — *A Treatise on White Magic* would be one. Look up 'fear' in the index and you will get many suggestions. But they are simply indications to help you along a very difficult path. DK, I am sure, is as aware of that as I am and He will know, I am certain, that they are not to be taken as the answer or the cure of fear. They are simply techniques of amelioration when the fear is such that you cannot do anything else.

If your fear is so overwhelming that you are totally devoid of impulse or control and just cannot carry on your life, then maybe you should see a psychiatrist for help.

If we tackle one fear, does it help to overcome fear in general?
Is there such a thing as one fear? Fear is a reflex of thought. Is it not true that all fears, being the result of thought, dissolve in the overcoming of thought? If you can go beyond thought, then you go beyond the mechanism that brings fear about in the first place. So if you can tackle and overcome what you call one fear by going beyond thought, then you have gone beyond all fear. There are not separate fears, there are different manifestations, fears connected to different situations, but the mechanism is the same in every case.

Are good desires necessary or do they get in the way too?
What is a good desire as distinct from a bad desire?

To get away from fear, that is a good desire.
If you wish to be fearless, does that make you fearless? The desire to be fearless is still caught up in the pairs of opposites, as you are still in conflict, are you not? If you say: "I am not fearless and I am going to try like anything to be fearless, and I am going to put every ounce of my energy into having the good desire to be fearless," you can be sure you will be fearful to the end of your life. The more energy you put into it, the more energy you are giving to this state of fragmentation, this conflict, which is the result of fragmentation, the worse the situation becomes. Of course, that is simply the other side of fear, the desire not to have fear. Wherever there is desire, there will be fear, because that desire will never be met or you will be afraid it will not be met. You are afraid that, if you do not get what you desire, which is fearlessness, you will know fear. Of course you will. But even if you desire not to experience fear, you will still experience fear. You have not changed anything. You have changed only the words.

You said you can achieve this state in a flash. Can you arrive at it by stages, can you practise this thing, sometimes succeeding — sometimes you have been objective — detached — over something, or do we have to take a quantum leap?
If you practise something are you actually achieving it? If you practise riding a bike, you will achieve riding a bike. That is physical-plane conscious knowledge applied to an end. If you practise learning French for long enough, you will learn French. It is possible on the physical plane by sheer practice to achieve any of this mechanical knowledge. That is what knowledge is for. Unfortunately, we imagine that that knowledge is ourself. It is not. It is a function of the mind, and the mind's function is to utilize thought and therefore acquire knowledge, to manipulate life on the physical plane by practice, but if you practise getting rid of fear till you are blue in the face you will never get rid of fear.

As soon as you attempt to apply the thought process of the mind to the experience of reality you will have an incomplete experience of reality. That is inevitable because it is a product of thought. But you can never know reality by thought. You can only know reality when you go beyond thought, when you allow thought to go. When you allow thought to go 'you' die, because 'you' are a product of thought, of memory. If you say: "Can I practise this and get to it bit by bit?", I have to say, no, you cannot, because you are still involving thought. You are simply prolonging the agony. You may mitigate the effects of it momentarily and think: "Ah, I've got there," but it will rise again, the many-headed Hydra will have grown two heads by the time you have turned your back. It has to be seen as it is. You cannot see reality through thought; it is impossible. Thought is not concerned with reality. You have to go beyond thought and see it by the light of the intuition, which has nothing to do with thought. It is direct perception, straight knowledge, direct knowing.

While we are experiencing the fear, what can we do about the fear?
Ask yourself: "Who is afraid?" Find out who is experiencing it. Ask yourself: "Who am I, who is experiencing this fear? I am experiencing it, then who am I?" Find out who I am, trace that thought back and find out who is doing it. That will relate you to the Self, shift your focus away from identifying with the fear, but you have to detach yourself from it; it is a process of detachment. You do not say: "Oh I've got to detach"; it does not work that way. You cannot approach it by thought, but you can think the thought, Who am I? The 'I' is the thing to hang on to, who am I, who is feeling this fear? Am I this fear, is this me? Well, it is obviously not. These are events that have nothing to do with me. They happened, but not to the same person. I did not feel it yesterday, I probably will not feel it tomorrow, so it is not me. If I am a continuous entity, going on from day to day, then I should feel this fear all the time, every single moment, so it cannot be me, it is not logical. So who is experiencing it, who is feeling this fear? Find that out, and you will find that you will detach yourself from the fear, the fear will just drop away, because you have not given it any energy.

THE OVERCOMING OF FEAR

*At the very moment one experiences fear, one cannot detach —
there is just fear and nothing else. I cannot ask who is
experiencing fear; but just know there is fear and that is it.*
Try it, try it.

Fear and Ray Structures

*How should people deal with fear in relationship to their
particular ray structure?*
Some rays are more prone to the glamour of fear than others.
Fear is one of the major glamours of the 2nd ray, whereas for
the 1st ray fear is almost non-existent. It has other glamours,
but not fear. Working with power, the 1st-ray type senses that
power, utilizes it easily, and is, relatively speaking, fearless in
all situations. The 2nd ray, on the other hand, is working with
the life aspect, rather than with form, and has such a deep,
intuitive sense of life and of the whole, that when it tries to
deal with the fragmented form through which to express that
life, it feels inadequate, and so is afraid. It is also able to
empathize, to see all points of view. This inhibits action and
so, again, it feels inadequate, because it cannot act, cannot
create form. It has such a sense of this tremendously powerful,
meaningful life, that the 2nd ray cowers and crumbles where
others, who do not have that direct intuition of the profundity
of life do not. Therefore, for the 2nd ray, a major problem is
how to lose the fear of the power and grandeur, the
unknowable nature, of life itself. It does not feel able to
construct the forms through which that immensity can be
demonstrated. The 1-3-5-7 line, less aware of the life aspect,
on the whole relates better to the outer world.

Second-ray types tend to be naturally timid, fearful,
anxious, lacking what is generally called self-confidence.
There is no such thing, actually, as self-confidence; there is
simply fear or absence of fear. Self-confidence is not
confidence in the Self, but the confidence of a person who is
used to doing something out of experience (therefore out of the
past, out of knowledge, from learning of techniques), who is
able to deal with his limited knowledge of life, his limited

capacity to experience life in its fuller sense, and is able to give that limited experience expression in some form on the physical plane, relating easily, then, to people, to circumstances, to events and structures in the world. That is the extroverted person with a rather limited contact with his or her own soul.

Of course you get mixed types. You get people whose major rays might be along the 1-3-5-7 line but from some sub-ray influence find the same inhibitions in dealing with people as the 2nd-ray type might feel. Because of the 1-3-5-7 rays in the rest of the make-up they can function perfectly well in a practical manner and do their work extremely efficiently. But as regards human relationships, they come into the same category as the 2nd-ray type who is full of fear. It is all to do with personal relationships. It is life itself, but life as we know it is largely relating to other people. It is each other we fear. We also fear events, but usually as they are expressed through others, the 'Other One', the big man or the boss who is not going to give us a rise, who is going to sack us for little or no misdemeanour , and so on. These fears usually relate to other people. There are, of course, fears of death, fears of catastrophe, and many others. The 2nd ray tends to fear life itself, because it does not handle well the forms. The forms are the means by which the life expresses itself, but these forms are changing. Life itself does not change, it eternally is, and only when we rid ourselves of fear can we see that life never changes.

Do 4th- and 6th-ray types have similar problems to the 2nd-ray types?
Yes, to a degree, since they come out of the 2nd ray. But they bring in their own particular qualities and one of the characteristics of the 6th ray is courage. Because of its often fanatical belief in its own ideals, the 6th-ray type usually has the courage of its convictions. Its convictions may be about something nonsensical but it has the courage to fight for them: 6th-ray types are sure, not of themselves but sure of being right, that their ideas are the only ideas fit to be held by

humanity, that their view of life is the only possible one that has any meaning or purpose at all (even though they might have held a different one last year and in two years' time will have a completely different one again); that each one is the total, absolute answer to all the problems of life is the fanaticism of the 6th-ray type, but that fanaticism has about it a kind of courage. Sixth-ray types are not afraid to lay down the law, to impose their view of life and the laws governing it on everyone else, so you get the fundamentalists of all the religious and political ideological groups. Ideology, religiosity, are products of 6th-ray fanaticism, and it takes courage to express it in that way, but the courage is out of the conviction — not really, I believe, the result of fearlessness. The same fear lies behind 6th-ray fanaticism. The 6th-ray type is a fanatic because inwardly he is afraid he could be wrong.

The 4th ray has a peculiar attitude to fear. The 4th ray is a very mercurial type. It is not by accident I say mercurial because Mercury is the planet which focuses 4th-ray energy in our solar system. The 4th ray has the capacity to go from the highest to the lowest and back again. It is the middle ray, embracing all the rays in a sense. The 4th ray is always used by Hierarchy in the transmission of Their energies as a harmonizing factor.

The 4th ray takes the pairs of opposites on every level and brings them together, and through the conflict of these pairs of opposites a new unity, a new harmony, is achieved. Fear is the result of conflict, of competition, of comparison, of choice. The resolution of the pairs of opposites the 4th-ray type sees instinctively, intuitively, as its task, thus producing harmony. The 4th-ray type is often fearful but if caught up in some high aspiration, service to a cause, something that inspires him to action, he can be totally fearless.

The 4th-ray type can be as fear-ridden as any 2nd-ray type, abject with fear, lying on the ground or in a bed unable to move, just waiting for something interesting to happen that will divert his mind from the fear. The beauty of the 4th-ray type with its mercurial nature is that he can be quickly diverted. It only needs a war or something like that to come along and he is immediately activated, joins the army, and is up there in the front where all the guns are, but on a horse. He hears: "Charge!" and all his fear is gone. Once up there, on the horse, nothing can stop the 4th ray. He is able to rise on wings above all fear while caught up in this great emotion, because of course it is an emotion of elation. The esoteric books say that the 4th ray is peculiarly equally divided between tamas and rajas. Tamas is inertia, non-movement; the other side, rajas, is the hussar at the head of his regiment with his sabre above his head, charging the tanks and guns on the other side. The 4th ray overcomes the fear to which he is as prone as is the 2nd ray by the glamour of exalted emotion. That exaltation makes him able to rise above it.

When you say a 2nd-ray type, for example, do you usually mean someone who has a lot of 2nd ray, or do you usually mean personality, or astral, because we are talking about fear?

It depends. It means an individual where the 2nd ray is largely dominating the structure whether that is the personality (it would tend to be a personality) but if that person were astrally polarized and had 2, 4 or 6 — the most usual — on the astral, then that astral nature would be dominating the personality.

If the person were mentally polarized, had a 2nd-ray personality, and a 5th-ray mental for instance, the expression would be completely different for that 2nd ray. It depends whether one is astrally, mentally or spiritually polarized; if one is spiritually polarized it does not matter what the ray structure is. It is the other side of the coin of that divinity, that virtue, which we are seeing when we are dealing with fear. The rays themselves are spoken of as 'shining through'. A person's rays are shining through when they are demonstrating the higher or virtue aspect, the soul aspect, of the ray.

A lot of us in our group are 2nd-ray souls, but the soul 2nd ray is not what we are talking about.

It is generally the personality expression. That can be influenced by the mental and the astral and very often by the brain, the quality of the brain. Someone with a 2nd-ray physical will have a 2nd-ray brain and that, too, brings in its own particular fear reactions to life because the 2nd-ray physical tends to be hypersensitive. That hypersensitivity makes the 2nd-ray physical type oversensitive to the world as a whole, and therefore fearful.

Somebody who had a 2nd-ray mental as well as a 2nd-ray astral might be having 2nd-ray astral thoughtforms, but if they are becoming mentally polarized would some of the virtues of the 2nd ray from the mental be starting to really take form?

Indeed, yes. The soul will demonstrate itself most through the mental plane. Although in a disciple it will galvanize all levels, its expression and its influence work through the mental plane. That is why when mental polarization begins (that occurs around 1.5), even only a little bit, 1.55 or 1.6 — which you cannot say is really mentally polarized but is the beginning of mental polarization — you can do enormous amounts in your life. Some of our world leaders, today, are 1.6, not higher. They are leading their nations and are highly mentally-focused individuals who do an enormous job, well or badly, but they do it, and they have been elected to their posts, most often, because of their outstanding ability in one way or another. I am sure if they had been 1.5 or less that would not have happened; they would be so glamour-ridden that they would not be able to cut a finely-chiselled-enough intellect to demonstrate their capacities. It would be fragmented into all the astral morass.

[For further information on rays and ray structures, see *Maitreya's Mission*, *Volume One*, Chapter 6, and Part III, Chapter 13, of this book.]

Experiences during Meditation

Talking about Being/becoming, some of us were saying that in meditation, say, it is quite easy to experience Beingness, and just be and have the awareness and all the rest, but as soon as you get up, walk across the room, start interacting with people, go to work, you lose it. There seems to be some kind of mystery there, bringing that being out of your meditation chair. Is that something you can talk about?

Meditation is the result of Self-awareness. True meditation is the living in the state of Self-awareness. It is a moment-to-moment experiencing of what is, and what is is the Self.

If you are sitting down to meditate in order to come to the Self you will never come to the Self. You might come to all sorts of other interesting experiences, but not the Self. You are either aware of the Self and living in the experience of the Self, or you are not, it is one or the other. And where it is at all relative, it is relative, and that relativity is the illusion under which we all live. People learn to do all sorts of formal meditation techniques, asanas, yogic practices and so on, which give them all manner of experiences, but these experiences are psychic, they are not the Self. All you need is the direct experience of the Self and then you are in meditation. Meditation I believe to be the direct experience of what is — that is the Self — without the intrusion of anything else, without a single thought coming between you and that experience.

Meditation, as a formal exercise, is not truly meditation. It may be concentration or contemplation, it may give illumination, but it is not, strictly speaking, meditation in the sense of unbroken awareness of the Self. Meditation is the result of Self-awareness and there is nothing formal about that. It is really a way of looking at what is, and when you look at what is, as it is, you are meditating.

If you really do meditation, I mean in the deepest sense of the word, in a continuous state of awareness, you come to realize that you do not exist at all. To say that sounds scary, fearful, so people do not do it. It is terrifying to some people even to contemplate the idea that they actually do not exist, that everything they see, everything they experience, is really an illusion, a dream, a shadow play, as real, in itself, as our dreams are when we wake up. All that phantasmagoria, all these extraordinary happenings, these people we talked to so wonderfully, all the marvels that happen in our dream, disappear in a flash as soon as we wake up. Where do they go to? They do not go anywhere, because they did not exist. They are purely a succession of thoughtforms which we created.

That is what the world is, that is what 'you' are. Your sense of 'you' is a bundle of thoughtforms which started when you were a baby and which you have added to through every experience. Every action, every belief, everything you have been told, have read, everything that has ever happened to you has built up in your waking consciousness an image of yourself which you carry around and think is you. It is not real. It is only a thoughtform. You are no longer the person who was sitting in the pram, who went to school. You are no longer the person who took the first job, got a rise at 25 and the sack at 30. You are no longer these people. There is nothing that you can say is a solid person who came together as a result of all those experiences. It is simply an image, and an image is a thoughtform. We construct an image of ourselves and then we project that everywhere. We make it the focus for comparison with everything and everybody: how do I, my image of me, relate to that image I have of him or her? I think they are better than me. There the fear begins.

If you can let go of that image, this, I believe, is what you have to do: you have to learn to not be, because you are not. If you can accept that fact, if you can look at yourself and think clearly about the reality or the unreality of that image of yourself, how it has really come about by a linking together of memories, that is all 'you' are, a bundle of memories, memories of when you were in school, when you got married, when your first child came, when they grew up. These are all memories. Are you memory? Why are you frightened if you are only memory? How can memory be frightened? But if you identify with the memory, then you are the memory. If you identify with the fear, you are the fear. So what you have to do is recognize that you are really looking at something which is not there. I am not here. I do not exist. So what is there? This is the beginning of meditation.

What does exist, if I do not exist? Is there a way I can look at what does exist without bringing in this memory, which I thought existed, but have now come to realize does not exist, and can I look at that which does exist in a way which does not try to enlarge it, prolong it, maintain it, keep me secure in it, but just look at it as it is? Can I be subtle, because it needs subtlety; subtlety and energy, you need both. You need the subtlety to recognize the movement of the mind which, all the time, is trying to bring you back to identifying with that thought and the next , and so on. So you have to be very subtle and recognize that that thought is not you. Thought is a mechanism by which we give shape to the ideas created by the mind. But we are not the mind; the mind is only a vehicle. A vehicle for what? The thing is to find out what that is, and you can only do that by experiencing it. It is not something you can talk about, but you can experience it, and when you do experience it, when you allow yourself not to be, when you are ready to die, to give up this tension which you take to be you — which is simply a desiring of this comfort, that fulfilment, that experience, that pleasure; avoiding that pain, that fear, that is all that we are doing — as soon as we allow that to drop away and just be quiet and still — suddenly we are filled with love, with the nature of our own Being. That Being illumines us and we see that that is all there is. There isn't anything else. We do not exist as separate from That. It is love. You can call It what you like — love, joy, bliss — it is the nature of reality, and we are, each one of us, That, eternally, moment to moment, as long as we dwell there. But we have to dwell in It.

How do you dwell in It? You dwell in It by dying to what is not It. Be prepared to die to everything else, to all you think you want, long for, hope for, aspire towards, let it all go, and when you do that something extraordinary happens. You see that you are everything, everything that there is. If you look around, you see people, sky, trees, bushes, houses, but you have disappeared as a separate form. That is what you are. I AM THAT. The great, slow movement of Beethoven's Choral Symphony is about That. He even spells it out: I AM THAT, I AM THAT. That movement is about the nature of love, of cosmos, of Beethoven, of all Being. You must be able to die to that which you are not. Give it up. Let it go. Ask absolutely nothing of life, no fulfilment, no longing, no pleasure, no avoidance of pain, avoidance of fear, and when you do the mind lifts out and up and you see that all of That is you, and

322

That is all there is. You are not separate. Separation is an illusion, and you will be afraid as long as you identify with yourself as separate from That. There is nothing but That which is everything, which is in a grain of sand, is huge, immense, endless; it has form and no form, and from that level everything that is happening here is a dream, a play; God playing, creating. We think it is real. It is not real, not for a second. We make it real and therefore we suffer. Our suffering is the result of our desiring. It is as simple as that. If we would give up suffering, pain, give up, in a moment, all types of fear, then we have to stop desiring, because the fear, the anguish, the pain, all of that, is a direct result of our desire. The desire principle rules us or it does not, whichever way we will have it.

If we stop thoughtforms, or if we don't see ourselves as our thoughtforms any more, why doesn't our body change?
How do you know it doesn't? Maybe it does.

It would seem that similar experiences to what you are describing can be achieved through drugs but that experience does not last. It does not leave you free of fear, but the words would describe it in that way. What is the difference, why is it that this lasts and the drug experience does not?
They are not the same experience at all. Drugs take you no deeper or higher than some level of the astral planes, and in the astral planes you are still dealing with thought. The astral planes are the result of the thoughtforming capacity of the human mind and the experience of the drug-taker is simply the phantasmagoria created by his own thoughts, nothing else. Therefore it is limited, temporary, a glamour through and through, not a spiritual experience. The experience of the absolute, the Self, as the spiritual base of life, the nature of reality itself, has to be achieved on the soul level.

Who uses the mind, that is the question to ask. Who uses the astral body, the physical body? That which we call the Self, divinity, which manifests itself through these vehicles, and thought is simply one of the mechanisms. It is the agency of the mind, whereby that which is not the mind can experience the movement of life, the becoming of itself at this level. That becoming is not Being but its becoming, in time and space.

That is thought's limitation, that is why you have to go beyond it to know that which is beyond time and space. Then you obliterate time. You experience that there is no time, no me. We disappear in That, and yet we have total consciousness, but the separate sense of 'me', this image which is simply a thoughtform built up by memory over countless years, totally disappears. We are clouds, other people, trees, everything, but we are nothing, because they too do not exist, but are only a mirror image, down through the planes, by which That which is — the only thing that is — makes a shadow on the physical plane. Seen from the point of view of the Self that shadow is paper-thin, like an image on a screen. It looks real, just as a figure on a screen looks real, but we know it is just a projection of the light.

Detachment vs. Non-Involvement

Can you contrast the difference between detachment and non-involvement?

Detachment is involvement without attachment. Non-involvement is attachment. You cannot be non-involved in something without being attached to it. You are involved in life, you cannot escape being involved in life. You could be a hermit in the Himalaya, live in a cave, and not be involved in life but you would still be attached. That is why you have to go into a cave. As soon as you are avoiding something there is conflict. That conflict is your attachment. Detachment is something completely different. Detachment is being able to live in life and not want to possess it, not desire anything in it.

That does not mean you do not want to eat, because of course you have a physical body that needs to eat. It does not mean you do not want money, because you have to pay the rent and the bus fare and your children's school fees. It does not mean being unaware or unintelligent, it means not being possessive, not clinging to things and owning them. You cannot really ever own anything. That kind of owning, of possessiveness, whether it is of people or things, is attachment. Detachment is, if you like, the opposite of that. It is being able to say no, to give up, to walk away from, to not desire, even the best pleasure in the world. That is non-attachment.

Non-involvement is one of the pairs of opposites?
Of course, yes. Non-involvement is making a choice. If there is a choice there has to be conflict. Otherwise there would not be a choice.

How can we raise a child, without creating fear? How do we do it without making the child feel emotionally suppressed?
Surround the child with love and trust in its instinctive, self-preserving mechanism. Every child, every animal (and of course a child is a little human animal) has built in an instinctive, intelligent means of self-preservation. Trust that. You have to trust that the child is a son of God and has this in-built mechanism for self-preservation and development. Surround it with love but do not over-coddle it, do not force your attention on it 24 hours a day. Let it be, give it space. We all, and of course all children, need space. They need an area to be themselves and to experience themselves inside. To be yourself is to experience your own Beingness. If you do that you will find the child will grow in that experience, constantly aware of itself as the Self.

Of course it is very difficult because all of us are conditioned. We are conditioned by our parents, and they by their parents, and so on, it has gone on for millions of years. It is very difficult not to project your own fears on to the child. There is no shortcut, there is no easy thing I could tell you to do; it is partly common sense. It needs a constant vigilance, and if you can focus your attention on the Self, actually shift your own identification, then naturally you will not project your glamours, your fears, on the child. It is a question of your changing in order not to harm the child. It is difficult; if it were not difficult we would not be here. It is quickly said, but it is the most difficult thing to do, it needs enormous discipline.

But that is why you are called a disciple. A disciple is someone who accepts the disciplines of life. You have to build in the disciplines which lead to Self-realization. The way is to die to your own desires. The route for most people is by self-sacrifice.

Why do we hold on to, or why are we so attracted by, fear? For example expressed in Hitchcock films or horror movies?
I believe the function of such movies is like that of Greek tragedy; they are supposed to be cathartic. As we watch them, we go through the fears latent in everyone's astral nature, waiting for a situation to arise which brings about, like a trigger, a reflex, an emotional reaction to the stimuli. These fear reactions are built in to the subconscious computer. It is like putting in a disk, typing out a question and out comes fear, inevitably, in that situation. The film presents the situation but at one remove from reality. It produces the facsimile of the reaction but in a safe environment. The cinema is comfortable and warm, we have some chocolate to eat, it is nice and cosy and we know that this film is not real, only illusion. We suspend judgement of it for the time being and let it get to us a little bit to give the *frisson*, but in a safe, secure way. It is still pleasure, it is experiencing fear as part of the pleasure of cinema — the fear becomes pleasure because it is safe here, that is the attraction. Like Greek tragedy itself. We do not know how many wars the Greek tragedies prevented from actually taking place; likewise, we do not know what horror of the astral planes and what violence of the physical plane have been diverted by this semi-expression of the fears, the astralism, the violence, which we see in the film.

It also has an infectious quality. I believe that much of the violence which takes place in the world is, at least in the form it takes, stimulated by film and television violence. I do not think they have no effect at all. If they have a cathartic effect, they also have a stimulating effect, depending on the person who is viewing them. If people are very susceptible, very impressionable, they can be highly stimulated; if they are rather more sophisticated, they can have the cathartic effect. It is really violence and fear by proxy.

You said everyone has to overcome his own fears, but there are people whose fears have grown into an illness, like a phobia, and I would ask you how can we help those people, and has this fear the same source as other fears?

Some people are so overcome by fear that their fear has become an illness. They are so phobic, so concentrated in one direction, a one-pointed fixation on one particular fear, that they are in an ill state. The only way for such a person to be rehabilitated, in the short term, is, I believe, by some form of psychotherapy. The phobia results from the Self being trapped in a particular vehicle. Perhaps it is a physical phobia, a fear of heights to such a point that they could not come on a platform a foot high, or such a fear of the world and of other people that they dare not leave their house, or a fear of open spaces. These are particular phobias to which some people are prone, and they are, I believe, the result of such a 'locking' of the Self in one particular vehicle that a total imbalance is created.

You can create mental illness by this kind of unbalanced focus or total absorption of the Self in the energy, caught in the net of the energy of one vehicle or another. Very often, it is just one, either the physical, the astral, or the mental, although in severe cases it can be all three. In every mental hospital, you will find people whose awareness of the Self is so distorted, the connection so tenuous, that the Self is caught up in the net of energy of the particular vehicle and locked in there.

The Legend of Hercules

What is the meaning behind the legend of Hercules, when having lifted the by-now 18-headed monster up into the light of day, the sunshine, they all died except for one head which he cut off and put under a stone?

The monster really represents the astral nature of man (and woman). Since it represents the astral nature, it also represents (as the other side of this coin) the higher aspects of man. Every lower manifestation is a reflection, distorted in time and space, of a high spiritual reality. The perfection of reality itself is constant, unchanging. It is will, love, intelligence, and

327

goodness knows what else besides for which we have no names as yet. That spiritual reality, which is all good, is reflected through matter until it becomes the very opposite of that: the nine-headed monster.

In the esoteric teaching there are nine major initiations of this solar system. On this planet we need take only five. The others are cosmic, so there are five planetary initiations and four cosmic initiations. The first three of these cosmic initiations can be experienced on this planet. The ninth is always experienced outside the planet. The nine heads of the monster are the correspondence, in matter, of these nine initiatory experiences which are really states of consciousness. An initiation finalizes, fixes, a state of consciousness, of awareness. There is a gradual expansion of consciousness which the ceremony of initiation consolidates.

The symbology is that the one head synthesizes all that. They were all shown in their imperfection; this is a monster, expressing our astral nature. Our astral body, however, is not a monster, but has a very important function if it could perform it correctly. Of course, eventually, when purified, it does.

We can begin by controlling the astral elemental and therefore the glamours of the astral plane. The process from the first to the second initiation is this gradual controlling of the astral nature. It begins around 1.5 when a shift is made from astral polarization, in which the astral plane is the main focus of consciousness, to gradually becoming mentally polarized. That goes on until 2.5 when there is another shift from mental to spiritual polarization. The person is then polarized on the soul plane; that becomes his normal focus of consciousness, even while living and working in the world.

This is symbolized in the legend of Hercules because these nine states of consciousness are reflected through the astral body itself. As above, so below, this is the basic occult axiom. As is the spiritual reality, so it will be mirrored, however distorted, on the lower planes. Every glamour is a perfect virtue of the soul, in reverse, in a distorted, imperfect form. The astral body as a vehicle in the evolutionary process is meant to be the reflection of the buddhic nature, the second of the three aspects of the soul itself. The nature of God as we know it is Will, Love-Wisdom and Intelligence. These states of consciousness are qualities of deity and are reflected as the Spiritual Triad, which the soul focuses on its own plane. The first, the Atmic, is spiritual will. A little lower is buddhi or love-wisdom. Below that again is the manasic or higher intelligence. The head which is cut off and put under a stone represents the soul, although it is part of the monster. It is that part which has, intrinsically, the mode of perfection of all the sins of the astral nature, of all the glamours and distortions, the horrors, the evils of this monstrous creature with all these heads, which nevertheless has the potential of all deity within it. That is symbolized by the one head, which is cut off and placed under a stone, because one day that stone will be lifted and that head will be seen as pure soul, pure Self. When all the rest is conquered, that Self shines.

CHAPTER 11

EVOLUTION

Evolutionary Process

Evolution of Consciousness

With the manifestation of Christ-consciousness coming into the world, do you see, or do you feel, that there will one day be a Utopia with none of the destructive energies that obtain today, and if you see it as a Utopia, how do you and I know that this Utopia, this 'Garden of Eden', is not just a product of a desiring mind? (March 1992)

You have given your answer yourself in the second part of the question. I personally do not believe in Utopia. I believe in evolution but I do not think that evolution is Utopia. We have come from early animal-man to the point where we find ourselves today; we are fantastically evolved compared to early man, but if you compare us with what we will be when we are all Masters we are very far from that state now.

If all of us were at least third-degree initiates — that is, three-fifths of the way to becoming Masters — then the world would be a very different place but still not perfect in the utopian sense. I do not believe in Utopia because I believe that evolution is a creative process, not static. There is a blueprint for that perfection but that perfection itself is not static. Evolution proceeds under the Law of Cause and Effect, and is manifest through that law. This is fundamental and is the basis for our responsibility, because every thought and action we have sets into motion a cause. Those who are destructive wreak destruction on themselves but, at the same time, temporarily, on those around them.

That will be controlled more and more as humanity begins to see itself as one, as it creates structures — political, economic, religious, social, scientific — which demonstrate that inner oneness. This will rid us of much of the separative tendencies which today divide the world. Humanity, at any given time, is a gradation, it is not at one level. There are people coming into incarnation now who, as far as modern humanity is concerned, are just beginning. They are low on the ladder of evolution and have a very long way to go, but humanity is changing fast. Everything that happens speeds up the rate of change, and this will get faster and faster. There will never be perfection until everyone in the world is a Master, and therefore perfect, so there will never be what I think is meant here by Utopia — a state in which there is no demonstration of any negative or destructive energy — until the end of the whole process of evolution, which is so many millions of years ahead that there is no point in my talking about it.

What is the idea of perfection? (June 1992)
Perfection, as far as this Earth is concerned, is the state of enlightenment in which there is nothing more you can learn on this planet and are free for ever from the pull of matter. Your body has become a body of light.

There are five planetary initiations, each a great expansion of consciousness. These allow deeper and deeper access to the mind of the Logos of the planet. In this way, you come to know the mind of God, the Plan of God and your part in that Plan. When the fifth initiation is taken, you are free to leave the planet; planet Earth is finished for you as a school. There are nine initiations in this solar system, but only these five are obligatory on this planet.

When we talk about perfection on this planet, it is always a very relative perfection. Perfection is the result of raising the consciousness to the point that you are no longer subject to the pull of matter. The Masters have consciousness on all planes, from the lowest physical to the highest spiritual. That means They are free from the pull of matter — it does not affect Them. They have nothing which we would call 'emotion', for example. They have not only consciousness but also control — a different thing — on all planes. They can appear and disappear at will, They can be anywhere They like by thought alone. They have given total expression to the spark of God, which They are: the Self, as Maitreya calls it. They are totally God-infused individuals — that is perfection.

They do not need to incarnate. When They do incarnate They do so simply to serve the Plan, but there is nothing to pull Them into incarnation; They make no personal karma (They have no sense of the personal self). It is personal karma that draws us again and again into incarnation.

Why do we need to manifest on the physical plane? (April 1992)
To quote the Master Djwhal Khul: "Love was the impelling motive for manifestation, and love it is that keeps all in ordered sequence; love bears all on the path of return to the Father's bosom, and love eventually perfects all that is."

The soul takes incarnation at the behest of the planetary Logos — God. The Monad, the spark of God, the Self, reflects itself as the individual soul — the divine intermediary between spirit and matter, the Christ Principle — which in turn reflects itself through the Personality. The aim is the spiritualization of matter. Through the descent of spirit into matter — the involutionary process — matter can be occultly 'lifted up' back to spirit, the duality of the pairs of opposites reconciled and synthesized. Through the Law of Rebirth (Reincarnation) and in relation to the Law of Cause and Effect, we gradually spiritualize the matter of our sequential bodies until, as a Master, we are free from the pull of matter for ever. We are liberated and enlightened. The agency of this perfecting process is love.

When a person comes out of the sequence of birth and death what is the next stage of evolution? (May 1992)
Such a person has become a Master Who is someone Who has expanded His consciousness to include the spiritual planes. For the Master, there is one of seven paths — the Way of the Higher Evolution — which He must choose.

These are: the Path of Earth service, which, luckily for us, many Masters take; the Path to Sirius — many Masters go directly from this Earth to Sirius on which very fast progress can be made; the Ray Path; the Path the Logos Himself is on; the Path of Absolute Sonship, on which Maitreya is, and which culminates in the Cosmic Christ; the Path of Magnetic Work; the Path of Training for Planetary Logoi.

If, as suggested by esoteric studies, there is no highest entity or Logos beyond which there is no further need to evolve, is not the implication that all beings on the endless chain of being — and therefore all kingdoms — are of equal importance, and therefore attaining the stage that lies ahead is no better than simply 'being here now'? (April 1990)

Indeed, in the Plan of evolution all kingdoms are of equal importance, all their given levels of appearance are reflections, more or less involved, of the Creator. However, in posing the question, the questioner leaves out the factor of consciousness. It is precisely through an expansion of conscious awareness that evolution proceeds. It is the difference in conscious awareness that denotes the difference in radiation — and therefore ability to serve the Plan of evolution — between a rock, a rose, a man, a Master, a solar Logos, on into infinity.

Is the coming age the time when the 'Divine Plan' will be fulfilled and thus humanity will fulfil its destiny? If not, how long will it take till this goal is reached? (March 1988)

The Divine Plan covers the whole of the evolution of all kingdoms on the Planet. This perfection will not be achieved until the end of the seventh round (we are now in the middle of the fourth of seven 'incarnations' or 'rounds' of the Earth cycle) which is millions of years ahead.

In this coming Age of Aquarius a part of the Divine Plan will be fulfilled, and humanity will enter consciously into a co-partnership role with the creating Logos in the working out of the Plan.

Will the fulfilment of this goal conclude with the seventh initiation of the planet Earth? (March 1988)

In cosmic terms, of the Logos, yes.

Man will develop his spirituality during the Aquarian Age, he will attain divinity. But after the Aquarian there will be other ages. Will humans fall down in their evolution or will they maintain their divinity? (April 1989)

Evolution proceeds in cycles, spirals. Of course man can misuse his free will and fall back, but once a certain degree of divinity has been manifested, certain peaks reached, the likelihood of such a fall becomes remote. Divinity, our intrinsic nature, once achieved, realized, is not likely to be lost. The momentum of evolution has an upward current and the Will of God eventually achieves its goal.

It is said that the dawning Age of Aquarius will be a time of great progress in many ways, in which love and understanding will at last take precedence over the strife and separation that have so long predominantly held sway. If possible, would you please give some information on what the next step might be, that is, what work might then be undertaken, what type of activity take place during the succeeding Age of Capricorn? (April 1988)

There writes an impatient man; he has not yet experienced the Aquarian dispensation but is already curious about the next! We still have to manifest the love and understanding, the synthesis and brotherhood which should characterize the Aquarian Age. It will not happen automatically, by itself, but only if we make it so. Theoretically, according to the Plan, Aquarius will be the age in which the Love nature of God, revealed by the Christ in Jesus, becomes manifest on a world scale. In Capricorn, the Will aspect, to be revealed in this age by Maitreya, is expected to become manifest on a world scale. The Will embodies the Purpose of God. What that will be like — in world terms — in Capricorn remains to be seen. We can only — I believe fruitlessly — speculate about such things. One thing I believe we can say with confidence: humanity will be demonstrating such control over the forces of nature and of cosmos as to justify being called gods.

The aim is that at the end of the Aquarian Age the bulk of humanity will have taken the first and many the second initiation. The more advanced units, responding to the Will aspect, will take the third. In Capricorn, humanity as a whole will take the third initiation. This will make possible a great cosmic initiation for the Planetary Logos.

Mankind never reached such a far step in its evolutionary process until this Age. How does this fit with the fact that the problems in the world have never been so great? (March 1988) I have little doubt that at the end of every age the problems for humanity have loomed especially large. Today, precisely because of the evolutionary advance of mankind, our problems are focused as never before. For the first time in history, the whole world is caught up in a process of change, and at the same time there is the possibility of total annihilation. This is unique to our time. Worldwide communications, too, have made us aware of the global extent of our difficulties. Our complex and sophisticated social structures place enormous pressures on every country, while our inability (so far) to share resources and rationalize distribution increases these pressures. Also, for the first time in history, 5 billion people are competing for space and sustenance on the planet at the same time.

How did the energies of the last Aquarian Age affect the humanity of the time? (May 1990)
At that time (roughly 26,000 years ago) humanity was, for the most part, scattered in small groups throughout the planet. Apart from some late-Atlantean remnants (Poseidonos and some South American cultures and city states), most of these groups were hunters, often nomadic, following the game on their seasonal migrations. Some were pastoral shepherds or fishers.

The Aquarian energies had the effect of uniting many of these groups into larger units which made hunting safer and more effective. In Europe, the cave paintings of Spain and France, for example, bear witness to the high standards reached in both artistic and magical expression. These larger units gave the possibility of lengthy stays in one place (cave or otherwise) and led gradually to the agrarian society and the establishment of farms, villages and eventually towns and cities.

What is the meaning of the different human races?
(January/February 1991)
Each race is given the task of perfecting a particular instrument of consciousness. For example, the first truly human race, the Lemurian, had the goal of perfecting the physical body and giving early animal-man physical consciousness and polarization. The next race, the Atlantean, had the goal of perfecting the astral, feeling, sensory vehicle. This is now the most powerful vehicle of average humanity who are still astrally polarized.

Our present race, the Aryan (no connection with Hitler's distorted beliefs) has the long-term goal of perfecting the mental vehicle. At the moment, only lower, concrete, aspects of mind are much in evidence (our present science and technology demonstrate this achievement). The sixth sub-race (we are the fifth) of the present Aryan race will demonstrate the higher aspect of mind which we call intuition.

The various human races in incarnation at the present time are partly a result of this process (the Mongol peoples are in Atlantean bodies), and also the result of the play of various rays on humanity over long ages. This has created the multiplicity of types and qualities by which the races are distinguished. Unity in diversity is the basic aim of the evolution of races.

What happened 95,000 years ago which caused the Masters of the Spiritual Hierarchy to withdraw from the world?
(December 1992)
There was a great war in ancient Atlantis between the Spiritual Hierarchy — the forces of light — and the forces of evil — the forces of materiality, as the Masters call them. That destroyed the last of the Atlantean civilizations, which had lasted for about 12 million years, and also the Atlantean continent, of which the Americas, North and South, are the remnants. That war ended in a stalemate; neither side really won. The Masters of the Spiritual Hierarchy retreated from the physical plane into the mountains and deserts, where Their successors are (except for 15 of them) to this day. A few of Them have come

out into the world from time to time — one very well known case is the Comte de St Germain Who was known throughout the 18th century at all the courts of Europe. We owe a great many of the inventions of modern times to His inspiration, including the railroads, gas and electricity. He is now the Master Rakoczi, in a Hungarian body, and lives in the Carpathians. He is the 'Regent of Europe' and is one of the Masters Whom you will see working openly in the world, among the first group to come out with Maitreya. During the Atlantean period, early, mid and late, there were times when the Masters of the Spiritual Hierarchy retreated, more or less, but there were long periods when They lived openly in the world. They were the Priest-Kings, the Godlike beings, Who created and gave as a gift to Atlantean humanity a series of civilizations where the technology was far more advanced than ours is today. They had silent, aerial flight — not inter-planetary or inter-stellar, but flight from one part of the Earth to another — and this without obvious propellants. They had the means of reversing gravity, a technology which our science fiction writers write about and which we would envy today. But it was not created by Atlantean man, who could not even think. Atlantean man's evolutionary aim was to develop and perfect the emotional body. So well did he do it, and so long did he take to do it, that it is still the most powerfully developed body of humanity.

Which came first in human evolution — music, speech or dance? (July/August 1987)
Speech, then dance, then music.

Evolution of Form

Does matter remain eternally spiritualized or does it need continual boosts of spiritual energy to sustain its spirituality? (December 1986)
In the eternal process of involution and evolution, spirit, at every level, is involving itself in matter (its polar opposite) and matter is evolving back to spirit. This process takes place spiritually; there is not one level of spirit but infinite levels.

Matter, spiritualized through the evolutionary process, therefore, moves through higher and higher levels of spirit, losing more and more of its 'matter' aspect in the process. We should remember that what we call 'spirit' is still part of the cosmic physical plane. In other words, spirit and matter are relative terms.

You say that love is the energy which holds the particles of atoms together. You also say that the task of the forces of evil is to uphold the matter aspect. How do you reconcile these seemingly contradictory statements? (April 1987)

There is really no contradiction. The energy of Love is the cohesive, magnetic force which holds the particles of an atom to its nucleus and thus forms the 'building bricks' of matter. These 'bricks' of matter come under the activity of the Lords of Materiality, who control the elementals to fashion the forms, gaseous and physical, of the body of the planet. The energy of Love, itself, is totally impersonal, neither good nor bad, conforming to the motive of those who use it.

You say the forces of evil will be destroyed in the middle of the Age of Capricorn. How will this affect matter? (April 1987)

Not at all. The forces of materiality are on the involutionary path. The evil results from the overflow of their activity on to the evolutionary path on which we, humanity, are. The destruction of the forces of evil in Capricorn is the destruction of their activity on the physical, astral and mental planes of the evolutionary arc. When this occurs, the planetary logos can take a cosmic initiation (the correspondence of the third initiation in man) which will make ours one of the sacred planets.

If souls are indestructible then why would it matter if the planet is blown up or not? (June 1987)

Only a human being could ask such a question, taking it for granted that the human kingdom is the only important factor in evolution. In fact, this is not only untrue, but the human kingdom is not the most important one at this time. The planet is the body of expression of a 'Heavenly Man', a cosmic

Being, and from His viewpoint, the kingdoms are parts of an integrated whole. The planet, too, is a centre in the body of expression of the Solar Logos and its integrity is vital to the evolution of the whole system.

Devic Evolution

How do devas evolve, and what is the connection with our evolution?
Devas evolve through the evolution of feeling, of sensory awareness. We evolve through the development of mind. We are the sons of mind, they are the daughters of feeling. Their evolution proceeds through the ever-growing awareness of what is, here and now, what exists in life, in matter, in vibration, in everything that you could think of as creation. That is their experience; moment to moment they are sensing life and matter and growing in awareness of what they are like. We are doing the same thing through our sensory apparatus, but we go further than that. The devas, at least up to the human level, do not think about it, they do not 'mentate'. Mentation is not part of their activity. But sensory awareness, a heightened, extreme sensitivity to the slightest alteration of vibration, becomes theirs as they evolve. Gradually they evolve to finer and finer perception of what is, now.

Of course we share this to some extent. An artist, a painter, a musician, has, too, to develop this type of extremely fine sensory awareness; if a musician, to sound; if a painter, to the slightest difference between two reds — an orange-red and a blue-red, for example. All that awareness is refinement of our sensory experience.

For the angelic or devic evolution, there is no limit to this process; that is the nature of their growth. The more that is experienced, the more they evolve. For us it is simply one level. We have the harder task of intuiting that which does not exist in creation, which is as yet unmanifest, has yet to be, could be, may be, that which is created through the action of the mind. The devas are not involved in that at all, unless they are super-human (some devas are super-human). But for the average deva, the process is one which does not involve that kind of mentation. By bringing in the faculty of the mind, humanity, man, can evolve into a kind of creation impossible for the devas. These two evolutions are parallel, they are moving forward in evolution together, and the plan is that one day the sons of mind and the daughters of feeling will come together and the Divine Hermaphrodite will be created. That is way, way ahead.

We are told in the Alice Bailey books that all members of the angelic or deva evolutions pass through the human stage at some time. Does this mean that at any one time some people are on the human and some on the angelic line of evolution? (March 1991)

No. All people are on the human line. What is meant is that life, in all its forms, is on the way to becoming human, is human, or is going beyond the human. For the angelic or deva evolutions, therefore, there are those (myriads) who are sub-human (nature elementals, etc) and those which are superhuman (the archangels, for example). All our bodies, physical, astral and mental, are made of devic substance. In this way they gain experience on the way to becoming human.

(1) Do souls from the devic (angelic) realm incarnate as humans to serve the planet? (2) Do they have a karmic relationship with Earth? (July/August 1987)

(1) One cannot speak of members of the devic or angelic evolutions as 'souls' in the sense of individualized human souls. They are scattered fragments, as it were, of many different kinds and degrees, of great angelic Lords, both sub-human and super-human. They evolve through the development of feeling while we evolve through the development of mind. They do not, therefore, incarnate as humans at any time. (2) Yes.

In your books you mention tiny little things called 'pitris'. Can you tell us what they are? (October 1992)

There are two levels of 'pitris' — solar and lunar. The matter of our bodies is made of one or other of these. The lower vehicles — physical, astral and mental — are made of lunar pitris; the vehicle of the soul — the causal body — of solar pitris. The lunar pitris are the elementals on the physical, astral and mental planes.

The path of evolution is the means whereby you gain control over these elementals. For long ages the life of the individual is controlled by their activity. Even your physical body, which seems so solid and physical, is, as you know, really energy. That energy is the result of the activity of these tiny pitris or elemental, devic lives.

As humanity evolves, it gains consciousness on each plane: firstly, on the physical plane, then, gradually, on the astral plane. Now, all humanity has consciousness on the physical plane, the astral plane and, to some degree, on the mental plane, but consciousness on the astral plane is not complete — so you can see how far humanity has to go.

Consciousness on a plane and control on a plane are very different things indeed, and only the initiate is gaining control, as well as consciousness, on the planes. The last part of the evolutionary process is marked off by five initiations which demonstrate that control.

Soul and Incarnation

How is a soul born, how does an individual soul emerge from the unboundedness, unmanifest? (April 1988)
Souls are not 'born'. The Spirits, Sparks of God, or human Monads (in Theosophical terminology), identical fragments of Himself 'thrown off' by the Planetary Logos, reflect Themselves as the human souls at the 'causal' plane, the two highest sub-planes of the mental planes. The soul uses a body — the causal body — during its incarnational experiences. This is shattered at the fourth initiation and the soul is re-absorbed by the Monad. Its role as 'divine intermediary' between the Monad and the man or woman in incarnation, the personality, is finished. The personality is totally ensouled.

Could you please explain: what is the relationship between the Greater Triangle, referred to as the Ego or Soul, and the lesser triangle, also called the soul? Is the Triad the higher triangle? Are the Triad and the soul one and the same? (November 1991)

The Monad, or Divine Spark, reflects itself on the soul plane through the Spiritual Triad — Spiritual Will or Atma; Love/Wisdom or Buddhi; and Higher Mind or Manas. That is the Greater Triangle. The Soul reflects itself in the man or woman in incarnation through the two head centres and the heart centre, the lesser triangle. The soul as the Divine Intermediary synthesizes the three planes of the Spiritual Triad.

In esoteric teaching, we exist for the purpose of the evolution of our souls. In Yoga teaching, Atman is omnipotence; then why does it need to create us? Shankara said there is nothing but Atman and there are mirrors. (September 1990)

The questioner is asking why God created the universe, and the complete answer only God knows. We exist for the purpose of the evolution of our souls in incarnation. If Atman is absolute, total unity, that unity can only be known through its diversity. We are the reflections, as in mirrors, of Atman in time and space. In this way Atman observes the process of its becoming.

Would you explain the actual process by which the soul chooses the ray nature of the lower sheaths prior to incarnation. Specifically, how are the permanent atoms brought into manifestation along a particular ray line? (July/August 1987)

The soul, existing out of time, knows its long-term goal and sets purposes (achievements of qualities) for each incarnation. There are usually three, sometimes four, such purposes to be fulfilled. The soul chooses the rays, major and minor, of each vehicle, to give the opportunity for the building-in of the qualities in line with its purposes. This it does magically (in advanced individuals, with the Master's co-operation and advice), bringing together matter from each plane — mental, astral and etheric physical — of the required ray type. The permanent atom (carried forward from the previous incarnation) on each plane sets the rate of vibration of the various bodies. Through the Law of Attraction the soul brings together only that matter which corresponds to the vibrational rate of the permanent atoms. The soul is thus a creative, magical worker on its own plane.

Is it possible to 'fail' an incarnation — to keep the consciousness but lose the development of a former existence? (November 1992)

If I understand the question correctly, then yes. We cannot lose what we have, but we can stand still or we can backslide by taking on karma. What holds us back in development is the acquiring of karma. All actions create karma. People think of karma always as 'bad' karma, but we are creating both good and bad karma all the time: it is only 'bad' if it is painful and 'good' if it is not! Every action, every thought, creates a reaction, sets in motion a cause. The effects stemming from these causes make our lives for good or for ill. What holds us back are powerful actions of harm which create major obstacles to progress. When it comes into incarnation, the soul sets its vehicle — the personality in which it is incarnating — four goals (if he has a special mission, otherwise three) in its life, one of which is always the establishing of right human relations.

Whatever the situation, the soul is always creating a repetition of family relationships: children can be mother or father, mother or father could be sister or brother, and so on, over and over again, recreating the same family situations so that the karma can be resolved. In this way the soul makes possible the creation of right human relationships. Each of us comes into life on certain streams of energy, called rays. The soul ray is always the same a world cycle, but the personality ray and the mental, astral and physical-body rays may change over and over again during that time. In this way the soul 'rounds off' the personality, enriching it with all the different ray qualities.

All rays in their perfect expression have virtues, but the opposite of these are the 'vices' or 'glamours' of the rays. Some rays are more prone to vices or glamours than others. Until we are more evolved, it is always easier to express the vices than the virtues. At certain times we might enter a cycle of incarnations in which everything goes smoothly and then suddenly we meet an obstacle that we cannot surmount — perhaps we do not make the right effort because we are not used to making effort, having always taken the line of least resistance. Suddenly, it does not work any more, and we might find that although we have reached a certain point we are not making any further progress. The soul might then bring in a series of very restricted lives, very hard, simply to overcome karma and speed up the next incarnation. It is difficult to explain this, but the answer to your question, basically, is: "Yes."

Buddhist teaching says that almost all people will be reborn in the form of an animal or in hell, or as some greedy entity, after spending this human life on Earth. What does Maitreya say about that? (July/August 1990)
I am unaware of anything Maitreya may have said about this, but, without claiming to speak for Him, I believe He would smile at such a suggestion. It certainly does not accord with my understanding of the Buddha's teaching. We do not return as animals, as "greedy entities", or end up in any hell (other than that of our own making). We are reborn again and again as humans until we make no further personal karma and are released (as Masters) from the necessity of rebirth on this planet.

Does reincarnation happen in serial time form or can we have lived lives occurring in a future time, say the year 2000? (September 1989)
Outside the physical brain time as we know it does not exist; past, present and future are one. However, one's physical incarnation relates to our physical time experience. One cannot have been alive (incarnate, that is) in a 'time' yet to come.

As you believe in reincarnation, do you believe that with free will we choose our next incarnation or that a supreme power is responsible for choosing the incarnation which He/She thinks is suitable for our spiritual development? If you think we make the choice then why did Hitler — or Jack the Ripper — choose that particular incarnation? Surely one would not choose willingly a life of evil? (April 1991)

The choice of incarnation is made by one's own soul — it is the soul which incarnates, in all forms. However, the soul does not choose a vehicle — an evil man or woman — as a deliberate act. The soul is divine and perfect and its aim is the creation, eventually, of a vehicle through which that perfection can be fully expressed. Under the Law of Free Will, the man or woman makes choices, selfish or altruistic, which hinder or help the soul's purpose. A deeply evil personality — a Hitler or mass murderer — is not carrying out soul purpose but indulging his own separative instincts. Most such people (Hitler was a special case, a medium, obsessed by certain members of the Black Lodge, or forces of evil) are emotionally and mentally unbalanced and quite often responding to destructive thoughtforms already in the 'mind-belt'.

What causes being cut off from one's own soul, like in the case of Hitler? (March 1988)

Giving expression to the lowest, evil impulses of the personality. Hitler was a second-degree initiate but was a deeply evil personality who, being a medium, was able to be obsessed by the forces of evil. Had he been influenced by his soul, this would not have been possible.

As the population of the world grows, where are the new human souls coming from? (March 1990)

There are only about 5.5 billion of 60 billion souls in incarnation. Those not in incarnation mainly wait in 'Devachan', somewhat similar to the Christian idea of paradise.

You say that there are 60 billion Monads associated with this planet. Are they all human Monads or does this number include deva Monads and the Monads in sub-human kingdoms? (September 1987)

The figure of 60 billion refers to human Monads.

Is there any connection between the taste of a certain food craved by pregnant women and the qualities of the incarnating soul? (December 1988)

No. Unless it shows whether the incarnating soul is a person of good taste or not!

Helena Roerich refers in her letters to the "great truism of twin souls". (1) What actually is it that makes two human beings twin souls? (2) On Swedish media recently, someone claimed that during the next 20 years, 95 per cent of the Earth's population will meet their twin souls. Is this true; a fragment of the truth; or all glamour? (July/August 1988, May 1992)

(1) It is the result of a decision taken by the Monads of the individuals. This ensures a close relationship on soul levels (not necessarily reflected on personality levels) which will keep these souls together however their incarnational cycles may tend to separate them. For many people, the idea of meeting (and marrying) their twin soul has a powerful romantic appeal. It is easy to see why there has been developed much glamour and misunderstanding about this subject.

Just as, on the physical plane, by the division of cells, twins are sometimes created, so on the soul plane, some souls decide to divide and take two physical-plane expressions. These incarnations may be simultaneous in time or not. In any given life they may be of the same or opposite sex. The individuals may meet or not, as karma and destiny dictate. In any event, they will eventually reunite near the conclusion of their evolutionary experience on this planet, when the soul, the Divine Intermediary, is reabsorbed into the Monad.

(2) This is just nonsense; only some 25 per cent of people have twin souls.

Do animals have souls? (July/August 1992)

Individually, no. Animals are expressions of a group soul — there is the soul which is 'cat', or 'dog', or 'horse' or 'camel', but they do not have individualized souls in the way humans have. The individualization of humanity occurred, according to esoteric teachings, no less than eighteen-and-a-half million years ago.

(1) Are the large-brain dolphins and whales individualized entities, individualized souls, in the same way human beings are individualized entities? Or are dolphins and whales members of a group soul? (2) If the large-brain dolphins and whales are not individualized, what specifically/technically is it about the design of the human brain (smaller in some cases than the cetacean brain) that sets us apart as individualized souls? (January/February 1988)

No, dolphins and whales, like all animals, are not individualized but part of a group soul. The crisis of individualization for the human kingdom occurred in Lemurian times eighteen-and-a-half½ million years ago.

It was not the result of some technical design of the human brain but of the Plan of evolution which brought the human souls into incarnation. When early animal-man (not yet individualized) had developed a co-ordinated physical body, an astral feeling or sensory body and the germ of mind, an incipient mental body (not brain), the human souls could then individualize on the physical plane. As a result of that individualization, the human brain has since developed (this is unique to the human kingdom) various centres in the brain which the soul eventually uses to reflect its presence on the outer plane. These centres are gradually awakened as the person advances on the evolutionary path.

Experience at Physical Death

In the literature about people who have had near-death experiences, one aspect of the core experience involves a profound encounter with a "being of light". Rarely does anyone attempt to identify these "beings of light" beyond saying that they are clearly divine personages channelling unconditional love and acceptance and radiating unfathomable peace. Are any/all of these "beings of light" (1) one of the Masters, or (2) Maitreya Himself? (November 1991) It depends on the point of evolution of the one going through the near-death experience. In the vast majority of cases, where the person is not yet a disciple, they are seeing their own guardian angel in the astral thoughtform in which they have habitually envisioned that entity.

If the person is a disciple and therefore in a Master's ashram, then the "being of light" is an emanation on the astral plane of their own Master. The "being of light" is never Maitreya.

How accurate is the **Tibetan Book of the Dead**? (September 1992) Allowing for the changes in language and expression since its compilation, its accuracy is remarkable — 85 to 90 per cent.

Are the images described in the Book symbolic or should they be taken literally? (September 1992) Some are described in a symbolic manner while others may be taken quite literally.

How is one to understand all the phases described in the **Tibetan Book of the Dead**? *(September 1992)* They are descriptions, symbolic and/or literal, of the experiences pertaining to each of the seven planes of the astral plane. On death, the individual spends a greater or shorter 'time' (depending on his or her point in evolution and karma) in the bardo or astral planes.

(1) Does everyone go through these stages of death or (2) do some people 'skip' some phases? (September 1992) (1) No. (2) Yes.

During the last years many books have been written (in a normal or mediumistic way) which bring the 'real knowledge' on birth, life, death and life after death. Some say this, some say that. People like Blavatsky, Alice Bailey, Yogananda and

Aurobindo each tell it in their own way. What, according to your Master, is the real course of events and in which books is this described? I prefer to spend my valuable time to study that which approaches the truth as nearly as possible. (October 1987)

No doubt the people you mention would consider that they were telling the truth of these life and death events. Certainly they were all high initiates and might know. Without claiming to be the repository of ultimate truth on these subjects, may I recommend to you the chapters on them in my book *Maitreya's Mission, Volume One*. There subjects such as incarnation, rebirth, and life after death are dealt with in some detail.

Initiation

In Message No. 69, given through you, Maitreya says: "I guard the Gates through which all pass to Him." What does this mean? (December 1990)

The last phase of the evolutionary process on this Earth is covered by five great expansions of consciousness called the Five Planetary Initiations. The fifth of these initiations confers control on all planes and frees the initiate from the necessity of further incarnation on this planet. All the Masters of Wisdom have taken these five initiations. Maitreya is the Hierophant at the first two initiations which are seen by the Masters as preparatory, only, to the third (the first true, soul, initiation, at which a man or woman really demonstrates divinity) when the Hierophant is the Lord of the World Himself. In this sense Maitreya "guards" the Gates of Initiation.

The first initiation only becomes possible when the Christ Principle or Consciousness is awakened in the human heart. Maitreya embodies this Principle. In this sense, also, He "guards the Gates" to God. As the Christian Bible puts it: "No man cometh unto the Father except through Me." Unfortunately, this has been interpreted by Christian groups to mean that a person can only know God (realize his own divinity) by becoming a Christian and accepting Christian dogma and doctrines. This is emphatically not the case and was not meant by Jesus to be understood as such.

Could you explain what the Christ meant when, speaking through Jesus, He said (or is reported to have said) "I am the way, the truth and the life; no man cometh unto the Father but by me"? Christians have interpreted this to mean that all other religions are barking up the wrong tree. (September 1987)
The Christ embodies the energy we call the Christ Consciousness, the energy of evolution *per se*. It is the awakening of the energy of the Christ Consciousness in the human heart (the spiritual heart centre at the right side of the chest) which begins the Path of Discipleship and Initiation — the Path to the Father, or God-consciousness. The Christ is the Hierophant at the first two initiations which are necessary to take before coming before the Father (Sanat Kumara on Shamballa) at the third and higher initiations. In this sense the Christ is indeed the way, the truth and the life and the gateway (through initiation) to the Father.

Of course, men and women of every and no religion eventually awaken to the Christ Consciousness and pass through the doors of initiation.

Is there a relationship between establishing soul contact and the degree of initiation? Can someone who is not yet a first-degree initiate establish soul contact (through regular meditation practice)? At what point is soul contact essential before any further initiations can occur? (December 1987)
Soul contact is essential before even the first initiation can be taken. The degree of soul contact and at-one-ment determines which initiation it is possible to achieve. The soul is first contacted as the first initiation is approached, around 0.7. From 0.7 to the first initiation will usually take several lives in which the soul seeks to influence its reflection (the personality) towards meditation and service. Several more lives will normally separate the first and second initiations, the soul seeking all the time to 'grip' its vehicle, and infuse the bodies, mental, astral and physical, with its energies and purpose. Each

initiation registers a degree of soul infusion until full at-one-ment is achieved at the third, the Transfiguration.

Is Initiation the same as enlightenment as described by many Eastern Masters? (March 1988)
This is a difficult question to answer directly and simply. Each initiation brings a degree of enlightenment. By enlightenment, a Master would usually mean the equivalent of the fifth initiation of (for Him) Revelation, but an Indian guru might mean the equivalent of the third initiation (the Transfiguration) which demonstrates the integration of the lower man (physical, astral and mental) and the appearance of the soul-infused personality. This initiation, when taken, presupposes the conquering of illusion and so achieving enlightenment. On the other hand, some Indian Masters use the term to describe God-realization, the equivalent of the fourth and fifth initiation experience.

When we have reached the Christ-state are all the cells of our body regenerated? (July/August 1991)
Throughout the last phase of the evolutionary process — the Path of Initiation — a transformation takes place in the cellular structure of the successive bodies of the initiate. More and more matter of sub-atomic nature (ie light) is absorbed which gradually replaces that of atomic substance. At the fifth initiation — the Resurrection — the process is complete and the God-realized Master has achieved His goal on this planet — He, and His body, are perfected and 'incorruptible', as it is called in the Christian Bible.

(1) What is the lowest degree of initiation one has to be in order to be overshadowed by Maitreya? (2) How many politicians currently in power are at that level? (March 1991)
(1) 2.5, at which point spiritual polarization begins. (2) One only. The average world leader today is around 1.6.

At what level of initiation must one be before one can respond to the mental impress of a Master? (March 1991)
1.6, when mental polarization commences.

Are there some specific astrological configurations to look for in the individual birth chart to see if one is ready for initiation or approaching such a time in their own life? (January/February 1988)
There are two gates, one into and one out of manifestation. These are Cancer and Capricorn respectively. Initiation is really the process through which, by sequential renunciations, one 'dies' to a lower state and goes out of manifestation. In initiation, therefore, the energy of Capricorn is always involved and must be present in the chart if an individual is to take initiation.

I have read that the mental body is not fully attached until the age of seven, that it is not fully active until the age of 14, and that we catch up to our point of evolution of the last life at ages varying from 14 to (from memory) 35. Is this so? (May 1988)
It is true that the mental body is not fully developed until the age of seven, and not fully active until the age of 14. We catch up to our point of evolution of the last life at ages varying from four years to 63.

Does the age at which we catch up depend on our point in evolution, more time being required for more evolved people? (May 1988)
Yes, except that the reverse is true: the more evolved the person the sooner he or she catches up.

Is it true that, by their actions, people can lose their present level of initiation and so fall to a lower level? (June 1988)
It is true that initiates can 'fall' — it is said that even an Arhat (fourth-degree initiate) can fall. However, the fall is in behaviour and actions and not in the degree. Once the karmic effects of the 'fall' have been resolved (however many lives that might take) the initiate starts again at the degree already achieved.

If an initiate has regressed badly, it is evident that he has to work his way up again. Does such a person take initiation a second time when he has evolved back to the same point? (December 1990)

No. Once he has worked off the negative karma involved in his regression, the initiate (of any degree) begins at the point he had achieved before. You cannot lose initiate status — which designates a particular state of consciousness — once achieved. You can only retard, or speed up, future progress.

In your book **Transmission: A Meditation for the New Age***, you say, in relation to those participating regularly in Transmission Meditation groups: "Every disciple who speeds up his evolution contributes to the speed of evolution for the rest." How does one individual's "speed up" affect the evolution of others?* (May 1988)
I would have thought that this was self-evident. We see the same principle demonstrated in every field of endeavour — for example in sports and the continual breaking and resetting of records.

When a disciple advances, he does so by becoming more and more radiant (of energy). Each initiation confers greater radiation to the aura and thus to the spiritual reservoir of the world. From this reservoir all are stimulated and thus the evolution of all is speeded up.

A few years ago you gave the number of first-degree initiates then in incarnation as approximately 800,000. Has this figure changed much over the last year or two? (September 1991)
The figure is now about 807,500. It is roughly 12 years since I gave that number of first-degree initiates.

What happens to people who do not know anything about initiation? Will they, too, have a chance? (2) When do they have to change? (January/February 1991)
There are many disciples (probably the majority) in the world who know nothing consciously about initiation. It is not required knowledge but happens when the disciple — in the normal process of life in the world — equips himself or herself for that experience.

It depends very much on the ray structure and life activity whether an interest in esotericism, as such, demonstrates itself in any given life.

Is a person aware of what level of initiation they have reached — for instance someone like Plato or Mozart? (October 1992)
I have no doubt that Plato and Mozart were aware, but, generally, people below their level are usually unaware.

Is it correct to talk about people as a first- or second-degree initiate? Does not that mean that you give them a stigma? (November 1988)
I do not go up and down the streets saying: "Sir, do you know that you are a first- or a second-degree initiate?" One only talks about initiation to those who are interested in initiation,who know about it and who are concerned about their own point in evolution. It is important to know because it gives you a sense of perspective. It is important to know that people like Gandhi, Freud, Einstein and Schweitzer were only second-degree initiates. If you have not yet found your own point in evolution and are wondering whether you are a third- or fourth-degree initiate, think about what you have as yet contributed to the world in service. It is not so important to know you are 1.5. However, it is important to know that you are not 4.5!

Does the initiate status you mention, such as 2.0 or 1.7 degrees, refer to major initiations? (June 1990)
Yes. These figures refer to the five planetary initiations to Mastery.

Why are the majority of the published list of initiates male? (July/August 1991)
While many women must have achieved some degree of initiate status, the circumstances of most women's lives, down the centuries, has militated against their becoming known and so entering our list. By the same token, most initiates would tend to take male bodies simply in order to be more publicly effective along their given line of service.

Do any of the initiates in the list given by your Master appear twice as having incarnated again as another famous initiate? (April 1989)

Yes. There are many such examples. One which comes to mind is Count Cagliostro (3.2) who incarnated as H.P.Blavatsky.

How can an initiate of the third degree or above be famous in one life (ie Mozart) but obscure in the next? Surely the special qualities would manifest themselves to an extent that he or she would stand out as an outstandingly evolved being. (April 1989)

It is important not to equate evolutionary achievement with public recognition or fame. It depends very much on the destiny of the individual. Mozart, for example, was an obscure violin-maker in his subsequent life, but much loved and revered by those who knew him. At the present time, the initiate who was Abraham Lincoln (third degree) is in incarnation again (fourth degree) as an unknown worker in government administration — a bureaucrat — in Washington, DC.

You recently gave the ray structure and point of evolution of Mikhaèl Aïvanhov, founder of Fraternité Blanche Universelle. How did he get the information which allowed him to give his teaching? Was he in touch with a Master? (December 1989)

I seem to have stirred a hornet's nest in France by giving Aïvanhov's point in evolution as only 2.4, since most of his followers consider him to be a Master. Indeed, letters received from some French readers state that my credibility *vis-à-vis* Maitreya Himself is dependent on my correcting that information.

I am sorry, but my Master's information is that the given point, 2.4, is correct, and that of his teacher, Danilov, from whom he received his training and teachings, was 3.2. These are high points on the evolutionary scale and I really do not understand why some people find them so controversial. I must say that, from my reading of Mikhaèl Aïvanhov's books, translated into English, I would have no hesitation in placing him somewhere between initiations two and three.

It seems to be inevitable that devotees and followers exaggerate the status of their teacher or guru. This is as true of

Maharishi as it is of Rajneesh or Maharaji. These gurus are so obviously more advanced than the average devotee that they are seen by their followers as Masters or God Itself. The teacher, of course, if he is wise, should do his part to help the devotee to rid himself of that glamour. It would seem, on the contrary, that many foster it.

(1) At what point of evolution did Krishnamurti come into incarnation and (2) at what age did he take the fourth initiation? (November 1989)
(1) Three. (2) Forty-nine.

Can you say at what age Mozart took the third initiation? (November 1988)
At the age of 30.

Visiting a mediumistic friend some years ago, I was told that my path lies towards the planet Saturn which she described as a planet to do with nature. Putting aside whether or not she was correct, I have read that the outer planets, Jupiter, Saturn, Uranus, Neptune, are synthesizing planets for the rest of the solar system. (1) What attaches people to one or other of these planets? (2) Do people go there before attaining Mastership? (3) Can they complete their initiations on these synthesizing planets? (June 1990)
(1) The phrase your "path lies towards the planet Saturn" has no meaning for me. I do not think it means anything at all. People are influenced cyclically by the energies of all the planets, according to their point in evolution and individual destiny. The list you give (outer planets) is only a partial one of the seven sacred planets in our system. The others are Venus, Mercury and Vulcan. (2) Frequently, yes, for a longer or shorter sojourn. (3) No.

Control over the Various Bodies

When initiation was introduced to help speed up our evolution why was it decided that one is ready for initiation on the basis of control over the various bodies (physical, emotional, mental) and not also on the basis of virtues like love, righteousness, truth, etc, since the initiatory process was decided upon by the White Lodge and not by the Black Lodge also? (July/August 1988)

The point is that it is precisely the cultivation of the virtues like love, righteousness, truth, etc which brings about the controls necessary for initiation on each level. Life is really teaching us the necessity of right human relationships. When these are achieved, the virtues are expressed naturally and initiation becomes possible. Initiation is really about expansion of consciousness which results from correct life activity.

We are told that Beethoven was a third-degree initiate, which presumably means that he was at least a second-degree initiate when born in that life. We are also told that he was, even before becoming deaf, hot-tempered. We are led to believe that second-degree initiates have control of their emotions, and I was wondering what "control of their emotions" means? I would have thought it precluded hot temper. (March 1987)

Beethoven was indeed born initiate of the second degree and took the third initiation at the age of 40. He was, therefore, mentally polarized and in control of the astral/emotional elemental from an early age. This does not mean that he did not emote, had no emotional reactions, but that he was no longer dominated by the desire principle and the emotional reactions to which it gives rise.

Does achieving emotional control mean that one no longer cries? (March 1991)

No. One has to differentiate between the stimuli to crying: emotional reaction or heart response. The tears (of bliss) of saints and yogis are well known.

Is there any correlation between a person's IQ or general level of intelligence in this embodiment and his or her level of initiation? (April 1988)

Yes. The higher the degree of initiation achieved the higher and more creative will be the intelligence manifested. With the higher initiates it is the intuition which demonstrates rather than lower-mind ratiocination.

Speaking generally, is it true that most people with a good level of intelligence have taken the first initiation? (I accept that one can argue about what 'intelligence' is!) (April 1988)
No, by no means is a 'good' level of intelligence a sign of having taken the first initiation. This comes about as a result of the control of the physical elemental achieved through soul contact and stimulus. These people would be intelligent, of course, but many very intelligent people, while nearing the first initiation, may well not have gone 'through the door'.

At what point of one's evolution does one have to transcend or 'overcome' one's sexual desires in order to reach the next initiation, after the third initiation? (May 1988)
At the fourth initiation. The fourth-degree initiate is free from the lure or pull of matter entirely (that is matter of the physical, astral and mental planes).

CHAPTER 12

GROWTH OF CONSCIOUSNESS

This article is an edited version of a talk given during the 1992 Transmission Meditation/Tara Network conference held in San Francisco, USA. The section of Questions and Answers also includes material from the 1992 conference held in Veldhoven, the Netherlands. The talk was based on the article 'The Growth of Consciousness', written for **Share International** *(September 1992) by my Master.*

The Growth of Consciousness
by the Master —

Throughout the world, there is a growing understanding that humanity is undergoing a profound change in consciousness. This reflects itself in many ways, not least in the efforts being made to explore the nature of consciousness itself, to investigate the connection between consciousness, mind and brain, and to study the effect that these three, singly or in unison, may have on matter and the natural world.

The old, mechanistic views of nature and of the forces at work within her are fast disappearing and a new awareness is dawning of the unity underlying all manifestation. More and more, the concept that all is energy, that energy and matter are different states of one reality and can be affected by thought, is being accepted on a wide scale and is changing men's view of life. Enlightenment is growing apace and soon the methods and technology will be found to demonstrate this fact. This is of profound significance for the future evolution of the race.

As we enter the new age, a new urgency is being felt to explore the outer and the subjective worlds, and to understand the relation between these two aspects of creation.

Many scientists around the world are bending their inquiries in that direction, prompted by the need to demonstrate and prove their intuitive belief that all is interconnected. The acceptance of a super-personal self or soul is gradually gaining ground and is leading to a new synthesis in men's view of reality. Eventually, the common ground of all such investigations will exist in the awareness that consciousness is the attribute of the soul, that mind and brain are conduits, vehicles for its manifestation, and that there is no break or separation in the connecting links between them.

Until now, the nervous system has been seen as the pathway for signals, electrical in nature, from the brain. Brain, the command post of that intricate system, initiates the actions and reflexes, mental, emotional and physical, by which we recognize and demonstrate our livingness.

To a limited degree, this, of course, is true. The complex computer of the physical brain does indeed co-ordinate and organize the multifarious information and stimuli streaming from moment to moment through that sensitive apparatus. However, as understanding grows of the nature and source of consciousness, a truer picture will emerge of the status and function of the brain, as the focal point for the infinite variety of impulses reaching it from higher principles.

Identification

For many, too, the mind is the man. They see themselves, through identification, as mental beings, capable of thought and action, completely autonomous and separate, whose very existence stems from the ability to think and measure. This, likewise, is but a shadow of the true relationship existing between man and mind.

Man's mind is an instrument, a body, more or less sensitive, depending on the person, by which the mental planes can be contacted and known. The plane of mind, the mind-belt, is infinite in extent and serves as the conduit for all mental experience.

When men realize this, they will understand how telepathy is the natural result of this relationship, and a new era of mutual communication and understanding will begin.

362

The nervous system will be understood as the connecting link between the soul and its vehicles, the means by which the soul in incarnation grips and demonstrates itself through its reflection.

In this way, consciousness, the nature of soul, expands and grows, shedding its light through all the planes, awakening man to his destiny as a Son of God.

It is a truism to say that, as we enter the New Age, a great change in consciousness is taking place in humanity. Maitreya Himself has said in one of the messages He gave through me: "My coming means change. The greatest change will be in the hearts and minds of men."

This is the essence of the New Age. It is, of course, about the construction of a new civilization, about new political, economic, religious and social structures, about living together in harmony, in peace, on a world scale for the first time: no longer having millions of people starving to death in a world of plenty; no longer having countless poor in the world. Jesus said: "The poor are always with us." What about sharing, then, you might say, is it necessary? We have the poor with us because we never share. If we shared, there would be no poor. Jesus knew clearly, correctly, the mind of His time, which exists to this day, 2,000 years later. The poor are still with us.

The change of consciousness which is taking place is even more profound than any outer changes in the world might suggest. Obviously, they are necessary; but they are outer. However, the outer is always the reflection of the inner. If inwardly we are distraught, in disharmony with ourselves, with our environment, with our friends, our family , and so on, then the outer forms which we make, what we express, the conditions which, moment to moment, we create around us, will be disharmonious. They will not have that kind of easeful, harmless relationship which is the essence of equilibrium. The more we are in equilibrium, the more our environment is in equilibrium. This is the basis of the need for harmlessness. Through harmlessness, we create the conditions in which we make no negative karma. What holds us back in expansion of consciousness on our evolutionary journey is, precisely, karma, the weight of our own individual karma. Everything, therefore, that can be done to lighten our karma is an aid towards the completion of our journey to perfection.

The experience of a shift in consciousness, of course, is not new, it occurs at the beginning of every new age. As the new energies, this time the energies of Aquarius, make themselves felt in human life, they necessarily affect our consciousness. I quote a statement from the Tibetan, DK, through Alice Bailey, which is, He says, an immutable law: "Consciousness is dependent upon its vehicle for expression and both are dependent upon life and energy for existence." Consciousness can only be seen and demonstrated through a vehicle. That is why the source of consciousness, the soul, finds it difficult to demonstrate consciousness in time and space, in the physical, emotional and mental apparatus of the human personality. The inertness of the matter which constitutes the bodies of these three vehicles inhibits the expression of the consciousness of the soul at this level. That is why we have to incarnate over and over again. Gradually, we evolve a more sensitive apparatus or vehicle, expressive of the perfection of the soul which itself reflects the Monad, the Spark of God, the Divine.

The evolutionary process, the return journey in growth of consciousness, is a series of unifications, each higher than the one before. First, at-one-ment with the soul, then at-one-ment with the Monad, with the divine. The Monad reflects itself as soul, the soul reflects itself as the man or woman in the world, and the return journey re-enacts that process in the opposite direction. At-one-ment only comes about when the soul in any given incarnation is able to create a vehicle sufficiently sensitive to its impulses and impression. That is why, as one nears the first initiation, the first of five great expansions of consciousness which makes one a Master, the soul brings its vehicle, the man or woman, into meditation of some kind. Meditation is a method, more or less scientific (depending on the meditation), of coming into contact with the soul. The soul brings its vehicle into meditation to construct a sensitive instrument for its purposes, for the carrying out of its plans on Earth.

The plan of the soul is sacrificial service to the Plan of evolution, which, as far as humanity is concerned, is the spiritualization of matter. Our task is to spiritualize matter. We do it through the spiritualization of our own successive vehicles or bodies of expression, sometimes as a man, sometimes as a woman, but always (all else being equal) evolving a more sensitive instrument for the soul to use. The ability of the soul to express itself is absolutely dependent on the quality of that instrument. Therefore, the path of evolution is the growing awareness of what the soul is, wants, and is seeking to express through the man or woman in incarnation.

All souls are individualized. Each is an individual unit or ego and has its own unique purposes. However, these purposes will relate to, and be dependent upon, group purpose, ray purpose, the evolutionary purpose, planetary or solar, of the Monad. The immediate soul purpose in any given life requires the creation of a body sensitive enough to bring that about.

As above, so below. We are made in the likeness of God and every human being has within himself or herself the necessary apparatus, if as yet only potential, for the complete expression of the soul in incarnation. There are centres in the brain, and throughout the body, by which means the soul can grip its vehicle and express itself through it. Gradually, in the course of evolution and especially through the initiatory process (which is an artificial process to speed up the evolutionary process; it is a temporary measure for this particular round), these centres are awakened in the disciple as he progresses through the initiatory degrees back to complete at-one-ment with the soul and, eventually, complete at-one-ment with the Monad and the divine. Then, of course, he is a Master.

Changing consciousness

The first thing to bear in mind, I would say, in this question of changing consciousness, is that it demonstrates itself in concerns. Scientists, philosophers, thinkers of all kinds, teachers, investigators in all fields, are now seeking, along their own particular paths, various means of understanding the nature of reality. That reality is changing under the microscope, under the power of thought, through the individual experience of meditation or whatever, of various thinkers, philosophers, and scientists.

Modern quantum physics has, I would say, led the way in this, and has brought the modern scientific mind to the acceptance of ideas — no longer simply as speculation — which have been esoteric axioms for countless thousands of years. Ancient Rishis, Masters of the Ancient Wisdom, have postulated various relationships, correspondences and connections between the divine and its expression in humanity, in nature, in the various hierarchies and kingdoms which only today is modern science beginning to investigate — and to find to be true. That is what is causing this change in consciousness. It is both the result of a shift in consciousness by the leading units of the race in the first place and, as a result of their investigations, writings and teachings, a gradual outflow of this awareness into the world, taken up by publications and media of all kinds. This is gradually saturating the mind-belt of the world.

We are living in an era in which what was once magical, mysterious and mystical is now taken for granted as facts in nature. Our modern communications — television, radio, electrical communications through computerization , and so on — are leading us to see the interconnectedness of all aspects of life. The investigation of the nature of consciousness itself is, as the Master says, "going forward apace." People are beginning to discover that you cannot separate the man looking at the world from the world, from his experience of the world. The inner and the outer, the subject and the object, are closely related. You cannot look at the world except through your own individual sight. The *quality* of your experience of the world depends absolutely on your conscious awareness. Your conscious awareness depends on the quality of the instrument of awareness, your vehicles, physical, emotional and mental.

The difference between a Master and a probationary disciple, for example, is that the Master has an apparatus, a vehicle of conscious awareness, which allows Him an awareness of vistas of Being, of Reality, which we cannot even imagine to exist. So far are they beyond our everyday consciousness that we have no opening into them.

I am often asked: "If, as souls, we are perfect, and the soul has no need to be perfected, why does the Plan involve our incarnation? Why do we go through this whole wearisome task of the perfect becoming imperfect on the physical plane and then making this long journey back to perfection? Why bother? Why did God choose to incarnate in the first place? Why descend into matter?" These are questions, of course, to which there is no answer. We cannot know. We have to recognize in the beginning that, when we talk about consciousness, we are talking only about a tiny fragment of the possible states of awareness which exist in creation. By creation I mean the whole of cosmos.

If you remember that humanity has full consciousness only on the physical plane, an imperfect consciousness on the astral plane, and only the beginnings of consciousness on the mental plane — and then only the few — you can see how impossible it is to talk about consciousness in other than very relative terms indeed. When you read about consciousness in books, for example in the Alice Bailey books, you have to remember that DK is telling a lie with everything He says. DK is having to relate His (a Master's) awareness to that which we could, perhaps, by a stretch of our intuition and imagination, begin dimly to understand. And realize that that is relative.

Read a page of DK one day and you may understand not a word. You can recognize the words as words, but you do not know what they mean. Can you imagine what it means to have the consciousness of a Master and still write for our limited understanding? He has consciousness of levels of Being we do not even know exist. He is a God-realized Master and therefore the nature of Reality to Him (and to all the other Masters) must be something very different from that of ourselves. So that when DK, talking about consciousness, or probably anything else in the Alice Bailey teachings, attempts to bring them down to our level, He can only talk about them in relative terms. Whatever is relative is, seen from the higher point of view, not true. It is a lie! I do not mean it is a deliberate lie to mislead us; not at all, DK is trying to lead us into some light. But it is an attempt to relate what is really unrelatable to the low level of consciousness of even the most aspiring, advanced human being; someone who could, with a certain realism, call him or herself a disciple. So relative is our state of consciousness that it is impossible for us to know the truth. That is something we have to accept. This is very difficult for some people because it makes them feel insecure. Everybody wants security. We want to know that what we know is true, and that it is going to remain true, not a truth which is true today but next year is going to be completely wrong, different.

People who want absolute truths, total, immutable truths will not find them in esotericism. The very nature of esotericism is that it is fluid, mobile, is always relative because, from the state above that where any individual is, it is untrue. This physical plane, seen from a higher state, from the view of the inner man, the soul, is a shadow. It is not real. For us, the physical plane is real, but for the soul only relatively real. In the same way, what we take to be so important, the action of the emotional body which churns us so powerfully and leads to such terrible heartache, disease and misery, pain and suffering, is unreal. It is as unreal as our dreams.

When we awake in the morning, even from the most awful nightmare, drenched in perspiration, our heart beating fast, we realize it was only a dream. Only a dream! If only we could say the same thing to all the feelings of the astral plane: every state of anger, fear, every negative emotion. If only we could say: "It was only a dream!" and wake up to reality, physical-plane reality, that is. Then, of course, our life would be easier. But for some reason we accept that our dreams are unreal while our emotions are very real, a different thing altogether. But what are our dreams? Our dreams are really our emotions, the figments created by our astral imagination when in light sleep. In deep sleep we do not have dreams. So in deep sleep something entirely different is experienced — the soul is experienced in deep sleep. But in light sleep, where all our dreams occur, it is the activity of the astral plane and the lower mental plane that creates these extraordinary visions, experiences, people, cities and all the fantastic glamours which we experience in our dreams. Our emotions are no more real than these figments of our astral imagination during sleep. That is something which we should consider and realize. It will help to free us from identification with our emotional body.

When, as esoteric students, we think of evolution we have to remember that we are not really thinking as most people think of it — in Darwinian terms. People generally think of evolution as the evolution of the species, of the form. The evolution of the form has taken place, but also, and more importantly, there has been the evolution of consciousness.

The aim of evolution in the physical sense has been to evolve a body sensitive enough to allow the soul to manifest. That is what evolution is for, why the kingdoms have been created. The mineral kingdom, the vegetable, the animal and then the human kingdom: these have been formed so that ultimately the soul can have an instrument in which the divine and that which is as yet not divine can come together. That is the unique position of humanity. We stand at the mid-way point: the highest of the lowest, the lowest of the highest. Through us, divinity can come into animal and man, and the Christ is born.

The Christ is the consciousness aspect. The Christ, Maitreya, embodies the consciousness aspect of creation. He is the embodied soul of humanity. The soul aspect is, *per se*, the consciousness aspect, but, needing an instrument through which it can express itself on the three lower planes, it has to incarnate. That is why incarnation takes place. That is the answer to the $64,000 question, why God incarnated in the first place: Because God, reflected as the soul, needs a vehicle perfect enough, sensitive enough, to allow divinity to be expressed, and therefore the purpose underlying this whole process to go forward — the purpose fully known only to the Logos of our system and of our planet.

Traditionally, the soul was seen (specially by Christians) as a divine, holy being "up in heaven". It never occurred to Christian writers after the 6th century to write about incarnation. The doctrine of reincarnation was expunged from the Bible at the instigation of the Emperor Justinius.

The churches quickly dropped this unpleasant notion that we incarnated and reincarnated because, if we did incarnate again and again, we had time to evolve; there was not such a pressure on us to be 'good' and to pay our dues to the church. If for any reason we chose not to be good, to be a heretic, what the church called 'bad', we would have another time, another chance. That does not make for good priesthood. Priests need power and you do not get power by saying: "Do not worry! You have time. Do not bother! Free will! You just go on, my boy!" That does not give the priest power. It may make him very popular, but power and popularity do not often go together. The church has forgotten about the doctrine of reincarnation (which the early church fathers taught) and hence has come the idea colouring modern Christian thought: the soul, if there is such a thing at all, is up there, in heaven, and we see it when we die.

Most modern scientists would question the whole idea of the soul. The separation of science and religion has led to this denial of the existence of anything so super-mundane as the soul or super- personal self. This is changing. A group of scientists around the world are focusing very much upon this question of a super-personal self and the idea is gaining ground with enormous speed. But until very recently the notion was that, if there was a soul at all, it was unknowable, unreachable, until you died and went to heaven.

What was left was the man with his mind — able to formulate certain ideas and give them expression, count figures and get a bottom line which added up — and also a brain which gradually came to be understood as the focal point of our existence. What you thought, you were. The very fact of thinking is what made you a man. There is a certain truth in this. The difference between humanity and the nearest of the lower kingdoms, the animal, is that humanity thinks, and as far as we can discover, if an animal thinks, it is a very rudimentary form of thinking indeed. It is probably not thinking at all, but instinct — instinctive knowing — and, at the very best, an emotional response to stimuli built in by reflex *à la* Pavlov.

Now we are beginning to understand that consciousness, mind and brain are separate but connected. The study of kinetics, especially in the Soviet Union, has led to the demonstration of the power of thought over matter, and people have been found with the ability to so focus their minds that they can move objects from one table to another in a controlled experiment.

In the 1940s, I subscribed to a magazine *Mind and Matter* published by the De la Warr Foundation, the originators of the 'black box' and radionics at Oxford in England. They made many experiments of the power of mind. One was to use mass telepathy, and to photograph the thoughtforms created telepathically. They would have a group, for example, in Manchester or Birmingham, several hundred miles from London, and another group in London. At an agreed time, the group in Manchester would focus their attention on a thoughtform 'sent' by the group in London, who would focus their attention on an object — a penknife, a comb, a cross, various objects of that kind — simple, clear-cut visual symbols which were easy to memorize and to focus on. These thoughtforms were photographed on infra-red film and shown, printed, having gone instantaneously by thought on the mind-belt from London to Manchester. Transference of thought is provable, demonstrable, in this way. More and more, we are beginning to realize that we have the ability to impress our thought on matter.

It is a fundamental occult axiom that all is energy, that nothing exists in the whole of the manifested universe but energy, vibrating at some frequency, some wavelength, and that the particular frequencies and their interrelationship make the forms of what we call matter. This is now so accepted that scientists build models of atoms. Every school, probably, in the developed world at least, has models of the patterns of these energy systems — usually balls on stems which are joined together and create most complex, often very beautiful, structures which are a nerve end, or globule of blood. We can make models of the structure of the tiniest sub-atomic particle up to very complex forms indeed. We can now demonstrate energy in form.

Gradually, we are beginning to understand this relationship between energy and matter. Of course to a large extent it stems from Einstein's theory of relativity in which mass can be demonstrated as energy, and vice versa. This is unbelievably important to the world in general, which is why it is a fundamental occult axiom. It is *the* fundamental axiom. There is nothing else but energy.

The Bible says: "God is a consuming fire." By God, the Bible does not mean an old man up in heaven. It means that the sum total of everything in the universe is fire. What is fire but energy? Everything within that complex cosmic Being is vibrating energy and the differences in forms in all the kingdoms are so vast, so incredible, that even if we take only the insect world, we cannot grasp the variety that exists in that part of the natural world. If we think of the variety of forms in the insect world, in the animal world, we humans seem to be the least variegated of all the kingdoms. Consider the mineral kingdom, the vegetable, the animal — tremendous variety. As you go up the scale, you get a lessening of that variety, a coming together, a coalescing of certain forms and tendencies. Consciousness exists in the atoms of all forms in all the kingdoms because it is the soul — the source of consciousness — which incarnates in all forms but the human kingdom is so important because in the human kingdom *consciousness* comes into its own.

The evolution of the *form* of the human kingdom has reached its ultimate. There are a few refinements still to come: the development of etheric vision, for example, and the awakening of certain chakras — force centres — in the human brain by which means the soul makes its presence strongly felt. The awakening of these centres, which until then have been quiescent, evokes a response from the vehicle, the man or woman in incarnation. We are very imperfect beings, and therefore very imperfect instruments through which the soul, the consciousness aspect, can demonstrate. The process of evolution is the development of that consciousness.

Human beings are the Sons of Mind, and our method of evolution is the development of the mind. That means that we cannot truly demonstrate the soul until the mental body is controlled. If we have perfected consciousness only on the physical plane, it is obviously going to be a very long time ahead until we can demonstrate on the mental plane with any kind of perfection. Also, consciousness on a plane and *control* on a plane are two different things. Everyone in the world today has consciousness on the physical plane, but how many people have control on that plane? — at this moment, in incarnation, around 850,000 people, a tiny fragment of the more than 5 billion people who exist in the world today. Of those who have control on the astral plane, there are only around 240,000 in incarnation, and on the mental plane, some 2,000-3,000 people. It is only those with control on the mental plane, the 2,000-3,000 third-degree initiates in the world, who have the possibility of demonstrating the soul correctly.

Evolution of consciousness eventually produces the apparatus, physical, astral and mental, sufficiently sensitive, vibrating at a sufficiently high level, synchronously, which is required for the soul to demonstrate in any real sense through the individual. When that comes about, the man or woman can take the third initiation, the Transfiguration — the first initiation from the Master's point of view. For us, it is a high achievement; for the Master, just the beginning. Everything is so relative that this is for us a major achievement: the creation of a vehicle sensitive, mobile, synchronous in its vibration, able to hold that vibration at a high enough level, for the soul to demonstrate its nature: will, love and intelligence. These three aspects of the soul become the property of the man or woman in incarnation, and they feel no difference between themselves as a soul and themselves as an individual in the everyday world.

Until that time our consciousness is necessarily not only divided, but also partial. We are aware all the time of our physical needs, of what we call our emotional needs (which are less needed than we might think). We are aware to a much lesser degree of the mechanism of our mind and how that takes a hand in this evolutionary process. As Sons of Mind, we develop through the evolution of our minds, the consciousness of the mental plane. It is through idealism and aspiration that the human being evolves, developing mind. It takes will, a mental decision, to do this. We cannot do this simply by *wanting* to do it.

The deva evolution, on the other hand, evolves through feeling. They evolve towards being more perfect (in fact towards being human, if they are subhuman devas) by the perfection of their ability to feel. They have an extremely sensitive sensory apparatus by which to know reality. This allows them to experience the material nature of reality in a way which for us is not alien, but not the path. The path for humanity is the path of the development of mind. That brings in the will and only by a conscious effort. It is the harder of the two ways. The way of the deva is relatively easy, for them a way of no resistance at all.

We, humanity, are tackling the path of most resistance because we are working in the unknown. We are trying to develop from below an aspect which can only come from above. This involves aspiration, and it is precisely aspiration, idealism, which controls the evolutionary process. We evolve as we aspire. We may think, perhaps, that aspiration stops at a certain point. It does not. The Masters aspire. There is no one anywhere in creation who does not aspire. When we think of aspiration, we tend to think of feeling: "I feel I would like to be better!" Every year we make resolutions at New Year to give up smoking or to drink less , and so on. Every year we make this list of resolutions, and, of course, if we kept them we would evolve so quickly! But the making of resolutions does not get us to the third initiation. They are only a symbol for the kind of aspirational idealism which is required to make the journey of evolution as a human being. This brings in the soul, actually evokes the soul whose nature is consciousness. We are really that soul reflected. The soul sits in the heart at the right side of the chest; we are never separate from our soul.

Evolutionary journey

I had a tragic letter recently from a man who said he had attended one of my lectures and read my books. To paraphrase, he wrote: "Would you please give me the method, the technique, of cutting myself off from all further incarnational experience, to have the soul destroyed for ever." He wanted to do it now; he no longer wanted to evolve. He said: "I hate the whole process! I hate God! I hate life! I hate incarnation! I do not want to be part of the Plan. Stop the solar system, I want to get off!"

I did not know what to write back except to say: I am sorry, there is no technique. You are in it for life. There is nothing that anybody can do — not me, not my Master. That is where free will stops. We have only relative free will. We have to go on with it. Sooner or later, we have to go on with it. There is no way off this boat.

A disciple is someone who is taking part in his or her own evolutionary journey. We do not have to do it, but once we start on it there is no way back. We have burned our boats. We could wait until the middle of the next round. I do not know how long that is, certainly not soon. In the middle of the next round, the process of initiation will be dropped. By that time, three-fifths of the world's population will have been what occultly is called 'saved', so they can go on. The others, the two-fifths who will be reckoned not to have made the grade, will either go to a lower planet or be kept back. So we can wait until that time and take it up then.

If we are serious as disciples we have to take a hand in our own evolution. The way we do that is to aspire. Aspiration is the force driving us onwards and upwards. It is really coming to us from the soul. Soul consciousness, the Christ Principle, is the principle of aspiration. It is that very principle which brought the animals, then aquatic, out of the seas on to dry land, created from these primitive reptilian types the mammals, and from mammals, the human kingdom. In that process the initiating factor to a higher form, in every case, has been through aspiration. Aspiration results from the downflow of energy from the soul, because it is the soul in all forms which incarnates. The energy, the consciousness of the soul, poured down into the instrument — man, mammal or aquatic reptile — brings about a response. With us it is immediate, eighteen-and-a-half million years. In the animal kingdom it takes countless millions of years. Gradually, over millions of years, aspiration grows, responding to the call, the consciousness of the soul, which is pointing to something higher. You cannot say, of course, that the soul impresses on the sluggish animal creeping out of the sea — alligator or whatever — a vision of divinity. For the alligator, the vision of divinity is a fat person swimming.

The soul, therefore, impresses the man or woman, and they feel the pull. They reorient their thoughts, their way of life to this call. They become what the conventional world would call a better person, not because the soul is 'good', because the soul is neither good nor bad, but because it is cutting down, refining the quality of its responses to life.

Evolution itself is a process of giving up, of renunciation. The symbol for this whole process is the Crucifixion, the Great Renunciation. This, the fourth, is probably the climactic initiation of all the five initiations to Mastery — not necessarily the most difficult, but the most climactic. The most difficult is said to be the second initiation, as anyone coming near it knows, dealing with the astral body and all its powerful mechanisms of response. It is very difficult to control that and so take the second initiation. But the climactic one, the one that really achieves the divinity to which we are aspiring, is the fourth initiation.

The very term for it, the Crucifixion, or better, the Great Renunciation, exactly demonstrates what is needed in this process. It is a renunciation. It is not being 'goody-goody'. The aim of the initiate is not to be better than anyone else, to be nicer than anyone else, to do better works than anyone else, to be recognizable as a very special, spiritual person. In fact, if you had met someone like Mao Tse-Tung or Winston

Churchill or Marshal Tito — three power men, great politicians, leaders of nations, all with a very powerful ray structure based on Ray 1 (Tito was 1-1-1-4-1; Mao Tse-Tung was 1-1-1-2-1; Churchill was 2-1-1-4-1) — I do not think you would think of them always as nice, harmless people.

Churchill gave the signal for the massacre at the Dardanelles (the massacre of Australians and New Zealanders mainly). It was slaughter and I am sure he knew it would be slaughter. During World War II he gave the signal for the Dieppe raid, before the real invasion of the Normandy beaches, in which 3,000 troops were sent as a trial run to see what would happen to them. Of course, they were slaughtered, every one of them; the bodies washed up on the shores of England for months. They happened to be Polish and Canadian and other non-British nationalities. Churchill also advocated the invasion of Russia in 1917 to forestall the Bolshevik revolution. Had that happened, the history of the world would be very different and probably the Nazi flag would fly right across the Soviet Union today. Whether that would have been the case or not, simple goodness is not the mark of the initiate.

Harmlessness

The evolutionary process is about the expansion of consciousness. This is not an invitation to get out all these glamours and air them, to throw all your harmlessness out of the window. Harmlessness is the primary need of all people, whether they are initiates or not. It has nothing to do with being initiate. Harmlessness is just sheer common sense because every thought, every action, sets into motion a cause or causes. The effects stemming from these causes make our lives, for good or ill. So you can see how harmlessness is an absolute necessity in our lives. It is not some special principle which only initiates can demonstrate.

Some of the most harmless people in the world are well below the first initiation, whereas many of the more harmful people have taken the first or later initiations. Hitler had taken two initiations; we would not call him harmless. Stalin had taken two initiations. Fanatics are not harmless. Fanaticism is not harmless. It is extremely harmful because it goes against the evolutionary process which is towards unity, synthesis.

Everything that works against that is evil, harmful, because it creates the separation which is the big lie of life. This is the great illusion — that we are separate. These divisions, that separatism, caused by fanaticism, anger, fear, create the conditions which we have to seek to overcome. We have to learn to build harmlessness, therefore, into our makeup. Harmlessness does not come automatically with initiation which results from control of the vehicle — control, actually, of the devic lives whose activity makes up the vehicle, whether that be physical, astral or mental.

The path of evolution is the growth of consciousness at succeeding stages. Each initiation taken increases that capacity because every initiation is the result of the focusing of the energy of the Rod of Initiation in the chakras of the individual. That awakens dormant chakras or centres in the brain. We have to be initiate before we take initiation. Our chakras, our whole body, must already be vibrating at a level where it can withstand the inflow of the energy from the Rod of Initiation. If that is not the case, we cannot take initiation. This is why the Lord of the World must give His assent that the initiation can take place, because if we were not ready, we would be dead. Literally. The initiate would be killed by the inflow of colossal fiery energy from the Rod of Initiation. This is true whether it is the first, the second, the third or higher initiations. The initiate must already be initiate. What happens at the initiatory ceremony, *per se*, is that the energy from the Rod of Initiation is focused on the initiate and awakens chakras which have been dormant. So initiation confers a kind of finishing touch, if you like, to a process which is already well under way. It is a kind of ceremonial concluding action on the process which the initiate has him or herself initiated through life and previous lives. It is a self-initiatory process.

People imagine that the Masters bring us to initiation. Actually, they do not. The relationship of a disciple to a Master is completely different, I think, from the general view which people have picked up by diverse reading of books by those who know little about that relationship, who have not experienced it, but have read about it in some manual. Initiation is always self-initiated. It is you, yourself, a soul in incarnation, who brings you to initiation. That means that the consciousness aspect, coming from the soul, must have done its work in the life which led up to the initiation, that the response to the soul has been sufficiently sensitive. This comes about through renunciation. It is not achieved by becoming good, or holy, or unholy or becoming anything except more aware. Initiation and the evolutionary process is to do with awareness, a growing expansion of conscious awareness *and of what might be*. Devas evolve through a growing awareness of what is, what reality — right this very moment — is. Our way is through a gradual expansion of our conscious awareness of the potential of what might be. That is what the soul is telling us all the time. The principle of the soul is so high in relation to the human mind, the human capacity to respond, that it is always holding above it a vision to which it can aspire. Aspiration gives us the sense that there is something higher than we know at this moment.

For the devas, the evolutionary aim is experiencing life as it is, this very moment, just how everything is now. The human path is the harder one because we are dealing with the unknown; we have to intuit. We do so because we are intuitive and we are intuitive because we are souls in incarnation. Intuition is a natural part of our make-up. It is more or less developed, of course, depending on our point of evolution, and, to a certain degree, on our ray structure. Some rays, the 2nd, 4th, 6th, tend to a more intuitive approach than the 1-3-5-7 line because they are more in-turned to the soul. Intuition comes from the soul. Buddhi, or intuitive knowledge, is direct knowing: knowing directly without having to think about it. That outflow of buddhi takes place gradually when the human being aspires towards that which is higher than he or she already knows.

The purpose of books like the Alice Bailey or the Agni Yoga teachings is not simply to teach the academic relationships and structures which baffle so many people and are difficult to remember (although they are important to know). The Master DK, in the Alice Bailey teachings, is trying to awaken the intuition; to hold before our minds, and so stimulate our intuition, our aspiration, our idealistic faculty, the notion that there is above us as souls areas of being, of knowledge, of awareness, of which we are as yet unaware. And we aspire towards that.

The process of evolution is awakened through aspiration towards higher levels of awareness. If we think back to various points of illumination, we will see that this is precisely what has happened. When we finish reading a good part of one of DK's works, we are filled with an illumined feeling. We have grown inwardly. There is more light in the real sense, in that the world has broadened, the vista of cosmos has broadened. We are aware of more possibilities in cosmos and in ourselves as part of cosmos. First of all, through the use of the lower mind, we put these things together, we think about them by pure mentation — but by the very way in which they are written, by the fact that DK is writing about things that the lower mind cannot really grasp and easily comprehend, He awakens the intuition. The soul's way of communicating is through the intuition. That illumines and suddenly we are aware of what before we were unaware.

Consciousness grows by aspiration towards that which lies above it. But of course we are lazy. This is the hard way and that is why the path of evolution is slow and long and arduous. The way forwards is precisely that of renunciation. Renunciation is another word for detachment. Maitreya uses the word detachment. I have not yet noticed if He has used the word renunciation, but detachment He uses all the time. It is the same thing. The path of evolution is the path of renunciation, is the path of detachment. The process, the technique, of renunciation is detachment. How do we evolve? What is the actual nature of the path? We cannot sit down and suggest to ourselves: "Today, I am going to overcome the astral vehicle. I am going to demonstrate my control of the mental vehicle." How do we do this? "Ah, the devas! I will control the devas! Will I get out a whip?" In the old days they did. Good Christian folks, every Lent, used to take out the whips and march through the town whipping themselves. What they were really trying to do was to control the physical elemental. Little did they know that every time they hit an elemental, two grew in its place! There are easier ways, the ways of detachment.

Detachment

Detachment is the difficult but absolutely essential process of evolution. It comes about through an expansion of consciousness as the soul grips its vehicle and the realization that we are not this physical body, these emotional reactions, these constructions of our mind — that the true man or woman is that which lies back of these and is using these vehicles for expression. The soul is a reflection of the Monad demonstrating the divinity of God. The path of evolution is a series of at-one-ments: first with the soul, then with the Monad and divinity itself: what Maitreya calls the Self, the Lord, the Absolute. The process is one of detaching step by step from identification with the unreal, the unreal being that which we take to be real: this physical-plane world.

The deva evolution evolves in matter and grows in consciousness through the experience of matter, of what is, now. We evolve through the renunciation of matter. When the fourth initiation (the Great Renunciation) is taken, we demonstrate our ability to renounce everything, even life itself, because then we realize that we are life, that there is nothing else but life, that we are that One Life. Firstly, we renounce the appetites, the apparent needs, of the physical body; the emotional reactions of the astral body; the constructions, the beliefs, the ideologies, the memories of the mental body, all of that conditioning.

The old, mechanistic view is that the soul (if it exists) is up there, the mind (us) is somewhere else — and our mind is the man or woman. The brain is the directing principle that knows all, remembers (or mis-remembers) everything and does the whole work in connection with the mind. This concept presupposes separate aspects of reality but in fact there is no separation. The soul is closely connected with the mind, the mind with the brain. It is a unitary mechanism through which the soul can work, demonstrating itself eventually in the most marvellous way.

To many people the brain is omnipotent. We even say: "We will one day make computers that are really superior to the human brain." The human brain, to most people, is the person. It is the brain, we think, who thinks. It is the brain who knows, who remembers or mis-remembers. The brain is the all-powerful mechanism directing the whole process of our living experience. This is not true. The brain is but a marvellous, wonderfully sensitive, intricate computer into which is fed all experience coming from the soul through the mental plane. Into this computer all information is fed, all the reactions of the nervous system, of the astral body and of the physical body are likewise fed into the brain.

When the body runs out of energy it gets hungry and sends the message to the brain. The brain says: "Go to McDonald's." The body tells the brain and the brain tells us to go and get something to eat. We feel hunger, want a drink. We experience cold or heat, the brain tells us, gives us the signal, that our body is feeling cold and we need to cover it with an extra blanket. These are all instinctual reactions by which the animal kingdom has evolved. The nervous system sends signals to the brain which computes this information from all levels. So the brain is an extraordinary instrument but it is physical. It pertains only to the physical plane, the physical body, and it dies at death. Using the brain is the thinker, using the mind is the thinker. We have to find out who that thinker is and identify with the thinker. As we identify more and more with the thinker, so are we imbued with the consciousness of the thinker. The thinker is the higher man or the soul, the transpersonal self, the ego, whatever you like to call it.

As we identify with that higher aspect we are imbued with its nature. Our consciousness grows and expands. Growth of consciousness comes about precisely through the awakening of ourselves to identification with that higher aspect. It is easy to read in a book that we are really a soul in incarnation. It is a very different thing in everyday life to remember that and to act as if it were true. It is a conscious, self-initiated process and brings us eventually to initiation. The way, therefore, is through awareness of the Self, identification with the Self.

When father/spirit and mother/matter come together, the Christ is born. Man, humanity, is born. We are, in a very real sense, the Christ. Divinity and the material world come together in the human species. That is why, throughout the whole of cosmos, everything is on the way to becoming human, is human, or has been human and has gone beyond the human. We are the midway stage through which everything passes. That is the unique situation of humanity. That is why the Christ Principle relates so directly to humanity. Through a gradual growth of consciousness we evolve to superconsciousness, to cosmic consciousness and beyond. What lies beyond the consciousness of the highest Being of our solar system we cannot even begin to imagine. Probably the highest Being in our solar system can know only the beginnings of what lies beyond.

The nervous system is seen as a mechanism of response by which the brain can know what signals it needs to send to the feet or the stomach or the digestive juices, the chemistry of the body. If left alone it does it marvellously. If interfered with by neurotic identification with our emotions, we can inhibit this mechanism and cause indigestion and various illnesses. These illnesses result from emotional disturbance of the natural, perfectly organized function of the brain to look after our physical body.

The physical body, in terms of principle, is inert: simply acted upon and responsive to impress from higher principles. That is why 'mind over matter' is a fact. You may have seen demonstrations of people walking on hot coals without burning their feet. You must have seen at least film or photographs of fakirs in India (not evolved at all) who can put a four-inch nail through their arm and bring it out the other side without drawing blood. Lying on a bed of nails is not just fanciful; it is true, people can and do lie on beds of nails. I have seen a man lying on nails and someone else putting a big lump of concrete, obviously very heavy, on his stomach. And then jumping on top of it! You expect to see this man pierced through with these great spikes, but he gets up without any help. And there is no blood, no mark. Mind over matter. The body can respond with training to any kind of misuse of that kind.

"I think therefore I am." It should be: "I Am, therefore I think." It is because we are thinking beings that we think. And because we have a vehicle called mind we are able to demonstrate that fact. It is the thinker who thinks, but we do not see the thinker, we see only the result of the process of thought because we have a vehicle called mind and another vehicle called brain which can give voice to the thoughts through the larynx. All of that is intricately interconnected. There is no break in these seemingly separate aspects of ourselves. The link is the nervous system.

The sympathetic and parasympathetic nervous systems have been known and analysed for a very long time. Today, nerve specialists know so much about the nervous system that the most intricate operations can be performed on different parts of the ganglia which would appal anyone who had not studied the subject. These are tackled with complete confidence — not to say nerve — without a qualm. The surgeons have been trained and they know their job. They think it is a mechanism like any other (which it is) but they think that it is part of the material world — which in a sense it is — but it is not only that.

We will come to discover that the ganglia of the nervous system is the most intricate mechanism by which the soul makes its presence felt through all the vehicles. In the tiny nerve conduits called nadis, gases from the soul (gas so fine that it is not detectable by any modern scientific method) flow through the nervous system. In this way, the impulses, energy, purpose, will, love of the soul make themselves felt in its vehicle. The more evolved the man or woman, of course, the more is this process taking place. In this way the soul grips its vehicle, pouring its energy into the physical plane. How does it do it? By what method?

Through the antahkarana, the bridge of light, the soul pours its energies into its reflection, the man or woman on the physical plane. The antahkarana is built downwards by the soul as the individual begins to meditate. Also, through meditation and aspiration, it is built by the individual up to the soul. It is a two-way process. It is a column of light, of three strands of force — Will, Love-Wisdom, and Intelligence — which enters through the crown chakra at the top of the head. From that chakra it flows through the nadis of the nervous system. That is the ultimate reason for the nervous system.

If we look at evolution from the purely material form aspect, we see the evolutionary process as one in which more and more complex nervous systems are created in the different species. The higher the species, the more complex; the earlier and more primitive the species, the less of this nervous system do they have or need because their reactions to life are very limited. When the reaction to life is to the life of the soul (and therefore to the consciousness aspect, because life generates consciousness and without it there would be no consciousness), we evolve in consciousness. In the human being the soul uses our very complex nervous system to distribute the gas at different temperatures, rates of flow, potencies, which become our awareness: physical, astral-emotional and mental awareness. All of this finally comes together at the third initiation. These three bodies vibrate together, synchronously, and the soul can then truly inhabit its vehicle. Until that time it is training, preparing its vehicle. At the third initiation it really takes over its vehicle in the fullest sense, because the nadis of the nervous system have opened up as pure channels for the flow of gas from the soul. It is gas, but it is the very livingness of the soul, the nature of the soul, poured down into its vehicle. It is energy. There is nothing else. In the end we evolve a vehicle so synchronous in its vibration on all three planes that the soul can truly inhabit it, and the divine Being is born; the Transfiguration initiation takes place.

Then begins in true earnest the path of renunciation. Then the individual, with will, love and intelligence totally dedicated

385

to the role which the Logos has designed for the human soul, divests himself of matter. Evolution for us humans is divesting ourselves of all that holds back light. We evolve through the absorption of light. Consciousness is light. Consciousness, the Christ Principle, flowing through the bodies of the individual initiate, floods them with light. Eventually, at the fourth initiation, three-quarters of his body is light. The process is completed at the fifth initiation, and the Master stands free from the pull of matter for ever. He has completely spiritualized matter on an individual basis. As everyone begins to do this, the world as a whole becomes spiritualized. Then the Plan of evolution of our Logos, for changing into light at the highest possible vibration of its ray energy, the ray shining purely through every kingdom, will be achieved, and we will have done our parts in this process.

Questions and Answers

Awareness and Consciousness

What is the difference between consciousness and awareness?
Awareness is the result of the action of consciousness itself. The physical brain, through its mechanism, allows that consciousness to be apprehended. That is awareness.

Awareness is the recognition that you are experiencing something. Consciousness is the faculty of the soul which makes us aware, which gives us the process of awareness. The Christ Principle is the principle of consciousness. It is light. It awakens and illumines. God said: "Let there be light." The light, in that phrase in the Bible, is the light of consciousness. Spirit and matter, father God, mother matter, came together, and the Christ Principle, the principle of consciousness itself, was born.

We come from light. All that we know and see in creation comes from light. Creation is the result of the action of light, which is consciousness. God, the father principle, is unmanifest. Mother God, the matter principle, by itself is unmanifest. When the two come together, you have manifestation — the birth of man, humanity, the birth of the Christ, the Christ Principle, the principle of consciousness. Awareness is knowing. Consciousness is the principle by which we know.

How can you recognize in yourself the difference between brain consciousness and soul consciousness?
The brain, like the physical body itself, is not a principle. The brain is really a computer, and a computer, as you know, will interrelate masses of material, but only in relation to what you put into it. It will not give out what you have not already put in. You can ask it questions and it will relate what it knows over here to what it knows over there, but what it knows both there and here was given by whoever programmed the computer. The brain, likewise, is an even more marvellous computer because it works on so many different levels: physical, emotional and mental. The brain consciousness is limited to what comes into it from higher sources. The soul illumines the mind with its consciousness, and the brain is at the receiving end of all the impulses from the soul downwards: from the mental body, the astral body, and the various sub-planes of the etheric and physical bodies.

Soul consciousness is impersonal, inclusive and synthetic. It illumines. Brain consciousness tends to be personal, exclusive and analytical. It separates. Brain consciousness is necessary for organizing physical-plane existence. Soul consciousness reveals the purpose of, and meaning behind, that experience.

Could you give examples of the differences between consciousness and control on physical, astral and mental levels, as illustrations of what you referred to in your lecture?
There is all the difference in the world between consciousness on a plane and control on that plane. All of us, without exception, on this planet now have full consciousness on the physical plane. The evolution of the physical body of humanity has reached its ultimate, apart from some minor developments, in particular the development of the eye and the achievement

of etheric vision. We have incomplete consciousness on the astral plane; for example, most people do not have continuity of consciousness, sleep to waking. There are refinements of feeling experienced by artists, musicians, and those who work closely in that area but which are not the average, the norm. Most people have only relative consciousness on the astral plane. The astral plane is the plane of feeling, but there are seven sub-planes of the astral plane, from the coarsest, the first sub-plane, up to the most refined, where the heart response is at its highest. These feelings flow either through the solar plexus or the heart. The lower aspects of the astral plane flow through the solar plexus, and all communications stemming from the astral plane tend to be distorted. At the very highest level, the sixth and especially seventh sub-planes of the astral plane, the energy is so refined that it is almost akin to the mental plane, and works through the heart. So when people say: "I feel such and such," they have to think about what it is they feel, in terms of emotion. Love is not emotion, as we think. The Masters call it pure reason. Most people feel it in the solar plexus, but then that is not love, but emotion. Love, in its more refined aspect, is felt through the spiritual heart at the right side of the chest. You can tell where you are experiencing the feeling, whether it is on the emotional level or at the heart level, depending on which chakras it is activating.

Very few people have real consciousness on the mental plane. There are four sub-planes of the mental plane and normally we know only the lowest of these four, the coarsest. That is the plane of mentation, where we think and calculate and order our lives and book tickets for planes and trains and so on. For most people, that function is the be-all and end-all of their mental activity. But the mental body is, *per se*, the organ through which the soul manifests itself in the man or woman in incarnation. Of course, it can only do so in so far as the mental planes are activated. If we are using only the lowest level, the soul is very limited in its expression on the physical plane. Therefore the person may be able to calculate, use a computer, send men to the moon and back, but have no consciousness of the spiritual nature of life at all. By spiritual,

I do not mean religious. I mean of the soul, using the higher levels of the mental plane. He may be totally unaware and never experience even a glimmer of that consciousness.

If consciousness is limited, control must be even more limited. If we have limited consciousness on the astral plane, and full consciousness only on the physical plane, then control on any of the planes must be very limited indeed, and so it is. Control denotes the initiate. It is the initiate, and only the initiate, who has control. The first-degree initiate has control on the physical plane. The control is not so much of the plane or body, but of the activity of the tiny devic lives who make up the matter of the body. This apparently solid physical-plane article, the physical body, both dense and etheric, results from the activity of tiny devic lives. The life activity of these devas makes the physical, astral and mental bodies of humanity. What we take to be mental is really physical from the cosmic point of view and is the product of the activity of the mental elementals; the astral body, of the astral elementals; and the physical of the physical elementals. They control our lives or we control them, it is either one or the other.

The average person, with consciousness on the physical plane, incomplete consciousness on the astral and very little on the mental plane, with no control at all on any of these, is swept along by the activity of the elementals on each plane. Their life is governed on the physical plane by the desire nature of these elementals. Their life is really dominated by the desire of the physical body for food, drink, sex, sleep, comfort, sunshine, for doing nothing or for over-activity, whatever it is.

The first initiation only becomes possible when the man or woman achieves a degree of control on the plane — which allows an individual to come before the Initiator and the Rod of Initiation, a powerful rod activated from the sun, from which tremendous energy is focused on the chakras of the initiate. The chakras are stimulated to a higher octave which means that, in reality, you have to be initiate before you can be initiated. Your chakras have to be vibrating steadily, keeping the vibration constantly, whatever it is, for a given length of time. The Masters know then that this person can stand the impact of the energy of the Rod of Initiation.

Control is the result of the control of the activity of the elementals. You are then in charge of your own body. It does not control you, you control it.

The same process is enacted later on at the second initiation, when you demonstrate control of the astral elemental. This is much more difficult. There are some 850,000 people out of over 5 billion in incarnation at the present time who have taken the first initiation. That is, they have control of the physical elemental — very few indeed. The rest have consciousness on the plane, but not control on the plane. Those who have taken the second initiation, now in incarnation, number about 240,000. The second is said to be the hardest of all the initiations to take, because the astral vehicle is the most powerful we have, and is the focus of the desire principle which governs the whole of the personality life.

What is the main impediment to our struggle to expand consciousness? Why did the Master choose 'The Growth of Consciousness' as the subject for this conference?
He chose it, I suppose, because He thought it would be useful, because the growth of consciousness is what evolution is about. That *is* evolution. When we talk about evolution, we are really talking about the evolution of consciousness, of conscious awareness. That is what life is, a gradual awakening to higher and wider vistas of Being and Reality. That is life at every level. So growth of consciousness started as soon as, for the very first time, we came into incarnation in the primeval swamp. When was it? Eighteen-and-a-half million years ago.

What is the main impediment in our struggle? The main impediment is karma. Every advance in evolution, and therefore every expansion of consciousness, takes place through the resolution of karma. It is karma that holds us back. Karma puts a weight of inertia on our evolution which, of course, as we resolve the karma, speeds up. The dynamic of service in relation to karma releases us to evolve. The process of evolution is through a gradual expansion of consciousness. The reason we do not expand our consciousness more quickly is because we are unaware. Consciousness is awareness. We have to be aware, consciously, to be conscious. It is really a question of perfecting or expanding the sensitivity of an instrument of awareness.

That instrument we already have — three bodies: physical, astral and mental. Consciousness cannot express itself except through a vehicle. It is the result of life and energy, and needs a vehicle through which to express or demonstrate itself. The instrument through which it does so is our personality, with these three bodies. Therefore, the way of producing or increasing awareness is to refine the sensibility of these three bodies. What prevents that? Inertia, karma — the inertia of matter itself of which the body is made, and, of course, the point of evolution. We cannot be beyond the point where one is at any time; we are where we are. If we are 1.3, for example, our area of response will be at that level. If we are 1.8, we will have an awareness of the mental plane which is not possible at 1.3, and a degree of control over the astral elemental which is not possible at 1.3.

Control of the vehicles makes possible the awareness which demonstrates as growth in consciousness. The control is, of course, over the devic elementals which make up the various bodies. We have a physical body with its appetites, needs and desires; an astral nature with what we think are its needs, certainly its desires; and a mental body which is out of our control. We must bring all three under control. It takes time.

I have found that many people are lazy but also ambitious and impatient. They want it all tomorrow, without doing any of the work. They are too lazy to do the work that brings it about but they want the results even before — if they had done the work — it would come about. They want it for nothing. It is the glamour of non-realization of the truly serious nature of life. Some people are heavy serious. We do not have to be heavy serious. We can be light-as-a-feather serious but we have to be serious. We have to do it! As Maitreya says:

"Nothing happens by itself. Man must act and implement his will."

What is the difference between activating the will and wanting something?
The will does not want; it acts. Wanting something comes from the desire principle, not the same thing at all as the will. The desire principle governs the astral nature. We want something because we desire it. The will plans and purposes, it does not want; it initiates certain projects, ideas, plans, purposes, and wills them into being.

That is very different from the desire principle, which simply wants what it does not have. The will deals with higher principles, with plans and projects, with purpose and the laws governing purpose. The desire principle acts to satisfy a sensed need, whether that need is real or purely the gratification of some astral whim, fantasy or glamour. The will does not want anything at all except the fulfilment of its plan and works dynamically to achieve this end. This attitude, of course, has its own glamours and brings about, very often, a state of arrogance and cruelty, riding roughshod over other people's needs and personalities. It is so powerful it can be very destructive and may cause much heartache to those around people who manifest this type of energy. But so also do those people who express the desire principle to such an extent that they, too, ride roughshod over other people's needs and feelings; and not for the fulfilment of the Plan but of their own self-will. When desire is powerfully focused in this way it becomes a major obstacle to progress because it is difficult to break the attachments. The 1st ray of Will has no such problem; it takes what it needs to fulfil its purpose.

Does the renunciation of something by will help the growth of consciousness?
It is only by the action of the will that any renunciation can be made. And, of course, the more advanced the individual, the more this becomes an habitual process. But you have to start in small things. The Great Renunciation becomes possible only when the little renunciations have been made. You cannot start

with the Great Renunciation. You can only lead up to it by building in the habit of renunciation. Of course, as we all know, by what we desire and receive, the appetite grows. Likewise, that which we renounce — it has to be done by an action of the will, otherwise it does not happen at all — is easily renounced, once renounced. Another renunciation can be made, and another, by the practice of renunciation.

The more you renounce, the easier it is to renounce. It becomes a habit. This starts with the application of the will. When you renounce in small things, you build in the instinctual, easy acceptance of greater and greater renunciations. They do not come automatically but need the will to bring them about. The renunciation of something by will, of course, helps the growth of consciousness. Anything that brings about renunciation of the lesser for the greater is, *per se*, a result of the growth of consciousness and leads to a further growth in consciousness.

What about service in relation to desire?
Desire controls the lower man. Service controls the higher man. When the individual controls the vehicles, he turns away from that simple, individualistic, self-indulgent, separative life, and desires to serve, because it is the soul's nature to serve. The soul impresses its vehicle, the man or woman, with the desire to serve, and as people get involved in service the lower is renounced, dies.

It happens naturally, because the involvement in service, if it is true service, pushes us forward faster than anything else in growth of consciousness. It helps to free the individual from karma, burns up karma. What, above all, holds us back in the evolution of consciousness is karma. The actions of the past, up to this moment, make karma. Every action, every thought, creates it. Thought is a thing; it creates that which holds us back in evolution. It ties knots which trap us, as it were, and until we sever these knots we cannot move forward. The moving forward, the growth in consciousness, is best achieved by completely forgetting about ourselves, involving ourselves in service to humanity, and at some kind of sacrifice to oneself. If there is no sacrifice, we can presume it is a glamour.

Many people enter service as a glamour. They know that it is a good thing to serve, but their attitude is not really coming from the soul, but from a desire of the self for betterment; that is the glamour. The will, the love and intelligence of the soul have to be involved. If so, if that is behind it, the service will be transforming.

As we get involved in service, we lose the usual focus on ourselves. We live then to serve the world. The initiate knows he has come into life for that. He has not come in to have 'a good time'. He can have a good time in serving the world. Mother Teresa has a great time, I am sure. It might seem a terrible time to some, but to her, I am certain, it is a wonderful time, the best possible time she could have. Service is the most powerful lever of evolution, but you must be truly involved.

Can you say something about the relation between service and growth in consciousness?
One of the fastest means of growing in consciousness is through altruistic service. Why? Because it frees us from concentration on the self. What holds us back in growth of consciousness is the fact that all of us, without exception, are indulging the desire principle. We are all at the centre of the universe, living greedily, selfishly, wanting what we want when we want it, as if it is written into the constitution of life; as if, when we come into life at birth, we are given a guarantee, a written constitution from God, saying that whatever this person wants should be gratified immediately: "All desires should be gratified, by order of the Lord." And we go around with this — "Look, it is written here, I got it from God, all my desires have to be satisfied, that is the law. That is why I am here. I know what my desires are, I know what my wants are, and I have a written guarantee from God that I am going to have them satisfied whenever I want, on demand." That is how we live our lives. Everyone does it. We do not, of course, recognize that that is what we do.

That is the desire principle at work. What irritates, what makes us angry, is when other people are doing the same thing, using us. That is the problem; we are all trying to use each other, manipulating, exploiting each other in various ways to get what we want, to have this written guarantee for satisfaction in life achieved.

We do not get it, of course, therefore we get angry, we get frustrated, we find we have to inhibit our desires. It starts with wanting to stab our father, and we cannot get away with stabbing our father. We cannot get up to our father to stab him, for one thing, because he is big and we are tiny, and from then on we live a life of frustration. Everyone is trying to stab their father, or us, in the back, and wanting what they want, when they want it. We all exploit each other, all the time. Service gives us the opportunity to detach from all of that.

What is the connection between consciousness and detachment?
Detachment is the result of the growth of consciousness and vice versa. If we do not have consciousness, we will certainly not be detached. It is the growth of consciousness, of what lies behind the outer appearances and what is restricting our awareness of life that brings about detachment. We see that as we detach we grow. People may think that if they detach they are losing something. On the contrary, they are gaining freedom — and in that freedom a greater intensity of life, a greater awareness of the living process, moment to moment, than one could ever have with the attachments.

We all have attachments because we are afraid of being left alone. We want to be loved. Everybody wants to be loved, or at least liked, accepted. Everyone wants to be made to feel comfortable, at home, safe. Everyone wants to be safe. Everybody wants security, all the time, moment to moment — but there is no security; this is the big paradox. Everyone wants the impossible. There is no security in life. Life has nothing to do with security. It is to do with movement, with consciousness, with transformation, with experience. Who said it is to do with security? Nobody said so. God did not write it into the contract. But we all long for it, for physical-plane, emotional, mental security. We want to know that what we believe is right. Everything in creation is relative. It must be so, otherwise there would be no evolution. Creation is evolving, and therefore changing. If it is changing, there is no static thing anywhere. There is no *status quo*, and if there is no *status quo*, there is no security.

We all want to protect ourselves from life. We do this by seeking comfort. We want life, but we want it in a package that we can handle and deal with and feel secure in. As soon as it acts outside that known parameter, we get scared, because it is frightening not to feel comfortable. We want people to love us so that we can feel comfortable. We know we can exploit whoever loves us — up to a point. We must not overdo it. Everyone instinctively knows that point is reached when they do not give us a smile as they let us walk over them. The more we are loved, the more secure we feel. Of course we cannot really feel secure, because we can never get enough love, and we cannot control that love. We all exploit to keep secure, to keep people liking us, loving us, being in the right comfortable relationship with us. In other words, we want to possess them. Possession is the opposite of detachment. So long as we are attached in that way, we will never grow, never evolve. It is the opposite of evolution. We can only evolve when we are free, and we can only be free when we are detached. While we are attached, we think we are in charge. We are not. We are caught up in the attachment, to whatever it is, whatever relationship, whatever situation, to our need for physical security, our job. That attachment keeps us from growing in consciousness.

Growth of consciousness comes, simply and purely, out of freedom. Nothing else. The given state of life is freedom. That is what Maitreya has come to teach. Freedom is the natural state of humanity. It is the divine as it demonstrates in our everyday life. That is what Self-realization is about. It has to be free of all attachment. Any attachment limits that freedom which begins to manifest, stage by stage, as we free ourselves from these attachments.

Psychotherapy and Consciousness

To what extent does psychotherapy help the growth of consciousness? Is there a danger in it?

The problem with psychotherapy, unless you are so disturbed you really need it, is that it focuses the attention on the lower self. Growth of consciousness is achieved precisely by losing consciousness of the separated self. No one enjoys psychotherapy more than the person being treated. They sit or lie down on a couch and talk about themselves. Have you ever met anyone who did not enjoy talking about themselves? All these memories should have been jettisoned long ago, let go, finished with, but are now allowed to grow and develop a life of their own. The result is a total concentration of the person on the couch on his or her self. Their attention is totally focused, not just as usual, but professionally focused (people are being paid good money to do this), on themselves: to perpetuate their illness.

I am not talking entirely against psychotherapy. We all know individuals who are, literally, too ill, who are psychotic or so neurotic and unbalanced in their personality that they do need professional psychotherapeutic treatment so that they can live in a reasonable state of balance. But apart from these, psychotherapy, in my estimation, does not do too much good for most people. It simply focuses their attention more than ever on themselves.

The quickest way to help, physically, emotionally and mentally, is not the psychiatrist's couch but the renunciation which comes from engagement in service. Nothing helps so much as service, losing yourself in service.

People think they find themselves on the psychotherapist's couch. They find only their memory. They find only a greater focus of their attention on their own problems. And of course they love it. It is a huge glamour. Everyone loves to focus their attention on themselves, everyone, without exception. The major illness of humanity is that everyone senses himself or herself as being at the centre of the universe. Well, we cannot all be at the centre of the universe; you just find your place more towards the periphery.

You can do that on the psychiatrist's couch, if you like — it will take longer that way — or you can get engaged in service and begin to lose the sense of having to yourself that place at the centre of the universe. You will not have that same desire, because you will be so involved in service, in acting with and through and for other people, and in serving the needs of the world, that you forget about yourself. You can, literally, for long periods, forget about yourself. It has been shown to be possible. The quickest way, the best way, is through service. You do not even have to pay for it!

What is the difference between a mental breakdown due to soul experience and a mental breakdown due to neurosis or psychosis?
Probably to the person experiencing it, not much difference at all. It depends on the degree of the breakdown. Breakdown, mental or emotional, can be the result of too great and sudden a downflow of energy from the soul into a vehicle relatively unprepared for the reception of that energy. These are some of the dangers involved in meditation. Every reputable meditation has always given a warning of the dangers of meditation: of how too much, too soon, too intensely practised or wrongly done, can bring about mental or emotional, and sometimes physical, breakdown.

Every downflow of higher energy brings about a temporary — it is usually very temporary — disequilibrium. Necessarily so, because every higher stimulus sets in motion a different situation, produces change. Change produces a greater or lesser degree of trauma or difficulty. If properly conducted, done under the correct safeguards, meditation is safe to do. (I am talking about meditation in general, not about any specific meditation.) Any upset, any disturbance of what we call the *status quo* is usually transitory, very temporary indeed, and the equilibrium, at a higher level because of the new stimulus, is usually quite quickly restored.

398

This happens cyclically throughout everyone's existence. It could not be otherwise. Every growth of consciousness is due to stimulus, however that stimulus comes. The stimulus usually comes as the result of invocation. Through aspiration, you invoke the energy from the soul. The soul responds, a downflow of energy takes place, and it upsets the *status quo*. If it is properly done, with proper safeguards, scientifically, there should be only a very slight, very temporary disturbance of the *status quo*, followed by the new equilibrium, set at a higher turn of the spiral. This is repeated again and again throughout all lives, until you become a Master. I am sure the same things happen to the Master, only He is dealing with cosmic forces.

So a mental breakdown can be, if slight and temporary, a disturbance of the *status quo* from a downflow of energy from the soul. If it is the result of a neurotic or psychotic condition, then it is the opposite of that: not the result of a growth of consciousness, but of denial of a growth of consciousness.

Neurosis comes, in the main, from inhibition. If you inhibit the bodily, emotional and mental functions, you bring about stasis. There is no absolute stasis, so we will call it a relatively static condition. On the physical plane, for example, an inhibition of the flow of energies through the chakras, the force centres in the spine, produces a stasis, in which there is not a correct flow of energy, freely, in and out of the chakras. These, when functioning properly, maintain the physical well-being of the body. A stasis will produce some disturbance of the endocrine system which, in turn, will disturb one or other organ associated with a particular gland. The result is ill health, dis-ease.

If you would maintain the health of the body, you must maintain the correct balance of the endocrine system which needs the correct, uninhibited flow of energy in and out of the chakras, in a balanced, co-ordinated way. Because of our wrong living conditions, of our badly-constructed and maintained environment, and because of all sorts of inhibiting factors in our education, our upbringing and so on, no one lives in a perfect state of total equilibrium. No one has perfect health. Everyone is inhibited because of the social norms within which we live, especially in our cities. Each of us suffers from the results of inhibition of one kind or another.

We repeat this on the emotional and on the mental level. The inhibitions on the mental level are very severe indeed; they lead us to become fundamentalist Christian, fundamentalist Jew, Muslim, Hindu, Buddhist, etc. These are mental straightjackets. They inhibit the free, thinking process of the mind. We cannot think creatively because it has all been thought for us. We are given a set of ideas, of beliefs, to believe in.

The same is true of the emotional body. We are taught not to show all these negative emotions. We know that they are not nice, and we are brought up to be nice; every little boy and girl has to be nice. So we learn a mechanism to keep all our bad, naughty thoughts in place. We do it by tensing the muscles. First of all, we tense the muscles of the solar plexus. Once we have got them really tight and hard, the rest take care of themselves. There is a group of muscles in the chest which inhibits our breathing, because we find that, if we breathe freely and easily, our ideas and gestures and feelings also come freely and easily, and we become dangerously spontaneous, a very dangerous thing to be, we have found, in the normal world among our parents and their friends.

Psychoses and neuroses are the result of inhibition of the life functions. Some of them are brought over from a previous life, and that is tricky, because you cannot go back to your therapist of 200 years ago.

All of that, of course, is to do with psychosis/neurosis, not with growth of consciousness or soul experience. There is all the difference in the world. They do not add anything to, but take away from, your life.

Inhibition, physical, emotional and mental, brings about a contraction of the life function. This can be so severe that we do, literally, end up on the psychotherapist's couch. We need the psychotherapist, or his pills or whatever he has to give us, to help us through that crisis. We all put ourselves, or have been put through, this inhibitory process, and we put our children through it. It takes a great deal of insight not to pass it on.

Where does the subconscious fit into all this?
I would say that, with most people, nine-tenths of our activity, emotional and mental, is subconscious. Certainly our emotional consciousness is nine-tenths subconscious, below the threshold of consciousness. It has its influence, and we can become aware of it from time to time, but if the emotions are painful, we tend to suppress them. They become subconscious. There are many fears which are inhibited. As soon as we inhibit something, we can push it down so far that it goes below the threshold of consciousness.

The psychotherapist has to get his pick and shovel out and try to bring up from these subconscious levels all those fears, inhibitions, hurts and so on. Sometimes they will come to the top, and then we get the fears all over again; we get a panic attack. We get over that, and the fears subside. They are still there, but they subside, until something else comes up — perhaps all the anger that we have repressed — and suddenly we get an angry, manic phase, and go around kicking everybody who has a moustache. We cannot keep everything down for ever, so it comes up from time to time.

This is the result, of course, in psychoanalytic terms, of keeping it all locked away, under the threshold of consciousness. The aim of the therapeutic, psychoanalytical process, is to bring it up into consciousness. As soon as we realize that we really wanted to stab our father in the back, we are free of that. (That is what they say. We go on wanting to stab our father forever, as far as I can make out.) The theory is that we bring that repressed intention, fear, or whatever, up into consciousness and it disappears. It would, if we *realized* it. Unfortunately, just bringing a thing up into memory and realizing it, in the sense of experiencing it as the 'not-you', detaching from it, are two different things. Just to bring the idea, the event, up into memory satisfies the therapist (he might be sorry because you are not going to pay him any more) but it satisfies him; he has done his job, but we are just the same, unless we go through what we have to go through every day, the process of detaching.

It is no different whether it was in the past or is happening now. We cannot deal with a negative emotion, either now or from infancy, on the psychiatrist's couch, unless we detach from it, either now, moment to moment as it is occurring, or having dredged it up from our subconscious. If it is in the past, of course, it is more difficult, because certainly we have to bring it up, but we will find that, as we detach, we become freer; we open up again the spontaneity of the emotional body.

To a greater or lesser extent, our conscious mind is fragmented into the subconscious; it is partly conscious and partly subconscious. It is all mixed together, and we do not know which it is. The therapist knows even less which it is. (Why we pay him, I do not know.)

If we detach, moment to moment, from negative emotions, consciously, every day, watching oneself, watching our experience, realizing that that negativity is not us, detaching and detaching, we free the subconscious inhibited desires and can resolve them.

This is the experience of the advancing disciple. He thinks: "I am so changed, I am so clear, I am no longer the same haunted person full of fears and inhibitions. I am living, I am breathing, like I never could before." Suddenly, something triggers it, and the whole thing starts all over again, because it is all there. Every time it happens, it is easier for it to happen again, and every disciple knows this experience, of reliving what we thought we had finished with long before. He thinks: "I am on the verge of the second initiation. I am sure I am in control. I do not feel anything. These people are hammering at me and they do not make me angry, they do not upset me, I am above it all, everything is clear, simple." They are walking on air. It is all glamour, of course; the glamour of the semi-clear, semi-free state.

This sense of being free is very short-lived, until this poor wretch, who thought he was on the verge of the second initiation realizes, he is not yet mentally polarized, so how could he stand before the Initiator?

It is an ongoing process, and once started has its own momentum. Just as we reach the Great Renunciation by an accumulation of small renunciations, so we find, in overcoming these repressed emotions, hurts, all the terrible things that people go around with all the time, that they come up over and over again, but each time we are able to deal with them more easily. Every time it happens we are freer, stronger because we are loosening these desire-principled fears and inhibitions. Then we grow into an inner calm, an inner awareness, a really conscious awareness.

The Nervous System

Are there physiologically things we can do to enhance the relationship between the soul and the nervous system?

You can always strengthen the nervous system. Of course, the stronger the nervous system, the more potently the soul can use it as its mechanism through the three vehicles. I do not want to carry this too far. Some of the greatest initiates of the recent past: people like Alice Bailey, H.P.Blavatsky, Helena Roerich — I do not know about Helena Roerich, but certainly Alice Bailey and H.P.Blavatsky — had very ill bodies. They suffered extremely. Alice Bailey was ill for 30 years. HPB was ill with kidney disease for the last 13 years of her life. Therefore, their nervous systems from a physical point of view could not have been perfect but their souls worked pretty well through their vehicles because they were advanced enough. They were both soul-infused individuals; Helena Roerich too, although I do not know if she had any illnesses or not. So, I do not want to carry this too far, but obviously, whatever you do to strengthen the physical body and its apparatus makes it easier for the soul to use it.

In regard to the nervous system, is it more important between the first two initiations than later in looking after it, protecting it and so on?

Yes and no. A third- or higher-degree initiate can do things to his or her physical body which a lesser degree cannot do with impunity, especially a first degree. The first-degree initiate takes the first initiation to prove control over the physical body, therefore a great deal of the attention of a person coming up to the first initiation is concerned with the body: strengthening it, therefore strengthening the nervous system. Anything that promotes health and well-being and therefore correct flow of energy in the physical body and nervous system will be along the evolutionary path. It will aid in creating a body which can stand the inflow of the energy from the Rod of Initiation. If the body is too weak, that cannot be done even if the person is ready. You need a body which is relatively free from disease and has a good strong nervous system to stand the strain before initiation can be taken. On the whole, the soul sees to that. The soul brings the person into the kind of disciplines that strengthen the physical body. That is why so many people become vegetarians, for example — why they stop drinking, if they have drunk, stop smoking, if they smoke, and so on. Later, you can do what you like, but at that point all these are out.

Since the nervous system provides the link between the soul and its vehicles, what can we do to strengthen our nervous system?
Certainly take Vitamin B, but that is not the answer. The thing is, do not misuse your nervous system. Get enough, but not too much, sleep. Avoid stress. That is, learn to relax. Stress is the effect of our crazy life patterns on our nervous systems. Do not take drugs, hallucinogenic or any other type of drug. People think that cannabis is a safe drug to use. It is just as harmful. It takes longer to do the harm and the harm is less measurable, but the effect on the nervous system is profound. The hallucinogenic drugs have a very stimulating effect on the nervous system and then, inevitably, the misuse of the system causes it more or less to collapse. That is what has happened with drug addicts who have gone 'over the top'. Their nervous system is, if not destroyed, at least severely harmed. Also drugs like aspirin have a bad effect on the nervous system. There is probably no drug, *per se*, which does not affect the nervous system somehow or other. Of course, some are more

and some less harmful. In life you have to balance. If you have to take a drug to ameliorate a certain condition, you have to weigh that against the effect that that has on the nervous system. You strike a balance. Sometimes, to save the life process, keep the person in the body, you may have to use a drug and that will affect the nervous system to some extent.

The nervous system is a highly sensitive instrument through which all the messages from all levels, from the soul down, reach the brain; so everything we do, every polluted breath of air we take, affects it. Our polluted water, polluted vegetables filled with DDT and the rest, that has a very bad effect. Many of the illnesses arising now in the world, the viruses which result from this disturbance, are profoundly affecting the nervous system of humanity. Coffee is very bad for the nervous system. This country (the USA) lives on coffee. Luckily, you do not know how to make it! If you drank as much coffee as you do the way Italians drink it, you would be worse off than you are! I think possibly one of the reasons why, in America, during a Transmission Meditation, no one can sit still for more than a few minutes is because you drink so much coffee. Coffee is very much a stimulant, and anything that over-stimulates the nervous system can only be to our detriment in the long run.

If someone has used psychedelic drugs in the past, like in the 1960s when a lot of people used them, what kind of damage was done to his system? Is there a healing?
Often the whole system is so disrupted that in a sense their incarnation is lost, wasted. The person might go on living but from the soul's point of view it cannot really stimulate its vehicle. This is the extreme. Also, there is healing. Maitreya can revivify a system; and the person, by becoming aware of the Self, can do the same thing. Becoming aware of the Self brings in energy from the Self, from the Monadic level through the soul. This can be so powerful as completely to regenerate the system. The Masters, however, do not look on death in the same way as we do. It is only temporary.

You have said before that a small amount of alcohol is OK.

That remains true. A small amount. But it is so small it is hardly worth drinking! A small amount of alcohol is a tonic. Anything more than a small amount is harmful to the nervous system. Again, you have to weigh it up. Which is more important — the effect of the alcohol or your nervous system? You have to take a long-term view of this.

What kinds of things harm the nadis and what can we do to restore them?
Above all, drugs and stress. Stress is the result of the nervous system being overstimulated and attacked from all sides. It is the effect on our nervous system of our neurotic way of life. We have to learn to relax and go with life instead of resisting it. Many people resist the impact of life. The thing to do is go with it: for example, if you are walking along the street and the noise is deafening and you resist it and are aware of it all the time, you become stressed; if, on the other hand, you go with it and allow the noise to be, aware of the noise but without resisting it, you find that suddenly you relax and noise is not having the powerful effect — which it normally would have — on the etheric body and therefore on the nervous system. It is the same in every situation which would normally cause you stress through emotional reaction — look at it and do not resist it and do not try to change it. Just look at it. Do not swallow and ask yourself to bear it; but do not, on the other hand, try to get rid of it. Just look at it, allowing it to happen without reacting to it, detaching yourself from it. Whatever you can detach from does you no harm. That is the thing about detachment. Try to be detached from these reactions to outer stimuli of that harmful kind. Noise is one of the major sources of stress and therefore of fatigue.

Why did the Master choose to emphasize the importance of the nervous system in the growth of consciousness at this time?
It is not at this time any more than another time. Perhaps he thought it was high time people understood the connection between the soul and its mechanism. Read Alice Bailey, *The Soul and Its Mechanism* — very illuminating, probably, in answering that question.

How is it related to the Reappearance work and/or the special emphasis on making Maitreya's presence known at this time?
Anything that increases your conscious awareness will help you in making known the Reappearance, obviously. Develop the intuition, develop your intelligence, your skill in action, your objectivity, your detachment. All of that helps in making known the Reappearance.

Telepathy

What is the difference between telepathy as known to the Masters and what most people call telepathy?
There is really no difference except that what most people experience of telepathy is haphazard. It is an emotional-astral response, through the solar plexus, one which we share with the animal kingdom, and one over which people have no control; it just happens. A mother often has a close, telepathic contact with her child: if something is harming the child, the mother will know.

Telepathy as described by the Master and as known and used by Hierarchy is of the same nature but of an altogether different order. It takes place on the higher mental planes and uses the mind-belt as medium. Our mind is an instrument or vehicle which tunes in to that mind-belt and extracts from it all the mental impressions and experiences that we have. The Masters do not use speech. They might if They came before a disciple physically but the normal way for a Master is by telepathic contact. The Masters have group consciousness, so Their telepathic contact with each other is complete.

Telepathy is really one aspect of the total contact experience of humanity which can be on many different levels, all of which come under the heading of telepathy. It might be simply the haphazard emotional response which a mother might have with a child, or a husband with wife; people who know each other very well, who live together, develop this kind of emotional contacting instrument, using the solar plexus.

On the mental plane it has to be trained. The Masters train Their disciples in telepathy and form, if necessary, a telepathic link, if the disciple has that ability. We all have it potentially, but a disciple who already has the ability can be contacted. This faculty can be developed, trained, and becomes a powerful instrument of contact. Of course it saves the Master from having to visit a disciple and make an actual verbal contact. He can just flash an impression or a thought and He knows that the disciple, either there and then, or later as it filters down into the brain consciousness, will carry out the Master's wishes.

The impression or instruction flows from the mind of the Master to the mind of the disciple through the medium of the mind-belt and thence to the brain. The brain registers it and changes it into the spoken thought. If you are English, you hear it in English; if Dutch, in Dutch, if French, in French , and so on. This is conscious, trained telepathy on the mental plane.

As soon as your aura becomes magnetic, which it does through the process of evolution, telepathy opens up. It is natural. You simply become telepathic. The innate telepathic faculty of humanity shifts from the astral to the mental plane (where it should reside). As you become magnetic, you develop an aura which is like radar and you can be either 'radar-ically' telepathic or mentally telepathic. Your telepathic impressions can come through every part of your aura or into the mind from the mental planes. It depends on your type.

You say telepathy naturally opens up when one's aura becomes magnetic. When will one's aura become magnetic?
When we have developed the vibration of the different vehicles, physical, astral and mental, and they are vibrating synchronously, the effect of this in the aura is radiation. It radiates light. When this radiation has reached a certain degree, the aura becomes magnetic. It attracts. Then the aura attracts whatever thoughtforms are being projected to it, because telepathy takes place through thought. The thought of the Master, for example, can become the thought of the disciple. Eventually, humanity will develop its innate telepathy when

we realize that there is a mind-belt which reaches everywhere and which is the basis for communication from one planet to another. The Masters of our Hierarchy are in constant contact with the Masters on Venus and Mars , and so on. The mind-belt is the common denominator on which all thought can be carried. It is the conduit for the transference of thought even from one solar system to another.

Is it not more difficult to make contact at such distances?
For the Masters, no. The Masters work on the soul level. All of this, for its development, requires mental polarization. If there is soul polarization as well, it is much easier because the Masters work on the buddhic plane all the time. My Master gives me His article for *Share International*, for example, from the buddhic plane and so I have to focus on the buddhic plane to take it. But He can bring it right down until He is thundering in my ear, so to speak. That is because of the moment-to-moment focus. If you are polarized there, for the Masters, you are working on the same level. It all takes place on the soul level. Telepathy is the natural means of contact from soul to soul. The buddhic level includes the higher mind or manas (at the manasic level) below it. So the Master can bring the thought down to the manasic level but He would normally, contacting another Master, use the buddhic level.

Can our groups do anything to develop and enhance our facility with telepathy and the mind-belt; specifically in relation to the Reappearance work?
You can develop telepathy because it is already there. In the early days of the London group, some of the people would set up experiments in developing their telepathic ability. They would agree between themselves that — at a certain time — one of them would concentrate and visualize a certain thoughtform, a silver disk on a yellow ground or a letter 'A' or a boat or something like that. The other one would tune in and try to apprehend that thoughtform. Apparently they had quite a large degree of success.

You can develop telepathy by experimentation. The thing is to focus on the ajna centre and send the message from there to the throat centre of the other person. The person receives it through the throat centre and it goes from there to the brain and becomes the image or the thought. But always make it very simple: a few words, not a long sentence. That is difficult. Images are easier to convey, but we are aware of images so often that you may miss them. If you concentrate too hard you will block it. A relaxed, nonchalant state of mind is necessary. The thing is to be aware without pushing it. Do not strain.

It is easy, if you strain too much, to give yourself false messages. It is easy, if you are too tense, to miss the whole thing. You have to be absolutely nonchalant, but aware, with an uncaring, relaxed but very positive awareness. It is being aware without trying. Then you will find the message or the image will just float into your consciousness without any effort at all. It is a natural faculty we all have.

When you are sending, visualize the other person. Just visualize them and send it from the ajna to the throat chakra and they should receive it. You send it from the ajna and they receive it through the throat.

Is it necessary to do this as a kind of practice, since people in this network do tend to tune into the same thoughtform and they all start having the same idea, more or less at the same time around the world?
It simply improves the system. If you practise it individually you will find that you can do it and that is encouraging. It is encouraging to know that you are telepathic. It is natural. It can be mental telepathy, not instinctual solar-plexus telepathy which everybody has, even dogs and cats. This conscious mental telepathy is very useful if you want to send a message and the post has gone!

Energy and Thought

How does energy follow thought?
All is energy. Thought itself is energy. Thought is really energy directed. It is focused and directed and therefore can have an effect on a less focused area of energy. Wherever you place your attention, your energy will follow. This is one of the

basic occult axioms. That is how worlds come into being. "In the beginning was the Word. The Word was with God. And the Word was God." God sounded the Word and all things came to be. That is focused thought. The Word is focused thought.

When a Master wishes to create a pool of energy, a power centre, He might use a rod; They have rods of power. Or He might use a combination of that and a mantram. The mantram focuses, charges, the thought and makes it into an instrument to activate centres of energy. Of course, He uses His creative imagination to do this. He probably does it in seconds. He visualizes it, activates it, and usually has a host of devas to keep it energized afterwards. All of that is done by thought.

One day, according to my Master, we will create factories filled with instruments made by thought, and the information in them will be organized by thought. Just as we programme a computer we can programme a robot or other instrument by thought. Whatever we can do on the physical plane we can do by thought. We will create these instruments and programme them by thought to create all the artefacts we need to live by: chairs, tables, etc. All things will eventually be made in this way.

You can see how powerful thought can be when it is focused. Energy is everywhere and thought is simply that same energy but focused by a mind. By the focused power of the mind, it is given an intensity and a vitality to create something or to move or lift an object.

Wherever you put your attention or your thoughts, the energy will flow. Make an experiment. Think of your right foot. Put your attention on your right foot and you will find it is charged with energy. It will vibrate in a way you did not notice before you put your thought there. Now withdraw it from your foot and put it on your left elbow. As you do this you will find that your left elbow will begin to vibrate. It will heat up. Do it now and you will see. Wherever you put your attention, your energy will flow. It is a law, a basic occult axiom that never fails. You see how important thought is and how important it is to gain control of thought.

How can we implement this process in practical life?
That is up to you, the implementation. The implications, of course, are obvious and enormous. Thought is a weapon, for good or for ill. We can create by thought and we can destroy by thought. This is why every book coming from the Masters has the injunction of harmlessness. Wrong thought is harmful, destructive thought, critical thought. We all indulge in it, of course, but that is why it is so harmful. The more powerful the wrong thought, the more destructive it is. So we must learn to control our thoughts and to be non-critical, which is very difficult. Some people find it easier than others. Some people are just nice and uncritical. Others work so much from the mental plane that they are very critical.

Which ray types are the most critical?
Fifth-ray types are very critical, as are 1st-ray types. I have found 6th-ray types to be either very critical or very uncritical, depending on the individual. Third-ray types are extremely critical. I think the worst are the 5th and the 1st. The least critical is the 2nd-ray type of mind.

Since energy cannot be destroyed, what eventually happens to all these thoughtforms?
We are responsible for every thoughtform that we have ever created. There comes a time before we can become a Master when we must take back into ourselves all these thoughtforms. Every destructive thoughtform we ever created in our long series of lives has to be taken back in and resolved. Otherwise we cannot take the ultimate fifth initiation. In every life we have created incredibly destructive thoughtforms. They have built a heavy burden of karma. The 'Dweller on the Threshold' is the result of those thoughtforms. That weight keeps us back. We have, eventually, to re-absorb and nullify these destructive thoughtforms, to stop making more destructive thoughtforms by detaching ourselves from wrong emotional response, wrong mental attitudes.

Can you give examples of wrong mental attitudes?

Prejudice is a wrong mental attitude. Why is it wrong? Because it is separative. It is non-inclusive. It is taking our own little separate view of life as the whole. It is judgmental. These restrict conscious awareness. We cannot be conscious of what is if our mind is filled with prejudice. If every black man is to us less than human, how are we going to cope with our next incarnation as a black man? If, for us, every Jew is a Shylock, how are we ever going to come into correct relationship with Jewry? Or cope with being a Jew in our next life? These are simply prejudices which block the flow of awareness — and we all have them.

These are the obvious racist ones, but there are thousands of others. The fundamentalist Christians have a prejudiced view about Maitreya: they think He is the Antichrist. That prevents their awareness that the Christ is in the world. It will probably prevent many of them from recognizing Him when they see Him on the Day of Declaration.

We cannot be blocked and prejudiced, and therefore unfree, and be free. We are either free or not free. If we are prejudiced in any way at all, and if we clutter our minds with these *a priori* conceptions of life which have nothing to do with our experience of life, but are simply conditioning (and it is conditioning above all which prevents conscious awareness), we have to get rid of our conditioning. The way to do that is to detach from it. Detach from that which, up until now — in every respect, physical, astral and mental — we have taken for granted. It is so taken for granted, so much part of us. Conditioning is like our skin. It is close to us, part of us. We do not even recognize it as conditioning. We have to become aware of what conditioning is in the first place. That is how we get through the glamours.

Glamours are the result of conditioning. While we are in the fog of the illusions, the glamours, we do not even see them as glamours. But as we do Transmission Meditation we become more and more mentally polarized. Then the light of the soul, through the mind, can throw its light on the glamour and reveal it as the conditioning which it is. We become aware. Awareness is the result of going back to a less conditioned state. The only truly unconditioned, free, state is Self-realization. So, the first step is the detaching process. That leads to greater awareness and, eventually, to Self-realization.

What activities will increase sensitivity to Transmission energy? What activities will decrease sensitivity?
An activity which will increase sensitivity to Transmission energy is to do more of it. Obviously. The more you transmit, within reason, the better you will be at doing it. But you have to do it in a particular frame of mind. You cannot do it as if it does not matter how you do it. You have to do it seriously. When you are sitting still, sit still. If you are making a noise, even to yourself, how can you be focusing? When you are getting up and stretching all the time, when you are chatting, when you are moving about, or having a cup of coffee and so on: all of that disrupts the concentration.

You think it helps you, but all it helps is the body. The body has nothing to do with it! The body will do whatever you make it do. If you make it sit still for three hours, it will sit still for three hours. If you make it keep up straight, then that is what it will do. If it is sitting on the most uncomfortable chair it will still do it if that is what you make it do. But so long as you are conscious of the discomfort, you will take all steps to get rid of that discomfort — and will not be transmitting. Transmission only takes place when your attention is held at the ajna centre. That forms the link, the alignment between the physical brain and the soul. As you know, it is from the soul planes that these energies flow. You have to learn to hold your attention there all the time. And take it seriously.

To improve our service during Transmission Meditation is there an instrument which could be made to measure soul/brain alignment similar to a biofeedback machine?
You could use a biofeedback machine. It is not worthwhile. It is so easy to know whether you are aligned or not. Where is your attention? If your attention is at the ajna you are aligned. If the energy is flowing through you, you are aligned. But as soon as your attention is down at the solar plexus you will realize the energy is not flowing through you because you are

not aligned. You do not have to build a machine to measure it. Someone else, a scientist, might be interested in testing in a Transmission group what is happening to the brain patterns of the individuals involved, but for the groups themselves to construct machines to test whether they are aligned, no.

Does the global Transmission Meditation Network function within humanity in a way similar to the nervous system within a human being?
That is an interesting question. There is a relationship there. The global Transmission Network allows the energy from the Masters to travel throughout the world and feed not only the individuals taking part in it, but humanity in general, with this spiritual nourishment. That energy might be to stop a war in a particular country, but it might also be to top up the bank or pool of spiritual energy in the world.

The energy coming through us in Transmission groups is utilized above all by the New Group of World Servers. It is they who, responding to that energy, make the changes in the political, economic, religious and social structures. So what we are really doing is acting as a sub-station for the energy of Hierarchy to stimulate, galvanize and keep nourished the New Group of World Servers, who are several millions strong in the world and in every country. So, yes, there is an analogy between these two.

Are the light triangles between us macro-cosmic to the nerve ganglia within us?
Do not carry it too far! It is not quite as straightforward as that, but there is an analogy and the mechanism is very similar. The nerve ganglia are the means by which the gases from the soul can penetrate right down to the physical plane, going through the mental and the astral planes, permeating the whole of that threefold system with the energy of the soul. This is the way in which the soul grips its vehicle. You could say that the worldwide network of light, created by the Transmission Meditation Network (among others), is doing a similar thing for humanity. The analogy is certainly there.

How can we utilize this information better and what are we not doing presently to do this?

Think about it more, put it into action more, take it more seriously, study it more, go back to the books more, read it over and over, listen to the tapes. *Put it into practice.* Whatever we hear does us no good at all — it can be the most wonderful words of wisdom and truth coming from the most exalted Master — unless we make it part of our life. We have to make it our own. It is only valuable if it awakens something in us, if it throws light. Otherwise it is just words. But if we can respond to those words, actually put them into effect in our life, then we change. That is the value. The value does not lie in the words, in a book or a tape.

This is being called information, but it is not information. It is stimulus. People take everything as information. I think this is a product of the 5th-ray tendency at the moment throughout the world. We are in a period in which we have been given a very short but very intense 5th-ray stimulus. The ray was brought in late last [19th] century for a short period and it has produced two things: a healthy scepticism of mysticism, the mystic approach to life which has saturated life for the last 2,000 years of Christendom. It has focused attention on the area in which the 5th-ray mind can best work: the physical plane. The concrete mind can work on the concrete plane. At the same time it has closed off certain areas of experience. What has resulted is that information, which the 5th-ray mind loves and the 5th ray in general is good at conveying, is taken for life, for experience. But it is not experience. It may be information about the nature of reality but reality has to be experienced. It is through conscious awareness that you experience life, not through information.

Everywhere I go, people are greedy for more information; more tools, more techniques. All the tools, all the techniques are at their finger tips. They have more than enough. What is missing is the experience, the ability to take even a little bit of information that will guide one to putting that information into effect in an experiential way. Because information is only a conveying of information, it is not experience. We cannot convey experience. We can only experience experience. Information can only guide us in that direction, throw some light and thus awaken the intellect and the intuition. Conscious awareness comes from the soul plane. It is the nature of the soul, and the more detached you can become, the more that conscious awareness becomes you. The more your intuition functions the less information you need.

Aspiration and Imagination

What is the difference between ambition and aspiration in the day-to-day life of the disciple?

Ambition is attachment to a desired result. Ambition is always related to the personal self. It is gain for the personal ego. The personal, separated, ego is the one who is ambitious, who wants to be better, to be better at this, to be recognized as that, to achieve the other. Being ambitious makes one competitive. There is even such a thing as spiritual ambition. Spiritual ambition is a glamour. To want to be a Master is a glamour. To want to make tremendously fast spiritual progress is a glamour. To do it is not a glamour, but to want to do it is a glamour. It always relates to the separated self.

Aspiration, on the other hand, coming as it does from the soul, is always altruistic, towards betterment for the world: peace, justice, closer relationship to the soul. Aspiration is what drives us onwards and upwards. I think we know instinctively the difference between separate, individualistic ambition and a truly aspiring attitude. That attitude should be one of simplicity, and a recognition of the spiritual nature of life. That is what we are aspiring towards, a greater experience, consciously, of the spiritual nature of life.

Some people see it in religious terms. They want to know God better, to go to church more often, and there is nothing wrong with that. They experience there an inner stillness, an inner concentration of silence, of Beingness, which is God. That you can experience anywhere, you do not have to go to church. Aspiration is a word for the tendency of all evolving beings to become what we essentially are, which is God.

417

Ambition is desire for a result and attachment to achieving that result. Aspiration is not desire at all. It is a response to a pull from above. That pull is the nature of life itself and it draws all creatures. It draws all humanity up towards what we are as souls: divine Beings, absolutely perfect reflections of God.

The soul has its seat in the body in a chakra at the right side of the chest. This is what gives the feeling we call aspiration. Aspiration can be on different levels, of course — mixed. In an emotionally polarized individual, it will be somewhat of an astral nature and therefore impure in that sense. Not impure in any derogatory sense, but impure in that it will be mixed. It will be both personal and impersonal. You can feel the difference. Where is it coming from? Is it coming from the solar plexus? Or is it coming from the heart chakra? There is a difference, you can feel it. If you feel it at the right side of the chest, it is aspiration. If you feel it at the solar plexus, it is emotional aspiration which will be, to some degree, glamour. But that is only a stage. Then we find that it will shift and it will be mixed. There will be a mixture of astral and heart response to the need of the world. And then we find that it will dwell in the heart only.

Does this aspiration exist in the animal kingdom?
Yes indeed, it is precisely aspiration which drew the early animal forms out of the sea on to dry land and the mammals began their evolution. Everything evolves in answer to the call of life from above. That we call aspiration. It is a growing awareness of what can be even if we have not created a thoughtform of it; we have a sense, every kingdom has a sense, that above it is something greater, something vaster, truer, more perfect. The response to that inner sense we call aspiration. In the animal kingdom there is nothing conscious about it. It works by instinct. Every kingdom has this instinctual aspiration — because it is the soul which incarnates in all forms.

What is the difference between creative and astral imagination?

There is all the difference in the world between the creative imagination and astral imagination, but often people do not recognize the difference; because, if we are astrally polarized, there is no difference; our creative imagination *is*, then, our astral imagination. Of course, there are many people who are astrally polarized, whose imagination is astral, but who, to some degree, achieve true creative imagination. Creative imagination comes from the soul; astral imagination from the solar plexus. I do not mean that the soul has nothing to do with the solar plexus, but there is a yard or two of difference. The soul stimulates the astral nature, too, and this is one of the problems for disciples, being stimulated on physical, astral and mental levels, all at the same time.

The creative imagination, stemming from the soul, brings into play the will. We invoke the will in this way. We aspire. The Christ Principle, the consciousness of the soul, *per se*, inspires us to aspire. We evoke from the soul through our meditation, our service, our creative work in whatever field, an aspiration for something higher, finer. We use the creative imagination if we are creative at all. Whatever the concept, it requires the creative imagination to put it into form, a structure. That invokes the energy of the soul to bring it about.

The creative imagination uses the antahkarana, the channel of light between oneself and the soul, and as we use it we create it. As we create it, we can use it. It is a two-way process. This brings in the light, the consciousness, of the soul, the aspiration which inspires us to see something that we do not yet see.

There is an occult statement: "And in that light will you see light." In the light of the soul, we can see a higher light, a brighter, a more dynamic, a more creative light. Everything we receive from the soul fulfils the immediate need, the point that we have reached. But in receiving at the level where we are, we also receive from the soul the intuition that above it there is something else. In the light of the soul we see a further light. Through aspiration, the soul gives us the awareness of something higher even than itself.

419

We talk about the creative people who make the culture of a society: the painters, musicians, writers, singers, politicians (one or two), educators, scientists. Those who use creative imagination in their work do so because they are disciples. The culture of any civilization is always created by the disciples and initiates of the time. This leads eventually to the creation of a civilization based on that culture. The civilization comes out of the culture which is made by the creative imagination of the initiates and disciples of a given time and nation.

Self-Realization

Do the Masters teach you to become initiate?
The path of initiation is self-initiated. No one is doing it for you. Not because no one would like to, but because no one can. You have to do it yourself. Only if you do it yourself is it yours. No one can live your life for you. No one can tread your path of initiation. You cannot become a Master if all the time you are being spoon-fed. You are just thrown in and left to yourself. If you are lucky you might get a little hint now and again to guide your path a bit. But these are only hints, impressions.

People imagine that you have a notebook and the Master gives you answers to your questions (well, He might for *Share International*) — personal questions about your evolution and so on. It is not like that at all. The Master is not telling you to do this or that or the other. There are books written by Masters which, if sensitively read and understood as being broad and general in principle, and not individualized, can be extremely helpful. When they are taken as gospel which you have to apply to whomever and wherever you are, then it is a misuse of the information. The information has really to be sought by yourself through your day-to-day experience. That can only happen if you do it, if you set yourself to become more aware. Nobody can teach you. You can use the mantram of the Prayer for the New Age given by Maitreya to develop an awareness of the Self. The awareness of the Self is conscious awareness.

There seem to be two opposite ways of describing Self-realization: a gradual process of evolution, and instantaneous enlightenment. Many Avatars refer to the possibility of realizing oneself in this life, and other teachings speak of stages. What is the truth of it?

There can be both gradual Self-realization in stages and instantaneous Self-realization. In effect there is only instantaneous Self-realization, but it is the end-product of a series of stages. There is partial realization. Self-realization begins with Self-awareness. We cannot realize the Self if we are unaware of the Self. And we cannot be aware of the Self if we are only aware of the vehicles of the Self. If our awareness and identification is with the vehicles, the physical, astral and mental bodies, then we are not aware of the Self. But if we can get through this barrier and end this identification with the vehicles, detach ourselves from that, there begins the growth of awareness of the Self.

There are ways to enhance that, there are meditations which are given; they help in the growing awareness of the Self. Some awareness of the Self leads to greater awareness, because in growth, in evolution, there are always degrees. When an Avatar talks about 'moksha' — liberation, release, Self-realization — in this life, it means that in this life you have reached a point of readiness for Self-realization. That would mean you were a fourth-degree initiate, of whom there are only 450 in incarnation.

This is the problem with Avatars: they never say what they mean, or they never really underline it. They say it in such broad, simplistic terms that the poor, simple devotee thinks that he means it literally — that the first-degree initiate can suddenly become a God-realized Master. It is not possible. This can only be done in stages. But if you are on the very point of becoming a Self-realized Master, in one life that is what happens, you become a Self-realized Master. The Avatar was right, you can gain it in this life.

There are many degrees of awareness. A child is aware of the Self. A baby of a few months old, lying in its cot, chuckling to itself, looking around, watching the sky, the trees, can be totally, moment to moment, aware of itself as the Self, but he cannot tell us anything about it. As soon as he grows to a certain age, he will have forgotten it. It pertains only to babies. Only if we get back to being a child would we have that awareness. We can only get to that readiness when we detach from all our conditioning. Then in this life, if we work on ourselves, physically, astrally, mentally, on our conditioning, that age-old conditioning which inhibits our spontaneous response to who we are, as a baby is doing lying in the cot, we could know Self-realization in this life. The reason that we do not do it, or almost no one does it, is because our conditioning prevents us. While we are attached to the body we are attached to the conditioning, attached to our feelings, our diseases, our memory, our ideas. We are either aware of ourselves as the self, with a small 's', or aware of ourselves as the Self with a big 'S'. It is one or the other.

The Avatars are right. We can know, instantly, in this life, Self-realization. But almost no one can do it, because it means being free of all that conditioning. That is the hard thing; we have to do it by stages. By stages, we grow in awareness of the Self. But if, by some blessed chance, we were the kind of person who could break through the conditioning, break through all these glamours and illusions and gain total detachment, we would realize the Self in this life. Theoretically, it can happen at any moment, but in practice does not.

CHAPTER 13

THE SEVEN RAYS

Rays

*This chapter has been compiled from articles which appeared in **Share International**, along with questions from the magazine's Questions and Answers section. Included are edited transcriptions of discussions on the rays by members of a London study group led by Benjamin Creme. For further elucidation, readers are referred to the Alice Bailey teachings and **Maitreya's Mission, Volume One**.*

The 1st Ray

The Ray of Will or Power

The 1st ray demonstrates largely through government and has to do with purpose, power and will. Many people equate the 1st ray only with dictatorial types of government and the 2nd ray with democratic types, but this is not the case. There are many exponents of 1st ray working in 2nd-ray democracies — Winston Churchill is a good example. He was a very powerful 1st-ray type with three 1st rays in his ray structure. In fact, 1st-ray power can be used in different ways — authoritarian, democratic, totalitarian, dictatorial.

DK says that the 1st ray governs the cycle of initiation, whereas the 2nd ray governs discipleship. This 1st-ray focus on the initiatory process relates to the need of the 1st ray to work through initiates. So one of the objectives of Hierarchy seems to be to bring increasing numbers of human units under the influence of the 1st ray on the path of initiation thereby enabling it to come again into a cycle of incarnation. This is made possible by the number of people in the world who are able to respond to its influence. If the 1st ray were in incarnation without this group of initiates to work through, would the effects be very destructive?

Yes, that is the whole point. The 1st ray is a very destructive ray unless it is working through disciples who are already in control of themselves. An initiate will exhibit a degree of control, wisdom and love which broadens the base of the 1st ray. Otherwise, it only expresses itself on the personality, not the soul, level.

According to DK, in 100 years 1st-ray force will begin to manifest on the astral plane, and then 1,000 years hence will begin to influence the physical plane. What effects will demonstrate?

You can imagine the effect on the astral plane. The 1st ray will have a very destructive effect on the astral thoughtforms of man. In fact, DK talks about the presence on the astral plane of three very powerful 1st-ray exponents from Shamballa whose work is the destruction of thoughtforms preparatory to the Reappearance of the Christ. They have been very active for the last 40 years. Their work is to release humanity from a great fog of glamour or illusion.

Are there certain rays only given at a certain point in evolution?

Yes, this is true for the 1st ray and the 5th ray. There is no point in giving a very unadvanced person the 5th ray — he would not know what to do with it. Once a person can make use of the mind, he can utilize the qualities of mind which the 5th ray confers, or alternatively, the global vision and power of the 1st ray.

One interesting example of the 1st-ray quality of brooking no opposition is Helen Keller. She had a 1st-ray soul and personality by which she overcame the incredible frustration of being without the faculties of hearing, sight or speech. She was able to express her 1st-ray talents in the world by teaching other handicapped people.

Yes, she epitomized the 1st ray and made a great impact on the world despite what to most of us would be insurmountable obstacles. The 1st ray does not just overcome obstacles; typically, it does not see opposition, but sweeps over it in the drive towards fulfilling its broad vision.

Does the 1st ray only come into planetary incarnation in order to initiate a particular cycle or to end one?
Yes. It is an initiator or a destroyer of the age. It is the Shiva force. The 1st ray is the only ray today that is entirely out of incarnation, working only behind the scenes.

If the 1st ray is not in incarnation at present, how then is it being released into the world?
Since 1975, the 1st ray, or Will-to-Good which is the highest aspect of the 1st ray, has been released directly into the world by the Christ without going through Hierarchy. Normally, 1st-ray energy from Shamballa would be stepped down and diluted to make it easier for the world to cope with. At the same time, since 1942, the energy of the Avatar of Synthesis has been released through the Christ. This is also 1st-ray energy, but is a synthesis of will, love, intelligence and another aspect for which we do not yet have a name. It is 'the principle of directed purpose'. These two 1st-ray energies are released consecutively for a period every year. The Shamballa force can be destructive but is also immensely galvanizing. This is released by the Christ in a blend with other rays (4 and 7) and also with the energy of the Spirit of Peace or Equilibrium. The 1st ray of the Avatar of Synthesis is slower in action, but safer, and is released for the remainder of the year till the Wesak Festival. Then the Buddha again brings the Shamballa force for the Christ to distribute.

It is difficult for people with 2nd-ray natures to come to terms with the destructive aspect of the 1st ray. To them, it is anathema.
It helps to analyse clearly the function of 1st-ray destructiveness. The 1st ray is deliberately used as the destructive agency which makes way for new forms. Destruction is not necessarily a bad thing when seen from the consciousness angle. We see everything from the form angle

and so destruction seems bad. DK states that it was a deliberate act of Hierarchy to prolong the First World War to 1918. The destruction of the animal bodies of man allowed the blood of man — representing animal life — to be poured into the earth. This was a great initiatory experience for the animal kingdom, including the animal nature of man. This seems to us a horrific idea because we place such enormous emphasis on preserving the form life. But from the angle of consciousness and the Plan working out, this was a great beneficent opportunity for humanity.

If you think about ancient religion, many had a blood sacrifice involving either humans or animals. Was this related to 1st-ray activity?
Absolutely. This practice stems from ancient Atlantean times when the purpose of the sacrifice of the form was known and understood. Later this was misinterpreted to become just a sacrifice for its own sake — such as to ensure a good harvest or to appease the 'gods'.

Animals are still slaughtered daily in their thousands all over the world to provide food. This seems not only unnecessary but cruel.
There were long ages when man was as subject to slaughter by animals as the animal kingdom is today subject to slaughter by man. The impact of the carnivorous dinosaurs, such as Tyrannosaurus Rex, on early man was devastating. Whole communities were wiped out in a short space of time by the unbelievable ferocity of these animals. The destruction today of animals by man reflects the instinctual knowledge by humanity that the animal kingdom is making karmic reparation for the slaughter of the human kingdom in the past. This seems appalling to us from the form angle, and incredibly cruel as well. But the 1st ray can be cruel. This is one of its qualities. God is not just nice and sweet — God is the opposite of that as well.

There is still a lot of blood flowing on the battlefields of the world. So this sacrificial process is not yet over?

No, it is a cosmic process; the real battle is in heaven, not on our battlefields.

DK says that cancer, one of the major planetary diseases, is caused by 1st-ray influence. Cancer is a mysterious and subtle reaction to the energy of the 1st ray, the will-to-live. It works out in an overactivity and growth of body cells whose will-to-live becomes destructive to the very organism of which they are a part.

This epitomizes 1st-ray independence which is so little influenced by or subject to the restraints of its environment that it can completely dominate it. The cancerous influence is so powerful that it totally disrupts the normal cellular activity of the body.

Would the personality type who is prone to cancer be someone in whom the strong will-to-live is not being expressed?

Yes, the 1st-ray type himself would probably not get the cancer. It would be the 2nd- or 6th-ray type who has a great awareness and vision of life but who cannot express it.

When considering this cancerous aspect of 1st-ray activity, it is surprising to realize that the major quality of the 1st ray is actually synthesis.

It is always a question of the level of application. Used at the highest level, the 1st ray produces a synthesis out of many disparate elements. This is where 1st-ray leadership comes in. A leader is someone who can take many points of view and synthesize them. He or she can lead a varied group in a certain direction — for good or ill. The 1st-ray leader can weld and blend many individuals together, creating not a mixture, but a true synthesis. The 1st ray dominates all other aspects in its drive to synthesize them into a cohesive whole.

I suppose this is how the British Empire originated?

Absolutely. It is the 1st-ray personality of Britain which created the British Empire. Under the influence of its 2nd-ray soul this became the British Commonwealth. Given a chance, the 1st ray will always conquer and then synthesize.

427

Are all politicians governed by the 1st ray or only the leaders? Are they on other rays, too — for example the 2nd ray, like U Thant? (June 1991)

The rays which most strongly influence the politicians are rays 1, 3 and 6. Ray 1 gives power, influence and authority. Ray 3 gives the adaptability (some might say deviousness) characteristic of many professional politicians. Ray 6 gives the idealism (characterized by ideological affiliation) which attracts many into political parties.

What are the qualities of a 1st-ray astral?

It is rather like the domination of the astral plane by the will, so that the astral vehicle is at the service not of the buddhic level, but of the will aspect. The astral body is planned to be, and eventually becomes, the vehicle for the buddhic vehicle, the second aspect of the Spiritual Triad. The domination of the astral vehicle by the will is a correcting device which the soul takes on, to correct a misuse of the astral vehicle — probably by a double 6, or a double 4, in a previous life.

The 1st ray on the astral creates a kind of neutralism. The former US President Hoover had a 1st-ray astral, and he had all the will in the world but no contact with the people, no sense of how far removed he was from responding to the needs of the time and the demands of the people.

Ray 1: Will or Power — Virtues and Vices

Virtues: Strength, courage, steadfastness, truthfulness arising from absolute fearlessness, force of will, singleness of purpose, power of ruling, vision, power-to-good, leadership.

Vices: Pride, ambition, wilfulness, hardness, arrogance, desire to control others, obstinacy, anger, solitariness, power for evil.

Virtues to be acquired: Tenderness, humility, sympathy, tolerance, patience.

Reference: Alice A.Bailey, *Esoteric Psychology, Vol. I.*

The 2nd Ray

The Ray of Love and Wisdom

When we say 'a 2nd-ray type' do we mean 2nd-ray souls, or personalities, or minds or brains?
DK always means that body in which the particular ray is at its most powerful — which with most people is the personality because they are centred in their personalities rather than their souls. So when He says '2nd-ray types', He does not mean necessarily 2nd-ray souls, but perhaps more often 2nd-ray personalities who are exemplifying 2nd-ray qualities, but they might be 1st-ray souls or 5th-ray souls, or whatever.

They would still have that magnetic quality about them, would they?
I think one needs a proviso here. This "magnetism" of the 2nd ray only works in an occult sense. It is the energy we call Love, that magnetic, cohesive energy which — under the Law of Attraction — draws the particles of matter together and creates the building forms, the tiny little bricks of matter through which the creative process can take place. But as it manifests through most people I would say the major quality of the 2nd ray is not so much magnetism as inclusiveness. It gives the ability to see all round a subject, everybody's point of view — so 2nd-ray types tend not to have a point of view of their own. They have a kind of timidity and hesitancy simply because they can see the other point of view — empathy rather than magnetism. When it demonstrates from the soul level, then it is magnetic.

Would people who produce new thoughtforms for institutions or new ways of living tend to be predominantly 2nd-ray types?
Let us remember the ray lines — 2-4-6 and 1-3-5-7. Basically, 2-4-6 exemplify (more or less) the consciousness which is turned in to the soul, and therefore bring out what we call the 'quality' of life, whereas the 1-3-5-7 are concerned with the forms of life. They create the institutions, the political and economic structures (money is concretized 3rd-ray energy, the

lower aspect of the 3rd ray). The 2nd, 4th and the 6th ray are to do with the quality of the life which is expressed through the forms — I think that is the distinction you have to keep in mind all the time.

Therefore those on the 2-4-6 line would be more concerned with the inner life and those on the 1-3-5-7 line more concerned with the outer form.
Precisely that, yes.

The 2nd-ray has the ability to persist; it is possessed of a doggedness — the quality of determination, never giving up.
This is probably based on understanding, of a goal to be reached or a plan to be worked towards, and therefore the persistence is part of that understanding — it is not a will-based persistence.

The 2nd ray also suffers from the handicaps or glamours of fear, and sensitiveness to this fear.
The 2nd ray inevitably has this quality because it is turned in to the soul; it is an introspective ray, and therefore it finds it difficult to handle the outer life of form. People are either introverted or extroverted. If they are strongly influenced by the 2-4-6 line they will tend to be introverted, turned in to the reality of the inner, spiritual life. If they are along the 1-3-5-7 line they will find it easier to work in form, and will therefore be more effective in the everyday life, in creativity along some outer work in the world of form, but will probably lack the immediate, intuitive connection with the soul which the 2-4-6 line finds very easy.

However, because of that, the 2nd ray can suffer from an inability to work effectively on the physical plane, and so finds relationships more difficult even though the 2nd ray, being very empathetic, seems to understand people and people turn to them for sympathy. But they are often ineffective, and lazy, because they lack initiative and, if they have nothing of the 1-3-5-7 line, they tend to lack energy — and they tend to lack love even though the 2nd is the ray of Love/Wisdom.

The 4th ray has a natural performing quality, and the 6th ray has the driving sense of purpose which makes them do what they have to do willy-nilly, whereas the 2nd ray has neither of these — that is why I still doubt the magnetism — it is much more inclined to be placid, flaccid, in performance.

I think the 2nd ray tends to be receptive rather than active, receptive to stimulus from outside. If it does not have stimulus from rays 1, 3, 5, 7, then it does not act, unless the fanaticism of the 6th gets hold of it, then it can be very active. Why is the 2nd ray so prone to fear? It is partly the ability to see all round, and also the difficulty of relating to the external world, to people, things and events — so that every outward movement is an effort. There is an over-sensitivity. People on all the rays, except probably the 1st, experience fear. Only the 1st ray has real fearlessness. Fearfulness is part of the human condition. It is exaggerated in the 2nd ray, that is all.

Re-reading **Discipleship in the New Age** *(Alice Bailey), I found the amount of 1st ray among the disciples absolutely staggering — I didn't realize that years ago when I first read it.*

If you look at the list of initiates in *Maitreya's Mission, Volume One, Two* or *Three*, you see the tremendous predominance of 1st ray in the world's initiates, either as souls, or personalities, or above all on the mental plane — because they had to influence their time and they became really effective in world history because they could so influence it. They needed the fearlessness and the broad overseeing outlook and sometimes the ruthlessness, if necessary, which world leaders, for example, very often need, just to do their job: if you are going to think in terms of individuals, then you cannot do major work. Mao Tse-Tung could never have created modern China if he had been concerned with niceties of whether somebody should be shot or not — for stealing the food of the whole column, for instance. That is something the 2nd ray is appalled by; it sees that sort of thing as the cruelty and violence of the 1st ray — it does not see the broader view, because it is attuned to the soul quality of love. Whether it can demonstrate that or not, it is attuned to it. It is frightened by the impact of 1st-ray power.

The 2nd ray brings in the intuition, and the intuition brings in the nature of the soul, either from the manasic level, that of higher mind, or from the buddhic level from which true intuition, which is group consciousness, comes. So the 2nd ray finds it easy to be intuitive. Ultimately, whatever ray people are on they will gradually demonstrate what we call intuition, which is direct knowledge from the soul without the process of ratiocination we go through today when we think, analyse, put two and two together and get five or whatever we get. This is the function of the lower mind. Gradually that will drop below the threshold of consciousness. The Masters do not think in this way, They just know. They directly intuit, because They are working at the buddhic level. People normally take a problem, look at it from all sides and then arrive, through common sense or rational thought, at some conclusions or theories.

This is why you can have conclusions of a right kind, in science and technology and so on, by people who have no control even of their astral nature let alone of the mental nature. It does not bring in the intuition at all — although there may be sparks of the intuition, leaps ahead. Then you get the really creative scientists who will be already initiate at some degree. Always, when the intuition is functioning, you have some degree of initiation. Obviously that is not true for thousands of people who are working in engineering firms and science laboratories throughout the world who are doing the most wonderful science using ratiocination, just the quality of the lower mind, perhaps with insights stemming from the intuitional level from time to time. A 2nd-ray type will be more intuitive than, say, a 5th-ray type. The world-shaking discoveries are made from the intuitive level, as a result of the opening up of the form that the lower mind looks at and studies.

The 2nd-ray scientist would intuit the answer, and then prove it.

Yes, like Einstein: he intuited the theory of relativity, but it took him years to prove it. He could not do arithmetic — but it was an intuitive leap of understanding about the relationship between energy and matter. It is phenomenal. There is no way you could arrive at that by ordinary ratiocination.

But to be able to put it to some use you need your lower mind.
To put it into effect in our technology, you need the insights of the lower mind, of the 5th-ray concrete mind. That is why the 5th ray has come into a short incarnational period, when it is not due, to stimulate the lower mind of man. This has led eventually to the discovery of the nature of the atom and the identity of energy and matter.

DK says of the 2nd ray that: "A clear intelligence and wisdom when dealing with matter is a capacity to express a true view of things and of impressing them on others."
That is what makes 2nd-ray types good teachers, because they see the truth and can usually communicate it.

How can people with 2nd-ray souls determine whether they are on the love line or that of wisdom? (November 1986)
They come to know in due course.

(1) Maitreya is said to be the "Nourisher of the Little Ones" — that is, second-degree initiates. Would it be true to say that these people, apart from receiving love and light from Maitreya, also receive, via Him, Ray 1 from the Avatar of Synthesis, and peace from the Spirit of Peace? (2) Can the "little ones" find the 1st ray difficult to handle? (September 1991)
(1) The "little ones," that is, those who have taken the first two initiations, do receive the 1st ray, not from the Avatar of Synthesis, but via Maitreya, from Shamballa. They do receive, not peace, but the aspect of the 2nd ray which the Spirit of Peace or Equilibrium embodies, and which, under the Law of Action and Reaction, creates equilibrium and balance. (2) Not especially, if at the right potency.

Is the Christ energy, so far as you understand it, universal and coming from the galactic beam to all galaxies in the universe? (November 1988)

To my understanding, the Christ's energy or ray, the 2nd ray of Love/Wisdom, is universal. It is the magnetic, binding force which holds all particles together throughout cosmos.

I was interested in the role of the 2nd ray in animals and their individualizing — that it is a 2nd-ray experiment.

Some animals have been chosen and put into a group (a kind of spiritual 'pen') and they are individualizing as a result of their relationship with man, but this has nothing to do with the love of man. It is to do with the energy of man's mind. People think that animals grow to be humans if you give them a lot of love and coddling and so on, but it is not that. It is the influence of the energy of man's mind. That is the true way in which the animal kingdom will individualize and come into correct relationship with man.

Eventually, DK said, animals will be used as mediums. Their minds will be stimulated to the point where they will think as man now thinks, with the lower mind, and man will move on to intuition. The intelligence factor of animals will be stimulated to the point where they will use what you could call the beginning of the will aspect. No animal at the moment can direct its purpose, it works purely from instinct. As man brings in the will aspect, so the intelligence and directed thought of the animal will begin to flower and they will then be able to work purposefully side by side with man. The love relationship, the devotion through the 6th ray which is built into the astral nature of the animal, has brought it close to man, but the true individualization will take place through the stimulus of the mental — just as did the individualization of humanity itself. That again was an experiment on the part of the Logos.

Ray 2: Love/Wisdom — Virtues and Vices

Virtues: Calmness, strength, patience and endurance, love of truth, faithfulness, intuition, clear intelligence, serene temper, divine love, wisdom, tact.

Vices: Over-absorption in study, coldness, indifference to others, contempt of mental limitations in others, selfishness, suspicion.

Virtues to be acquired: Love, compassion, unselfishness, energy.

Reference: Alice A.Bailey, *Esoteric Psychology, Vol. I.*

The 3rd Ray

The Ray of Activity and Adaptability

The 3rd-ray type is epitomized by DK as being the spider in the centre of the web. Does this have to do with the manipulative elements of the 3rd ray, spinning intrigue, plotting and scheming — wanting to be at the centre of events and to orchestrate everything around them? But for what reason?

It is because, if he stops concentrating on the form life in that busy way, the 3rd-ray type finds it difficult to find other resources within himself. He finds it difficult to be still, to look inwards, to deal with the point at which form is no longer real. This is the essence of it. The busyness, to some extent, is a cover for having to stop and face what is behind the life of form. The 3rd ray finds it difficult to contact that. The crisis for the 3rd-ray individual is the realization of what lies behind the form. All its energy and motivation is directed towards creating forms — following the creative movement of consecutive forms. This entails thinking and planning ahead, even building a great organization, so that eventually it can see and recognize a form, and know by this that its life has been worthwhile.

But isn't that a valid type of creativity?

Of course it is creative. But it is limited specifically to the creation of the form. The basic problem of the 3rd-ray type, until the third initiation, is that his main focus is on the form rather than the life within the form. The third initiation, which is the 'crisis of the life' or the Transfiguration, involves entering into a relation with the soul and through the soul with the Monad. This always presents a major hurdle for the 3rd ray. For the other rays, it is the second initiation which is the real hurdle. This represents control of the astral vehicle. However, for the 3rd-ray type this is not such a major difficulty. It is the third initiation which is difficult. You may have noticed that the list of ray structures of initiates in *Maitreya's Mission* contains practically no 3rd-ray souls above the level of the third initiation.

As a 3rd-ray soul with a 3rd-ray mental, I have analysed the typical 3rd-ray approach to the truth, especially in comparison to how other rays regard truth. For example, it seems to me that the 1st and 2nd rays value truth highly, though for the 2nd ray fear of the results of speaking the truth may colour this. However, from my experience, the 3rd-ray type never speaks the truth. Not because it is afraid, but simply because, adaptable as it is, it gives the answer which it supposes to be in its best interests. This is instinctive. The interesting thing is that these 3rd-ray types do not even perceive this as a lie. It merely sees this as using a tool to further its own interests without being bothered by any moral implications.

This reflects the 3rd-ray focus on the outer form or effects of behaviour and not the life within the form. So truth is something which can vary — this is 3rd-ray manipulation if ever it was!

I have read in DK that the 3rd-ray type, after many busy, manipulative lives, may have a given life in which it has an inhibition to speak — either having a colossal stutter or being completely mute. This is in order to teach itself the lessons of how to work with truth, to observe, to be still.

No wonder it is the best ray for politicians! It is also interesting to note the attitude of certain countries with 3rd-ray personalities, who handle the truth very lightly, who see the object of any interaction as being to win. They feel that to play the game by certain rules is just plain unintelligent!

What about another facility of the 3rd ray — the capacity for abstract thought. Does this manifest as philosophy? If so, then it seems to counteract this disregard for the truth. Surely philosophy has a high regard for truth as expressed through different abstract theories?

This is still to do with the creation of forms, though on a more abstract level — as thoughtforms. It is interesting that, of all the rays, the 3rd ray has the longest cycle. This is because it takes a long cycle to produce the forms, which gradually evolve and then give expression to the higher levels. Earth is a 3rd-ray planet, embedded in form, and therefore is known as 'the planet of suffering'. Being deeply materialistic at present, we find it difficult to give expression to the life within the form. We are still very responsive to the energy of matter. This is a hangover from the previous solar system when the 3rd aspect, the matter aspect, was the divine expression. We are still very much influenced by that. Through the purifying force of the suffering in the world of form and matter, a transmutation will eventually occur enabling planetary expression of the 1st aspect, the Will-to-Good of the Planetary Logos.

It is interesting to look at the nations which exemplify 3rd ray. China and France both have 3rd-ray personalities, and interestingly both are renowned for their cooking. Sweden has a 3rd-ray soul and Switzerland has a 3rd-ray personality, and both were neutral in the war.

Yes, it is a kind of 'looking after number one'. The one who really looks after himself is the 3rd-ray type — it is instinctive and automatic. He has to make opportunities happen for himself, instead of going with events. This quality is typical of France and China in their dealings with other nations. In Switzerland, there is a busy focus of wheeling and dealing — accruing money from all over the world, whatever the source. Greece with its 3rd-ray personality and 1st-ray soul is notorious for the wielding of power and money and has a reputation for endemic bribery. Sweden with its 3rd-ray soul and 2nd-ray personality is seen as the exponent of a fair and just social welfare system with the highest democratic ideals in the world. This reflects the organizational ability of the 3rd ray on the soul level, manifesting through a caring 2nd-ray personality.

Can you give the rays (soul and personality) governing Israel?
(May 1990)
Soul 3; personality 6. The 3rd-ray soul is responsible for the pronounced intelligence and creativity of the Jewish people, for their adaptability to circumstances (which has ensured their survival over thousands of years) and also for their materialistic bent. Their 6th-ray personality is expressed in their stubborn dogmatism and separativeness, the sense that they are always in the right, and also for their marked religious and mystical yearning (not necessarily expressed in truly spiritual terms).

Ray 3: Activity and Adaptability — Virtues and Vices

Virtues: Wide views on abstract questions, sincerity, clear intellect, capacity for concentration, patience, caution, absence of the tendency to worry him/herself or others over trifles, mental illumination, philosophic viewpoint.

Vices: Intellectual pride, coldness, isolation, inaccuracy in details, absent-mindedness, obstinacy, selfishness, critical, impractical, unpunctual, idle.

Virtues to be acquired: Sympathy, tolerance, devotion, accuracy, energy, common sense.

Reference: Alice A.Bailey, *Esoteric Psychology, Vol. I.*

The 4th Ray

The Ray of Harmony, Beauty, Art and Unity

The 4th ray is the ray above all others which controls human evolution. Other rays exercise an influence, like the 3rd or 5th for example, but the 4th ray is always strongly affecting humanity whether in incarnation or not, because it provides the conflict which makes for fast progress. (And it seems to do the same thing for the deva evolution; the Chohan of the 4th ray, the Master Serapis, is probably more engaged in work with the deva evolution than He is with the human evolution.)

Does that mean that there are no or few 4th-ray souls in incarnation?

There are many 4th-ray souls in incarnation, particularly in certain countries: in Germany, for instance, there are many 4th-ray people — artistic, philosophical, musical — because Germany has a 4th-ray soul, and in Japan, with its 4th-ray personality.

I was interested in its being a double sign, a double energy. The task to be done, according to DK, in the 4th-ray method of approaching the Path is: "First the acceptance that we are, or may be, much of the time at war with ourselves and with the environment. Second that there is an opportunity presented to work consciously or deliberately to reconcile the many conflicts. Third that the gaining of a sense of balance, equilibrium, amongst the many warring forces is, par excellence, the art of self-control, since conflicts do not resolve themselves by themselves, they have to be consciously approached. This means lots of tedious painstaking work to be done as both sides of every question have to be considered and the good extracted from both."

You can see why that applies so much to the human kingdom because we are, of all the kingdoms (at least up to the human kingdom), the ones who can make decisions. What you just said involves human thought, speculation, adjustments, decision-making, establishing control and so on. It takes the thinking man to do that.

I had always thought 4th-ray qualities would be inaction and inexactitude, but in fact they are exceedingly powerful and useful, and very specific in operation — in terms of the disciple — giving him/her the opportunity to make a stand. DK says the word that is presented as a key to the 4th ray is 'steadfastness' — which I would never have thought was appropriate and yet it is, because it gives the opportunity to become steadfast.

The 4th ray is in the middle, between the first three rays — the Rays of Aspect — and the Rays of Attribute, and somehow sums up all of these in itself, having the peculiar quality of harmonizing all of them. The 4th blends all the rays together, the 7th grounds them, brings them onto the physical plane. The 4th is always used to blend into a harmony, a unity, the resonances of all the different rays, so it has a very specific role to play in harmonizing the whole. That means it has the capacity to be the whole, and in my experience the 4th ray has a chameleon-like quality; it can be anything it likes. This is why you will find the great actors on the 4th ray — the great playwrights, the writers, poets, painters, sculptors — artists of all kinds. To be an artist you have to create, visualize the thoughtform of that which you are depicting. You have to imagine yourself to be 'God', in a sense, to be placed in the position of creating, to see the creation and identify with it — all of which is a kind of becoming the thing. Just as an actor, by a sheer chameleon-like empathy, has to grow into the likeness of a character, become the character on the stage. All artists do this: it is an act of the creative imagination to become not other than you are, but all possibilities. In a sense, the 4th-ray person is not there him/herself, but has the possibilities of all. That is the essence of the 4th ray, that it can lend itself, blend, bring together and fuse all possibilities — therefore, all rays.

What is the effect when a person really falls into the 4th-ray category?

It depends on the point of evolution. If it is a Danny Kaye who has two 4s on the personality, 4 on the mental and 4 on the astral, or Mozart who has a 4th-ray soul, 4th-ray personality,

4th-ray mental, 4th-ray astral — he was 4 personified — then you have a very exaggerated expression of the artist. You see it in Danny Kaye though he is only 1.55 (from the point of ordinary humanity that is rather evolved; he is already a disciple). When you see it in Mozart, who was a third-degree initiate, everything was focused to give the greatest expression to his 4th-ray ability to comb the heavens for beauty — because that is what the artist does; he searches the heavens and looks for that vibration of reality which, when expressed in form, creates beauty.

Don't we think of mathematics to do with the 'harmony of the spheres'?
When you think of musicians and the relationship between mathematics and music then you see a clear connection. The higher maths is intuitive maths and the mind of the 4th ray is intuitive. It is also a highly individual ray. I think of all the rays it is probably the most intuitive coming out of the 2nd-ray intuitive faculty but with vivid imagination. This makes for a very high degree of intuition of an imaginative kind which can lead to a real understanding of the mathematical basis of the universe, which is reflected in music, in architecture, and so on.

Einstein had a 4th-ray mental body. His soul was focused through the mental body. He could not do simple arithmetic, but the intuition of the 4th ray at that level (he was a second-degree initiate) produces the direct intuitive faculty to understand and reveal the form of the universe. Beauty is the nature of the universe, of reality, embodied in some form — mathematical, musical, artistic. It is the response to vibration, and the encapsulation of that vibration of reality in some form or other. Bad artists are those who cannot give form to their vibrational response. Good artists can give form — colour form, plastic form, mathematical form — to their experience of reality. The point in evolution determines the quality of that response.

The 4th ray needs to be more contemplative, I suppose, to have a sense of history. I get a feeling from the 4th ray of it being very spontaneous, it has a very quick intellect and produces things very quickly and makes rapid decisions.

The 4th ray is tied up with the creative process, which is cyclic. You have to be nourished by the experience of life over a period and then give expression to it. When that is played out you need another period to lie fallow, again to imbibe and give expression to the new experiences, and so on. So 4th-ray people, in my experience, seem to act more cyclically than other people. That is why you get artists who for months do nothing and then will work day and night. This gives a sense of recklessness, of lack of rhythm, but that itself is a rhythm, the rhythm of cycles, and I do not know any artist who is not aware of that. It is this peculiar quality of the 4th ray of being tamasic-rajasic (ie inertia on the one hand and intense activity on the other) in equal measure.

I think it is the most charming of all the rays, almost everybody's favourite, except of 4th-ray people. If it is in a reasonable amount it is very attractive; if there is too much it is repulsive. A 4th-ray personality with a 4th sub-ray is often over the top in my experience. I think the 4th-ray personality, if it is powerful, really needs a qualifying agent, like a 7 or a 1 or a 2, to tone it down a little.

Indolence is probably one of the worst vices resulting from the peculiar balance of the 4th ray, so every action is an effort. His will to serve, to create, his will to sacrifice has to be fired and then nothing can stop him; it is getting him fired that is the problem.

It is surely difficult with our present social and educational set-up because if the 4th ray is proceeding according to his/her rhythm it doesn't fit in with the rhythms imposed by everyday living.

That is why you get a lot of 4th-ray ne'er-do-wells. But the pressures of life must have their validity too — the 4th-ray person cannot expect life to be carried on just to suit him, as he tends to do. The 4th ray will always find a way round the exigencies of life and make his own rhythm, nevertheless, because he has no alternative. He has to live his own rhythm, it would be against his nature not to.

It raises interesting questions in bringing up children. For instance, if you have a 4th-ray child how far would you try to push it to fit in with everything that it is coming across? How far should one attempt to impose discipline on children or allow them to create their own discipline?

A lot of 4th-ray types under-achieve because they do not build in the discipline. The 7th ray is a great help here because that produces the highest apparatus with the 4th ray — then you have the combination of 4th-ray inspiration, response to the vibration of music, of colour, and the ability to create it, and also the response to measure, to rhythm, to imposed discipline — so you get colour and form.

I was interested in the glamour of war, in that often if you have this inertia and then violent activity you get caught up in the glamour of the violent activity because it gives you a sense of direction.

I think it is on a higher level than that, to do with a cause. The glamour of war is the glamour of a cause, and the 4th-ray type will always respond to a cause. The cause of war inspires him — love of country, patriotism, establishing himself as a career officer — it could be personal or impersonal but it is a glamour, the glamour of that activity which has a brilliance and drama — because war is dramatic, the drama of identifying with one side or the other.

Is that to do with the glamour of the pairs of opposites, always seeing the dualities and not seeing the possibility for harmony?

Very much so. The lower pairs of opposites refer to, for instance, good and bad, right and wrong, day and night. In the higher sense the 4th ray deals with the pairs of opposites — between one group and another, soul and personality, spirit and matter; we live in that duality. From one point of view that duality is unreal, but we live eternally in the duality of spirit and matter because they both meet in us. That is the position of the 4th ray — everything meets in the 4th ray.

There is also the glamour of conflict with the objective of imposing righteousness and peace, isn't there?

That is typical 4th-ray idealism. India, as a nation, is a good example, I would say: the syndrome of desire for peace but imposed with conflict and disharmony; and the 4th ray loves the conflict. It sees the end result as peace and any means that produce it, the more conflicting the better, are found. The 4th ray likes the process, it is not the result it is after, it is the drama, the acting, the conflict it likes.

Just look at their vices: self-centredness, worry, inaccuracy, lack of courage, strong passions, indolence and extravagance. Who would want to live with all that? Moodiness — nobody quite knows where they are with a 4th-ray person. Changeability of temperament.

On the other hand, I would say the 4th ray, probably, of all the rays has the best inventiveness of humour. The 4th-ray mind seems to me to be an inventive type of mind, imaginative therefore inventive. Quick in imagination, it likes plays on words, likes developing ideas and so on, seeing the humorous side — and because it is looking for harmony, probably more than many, has a sense of humour, because humour produces harmony.

How does the 4th-ray compare with the 3rd-ray mind, which is very much dealing with ideas?

It is the difference between imagination and thought, I would say. The 4th ray works through intuitive imagination; the 3rd ray through thought — a thinking rather than an intuitive process.

Ray 4: Harmony, Beauty, Art and Unity — Virtues and Vices

Virtues: Strong affections, sympathy, physical courage, generosity, devotion, quickness of intellect and perception.

Vices: Self-centredness, worrying, inaccuracy, lack of moral courage, strong passions, indolence, extravagance, veiling of intuition.

Virtues to be acquired: Serenity, confidence, self-control, purity, unselfishness, accuracy, mental and moral balance.

Reference: Alice A.Bailey, *Esoteric Psychology, Vol. I.*

The 5th Ray

The Ray of Concrete Knowledge or Science

Benjamin Creme was not present at the discussion on the 5th ray, in which members of the London Transmission Meditation group took part. Questions, answers and further statements are all by members of this group.

Group Member: Broadly speaking, how does the 5th ray influence humanity now?

Group Member: DK says that the 5th-ray approach to service involves an investigation into form in order to find the hidden idea that is the motivation behind the form. The 5th ray is now more active on our planet than at any other time in history. This approximately 100-year cycle started around the turn of the 20th century. The 5th ray is always the most powerful influence on humanity even when it is not in incarnation. It is fundamentally the most potent energy at this time on the planet — although not as potent as it will be later. It is the energy that creates thoughtforms. The purpose of this short burst of 5th-ray energy is to stimulate the lower mind of man. This is reflected in the rapid developments this century in the scientific and technological fields, and also in the rise of the sciences of mind such as psychoanalysis, psychology and philosophy in general. It is also the energy which relates the divine idea to the human ideal and is thus the agent for the creation of the various modern ideologies such as fascism, communism and democracy.

GM: How does 5th ray manifest on the personality level?

GM: DK lists the virtues as follows: strictly accurate statements, justice without mercy, perseverance, common sense, uprightness, independence, keen intellect. The vices are listed as: harsh criticism, narrowness, arrogance, unforgiving temper, lack of sympathy and reverence, prejudice.

GM: I think we should bear in mind that the personality ray is always the sub-ray of the soul ray. So if one had a 2nd-ray soul, this would colour the 5th ray on the personality. There is an automatic connection between the Monadic ray, the soul or egoic ray and the personality ray. According to DK, this is the key to understanding your path of least resistance and therefore of advancement.

GM: There is a special relationship between the 5th ray and the 2nd ray. The 5th ray is particularly receptive to the energy of Love/Wisdom, especially the wisdom component. The 5th ray augments and highlights the wisdom aspect of the 2nd ray when they are working together. DK defines wisdom as follows: "All wisdom is knowledge gained by experience and implemented by love." I see that in terms of knowledge being gained by 5th-ray experience and being implemented by 2nd-ray love.

GM: On the personality level, I perceive the 5th ray and 2nd ray as having similar characteristics. Both types are rather restrained and it is often not easy for them to make contacts. Firstly, they need to know that they are accepted already and this facilitates their movement outwards to others. For example, on public transport, the 5th-ray or 2nd-ray types would be unlikely to make contact with a stranger sitting right next to them, even if they would really like to. They do not know how to approach them. Whereas the 4th-ray personalities simply start talking. Also, strangers might be more likely just to start talking to a 4th-ray type. In my experience as a 5th-ray personality, strangers would never just chat with a 5th-ray type. Perhaps there is one characteristic which distinguishes these two personality types at first glance: the 2nd-ray personality, though distant, can fairly quickly be dominated whereas the 5th-ray personality, though equally reserved, will not tolerate being bullied. It is self-sufficient and does not necessarily follow orders.

GM: The 5th-ray person often experiences initial difficulty in relating to people. This is because the automatic 5th-ray approach to someone is immediately to analyse and, since the 5th ray throws such a clear light of knowledge, to criticize them. This first impression inhibits one from relating to people spontaneously or empathetically. This leads to a kind of isolation through non-engagement. It cuts off and divides into compartments and throws a bright spotlight on a small area, for good or bad.

GM: I have read in DK that the 5th ray is able to be extrovert or introvert as occasion demands. But DK also mentions the quality of constantly analysing people or situations around them. They are over-discriminating in practice.

GM: What are the 5th-ray qualities on the mental level?

GM: The 5th-ray mental body could be described as being extremely sensitive to matters which involve perception of the truth; philosophies must have some sort of foundation that can be checked against scientific fact. The 5th-ray mind is unremitting, and will not let a thing lie until every aspect of it has been thoroughly investigated and its source illuminated. It pursues the frayed edge of some problem through to its ultimate resolution. Though artistic appreciation is there, it is secondary to strict accuracy. Gauguin is a rare example in our list of initiates of a painter with a 5th-ray soul. I think he painted despite his 5th ray under the influence of the 4th ray which features strongly in his make-up.

GM: DK mentions that one of the glamours of the 5th ray is to make up its mind too quickly without actually looking at the broad view. It is a kind of tunnel vision.

GM: In *The Rays and Initiations,* DK says that the 5th ray is instrumental in bringing people to initiation — in particular the first and third — precisely because it is the energy of mentation, illuminating and revealing the real as distinct from the unreal. This is especially so where the third initiation is concerned. In this case, the 5th ray acts as the agent for the illuminating factor of the Spiritual Triad reflected through the soul. This is true not only for the individual disciple but for humanity in general. The 5th ray has the ability to dissipate the fogs of glamour by throwing light on them. Under its influence vast numbers are being brought to the door of initiation. This is referred to by DK as man being admitted to "the mysteries of the Mind of God".

GM: DK describes the 5th ray as being "the receptive agent of illumination". He points out that this can also be poisonous in effect, because the mind can be the "slayer of the real".

GM: The 5th ray takes knowledge and creates thoughtforms. It does this by receiving the impact of all the various energies, synthesizes them, produces order, interprets them and thus "creates the multiplicity of forms to which we give the name 'world thought'". Out of this process has come, in particular, our science this century, and the profusion of material products which flood the developed world. DK describes the 5th ray as being "sadly concrete in the Aryan race", referring to this over-emphasis on materiality.

GM: It seems to me that DK Himself has a 5th-ray mind, and the Alice Bailey teachings exemplify precisely 5th-ray quality at its highest. [Benjamin Creme's Master has confirmed that DK does have a 5th-ray mental body.]

GM: In my experience, when 5th ray works with 6th ray it makes an odd, prickly sort of combination. They seem to work across each other in many ways.

GM: It can be a useful combination, in that the 6th-ray ideal is taken up by the 5th ray and pursued to its logical conclusion. It can then be made concrete, something the 6th ray, impractical as it is, finds very difficult. The 6th ray helps the 5th-ray type to accept an initial hypothesis without rejecting it immediately out-of-hand.

GM: On the soul level, there are great 5th-ray exponents, like St Paul. As a third-degree initiate he was instrumental in organizing the early Christian church, a fundamentally 6th-ray organization. Though involved with a high ideal, his task was to take it to its logical, concrete conclusion thereby making it a reality accessible to all. St Paul is now the 5th-ray Master

Hilarion, Who inspired the growth of spiritualism last century. This was in order to 'thin the veil' between the worlds of inner and outer living and so prepare humanity for a better understanding of what we call death.

GM: DK also talks about the 5th ray as being the major ray influencing the animal kingdom. Under its stimulus the mind quality of animals will develop. Man will act as the agent to make this possible.

GM: DK comments that 5th ray and 3rd ray together produce the highest type of mind. 5th ray and 3rd ray work well together because the 5th ray helps to make concrete the abstract ideas and concepts of the 3rd ray. The inventor James Watt had both these rays on the mental level as well as a 5th-ray personality.

GM: France has a 5th-ray soul and a 3rd-ray personality. As a nation they value intellectual activity more than most. Holland also has a 5th-ray soul, but with a 7th-ray personality.

GM: DK makes the interesting comment that France is not yet correctly manifesting her 5th-ray soul because the 3rd-ray personality still dominates: "The scintillating and brilliant French intellect with its scientific bent is accounted for by the interplay of the 3rd ray of Active Intelligence with the 5th ray of scientific understanding. Hence, the amazing contribution of the French to the knowledge and scientific thought of the world. When the separative action of the 5th ray is transmuted into the revealing function of this ray then France will enter into new glory. Her empire will then be of the mind and her glory of the soul."

GM: DK also talks about the French being the nation who will ultimately prove scientifically the existence of the soul. One French scientist, Jean Charon, has used computer mathematics logically to prove that the soul must exist. It took him eight years using computers to prove mathematically what he intuitively knew to be the case — that the existence of the soul is a reality.

Ray 5: Concrete Knowledge or Science — Virtues and Vices

Virtues: Accuracy, justice (without mercy), perseverance, common sense, uprightness, independence, keen intellect, truthfulness.

Vices: Harsh criticism, narrowness, arrogance, unforgivingness, lack of sympathy, prejudice, tendency to isolation, mental separation.

Virtues to be acquired: Reverence, devotion, sympathy, love, wide-mindedness.

Reference: Alice A.Bailey, *Esoteric Psychology, Vol. I.*

The 6th Ray

The Ray of Abstract Idealism or Devotion

How do the 'outgoing' 6th ray, and the 'incoming' 7th ray, influence us?

These two rays above all control everyone, today, whatever their individual ray structure might be. So it is useful to take the study of this ray from an individual to a more universal application. The tension that exists between these two rays has a definite world effect, which is the reflection on a broader level of their manifestation in any individual. For example, 6th-ray devotion to any ideal, even to making money, examined on a large scale, can be seen as the basis of our competitive society.

I read that the 6th ray, although 'going out of manifestation', is only to be replaced by the 7th sub-ray of the 6th ray.

Yes, the 6th ray, in the major cycle, will be in manifestation for the next 21,000 years! What we are being influenced by is the 6th sub-ray of the 6th ray, which precedes the incoming 7th sub-ray. But the 7th ray is now very potent so the excesses of the 6th ray are now starting to recede. For example, the religious fanaticism that led to the upheavals of the 16th and

450

17th centuries probably represents the period of the 6th ray's greatest potency because the 6th ray and the 6th sub-ray were in manifestation simultaneously.

At the moment, our history demonstrates the interaction of the 6th and 7th rays. We are seeing the upheavals, turmoil and conflict inevitably resulting from the tension existing between these two different approaches to reality.

It seems to me useful to consider this broad pattern of incoming rays and their effect on the planet and humanity. It places one's own personal tussles with rays like the 6th in perspective, and in a sense defuses the struggle. This aids in combating glamours by attrition.
Yes. To take that further, if we could see the rays from the level of the Solar Logos, manifesting in His body of expression which is the Solar System, you would actually see streams of energy moving at fantastic speeds through space. The impulses creating the outflow are rhythmic; thousands of years later, the impact is experienced on Earth. The Solar Logos would know that, at a certain point in the rhythm, a given pattern of cause and effect would manifest on Earth. It is preordained on a scale beyond our capacity to assimilate. In fact, all our trivial personality and emotional desires are totally and absolutely irrelevant. They are not real in any sense whatsoever. From the point of view of the cosmic Being, they do not exist and never will exist. What does exist is the impress on life-in-form of these great cosmic forces which have inbuilt in them a certain plan. It makes rather insignificant our approach to the rays, with all our personal reactions to the defects and attributes. It is of total irrelevance to what is actually going on in terms of the interrelation of the rays according to cosmic purpose. It is all prearranged.

This doesn't mean that our lives are prearranged?
No, I do not mean that. We either go along with this prearrangement and so do not suffer, or we resist it by imposing our tiny little desires on karma. That is what karma is. We either impose our felt need, or desire, on the karmic pattern which is unfolding and making our life, or we accept it

as it happens, day by day. By doing the latter, we live according to the cosmic Law of Karma, Cause and Effect. A time comes when we are able to translate that into its highest meaning or ideal. If we resist it, or impose on it, then we will suffer. This is what the Buddha and Christ talked about, and it is what Maitreya will address. It is the process of, and shows the need for, detachment.

So the rays as they impose on us are only directing us into this stream?
Yes. They give us the energy to flow with the stream or to resist it. It depends how strong our personal desire is. One of the problems of our time, dominated as it is by the 6th ray, is that this ray represents the desire principle. It flows through the solar plexus and is activated on the astral plane. It is for most people an astral manifestation. This is the problem for the world. It is a huge world glamour, the result of our response to the 6th ray which has been in manifestation for millennia.

DK says that one major problem with the 6th ray is that it stands alone. What exactly does this refer to?
It is exclusive. It does not work — of its own volition — with other rays. It is so devoted to its own vision of reality — however fragmentary or impractical — that it stands apart. Personalities on this ray, highly individualistic, usually find it difficult to work in groups. They can work with a will for the group but not with the group. For this reason they are often very destructive to group life.

Although the 6th ray performs the necessary task of intuiting and formulating ideas, it is happy to occupy itself solely with that process. There is no impulse to put the ideas into practice and to make them happen. For the 6th-ray type, it is enough to have experienced and formulated the idea. It is a totally impractical ray. Of course, it is ideation and idealism that are needed because they give great driving force and vision, but the trouble lies in the non-implementation. Often, fanaticism is the impulse behind any practical realization of the basic idea. The 7th ray grounds 6th-ray energy and relates it to the physical plane and therefore makes it practical and useful.

452

The Master DK seems to say that the Lords of the other rays have difficulty understanding and working with the Lord of the 6th ray.

Yes, there is some slight disharmony at that cosmic level which works out at our level as evil. But you would have to get up to that level of expression to understand it — after all, these are expressions of stellar lives in Cosmos.

In everyday mundane terms, what does someone who has 6th ray try and do with it? I am trying to apply all this to my own life.

Well, let us see what are the special virtues, specific — though not exclusive — to the 6th ray. The following qualities would manifest from the soul level: devotion, single-mindedness, love, tenderness, intuition, loyalty, reverence. These qualities tend to manifest on the personality level as selfish and jealous love, over-leaning on others instead of single-mindedness, partiality, self-deception, sectarianism, superstition, prejudice, over-rapid conclusions, fiery anger. These are the opposites to the virtues. Now let us consider the qualities to be acquired for the virtues to manifest. If you acquired strength, you would get that single-mindedness; if you had self-sacrifice, then you would get tenderness, loyalty and reverence; if you had purity, then you would overcome the rapid conclusions and the fiery anger; if you acquired tolerance, you would not get the sectarianism, self-deception and partiality; serenity would overcome the fiery anger, and so on. So certain qualities have to be acquired in order to overcome the vices and achieve the virtues.

The best manifestation of 6th ray is the saint.

Yes, this is the highly developed quality of self-sacrifice. The essence of becoming a saint is the sacrifice of the lower for the higher; it is actually personality sacrifice. One sacrifices the separate sense of oneself and one's personal desires for the higher which is the spiritual reality of the soul. When you can do that, you become a saint. That is why none of us here are saints! The Master Jesus was able to make His extraordinary sacrifices through His 6th-ray soul, highly developed as He was as a fourth-degree initiate. He could do it at that level. Of course, when He was a first-degree initiate, even He could never have done it. It is a quality that comes with evolution, it has to be built in. But the point is, if you are a 6th-ray soul you have the potential for these qualities.

Am I right in thinking that as the 6th ray goes out of incarnation in the Age of Aquarius there will be a relative scarcity of 6th-ray souls during this coming age? (May 1988)
No. Few new 6th-ray souls will come into incarnation during the Age of Aquarius but those who are members of fairly advanced humanity will continue to incarnate until they reach perfection. Only very undeveloped 6th-ray souls will remain out of incarnation during that time.

Ray 6: Abstract Idealism or Devotion — Virtues and Vices

Virtues: Devotion, single-mindedness, love, tenderness, intuition, loyalty, reverence, inclusiveness, idealism, sympathy.

Vices: Selfish and jealous love, overbearing, partiality, self-deception, sectarianism, superstition, prejudice, over-rapid conclusion, fiery anger, violence, fanaticism, suspicion.

Virtues to be acquired: Strength, self-sacrifice, purity, truth, tolerance, serenity, balance, commonsense.

Reference: Alice A.Bailey, *Esoteric Psychology, Vol. I.*

The 7th Ray

The Ray of Ceremonial Order, Magic or Ritual

Group Member: With the 7th ray coming into manifestation now (beginning in 1675), the tendencies towards dictatorships and imposed control, the organizing of systems, are more and more evident in society. Take the example of Spain, which has a 7th-ray personality and exemplifies the 7th-ray virtues and vices listed by DK: strength and at the same time excessive emphasis on formality; rather rigid modes of life; bigotry, intolerance of others' points of view (fanatical 6th-ray soul plus the bigotry of the 7th ray) with an inflated idea of their own opinions. A favourite Spanish expression at the end of giving an opinion is: "I'm saying it to you." It is a common expression in the language. At the same time they are people of great courage, courtesy, strength and endurance; qualities which can be seen in the history of their dreadful Civil War.

It is interesting that Spanish art is largely magical, ritualistic, and incantational — that is one of the positive aspects of, especially modern, but of all Spanish art. It has always had this quality.

I don't understand the application of the term 'incantational' to art.
It is like creating art as a means of contacting higher forces, a sort of conjuration. All Spanish painters have it to some extent. It is the mixture of the 6th-ray soul and 7th-ray personality. The 7th-ray personality colours the art of Dali, Miro, Picasso, Juan Gris. There are many more but these are the very well-known ones. In earlier days, Zurbaran; Goya too.

What is the difference between magic and incantation?
I think it is a question of creating a process of invocation, or the very thing itself is the ritual of magic. The work of an artist like El Greco, who was actually Greek but was totally saturated in the Spain of his time, was both magical and incantational, and certainly ritualistic.

Every ray has a higher and a lower expression, and DK indicates that the higher expression of the 7th ray works out in white magic. Magic is part of the ritualism of the 7th ray — it is the ray of the ritualist in discipleship terms. The lower expression is spiritualism, in all its lower aspects, which grew up in the late 19th century, curiously enough under the stimulus of a 5th-ray Master, the Master Hilarion, in a nation — America — strongly influenced by ancient 7th-ray force from Atlantean days. Spiritualism was the religion of Atlantis. In nations influenced by the 7th ray — it is certainly true of

Russia — you have enormous interest in psychic activity, high and low, but especially low, because it is the easiest of access. That is a direct result of 7th-ray influence — an increase of interest in 'psychism' on all levels.

Group member: That influence is very strong in Spain: it is very easy to arrive in a place like Madrid and meet people who are busily tying knots, making spells. In South America you have that because of the Indian cultures that have a left-over element of Atlantean civilization. In Spain the influence is directly 7th ray, and it is very easy to talk with almost anybody about psychism, whether lower or higher — the whole society is entirely open to that vein of enquiry.

Perhaps the growth of acupuncture and working in healing with etheric energy is a 7th-ray activity?
Yes. The discovery of the etheric level of energy is a direct result of the 7th ray — I am thinking of the work of Wilhelm Reich, of Kirlian photography and the general interest in the science of the chakras; all of that is a direct result of the 7th ray. It is the energy which galvanizes the etheric vehicle, through which it works to organize into form the spiritual life seeking expression. Its nature is to relate the spirit to the matter aspect, it is the 'relating ray'. It acts as a kind of conductor of the nature of God, of the spiritual reality, on to the physical plane to give it form.

The 7th ray works through ritualized movement, through time, sound, organization — anything which is ritualized, which means 'number' and 'time'. These are the two factors which give rhythm and through which the 7th ray makes its impress on the outer physical world. It does this in a quite different way from the actual manipulation of form of the 3rd ray. Through rhythm, sound, time, it organizes and gives order to the inner idea, the planned expression of Divinity, whatever that happens to be. To the ideals of the previous cycle, which are held as ideals and remain as such, it gives form. It brings them from the astral plane on to the physical plane where they become structures. It organizes — and nearly always the 7th ray and the 3rd ray work together in this respect: the 3rd, manipulating matter, and the 7th, impressing that matter through time and rhythm, bringing the idea as a structured entity onto the physical plane.

The problem for 7th-ray types is that that activity is so magnetic for them that they get caught in its rhythm and find it very difficult to change rhythm. So 7th-ray structures tend to be monolithic, insensitive to change, open to crystallization, rigid — it is very difficult to get 7th-ray people to change their rhythm. They fall into habits so quickly; order is established through 7th-ray activity which may be logical as order but inhibits the expression of the life. Rather than give it expression, it can inhibit its expression. The 7th-ray person tends to love and impose order for its own sake, not because it relates to the need of the indwelling life but because it finds structuring the path of least resistance. You get it, as somebody mentioned, in dictatorships. The sense of the need for order and the imposing of it from above is the action of the 1st ray through the 7th. The 7th in itself is a vehicle for the 1st ray, at its highest and lowest; it is really the energy of the mineral plane and has imposed its extraordinary order on the mineral plane. Crystals are an exact example of rigidity — there is no way a crystal can break out of its mode (not that it should) but a human organization has to be open and adaptable and responsive to new needs.

The 4th ray is also very much in manifestation at the same time as the 7th ray, isn't it?
Where humanity is concerned, the 4th ray is always subjectively present, whether in incarnation or not. It will come in early next [21st] century.

Wouldn't the 4th ray help to loosen up the tendency towards crystallization of the 7th ray?
The 4th ray does not "loosen up" the 7th ray, it blends together and harmonizes disparate elements. What the 4th ray ideally and perfectly does is to give us an image of the beauty of God. The beauty of God is many things: what we call colour, beautiful sound, melody; that which is radiant, harmony — all these are the beauty of God. The 4th ray tends to enrich and

blend and bring together all disparate elements and in that blending of these opposites another new and beautiful reality is revealed. It is that relating and blending and harmonizing of opposites that gives a dynamic beauty and therefore radiance to art and, when applied, to life, to a civilization.

How would its influence work?
By giving humanity a sense of the beauty underlying the spiritual life which we call God, and how we can express that beauty in every aspect of our life — in our cities, our day-to-day living and relationships (art, music, architecture). What the 7th ray does allied to the 4th ray is to bring order into that radiance, it gives a structure through which that radiance can express itself. The 7th ray is a conditioning factor on the 4th and the 4th is a conditioning factor on the 7th, and when they are working together you get a structured beauty which is open at the edges — which is not so structured as to be rigid and therefore sterile, but not so unstructured as to be chaotic; which is ordered, structured and at the same time mysteriously beautiful and radiant of a reality which otherwise we could not see. The Master DK says that the combination of the 4th and 7th rays makes for the highest type of artist (given a high point in evolution, of course).

Where the 7th ray is to do with organization and structure, it tends to get bogged down in that. It is because of the imbalance in humanity — it is as if everything we touch, we take to excess. Once we get a structure that seems to work, we enforce it until it no longer works. But it is nothing to do with ray. The 7th ray is not, in itself, unbalanced.

Do we see this demonstrating in Egypt, with a 1st-ray soul and 7th-ray personality, which it has no doubt had for centuries? I see the ancient Egyptian civilization of the Pharaohs as a symbol of the 7th ray, but in modern Egypt Sadat tried to change things; but Egypt seems to have fallen back into its rigidity.
I would not say it has fallen back — I think Egypt is in a no-man's-land at the moment, it is waiting to be awakened to its spiritual purpose and ideal. But I think it is absolutely true to

say that the Egyptian civilization, going back 4,000 years, has been dominated by the impact of the 7th ray. Spiritualism has been its religion, which it got from Atlantis. There is no society on Earth, not even the Chinese, which has been so rigid, so stereotyped, so unchanging for thousands and thousands of years; which had dynasties going on for two and three thousand years without any change in the social structure, and it is a clear expression of the wrong use of the 7th ray. In its case, probably behind the scenes, is the influence of the 1st-ray soul of Egypt which has a tendency to conservation, to rigidity itself: it is a very preservative, conservative type of ray. No wonder this 1st-ray nation is so conservative in its social traditions.

The 1st is a very dynamic ray, but it is also a very conservative ray as it works in society. There is a tendency to preserve the present — and that means the past — which makes for inertia. In the combination of 1 and 7, the soul is all the time influencing the process towards conservation and the personality is on the treadmill. Egyptian art did not change in thousands of years, nor did Egyptian society.

It was also known by other ancient civilizations as the society that really knew about magic; they were the great magicians.
They were, and they will be in the future, too. When the Mystery Schools are opened, one of the most advanced ones will be in Egypt, and the 7th-ray magic will rise to the surface. There are even today in Egypt sources of magic which have remained untouched since Pharaohic times — still intact and uncontaminated for 3,500 years, still undiscovered — and which may not be touched. The magic preserves them from being discovered. When that magic is relearned, on a higher turn of the spiral of course, then everyone will make their own mayavirupa. There will not be this intention to keep a body as a mummy for thousands of years. There are bodies which are totally intact and preserved, looking exactly like the day they were buried, thousands and thousands of years ago. There is no real need to do that; it is part of the religion, but when man sees that he can create a body which is deathless, he does not

have to make himself deathless on the physical plane. In that ancient ritualistic magic you have a premonition, as it were, of the magic of the future in which man will create his body of manifestation, give it up at will and recreate it at will. It is the same magic, only spiritually on a higher turn of the spiral. Modern Egypt is a different story. It has lost its way; it has yet to find its purpose.

Australia has a 2nd-ray soul and 7th-ray personality.
Australia, too, will be one of the seats of an advanced Mystery School. I think a most interesting aspect of the 7th ray that you can actually see is the physical body, the ray of which for most people in incarnation is either 7th or 3rd — either 7 and 3, or 3 and 7, or those rays combined with any of the other rays.

There is a typical 7th-ray look, quite apart from the shape, which is a quality of the mineral — dry, sometimes leathery. There is no moisture on it. Touch a 7th-ray skin, and it is either velvety or feels like suede. It can be smooth or rough but it is dry, as minerals are dry. It is the quality of the mineral world, as a whole, that is created by 7th-ray activity, and mineral bodies have that same dryness. When you really need stamina and staying power — which is what the mineral has — the 7th ray has that.

A 7th-ray astral body is inconceivable.
It is very rare. The normal astral line is 2-4-6, but occasionally you get 1st-ray and 3rd-ray astral bodies.

Can one see a manifestation of London's 7th-ray personality?
Yes, in the organizing genius. London basically has organized the financial houses of the world — now it is just one of many, but why are Lloyds the great underwriters of the world? It was all organized from London. Some of the major financial organizations still stem from London; not that London is the only place where money is made, of course not — there is Tokyo, New York and so on — but London has organized the means and presented it to the world. Britain organized the parliamentary system, then presented it to the world. It is organization.

The 1st ray would give power to that organization?
Yes. It makes it work. Nothing can really stop the 1st ray; it brooks no interference, and eventually its power destroys or creates — one or the other — and where it cannot do either, it preserves and maintains. Its instinct is to preserve. It is creative in a dynamic sense, but it is creative in form and very often it destroys as much as creates because of that. Where it conserves, it tends to conserve the form, but of course it is always the form of the past — you cannot conserve the form of the future, because it does not exist yet.

Self-preservation is the first instinct of man. That is the life within the 1st-ray impulse of will — the will to be, which is essentially behind all manifestation, and everyone and every nation acts according to it.

When the 1st ray is present in the personality structure of a person, it seems to me that they have a fund of tremendous energy and staying power which augments all the other rays that they may have in their personality. If you have 7th ray you would also have that staying power.
The 1st ray can work through the 7th ray. The 1st ray always rises to the top because of the impulse of its will, for good or ill, creating or destroying; it will always come to the top of its class, its milieu.

The 7th ray may or may not, but what it will always do is give structure to its milieu. The 7th ray is only happy when it is structuring and organizing, and that can be fetishistic.

(Speaking as a Dutchman) Holland has a 7th-ray way of organizing the whole of society. We had a 6th-ray personality before having a 7th-ray. Ours was a rather religious country so we started to organize religion in a way it has been organized no place else. There are probably more Protestant sects in Holland than in any other country in the world. We have managed to organize religion into every other aspect of our society, to the extent that we have 'columns' of our 'broadcasts' [ie radio and television programmes] representing the religions. Also the sectarianism itself is a 7th-ray problem.

Sectarianism is one of the glamours of the 7th ray, because of its rigidity. It can organize itself, but it falls foul of its own organization and then devotes itself to the upholding of the organization rather than what the organization is supposed to be about — that makes for sectarianism.

DK says that the Great Invocation was the inaugurating mantram for the 7th ray.
Precisely. That is it: invoking. The 7th ray works through ritual, incantation, magic — ritual that invokes the energy, in this case, from the Buddha, from the Christ and from Shamballa. These forces are invoked into the world to bring about the transforming process of creating the new structures, so that the will, the plan, the purpose — all the ideas of brotherhood, justice, sharing, right relationship and co-operation, which remain ideals — can take shape on the physical plane, creating the new structures, and be made manifest by 7th-ray energy. When that energy is there, it can happen. The function of the 7th ray is precisely to make the ideal manifest. It synthesizes by relating spirit to matter; it is utterly, totally practical.

I've seen on our ray list that most of the sculptors and architects have quite a few 7th rays.
They would have to. Sculptors, who are working with the mineral world, would have it, and architects, who are working with form. It is the energy behind architecture, that abstract form which embodies an ideal of an age or a time. And so you get distinctive architectural forms. Architects of the time embody the idea of the time — whether it is grandiosity, splendour, domesticity or whatever — in an architectural abstract form.

Would you say that cathedrals were a 6th-ray form ?
They are a combination of 6 and 7: it is the 7th ray giving form to the 6th-ray ideal of reaching up to heaven. That is why they are built up, up, up to heaven — the Gothic ideal.

What about modern office blocks?
That is pure 7.

With the coming in of the 7th ray will there be a problem with more black magic?

That problem is now, because we are in a transitional phase — a lot of people are responding to the incoming energy of the 7th ray, the lower aspects of it, but gradually that will change as the higher aspects begin to dominate in the life of humanity under the Christ.

So that in fact the incoming new ray, because it is the new ray, is in its purest undiluted spiritual form, and will displace the old energies of the 6th ray?

It is already displacing the 6th ray. The 6th ray has been withdrawn as a source of energy, but all the structures in the world are saturated by it, so the two are really in balance.

Gradually the 7th-ray influence will supersede the 6th-ray form of working. As 6th-ray souls go out of incarnation so the hold that the 6th ray has in the world will be less and less. The stimulus is already fast fading anyway.

One of the aspects of the Christ's work is to focus that 6th-ray energy for humanity. He set it in motion 2,000 years ago and He will focus the highest aspect, the idealism of the 6th ray, but with the 7th ray coming in, that idealism can be given form.

You have said that the 7th ray is the ray of the sex centre. However, Alice Bailey says in **Esoteric Psychology, Vol. II** *(p521) that the sex centre is connected with the 5th ray. So who is right?* (September 1988)

Both of us are "right". As always in esotericism, it depends on the angle from which one is viewing. Thus the many paradoxes (very much disliked by certain 'tidy' minds) in esoteric teaching. It is true that from one point of view the sex centre is connected with the 5th ray but it is even truer to connect it with the 7th ray which works through the base and sacral centres, and in the dense-physical, through the gonads.

Ray 7: Ceremonial Order, Magic or Ritual — Virtues and Vices

Virtues: Strength, perseverance, courage, courtesy, meticulousness, self-reliance, creativity, thoughtfulness, organization.

Vices: Formalism, bigotry, pride, narrowness, poor judgement, arrogance, over-stressing of routine, superstition.

Virtues to be acquired: Realization of unity, wide-mindedness, tolerance, humility, gentleness and love.

Reference: Alice A.Bailey, *Esoteric Psychology, Vol. I.*

General Questions on the Rays

Why do we have the same soul ray but different personality rays from life to life?

Because the soul, in its wisdom, is building in the quality of all the rays, creating a unified whole, fused and blended by the basic soul ray which eventually will dominate. As far as the soul is concerned, the personality rays are just reflections of itself on the personality level. It gives its reflection certain rays for its own purpose. This is either to build in qualities which are not yet in its structure, or to purge qualities which, through illusion or glamour, are over-expressed. This is done by bringing them to such an acme or crisis point of expression that the individual, saturated as he is in these glamours, can at last see them and overcome them. In order to bring this fact to absolute clarity in the mind of an individual, from which point he or she can begin to deal with the glamours, a 6th-ray soul may provide itself with a 6th-ray personality, a double 6th-ray mind and a double 6th-ray astral.

In fact, to my mind, 99 per cent of people in the New Age movement are saturated with 6th ray, however much they would prefer to think of themselves as 7th-ray types responding to incoming 7th-ray impulses. The 6th ray gives them their idealism, that is why they are in the New Age movement. Their souls provide them with these rays for two reasons: to bring about their usefulness at this time, and to bring their glamours to such a point that they can be recognized by the individuals. Most such people are on the verge of mental polarization, at 1.4 or 1.5 degrees initiate, and at this point the soul often provides itself with a vehicle which exaggerates the negative qualities of a particular ray — it need not be the 6th ray. If on the other hand, the individual is a highly advanced initiate like a Leonardo or a Mozart, the soul may choose an exaggerated personality structure to provide it with a very potent vehicle. For example, Mozart was 4-4-4-4-3 and Leonardo was 4-4-7-4-7. These are very simple, straightforward vehicles, but potent at that level, Mozart being a third-degree initiate and Leonardo a fourth-degree initiate. The study of the rays is a totally new science. Many people who work with me are in the fortunate position of knowing their ray structures and this information is invaluable in focusing the mind on the glamours.

You have explained that the personality and mental, astral and physical bodies will be on a particular ray but with an important sub-ray in each. During the lifetime, as the person evolves or backslides as the case may be, might these sub-rays change? (May 1987)
No.

With reference to the rays and sub-rays of a particular body, you state that there are percentages of influence or activity of a main ray and of a sub-ray. As a person grows and changes through life, do these percentages change? (May 1987)
Yes. Very frequently the percentages will change as the major ray absorbs the influence of a sub-ray. To illustrate: I know a woman whose physical body is on the 7th ray of Order with a 6th sub-ray, which for many years was the major influence. Throughout childhood and early womanhood she was always ill, had many operations, and displayed all the characteristics of a not-very-strong 6th-ray vehicle. Over the last two to three years, however, the 7th ray has begun to absorb the 6th-ray influence and her health has improved dramatically and should

continue to do so. The reverse may also happen, the major ray weakening relative to the sub-ray.

In the books of Alice Bailey the Master DK often refers to "the line of least resistance". What does He mean by that line? Is it the ray structure? Please explain. (June 1989)

"The line of least resistance" is that direction in which a given flow of energy finds the least obstruction. Depending on circumstances, the effects of this can be either constructive or destructive.

In relation to a ray structure, for example, a 2nd-ray soul would find in a 2nd-ray personality such a line of least resistance, and so could make its impress more easily, while the same 2nd-ray soul might find in a 1st-ray personality a major obstruction to its expression. Likewise, a 3rd-ray mind would find little resistance in using a 3rd-ray physical body (and therefore brain). Like rays produce, therefore, a line of least resistance to their expression.

On the personal or psychological level, however, the line of least resistance, if taken, might not produce the necessary friction and effort for worthwhile achievement and advance. This factor is important in selecting life work or service and requires a rather mature knowledge of the art of living.

In our group, people's soul focus is always either on the personality or mental body. Is it correct to say that in former times of mankind's evolution the soul focus was on the astral or physical body? (June 1989)

In a broad, general sense it would be correct to say so but this was by no means universally the case. Likewise, it would be incorrect to assume that everyone's soul focus today is on the personality or the mental body. There are many instances to my knowledge where the soul focus is on the astral vehicle. This would most likely occur where a degree of astral/emotional warmth was required to correct a certain mental coldness resulting from a previous life's mental over-emphasis.

The Master DK has written (through Alice Bailey) that the mental body is always on the 1st, 4th or 5th ray; the astral body on the 2nd or 6th; and the physical body on the 3rd or 7th. Deviation to this rule is only made in the case of an accepted disciple, or, as pointed out by your Master, in someone who will become an accepted disciple in his or her current life.

According to your information — Marilyn Monroe (0.9) and Duke Ellington (0.6) had a 6th-ray mental body, and Elvis Presley (0.8) had a 1st-ray astral body. It is hard to believe that these people were accepted disciples or would become so in that incarnation. Can you explain this? (June 1989)

The above statement by the Master DK is a broad generalization, not a hard-and-fast rule. The confusion arises from a misunderstanding of what the term 'accepted disciple' means. It would seem that most people take this to mean someone, sufficiently advanced, who has been accepted by a Master for training. This is not the case. It means someone who has accepted the discipline which will lead to initiation. A better term might be 'accepting' disciple. The people named above, except for Duke Ellington, were all on the verge of the first initiation, which is precisely where people make their acceptance of the disciplines which will take them over that hurdle.

Can rays work out on a national level, too, through the leaders of a country?

Very much so. Look at very exaggerated types of leaders like Mrs Thatcher or Ronald Reagan. People like them represent national glamours at such a peak that these extremes of expression can be recognized by the populace. These two leaders were strongly separative, exclusive and divisive.

Inevitably, political leaders synthesize in themselves the qualities of a nation — usually the personality ray qualities, but sometimes, with really great leaders, like Roosevelt or Mao, the soul quality.

Why do some people seem to have a fine inner quality but a poor memory or outwardly seem rather dull? (April 1988)

467

There are a number of possible reasons or combination of factors involved. The ray structure, particularly the ray governing the mental body, is a conditioning factor. Also, whether the person is, generally speaking, introverted (to the soul) or extroverted (to the outer world). The body (and therefore the ray) on which the soul is mainly focused is also important.

What are the advantages and disadvantages (if any) of parents knowing their children's ray structures? (December 1987)

A knowledge of ray influences forms the basis of the new, soul psychology and the knowledge of a child's ray structure affords a parent an insight into the child's nature, limitations, line of least resistance and possible area of activity which is otherwise unobtainable. It helps the parent to see the child as a whole, the expression of particular forces provided by the soul at birth and therefore subject to soul purpose and plan. This helps to 'objectify' the child in the parent's eyes and increase understanding and tolerance.

The disadvantage is that with partial or superficial knowledge of the rays and how they may interact, or where a parent may have too rigid an approach to the ray qualities, they may see the child in too narrow a way and seek to impose certain attributes which they believe should be inherent. They thus may push the child in directions for which he or she is unfitted. Crucial, of course, in any such considerations, is a knowledge of the point of evolution of the child.

Do identical twins have the same ray structure and point in evolution? (September 1988)

No, not necessarily. They would usually tend to be at the same evolutionary point, more or less, but may have a similar or quite different ray make-up.

Is it possible to determine a person's ray structure from a person's horoscope? For example, does Mars in Scorpio tell us which ray is governing a particular body? This would presuppose that only seven of the planets govern our ray make-

up in conjunction with only some of the zodiac constellations.
(September 1991)

Many people try (and many believe they have succeeded) to
find ray structures through astrology and personal horoscopes.
Some even try to find their rays with a pendulum. I am assured
by my Master that it is impossible to find one's rays through
astrology, pendulums, or anything other than personal insight
into one's own nature and a study of the ray qualities.

For personal counselling, is an understanding of the Seven
Rays more useful than esoteric astrology? (July/August 1988)

To my mind, yes. The ray structure (if known) gives an
immediate insight into the forces governing the various bodies
of an individual and also of the harmonies or imbalances which
might result from such a structure. With astrology, there are so
many unknown factors which, in the nature of things, cannot
be taken into account.

Rays of the Nations

In *Esoteric Psychology* the Master Djwhal Khul indicated,
via Alice Bailey, which rays govern a number of important
countries. My Master gave out further information a few years
ago (published in *Maitreya's Mission, Volume One*) and has
now, again, filled some gaps in our knowledge.

The rays of Europe as a whole are 4th-ray soul and 3rd-ray
personality. The soul ray therefore is the same as that of
several of the countries in the old heart of Europe: Germany,
Austria and Czechoslovakia. The personality ray corresponds
with that of France — for long one of the major powers on the
continent — and Switzerland. Further, it is apparent that the
'birds of a feather' idea applies also on the soul level: besides
the 4th-ray bloc in the heart of Europe, there is a 5th-ray area
on the west coast (France, Belgium and the Netherlands), and a
large 6th-ray bloc in the South and South East (Portugal,
Spain, Italy, Yugoslavia, Bulgaria and Romania).

Scandinavia as a whole has a 3rd-ray soul, while in the
bloc of Nordic countries Norway has the 2nd-ray soul in

common with Great Britain. This pattern, of countries sharing borders sharing also the same soul ray, is not coincidental: it mirrors earlier migration waves of peoples with like soul rays, who ended up in areas that later fragmented into different nations. While Scandinavia as a whole is characterized by a 3rd-ray soul and a 2nd-ray personality, Great Britain is governed by the 2nd (soul) and 1st (personality) rays. Yet peoples within these great groupings have again their own rays: the Norwegians are 2nd-ray on the soul level and 4th ray as personality. The Irish have, as a people, a 6th-ray soul and also a 6th-ray personality. Indeed, this fact throws some light on the difficulties that the Irish have in solving their problems on the basis of compromise and, besides, explains well why they are exceptionally drawn to religion and mysticism.

It is not surprising that the Irish are matched in this respect only by the Poles who have the same ray combination at present. Those familiar with the Bailey books will know that, according to the Master Djwhal Khul, the personality of Poland was of the 4th ray, that of Harmony through Conflict. This was correct at that time. However, my Master revealed that Poland has comparatively recently been through a change-over phase and has now begun a new cycle in expressing its personality, with the 6th ray of Abstract Idealism now the dominating factor. For this reason we have given both rays.

Shifts in personality ray occur relatively often in this fast-changing world. My Master points out that a number of other Eastern European nations (Yugoslavia, Albania, Romania and Bulgaria in particular) are also between two cycles and that their present personality rays will not necessarily remain the same for long.

Table of Rays of European Countries

The recently announced rays have asterisks. The left-hand figure is for the soul ray, the right-hand for the personality ray of the country concerned.

Albania*	2	7
Austria	4	5
Belgium	5	7
Bulgaria*	6	7
Czechoslovakia*	4	6
Denmark*	3	2
Finland*	3	2
France	5	3
Germany	4	1
Greece	1	3
Hungary*	6	4
Iceland*	3	4
Ireland*	6	6
Italy	6	4
Yugoslavia*	6	7
Netherlands	5	7
Norway	2	4
Poland	6	6* (4)
Portugal*	6	7
Romania*	6	7
Soviet Union	7	6
Spain	6	7
Sweden	3	2
Switzerland	2	3
Turkey*	3	6
United Kingdom	2	1
Scandinavia as a whole	3	2
Europe as a whole*	4	3

Table of Rays of Asian Countries

Afghanistan	6	4
Bangladesh*	7	6
Bhutan*	6	2
Burma*	4	6
Cambodia*	6	2
China	1	3
India	1	4
Indonesia	6	2
Japan	6	4
Korea*	6	4
Laos*	4	6
Malaysia*	3	3
Mongolia*	3	6
Nepal*	6	3
Pakistan*	6	4
Philippines*	6	2
Soviet Union	7	6
Sri Lanka*	6	4
Thailand*	7	6
Tibet*	7	4
Vietnam*	4	6
Asia as a whole*	6	4

For the rays of other nations, refer to *Maitreya's Mission*, *Volume One*. For a more detailed discussion on the rays of the nations, see *Destiny of the Nations* by Alice A.Bailey.

Glamour in Group Work

This article is an edited version of a talk given by Benjamin Creme on 27 February 1988 in Ubbergen, the Netherlands.

In New Age circles there is a great deal of talk about the subject of glamour. New age groups, the esoteric and occult groups, fondly imagine, of course, that they are without glamour. They tend to see themselves as the most advanced groups in the world, above and beyond the glamours which beset ordinary humanity, and as particularly fitted to guide the rest of us into the same, blessed, glamour-free state in which they happily reside. This is one of the biggest glamours of these groups. The Tibetan Master DK, Who gave the Alice Bailey teachings to the world, has written that the esoteric and occult groups, so-called, are the most glamoured of all the groups. And, I must say, that is exactly my experience.

What is glamour? We can more easily answer, what is not glamour? There seems to be nothing which enters our mind, comes out of our mouths or concerns us in any way at all, which is not saturated with glamour. Glamour is illusion on the astral or emotional plane. There are three levels of illusion, all pertaining to the personality. Illusion on the physical plane we call maya. On the astral plane we call it glamour. When it is on the mental plane, we call it illusion. The vast majority of us live constantly in a state of illusion, the result of not seeing reality as it is. Eventually, we come to an understanding that this physical-plane world, our astral and emotional life and even our mental ideas are nothing more than illusions of one kind or another. The real world, which we can only know through the development of soul consciousness, we have to reach and experience through the practice of meditation and service. Through meditation we gradually form a contact and eventually an alignment between our personality self and our true Self, our soul. When this is established the soul can throw its light on to this illusory life, physical, emotional and mental, in which we have up till then lived. That is evolution. We gradually evolve out of the darkness of our illusions, physical, astral and mental, into the light of the soul, the true reality.

Before this process of change takes place we do not see the harm that maya, glamour and illusion do to us and the world. When we are in a state of glamour, of illusion, we are quite content because we do not know anything else. Our glamours, our illusions, are very comfortable for a long time. We have illusions, glamours, because they are comfortable. They help to bolster our ego, or denigrate our ego, depending on what we wish to do.

Many will have heard of the Seven Rays, energies from Cosmos, which control our lives. These ray energies have very definite and, in many cases, quite different qualities. The 1st ray of Will or Power or Purpose, for example, has strength, perseverance and breadth of viewpoint. The 2nd ray of Love and Wisdom has the qualities of love, of empathy, the ability to see the other person's point of view. Therefore it brings understanding, inclusiveness, sensing inwardly the reality of unity, which is the essential nature of the human race.

All of us, as you probably know, are 'on' particular rays. Our soul is governed by a particular ray; our personality, our mental body, our astral body and our physical body are all governed by particular rays. Therefore, we have (or may have potentially) the qualities of these rays. The differences in our personalities, in the effect which we have on each other, is to do with the differences in the quality of the rays on which we find ourselves. This also accounts for the differences between nations. The differences in the way the Dutch, for instance, govern their life and, let us say, the Americans, Russians or the Chinese, are the differences in the rays of those countries. Nations whose rays are the same or similar tend to understand each other and become friends and probably trading partners. Nations whose rays are very different have very different approaches to politics, economics, international affairs and so on. If we were perfect enough always to demonstrate purely the qualities of our ray structure, we would have no maya, no glamour, no illusion. Unfortunately we are not. We are all of us rather unevolved and so demonstrate these ray qualities in their obverse effect — not the virtues but the vices of the rays. All of us have the vices of our rays, without any doubt at all. And those who are in the process of trying to find out their ray structures are best instructed to do so through the recognition of the vices of their rays. You may have some of the virtues; you will certainly have the vices. Not because you are any worse than anybody else, but because you are human. Humanity lives under a great pall of murky darkness, which surrounds us even if we do not see it. It interpenetrates all our being; it is called glamour. Glamour is the result of not seeing reality as it is. As groups form and work together they demonstrate, necessarily, their ray qualities: some of the virtues and certainly most of the glamours of those rays.

There are seven rays and seven times a multitude of glamours. Rather than going into individual ray structures and individual glamours and how to handle them, I would like to talk a little bit about how these glamours affect the interaction of individuals in a group formation. An esoteric group comes together under karmic impulse, ashramic necessity and soul purpose. If this is the case let us assume therefore that we are talking about a serious group with a serious purpose in coming together and not on some kind of whim. This being so, it will be very important how that group actually works, each member in relation to each other member. The group dynamics become very important; they matter. If a group is to function properly, each member will have to give of his or her best.

In New Age and esoteric groups, there is no lack of desire to do one's best. These groups are saturated with idealism. There is no lack of idealism today. How is it then that we have such a rotten world? Because the idealism never results in any kind of action. It remains a vision, an ideal. This world is filled with great idealistic notions of bringing peace, joy, the end of suffering to the world. Yet every day we have suffering, we have war and starvation in the world. So what about the idealism? It is glamour, unreal. New age groups, probably more than anybody else, are saturated with this unreal idealism. There are registers, thousands of names long, of groups with wonderful names: "The Universal Brotherhood and Sisterhood of World Servers in the Light", or: "The Universal Brotherhood and Sisterhood of Creators of the New World". They are all 'Universal'; they are all about 'transformation'; they are all full of 'Light' — and a lot of hot air. They come together regularly and talk about transforming the world and creating conditions of love and light throughout the world. That is done, they believe, by talking about love and light, by recognizing that the most important things in the world are love and light, and that if only enough people in the world knew that the things that really matter are love and light, we would have a wonderful world. There are thousands of such New Age groups all over the world. And of course they are not wrong. The world does need love and light. But they do not do anything about it. They do not address the problems of creating the conditions in the world in which love and light can come into manifestation. This, I think, is the major New Age glamour. There is a particular glamour which assumes that if you can name a thing, you have it in your pocket. Let us name the most blessed state for humanity: peace, love, brotherhood, wholeness, unity. As soon as you can see it or name it, you have it. All the world needs is to see that it needs peace, love, freedom, and unity. This glamour imagines that, if you have the vision of a thing, you have the thing itself. That is the major New Age glamour, I believe. It is, of course, total self-deception, a purely astral idea.

The vision is seen on the astral plane, imagined as a vision of love and light and peace, and just having the ability to envision that is deeply satisfying. You do not have to do anything more. That is glamour. Glamour is taking the unreal for the real; the vision for the reality. Of course, you have to have the vision. If you do not have the vision, you cannot create the reality. But you have to make the vision real on the physical plane. Otherwise, it is glamour.

Some people imagine that they have come into this world with a great mission, a great role — not an ordinary mission, an ordinary role, like growing up and having a family and doing your best in the world, but a great mission, a great responsibility. They have not yet done anything about it, but they will. That is a typical New Age glamour. The New Age groups are full of individuals of that kind: nice, sweet, full of idealism and absolutely, totally impractical. As soon as you contact the soul you want to serve. Today, millions of people, through meditation, are contacting their souls and desire seriously to serve. They come into a group and say: "Is there something useful I can do?" They are told: "Yes, we have a mailing going out tomorrow. All these envelopes need to have a name and address and a stamp," and so on. "Well, actually, I don't happen to have so much time tonight. Perhaps some other time." Or they say: "Yes, I could do that, but I have a very, very good way of talking to people and I feel I can be more useful in talking about the work to people and spreading the message." Or: "I have done esoteric work, and I have been in groups for so long. Well, you begin by licking stamps and addressing envelopes, but it is a waste of my qualities, my experience, my point in evolution, to be used in such work." How many people can put their hand on their heart and say that they have never felt or thought in this way?

One of the most difficult things in a working group, a group really working seriously on the outer and the inner plane, is to get people to accept any level of work, any level of job. Everybody wants to do what they think they are good at. Whether they are good at it or not (usually they are not), what they want is to do something that they enjoy, not something that is boring, run of the mill. All of that is glamour. The idea that one job is more important than another in a group activity is glamour. The idea that anybody is better fitted than another person to do more important work, or too important to do a lesser work, is glamour. One of the major glamours in group activity is to take on jobs and then not to do them. People do not recognize these as glamours, but they are.

It is very difficult for people to work in a group with impersonality. And yet that is precisely what is needed for correct group activity. I wonder how many people really, honestly, with hand on heart, can say that they do not enter a group of this kind, for instance, without a motive of personal gain. I do not mean of money, but a personal gain in some way or another. I wonder how many people can say that they enter this work out of a pure, simple desire to serve the world to the best of their ability. That there is no personal ambition to be in a position of some importance, some desire for recognition for doing certain work, a desire for a situation in which they can advance themselves, become more powerful, more knowledgeable, more important. I wonder how many people can say in all honesty that there is none of that in their approach to service. I think that, if we are honest, we have to admit that in all groups perhaps the majority of people have approached the work for these personal reasons. That is glamour. And that is one of the major hindrances to real advance, personally and in a group relationship. To advance individually and in group formation there has to be complete impersonality in relation to each other and to the work. Sooner or later that impersonality has to develop.

The problem with glamour is that when we are in the glamour we do not see it as glamour. That is why we like the glamours: they are comfortable; they keep us from seeing reality as it is. They are protective devices. As soon as the light of the soul through the more focused mind begins to recognize the glamours and show them for what they are, a very uncomfortable situation develops. A glamour which is seen and recognized, but still lived within, is a very uncomfortable thing. It can only be overcome by not giving it any energy, by withdrawing the attention from it.

Our glamours are maintained by the effect of the basic law of occultism, that energy follows thought. Wherever we put our thought we put our energy. If all our thought is directed to ourselves, then all our energy is directed to ourselves. And if all our energy is directed to ourselves, there is no interplay with the other, that which is outside ourselves. Then we feel unloved, alienated; we feel isolated, miserable, because all our attention is directed to ourselves. All of that is glamour. It is the illusion that we are separate. If we could only recognize, and live, the fact that there is no separation, there would be no glamour. If we have a pain in the physical body and we direct our attention to it all the time, we will continue having the pain and we will make the pain worse. We will create inflammation and make the whole condition worse. If we direct our attention to the world, to the needs of the world, our energy will flow from us out into the world. In meeting the needs of the world, we forget about ourselves. And when we forget about ourselves, the glamours go, because we have taken our attention, and therefore our energy, away from them. So, too, goes our misery, our pain, our isolation.

The great secret in transformation is the re-direction of thought, away from ourselves to the needs of the world. The more we are engaged in serving the needs of the world, the healthier and the happier and the more serene we become. The fears, the jealousies, the unhappiness fade away from lack of energy. These glamours are only held in place by the energy with which we feed them. The first thing is to recognize them, to look at them. That is all; do nothing about them. Do not judge them or condemn them, do not try to change them, but do not try to repress them, do not try too hard 'to be better'. Every undue effort you make to overcome a failing, a glamour or whatever, simply makes the condition worse. The way to deal with a glamour is, first of all, to recognize it. Just look at it and do nothing about it. Do not identify with it. Just withdraw your attention from it and it will die of starvation. The major thing is recognizing and not identifying, both in a personal sense and in a group relationship.

One of the most destructive forces at work in group relationship is competition. In most groups you will find a number of people competing with each other — competing for influence, for power, for recognition, if there are offices, then for offices. This is highly destructive of group unity and of any correct group work. That is probably the first glamour that should be recognized and has to go for the correct working of any group. Competition is deadly; it is always destructive.

Are there no good glamours? No worthwhile glamours? Are there no good illusions? No. There are no good illusions and no good glamours. Some are more destructive than others, that is all. The worst glamours are other people's glamours! Our own glamours we can put up with. Of course, the glamours of people with the same rays as ourselves are unbearable. It is amazing how quickly we recognize other people's glamours when they are the same as our own. A key to knowing what your worst glamours are, perhaps, is to recognize what you hate most in other people. That is an eye-opener.

The Master DK wrote about a most unusual glamour which He had for many years and which kept him back for years. There is a lot of it about. It is a glamour which saturates the New Age and esoteric groups. It is called "devotion". The Master DK had an intense devotional attitude to His Master, the Master KH. He was absolutely devoted to that Master and was certain that that, at least, was His major virtue. But that devotion held him back for years. It was not His greatest quality; it was His chief fault. Devotion can be a glamour. Anything can be a glamour, if it is 'over the top'. Devotion can be the chain which keeps us from initiation. At the same time, lack of devotion can be the chain. It works both ways. What is needed is total impersonality — not devotion or lack of devotion, not idealism or lack of idealism, but a correct balance of recognition of the needs of the world and, using whatever faculties we have, serving those needs. Otherwise our devotion, our idealism and so on, are chains. It is the easiest thing in the world to be a devotee, but it is of no value to the world and may be a hindrance to ourselves. There is no Guru in the world, high or low, who needs our devotion, not one. No one on Earth needs our devotion except the old ladies who need help across the road, or the starving millions who are, right this moment, dying in Africa and Asia. The needy of the world need our devotion, no one else. The pain, the suffering, the anguish, the terror, the fear of the world, that needs our devotion. All the rest is glamour.

Is it possible to take stress from other people or is this glamour?
It is possible, because stress is infectious. It is precisely one of the problems with glamour that some are very infectious

indeed. The glamours of anger and violence are infectious, and above all the glamour of fear is extremely infectious. All you have to do is to create a fearful idea, about catastrophe or disaster, and that fear will spread as a rumour throughout a continent. America, for instance, is a great 'rumour land'. The Master Morya writes about one of the major glamours, that of anger, of irritation, which He calls 'imperil'. Anger imperils the world; it enfolds the world in a fog which surrounds humanity and is released in all kinds of violent acts. We create it all the time. One of the major tasks of the Christ in this New Age is to free humanity from glamour, above all the glamour of materialism and the illusion of separation.

If I feel someone else's fear, is that because I have that fear in myself?
Absolutely. If it were not present in you you would not feel it. You might recognize it and see it, but you would not feel it yourself. One of the major disservices given to the world by so-called 'Masters' (communicators 'channelling' through astral sensitives, either trance mediums or not) is that from them is pouring into the world the threat of destruction and catastrophe. These are the ones I call 'the prophets of doom'. Humanity has enough fear, without these induced fears. They are playing on the insecurity of humanity. People have those fears, so it simply strengthens them. I am amazed that people are so glad to receive these fearful warnings, happy to pay any amount of money, to buy any number of books, if they have these forecasts of doom and catastrophe in them. One of the dangers is that, if people hold on to a thoughtform for long enough and make it powerful enough, they can precipitate the doom, the catastrophe. We do it to ourselves all the time. We precipitate our fears, our anger, our neuroses. We are projecting them as thoughtforms. In doing so, we create our own lives with pain and suffering, much of it unnecessary.

Why does glamour exist at all?
Because we are spirit immersed in matter, which is so inert that the spirit cannot manifest purely, correctly, at this level. We are perfect spirit, complete, perfect Gods, as any 'New Age'

group member will tell you. That being the case, they will say, there is no evil in the world; there is nothing to worry about. Only a few millions starving in the world, but that is not evil. There is nothing we need to do about that, because we are all perfect. The starving millions are perfect, too. If only they would realize that, they would not starve. People actually believe that.

Glamours result from our inability to think. Responding largely to events of life with our astral/emotional body we cannot see the reality which exists outside this fog. We are in incarnation in order gradually to change this equipment, evolve it, until we have bodies which correctly demonstrate the nature of the soul, which is will, love and light.

What is the difference between glamour and goodwill?
With goodwill, you will want the best for your family, community, nation, world, and humanity in general. That is generalized goodwill, which is a positive and absolutely necessary quality, the lowest aspect of the energy we call love — the aspect that humanity can, at this stage, demonstrate. It should not be confused with the desire principle. If you say: "I wish that my friends would join in this work which I hold to be so good and useful," if you wish for it, not as generalized goodwill for their betterment, but as a desire that they work with you, share your enthusiasm for the cause, then you are bringing in the element of glamour. Glamour is your lack of liberation, or lack of detachment from the desire principle. Attachment and desire are the same. That is what glamour is. The desire is the outcome of the attachment — to an end result, a desired object, or whatever. It produces glamour, the non-detachment. Only detachment from the desire itself will bring about mental polarization and eventually liberation. The process of evolution is a process of freeing oneself from the desire principle.

Is glamour recognized by life experience, by meditation or both?
We are in the midst of glamour until we have taken the first initiation and are approaching the second. Around the point

1.3–1.5 the soul energy becomes more and more potent and the light of the soul strengthens the mental body. This will throw a new light on every situation, which reveals the glamour. Up until then, when one is completely in it, one does not even see it. But then, even when we have never heard about glamour, we will realize the inconsistencies, see the glamours in our make up. We cannot do anything about them at first, they are just painful. We experience it as the not-self. As not us, and yet they are us. Our fears are us; our anguishes, our jealousies, the timidities, all of these are glamours. As long as we identify ourselves with the glamour, we are as good as being that glamour. The more we can identify with ourself as a soul, the less we will identify with a glamour. Through meditation, the soul pours in its energy and, through the mind, reveals the unreality, the glamour. The mind looks at this glamour and asks: "Is that me?" That fear, that ambition, that pomposity, is that me? Well, of course not. The nature of humanity is joy. Everything that inhibits that joy is a glamour. If we condemn the glamour, we are giving it energy and only strengthen it. Whatever we inhibit, we will strengthen. On the other hand, if we indulge in it, we will strengthen it too. So there is only one thing left and that is just to look at it. Look at it without condemning, without indulging in it. Just look at it, recognize it, and gradually you will withdraw from it the energy which keeps it going. The second initiation can be taken only when we have really demonstrated our control over the astral elemental which creates the glamour. We have illusions, glamours, because they are comfortable.

During the last year, several people in our group have experienced an increase of their fears. Is there an objective (energetic) cause behind it? Or have they simply become more sensitive to or aware of their fears? (March 1990)
In response to the higher spiritual energies, they are gradually becoming more aware in themselves of the glamour of fear.

Could you please explain what is meant by the glamour of (a) the pairs of opposites, in the higher sense; (b) the lower pairs of opposites; (c) the relation of the opposites. (May 1987)

These questions are too vast to be dealt with succinctly in these columns. Suffice it to say that the very notion that there are 'pairs of opposites' is — from the highest viewpoint — the result of glamour. There are various resolutions, or partial resolutions, of the 'pairs of opposites' into (relative) unities, each 'unity' dissolving into apparent opposites — viewed through glamour — in their turn. In the relation of the opposites — really a unity of differing forces — lies the dynamic, creative impulse of life.

Is it recommendable to entertain 'high goals' or might it only be an expression of lack of humility? (March 1988)
'High goals' are the magnets which attract our aspiration. The question is whether these goals are of a personal and selfish nature — of the personality — or are truly altruistic and from the soul. If the former, the 'high goals' are only an expression of spiritual ambition and must sooner or later be recognized as such.

Is a strong identification with classical music and a desire to be a composer or conductor a soul stimulus through inspiration or is it an emotional aspirational response to physical-plane dualities? (April 1989)
If there is only the desire to compose or conduct music but no actual achievement, I think we can safely identify that as emotional rather than soul stimulus.

Would it be possible to advance in spiritual evolution in service to humanity without being concerned with esotericism and so on? (September 1988)
Of course, yes. The so-called esoteric and occult groups imagine that they are the most advanced of all groups. This is not true; it is just their glamour. The higher initiates today are often working in other fields. The real changes are taking place on the political, economic and social level. 'New Age' people, reading about esotericism in books, suppose they are esotericists. They are not necessarily so at all. Esotericism is not a study you can take an examination in. It is a state of Being, or rather: the science or the philosophy of Being. Can

you imagine that Mao Tse-Tung knew anything about esotericism? Or Churchill, or Roosevelt? No, not at all. They would perhaps have been much less effective as statesmen had they done so. But Mao was a third-degree initiate. So was Churchill. Roosevelt was 2.7. They probably never heard of the New Age, but they were doing the real work.

Does it make sense to inform people in the political and economic field about esotericism? (September 1988)
It depends on the person. Some are responsive, some are not. In my experience there is a change taking place in strictly political and economic groups. More and more people are becoming aware that there is a level of reality above the dense-physical plane. Ideas which so far have attracted only New Age groups are now beginning to infiltrate all strata of society. Educational groups, which until now have been probably very strictly academic, are increasingly more open to what we might call 'New Age' approaches. What for many was just a joke 10 years ago, is taken very seriously today. So, though they are not necessarily the most advanced group, the ideas of the New Age groups are potent and influential.

CHAPTER 14

TRANSMISSION MEDITATION

Transmission: A Potent Method of Service

*This article is an edited version of a talk given by Benjamin Creme at a Transmission Meditation/Tara Network conference held in Nagoya and Osaka, Japan, during his lecture tour in March 1989. For further detailed information on Transmission Meditation, see **Transmission: A Meditation for the New Age** (4th edition, February 1998).*

Meditation is, depending on the meditation, a more or less scientific means of contacting the soul, and of eventually becoming at-one with the soul. That is the basic purpose of meditation of any kind.

Transmission Meditation is a way of serving the world. Unlike many other forms of meditation, it attracts to it only those people who have a desire to serve. This desire to serve manifests itself in an individual only when that person has made some degree of contact with his or her own soul. This is because it is the soul which desires to serve. The nature of the soul is to serve. The first response to soul contact (whether it is followed up or not) is a desire to serve the world in some way. Transmission Meditation provides a simple, easy form of very potent service to the world which at the same time is an extremely potent, fast method of personal growth. This personal, evolutionary result is a side effect of the Transmission Meditation process.

The Masters have at Their disposal tremendous spiritual energies. A major part of the Masters' work is to distribute these energies in the world to produce the effects, the fulfilment of the Plan of evolution which They know to be envisaged for this planet. The Masters are the custodians of the

Plan and the custodians of the energies which bring about the fulfilment of the Plan. Many of these energies are cosmic in source and if they were released directly into the world they would be too high, and would simply bounce off the mass of humanity. Transmission Meditation groups act as sub-stations. The Masters send these spiritual energies through the chakras of the individuals in the groups. This automatically transforms the energies, making them more accessible, more usable by humanity. The Masters then direct the energies into the world wherever they are needed.

There are several hundreds of Transmission groups, all over the world, and they meet regularly at a particular time and day, whatever is suitable for the individual group. This can be once, twice or three times a week. The groups can be anything from three people upwards. Three people form a triangle; that is the basic group.

The group meets and sounds together, aloud, the Great Invocation, which has been given to humanity for this purpose. This Invocation was released to the world in 1945 by Maitreya to give us a technique for invoking the energies which would transform the world and prepare for His coming. By the sounding of this great mantram with the attention focused on the ajna centre (between the eyebrows), a conduit is formed between the group and the Hierarchy of Masters. Through that conduit the Masters send Their energies.

These spiritual forces are precisely the energies which are transforming the world right now. Maitreya fills the world with the energy of equilibrium, for example, and national leaders find that they can work together, can compromise, can reach some kind of consensus, almost overnight. Suddenly, nations who have been enemies for centuries, perhaps, find that they can talk together round a table, and peacefully work out a solution. They are simply responding correctly to the energies which the Hierarchy of Masters are sending out into the world.

That is the service which the Transmission groups perform for the world. It allows you to move away from simple contact with your own soul to a working relationship with the Kingdom of Souls, the Spiritual Hierarchy of Masters.

It is not possible to work in this way, to have the energies sent through the chakras, without the chakras themselves being stimulated, galvanized and transformed. The Masters measure the point in evolution of any individual disciple by the quality of light emanating from the chakras. People talk about auras — brilliant auras and rather dull auras, wide auras and narrow auras. The auras are really the synthesis of all the energies emanating through — into and out of — the chakras up the spine. The more active, the more stimulated these chakras are, the greater the radiation, the wider and more brilliant the aura. This designates the degree of the disciple.

In Transmission Meditation, your chakras are stimulated in a way that would be altogether impossible otherwise. In one year of consistent, intensive Transmission Meditation, you can make the same kind of advance as in 10 or 15 years of personal meditation. It is a hothouse, a forcing process. For this reason, it is not for everyone. Only those who wish to serve the world in some way would be bothered to do Transmission Meditation, because nothing seems to be happening during the meditation. You may or may not be aware of the energies; some feel the energies very clearly and powerfully, some do not feel them at all. This has little to do with your point of advancement, but, in the main, with your particular type of physical body.

This work, however, leads to very profound changes in the individual. Most people, within six months or a year of starting Transmission Meditation, realize the changes in themselves, recognize that they are becoming a different, a better person. People find that they can experience, and demonstrate, love more easily. They find that their minds are more stimulated and creative. They may find that they have more discipline, more determination, more consistency in their approach to work. People see their group members become more radiant, softer, more loving — in a word, more spiritual. A large number of people receive healing, spontaneously, during the Transmissions.

The technique involved is very simple and is applicable to anyone above the age of 12. Transmission Meditation does not interfere with any other form of meditation which you might do. On the contrary, it can only potentize, make more valuable, any other meditation. It is absolutely safe because it is in the hands of the Masters, the Master scientists of the planet. It is potent, safe and scientific because the real work, the major work, is done for you by the Masters Themselves. All that you are asked to do in a Transmission Meditation is to hold your attention at the ajna centre between the eyebrows. That is all. You will find, however, that your attention will wander from this centre. When you realize that this has happened, you sound, inwardly, the mantram OM, or think OM, and your attention will come back automatically to the ajna centre. Holding the attention at the ajna centre produces an alignment between the physical brain and the soul. The energies are sent from the level at which the Masters habitually work: the soul level (the buddhic level, to be precise). While that alignment is held, the Transmission will take place.

I can assure you that there is no more potent service that you can give so easily, with such little expenditure of effort, to the world. Nor will you find a technique of personal growth so potent, so far-reaching, for such little effort. All the Masters, perfect as They are, spend 24 hours a day in transmitting Their energies. There is no Being in cosmos not involved in transmitting energy from levels above to levels below Them. We live in an energetic universe. That energy, from however high a level, is being transmitted, stepped down, received; transmitted, stepped down, and received, throughout cosmos.

If you find that Transmission Meditation is for you, then you have a mode of service which will last until the end of your life and through all future lives.

Mantrams and Prayers

At the end of the Transmission Meditation conference in Kerkrade, Holland, you asked all of us to say together the Mantram of Unification. I found this to be a very moving experience even though I had known nothing previously about it. Could you please publish the words or tell us where to find them and also explain something about its use? (November 1988)

The words of the Mantram of Unification are to be found on p142 of Alice Bailey's *The Externalization of the Hierarchy*. I cannot do better than quote the Master DK as He introduces this mantram to the disciples of the world:

"Endeavour to use the following formula or mantram every day. It is a modernised and mystically worded version of the one which was used widely in Atlantean days during the period of the ancient conflict of which the present is an effect. For many of you this mantram will be in the nature of a recovery of an old and well-known form of words:

> The sons of men are one and I am one with them.
>
> I seek to love not hate.
>
> I seek to serve and not exact due service.
>
> I seek to heal, not hurt.
>
> Let pain bring due reward of light and love.
>
> Let the soul control the outer form and life and all events, and bring to light the love which underlies the happenings of the time.
>
> Let vision come and insight; let the future stand revealed.
>
> Let inner union demonstrate and outer cleavages be gone.
>
> Let love prevail. Let all men love.

"These words may seem inadequate, but said with power and an understanding of their significance and with the potency of the mind and heart behind them, they can prove unbelievably potent in the life of the one who says them. They will produce also an effect in his environment, and the accumulated effects in the world, as you spread the knowledge of the formula, will be great and effective. It will change attitudes, enlighten the vision and lead the aspirant to fuller service and to a wider co-operation based upon sacrifice. My brothers, you cannot evade the sacrifice in the long run, even if you have evaded it until now."

(1) Would you be able to clarify, in the text of the Mantram of Unification, the fragment "and bring to light the love which underlies the happenings of the time"? In what way is love underlying the happenings of the time? And are we supposed to read "our time" or "all times"? It cannot mean that love is at the basis of all these nasty things we see happening around us, I assume? (2) What is the most effective: to say the words aloud, or to say (think) them inwardly? (July/August 1989)

The nature of God, in this solar system, is love. Whatever the outer cleavages, that love underlies all events and is inherent in the Plan of evolution of which these events are but the passing effects. The aim of the disciple, working consciously (more or less) with the Plan, is to 'bring to light', to recognize and manifest the love behind the outer happenings of our time.

The "nasty things we see happening around us" are the result of man's ignorance of his inner divinity (whose nature is love) and his resulting inability to reflect his true nature in a meaningful way. These are temporary and will pass away.

The most effective way to use the Mantram is to say it aloud, the attention fixed meanwhile at the ajna centre (between the eyebrows).

Should we actively use the Mantram of Unification at present or is it more appropriate for the present time and age to use the Great Invocation and/or the Prayer for the New Age which was given to us by Maitreya recently? (January/February 1989)

These three prayers, invocations or affirmations have quite different effects on the user so that there is every reason why all three should be used daily. I would recommend that people use these powerful invocations at different times of the day rather than one after the other.

How does one deal with and change separative tendencies in one's thoughts and actions? (January/February 1990)

(1) Meditate and bring in the soul's inclusive energy. (2) Use the Mantram of Unification and constantly remind yourself that "the sons of men are one". (3) Become engaged in some service activity, thus decentralizing yourself. (4) Use daily the Prayer for the New Age given by Maitreya. (5) Remember that

you are evolving towards perfection so that some separative tendencies are inevitable at this stage.

Why do people discriminate? Why do men feel superior to women? Why do some races feel superior to others? Why do some social classes feel superior to other ones? (June 1991)
The answer lies in the sense of separation — the great heresy — which so enthrals humanity. It is for this reason that Maitreya says (Message No. 11): "Firstly, men must see themselves as brothers, sons of the one Father. This is essential if they would progress one step nearer the Godhead."

It is said by some that NAMASKARA, a Hindustani word meaning "I salute Divinity in you", may be used aloud, silently or written as a special type of all-purpose greeting that has the effect of evoking our essential spirituality, helping us to recognize each other as souls and not just as personalities. Used deliberately and with focused intent, may it have as potent an influence as is said? If so it would seem to behove those who know of it to help make it more widely used and known? (June 1988)
Yes.

Please explain how prayer works esoterically.
Prayer is a stage of the great science of invocation and works by setting up a telepathic link or conduit through the common denominator of mind. The stronger the mental focus, the greater degree of mental communication is achieved. Most prayer, however, is astral/emotional in focus and so less 'sure' of response.

Does it matter to whom one prays? I am confused as between God, Jesus, Sai Baba and Maitreya. Presumably the important thing is to believe in Whomever one chooses: I believe in Them all. Perhaps the best thing is to pray in a blanket sort of way, addressing one's prayer to no one in particular, without personalizing? What about the saints, and one's guardian angel? I'd appreciate your help on this. (November 1990)
It really does not matter to Whom you pray; the important thing, as you say, is to believe in the one you choose. The more

conscious the approach, the more mental, the more the will is involved, and the greater the faith of contact, the more the likelihood of the prayer being heard and, within karmic law, answered. My recommendation is to pray to Maitreya, as Representative of God, Divine Intermediary, not least because He has promised to answer the prayers of those who need His help. I would suggest that we should not pray for, and expect to receive, material goods or solutions to life problems, which it is our responsibility to find or work out for ourselves.

When I pray, what name should I give to the Christ? (July/August 1991)
By the name most familiar to yourself: Christ, Jesus, Maitreya Buddha, Messiah, Imam Mahdi, Krishna. He Himself prefers to be known as the Teacher.

Do you think there's a parallel between all the invocations and prayers during the Second World War which led Maitreya to decide, in 1945, to come into the world and the prayers which are released at this time? (May 1991)
The prayers and cries for help which rose to Maitreya from humanity throughout the First and Second World Wars led to Maitreya's decision (in 1945) to return, Himself, to the world, not to end the war and, therefore, the suffering, but to show us a new way, the way of peace. In other words, He did not come to end war but to inspire us to end war — through sharing and justice.

The prayers released at this time are for divine intercession to end the Gulf crisis — to prevent war or limit its effects.

I believe (with Maitreya) that: "Nothing happens by itself. Man must act and implement his will." (Message No. 31) I do not think we get peace simply by praying for it. We get peace by removing the causes of war — injustice, greed, selfishness, competition, market forces, national pride.

After what happened in 1945, was it not the prayers that brought Maitreya to London? (May 1991)
No, it was not the prayers; it was the call, the cry, for help. People cried for help in every language, not to Maitreya

particularly but to God, to 'up there', just crying out "Please! Please! — Reality, God, Cosmos, help us, help us!" Maitreya answered the cry for help; He will also answer the prayers. We can pray for peace but Maitreya cannot just give it to us on a plate — that is the point: we have to do it — we have to put into motion the things that bring about peace. We have to do it ourselves. When we pray to God, to Maitreya, or Whomever, for peace — to my mind it is going about it the wrong way. We have to do it ourselves. Pray for help, for energy, for guidance, for inspiration to bring about the peace, but we have to make the peace. We cannot just sit back and think God will make peace. God has peace, God is peace. There is already peace but we disturb the peace. We are disturbers of the peace, we should be in jail.

Is prayer enough to maintain peace in the world? What more can we do? (November 1990)
In my opinion prayer, by itself, will not maintain peace. Work for balance and equilibrium in the world — political, economic and social — and you will work for peace.

Transmission Meditation: Its Role in the Development of The Disciple

The following article focuses on the role of Transmission work in the development of the disciple, with special attention to the experience of the disciple as he or she moves forward on the evolutionary path. It is edited from a talk by Benjamin Creme at a Weekend Transmission Workshop in the Netherlands in 1987.

A disciple is someone who is consciously taking part in the evolutionary journey. It goes without saying that all humanity is evolving, has evolved, from early animal-man to the point where we are today. For untold aeons, that process takes place more or less unconsciously; the individual soul comes into incarnation again and again, swept into evolution by the magnet of evolution itself. The disciple, on the other hand, takes a very conscious role in this process, leading to a very specific goal.

The disciple is someone who knows there is a goal and who seeks to further his evolution himself in a highly conscious manner. The goal he sees is, of course, perfection — liberation from the necessity to incarnate on the planet at all. The disciple willingly and consciously submits himself to the necessary disciplines — that is what being a disciple is — to arrive finally at that goal.

Until now, I have, on the whole, emphasized the service aspect of Transmission Meditation. By the simple act of sitting in a Transmission group and allowing the Masters of the Hierarchy to transmit Their energies through the chakras of the group, service of immense value is carried out.

But there is even more than service to Transmission Meditation. It is not possible for these spiritual forces to be transmitted through the chakras of the individuals in the group without these individuals becoming transformed by them. As the energies pass through the chakras, they stimulate, heighten the activity of, the various chakras, usually the heart, the throat and the head chakras. Because of this, besides being a service to the world of tremendous importance and value, Transmission Meditation is at the same time probably the most potent method of personal growth open to any individual today.

Laya yoga

The Tibetan Master, Djwhal Khul, Who gave to the world the Alice Bailey teachings, wrote about a specialized form of laya yoga — the yoga of energies — which, He said, would emerge in this coming Age of Aquarius.

Transmission Meditation is that specialized form of laya yoga. It is really a combination of two yogas: laya, the yoga of energies; and karma, the yoga of service. It brings together the two most powerful methods of evolutionary advance known.

It is a group meditation, and for its correct carrying out it needs the formation of groups. It has been possible to introduce it to the world only now, at the dawn of the new Age of Aquarius, because only now are disciples beginning to work in group formation.

All forms of meditation developed over the last 2,000 years of Pisces, and therefore under the influence of Piscean energy, have been individual meditations. They have been designed to bring the man or woman into soul contact, leading eventually to at-one-ment with the soul. When, through meditation, the soul is contacted, it can stimulate and eventually 'grip' its vehicle — the man or woman in incarnation. Through meditation, a channel called the 'antahkarana' is built between the personality and the soul. Simultaneously, the soul, itself, is building that same channel downwards to its reflection, the personality. This process starts just before the first initiation.

There are five great points of crisis which mark out the evolutionary process. These are the five initiations to Mastery or Liberation. Having taken them, you do not need to incarnate on this planet. These five great expansions of consciousness, which is what initiation is, cover only the last few lives of the

497

evolutionary journey from animal-man to the totally liberated Master.

It takes literally hundreds of thousands of incarnational experiences to bring a person to the point of the first initiation. As the soul sees its vehicle coming close to that point, perhaps four or five incarnations yet away from the first initiation, it brings its vehicle, the man or woman on the physical plane, into contact with some form of meditation.

In that first instance, the contact might be very slight indeed: the person hears about meditation, tries it for a bit, perhaps spends a little part of his time doing it. Eventually, there comes a life in which the person will spend a considerable part of his or her time devoted to the practice of some form of meditation. It is not the personality who seeks meditation; it is forced into this process by the impulse of the soul itself. In this sense the soul is the first Master.

Great expansion of consciousness

When, through several lives passed in a more serious approach to meditation, the person becomes ready for the first initiation, the Master steps in and guides, tests and prepares the person for this first great expansion of consciousness.

In incarnation (of course there are many out of incarnation who have also gone through this experience), there are roughly 800,000 people who have taken the first initiation. Out of 5 billion people, it is not very many. Of those who have taken the second initiation, there are only some 240,000 in incarnation; of the third only between 2,000 and 3,000. Of those who have taken the fourth initiation, there are only about 450 in the world at the moment. The numbers are very small indeed. The interesting thing is that the process is speeding up extraordinarily. Today, several million people are standing on the threshold of the first initiation. This is why the Hierarchy, for the first time in countless thousands of years, are returning to the everyday world — the disciples are drawing them magnetically into the world.

The probationary disciple is watched and tested by the Master, at the fringe of a Master's Ashram. When he has passed his tests and is ready, he enters through the gate of initiation into Hierarchy, and becomes a disciple. That is the beginning of a journey from which there is no return, it is the burning of the boats behind the disciple. He can waste many lives, hold himself back, but he really cannot ever turn back against the tide of evolution.

Then begins a period where a great battle is fought out between his soul and his personality. The man or woman on the physical plane becomes the arena of a battle for possession between his personality desire life and the spiritual life of the soul. Eventually, though it may take time, the soul (because it is stronger) wins.

The battle can rage for many lives. There is an average of six or seven lives between the first and second initiation. It is a hard struggle, and often a painful one, in the beginning.

The disciple finds that he is being stimulated on all fronts — mentally, emotionally and physically. His three bodies are stimulated as never before. The battle has to be fought out simultaneously on all these fronts. As he thinks he is coping with the 'enemy' attacking his physical frontier, he finds himself invaded on the emotional front. He brings all his personality forces to bear to thrust the 'enemy' back, and he finds that on the mental plane and on the physical plane, again, there are forces attacking him from behind. Eventually, by the sheer exhaustion of the battle, he gives in, he accepts the dictates of his soul.

He becomes an accepted (accepting) disciple, working closer to the centre of a Master's Ashram. Then he discovers that he is not alone, never has been alone, as he thought, but that he is really part of a group, the members of which he has probably never met on the physical plane. He works under the supervision, not immediately of a Master, but of a disciple of one of the Masters. He finds the battle raging more and more fiercely until he comes to a point about half way between the first and second initiation.

A little glimmer of light

Suddenly, he sees a little glimmer of light at the end of a long tunnel. He finds that the physical body is obeying his will, and that the most unruly body of all, his astral body, is beginning to be controlled. He finds this very encouraging — he sees the way ahead. It is still a fight, but he sees that, if he keeps at it, there is hope.

Then he finds that he is put in contact with other people in some group work. He finds that these other people have the same experiences, the same difficulties, and he realizes that this is part of growing out of his ignorance, glamour, illusion, seeing the world and himself as they really are.

To bring all of this about, meditation has been given to the world. It is the catalytic process which allows the soul to create this situation *vis-à-vis* its reflection. It 'grips' its vehicle, mentally, astrally, physically, more and more, making it a purer reflection of itself. Its aim is to bring its vehicle into a perfect reflection of itself. It does this by stimulating the vibrational rate of each of the bodies, physical, astral and mental, until all three are vibrating at more or less the same frequency.

The soul is in no hurry. It has aeons of time because it does not even think in terms of time. It is only the personality who has the feeling that this is taking forever. It seems to us that we will never be free of these physical, astral and mental controls which prevent us from expressing ourselves as the Soul, the spiritual being we know we are, whose spiritual intelligence, love and will is demonstrating and radiant. When that point is eventually reached, the third great expansion of consciousness can be taken.

This is a watershed in the evolutionary process. From the point of view of the Masters, this is the first initiation. The first two are seen by Them as preparatory to this first, true soul initiation when the man or woman really becomes ensouled — and therefore truly divine — for the first time. Until then, the divinity is there but it is only potential.

Two factors

Two factors bring this about: meditation of some form or other, bringing the man or woman into contact with the soul; the other is service — some form of altruistic service.

Why service? What is so important about service? Perhaps it is easier to see the value of the scientific aspect of meditation, but why service? Service is the impulse of the soul. The soul knows only service; it is its nature. The soul comes into incarnation to serve the Plan of evolution of the Logos, the Heavenly Man ensouling the planet. As soon as a man or woman comes into contact with the soul, that person, spontaneously, wants to serve in some form or other. The person might or might not actually do the service, but the soul will impel it towards service. If, under the impulse of the soul, the person serves, all goes well; the purpose of the soul is being carried out, soul energies are being properly used. If, through meditation, the person receives the stimulus from the soul but does not use it in service, the soul energy 'goes bad' on him or her, produces stress, stasis. The person becomes ill or neurotic. The illnesses and diseases of the world, in particular of disciples, are largely the result of the misuse or non-use of soul energy. You can see how important it is, therefore, in response to soul stimulus which meditation brings about, to use the contacted energy in service.

Transmission Meditation provides both of these requirements. The service, the act of sitting in a Transmission group and having the energies transmitted through you, allows the Masters to oversee your meditation. It is not possible to do Transmission Meditation without carrying out an act of service — that is its nature. It is not possible to serve in this way without at the same time advancing along the evolutionary path because Transmission Meditation brings together the two yogas — the yoga of service, karma yoga, and the yoga of energies, laya yoga. The beauty of Transmission Meditation is that the laya aspect of it is done for you by the Masters. The karma, the service aspect of it is simple and minimal, in terms of the time and energy involved, so that the laziest person in the world can still act in a powerful way and benefit the world.

Considering the laya aspect of it, the laziest individual can make a potent advance along the evolutionary path because the Masters do all the work. They are Master scientists. Every second of every minute of the day, They are transmitting and transforming energies from one or another extra-planetary source, and protecting humanity from those which would be harmful.

Can you imagine having such advanced scientists actually overseeing your own meditation? Everyone who takes part in a Transmission group enters a field of service so simple that a child of 12 can do it, yet so scientific that the most incredible advance along the evolutionary path becomes possible. It is literally a gift from the Gods, and it is released into the world at this time because only now are being formed groups of disciples able to handle these energies and to work consciously in group formation.

Transmission Meditation brings together, therefore, these two most potent levers of the evolutionary process — laya, the yoga of energies, and karma, the yoga of service. They impel those involved in it fast along the last phase of evolution which we call the path of initiation. The underlying purpose behind Transmission Meditation is to make it possible for the groups involved to pass quickly along the path of initiation.

[*Note*: For further information on the underlying purpose behind Transmission Meditation, please refer to Chapter IX in *Transmission: A Meditation for the New Age* (4th edition, February 1998). More information on initiation is to be found in *Maitreya's Mission, Volume One*.]

CHAPTER 15

DISCIPLESHIP AND PRACTICE

This article is an edited version of a talk given by Benjamin Creme at the 1990 Transmission Meditation/Tara Network conference held in San Francisco, USA. The section of Questions and Answers also includes material from the 1990 conference in Veldhoven, the Netherlands.

It is a truism in occultism that no new teaching can be given until that already given has been put into practice. This is a law. There is no way you can take in anything higher until you have put into practice what you have already received. Mainly, people approach esotericism as if it were an academic subject in which you take exams and get a degree. It is not like that at all. Certainly there are degrees, degrees of initiation, but you can become an initiate without knowing anything about esoteric theory or practice at all, by living naturally, intuitively, the life of a disciple.

You have to do it one way or the other. You can do it intuitively, or through the acquiring of knowledge and the application of the rules and precepts in your life, moment to moment. It is an all-day affair. In my experience, most people set about being a disciple in a very lukewarm way. He/she fits it into their everyday life when there is a moment to spare. The average disciple does not realize that the disciple is a different person from the rest of humanity. The rules and laws which apply — even the Laws of Cause and Effect and of Rebirth — which affect humanity willy-nilly — affect the disciple differently, according to his ability to work within them and to manipulate them to the soul's needs.

A disciple, or anyone who has the aspiration to become a disciple, must recognize first of all that he is an ordinary human being who has made a pledge and has taken in hand the development of his own evolution. He is learning to work with the soul and to carry out its purpose. The soul's purpose, whatever other purposes it may have, is, under the Law of Sacrifice, to work with the Plan of evolution in so far as the disciple can intuit it and put it into effect in his or her life. Only the rudiments of the Plan may become real in his or her consciousness, but in so far as these aspects do become real, it behoves him or her to put it into effect in life. Actually doing this is very rare indeed.

It is not the forces of evil that worry the Christ and the Masters of the Hierarchy. They can cope with the forces of evil rather well. Most people think that the main obstacles to the externalization of the Hierarchy and the spiritualization of the life of humanity are the problems involved with the forces of materiality. There are such problems. But some of the quickest responders to that materiality are the disciples of the world. It is the ingrained materiality and, above all, inertia, of disciples as well as everyone else that keeps humanity in thrall to the forces of materiality, the forces of evil as we call them.

Disciples are doubly responsible. They have the responsibility of ordinary humanity but extra responsibility because they know some aspects of the truth. They have taken upon themselves to do something about changing the situation in the world, and to change their own nature in such a way as to work intelligently with the Plan. Yet people are so steeped in materialism — it is so ingrained in the vast body of even the world's disciples, that little or no action is taken by any of us to remedy the situation. We remain as engrossed in materialism as anyone else. That is the problem for the Christ and the Masters: not the forces of evil, but the inertia, the crippling inertia of the disciples of the world.

I learned recently from my Master that the average number of minutes in which people in the Transmission Meditation groups around the world are actually aligned, in which the physical brain and the soul are aligned — and so they are being transmitted through and therefore doing the work of Transmission — is astonishingly small.

Why is this? There has to be a reason why, after 10 years, you are still doing so poorly — for example, this is the 10th year in which I have come to the United States and the 10th year in which some of you have been doing Transmission Meditation.

"What have you been doing all these years?" I ask myself. Of course it is a question of polarization. If one is astrally polarized — and the majority of people in these groups are — it is more difficult to hold the attention at the ajna centre and so be aligned for longer than a few minutes at a time. Also people do not seem to know the difference between being aligned and not being aligned. They really think they are aligned. I am sure all of you are shocked by this statement. You imagine you are aligned yet, quite frankly, most of the time you are not.

What are you doing if you are not aligned? I suggest that you are in a state of reverie. You are ruminating. You are in a state in which your attention is hovering around the solar plexus. But since you know that Transmission Meditation involves focusing your attention at the ajna centre, and since from time to time, when you remember, you can bring the attention back there, you forget that it has dropped. But within a few minutes it has dropped. If you add up the few minutes in which it is really held at the ajna centre and in which you are transmitting, it comes to — on average — four to five minutes in the hour. Some people do only an hour's Transmission in the week. That is four to five minutes in the week. It is not a lot. "The Role of Transmission Meditation in the Development of the Disciple" [the title of a previous talk; see Chapter 14, p484 of this book] is something which does not apply to people who are doing four or five minutes' actual Transmission in the week. Little can be expected to happen in that time.

Nevertheless, enough happens to make Transmission Meditation a powerful way to serve. If you are transmitting four or five minutes in the hour even for only one hour a week, you are receiving the benefit of these spiritual forces through the chakras in a way still more powerful than you would have achieved by any other method, given the same amount of time and effort.

The point is, people do not make much effort. They think they do. They mean well. Everyone means well. Everyone imagines that they are working quite hard. But from a Master's point of view they are only playing at being in a Transmission group, playing at helping the world. A Transmission Meditation group contacts spiritual energies which transform the whole world — politically, economically, socially and so on. Most people are contributing to this only for a few minutes a week, yet they feel that they are in a very potent, powerful situation — which they are; but only because these energies are so potent, so powerful, are these short minutes of actual Transmission worth anything at all.

Discipleship, for most people, is an activity which they fit into their general life. They go through the motions. Their first priority is to earn their living. Everyone — almost everyone — has to earn their living. That is true for everyone at every level. That takes precedence, it would seem, over everything else that people do. Then you must have vacations. That is the second priority. If you have family, you have to look after them and clothe and feed them and take them on vacation and so on. People will spend enormous amounts of time, energy and money on vacations, on restaurant meals, on having a nice, pleasant, civilized time. There is nothing wrong with that. Except that it has nothing to do with discipleship.

Commitment

Discipleship means commitment to the life of the disciple and that is distinctly different from the life of the average human being. He is in the world, part of the world, totally identified with and serving the world, and yet, in a curious way, he is isolated from the world. He is in the peculiar position of isolation amidst the maelstrom of everyday living. And the disciple feels things more powerfully, more painfully than other people. Everyone can see the pain, the suffering of the world — the starving millions, poverty, earthquakes, the terrible diseases which ravage humanity. Everyone is moved by that. But the disciple very often sees it more clearly than others. And being more sensitive to that suffering because aware of being a soul in incarnation and committed to serving and relieving it, he/she feels it more than most people.

So why does he not act on it? Well, of course, people do act on it. Many people devote themselves totally to the service of the world, to removing the agony of the world. But they tend not to be students of esotericism. They tend to be people who could not care less about esotericism, who have no sense of being anything very special, but are simply committed to service. They are disciples carrying out the actions and undergoing the training of discipleship through service without even giving it a thought.

How much more can you do when you do give it thought, when you do know yourselves as disciples, consciously seeking to fulfil the requirements of discipleship. What is missing in the life of the average disciple is a sense of vocation — of vocation as a disciple. Discipleship in a sense is a vocation. You are called to it, not by God, but by your own soul. Your own soul makes you a disciple. You are a disciple as soon as you contact your soul and your soul drives you forward.

The average disciple, however, simply fits his vocation into his everyday life. He does not see it as the aim of this particular incarnation. He does not, therefore, generate the fire which makes discipleship what it should be: a path which will take him as fast as possible to the door of initiation.

You cannot enter the door of initiation lukewarm; it has never been done. Sooner or later that lukewarm attitude has to change, if not in this life, then in the next or the one after. The soul is in no hurry. The soul has endless time, all infinity. But if you are in a hurry, if you sense the world need, you can be sure that just being a disciple when it is convenient, when there is nothing better on television, when you are feeling better, when you are no longer in pain or your stomach is not upset, is not enough. People allow all sorts of little things to prevent them from being a disciple; the fatigue of the physical body — which everyone shares — is nothing special. Everyone's body is deficient in some way and they have pains, illnesses, suffering of all kinds. The point is not to let it get you down or prevent you from carrying out your actions.

Two of the great disciples of recent years known to us — Helena Petrovna Blavatsky and Alice A.Bailey — were ill for a great deal of their lives, but they never let illness prevent them from serving the world as few have done. As you know, for 30 years Alice Bailey served as the amanuensis of the Master DK. For much of that time she was ill and sat up in bed writing until she could not write any more, literally could not write another word. Then the Master changed the procedure and she was able to read His teaching on a kind of internal screen, which she read out and recorded on tape for someone else to type from. For years she worked under extreme disability.

Madame Blavatsky was ill with kidney and half a dozen other diseases for the last 13 years of her life. Only her Master, the Master Morya, kept her in the body so that she could finish her work: bringing to the world *The Secret Doctrine.*

These two initiates brought the will to bear on the work. They ignored the physical body. They ignored their upset emotional states brought about by family discord and very often calumny and treachery from those closest to them. They ignored all that and got on with the work of being disciples: doing their work for the Plan. If they could do it, others can do it. Of course, being third- and fourth-degree initiates, respectively, made it easier for them. They were not only mentally but spiritually polarized. If you are spiritually polarized you are living and working as a soul and the soul's energy is propelling you forward all the time and carving the path for you. But the will still has to come into play — especially if the physical body is disabled or the emotional body disturbed.

If you are polarized on the astral plane, however, as most people are, you are subject to all the limitations and illusions of that plane. What can you do about it? You must bring the mind to bear. It is the light of the soul focused through the mental body, through the mind, that dissipates the glamour. You must look at the glamours, not be content with them but work continuously to overcome them, instead of saying: "That's how I am, I am afraid, what can I do but live in fear?"

You do not have to live in fear. No one has to live in fear. Fear is a glamour like every other glamour, the worst there is, underlying, I believe, most other glamours. It must be overcome by anyone who has any hope of standing before the Initiator.

You cannot take initiation, become initiate, while you live in fear. You can never become a Master until you have, not just courage, but the total absence of fear. You need courage to tackle the fear and to demonstrate in your life that forward looking, advancing impetus and effort of a true disciple.

Let me quote a few statements which the Master DK gave through Alice Bailey to show you how the Masters have always looked on this matter:

"When the Self is known and not simply felt, and when the realization is mental as well as sensory, then truly can the aspirant be prepared for initiation. I would like to point out that I am basing my words on certain basic assumptions, which for the sake of clarity I want briefly to state. Firstly, that the student is sincere in his aspiration and is determined to go forward no matter what may be the reaction of and upon his lower self. Only those who can clearly differentiate between the two aspects of their nature, the real self and the illusory self, can work intelligently. Secondly, I am acting upon the assumption that all have lived long enough and battled sufficiently with deterrent forces of life to have enabled them to develop a fairly true sense of values. They are not to be kept back by any happenings to the personality or by the pressure of time and circumstance, by age or physical disability. They have wisely learned that enthusiastic rushing forward and a violent energetic progress has its drawbacks, and that a steady, regular, persistent endeavour will carry them further in the long run. Spasmodic spurts of effort and temporary pressure peter out into disappointment and a weighty sense of failure. Nevertheless, intention and effort are considered by us (the Masters) of prime importance and are the two main requisites for all disciples, initiates and Masters. Plus the power of persistence. The whole secret of success in treading the occult path depends upon an attitude of mind. When the attitude is one of concrete materialism, of concentration upon form, and a desire for the things of the present moment, little progress can be made in apprehending the higher esoteric truths. The moment a man becomes consciously powerful on the mental plane, his power for good is a hundredfold increased. Most men do not yet distinguish with accuracy between themselves as the thinker, persistent in time and space, and the vehicle through which they think, which is ephemeral and transient. One of the first lessons which a disciple needs to learn is that where he is strongest and where he finds the most satisfaction is very frequently the point of greatest danger and weakness."

Everyone wants higher teaching. Everyone wants something they have never read or heard of before — whether or not they have put into effect what they already know. People are greedy in their curiosity. They want more sensation, the sensation of the new. But the sensation of the new will never take you to the door of initiation — only the application of certain laws: the Law of Service, the Law of Sacrifice, the building of the antahkarana, the removal of all perception that the physical, emotional or mental bodies are of any consequence at all to the soul, except as vehicles of expression. Once understood, this relates you to the path of discipleship, and will bring you to the door of initiation more directly than anything else. It is not a question of more teaching, though everyone wants more teaching, more techniques, more tools. They have all the techniques, the tools, the teaching, more than enough, more than they could ever use, or ever do use. Most do not put into practice the teaching already given.

There is no higher teaching than that which we can actually put into practice. If it cannot be put into practice, it does not matter whether it is so high that it can be understood only by eighth-degree initiates. It does not mean anything to you unless you can put it into practice.

Use the teaching which has already been given. Put it into practice and you will advance faster than your greatest expectations. When you do this, when you put teaching into practice in this way, it becomes your own, no longer an abstract teaching, an academic subject. It becomes yours. You become the path. The path unfolds before you as you practise the requirements of discipleship. The path is not over there, or in that book, or in this technique — it is something which unfolds out of your consciousness. The path for everyone is unique.

Of course, there are certain basic, fundamental requirements which never change, which are of the nature of deity itself. Remember that the path of discipleship leading to initiation, and the path of initiation leading to Mastery, is the path to God. It is the path of the unfolding of one's divinity. That is what it is about, and one should never forget that.

Most people tend to forget it. It becomes peripheral to their lives, which is like saying that my very nature is peripheral to my life; my life peripheral to me. But I am my life. If I am not my life, I am nothing. How can your own life and the movement towards the expression of that divinity be peripheral to your day-to-day life?

You have to make it your vocation. If you want to become a disciple, you must become fiery with enthusiasm. You have to move in a state of joy, of commitment, of high expectation that you are following a path which will lead you to initiation. Otherwise your action will be so lukewarm it will take the next 50 incarnations to reach what you can reach in this incarnation.

Referring to your statement that we must be on fire to achieve initiation, is there a starting point to kindle that fire? A meditation, an attitude, an activity?
There is a meditation, there is an attitude, and there is an activity. The meditation is called Transmission Meditation, together with any other personal meditation you may do. The activity is service of whatever kind that you feel strongly drawn to do, and the attitude is one of commitment, absolute commitment to playing your part in the Plan.

The Master DK, through Alice Bailey, put it this way: "Every man who liberates himself, who sees clearly and who releases himself from the glamour of illusion, aids in the great work." That is the kind of ideal which I think you have to generate in yourself to bring fire into your belly. (It is actually the heart, but we say "fire in the belly".) Fire in the heart drives the disciple forward. It is a fiery aspiration to move forward, not just as fast as possible, but without hindrance, no matter what, overcoming all obstacles — health, age, family commitments, whatever your personal circumstances — none of that must stand in the way. We do not let these things stand in the way of other things we — as the personality — like to do.

The personality and the soul are at war. It is very painful for the personality to give up its dominance, but it has to become negative to the soul if the person is to take initiation. This is the process behind the initiatory experience. Unless you are really determined to go through the pain of renouncing personality desires and so carrying out the soul's purposes, you will not do it. The personality does not do it by itself. The personality has no intention of giving up the fight. It is a fight! You take the side of the personality or you take the side of the soul. Of course, mostly we take the side of the personality, but we suffer thereby. You either overcome the personality or you suffer.

It is a question of overcoming, of relinquishing. You come into incarnation under the Law of Sacrifice. That law drives the soul into incarnation. The life of the disciple is governed by the Law of Sacrifice. If you are not prepared to make sacrifices, then you are not prepared to enter the path of discipleship. So, forget about it, or leave it till the next life or the one after that.

If you want to become a disciple, if you want to enter the initiatory gate, then you must make the sacrifice of the lower for the higher. It has to be done willingly, gladly, from your own choice. Eventually, by gripping its vehicle more and more powerfully, the soul brings it about. But the battle is on for years. If you really wish to act as a soul, to be of service to the world, and to progress as fast as you possibly can, you must use your will.

Will is the focused intent behind your mental idea — to become a disciple, to make it work, to serve the world, whatever it is. You bring your will to bear as a focused, immovable intent to do it. Of course, we allow things to move us. We make up our mind and then we unmake it. You have to make up your mind and stick to it.

The meditation, then, is Transmission Meditation, the activity is service and the attitude is one of focused intent and commitment.

How does one bring the will to bear upon one's impediments and inertia?

You have to carry out your intentions. It is like every New Year when you give yourself some New Year's resolutions and then you work at them. You work at transforming your character. And if you do it day by day, in little bits, then when some big thing comes along you have the habit of coping. It is building into yourself instinctual habits, habitual right action, of doing whatever the duty happens to be, honouring commitments and responsibilities without liking or disliking. Just doing what has to be done, answering to the necessities of life. As you do that in small things, you find that you can do it in big things. It is more than habit; it is a built-in instinct to do what is right. Then you have discrimination.

Discrimination grows from this instinctual habit of doing the right thing, without thinking about it. You do not say: "Now what is the right thing in this case? What should be my response?" You just do it. That is the sign of the disciple who has built into himself or herself instinctual right action in each situation. Of course it takes time to do this, many lives. We are talking now in terms of perfection. The real disciple will have built into his or her character right action as an instinctual, habitual reaction to life. First in the little things, bring your will to bear on the little things, then the bigger things become automatic. There is no difference, just an intensification of habitual action.

Would you recommend setting aside a period of time each day for an honest and detached evaluation of whether or not one has lived as a soul during the day's activities?

Yes indeed. If you can do that, you are half-way there. It is a very useful thing to do. Go through it every day, and say: "How did I measure up? Where did I go wrong? What did I do that was not up to my own notion of what I have set for myself? Was that the soul or was it the personality? Was that glamour?" Go through it. It is the best thing you can do.

Could you identify the glamour that most inhibits our service now? Anything more specific than fear.

Fear is the worst glamour. It is the number one glamour for all people, and of course all disciples. Average humanity is filled with many fears, stemming from all sorts of conditioning, like superstition and so on. But the problem for disciples is more crucial, because they are taking a conscious hand in speeding up their own evolution, training themselves to serve the Plan, in so far as they are aware of it. That requires courage. You cannot do it if you are afraid. You become impotent if you are afraid.

Fear imposes limitation. If you are impotent, how can you serve? How can you be potent if you are impotent? Every reflex of fear imposes a limitation on consciousness and therefore on the energy which would lead to action. If you put a block, caused by fear, between your impulse and your action, that action will be distorted and limited in some way. You will not be able to generate the energy which will take you through the obstacles, and life is full of obstacles.

The disciple is also under test. These tests and obstacles are sometimes put in the way of the disciple by his own soul or his Master. Overcoming them leads to higher, more potent, service. But if the disciple is filled with fears, he cannot overcome the obstacles, they seem too great.

One should remember that no one is ever given more than they can do — never. It is a law. No one is ever required to do more than they are constitutionally able to do, that is in terms of their ray structure, point in evolution, awareness, health, age and so on. That is something you should remember. The only things that may prevent you from actually doing all that you can do are fear, laziness, inertia, sense of inadequacy — which is another name for fear. Lack of courage is another name for fear. Fear is the big one.

However, a great many people inhibit their service activity now because they think they are already serving. They have the glamour which says: "Because I have the ideal, it is already happening." If they can visualize something, it is. But it is not! It is only a visualization. Many people do this, strongly motivated by their ability to sense an ideal, a concept which they take to be true. Whether it is or not is beside the point. They have an ideal, but it remains astral. They immediately think: "That's it! I've done it! I'm there!" This is one of the major glamours of disciples, one of the major glamours of 'New Age' groups which are dominated, not by 7th-ray souls, as they imagine, but by 6th-ray personalities. The 6th ray has this self-deceiving quality because it remains astral; the vision remains on the astral plane. It satisfies. Just to have the idea is so satisfying in an astral sense. It feeds the emotion of satisfaction and kindles that glamorous feeling of "The work is done, that was a wonderful experience." The "wonderful experience" may be the ability to envision a beautiful future, a plan, an ideal of some kind: link up at nine o'clock every night for half a minute praying for world peace and Hallelujah!, you have world peace. It is not useless, but world peace does not come that way. World peace comes from getting rid of the conditions which lead to war.

There is nothing wrong with the idealism, but that glamour leads the idealist to believe that just to enunciate it, to envision it, is already enough. That is one of the most inhibiting factors in service. So it is a mixture of fear and the glamour of "It is already done. We do not need to do any more." But as Maitreya says: "Nothing happens by itself. Man must act and implement his will." You have to put the ideal into effect. You have to create a form which allows the idea or ideal to take outer physical shape. Otherwise, it remains stillborn and an inhibiting factor for the development of the individual because he thinks he is active, he thinks he is evolving. He is not; he is simply idealizing. We have done that for thousands of years with all sorts of wonderful ideals and few of them have ever been put into effect. That is why we have the world we have.

How does one marry together the more spiritual and the everyday world? (July/August 1991)
That is precisely the role of the disciple, and for that reason the role of the disciple is tough. You have to remain integral in the spiritual reality, in touch, moment-to-moment if possible, with your divine nature, and at the same time live the ordinary life of a person in the world. That is why it is not easy to be a disciple — why there are not too many of them around. Only 800,000 people out of the 5.5 billion now in incarnation have taken the first initiation; only about 240,000 the second initiation; only 2,000-3,000 the third and only 450 who have taken the fourth initiation.

But as the world is changed for the better — based more on spiritual values of justice and sharing — the task of the disciple will become easier and the numbers will increase dramatically.

Given the number of initiates in incarnation above the second degree, say, who have ongoing contact with an externalized Master, why are not some, at least, making known in some way the fact of the Reappearance? (November 1986)
This question shows a basic misunderstanding of the relationship between Masters and second-degree disciples, and also about the role of disciples in general in the externalization process.

There are around 240,000 disciples of the second degree in incarnation at present. They are to be found in all fields. Of these, only a tiny minority have "ongoing contact with a Master", externalized or not. The vast majority do their work, in politics, industry, science or wherever, without necessarily knowing anything about Hierarchy or Masters, far less the facts of the Reappearance. And if they heard of these facts (as some of them must have done) they would not necessarily believe them. Almost all disciples of the second degree and many of the third work under subjective (soul) stimulus and inspiration.

Also, where disciples do work consciously in contact with a Master, they would know their particular role and be inclined to stick to that. Each to his task.

*In **Discipleship in the New Age**, by Alice Bailey, DK speaks of psychic powers developed by the disciple. This is a totally different approach to what the average person understands as 'psychic'. Can you explain this higher level and how it relates to the lower?* (June 1987)
This is a vast subject, too large to deal with adequately here. Very briefly, what most people understand as 'psychic' is the lower psychism of the astral apparatus — astral clairvoyance, clairaudience, and the like — developed over the millions of years of the Atlantean root race and now an atavistic trait. The higher psychism of the mentally- or spiritually-polarized disciple is the outcome of the ability to register not astral but soul contacts and qualities. This may demonstrate as true, conscious, soul telepathy, for instance. A magnetic attractiveness, spontaneous and unconscious, is such a psychic enfoldment. The disciple radiates, and this radiation has varied subtle effects. An interesting example of this is given by DK in *Discipleship in the New Age*, in which He draws a disciple's attention to a quality which he radiates quite subjectively: "the power to hold others steady by the nature of your understanding; this they feel, even if you do not consciously express it."

Much information has been given about the disciples and initiates, but is it not true to say that many non-initiates are actively helping the Plan of Hierarchy, and may indeed be of more service if they are in an influential position in society? (June 1987)
I am sure it is true that hundreds of thousands of people are actively helping the Plan of Hierarchy without being initiate or having heard of the idea of initiation; but if they are "in an influential position in society" it is more than likely that they will be on the threshold, at least, of the first initiation. From

the point of view of the Masters, to be 'initiate' means to have taken the third initiation.

If classes (out-of-the-body instruction by Hierarchy) are held between 10pm and 5am, what happens to disciples and aspirants who don't sleep till after midnight? (1) Do they arrive at classes late? (2) Do they miss vital lessons? (3) Can their curriculum be adapted to their own sleeping hours? (June 1987)

(1) Yes. (2) No. (3) Yes.

Modern living and working habits (to a large extent due to the advent of electricity) have necessitated a change in Hierarchical teaching procedures.

We feel love for our family. From the Self's point of view is that an illusion? (April 1991)

No. Love is the nature of the Self.

Thoughts on Group Work

This article is an edited version of a talk given by Benjamin Creme at Tara Network group meetings held in Tokyo and Okinawa, Japan, in 1987. The questions and answers have been compiled from these two conferences.

Group work is the way of the future. Every activity in this coming age will proceed through groups — group affiliation, group thought, arriving eventually at group consciousness. This is in line with the quality of the energies streaming in from Aquarius, which can only be known, apprehended, and used, in group formation.

Group activity of the past Age of Pisces has always come from one individual, a leader, making his intentions and vision known, and having his instructions carried out by the other members of the group. This has been the norm over the past 2,000 years. To respond correctly to the quality of the energy of Aquarius and to the intentions of the Plan of evolution for humanity, this approach has to change. Rather than the group of individuals, however devoted, following the orders of one, perhaps more potent, individual, each member must take full responsibility for the thoughts, ideas, intentions and purpose of the group.

In London we have a group active in the work I have been doing since March 1974. This group was formed at the instigation of my Master. The first thing the Master said about the formation of this group was that it should have no name. Thus in no sense should it put a fence around itself and its ideas. When I am speaking publicly, I can speak directly to any group. I am not coming from one precise direction which is 'that group' under 'that name', 'that association', 'that society'. He also said that it should have no offices or officers, no one in any particular position. Each member of the group should have equal position and equal responsibility. Of course this concept is easier to carry out in a small group. This group was formed by 12 people plus myself, 13 in all. Although many have left, other people have come in and numbers have grown, the concept remains the same and this method of working continues in the London group.

We are in an age of transition between two ages. The old does not work very well, but there are not yet new forms; we are 'in between'. Those who work in the old individualistic way, obeying the leader, will find themselves becoming less and less effective, because this approach is not true to the quality of the energy of Aquarius.

The ultimate aim is group consciousness. This is very subtle, and difficult to achieve, and is unknown today except in Hierarchy. The Spiritual Hierarchy know *only* group consciousness, They have no sense of separate personality consciousness at all. That is perfection, and it is something which we should aim at, but not be too despondent about if we do not have it as yet.

Group consciousness is the expression of buddhic consciousness, but at our level we might say it is the synthesis of thought that evolves from the total absorption of all the members of a group at an equal level in the group work. This type of consciousness, synthetic thinking as a group, evolves rather slowly, depending on circumstances. Just as a plant grows and flowers correctly in due time when you give it the right soil, right water and the right amount of humus, so does a group grow when you give it the right kind of stimulus. Although it takes a long time to evolve group consciousness, the way towards it is to create the mechanics, the form and the structure by which that consciousness can grow. The form needed for the creation of group consciousness is that structure which will allow the fullest participation at an equal level of all the members of the group. This is the most complete democracy.

Some nations and cultures provide the right environment and find this process easier than others. For instance, Americans find it not too difficult to create groups in which there is a reasonable degree of democracy, because they aim quite consciously at the democratic participation of all the members, and they have the habit of it from school days. Likewise, the French groups have little difficulty in creating a situation where every member of the group feels totally free to give his or her opinion on any particular aspect of the work. I do not know what it is like in Russia, but it is certainly true of France and America where the first revolutions took place aiming at individual liberty. This is not so prevalent in Germany, fairly prevalent in Holland and reasonably so in Britain. However, for centuries in Japan there has been the authoritarian approach: the law, the instructions coming from above, with other people carrying them out.

I would say that the greatest need here in most countries is for a greater involvement of the women in the group. There are usually more women in so-called New Age groups and Transmission groups than there are men. Yet it is usually the men who make the decisions and the women who make the tea. But in my experience, if we want a job well done, let the women do it. Most women have an extremely well-developed practical sense. Many are used to bringing up children, getting them to school, fetching them home, making meals on time, and often doing an outside job as well. They have to have their feet on the ground and know exactly how to find what, where and when. This gives them a very good ability to work with form. Of course, people vary, but men tend, on the other hand, to think in broad, philosophical, abstract terms.

The coming age is the age in which the Mother Principle will come into its own. The Age of Maitreya is the Age of Tara, the World Mother. The mother nourishes the child, nourishes the family, and the female principle nourishes the civilization. For that reason alone the female principle must be given its full expression. That means that all women must have full and equal human rights with men. This is above all true in an active New Age group in which there are usually more women than men. To work correctly in the new Aquarian-age concept of group work, every member, male and female alike, should see him or herself as a full, equal, responsible member of the group, no one higher or lower than another. True democracy really means participation of all members of the group. Full participation is the future aim of all countries. Only in this way can every human being grow to his or her full potential, participating in decision-making and action to transform the world through a change of consciousness. That begins in a group situation; even in a family. Hence the need for full communication between all members of the group and the acceptance of the concept of individual and mutual responsibility.

The important thing is mutual respect and the absence of personal ambition. If someone has an ambitious personality, he or she can completely ruin the work of a group. That person will always be working for his or her own personal ambition and not for the good of the group or cause. People have to be very honest with themselves and honest with each other. Everyone working in the group must see what they are doing as serving the group purpose, and in no sense as serving their own ego, their own sense of self-importance. In this way there will be true communication between all members, no one withholding information from a sense of power; but everything that is known, everything that can be communicated, will be communicated.

For any project or work, there will always be different ideas or different ways of doing things among group members. If everyone in a group is equal and no leader is at the top to make a final decision, how do we make any decisions? Do we go by majority rule?

It is done by arriving at a group consensus, not by the imposition of the ideas of the strongest member or of the majority. In the old way, take for example a political party, there will usually be several factions, and they will debate and argue out the different approaches. Then they will take a vote, and you might have 15 votes for one idea, six against, three don't knows, and so on, and so you get the majority ruling. This is the old way.

The group in the sense of the New Age should try to work more in terms of coming naturally and intuitively to a consensus idea of how to proceed. The different points of view are the result of the different ray structures of the different individuals who make up the group, and this should be welcomed rather than fought against. Rays make the person work differently, see the world differently, have different lines of approach. The aim should always be to try to work from the soul aspect of the individuals.

On the soul level, every soul can work harmoniously with every other soul, whatever the ray. Hierarchy is made up of seven different groups, each under a different ray, and yet it works together in complete and total harmony, each particular ray contributing its own view of reality, which enriches the general view.

The difficulties in groups are always brought about by the differences in personalities. The aim must be to act from the higher level of the soul; to try to learn wise compromise. Much difficulty is caused by the lack of ability to compromise, to see a group vision and to aim at the fulfilment of the group intention. One must use the intuition, and respect the fact that everybody is working from a point of truth, from honesty, from sincerity, and is simply seeing things differently. All are useful because everybody brings a unique approach to the idea or problem.

Women are less competitive, more ready to see the other point of view, tend to be more tolerant, more ready to compromise. They generally have more common sense. I am not suggesting that male leadership should be superseded by the leadership of women. That would merely be changing roles without changing the situation. We need, not leadership, but full participation, which means everyone accepting responsibility.

It is important that when people take on responsibility for certain jobs or actions they should carry them out. They should not take on work and then not do it, or only do a half or a quarter of it. The group as a whole must be able to trust them to be responsible.

Most groups involved in this work are highly idealistic. That is why they are responding to this message. Idealistic people are very good at broad, vague, abstract conceptions, but they very often lack the ability to make these ideas manifest practically on the physical plane. The physical plane is just as real and just as important as any other plane; it is a part of God, like any other plane. A group which is working really well needs vision — a broad abstract ideal or cause — and the ability to work the whole thing out clearly, practically, in detail. The only way to bring this about is actually to do it. You learn it by practice.

It is very difficult to reach a decision which will reflect everyone's point of view or ideas. If we do not take a vote, we can keep discussing for ever without coming to a consensus. Should we still continue to try?

If you keep doing it, you will find that decisions are not 'reached', they evolve, they come out by themselves. It is best to try to work from the soul level, from the intuitive level. That is always right, under every condition. The soul knows only group consciousness, and is totally altruistic, has no personality ambitions. Decisions reached at that level 'over-encompass' all the different personalities in the group, all the different points of view.

Also, the factor of time comes into this. I do not think you need try to reach a decision on something too quickly. If you have a personal decision to make, you say: "Well, I'll sleep on it, I'll decide in the morning." When you sleep on it, you allow the soul to look at it during the night, so to speak. In the same way, the group can "sleep on it" as long as it takes to come to a decision. The fact that you have met together to make a decision does not mean to say that you have to make the decision immediately.

People have to become more subtle, more sensitive to their souls, the cause they are working for, the purpose behind the overall Plan. They have to learn to intuit their approach to the Plan, and allow the magnet of the Plan to draw them in the right direction.

When you meet together for a particular project, take a few moments at the beginning to link together at the soul level, as high a level as you can, and invoke the soul of the group to throw light on whatever decisions you have to make; invoke the intuition.

Remember, no individual is important; the group is more important than the individual. The groups, as a whole, are more important than any individual group. And more important than any individual, more important than any group, is the Plan for which all the groups are working.

That Plan involves the coming into the world of Maitreya and the Hierarchy of Masters and Their inspiration, through humanity, of a new civilization. If you keep this as the measure of where you are, who you are and what you do, you cannot go very far wrong. Then you work in the direction of the Plan itself. Invoke the aid of Maitreya — invoke His inspiration and guidance in your work. He says: "My help is yours to command. You have only to ask."

Group consciousness is very subtle, and difficult to achieve, and is unknown today except in Hierarchy.

The idea of Hierarchy seems to conflict with the modern democratic principles of one man, one vote. Should esoteric groups not seek to work as a fully democratic team in which no one has more influence or power than others and in which all the work is shared by everyone? (September 1988)

There is no real conflict between Hierarchy and democracy. An esoteric group should move towards a mode of work in which the Hierarchical process can be repeated and so become a miniature Hierarchy, without the glamour of somebody being more advanced or more important than another. Everybody should know precisely where he/she is in that Hierarchy and what one can and should do at that particular level. That is how Hierarchy works. The work should be shared by everyone but that does not rule out specialization to some degree.

(1) What is the relationship between self-will and God-will? (2) Are they both manifestations of ray 1? (3) How does the one become transmuted into the other? and (4) is there a way to hasten the process? (November 1988)

(1) God's Will is the Purpose behind the Plan of evolution for our planet and ultimately that of the Solar Logos for our solar system. Self-will is the desire principle of the separated personality which eventually must come into alignment with God's Will in order to evolve.

(2) Ray 1 embodies the Will or Purpose of God (although in the present solar system, which is 2nd-ray, the 1st ray is the first sub-ray of the 2nd ray). Ray 6, on the other hand, embodies the desire principle which must be "killed out". It is the desire principle which is behind the individualistic, separative tendencies of the 6th ray. (Hence the method of advance for the 6th ray is self-sacrifice.)

(3) The overcoming of desire takes place gradually, first through "transmutation" (purifying, stabilization of vibration) and then through "attrition" (withdrawal of the energy feeding the desires).

(4) Meditation and service, as always, hasten all evolutionary endeavours.

What comes first: a focus on the growth of the group or accomplishment of the task?

The purpose of the group is to accomplish the task, so it is clear cut. I would say that the priority is the accomplishment of the task. The group is not a group unless it is accomplishing a task. In so far as it does, the growth of the group will go forward in a natural way.

What is the process or responsibility of the group in helping the individual to (1) identify potential service activities and (2) to encourage sustained rhythm?
The group can help the individual members of the group to sustain a rhythm. That is what makes it a group. A group is really a group of people working together in a certain rhythm for a certain cause, with a certain aim or purpose. Individual rhythms vary, individual rays differ. Their point in evolution may be different — not by much, but different. Their habits of work are different. It is quite difficult for a group of individuals, who otherwise might never know each other but for the common cause, to sustain a rhythm. In this way, the example of the most active and intensely focused members of the group can be a great help to the individuals who might not be quite so focused. That, I am sure, is the case in most groups. The powerful ones sustain and provide an example for the less-focused individuals.

This responsibility is something which I do not think needs to be talked about. It is taken for granted that a group is a group of people, and each one has a responsibility for the other because the actions of every member rebound on every other member. You have responsibility for your own actions and for the group good. In this way the group can help some member who is losing faith, who is unable to sustain a rhythm, who is having problems in the outer work and life which prevent them from focusing on the work of the group. In those respects the group can be responsible and can help the individual. Group interchange, of course, leads to identifying potential qualities and opportunities for service.

How do you come to an intuitive consensus within group work instead of just a mental configuration?
You have to work towards it. It is not something which is ready-made. No groups have the experience of it. You do not have to use the mental process: working it out, putting up

hands, finding out where the majority lies. The majority might be wrong.

You can approach this work in another way, come to solutions which are the result of consensus. I cannot tell you how to do it. It is something which you have to practise doing until you come to it. It is a skill you have when you use your intuition and learn to compromise. Suddenly, by an intuitive, unseen process, the group, by consensus, knows that this is what they should do. It is commonsensical because it is intuitive. Common sense is the sense which few use. Another name for it is intuition. By intuition you know that this is the right way. No one has to tell you; figure it out. You may have to know data, someone has to supply the data on which you may intelligently base certain actions. It is common sense to use your brain when you can. But the brain alone may not be able to tell you what to do in a particular instance because you may have data which gives you competing answers. You have to choose. But the way to choose is not to choose but to use the intuition to make the choice. The intuition knows because it does not make a choice. It knows because it knows.

CHAPTER 16

DISEASE: CAUSES AND CURE

Disease and Death

How do we know that the soul is done with its vehicle?
Usually soon after the soul has decided it can make no further use of the vehicle — either the personality is not responding to the plan or purpose of the soul, or the vehicle itself is too old and devitalized for effective further use to be made of it — the soul withdraws. It breaks the two links — the consciousness link and the life thread — and the person dies. Dying is the withdrawing of the link with the soul and it is effected by the soul.

When both lines get severed, death is total and sudden. But if the consciousness link is cut, and the life line is not, then the person goes on in a vegetative state. That can be for a few weeks, months, or even 20 years.

The person may continue as a living person who is going through the motions of living, but from the soul point of view, there is no soul consciousness, no effective reciprocal relationship going on. The soul is not receiving any more back into the causal body from that life. It is like a vegetable existence as far as the soul is concerned. It is all personality. The life connection is still present, but the consciousness connection is severed.

You have said that the body can go on for a number of years.
Yes, because that body itself is strong; it has a momentum of its own. But if it is not responsive to the consciousness aspect, from the point of view of the soul, however physically strong it may be, it is not doing very much. The soul might decide to withdraw, and return in a new body, one more sensitive to the purpose of the soul.

Is disease karmic? (January/February 1987)

By 'karmic', I suppose, is meant the result of actions in previous lives or earlier in this life. All disease or ill health, except when it is hereditary, is karmic — the result of our misuse of energy from one level or another, that of the soul and, in astrally-polarized individuals, from the astral plane. Karma can relate to yesterday or last week or a month ago or last year, and not necessarily to much earlier in this life, or even in a past life. We are making karma all the time, good or bad.

What is the value of sickness which leads to death? (May 1987)

To quote from the Master DK (*Esoteric Healing* by Alice A.Bailey, p41): "disease is sometimes the working out into manifestation of undesirable subjective conditions. These, when externalized and brought to the surface of the human body, can be known, dealt with and eliminated. It is well to remember also that sometimes this working out and elimination may well bring about the death of that particular body. But the soul goes on. One short life counts for very little in the long cycle of the soul, and it is counted well worth while if a period of ill health (even if it eventuates in death) brings about the clearing away of wrong emotional and mental conditions."

If the new Technology of Light will eventually cure all diseases, does this mean that each individual will decide himself when to die, not as a result of physical decay? (September 1989)

The time is coming when each of us will know instinctively when to die and we will 'pass over' consciously. The new technology will make possible a much longer physical life (with greater efficiency) but eventually the organism will wear out completely and a conscious decision to die will be taken. We will know that there is no such thing as death, but simply a shift of consciousness from this to another plane. In the course of time (as we understand it) and according to our destiny, we will reincarnate in new healthier bodies to continue this process of perfection.

AIDS: Its Cause and Cure

AIDS is not a disease confined to the homosexual community but is one that presents a threat to the whole of humanity. Unchecked, this newly-discovered virus could decimate mankind. It constitutes a threat greater even than the plagues of the Middle Ages. How is it engendered and why are the homosexual groups singled out for blame?

To understand fully how AIDS makes its appearance at this time, it is necessary to understand somewhat the nature of the new energy or ray which, in mounting potency, is making its impact on our lives. I refer, of course, to the incoming 7th ray of Ceremonial Order or Organization. This great ray has been in incarnation, as it is called, since 1675 and is now very potent indeed. Its natural point of focus in the human body is the sacral or sex centre, and its physical gland correspondence the gonads. A tremendous new stimulation, therefore, is being brought to bear on the sexual life of humanity — hence the current outspoken interest in, and concentration on, sexual matters and activity. This is not by chance but is a direct result of the increased stimulation of the etheric counterpart body of humanity by the 7th ray. This has led in some instances to a neurotic and morbid concentration on this basic (and perfectly natural) human instinct. A pathological and unnatural sexual obsession in certain cases has taken the place of a natural, healthy sexual interest and activity.

The proper sphere of activity of the sexual impulse and function is the physical plane. The desire principle holds sway there and on the astral realms. The increasingly mental focus of humanity, however, has made it possible for the desire principle to enter the realm of the mind, with the greater concentration and potency which that higher level affords. The result has been devastating. Desire has entered the mind. The mind has responded with morbid obsession and magnetically caused the disintegration of the blood cells of the body, thus breaking down the immune system itself, and the creation of the AIDS virus (a virus is self-created). It is thus the result of wrongly-directed thought or misuse of energy, and emphatically not 'divine retribution' (as claimed by various fundamentalist groups and individuals) for 'unnatural' sexual practices.

A relatively few people, only, have actually created the AIDS virus in themselves. Its rapid spread (and danger for humanity) is the outcome of its being extremely infectious through the body fluids: the blood, urine, faeces and sexual secretions, and less readily through saliva. At the moment it is most prevalent in the USA and in parts of Africa. In the USA, so far, it is the homosexual groups which have taken the brunt. This is so, not because AIDS is the outcome of 'unnatural' or 'unlawful' sexual activity or practices, but because of the greater sexual experimentation which prevails in these groups. Despite the altogether freer social climate in which homosexuals now live, there is no doubt that they come under pressures, leading to frequent changes of sexual partners and the widespread use of prostitutes. In connection with the spread of AIDS, therefore, bisexuality and the activities of the 'oldest profession', male or female, represent major threats.

Carriers

Among the many problems in dealing with this disease is the fact that people can be carriers of the virus — often for many years — without a trace of symptoms. Mothers can pass it on to their children in the womb through the blood. Infected blood-banks have already taken their toll. This makes its containment difficult, and all the more essential.

The Hunger Project, in its interesting twice-monthly *World Development Forum* (Vol. 4, No. 20, 15 November 1986), has the following report: "Do mosquitoes and bedbugs carry the AIDS virus? The Pasteur Institute's Jean-Claude Chermann, a co-discoverer of the AIDS virus in 1983, says they do. A study in Zaire of 50 insects, reports *Asiaweek*, indicated that all — including mosquitoes, tsetse flies and cockroaches — were infected. But the reassuring news is that the 'insects don't carry nearly enough of the virus to infect a human. There is no way,' he said, 'that the virus could be transmitted to humans by mosquitoes or other insects.'"

Unfortunately, my information is that this is not entirely the case. In Africa — together with the US the continent most severely hit by the disease — the AIDS virus has made its appearance, for the most part, among heterosexuals; in this case, mosquitoes and other insects have played their part, as carriers, in its spread.

This fact may provide a means for its containment and control. To quote *World Development Forum* again: "Chermann explains that the receptor (chemical component of a living cell which combines with a foreign substance to alter the cell function) for the virus is 'very specific'. Hence, if the virus receptor in the insects proved similar to that in humans, 'we could make an antibody' to prevent the spread of the disease."

There is every hope that such an antibody, which will contain and control the spread of the virus, will eventually be discovered, but humanity must face the fact that AIDS is not easily eradicable and that every precaution must be taken to prevent its spread. Among other actions, saner and safer sexual attitudes are called for. This does not mean the cessation of all sexual activity (as has already happened with some groups in their initial fear-reaction) but of a wholesome respect for the virus and an awareness of its dangers. Greater caution and discrimination in the choice of sexual partners is obviously a priority. In this respect education is the key. A worldwide educational programme, outlining the dangers and exploding the myths, is required. Some governments have already set such a programme in motion but this must become a global effort if the true import of the disease is to be understood and the means of containing it are to be adopted.

New scourge

What part can the Hierarchy of Masters play in ridding the world of this new scourge? Already, several Masters, including my own, are lending Their experience and expertise to the healing of individuals but They may not overstep the bounds of karma to tackle the problem on a global scale. This must await the action of humanity on its own behalf. Shortly, however, due to the action (and intervention) of the Christ, Maitreya, many already suffering from the worst effects of the virus will find the disintegrative process spontaneously being reversed and normal health established. For karmic reasons, this is possible only for a 'sample' of those affected by the disease, but it will draw attention to the seriousness with which He views this new danger to the race.

In the longer run, only the correct use of thought (and therefore of energy) can rid the world of the diseases, including AIDS, which now afflict it. This presupposes a re-orientation of consciousness at present not possible for the majority, but one which will inevitably come as we enter into better relationship, one with another, by establishing the correct structures, political and social, on which our future well-being depends. This is the spiritual transformation which Maitreya comes to inspire.

(1) Are all viruses created initially by a few people, then transmitted to many? (2) Do these people have any special ability to do this? (3) Where does the momentum of contagiousness come from? (Surely not from the few people who have created it?) (4) Is a virus an effect of a collective energy imbalance of many people, some of whom create a vehicle for its expression (a virus) and transmit it to others? (5) Is the viral infection the balancing of energy? (6) Are the people infected by a particular virus only those who have contributed towards the collective energy imbalance? (July/August 1987)

(1) Yes. (2) No. (3) There is no simple direct answer to this question. It depends on the virus and circumstances. (4) Yes. (5) No. (6) Usually, but not always. Certainly not in the case of AIDS and some influenzas.

*I was fascinated to read (in the June 1987 issue of **Share International**) the interview with the AIDS sufferer who was 'miraculously' cured. He stated that he knew others who had been cured and believed there were still others unknown to him. In the light of this and the article "Maitreya's Forecast"* *in the January/February 1987 issue of* **Share International** *about Maitreya's intervention for a given number of AIDS patients, I wonder how many people have indeed been cured and why the media do not report on it?* (July/August 1987)

The number of people selected — for karmic and other reasons — for cure was around 370 and of these 96.5 per cent have been cured. The others are still in the process of cure. That the media have more or less ignored these happenings may be due to several factors: one is the lack of large numbers coming forward to testify. Mr Michael Click, the interviewee in the *Share International* article, stated that, while believing that many have experienced cure and 'a spiritual renewal', they were reluctant to talk about it, even superstitiously so, fearing reversal of the cure. Secondly, I am informed that in some cases, where cures and 'a vision of the Christ' have been reported to doctors or media, they have been sceptically received and/or ignored. Thirdly, many of the cures took place in Africa where reporting may be haphazard or non-existent. However, Tara Center *Network News* quotes a headlined story in the Pasadena, California, *Star News*, 3 June 1987, which states that five individuals "who tested positive for the AIDS virus inexplicably lost all signs of infection six to 18 months later". It went on to suggest two indeterminate possibilities for this.

What do you hold of the theory that says the deadly AIDS virus was artificially tailored and vaccined by scientists secretly working for the US Government in order to selectively wipe out undesirable segments of the world's population, such as homosexuals, drug users, blacks? (November 1989)

This idea is not so much a theory as pure speculation from a viewpoint almost of paranoia. The US Government has been accused, at different times and with a greater or lesser degree of justice, of all manner of misdeeds, but no government today would be so foolhardy as to initiate such an uncontrollable situation as the AIDS virus presents today. The virus is no respecter of persons. It is not — and cannot be — confined to "homosexuals, drug users and blacks", and surely no government is naïve enough to imagine that it could be.

What is the real cause of homosexuality, and is it something one has to 'overcome' if one feels homosexual? (March 1988)
This is not a subject or question one can deal with in a few lines in these pages. For a deeper understanding, I refer readers to the Master DK's insights on this subject in Alice Bailey's *Esoteric Psychology, Vol. I* in the chapter 'The Problem of Sex'.

Have you any guidance on the illnesses of the immune system? Are we overloaded with toxins and can we reverse this? In nature as well as ourselves? (December 1989)
There are many areas in man and in the environment as a whole in which toxic pollution is reaching a dangerous level. Some have already overstepped the limit of tolerance and have created the various viruses which attack (or place great strain on) the immune systems of man and nature. A complete reorientation is necessary to prevent major breakdown. Fortunately, both man and nature are very resilient, and given the right guidance — and the will to change — these problems should be overcome within the next, say, 20 years.

Myalgic Encephalomyelitis (ME), a Post-Viral Fatigue Syndrome (PVFS), has recently been the subject of articles in the press. Many doctors do not accept it as a disease and there is no orthodox treatment. (1) What is the esoteric explanation of PVFS. (2) How can such diseases be treated? (June 1988)
(1) PVFS is the result of a breakdown (to some extent) of the immune system. This in its turn is the result of wrong identification, wrong values, wrong modes of living and thinking, and, in particular, of conditions of severe stress. Its prevalence today results from the severe strain under which many people (most people?) work and live. Polluted air, water and food are powerful contributory causes.

(2) There is no treatment (cure) except a change of lifestyle and values on a large scale. Amelioration by homeopathic approaches would, I suggest, be most successful.

Can you comment on vaccines and their impact on the immune system — both pro and con, short and long term? (October 1987)

Vaccines, even in their present rather coarse form, have been of immense benefit to humanity and have all but eradicated many formerly killer diseases. Especially in (homeopathically) refined form they will have a long-term value in dealing with disease.

Cancer, Tuberculosis and Other Diseases

*In the book **Hierarchy**, in the Agni Yoga series, it states (stanza 285): "Cancer can be treated by psychic energy, since lack of psychic energy in the blood generates the disease. Often psychic energy is exhausted as a result of spiritual outpouring, as was the case with Rama Krishna and other spiritual Teachers.... Precisely, closeness to Hierarchy is needed in such cases, because even great Spiritual Toilers, in their self-abnegation, sometimes expend their forces beyond a legitimate extent...." For ordinary people it is not a question of exhausting psychic energy for others but simply of lacking it. How does one accumulate psychic energy?* (January/February 1987)

Psychic energy is the energy of consciousness which comes from the soul — the consciousness factor. Meditation and service are (as always) the activities which invoke soul energy and make it available for the health of the body. To say "lack of psychic energy in the blood generates the disease" may be true but begs the question of how the energy becomes insufficient. There are a great many reasons for that: hereditary weaknesses; fear of life and a too-ready resignation; stress produced by modern urban living conditions leading to devitalization of the etheric envelope. All these may inhibit the flow of energy from the soul. The misuse or under-use of soul energy is probably the greatest factor. Service and meditation, therefore, are vital!

(1) Is the cause of skin cancer excessive exposure to the sun's rays, or are there other factors involved? (2) I understand

sleeping under the sun is very harmful because your physical body is not protected by the etheric body; is that correct? (December 1988)

(1) Skin cancer is not caused by excessive exposure to the sun's rays. Several other factors are involved and have to be present. Chief among these is predisposition to the disease, without which no amount of exposure will bring about cancer. (2) No. That is nonsense.

Is it safe to apply 'feet reflex zone massage' in the case of a brain tumour? (April 1988)

It is safe but will do no special good.

When will there be an end to diseases like cancer and AIDS? (March 1991)

In the not too distant future, the Technology of Light will give the medical profession an entirely new approach to the cure of these and other diseases. In the meantime, many people are finding that through meditation, and the closer identification with the Self which ensues, direct self-healing can be achieved. A transformation of our lifestyles on a national and international basis is the key to the eradication of the imbalances which demonstrate as disease. As far as cancer is concerned the replacement of burial by cremation would speed this process.

*In **Share International**, March 1991, in a question about cancer, the answer ends with the sentence: "As far as cancer is concerned the replacement of burial by cremation would speed the process." Why? Does the cancer enter the soil and eventually become part of the food chain?* (October 1991)

Yes.

*In **Esoteric Healing** the Master DK states that the Earth, the planet and soil itself, are contaminated by three diseases — cancer, tuberculosis and syphilis. The conditions of senile dementia and Alzheimer's Disease seem closely to resemble the advanced stages of neuro-syphilitic decay. Are the origins of these conditions related to contamination of the Earth?* (June 1988)

Yes.

*Referring to Alice A.Bailey's **Esoteric Healing**, p232, in the section on tuberculosis, is it correct to assume that this was originally an artificially induced disease created by the Great White Lodge? If that is so, would it be correct to look on AIDS in the same way?* (December 1988)

The section mentioned above refers to the origin of tuberculosis in the breathing organs — by which men live. It was not so much artificially induced as imposed, as a penalty, by the Great White Lodge. It resulted from the promulgation of a new law for the people of Atlantis when the desire principle — and the ruthless use of magic to gain the objects of desire — had reached its height. To quote the Master DK: "This law can be translated into the following terms: 'He who lives only for material goods, who sacrifices all virtue in order to gain that which cannot last, will die in life, will find breath failing him, and yet will refuse to think of death until the summons comes.' "

This brought people to realize that attitudes and states of consciousness can have an effect on the physical body, for good or ill, and also, for the first time, to face the reality of death, brought about by men themselves through their own greed.

AIDS is an altogether different phenomenon, but, as always, is also the result of the wrong use of energy. It relates more closely to the Lemurian mis-use of sex energy, and is an effect of that mis-use rather than an imposed penalty to teach a lesson.

*In **Esoteric Healing** by Alice Bailey, p311, we are told that diabetes, which is so prevalent today, is the result of "wrong desires" which may originate in this life or be inherited from a previous existence. Could you please explain what is meant by "wrong desires"?* (July/August 1990)

While all illnesses can be ascribed to the mishandling of energy (particularly soul energy), and the consequent overstimulation of the astral vehicle (the focus of the desire principle), diabetes does seem to result from a rather specific aspect of this general problem: an unfulfilled desire for power or dominance, desire for attention through ill health, and, in some cases, an inner death wish resulting from a felt inability to cope with the problems of life.

(1) Please explain the (esoteric) cause(s) of Multiple Sclerosis. (2) Could you outline preventive measures, way of life, etc. (3) Are certain types of people more prone to MS than others? (4) How can this disease best be dealt with and/or cured? (January/February 1987)

(1) There is no simple separate cause or single factor behind the effect, Multiple Sclerosis. As in all diseases, it is the result of the wrong or inadequate use of soul energy. For this basic cause to manifest as MS, however, several other factors have to be present: a hereditary predisposition to this particular ailment — for example, an over-sensitive nervous system which is inadequate to cope with stress; a condition of strong stress or inimical environment or occupation for an extended period; the interior stress caused by frustration of a powerful creative energy; a sudden collapse of the life purpose and will. Some or all of these will be found behind the manifestation of MS.

(2) Ways of life should be found which give the greatest outlet to creative and service activities. This, of course, is true for all relatively advanced people. Creativity and the desire to serve are the result of soul contact and influence.

(3) Creative people with weak nervous systems who lose to some extent the will to live would be, at least theoretically, most at risk from MS.

(4) Through the strengthening of the nervous system and a restoration of the will to live and to be. The removal also of obstacles to creative work and expression. The strengthening of the desire to serve and the acceptance of service.

What exactly is senility? How should it be viewed and handled from an esoteric point of view? (January/February 1987)

True senility (and not simply premature senile decay) is the result of the gradual withdrawal of the soul's energy of consciousness. The life energy may persist for many years after the soul's decision to withdraw from that vehicle but the person really is a form of vegetable. The only way to 'handle' this condition is with tolerance and patience. It is not a disease (which senile decay is) and is incurable.

(1) Why are children susceptible to so many diseases: measles, mumps, chicken pox, etc? (2) Should they be exposed to them or protected from them? (January/February 1987)
Infantile and children's diseases are a mechanism which nature has provided to allow children to 'burn off' karma early in life. Therefore, they should not be especially protected from them. Many children, in any case, have inbuilt immunity to several of these diseases.

Why do we get colds? (January/February 1987)
Colds, flu, sinusitis, etc, are largely attempts of the body to throw off the toxins in the system. They may be, of course, if the resistance is low, often the result of infection or of getting chilled.

Are tonsils useful? (January/February 1987)
Tonsils focus toxins, usually affecting the throat, at the surface of the body where they can do less harm.

Recently there seems to be quite an outbreak of sinus ailments in this (America) and perhaps other countries. If possible would you please explain what the cause of this might be? (April 1988)
Personally, I would think the reason to be a combination of stress and increasing pollution of the atmosphere in most countries and cities.

Why does my husband hardly ever get sick at all and he smokes, and drinks coffee every day, whilst I try to eat a pure diet and always get sick? (January/February 1987)
Your husband has a 7th-ray physical body, which is very resistant. He takes a long time to get ill. Your physical body is sensitive and adaptable. You cannot have it both ways!

Is homoeopathy more effective on certain people than others? If so, what factors are involved? (January/February 1987)

At the present time homoeopathy tends to be more successful in chronic rather than acute cases. As deeper understanding of its processes becomes available this will not always be so. Also, children often respond better (probably because, having had less time to accumulate toxins, their bodies react more readily to the remedies) than adults to this form of treatment.

I have heard a lot recently about the ancient Ayurvedic treatment of Urine Therapy, details of which are mentioned not only in the Vedas but also in the Christian Bible ("Drink waters out of thine own cistern." — Proverbs 5:15). Could you please comment on this, and in view of the fact that Gandhi used to drink his own urine every day, is it to be recommended? (December 1990)

My information is that a very small amount, preferably in homeopathic dilution and potency, of one's own urine does have a homeopathic effect in stimulating the body to rid itself of toxins. A larger amount is not only disgusting but contraindicated. I do not accept that the Bible reference quoted, Proverbs 5:15, has anything to do with urine-drinking, but rather with warnings against covetousness.

(1) What is esoterically the result of the use of psychopharmaca as tranquillizers, medicines to lessen fear? Are they a hindrance to spiritual growth? (2) How do you get rid of them? (July/August 1989)

(1) Tranquillizers work precisely by cutting the person off from the awareness of his or her problem, fear, neurosis, or whatever. As a temporary measure, in extreme cases, they are valuable and even necessary at present. Long-term, since they do diminish awareness, they are a hindrance to spiritual growth. Nevertheless, they make life bearable for many people. (2) I take it that the questioner means how do you get out of dependency on tranquillizers? The answer lies in growing awareness of the Self and the habits of wrong identification with the fears of the personality.

What takes place subjectively during a deep hypnotic sleep? Is the soul out of the body along with the etheric body? (December 1988)

The conscious mind is submerged as in natural sleep and the subconscious, computing apparatus of the brain becomes open more readily to suggestion, either from oneself as in auto-hypnosis, or by some outside agency. In this trance state the computer can be retrained by feeding it more positive, desirable suggestions. It has nothing to do with the soul — in or out of the body — nor with the etheric body.

A recent German occupational health report ("Do computers cause illness?") states that little is known about the effects of computers, screens and printers, but that the risks to users are considered to be low. Can you give your opinion on the risks to health, and some guidelines for avoidance of harm? (July/August 1991)

There is certainly an outflow of positive ions from computers which can be reduced by using screens. The use, too, of a good quality ionizer is advised. I think that the general risk to health is, indeed, low.

In the countryside there is a greater percentage of negative ions in the air than in cities. Many studies show negative ions in the air to be beneficial to health although there is wide disagreement as to the exact benefits. Are there benefits to having a negative ionizer machine? If so, what are they? (March 1989)

High-tension electric cables and electric devices such as television sets and computers radiate positive ions into the atmosphere or room. A negative ionizer is useful in re-establishing a balance between positive and negative ions. The ones on the market are not all equally efficient, however. One should choose with care.

(1) Can Bovine Spongiform Encephalopathy (BSE) or 'mad cow disease' be transferred to humans as the symptoms of Creutzfelt Jacob's Disease suggest? (2) How many people in Britain have died of CJD? (3) Are pathologists conducting

post mortems on those suspected of dying of CJD in danger of being affected? (4) Is it safe to continue to eat British beef? (July/August 1990)

(1) Yes. (2) So far, 18. (3) Yes. (4) No. Of course, not all beef is contaminated, probably only a small minority of cattle are affected so far. The problem is that it is impossible to tell which is safe and which not.

Food preserved using gamma radiation is now becoming available in more countries although there are doubts about its safety. In the West, microwave ovens are ubiquitous. Is there any benefit or disadvantage to these two novel methods of food processing? (June 1988)

There are distinct disadvantages to both. Gamma radiation can so easily disguise as fresh food (for example seafood) which is unfit for human consumption. Microwave ovens have the effect of altering the molecular structure of the food being cooked and as a result diminishing the energetic, and therefore health, value of the food.

Some people say that it is harmful to use aluminium cooking utensils. Is this true? (January/February 1987)

Yes. Aluminium is a poison and food cooked in aluminium (including foil) absorbs the poison. Many allergies and various eczemas, skin rashes and stomach disorders can be traced to this cause. Stainless steel or, less expensive, enamel should be used.

Birth Control and Abortion

In the world of the spirit is abortion considered to be murder? (April 1987)

Phrased in the oversimplified manner here — the answer is no; indeed, it may be the lesser of two evils.

Why are some of us infertile? I am a male unable to have children and this has caused a disruption in my marriage. I ask myself often: Why did I choose this body? Has karma anything to do with this problem? (October 1990)

This problem usually has a karmic cause, in which case nothing can be done to change the situation (which is not the case in ordinary illness also of karmic origin). However, there are many cases of infertility which yield successfully to medical treatment, and I suggest to the questioner that he investigates (if he has not already done so) what may be done for him in that field.

My wife and I don't want any more children and I have thought of getting a vasectomy. How do the Masters view vasectomy? Does this retard one's spiritual progress? Is it seen with disdain? I am very confused about this issue. (September 1991)
The Masters view vasectomy with neither disdain nor approval, and to have one done does not retard spiritual progress. In cases where it would be dangerous for a wife to become pregnant it may well be indicated as an almost (but not quite) sure method of control. However, the Masters do warn that in some cases (where there is an existing predisposition to the disease) vasectomy can lead to a morbid cancerous, or precancerous, condition.

Does sterilization block the soul energy and thereby hinder spiritual development? (June 1988)
No.

If a woman needs to take hormone replacement tablets either because of the menopause or for any other reason, would this affect her body's ability to produce hormones in a future life? (September 1991)
No. That is not to say that such hormone replacement is always the best course.

***World Development Forum**, a "twice monthly report of facts, trends and opinion in International Development, published as a public service by The Hunger Project" (Vol. 7 No. 13, 15 July 1989), quotes a **Washington Post** editorial concerning the approval by the Food and Drug Administration of a long-lasting (up to five years) contraceptive which is implanted under the skin of a woman's upper arm and which can be* *removed whenever she desires to conceive. It claims a 99 per cent effective rate and greater safety than the 'pill'. The **Washington Post** comments: "It will be revolutionary because it is so easy to use. Implantation is a simple medical procedure, and healthcare workers all over the world can be trained to do the job... In the developing countries, overburdened with population and shortchanged in medical care and supplies, this technique can be readily explained, and five-year contraception can be offered in a single procedure ... and the new implants ... safe, easy, effective and long-lasting ... sound like the most promising development in this field in a generation." My questions are: (1) Does your Master know of this development? (2) Does He have the same high hopes for this new contraception as the **Washington Post** editorial? (3) Is it absolutely safe to use? (4) Is it really 99 per cent effective?* (October 1989)

(1) Yes. (2) With some reservations, yes. (3) There will always be some women for whom it would be contraindicated but, in general terms, if not absolutely safe, then very nearly so. (4) It is too early to be certain (tests are still going on) but the indications are that a very high rate of effectiveness will be achieved.

I have read several articles here saying that men maintain greater vitality and energy, not from abstaining from sex, but by abstaining from ejaculating during sex. Is this true physiologically and/or energetically? (December 1988)

This is true in general but not in every individual case. The sex technique of Karezza has long been known to maintain vitality without abstention from sex. However, it requires a fair degree of control — and therefore maturity — in the male partner.

For an organ transplant is it necessary that the donor and recipient have the same physical ray in order to prevent rejection? (March 1988)

No.

After one 'dies', is it OK to donate one's body to medical research? (May 1987)

Yes. It is a form of service.

Euthanasia and Suicide

(1) What is the esoteric view of suicide and euthanasia? Are they ever justifiable (for example to end the suffering of terminal illness)? (2) What kind of karmic consequences result from such actions? (3) Do they depend upon the motivation for committing the act, or upon the act itself, regardless of motivation? (October 1989)

Suicide and euthanasia are not the same actions and should be seen as having different karmic effects. In cases of extreme suffering in what is clearly a terminal illness (although no one can say with total authority that an illness is terminal), euthanasia can be seen as an act of mercy and doctors today frequently (and quietly) perform this 'service' for their patients. Nevertheless, from the esoteric standpoint, it is still the taking of life, and is fraught with so many dangers of misuse that it is not to be recommended.

Esoterically, the major objection to both euthanasia and suicide is that both interfere with soul purpose. It is the soul which, in service to the Divine Plan, incarnates, and it is the soul which terminates the incarnation. Pain and suffering, and most disease, are the result of the friction produced on the physical planes (including the astral and mental) by the inability of the soul to express its nature and purpose adequately, without resistance, through its reflection, the personality. The pain, suffering and disease, therefore, have a purpose and are 'the other side of the coin' of the soul's perfection. Suicide is really of no avail, since the person involved will come to the same point, the same necessity to fulfil soul purpose, in a later incarnation. It is not the terrible sin against life which earlier generations held it to be, but is a major interference in the soul's plans and has, therefore, its karmic consequence in holding back the evolution.

If someone does practise euthanasia on another at his request to help him avoid the pain of an agonizing death does this not place a heavy load of karma on his shoulders?

There would be a karmic reaction, certainly. Only the Lords of Karma would know how heavy or otherwise the load would be.

Is it acceptable from a spiritual point of view to take someone's life at their request to help them avoid a painful death process? (April 1987)
No. The problem here is not only a moral but also a practical one: who is to say whether the 'dying' person would, left alone, die or not? One never knows what the Lords of Karma have 'up their sleeves'.

If it is true that the time of one's death has been laid down before one is born, is euthanasia an infringement of God's law — or is my view too severe? (April 1987)
I do not believe that the time of one's death is 'laid down' before one is born. The question about euthanasia really revolves around the rightness or wrongness of helping someone to die 'artificially', so to speak. The time is coming when people will quite consciously relinquish an old or outworn body, sure in the fact of reincarnation and eternal life, but that time is not yet with us and the present safeguards are, I believe, necessary to ensure correct karmic harmlessness and to prevent criminal exploitation.

If a patient is on a life-preserving machine and a decision is made to let the patient die without being able to consult him or her, does the karmic law apply in this case? (April 1987)
The karmic law always applies but in such a case the doctors, given that they acted in good faith that no further benefit would result from prolonging the life processes, would be free of karmic responsibility. After all, they are not responsible for the need for life-preserving action, but simply administer to the result.

Healing

How soon will genetic surgery be introduced? (September 1989)

Already many scientists are involved in genetic engineering. This will develop to a point where all the necessary genetic information can be fed into an organ enabling it to 'remake' itself, sometimes in a matter of hours. This technique will be in use within a few years.

Does that mean there will be no such thing as karmic disease? (September 1989)
No. Karmic disease is the result, through the Law of Cause and Effect, of our wrong use of energy. So long as we misuse energy we will create the disequilibrium we call disease. The new technology will help us to deal with the effects of such misuse. What is required is a greater awareness of the causes of disease.

Throughout the Agni Yoga series they warn the disciples to guard their health. Was this emphasized particularly at that time (1924–1939) when the fight between the Forces of Light and of darkness was raging at its peak? Are we more protected now and do not need to concern ourselves as much with our health in the way Hierarchy was stressing at that time? (January/February 1987)
The emphasis on guarding the health does not relate more to that period than to today. The same precautions are needed by all disciples at any time. Disciples are expected to do more than other people — really to act on two realms, the spiritual and the lower world, simultaneously — and this puts a great strain on the physical apparatus. It is also important not to dwell too much on one's physical health.

Should one not attempt to heal (whether with prayer or laying-on-of-hands) unless one can discern whether it is karmically right to do so? (October 1990)
Only a Master can know, from the karmic point of view, whether healing should be given or not. The only thing for ordinary healers to do, therefore, is to proceed within their (limited) knowledge and skills, knowing as they do that if their healing runs counter to the patient's karmic situation, any

549

amelioration of the illness will be temporary and transient. That should not deter them from trying, nevertheless.

*In **Esoteric Healing**, by Alice Bailey, it is stated: "People on the 6th ray are advised to abstain from the healing art until they have arrived (consciously) at the initiate stage. (1) Does the initiate stage in this case mean above second degree? (2) Does the '6th ray' mean 6th-ray souls or people with dominant 6th rays in personality makeup? (3) Is the reason for this because people on the 6th ray tend to use their solar plexus centre?* (January/February 1987)

(1) Initiate stage here means those who have taken the third initiation. (2) It means 6th-ray souls. (3) No. The reason is that the 6th ray is moving out of incarnation and the 6th-ray approach with it. The fanaticism of this ray allows the healer a powerful command of energy but the 6th-ray type tends to use it like a 'blunderbuss' — to cure or kill! The third-degree initiate, however, acting with knowledge, can be more subtle and lawful.

When I do healing, if I play a tape where you are overshadowed by Maitreya does that (1) affect the process? If so, how? (2) Is the energy beneficial to children too? (3) Has it the same effect as the Christ Messages? (June 1989)

(1) You will find that the energy emanating from the tape (magnetized on to the tape during the overshadowing) will enhance and potentize the healing process. (2) Yes, to children and also to animals. (3) Yes, very similar.

Is the term 'aura' identical to the etheric body, the astral body, or is it something different altogether? (November 1988)

The aura is formed from the energies emanating from all planes, soul, mental, astral and etheric. It is synthesized by the etheric body. Its area and intensity of radiation depend on the development and activity of the etheric chakras.

(1) Can the opening of the chakras be forced? (2) Do healers (as many claim) open chakras? (3) Do Gurus open chakras? (4) What is the correct process? (5) Does the Earth have chakras? (September 1988)

(1) No. Chakras can only be 'opened' in the occult sense when the evolution of the individual makes it possible. This is a result of life experience, together with meditation and service. Any forcing process (breathing techniques, hatha yoga, etc) can stimulate the activity of the chakra (often in a harmful and unbalanced way) but that is not the same thing as occult opening. (2) No. (3) Yes, depending on the guru and the readiness of the individual. (4) A balanced awakening of the chakras takes place naturally in the course of life if correct living patterns are maintained. Right relationship, right meditation and right service assure the correct opening of the chakras in due sequence. (5) Yes. There are five major centres for the inflow of spiritual energy: New York, London, Geneva, Darjeeling and Tokyo. Two minor centres are Moscow and Rome. There are many more minor centres, some of which are the sites of great cities around the world.

What accounts for the variable responses of people to healing? Some people seem to get better right away and some don't seem to respond so readily.
The effectiveness of any given healing, even within the karmic pattern, depends to a large extent on the age and vitality of the physical body. A young child, for example, will make better use of a given amount of healing energy than an elderly person because the physical vitality, above all of the etheric body, is much greater than an old, devitalized body.

One of the factors in healing is the level from which a Master works. A Master always works from the level of cause — the causes behind the effects which we call ill health, or disequilibrium, in the body. Working at that level, a Master may effect a cure; the disequilibrium, the karma, is resolved, but the actual physical symptoms of the illness can go on. The person is cured, but it will require a new body, a change in consciousness, a new personality, for that cure to be noticeable even though the person's causal or karmic situation is entirely changed; that karma will not affect him in the next life

Likewise, by a change of consciousness, a person may make the greatest use of a Master's healing energy, and collaborate with the Master. What effects the best cure? Two things: the change of karma — the karma of the individual allows it; and the faith of the individual that brings about a greater cure. These two factors allow the person to make the best use of the energy which a Master or Avatar can make available at any given time.

When you say change of consciousness, do you mean consciousness about the disease?
No, consciousness in relation to reality.

When a person is devoted to the work of service, will that affect the karmic condition of the person? Will it help accumulate more energy that a Master can use for healing?
As the person devotes himself to service, he is creating conditions which we call good karma. The individual is creating an energetic balance which affects his own karmic situation. He is burning up the load of karma by service. It is not a reward, but an energetic balance. Every act of true, altruistic service, serving the Plan and the world, is at the same time re-creating a karmic situation for the better.

Does a person have to give his or her consent to receive healing? (January/February 1987)
Yes. It is important that the person involved has given his or her consent. Otherwise, no healing can be given; it would be against free will.

(1) Can an infant be placed on a healing list, even though the child is too young to give consent? (2) If so, does one need the consent of the parent? (3) If the parent specifically does not give consent, can the infant be placed on the healing list anyway? (October 1991)
(1) Yes. (2) Yes. (3) No.

If people are already on a Master's healing list, is it wise and/or useful to seek also the help of another 'healer'? Might the results be conflicting? (January/February 1987)
If people accept to be on a Master's healing list (and if they do not accept they cannot be on it, otherwise their free will would

be infringed), one can assume that they have some degree of faith in its efficacy. The idea of seeking the help also of a healer working on this plane is to me rather ridiculous since you cannot get healing from a higher level than a Master (except from the Christ or the Buddha).

Also, the efforts of the healer may well run counter to those of a Master Who works from the causal level. In that case, the Master would have to overcome the effects of the healer's 'interference' which is simply a waste of His valuable energy.

If one is on a Master's healing list, should one refrain from entering into other physical types of healing, too — such as the use of herbs, fasting, chiropractic, homoeopathy, etc? Would radionics and such forms of healing be categorized, then, as more physical, astral, etc, and should they be refrained from while the name is on the list? (September 1987)

There is no hard and fast rule here. Each case is different and it depends on the individual circumstances what other forms of therapy are acceptable while on a Master's list. Other forms of 'spiritual healing' are not acceptable and simply waste the Master's energy in countering. Usually, chiropractic, homoeopathy, radionics and so forth are acceptable; occasionally advocated. The wisest action is to use no other therapy unless advised to do so.

(1) If someone with a birth defect like cerebral palsy or muscular dystrophy, for instance, were to go to London and seek out Maitreya for a healing, would Maitreya honour that request? (2) Can and will He heal by the laying on of hands as the Bible said Jesus did when He was around 2,000 years ago? (September 1988)

(1) Possibly, but not necessarily. They would have to find Him, of course, and whether He healed them or not would depend on karma. He would know whether or not to interfere with the karmic situation. (2) I have no doubt that He can so heal but a look from Him, if He intends to heal, would be sufficient.

553

When miracle healings occur (on the Day of Declaration) will it be through new techniques revealed to people or directly as a 'laying on of hands' phenomenon? (November 1987)
The healings will take place directly as a result of the outflow of the Christ Principle which Maitreya embodies. Those whose karma permits and whose faith opens them to the energy of the Christ Principle as it flows from Maitreya will be healed.

CHAPTER 17

PRACTICAL PSYCHOLOGY FROM AN ESOTERIC PERSPECTIVE

Interview with Benjamin Creme
by George Catlin

George Catlin (GC). You have said that slightly over 1 million people presently in incarnation have taken the first or higher of the initiations to Mastery. With the world population at approximately 5 billion, that means 99.98 per cent of humanity has the first initiation still ahead. What kinds of steps in consciousness is this group, virtually all of humanity, trying to take?

Benjamin Creme (BC): The main step forward for the group on the verge of the first initiation is the becoming aware of the soul. That is why the soul brings the person into some connection with meditation during the two or three lives preceding the first initiation, usually beginning around 0.7 (if the first initiation is considered 1.0). Meditation is the process more or less scientific, depending on the meditation, of coming into contact with the soul.

The first initiation is about achieving the first aspects of soul consciousness. This reflects itself in the lower man — as a physical, astral and mental reality — in the gaining of control of the physical-plane elemental. That is the goal of the first initiation. It is achieved by raising the vibration to a point where the person is in control of the appetite of the physical body.

The physical, astral and mental bodies are made up of tiny elemental lives of the etheric physical planes. Their activity dominates our life or we dominate them. The vast majority of humanity are dominated completely by the activity of the elementals on each plane. The first step in gaining control is the reorganizing the life pattern. It is not the overcoming of desire (maya, or illusion) on the physical plane, but the overcoming of the activity by which maya manifests. When that is achieved, then the first initiation can be taken.

GC: It is hard to wake up in the morning and decide to work on controlling your physical elemental. What other practical steps besides meditation can people take at this stage in the path?
BC: The body longs for — more food than it needs, more sex, more drink than it needs, more comfort and sleep than it needs and so on. These desires are all part of the desire nature of the elemental itself. The training of the body becomes an important factor in the consciousness of the individual approaching this stage. Nearly always, the person becomes a vegetarian. They become food faddists. Food, especially the right food, becomes an essential part of their lifestyle. They will only eat what they know is good for the physical body and try to eschew what they know is harmful. This, of course, is intelligent, but there is often an element of fanaticism at this stage.

GC: Would exercise be part of this effort?
BC: Yes. Whatever strengthens the sense that you are in charge of your own physical body. Gradually you do become in charge, not only through meditation, although through meditation you come in to contact with the soul. This process demonstrates itself by a gradual gaining of control over the elemental. When it is complete enough, the person can take the first initiation. Then the same process starts with the control of the astral elemental, with all of its demands, and it is even more difficult.

GC: You have also talked about the awakening of the Christ Principle as part of the preparation for the first initiation.
BC: The Christ Principle is really the principle of consciousness itself; it comes from the soul. The Christ Principle is consciousness, *per se.*

GC: But everybody has consciousness, don't they?

BC: Yes, but on what level? It is a question of conscious consciousness. Most people up until that point really are only semi-conscious. They are conscious as a personality, but not as a soul. When we talk about the consciousness aspect, we are really talking about the unfolding of the soul nature in the personality. The soul, from about 0.7 onwards, grips and takes control of its vehicle (the man or woman with his or her bodies, mental, astral and physical) and gradually these are bent to the will and purpose of the soul. It is a struggle. But the will of the soul being stronger, it eventually wins the battle. Prior to this, there is sentient personality life, but little evidence of the soul with its own altruistic purpose and meaning of its own.

GC: How does this relate to free will?
BC: People have only very limited free will. They have the potential, but only initiates truly have free will. Until people are initiate, they are swept along by evolution. When the person is initiate, especially once they have controlled the astral vehicle and are thinking and acting as a soul, then one can really say that the person has free will. Then you can actually develop your own destiny and control cause and effect because you understand the Law of Cause and Effect; you live the Law. You are acting, not reacting.

GC: I am interested in the kinds of factors that make for faster progress at the early stages of the path. I will name just a few and hear whatever you have to say about them: the kind of family life and parenting that you come into.
BC: Of major importance in terms of the inspiration for a rich life-purpose and expression. A family who can give to their children a sense of the value of life, the sanctity, the spiritual nature of life, would be providing a good framework.

They do not have to teach the child about God. In fact, it is better not to teach the child about God, but to provide a broadly based, inclusive, 'spiritual' sense of the value of human life and of all life. That is needed, not a framework of belief, especially not a framework of belief.

GC: You think that is actually detrimental?
BC: To have a framework of belief imposed on a child is highly detrimental.

GC: Even if it is a relatively 'enlightened' framework?
BC. It does not make any difference. It is still a limiting factor on the child's consciousness. It is better that the child be encouraged to see the good in everything, and that their parents' belief or religion is not the only one. As soon as you get dogma, you limit the consciousness, the awareness. That is what is so harmful to children.

GC: I am also interested in the emotional experience of the child because it seems that some people emerge from childhood deeply scarred by what has happened, primarily with their parents. Do you agree with that? Also, at what stage in the path does this begin to matter less? It seems that for the more advanced initiates it does not matter what happened in childhood.
BC: Yes, it is very important. What you say about the initiates is also largely true, although they too can be scarred and limited by their upbringing. The more advanced an initiate is, the earlier he recognizes who he is in the spiritual sense, and the more independent will be his life appearance and demonstration. It would not be true to say: "It really does not matter how an initiate is brought up. He is going to be an initiate anyway." It does matter how an initiate is brought up. It matters how every child is brought up. They have to be surrounded by supportive, loving parents just like everyone else. The more that is the case, the better and the more quickly they will evolve. That is as true for initiates as it is for anybody else. For those less evolved, it becomes a crucial factor because they are more easily crippled emotionally and in terms of the expression of their true nature.

GC: What about education, the formal schooling that the child receives?
BC: There is probably no perfect education anywhere today. Everyone has a more or less limiting, and in some cases

crippling, education which thwarts their creative imagination, inhibits them as individuals, and builds fear complexes into them — fear of teachers, fear of examinations, fear of each other; it also overstimulates harmful competition.

GC: What would you say are the right principles to stress in education?

BC: The most important is that every individual should be seen as a soul. The whole of education should be geared to that. In addition, each child needs to be recognized as being unique, with a personal ray structure that is the outcome of their past incarnational experience and the soul purpose in this life — because the soul provides the rays for the various bodies.

Therefore, real education, and the education of the future, must necessarily take into account the ray structure so that each individual's education can be tailored to fit that person.

GC: What about IQ? There is a major emphasis on it, yet it does not really correlate with anything except academic success.

BC: It is not so important. Of course among initiates and disciples you always find a higher IQ factor than in less evolved people. But you also find lower scores in more deprived homes where the parents are not providing the stimulus, the conversation and the involvement which stimulates the individuality of the child. So they lose their sparkle. When children lose their sparkle they register an IQ which is probably below their actual level.

GC: That word "sparkle" seems to bring together much of what you have been saying. Maintaining the sparkle in the child is what we are trying to do.

BC: It is individuality. That is essential to life. It must never be put down. Unfortunately, in our modern society that is the first thing that is put down. Anybody who shows any kind of independence — on which sparkle depends — is immediately put down: "Don't do that. Stop that. Put that down! Naughty, naughty!" This goes on for little kids, one and two years old.

GC: There is a real push now to develop reading and cognitive skills very early in life. Does that inhibit the individuality?
BC: No, it will not inhibit the individual, but it might stimulate one factor above another; also, you might find that the child becomes stressed emotionally. You have to let the child take their own time and make their own demands for learning. Then you try to meet those demands, watching the direction in which the child is going.

GC: What about the overall stress of modern living?
BC: Colossal. But that is not just for children. Everyone is affected by the overall stress of modern life, because we are at a point of transition and transformation which is inevitably a point of tension. When as today, you have two great forces — one forward-looking, one reactionary — opposing and fighting, that builds up an enormous amount of stress because everybody is caught up in the energy which that generates.

GC: Returning to something we touched on earlier, the numbers of lives it takes to reach various stages of the path, I wonder if you could give me some numbers for each of the following intervals: the very beginning, which could be defined as the point of maximum involution, to 0.5 — half way in consciousness to the first initiation.
BC: Hundreds of thousands.

GC: Hundreds of thousands? I never imagined it was so many.
BC: Yes, hundreds of thousands of lives. I am informed that there are as many as 6 million people on the verge of the first initiation, which means from about 0.7 to the first initiation.

Between the first initiation and the second, the average is about six to seven lives. It could be 15, or it could be as low as two, which is rare. Maitreya did it in two, and only today are a few 'high flyers' doing it in two. Of course, that will speed up, more and more people will do it in two lives.

GC: From the second to the third initiation?
BC: One life. If you take the second initiation early enough in one life, you can take the third initiation in the same life. If not, you will almost certainly take it in the next life. And if you

take the third early on, you can take the fourth in the same life: many people come in as a third-degree initiate and go out as a fourth.

GC: And the fourth to the fifth is probably again one life?
BC: That depends. You might be initiate but not be able to take it in that life because the astrological conditions were not right. You would have to wait until the next life. You become initiate through your life experience. The initiate, necessarily, is initiate before the actual initiation 'ceremony' which requires the correct astrological influences.

GC: You have said elsewhere that during the period from 1.3 to 1.6 the fight is really on because you become aware that you have glamours, illusions.
BC: It is the becoming aware of the glamours, the pain that that creates, the sense that you are not being what you are, that hurts. The glamours get in the way. Before that time the glamours do not seem to get in the way because you do not even know they are there, you are quite at home in the fog of illusion they create.

GC: In light of this struggle, which, as you say, is unique to this particular stage of the path, I wonder if the standard definitions of mental health need to be adjusted. Usually people are considered healthy if they are stable in their job and relationships and have generally high self-confidence and self-esteem. But it seems to me that in this stage of the path all those criteria of mental health generally deteriorate as the individual struggles through their glamours. Is that so from your perspective?
BC: Glamours keep us functioning and reasonably at ease in the personality sense. In the soul sense, they create a condition of ignorance or non-functioning. Glamours prevent us from seeing reality.

When the soul energy pours in, it disturbs the *status quo*, and then the fight is on. At every stage in the path of the initiate, there is a shift in the balance of power of forces. These are tremendous energies, and every influx of a powerful, higher energy into any established situation transforms it. One's self-esteem, self-confidence, and ability to function as an integrated person is shifting all the time between 1.3 and 1.6.

It depends on the ray structure of the individual how more or less disturbing this will be. If they are along the 1-3-5-7 line, and, therefore, probably more extroverted, more at home in the world of form, their confidence would not necessarily be so affected. If they are along the 2-4-6 line, they will be more introverted, and, especially if they have a lot of 2nd ray in their makeup, may find this a period of great disturbance. The new energies galvanize but upset their emotional life. It is always like that; every influx of higher energy is temporarily disturbing to the *status quo*.

GC: It seems to me that a lot of people who seem to be doing very well in life are doing so because they identify totally with the form level of their achievement, and that is what is real to them.
BC: There are many very clever individuals who have not yet taken the first initiation, but who are extremely competent in their profession. There are also many people around 1.5 or 1.6, who have never done anything of note in this particular life, but who are actually as evolved as some of the present world leaders.

You cannot look at the outer and judge the inner. From the point of view of a Master, and of course from all of esotericism, it is the quality of the life that matters. The form is important, but the life within the form is more important.

GC: A tremendous number of the 'creative geniuses' who presumably had a well-developed inner life which they sought to express in art of one kind or another were once, or would now be diagnosed as, manic-depressives. What is going on with them?
BC: This is a result of imperfect liaison with the soul. Where you have a more perfect liaison with the soul, you might get the manic condition because the soul provides a galvanizing energy, but you will certainly get a very powerful, sometimes

obsessional activity along some creative line. This expression may be perfectly balanced depending on the other rays, the emotional balance of the individual, how successful he is, how much money he has, and his family situation. There are many factors which play a part in this, but generally it is to do with the solidity and extent of soul contact.

If there is a degree of soul contact in a cyclic, on-and-off kind of way, then you get periods of manic activity followed by corresponding periods of inactivity, and even depression.

But there is more to it than that. Any creative individual is living under stress. The stress itself creates a tension which manifests itself cyclically in these manic-depressive states. They can also be chemically-based, the result of chemicals in the system affecting the brain in a cycle of a manic, overactive state, followed necessarily by a depressed, underactive state. It is an illness, an imbalance. It may have a hereditary cause.

GC: There are drugs, lithium for manic-depression and more complex chemicals for schizophrenia, that try to balance all that out. How does that relate to the actual life of the soul and the person?
BC: It is always difficult for the soul to manifest itself perfectly through its vehicles. It depends on karma, on heredity, and on the chemical nature of the physical body through which it is trying to express itself. If you have a 2nd-ray soul, for example, with a 2nd-ray personality and physical body, then you have a very tender, over-sensitive vehicle through which energy and purpose of the soul can manifest. These over-sensitives are the people, who, on the whole, become manic-depressives. It is a question of over-sensitivity or vulnerability, which nearly always has a hereditary factor.

GC: In general then, do you think using therapeutic drugs can be beneficial?
BC: From a temporary point of view, yes. It can only be seen as amelioration, but to ameliorate a condition is worth doing. That is what any medicine tends to do. No medicine 'cures' but ameliorates conditions, and that is, of course, of value if it makes life more bearable, happier for the individual.

Relationships

*GC: The next thing I would like to discuss is relationships —
romantic love in particular. It too can make life "more
bearable, happier for the individual", but it has a funny way of
evaporating as individuals grow and come to know themselves
and their partners better.*

BC: The nature of being is wholeness — total oneness, the
coming together of Father-Mother-God. That is the given
nature of man and woman. But on the physical plane,
individuals have lost that sense of wholeness, and are
searching for it all the time. They find it, naturally, in an
attractive — to them at that moment — member of the
opposite sex. That longing for union is the same sense of
longing for unity on the highest spiritual level, but related to
the physical plane. It ensures the procreation of the species,
and is essential.

Romantic love is a relatively recent invention; it stems
from about the 12th century. There must have been elements of
it before that, but as an 'organized religion' romantic love
began around the early Renaissance. It is the result of the
idealizing factor of the 6th ray. The 6th ray reached its
strongest potency from about the 10th to the 17th century, and
just in that time what we call romantic love flowered. Before
that, there was no such thing as romantic love. There was the
coming together of the sexes naturally, based largely on
animalistic instincts.

But from then on, an idealistic notion of the beloved took
the place of this purely physical-plane activity. Essentially it
was created by men. The female was elevated into a position of
virginity reflecting the nature of the Christian Virgin — which
was an essential part of the belief in Jesus as God. The object
of romantic love was likewise lifted out of the carnal, desire
nature of real, physical-plane sex onto a level on which she
could be worshipped as the Virgin. That has brought about the
notion of romantic love. It is the mother, or the other, idealized
to the point of perfection, and is the outcome of the idealizing
faculty of the 6th ray. Had there been another ray in

incarnation, say the 7th ray or the 3rd ray, there probably would be no such thing as romantic love.

Romantic love is a stage in the recognition or expression of spiritual love. Spiritual love is total, unconditional love streaming from the heart of the unified being — asking for no love in return, simply an expression of the nature of being itself. But probably that love by itself would not have been sufficient, up to this point in the evolution of man, to guarantee the continuance of the species.

GC: Or the stability of society.

BC: Both are entailed. As societies evolve, there are always more and more sections of society who have the time and energy to play with the experience of sexual attraction and to develop different aspects of love. In sophisticated, leisured societies, you get a playing with the whole notion of love and the transference of love onto a romantic level where it is really a kind of game that intelligent, but essentially idle, people have the time to indulge in. It is the product of astral imagination. It is a glamour. While that glamour lasts, the love lasts. As soon as that glamour fades, the love fades. That is the problem with romantic love. The glamour itself decides the tenure of the love.

GC: Assuming the couple manages to work their way through the glamours involved in romantic love, surely there has to be something of substance remaining between them.

BC: It is called karma. The motivating force for couples to come together is sexual. But that 'sexual' may be on any level. It may be physical-plane sexual. It may be an astral connection — likeness or difference. It may be mental, personality or soul connection — likeness or difference. Or it can, at its highest and best, be a combination of all of these. The five-pointed star of relationship, on which the people meet correctly on all five levels, is relatively rare. The perfect marriage is rare. The problem is that people may be very well-suited on the soul level, in terms of personality may get on all right, mentally have no contact at all, emotionally perhaps, and sexually probably. Or mentally, on the personality level, and emotionally reasonably well, but sexually not at all. There are many such permutations.

The quality, depth and stability of the relationship will depend on these factors, but above all on the inner factor of ancient karmic ties which draw the people together despite their differences.

GC: When you talk about "getting on well" on any given level, does that mean essentially a positive-negative exchange that creates something better?

BC: It could be one of two things. It could be similarity of ray structure where like attracts like. Two 2nd rays or two 3rd rays, for example, will find it easy to look at life in the same way, and will tend to get on. They will want the same things from life; be interested in the same things. They have, as it is said, "a lot in common".

Where one ray structure complements the other, a similar thing happens but in a different way. Although they do not have much in common, they have needs which are supplied by the structure of the other person. For instance, if one person is all 2nd and 6th ray, and the other is all 1st and 3rd, one supplies what is missing in the other's nature. Together they make a good team. That is a team rather than a pair.

GC: A team for their own wholeness or a team for what they can do for the outer world?

BC: It could be either. It is a family unit. The family unit is the basis of all society. It is a negative step for any group to break down the family unit into group units, as they have done in the Israeli kibbutz. It is an absolute, basic necessity, and is the essential karmic crucible in which ancient ties are worked out.

GC: It seems to me that a lot of relationships and marriages dissolve prematurely from an evolutionary perspective simply because people are not having fun together any more. And that seems to do with the fact that the two people have gotten down to the real hard work, they have gotten down to what you are calling "the ancient karmic ties".

BC: Yes, people have reached a point where the glamours of the relationship are over. They have been together for so long, they no longer find anything fresh in the other. The problems of bringing up a family, making a living, all of that, impinge too strongly on their sex life, social life and personality relationships. Many couples give up. They give up either too early or too late. Some do not give up early enough, when the marriage has run its course and they have nothing more to give each other. They are living in a state of inhibition, pain and suffering. Others, on the other hand, give up far too early — not having reached the point of having established a relationship on a less glamoured basis. Having got through the initial glamours, they have to build the relationship on the connections which may or may not come from ancient karmic ties. The karma has to be worked out. That is why they have come together, nine times out of 10.

GC: I am interested if there are any keys in discriminating one set of circumstances from the other. The pain feels the same in both situations.

BC: It is very difficult. The thing is always to see it from the soul's point of view if you can, and answer the needs. The essential needs usually are the needs of the children, which generally supersede the needs of the parents. If the situation is not so painful as to cause constant strain on the life energy of the couple and the children, then the family unit should work out some means of living together under tolerable conditions. But if they are too intolerable, then sometimes the well-being of the children has to be, if not sacrificed, at least put in jeopardy by a more or less total break-up of the family. Most people imagine that it has to be a total break-up, but it need not be.

As to whether to stay together or not, you have to know the situation from the karmic point of view. I do not know the way, short of being a Master, that you can know this. You have to use your intuition and try to see it from the point of view of the soul, the need of the children, and your own sense of purpose and responsibility. You have to take responsibility, and grow in responsibility.

GC: One of the problems with relationships seems to be that individuals have failed to develop a sufficient sense of their own autonomy. In psychoanalytic thinking, autonomy is seen as the result of a properly resolved Oedipal conflict. Forgetting castration anxiety and the rest of Freud's elaborate view of this process, do you think that there is an important process of a child competing with the same-sex parent for the primary affection of the opposite-sex parent, ideally losing that battle, and ultimately identifying with the same-sex parent having gained a sense of autonomy in the process?

BC: I believe it is important, but I would not give it the importance which the classical Freudian would give to it. It does not seem to me that the possibility of right human relationships can take place until the Oedipal complex is more or less resolved in the individual, because, by analytic theory, one carries forward into all relationships the needs, desires and expectations which one has experienced in relation to one's parents. We are always repeating the same infantile situation if there is not a real resolution of this complex. The 'cure', I believe, is through growing detachment and not necessarily through psychoanalysis.

Many men see in their prospective wives everything that they expected from their mothers, unless they have resolved that conflict and can approach their wives in a much more adult way. This has been supported up until now by society itself — in which the wife is very much the mother. It is equally true that what many women look for in their husband is some big, strong, comforting, protective entity who is really their father. That has been supported up until now by society, where the man has been the breadwinner, the protector of the family, the person that everyone looks up to and relies on to meet every situation with calm and experience. These roles become stereotyped, and people fit into their roles very easily.

Many marriages are completely happy if these roles are satisfied. Sometimes these marriages last a lifetime, but I would think that the people involved probably make very little progress in their life demonstration. If that is the relationship that you have with your wife or husband, that must be a limiting factor in soul expression or even in personality expression. You cannot remain infantile and grow.

GC: It seems that a fair number of relationships get into trouble when one partner grows and the other does not.
BC: Yes, this is very common. My experience in relation to the groups with which I work — people more or less conscious of the nature of Hierarchy, and who are, or are trying to be, active, conscious disciples — is that women are changing more than men and coming into a new awareness of themselves, just as women more than men are becoming aware of themselves in the society at large.

GC: Do you see that as the result of the individual effort of the women involved, the women's movement, or the coming Age of Maitreya, the Age of the Mother?
BC: They are all part of the same thing, part of a process in which the female nourishing aspect of life will gain in potency in the New Age now beginning.

Western orthodox (Freudian and post-Freudian) psychology is based on certain basic premises which it posits are inevitable for all people. For example, the love/hate relationship with mother and/or father, Oedipal complex, etc. (1) Is this a valid standpoint? Is neurosis unavoidable or do such neuroses apply in some cases but not in others? (2) If Western psychology is only partially correct, what steps does it need to take to become more universally valid? Is it possible for modern psychology to begin to blend with esoteric psychology? (January/February 1987)
(1) Obviously the Oedipal complex exists: people did and do love and simultaneously hate their parents. They carry this unresolved dichotomy into all later relationships. This is Freud's basic clinical, objective finding. That it is inevitable and unavoidable is another matter. From the point of view of esotericism this need not be so — it is a socially conditioned

phenomenon, the result of wrong human relationships passed on from generation to generation. The degree to which it exists, moreover, depends on the point of evolution of the individual, in particular whether he or she is mentally or astrally polarized. For the advanced, mentally polarized disciple, this need not be the case at all. He is usually well able to cope with his conflicting emotions and bring about a resolution. The more advanced the individual the more will this be the case.

(2) The big gap in the thinking of modern psychology and psychoanalysis (a gap soon to be filled) is the omission (except in the case of Jung and his followers) of the concept of the human soul and its incarnational cycles. Of necessity, this position also neglects the fundamental concept of karma. The Seven Rays and their powerful conditioning influences remain as yet a closed book to modern psychologists. Until the nature of the threefold human constitution — spirit, soul, personality — is known and accepted; until the fact of reincarnation, the influences of karma and of an individual's rays are taken into account; until the soul's nature and individual purpose can be ascertained, modern psychology cannot further advance. At the moment, except for the pioneer work of Wilhelm Reich, which led him from the concept of the unitary basis of neurosis to the discovery of primordial energy, it is, generally speaking, at odds with itself. While doing much useful therapeutic work in amelioration of the effects of neurosis, it is waiting, albeit unknowingly, for the next great step forward — the 'discovery' of the human soul.

[Note: The above interview appeared in *Share International* in July 1992.]

CHAPTER 18

INDIVIDUAL INITIATES AND TEACHINGS

Esoteric and Spiritual Field

Bailey, Blavatsky, Roerich

Is an understanding (or lack of it) of the Alice Bailey books an indication of one's point of evolution? (May 1988)

A true understanding of (and not simply an interest in) the Alice Bailey teachings would certainly indicate that the person was 'advanced' enough to have taken at least the first initiation, perhaps even the second or third. A serious interest in and effort to apply them in life would indicate that one was near or had taken the first initiation. However, spiritual evolution should not be judged simply by an interest in or understanding of these esoteric teachings. There are many paths to Self-realization, and many advanced initiates know nothing of them. To quote the Master DK: "The disciple is known by his control of his environment. The initiate is recognized by the extent of his world service." It is service that counts, not book knowledge of any, however lofty, teachings.

*For several years, I have been reading **Share International** and I find the information on esoteric subjects quite difficult. Can you mention some simpler introductory books which explain esotericism for beginners?* (March 1987)

To be honest, I do not think esotericism can be approached more simply than we attempt in *Share International* and my books generally. The articles by Aart Jurriaanse, I believe, are particularly clear and illuminating. The problem is, of course, that by the nature of things we can present only fragments of a vast and all-encompassing teaching which requires much serious study to gain an overall vision and grasp of the whole.

The questioner might find Aart Jurriaanse's compilation from the Alice Bailey teachings, *Ponder on This*, a good starting point for such a study.

(1) Why (what is the evidence or authority?) should we believe the teachings of Helena Blavatsky, Alice Bailey, etc? (2) How does one discern the difference between (spiritual) telepathy and the delusional tricks of the mind? (January/February 1990)
(1) There is no reason at all why you should believe the teachings of H.P.Blavatsky or Alice Bailey. You are not asked to believe them unless from your own experience their truth resounds in you. (2) The only way is through correct discrimination which comes about naturally through correct experience.

*I can't help but wonder if I've stumbled across a mistake. On p163 of **Telepathy** by Alice Bailey, it reads: "In the Book of Revelation which was dictated 1900 years ago by the disciple who is now known as the Master Hilarion...." But on p59 of **Initiation, Human and Solar** it reads: "... we find the Master Hilarion who in an earlier incarnation was Paul of Tarsus." I do not believe Paul had anything to do with writing the Book of Revelation. Can you discuss this?* (December 1988)
You are quite right. Obviously, St Paul, later the Master Hilarion, did not dictate the Book of Revelation to St John, who was one of the closest disciples of the Christ. The Book of Revelation was not dictated by anyone but was the description, as closely as He could put it into words (which is not close at all), of a series of visions given to Him by Maitreya. Some of these visions relate to events of His own time, such as the downfall of Rome and the emergence of Christendom, some to events now taking place, others to events to take place in the Capricornian cycle, while still others relate to happenings at the consummation of our Earth's evolutionary experience.

In the Alice Bailey books, from memory, the following statements are made in various places. Can you say whether they are true or not? (1) The human eye is starting to develop sensitivity to ultra-violet light. (2) Hierarchy is holding back this development because we have been appallingly cruel to animals and They do not want us to be able to see etheric creatures. (3) The etheric body is the seat of disease and the cure of disease depends on recognizing it. (4) At death the etheric body and (presumably) the higher bodies with it leave the gross physical body through one of the chakras. (5) Late this century there will be photographic proof of survival after death and this will rid humanity of the fear of death. (6) Putting these things together, it seems to me that it should be possible to photograph or video etheric bodies of the dead (ghosts) by ultra-violet light. Is that what the Master DK had in mind? (7) How far into the ultra-violet region would it be necessary to go? Would one more octave of light do? (September 1988)

(1) True. (2) Not true. (3) True. (4) True. Through the crown chakra. (5) True. (6) Yes. (7) No. It requires four more octaves.

I think feelings of guilt can hinder people in approaching others with love and an open heart. In a book by Alice Bailey about sexuality, I found about 15–20 curse words about homosexuality. Since I live homosexually and express love in this way, I feel hurt and rejected. Isn't love more important than anything else? (January/February 1990)

I cannot believe that a book by Alice Bailey can have 15–20 curses of homosexuality. Certainly such a book would not be written (through her) by the Master DK. Perhaps the questioner is referring to some (biased) commentary by another writer. Homosexuality is not seen by Hierarchy as 'normal', and if it were universal it would lead inevitably to the ending of the human race, but, so far as I am aware, no curse words would be used by Hierarchy in commenting on it. As to the final question about love: while obviously of vital importance, love is not the only factor in life. The Laws of Life are complex, varied and mutually dependent. It limits understanding and produces imbalance to isolate and exaggerate one aspect.

Why has not the Lucis Trust, the organization promulgating the Alice Bailey teachings, accepted Maitreya's emergence? (January/February 1991)

Because it is not (yet) part of their experience.

When Alice Bailey died, her point of evolution was 3.2. With which degree did she enter into incarnation? (May 1989)
She was 2.0 degrees initiate at birth.

*HPB and Alice Bailey "had glimpses of the teaching" (**Share International**, September 1987, p10) but what did these two fail to see? Was it to maintain freedom of thought by refusing/transcending all outside authority like Krishnamurti did? If so, it contradicts Maitreya's comments on Krishnamurti published in Anrias' book.* (January/February 1989)
I think it is not so much that HPB and AAB failed to see certain things but that they got caught up in the process of teaching, thus making academic what has to be a moment-to-moment living experience.

Krishnamurti, on the other hand, inspired by Maitreya, went straight to the heart of the matter: our own individual experience, now, this moment, of reality. I do not believe the comments of Maitreya in the Anrias book to be authentic.

(1) Since they were in incarnation at the same time, did Helena Roerich and Alice Bailey know of each other and each other's work? (2) Why was it necessary to produce works at approximately the same time (though each may take a somewhat different approach, the basic underlying purpose, to prepare humanity for the New Age and the return of Maitreya, seems to be essentially the same)? (November 1987)
(1) It appears that they did know of each other and of each other's work although it seems they never met. (2) They each represent a different approach: that of the 1st ray in the case of Helena Roerich and of the 2nd in that of Alice Bailey.

If Helena Roerich received the Agni Yoga teachings from the Master Morya primarily for the purpose of informing the world of the fact of the Hierarchy, will she be in incarnation at the time of the Reappearance of the Christ to further help with the externalization of the Hierarchy? (November 1990)
I am afraid there are a number of misconceptions revealed in this question. Firstly, while the Master Morya gave the

574

majority of the teachings, other Masters, in particular the Master Koot Hoomi, also contributed, while the first book, *The Call*, is by Maitreya Himself. Secondly, these teachings were not given primarily to inform the world about Hierarchy but to alert the disciples to the dangers of the coming World War, and to galvanize them into constructive action in line with Hierarchical intention. Readers may be interested to know that they are not seen, by Hierarchy, as having been successful in doing this.

Thirdly, as any regular reader of this magazine should know, the Reappearance of the Christ has already taken place. Helena Roerich is not in incarnation at this time. It appears that the initiate who was Helena Roerich is still not decided as to the timing of a further incarnation.

Did Jesus overshadow Origen or incarnate as Origen? In **Leaves of Morya's Garden** *and in her letters Helena Roerich repeatedly refers to Origen as the greatest of Christian teachers, and in a letter of 6 May 1934 there is the following intriguing passage: "Not always have the Great Souls, who had to fulfil certain missions, entered the Community of the Brotherhood during their earthly life. For instance, Apollonius of Tyana was called to visit the Brotherhood, but he, in his incarnation as Origen, accepted the most difficult task of guarding the purity of the teaching of Christ, and for this he suffered imprisonment instead of dwelling in the abode of the Brotherhood and participating in the joyous work there."*

If Jesus incarnated as Apollonius, this makes Jesus Origen also, but you give Origen's soul ray as 2 instead of 6 and his initiation grade as 4 instead of 5. Was Helena Roerich mistaken? (December 1987)

My information is that Helena Roerich was, if not totally mistaken, then rather inaccurate. Origen was not an incarnation of Apollonius (the next incarnation of Jesus) but was overshadowed by Jesus (Apollonius). His difficult life was that of the fourth-degree initiate and he did indeed uphold the Christ's teaching on reincarnation which was later made anathema by the Church Fathers.

Is it true that the soul of H.P.Blavatsky reincarnated again this century in a male body working behind the scenes and died several years ago? (December 1986)
That is not my information. My information is that the entity who was H.P.Blavatsky incarnated again, in a male body, only three years ago. He will take the fifth initiation (and so become a Master) in this life. He is living at present in Leningrad (St Petersburg).

*I could not help noticing in the List of Initiates (**Maitreya's Mission**, **Volume One**) that the ray structure (at least as given, not including sub-rays) for Helena Roerich is the same as that of Helena P. Blavatsky, and wondered what significance there may be to this. I had read (C. W. Leadbeater, **The Masters and the Path**) that at her passing HPB had taken the body of another disciple, and wondered if in this sense she may also have been Helena Roerich. Would you please explain if this may have been the case, or, if not, who HPB became, if she did assume the body of another disciple?* (November 1987)
Notwithstanding his degree (2.4) C.W.Leadbeater was incorrect in stating that HPB "assumed the body of another disciple". After her death she remained out of incarnation until only three years ago. As already revealed in these columns, 'she' is now a young boy in Leningrad (St Petersburg). She and Helena Roerich were quite separate personalities (Helena Roerich was born in 1879 while HPB died in 1891) and the similarity in ray structure is quite coincidental. Their sub-rays were slightly different. HPB's were: Personality 7, Mental 4, Astral 6, and Physical 7; Helena Roerich's were: Personality 6, Mental 2, Astral 4, and Physical 7. They were both disciples of the Master Morya.

Would you please explain what significance there might be that this work (that of HPB, Helena Roerich and Alice Bailey) was all done by those then in female bodies? (November 1987)
It was pure coincidence that they were all women. They happened to be the best available vehicles at the time for the planned work. In fact, had HPB been in a male body she would

576

probably have met less resistance to her revolutionary revelations and statements than she did.

As most of the knowledge of the existence of Hierarchy has come from women (Blavatsky, Bailey, Roerich, Besant, etc), can you explain why you, a man, are at the forefront of the present wave of information rather than another woman? Is it because of your ray structure being the most suitable or that at present there are no women who would be able to present the information in a way suitable to Hierarchy? (December 1990)

The reasons for the choice of any given disciple for Hierarchical work are complex and little is to be gained by speculation. Suffice it to say that the sex of the individual is not important. The Masters were not looking for another woman, and, finding none suitable, settled on me. Nor is my ray structure the prime consideration, although useful in this approach to the public. The major considerations are: availability (which includes evolutionary development and, therefore, suitability by ease of contact); impersonality and objectivity; and karmic opportunity.

Are you now, or have you ever been, a part of the Masonic Brotherhood? Do you belong to the same Masonic Lodge as Charles Leadbeater? I believe it was the Co-Masons (with Annie Besant) and they spawned Krishnamurti? (July/August 1987)

I get the impression that the questioner does not think too highly of the Masonic Brotherhood which generally is getting a rather bad press at the moment. The Society of Freemasons is the oldest Society in the world (going back to Atlantean times) and contains hidden in its rituals (according to the Master DK) some of the secrets of initiation. I am not, nor have been, a member, but any group that could 'spawn' a Being of the stature of Krishnamurti would certainly have my vote.

You answer questions using phrases such as: according to my information; my information is; as I understand it; etc. Such phrases could make the reader feel that you, yourself, may not be fully convinced of what you say. If Maitreya, Himself, (at times) and your Master (always) overshadow you when you answer questions, how could there be doubts? (November 1991)

First of all, Maitreya does not (at any time) overshadow me when I am answering questions for *Share International.* My Master does at all times.

Not even the Masters claim to be infallible. That being so, it behoves a humble disciple like myself not to appear to claim such, even when I write with complete conviction and no doubts. In that way I acknowledge that others may have another point of view.

What is the experience of someone who is being overshadowed? In the case of Mr Creme, do you leave your body, are you fully conscious, do you remember the overshadowing afterwards? (July/August 1989)

There is no generalized answer to this question; everyone's experience will be, to a greater or lesser extent, different. We have no record of Jesus' experience, overshadowed profoundly by the Christ. For Krishnamurti, who called it "the process", the experience caused him terrible pain and migraine-type headaches. He had a double 7th-ray physical, oversensitive, and not very adaptable or resilient; this, I believe, was the reason for his painful experience.

In my own case, I appear to be blessed with a rather resilient physical body which quickly adapts to the inflow of the high-level vibration of Maitreya without too much trouble. Any pain (there is some in certain head centres, and in the neck and shoulders) soon goes when the overshadowing stops. I never leave my body, I am always totally conscious and of course remember everything I experience, see or hear during the overshadowing.

*In your book **Maitreya's Mission, Volume One** you seem to have a fairly deep awareness of the inner feelings and motives of Pontius Pilate. Are you the reincarnation of that man? (May 1990)*

No. The information about the feelings and motives of Pontius Pilate was given to me by my Master.

Why is the terminology used by the Hierarchy — as in the Alice Bailey books, the Lord Maitreya's Messages and your own references — primarily masculine, ie brotherhood of man, etc? Surely this just adds to the already huge division between the sexes? (March 1987)

Hierarchy uses terms that are in common use and readily understandable. There are no satisfactory terms yet for the concept of a brotherhood and sisterhood of man/woman which are not clumsy and stilted, and one cannot use 'humanity' *ad infinitum*. In the Messages from Maitreya and my Master's articles for *Share International* especially, the language is so structured and mantric in effect that simplicity of terms is essential, even if seeming to stress the masculine. It should be understood that Hierarchy is the stimulus behind the woman's movement and has no masculine bias whatsoever.

In the List of Initiates, the point in evolution was omitted in the case of Avatars. Yet, you say William Shakespeare and Leonardo da Vinci are human Avatars from Jupiter and Mercury respectively, and give their initiatory degree as 3.5 and 4.4 respectively. Can you please explain why you give their degree? (May 1987)

In the usual meaning of Avatar, He is a being called in (to answer human need) by Sanat Kumara, Lord of the World. In the case of human Avatars like Shakespeare and Leonardo, they had *fallen* to Earth, not come to serve it. They became part of our human evolution for around 3,000 years before appearing as Shakespeare and Leonardo da Vinci. For this reason their degree is given.

Krishnamurti, Steiner and Others

(1) Why do you think Krishnamurti rejected the Hierarchy, teaching instead that the only authority should be ourselves? (2) Is he a Master himself? If not, what degree initiate? (March 1987)

(1) With respect, Krishnamurti did not reject Hierarchy. Indeed, his teaching that the only authority should be oneself is precisely the age-old teaching of Hierarchy, from the Buddha

Himself to the Master DK, Who prefaced each book of His amanuensis, Alice Bailey, with the advice not to take the contents as an 'authority', Hierarchical or otherwise. That His advice has not always been taken by aspirants is another matter. (2) No, Krishnamurti was not a Master but a fourth-degree initiate.

(1) Has the soul who was Krishnamurti incarnated again? (2) If so, in which country? (3) If no, will he return by the end of the century? (March 1990)
(1) No. (3) Yes.

*On p10 of **Share International**, September 1987, Maitreya gave full approval to Krishnamurti's teaching. But if Maitreya's comment on Krishnamurti in the final chapter of David Anrias' book **Through the Eyes of the Masters** (3rd edition, 1947), are authentic (they are said to have been communicated to David Anrias telepathically), how should we interpret the difference in the two teachings?*
It is my information that Anrias' book is the result of communication from the 5th astral plane and not from the Masters at all. Personally, I would not give credence to the information contained in his book.

*In the book written by Gopi Krishna (1903–1984), **Path to Self-realization** (or similar title), there is a passage which sounds like a description of the Day of Declaration. It was said that this metaphysical dissertation was a work of inspiration. (1) Was the information in fact dictated by a member of the Hierarchy or by an entity on some lower plane? (2) What was the author's point in evolution?* (November 1989)
(1) It was dictated by the Master of Gopi Krishna. (2) 1.7. He was unusually sensitive to mental impression.

Joan of Arc said she heard "voices" giving her orders. According to her, these voices belonged to St Catherina, St Margaretha and even the Archangel Michael. Since she was 3.3 degrees initiate, we may assume that her "voices" were the result of telepathic contact with one or more Masters. (1) Are you allowed to reveal who these Masters were? (2) Did Joan of Arc herself know these were Masters and not angels? (3) Would you be able to tell if she is a Master now herself and if so in what field this Master is active? (4) May we know her sub-rays as Joan of Arc? (April 1989)

(1) She was in fact contacted by only one "voice", that of her own Master, the Master Hilarion. (2) She herself thought she heard the "voices" of the various saints and archangels to whom she was emotionally devoted. (3) She is now a Master, not in incarnation, but preparing to be so, in France, in the very near future. His work is, and will be, in the scientific field. (4) As Joan of Arc, her sub-rays were: Personality 7; Mental 6; Astral 6; Physical 7. (Her major rays, as listed in *Maitreya's Mission, Volume One*, were: Soul 5, Personality 1, Mental body 3, Astral 6, Physical 6.)

Did Rudolf Steiner (1861–1925) have any insights in relation to the Reappearance of the Christ? (July/August 1990)

Rudolf Steiner was a Theosophist who broke away to found Anthroposophy. He was a remarkable man, 2.2 degrees initiate, with fascinating and valuable insights into many areas, such as agricultural husbandry, education and medicine. However, about the Reappearance of the Christ he had, I believe, a blind spot. Although he was a Theosophist and would claim to be an esotericist, he is not to my mind a true esotericist but a Christian mystic. Somehow, his Christian mysticism got in the way of his understanding of the relationship of the Christ to the Hierarchy. Although theoretically he must have known that the Christ is the head of our Hierarchy, he still saw the Christ in rather mystical terms and maintained that the Christ cannot return in a physical body, but only on the etheric plane (which he called the spiritual realm).

As we know, in 1945 Maitreya made a decision to return at the earliest possible moment, and on the physical, astral and mental planes. As Steiner died in 1925, he did not know about this aspect of the Plan, but as a Theosophist he should have known that this was on the cards, and has been so since at least 1922 when the first Alice Bailey book (dictated by the Master

DK), *Initiation, Human and Solar*, was published. In *The Reappearance of the Christ*, the Master DK says quite emphatically that He was talking about the Christ's physical appearance in the world. This, He said, was one of the most important statements in the book. The Christ, He emphasized, will appear in a physical body, visible to all.

This somehow conflicted with Steiner's Christian mysticism. He maintained that the Christ could come only on the etheric. Gradually, he wrote, humanity will develop etheric vision in this coming age (which is true), and one by one they would recognize the Christ on the etheric. To my mind, this is a complete misunderstanding. It is Christian dogmatism that makes Steiner maintain that Christ cannot come in a physical body. It is as if to do so would somehow 'lower' the Christ, bring Him on to too low a level. Many Christians believe this, seeing Him only in His role as a Principle, not as an actual man embodying that Principle Who can work on all planes, including the physical plane.

*(1) Are the **Mahatma Letters**, written by A.P.Sinnett, genuine? (2) All of them?* (December 1986)
(1) Yes. (2) No.

When Gurdjieff spoke of a number four and a number five man, does that mean an adept and a Master as you describe them, or does it mean something different, like an integrated personality and what you call a disciple? (March 1990)
As I understand it, a number four man is one who is still working exclusively with the lower Quaternary, the Personality and its vehicles, mental, emotional and physical. The number five man is one who has expanded his consciousness to bring in some awareness of the soul. He is the disciple.

Some years ago, before his death, Swami Muktananda spoke of a great Being who is coming to this planet. He is known in Hindi as the Dharma Purusha. It was said that if there was a nuclear war, the Dharma Purusha would turn the bombs into water. Who is this great Being, is it Maitreya? (September 1991)

Yes.

I was interested to see that Life and ***Teachings of the Masters of the Far East*** *by Baird T.Spalding was included in the list of 'Suggested Further Reading' in your book* **The Reappearance of the Christ and the Masters of Wisdom**, *p254. Would you please comment on the accuracy of this work? Did all the events described actually take place? Did Mr Spalding actually experience all he wrote?* (March 1988)

The events described by Baird Spalding did take place and he did experience all he wrote about. His descriptions are very accurate. What he omitted to point out, however, is that some (the less sensational) of these happenings took place on the physical plane while most took place at different levels of the etheric planes (out of the body as far as he was concerned). That does not make the events any less 'real'.

Did he realize that these were 'out of body' experiences? Not at the time that they were taking place but he was later informed that this was so. Why, you might ask, did he not reveal this fact in the books? I believe he thought the material would be even less acceptable and believable if described otherwise than as physical-plane events.

In the book **The Boy and the Brothers**, *the Master would not let them play cards. Why? Was it because card games are competitive?* (September 1987)

No. It was a protective measure for 'the Boy', whose early upbringing in the slums of London had brought him into close contact with many 'cardsharps'. He was an expert cheat at cards.

Rajneesh has had himself announced as Maitreya. What do you say to that? (April 1987)

As I understand it, Rajneesh has not had himself "announced" as Maitreya but, following some 'inspired' writing by two devotees, has acknowledged that they could call him by that name. That is not to say that he actually believes that he is Maitreya. I cannot think that he could be so silly!

*Was **A Course in Miracles** (1) dictated by Maitreya and (2) is it to prepare people for the first initiation?* (September 1988)
My information is that *A Course in Miracles* contains the ideas and teaching not of Maitreya but of the Master Jesus. He 'conveyed' these ideas to a disciple on the inner planes (not incarnate) who 'conveyed' them to Helen Schueman, an unconscious medium (meaning unconscious of being mediumistic).

To my mind, its teachings — if put into practice — are one approach to the problem of overcoming glamour and therefore more likely to help prepare people for the second initiation.

The predictions of Nostradamus are very interesting. In many ways he reminds me of Leonardo da Vinci. Both men possessed incredible insight: Leonardo with his fantastic inventions and Nostradamus with far-reaching predictions. I've read that Leonardo was an advanced human sent from another solar system to teach humanity. Could this also be true of Nostradamus?

Also, how accurate can predictions really be, especially such far-reaching predictions as Nostradamus presented? One would imagine that our destiny is changing with every tick of the clock due to man's free will and initiate ability to alter destiny. How is it possible, then, for anyone to predict the future with any degree of accuracy? (May 1988)
Quite so, exactly. With respect, I must say I do not see very much in common between Leonardo da Vinci who was 4.4 degrees initiate and a human Avatar (not from another solar system but from the planet Mercury), and Nostradamus, only 1.7 degrees initiate (quite advanced to be sure, especially for the time, 16th century, but not yet even mentally polarized in the full sense).

To my mind, Nostradamus is accorded an altogether undeserved respect because some of his clairvoyance was accurate (and some inaccurate). The Masters Themselves allow for a margin of error of 300 years, more or less, in any forecasting of future events for the reasons you have given.

Kukai (774–835) is known in Japan as an expert in esoteric Buddhism. Is it true that he is now the Master Djwhal Khul?
He is not now the Master Djwhal Khul. He is indeed a Master, of the fifth degree, not in incarnation but working on the higher planes of the planet.

Is the great Venetian painter Lorenzo Lotto, who was 2.5 degrees initiate, now a Master? (July 1989)
He is now a Master of the fifth degree. He is not at present in incarnation but is planning to be so about 10 years from now. He resides (in etheric matter) in the Italian Alps.

Political Figures

Mao Tse-Tung, Castro and Kennedy

Mao Tse-Tung was a third-degree initiate, you say. How is that possible, since he was a Marxist and had a materialistic viewpoint? (September 1988)
What is a materialist? Study the life of Mao Tse-Tung and you will find the actions of a great initiate. Instead of being materialistic he was saturated with the will-aspect of spirit. Nobody who was not imbued with the will-aspect of God could bring 500 million people from nothing into a great nation. You cannot imagine what that man has accomplished. The fact that he did not believe in your God is something else. Everybody is concerned with beliefs. However, a belief in God or the belief that there is no God are essentially the same. Both are glamours. Belief is glamour. What is important is that we, as divine beings, demonstrate that divinity in every breath, every action we take. And if we do that, there will be no problems in the world. And no beliefs either.

In your last issue (March 1988), I was rather surprised to read that Castro was a highly evolved world leader — this was the implication of your answer. I have always thought of him as a warmonger and opportunist. Would you comment please? (April 1988)

The answer in the March issue was in reply to a question on why Maitreya does not manifest (presumably by overshadowing) through a world leader. I am not permitted to give the point of evolution of living people (especially if in the public eye) since this would be an infringement of their free will. Despite the reader's political prejudices (for that is what they are) Castro is the only world leader now in office sufficiently evolved for Maitreya to overshadow. That Castro (unlike Gorbachev, who does respond to the impress of the mind of Maitreya) does not appear to respond to world need rather than Cuba's need is a result, I would say, of his rather doctrinaire approach to politics.

Other major figures, evolved enough for Maitreya to use if that were His intention, are Chancellor Willy Brandt, ex-President Nyerere and ex-President Carter, all now, sadly, out of office.

Was Karl Marx inspired by a Master? (November 1987)
Yes. Although his own Master is the Master Jesus, he worked (and still does) very much under the inspiration of the English Master, a 3rd-ray Master. This 'lending' of disciples to other Masters (often of different rays) is quite common in Hierarchical work.

*Was Adam Smith inspired by a Master? His book **An Enquiry into the Causes and Nature of the Wealth of Nations**, published about 200 years ago, seems to have a lot of common sense and says, for example, that wealth will not make us happy.* (December 1987)
No, he was working under inspiration from his own soul. He was 1.7 degrees initiate.

In August 1963, when Martin Luther King gave his powerful "I have a dream" speech on the Washington Monument grounds, was he overshadowed by a Master? (December 1987)
Yes. It is this, probably, which makes that speech so powerfully moving.

President Kennedy was, I believe, a third-degree initiate. There are popular claims that he was a womanizer. (1) Would you be able to say how much a person's attitude towards the 'opposite sex' (as being part of his broader attitude towards other people) is taken into account regarding initiations? (2) Is it something which will be taken into consideration more in the future? (March 1992)

(1) President Kennedy was in fact 2.4 degrees initiate when he died. However, his exact degree has no bearing on the question. A person's "attitude to the opposite sex" is not a factor in achieving (or not achieving) initiation. Initiation is the result of the sequential control of the devas of the physical, astral and mental planes and not of the following of some particular Christian or other religious or philosophical ethic or code of conduct. (2) No.

Can you please give the ray structure and point in evolution of Willy Brandt, the ex-Chancellor of Germany, who died very recently (1913–1992)? (December 1992)

Soul 2; personality 1, sub-ray 4; mental body 5, sub-ray 7; astral body 2, sub-ray 4; physical body 1, sub-ray 3. He was 2.97 degrees initiate. With his rare combination of pragmatism and vision Willy Brandt made a major contribution to the world. His policy of 'Oest politik' led to the unification of Germany and speeded the end of the Cold War. Maitreya's first political/economic effort, after coming to London in July 1977, was to inspire the Brandt Commission in November of that year. Under the chairmanship of Willy Brandt, that Commission, representing all shades of political and economic thought, eventually, in 1979, produced their consensus Report: *North-South, a Programme for Survival*. With an eloquent introduction by Willy Brandt himself, this Report outlines and recommends the various practical measures which, if implemented, would go a long way to solving the present economic problems of rich and poor countries alike. At the Cancún Conference (1981), these measures met with the implacable opposition of the US, UK and other Western governments, and were rejected, despite their overwhelming acceptance by the Third World delegations who, incidentally, were in great majority. Reagan and Thatcher economic dogma prevailed and the world, in recession, now suffers the consequences. A decade has thus been wasted in the search for justice and reason. We have just witnessed the passing of one of the Great Men of recent history.

Was Rasputin overshadowed by any of the Masters? If so, were they trying to bring about reforms to defuse an explosive situation which led to the downfall of the Tsars and the ruling aristocracy? (July/August 1992)
No.

You frequently mention that Mozart was often overshadowed (by his Master) during his life and composing. You have also stated that some of the other famous composers were overshadowed for much or a portion of their work. Might you mention some names of well-known composers who also were overshadowed by a Master for some or all of their major compositions? (May 1987)
Bach, Handel, Beethoven, Wagner, Mendelssohn, Brahms, Haydn, Schubert and many more.

Channelled Information

In one of your books you say that the astral is only an illusionary level of consciousness. I don't quite understand that. (July/August 1992)
The astral planes, the emotional/astral planes, exist as energy. The function of our astral/emotional body is to act as a physical-plane expression or vehicle for 'buddhi'. Buddhi is the second of the three planes of the Spiritual Triad. The nature of Atman, of the Self, is spiritual will, spiritual love/wisdom and spiritual intelligence, and these are reflected in the soul as atma, buddhi and manas. They all need a vehicle, and the vehicle for buddhi (love/wisdom or group consciousness — intuition, group awareness) is the purified astral/emotional body in the advanced individual, particularly, of course, in a Master.

The average individual is still caught up in the desire, rather than the spiritual, principle. Desire governs the function of the personality and the vehicles of the personality (the physical body, the astral/emotional body and the mental body); but the physical body purified, the astral/emotional body purified, and the mental body purified eventually become the vehicles for atma, buddhi and manas. Until that point is reached the person is swept along by the illusions of the astral plane which are created by the thoughtform-making process of humanity.

We have a physical body with an etheric sheath. The physical body dies and is put in the ground or burned, but the etheric counterpart of that body is a sheath which, normally within three days, dissipates and returns to the ocean of etheric matter which surrounds us all. We are then left in our astral sheath in which we exist for a shorter or longer time on one or other of the seven astral planes (hopefully the higher planes, because the lower are terrible). The more advanced a person is the more he or she will be on the higher planes, and the less time will be spent on these planes.

On the astral planes there are 'facsimiles' of various Masters — the Masters DK, Morya, Koot Hoomi, Serapis, Jesus, Hilarion and various other Masters, created, as astral thoughtforms, by humanity. There are many mediumistic, astrally sensitive individuals who 'receive' from these 'facsimiles' so-called 'teachings from the Masters' which are more or less erroneous.

Originally, the teachings came from the real Masters through people like Alice Bailey, Helena Roerich and Helena Blavatsky, and which are reflected back on to the astral planes by the disciples of the world. They are then reflected back again through the astral sensitives with all the distortions of the astral planes — the planes of distortion. It is like what happens in dreams. Can you believe what happens in your dreams? The astral planes are your dreams because your dreams happen on the astral plane, are the result of the faculty of the lower mind during light sleep — in deep sleep there is no dreaming — to create astral thoughtforms. This activity of the lower mind goes on and on, the most fantastic things happen. Then you wake up. The astral planes are as real as your dreams; that is what I mean by the unreality of the astral planes.

Can you say precisely what a thoughtform is? (June 1992)
It is a form, a thing, which has been created by thought. A thought might be mental or astral/emotional. The vast majority of people are what is called "astrally polarized": the focus of their life experience is on the astral planes. Hence the fact that people believe that everything they feel is real. The desire principle is the basic principle governing their lives. This is true for almost everyone; it is the human condition. That is why we have the pain and suffering in the world.

The Master Djwhal Khul, Who gave the Alice Bailey teachings, wrote that the greatest gift you can give to the world is to raise your consciousness from the astral to the mental planes and so become mentally polarized. In this way you cease the process of discolouring the mind-belt of the world, which is filled with murky thoughtforms created by this 'thoughtforming process' of humanity.

Every time you feel something — fear, pain, disappointment — you create a thoughtform. These emotional thoughts continue their existence on the astral planes. There are deceased entities on the astral planes who every 'morning' go to the office or down the mines, because that is what they did in life. They do it because they have created the thoughtforms on the astral planes, so they think they have to go to the mines — they are sweating and stripped to the waist and dig up astral coal, which is unreal — everything about the astral is unreal. They are the planes of illusion, created by the thoughtforming faculty of humanity.

At its lowest level of desire, the thoughtforming process is a hindrance to evolution, but at its highest level it is a creative faculty. When it is used on the higher mental planes by the Masters or the initiates of the world — the great painters, writers, scientists and so on — you get inspired literature, music, painting, discoveries. On the ordinary level it is simply our pains, our hurts, our fears reflected onto the astral planes;

these are the dark, murky thoughts which surround people and keep humanity in thrall.

In this time when channelled messages/information/teachings are becoming so prevalent, we hear warnings that some material emanates from astral or lower-astral levels, or even negative or 'alien' sources. On what basis can we wisely evaluate these offerings to determine which to trust and heed, and which to reject?

Please address the channelling phenomenon in general: its purpose, the process itself, and how distortion occurs. (July/August 1987)

Channelling — that much-abused word — has been with us since Atlantean times, and is a result of our recognition of states of being and knowing above that of the physical body and the concrete mind. Modern interest in 'channelling' — at least in the West — stems from the growth of the spiritualist movement in the 19th century. Spiritualism, the religion of old Atlantis, revealed the fact of the continuity of conscious, intelligent life after so-called death and is helping to free humanity from the fear of death.

Spiritualists have tended to divide reality into two worlds: this physical plane and the after-death state, the realm of 'spirit', the denizens of which are all-wise, all-knowing, all-good — except for some mischievous and misguided entities on the 'lower astral' planes. Although, theoretically, various planes or levels of consciousness are known to exist, the average spiritualist tends to lump together everything coming through a medium or astral sensitive as guidance from 'Spirit' and therefore worthy of great respect and consideration. As a great many people have entered the more esoteric field from the spiritualist movement (many still use mediums or 'clairvoyants' for guidance and counselling) they tend to confuse the two activities and accept as bona fide 'channelling' whatever is brought through from whatever source: soul-level telepathy from a Master of Wisdom, as through Alice A.Bailey or H.P.Blavatsky; an astral entity or group as evidenced in the bulk of the channelling prevalent today; or simply from the subconscious of the 'sensitive' in response to his or her aspiration.

The vast majority of the 'teachings' channelled today come from the 5th astral plane (on occasion, at the highest level, from the 6th astral). These 'teachings' are as valid and as trustworthy as the astral planes — the planes of illusion — themselves. To my mind, that is, not at all.

The majority of people in the world today are astrally polarized and no doubt get a great deal of satisfaction from these 'teachings'. But that does not make the information authentic or valuable. Discrimination is, of course, the key to being able to evaluate these 'offerings' and that can only come from experience, a high degree of mental polarization and/or direct soul knowledge.

What then is the purpose behind the proliferation of information and guidance from the distorting mirrors of the astral plane? In the first place, a great deal of money is made by the channels for private 'guidance' or from the vast sale of books, while some of the teachings are generally 'uplifting' for the aspirational type. Above all, I suppose, a great many channels are confused as to the nature of their sources or 'guidance' and feel that they are performing some beneficial work of service. And people are fearful of the future and hungry for information, however dubious.

What future, if any, can you see for the spiritualist movement?
(May 1992)
The spiritualist movement, as far as I am concerned, has proved absolutely conclusively, to all reasonable, open-minded people, that something, after the death of the physical body, goes on and can make contact through mediums of one kind or another, can make its presence felt. That has been the success of the spiritualist movement — to tell the world that death is not the end.

It was stimulated by the 5th-ray Master Hilarion, in order to take away from humanity what is perhaps its greatest fear, the fear of death; after that comes fear of illness. Most people fear being ill, not seeing the function of illness, its karmic necessity, and also fearing death, the shift from one state of consciousness to another — for that is all death is.

The Masters have conquered death. They do not die (you cannot die once you are perfect). And they have sought in one way or another to show humanity that death is not the end. The spiritualist movement was inaugurated to prove that this was the case. It has, I would say, largely succeeded in doing so. It does not prove the fact of reincarnation, which, of course, not all spiritualists would accept anyway, but to me the fact of reincarnation is the reality, just as the fact of continuity of consciousness after death is the reality.

Inevitably, with the advent of the Masters and the Christ, working, teaching openly, the attitude of humanity to death will change profoundly, and therefore to movements like the spiritualist movement. Life after death will become a reality. For instance, when people see the Master Jesus, and the Master Who was St Peter, the Master Who was St John and so on, working openly with Maitreya as the World Teacher, the fact of reincarnation becomes proven. Then the teaching of the spiritualist movement, *per se*, will be less needed, and it will become more sophisticated, more esoteric.

When the Reappearance takes place will there be an effect on the astral and mental planes as well as the physical? I keep thinking about all the misinformation being given out by psychics (ie Ruth Montgomery and Ramtha); will these 'channelled entities' change their tune? Might they even disappear? (March 1987)
No, I do not think they will disappear. The majority of people are astrally polarized (ie Atlantean in consciousness) and find these astral-type communications immediately accessible and satisfying and probably for a long time will continue to do so. The 'entities' themselves will most certainly 'change their tune' in the light of events.

Why is there so much discrepancy in the information channelled through various sources? How can Masters disagree? (July/August 1988)

593

The Masters do not all think in the same way, or rather, the Masters have seven different approaches to Their work, depending on Their ray. But if They are real Masters there will be no discrepancy in Their teachings. Most channelled information comes through mediums, from some level of the astral planes. These teachings, therefore, are the result of glamour. Glamour is illusion on the astral plane. Many teachings coming from the astral levels agree in parts and disagree in other parts. This is the case because there is a kind of fashion, if you like, where no medium can afford not to be up to date with the latest prophecy of doom or catastrophe, or whatever it is. They cannot afford to seem not to know. But they also have to be a little bit original, so they have some other information. I'm not implying that this is contrived; it is unconscious, astral, glamour.

(1) A spirit guide I am in contact with called "Hareeb" through a channel medium says your man is not the Christ. I am confused — how can I find the truth? (2) "Hareeb" says there is no Spiritual Hierarchy. Is he egotistical in saying this? (January/February 1991)

(1) My first reaction is to say that if you believe any 'spirit guide' through any 'channel medium' you will believe anything. Since that is not very enlightening I would add that 'spirit guides', where they exist at all and are not the result of the medium's imagination, act on the astral planes (usually the fifth) and their teachings suffer from the distortion of these planes. The astral planes are the planes of illusion and, for my part, have no validity in ascertaining truth. My advice is to trust your own judgement and experience. If Maitreya is the Christ as I say, then He will be able to demonstrate the Christ Principle, the energy of the Christ which, I submit, He embodies. On the Day of Declaration, I suggest, you will have ample evidence that this is so.

(2) I do not know if your "Hareeb" is egotistical in saying that there is no Spiritual Hierarchy but I do know that he is wrong. Anyone who, in any degree, has had contact with the Masters of the Spiritual Hierarchy knows Them to be a fact,

and the Centre of Love on this planet. This alone, I would have thought, would tend to invalidate any comment made by "Hareeb".

Would you comment on the books **The Hidden Dangers of the Rainbow** *and* **The Planned Deception?** (October 1992)
These are by a Detroit woman lawyer and arch-fundamentalist, Constance Cumbey. They might well themselves be called 'the planned deception' for they consist of a violent, irrational attack on the New Age movement in general, and myself and my message of Maitreya's mission in particular. The technique used is to quote — and to misquote — New Age writers and teachers and to interpret their ideas according to her own fundamentalist prejudices, misunderstandings, and jaundiced view of the world. They are concoctions of misquotations, half-truths, distortions and downright, barefaced lies. A typical example is her 'warning' that Hierarchy intend to attack the Vatican with a nuclear bomb!

According to her, spiritual, New Age values like sharing, justice, freedom, co-operation, interdependence, tolerance, goodwill, brotherhood are simply 'ploys' used by Maitreya to 'take over' the world. In other words, she sees Him as the Antichrist.

The ironic thing about these books is that she is so irrational in her hatred of New Age ideas and ideals, and yet quotes so extensively from New Age writers, that she turns many people towards these ideas, perhaps for the first time.

Can we do anything to oppose the negative forces of matter, and so try to limit chaos, fear and war? (June 1987)
Yes. By the creation only of positive thoughtforms and a firm refusal to be influenced or depressed by 'fearful' events. By a clear realization of who we essentially are — ie souls — and a continuous effort to act, altruistically, from that level. By serving the needs of the world as we are able and remembering that everyone, without exception, is important to the Plan of God. By spreading the ideas of internationalism, justice, freedom and sharing, and working actively for their implementation. By making known to all who will listen the

fact of the Christ's presence in the world and the imminence of His emergence.

Do you know what the 'polar shift' is? Will there be significant changes on the face of the Earth? Where will the 'New Age' centres be where people will be safe? (November 1987)
They come into the category which I call 'the catastrophe complex'. People know that at the end of an age, as now, far-reaching changes take place which may (or may not) involve physical changes of the Earth's surface. The world is now flooded with prognostications of such violent Earth changes 'channelled' by countless people from countless inner plane 'guides'. Without exception, these 'channellings' come from the astral planes and are the reflections of humanity's (self-imposed) fears. Edgar Cayce seems to have started the fashion. Now, no self-respecting medium or 'channel' dares to appear not to 'know' of these impending catastrophes or can afford not to be up to date with the latest expected disaster.

A 'New Age group' twist to this phenomenon, implied in the question, is that there are certain 'New Age centres' (filled, of course, with very 'highly evolved' New Age people) which, because of their great spiritual contribution to the world will be safe from these catastrophes — so it behoves people to join them! This glamour is extraordinarily widespread but remains nothing but glamour nevertheless.

There are indeed certain Earth changes which will take place, but these are not scheduled to do so for some 800 years yet and, in any case, will not involve the huge loss of life usually predicted by the 'prophets of doom'.

How does Maitreya respond to or comment on the many predictions of great Earth changes? (September 1992)
My understanding, not only from Maitreya but in particular from my own Master, is that these predictions, 'channelled' through mediums and astral-sensitives all over the world, are enormously exaggerated.

As we come to the end of the age, or cosmic cycle, and the beginning of another, inevitably there are upheavals, but these are mainly within the psyche and structures of humanity:

political, economic, religious and social. The Earth destructions which do occur — the earthquakes, floods, volcanic eruptions, bizarre weather patterns and so on — are largely the result of the wrong thought and action of humanity itself and can be righted by us. For example, every underground nuclear test results in an earthquake — inevitably. Man's inhumanity to man through war and lack of sharing and justice results in destructive tensions leading to disasters which we call 'acts of God'. These 'acts of men' are totally preventable.

There will not be the colossal earth movements as predicted by many (it is so popular today!) where great areas are said to go under the oceans.

What they are doing, did those who spread such misinformation but know it, is playing into the hands of the evil forces of this planet whose aim it always is to keep humanity in thrall through fear. To quote Maitreya: "Fear not. All will be well. All manner of things will be well."

What does Maitreya say about the recent channelling of **Mary's Message to the World** *by Annie Kirkwood predicting the disappearance of great parts of the US and Europe before 2000, to cover up and seal great parts of the Earth for centuries to heal the toxic wastes we have created?* (May 1992)

Maitreya has talked of earthquakes and floods, which He emphasizes are man-made — the result of our destructive thoughts and actions. But, He assures, the warnings of major cataclysms have been exaggerated. There will be no such inundations or disappearances of large land masses. These portents of disaster come, by 'channelling', from the astral planes, and have the effect of arousing fear on a large scale. This is precisely the intention of the originators of these 'predictions' — the forces of evil, and those who believe and spread such misinformation play into the hands of those who would thwart the onward progress of humanity, led by Maitreya and His Group.

The prophecies of Nostradamus say that the Third World War will come in the last years before the year 2000. Do you agree? (January/February 1991)

No. I do not attach any importance to the 'prophecies'of Nostradamus, nor do I believe that there will be a Third World War. The presence of the Christ now is the guarantee that we have accepted world peace. Otherwise He could not be here. The new relationship evolving between East and West is the demonstration of this fact.

I have read two books of 'White Eagle' and I doubt that everything he tells us is true. He is said to be one of the Masters of Wisdom which I can't believe. What kind of personality is he? (April 1988)

'White Eagle' is the 'nomme de plume' of a teacher on the inner planes. He works on the sixth astral plane which ensures a high level of aspiration in the teaching, but, like all astral-plane teaching, is subject to the distorting mirror of the astral planes — the planes of illusion — themselves. He is not a Master but is 1.5 degrees initiate.

*In your book **Maitreya and the Masters of Wisdom**, you say that no Masters take female bodies. But there are a lot of Masters/Masteresses in female form: eg Rowena on the Rose Ray of Love from the Archangel Chamuel, then there is Nada, on the Red-gold Ray of Peace and Servers of Jesus and the Archangel Uriel, and let's not forget the Masteress/Mistress Kwan Yin, the Goddess of Mercy on the Violet Ray from the Master L. Saint Germain and the Archangel Zadkiel, to name but a few. Why aren't these Women Masters mentioned in your books?* (November 1991)

Because, according to my information, these so-called women Masters do not, in fact, exist. The titles of my books, by the way, are: *The Reappearance of the Christ and the Masters of Wisdom* and *Maitreya's Mission, Volume One*.

In your books you speak of higher and lower psychism. In many other books we read of teachings from the "Brothers of the circle of light." (1) Are these Brothers part of the

Hierarchy of Masters? (2) Do the teachings come from the astral or mental planes? (3) Would you advise people to join a group which is receiving information from other planes? (4) Does the Master Jesus 'come through' to such a group? (5) Does the Master Jesus inspire people, telepathically, so that they can give out His message? (6) Would the Master Jesus inform a medium that they were on the right or wrong track? (June 1992)

(1) No. (2) Astral. (3) They have free will; it is up to them. (4) No. (5) In certain circumstances, yes. (6) No.

What can you say about the book **The Cosmogony of Urantia?** *It is supposed to reveal great truths to mankind and the authors are said to be high entities not from the Earth. It says that reincarnation does not exist, that the Christ is the maker of the universe who comes to visit regularly the planets of his creation, and many other strange things.* (June 1987)

My information is that the 'Urantia' teaching comes from no higher than the fifth astral plane and is a kind of 'hotchpotch' of various teachings. It is about 20 per cent accurate only.

Jacob Lorber (19th century) wrote some important spiritual books, among others **The Youth of Jesus** *and a complete John Gospel. These books were dictated by "the silent voice under his heart". (1) Was this a case of higher telepathy? (2) Are his books fairly trustworthy?* (June 1988)

(1) My understanding is that these books came as a result not of the higher telepathy (soul level), but from astral sensitivity (5th astral plane). (2) The information, subject to the distortions of the astral planes, is fairly trustworthy. His ray structure was: Soul 3; Personality 2, sub-ray 6; Mental 5, sub-ray 4; Astral 6, sub-ray 6; Physical 7, sub-ray 3. He was 1.4 degrees initiate.

What is your information on the claims of Ramtha via J.Z.Knight? I am sceptical of some of these teachings such as Ramtha's advice to put away a two-year supply of food in preparation for America's disaster to come. (June 1987)

As is common in this astral type of communication, great emphasis is placed on fear-inspiring prognostication. The more sensational and alarmist the communication the more successful appears to be the 'channel' or organization peddling the information. Somehow, people love to be frightened — or have their worst fears confirmed or given voice. Good news they tend to disbelieve.

This 'channelling' also appeals to the most greedy and separatist instincts in people. America already uses, usurps and wastes the lion's share of the world's resources, including food. This advice of "Ramtha" is only confounding an already unjust situation.

*Can you give the ray structure and point in evolution of Lobsang Rampa, author of **Doctor from Lhasa** and other books?* (June 1988)
It is not possible because 'Lobsang Rampa' is an astral (5th astral) entity. The books are written through a medium. Despite the vivid realism of the writing the information contained in them has no more validity than the astral planes (the planes of illusion) from which they came.

Nevertheless, like many similar astral-plane communications and 'channellings', they have led many people into an interest in the unseen worlds and more esoterically 'sound' teachings.

It is thought that the late Vicky Wall, who was given the formulas for the soul colour therapy 'Aura-Soma' through direct channelling, has returned to Sirius. Could you confirm this please? (September 1992)
I must confess that this question makes me smile. Sirius is the alter-ego of this solar system and only Masters of the fifth initiation or higher may — if it is Their destiny — go to Sirius and, by the same token, only Avatars can come from Sirius to this planet.

The late Vicky Wall had not yet taken the first initiation; her point in evolution was 0.8. So much for "direct channelling", 99.999 per cent of which comes from the astral planes — the planes of illusion.

(1) Do you put any significance on the 11.11 (Eleven Eleven)?
(2) For example, what is your interpretation of the events of
11.1.1992? (May 1992)

(1) No, none whatsoever. To my mind, this is yet another example of the glamours and misinformation streaming from the astral planes through so-called 'channels'. (2) The sun rose and set as usual. The tides came in and out as usual. People were born and others died — as usual.

I have heard it claimed that Hitler and his followers listened a
great deal to Wagner's music and that therefore the music
itself has something evil in it. Could you comment please?
(November 1990)

It is true that Hitler (and probably his followers) listened to Wagner's music and found it stimulating and inspiring. This is something they shared with millions of music lovers around the world. Most probably they also enjoyed German beer and German sausage, again much loved all over the world. There is no such thing as evil music, only evil men.

Is the technique of astral or mental projection a way of
achieving continuity of consciousness? What is the difference
between astral and mental projection? Can either be
dangerous? Can it be used as a means of helping others? (May
1988)

Astral projection, of itself, will not bring about continuity of consciousness but may be a result of it, in which case the projection would be consciously initiated (with the purpose of service on the astral planes). Mental projection, as such, does not really exist. Conscious projection at that level is really soul activity and presupposes continuity of consciousness in the first place. Very much help is given on the astral planes in that way. Astral projection, without the help and guidance of a Master or experienced higher initiate, can be very dangerous.

I am quite confused about the concept of 'guardian angel' and
'guiding entity' and their relationship to higher initiates and
Masters who work on the inner planes. (1) Is a guardian angel
an astral thoughtform created by our own mind? (2) Does

everyone have a guardian angel or do only those who are focused on the astral plane — astrally-polarized people — create one? (3) Is it valuable to direct one's attention to the guardian angel and to try to listen to their advice? (4) What is the difference between 'guardian angel/entity (Japanese, Shugo-rei)' and 'guiding entity (Shidoh-rei)'? Is the latter a higher teacher or Master on the inner planes as many books claim? If so, how can we distinguish one from the other? (5) If we do not know them (have no communication from them), should we make an effort to direct our attention toward them? (December 1991)

(1) No. (2) Everyone has a guardian angel, which does not exist on the astral plane. What is seen in the near-death experience is an emanation on the astral plane of that entity. (3) No. (4) Yes. The guardian angel does not seek to make contact. The teacher may. (5) No.

CHAPTER 19

TOWARDS GROUP INITIATION

This article is an edited version of a talk given during the 1988 Transmission Meditation/Tara Network conference held in San Francisco, USA. It has been withheld from publication until now because of the private 'in-group' nature of much of the information revealed. However, with the publication of the present volume, my Master has recommended that this information be given out for the stimulus and encouragement of other groups working along truly occult lines.

Group initiation is incredibly difficult to achieve. So difficult, indeed, that it has never been achieved, not in eighteen-and-a-half million years of human history. For millennia, the Masters have seen the prospect, at some future date, of a group on the outer plane, through its own work together, bringing about a fusion with an inner ashram. This has never yet been possible. Many Masters, in different parts of the world, at various times, have made experiments, and every experiment so far has failed because the outer and the inner requirements have not been met. Only today, at this extraordinary time in human history, does group initiation become a possibility. It is a hope, not a certainty but a possibility. For the first time in the evolutionary history of humanity this possibility is now seen as becoming a fact.

What has prevented group initiation from being achieved before is that the Masters have never found a number of necessary factors coexisting. Only today are these important factors present together: the existence of a group of disciples more or less around the same point in evolution; never have the Masters been able to present to the groups involved, nor have the groups themselves found, some idea, some great controlling theme, which can bind the groups together in one unified purpose; a theme so powerful, so magnetic, that it can hold them in unison despite all personality differences and disunity. That theme is the Reappearance of the Christ and the externalization of the Hierarchy.

Many people have a rather vague idea of the externalization of the Hierarchy. Most people, I think, see it as the time when the Masters take up Their positions again in the world, and this in fact is true. This is happening now.

But the externalization of the Hierarchy is infinitely more complex than that. What it really entails is the externalization onto the outer plane, in working relationship, of the ashrams of the Masters. The groups of disciples will be working in a unified way on the outer plane, and *at the same time* fused, at-one, with the inner ashram of which they are a part, at the centre of which is a Master. The Master is a nucleus in an ashramic ring-pass-not. His radiance, His energy, forms the powerful nucleus which energizes, stimulates and encloses His group of disciples. These ashrams, as you know, exist on the inner planes, on the soul plane, but the aim, ultimately, is to reproduce them on the outer physical plane.

That is what preparing for group initiation is about: how to bring together a large group and present them with a field of service and techniques of self-development which will insure the fusion of the group on the outer plane with the inner ashram, established around the Master. Because of the work of the Reappearance — the work connected with the preparation for the Christ which provides this powerful, controlling theme — have we at last got an idea which can hold together a group of disparate individuals, highly individualistic disciples, scattered around the world, who can work together, focused on that idea which is magnetic enough to hold them despite the differences on the personality level.

Most of the people involved in the work of the Reappearance, in Europe and the Far East, in the Americas or New Zealand/Australia or wherever, would in the normal course of events never meet. They would have very little in common. They would probably find very little to say to each other. They come from different backgrounds and disciplines, and but for certain karmic ties it is unlikely that they would ever be able to work together. Karma itself would bring them together but apart from that these people are not necessarily those that in the ordinary course of life would have had very much to do with each other. This in itself presents problems: of personality differences, in points of view, in ways of looking at the world. People are governed by one or other of the seven rays and therefore approach reality in different ways; all of this colours their personality approach.

The Reappearance of the Christ, a powerful, magnetic idea, has brought these groups together on the outer plane. The work of Transmission Meditation has provided the stimulus to the inner work of the groups, producing the necessary psychological transformations, and building the inner relationship, first of all to the soul, then to the inner ashram, thus quickening the pace of evolution along that path. The work for the Reappearance of the Christ and the service technique of Transmission Meditation are presented to the groups at this time precisely to bring them together in such a way that inner and outer fusion can take place, and, hopefully, group initiation can become a reality for the first time. These are very important times in which we are living, in which all of us have the opportunity, if we like, to take on the work and to receive the spiritual energies of Hierarchy through Transmission Meditation. These energies will, if we make it possible, *if we will it*, bring about group initiation for the first time. It is a very extraordinary thing which is taking place.

Group initiation

There are certain very basic requirements for group initiation. This article is more about the requirements for achieving the outer fusion which makes the inner fusion possible, than group initiation itself. Group initiation is so subtle that there is not a lot I can say about it which would be meaningful to people at the present time, unless we had already achieved the outer fusion which is necessary to bring it about in the first place.

Let me say, very briefly, in terms of group initiation, that it is a process of transference: the transference of the lower to the higher. This transference, as always, takes place through renunciation. From the occult point of view, our whole life history is the history of minor renunciations which culminate in the Great Renunciation, the fourth initiation, the Crucifixion.

In a very precise, mysterious, and occult way, group initiation is really connected with the fourth initiation. The fourth initiation, of course, is taken by the initiate who has gone through the Transfiguration. The fourth initiation from the Masters' viewpoint is the second initiation, because the Transfiguration, from our point of view the third initiation, is from the Masters' point of view the first initiation, when the transfigured personality is totally at-one with, and infused by, its soul. At the fourth initiation, the soul itself, the divine intermediary between the life principle, the Monad, and its reflection on the physical plane, the personality, is no longer needed. In a very peculiar way, because of the occult correspondence "as above, so below", the same process is undergone by those aiming to go through the initiatory process together as a group.

This is achieved — I am speaking very broadly, partly symbolically — in the first place by a mounting tension. The outer work, the total, unalloyed focus on the given purpose of the group, creates an inner tension. This tension, in turn, creates a spiritual detachment, which sets up a stabilized rhythm. The rhythm constitutes an invocative demand to the soul, and beyond the soul to the inner ashram of the group.

This invocative demand is called "the word". It is a sound, a note, and is gradually sounded occultly by the group. Every individual sounds a certain note which can be heard (or seen as light) by those sensitive to the sound or the light's radiation. That sound or note is absolutely individual, both to the individual and to a group of individuals who make up a given group. When that note is strong enough, stabilized, intense enough, when the potency is so great that it can invoke the will aspect of the Monad, this, too, comes into play. At the fourth initiation, the causal body, the body of the soul, is destroyed and a new, direct relationship between the Monad and the individual in incarnation is established. The energy of the lower is transferred into the higher. The higher energy is invoked and establishes itself on the lower plane. These changing relationships, renunciations of the lower for the higher, take place throughout the process.

Through the Law of Correspondence, the same thing happens in group initiation. When the sounded note is strong enough to invoke the life within the Monadic vehicle, the correspondence, the group soul, is shattered, no longer needed, and the life aspect works directly through the physical-plane group. This process of transference, you will find, is the new approach, from now on, in all Hierarchical endeavour. It is essential for the establishment in group formation of the inner ashrams on the outer plane. We are used to thinking about evolution in terms of achieving a relationship with our souls, establishing soul love quality, on the physical plane. But once that union is achieved, there is a yet greater and higher union with that of which the soul itself is a reflection: the life, the Monadic aspect, which of course is also the destroyer aspect — that which destroys the obstructions to the life process. Where the life finds obstruction, it destroys in order to manifest itself on the physical plane.

This destructive process is the first thing which any group has to invoke. It has various aspects, it is not a simple thing. There are four rules, or absolute basic requirements, for group initiation. Until these four requirements are established as a norm in group unity, fused, working together, group initiation does not become possible. They sound really quite difficult, and in fact they are very difficult. They take time to achieve; their achievement is not an easy thing.

Non-sentimental relationship

The first requirement is the achieving of a non-sentimental group interrelation. Easier said than done, of course, but absolutely essential. It requires the elimination of all sentiment in group relation, the bonds of liking and disliking. No doubt, there are people in our group whom we tend to like very well and those whom we tend not to like. These are simply personality differences. It is not that we are better or they are a worse person, or the other way around. It is simply that because of different ray structures, of various prejudices to do with people's looks or accent or habits, we tend to like or dislike people. We all do it. That kind of relationship in a group must be totally eradicated before any kind of real group fusion can take place. We are talking about group fusion, not about taking individual initiation, but about group initiation, which can only come about through group fusion, working in unison. We have to realize that true group relationships are not based on personality or impersonality, on liking or disliking, on criticism or on non-criticism. None of these pertain in the type of true group relationships which make group initiation possible.

I suggest that if we look at our group we will think that we all like each other. But there are always some people that we find we do not like to work with. What does this do in a group relation, if there are such people whom we feel about in this way? We are always rebuffing them, we cannot meet them, cannot work with them. There are, of course, other people whom we want to be with and work with: we like being with them, we approach the work in the same way, we understand each other, we have the same ray structure probably — with all the faults, all the vices of that ray structure. But because we share these, we tend to find that we can work well together. We all want to work with those with whom we can work well, because it works, it is pleasant. It is always more pleasant to be with like-minded people than with people with whom we are always in a controversial situation.

We have to understand that true group work has to be based on a divine indifference. We must not like too much, and we must not dislike too much. In fact this liking and disliking, criticism and non-criticism, should not come into it at all. Non-criticism is just as bad as criticism; it is not a question of "you must not criticize", since *not* to criticize is just as bad. The positions of doing or not doing, of criticizing or not criticizing, of liking or disliking, are equal, and both are disruptive of group relations. The only thing that really counts in true group relationship is divine indifference, spiritual indifference or detachment. Of course, that spiritual detachment can only be based on some initial, profound, unspoken, but unwavering love. Love must hold the group together. But that love must not be expressed in terms of personality likings, nor lack of it expressed in personality dislikes. A deep, underlying love between the group members makes it possible for the group to work together, in unison, as a reflection of an inner ashramic relationship, because the soul *has* this divine indifference already. That is the first requirement towards group initiation.

The forces of destruction

The second requirement is that groups must learn to work with the forces of destruction in a constructive way. That may seem a paradox, but it is occultly true. The forces of destruction, which are basically the forces of the Monad working through the second aspect, the love/soul aspect, have to work through the group and bring about the required detachments.

Three things bring an occult group together: karmic law, ashramic necessity, and soul direction. Karmic law brings together, into incarnation, individuals, governed by particular energies, at, more or less, a given point of evolution, who are able to deal with the requirements of the time, whatever these happen to be. (That would depend on the particular group and their rays, and on what requirements at any given time they will be asked to achieve.) Ashramic necessity is the second thing which brings a group together. There are many different kinds of groups; they are not all working under ashramic necessity; some are and some are not. I am talking about those who are brought together under karmic law, working under some powerful ashramic necessity, and of course also under soul direction. The soul directs its personality reflection into a group, to meet the ashramic necessity under karmic law.

This bringing together of a group under these laws — karmic law, ashramic necessity and soul direction — provides the Master with an opportunity to train a group of aspirants. The forces of destruction have to be brought into play because of the mixed motives of everybody who enters such a group. If you study your heart and motives profoundly, carefully, you will probably find that your motive for entering this work has not been 100 per cent that of serving the world, even though that, no doubt, has been part of it, but is based to some degree on spiritual selfishness. All disciples are ambitious. They are ambitious for liberation. They are ambitious to become Masters.

In occult work all personality desires for achievement, for personal position, for power, for recognition, must be destroyed. The forces of destruction have to be invoked to carry out this desirable but painful work, and of course this takes time. Group initiation does not happen overnight. This killing out of individual desire must be the first destructive activity of the disciple.

The second is the destruction of the ties linking the personalities. These relations must be based on soul activity, joint pledge to the Master at the heart of the ashram, and of course, above all, united service to humanity. If these are not the basic aims and purposes of the group, they will never achieve group initiation.

The third thing which must be destroyed is all reaction towards recognition. This is difficult. Many people in the groups I work with all over the world have, to a greater or lesser degree, the desire for recognition of some kind. Some have the desire that the world, sooner or later, perhaps only after the Day of Declaration, will recognize the true, good service which this group has rendered; that others will recognize that they were there, in front, the first to do this, the first to tell the world that the Christ was in the world, the first to publish my books and so on. There is often a desire for recognition at the basis of some individuals and even some groups. That has to be totally eradicated.

There is also the desire for recognition by the other members of the group. This, I think, is one of the commonest traits in all the groups that I come in contact with. Everybody wants a pat on the back from everyone else, and many want a pat on the back from me. I am not a patter. I do not like to pat people on the back, it puts one into wrong relationship with people. It is as if (this is true in many groups) people think they are working for me. For example, someone will say: "What do you want done about this?" I say: "I don't want anything done about it." "But what are we to do?" "Well," I say, "what do you want to do?" They say: "But what do you want done about it?" I say: "I don't want anything done about it." They have the idea that what they are doing they are doing for me. Simply because I initiated this work, they think they are carrying out my desires. They are not right; I do not have any desires about it. I do not mind if people work or not, that is up to them. Of course, the more and the better they work, the more the information goes out into the world, and the better the world knows about the fact of the Reappearance of the Christ. But that is self-initiated work. It is initiated by the souls of the individuals and not by me.

The whole work that I am engaged in was initiated by my Master as His part of the Plan for the externalization of Hierarchy and the Reappearance of the Christ. In this way, Transmission Meditation was given to the world and the initial approach made to the public about the fact of the Christ's return to the world. But everyone who takes part does so under their own soul direction. They do it for their own soul purpose and not for me and I do not have to tell them how to do it or how not to do it. I am always available, of course, in terms of advice if I can give it, although I find that people know about co-ordinating the work in the world far better than I do, and so are better able to get on with it. It is important, therefore, that people do not look for recognition from each other, from me, or, above all, from the Master.

This question of recognition is very important because it is so subtle. It is so easy to want recognition for what you do. It seems self-evident that if you do something you should get praise for it, and the natural reaction to work of importance in the world is that people should recognize it. The media should recognize it, the people around you, other groups, should recognize it. Would it not be terrible if certain groups (who shall remain nameless) get all the credit for preparing the way

611

for the Christ? When we did all the work, we know we did. We were out there, right out in front, taking it on the chin time after time. You will see, after the Day of Declaration, other groups who did nothing will be reaping the benefits of our work. You have to be able to take that, because it will probably happen. You have to approach this work completely dispassionately, looking for no kind of recognition at all, not from the Master, not from me, not from each other, and not from the world. That is an absolutely fundamental requirement.

This kind of detached, focused work brings about in the group a united tension. When you work under this united tension, focused on the work, on serving the Plan — in this particular case the fact of the Reappearance, Transmission Meditation, the awakening of humanity to what is going on in the world — so focused, so absolutely concentrated, when that united inner tension is achieved, all these non-essentials fall away. That is the important thing. It is not a question of: "I feel like criticizing but I mustn't do that." Or: "I feel like liking them but I mustn't like them either. I can't like, I can't not like, what can I do?" It is a very difficult rule. All the time you are correcting yourself. If you are really focused, you will find that none of that happens. It never arises in your mind that you wish a pat on the back. All these non-essentials are purely personality reactions, this is what we have to understand.

We are not the personality. We are the soul. We are the life reflecting as the soul. We have to bring that life, reflecting as the soul, down onto the physical plane, and the personality must be transferred into that life. That is the achievement of the spiritual path. The way to do it is to focus completely on the work in hand and create that united tension in which all of these difficulties disappear. Not by overcoming them, but simply because you do not allow them to arise.

It is quite obvious that the Masters do not get any recognition for Their work. They do all the work, really — at least They set it in motion, They inspire the disciples, They formulate the Plan, They galvanize groups and individuals to carry out the work. The disciples take the full responsibility, they suffer the karmic reactions, good or bad, they reap the benefits and suffer the calamities which might occur through their wrong action. The Masters get no recognition at all.

The disciple, too, must seek no recognition. You can imagine the problems arising when a whole group of disciples, perhaps hundreds and hundreds of people, dispersed all over the world, are seeking that kind of recognition. Then the problems become very difficult indeed. Such a demand for recognition, at whatever level, delays the complete absorption of the energy of the group into the inner ashram which is what group initiation is about; that, and the reflection of the inner ashram, precisely, perfectly, on the outer plane which is what the externalization of the Hierarchy is really about. This requires complete absorption in service.

When a group does this, it brings into play the group will. When the group will is invoked, all of this takes place in a natural way. This only makes itself felt when the group is working intelligently and demonstrating love adequately. We all know that the will aspect is always the third aspect to be invoked. First is the intelligence aspect, which dominates throughout the life up to the first initiation. Then the love aspect comes into play, the second aspect of the Triad, spiritual love, or buddhi. That eventually makes possible the appearance of the highest aspect, the Atmic or spiritual will. This galvanizes the vehicles, now infused with the intelligence and the love of the Triad, and the work proceeds quickly and correctly. The forces of destruction, of course, are utilized to bring all of this about.

Mini-hierarchy

This leads to the third absolutely essential requirement: the attaining of the power to work as a miniature Hierarchy, and as a group to exemplify unity in diversity. This is a very difficult one for most groups to achieve, and yet if you think about it, it is perfectly natural. A group is made up of individuals at different points in evolution. I know I said earlier that one of the requirements for group initiation is that there should be a group of disciples all roughly at the same point of evolution. That is a general statement. In actual terms, every group is

613

composed of people at varying stages. There will be those, the majority, who have taken the first initiation. There may be a few who have taken the second, perhaps, even, the third. For group initiation to be a reality, the *presence* of a fourth-degree initiate is essential although not necessarily *in* the group. So you can see there is a fair range of initiatory status. This is essential as you need a broad field of performance and the correct approach to different levels of work.

We talk about group initiation, and so it is, but not all of the disciples involved in the group are being prepared for the same initiation, some perhaps being prepared for the first, most for the second, a few for the third, and even for the fourth.

The work requires a diversity of qualities and potencies to be effective on the outer plane. It needs an initiate or initiates who are in close contact with a Master. This means initiates of a certain status, giving the inspiration, the purpose, for the group. It needs some fairly senior disciples who are able to take this inspiration, co-ordinate it, and relate it to the outer world. It requires those not so advanced who can establish a close contact with ordinary outer humanity. In this way, the requirements for true group work can take place.

The greater the diversity, the richer and more effective is the group work. Just as the more rays involved in any group, the richer, the more effective — when they are working correctly in a true group way — is the work that group will do. Where they are not working correctly, of course, the differences in the rays, the differences in point of evolution, create problems. But when people are working in the detached way I have outlined, you have the best possible means for the group work to go forward: one, or a group of initiates, with a close contact with the inner ashram, with the Master from Whom the inspiration is received; some senior disciples who can intelligently co-ordinate the work; and those who can establish a close connection with ordinary humanity and relate the work to the outer plane.

When this is achieved, and when the work is working potently on the outer plane, this sets up an invocatory power of its own, and the invocative demand, or "the word", of the group can be heard by the Master. He can galvanize and potentize the work of the group. Hierarchy exists in its various degrees in order to permit of a wide range of effective relationships. Hierarchy exists throughout cosmos.

Many people today are concerned about democracy. Democracy and Hierarchy are not mutually opposite or opposing ideas. There can be democracy and Hierarchy existing side by side or one above the other. In the future we will have democratic forms of government with a degree of Hierarchical supervision. People will understand that there are those with greater experience of life, of the evolutionary process, who, by dint of that experience, have the spiritual intelligence and wisdom to oversee the development of the rest of us. This will be democratically enacted, from our own free will. Free will, as always, is sacrosanct.

Most disciples are very individualistic. You cannot become a disciple except by being individualistic. The 6th-ray experience of the last 2,000 years has prepared groups of disciples for group initiation. It is precisely the individualizing quality of the 6th ray which will enable disciples to give it up. You cannot give up what you do not yet have. The potency of the individual gives the possibility of going beyond the individual and gaining group consciousness.

What I am really talking about is group consciousness. It is the expanding of group consciousness which constitutes group initiation. A group must accept that there are those who are somewhat more advanced than they are, and those who are somewhat less advanced, but that all are heading in the same direction towards the goal of initiation, whatever that initiation might be. This requires a conscious recognition of these differences and their acceptance, without jealousy, without personality reaction. This is absolutely essential for a group to work together properly in a unified way.

It is not for nothing that those who have ascertained, and had confirmed, their point in evolution, have been told to keep it to themselves and not in any case at all to share it, even with their husband or wife. This is because of the danger involved of jealousy, the glamour of advancement, of non-advancement, of ambition. Everybody wants to be more advanced than they are.

We have to get rid of competition and accept that there are those we work with who do things that we cannot do and that we can do things that they cannot do. The Master cannot go to the bookshops or tell everyone that the Christ is in the world. Those who can take the inspiration of that idea and co-ordinate it and get books published, and take the books to the bookshops and make it known in that way, are doing the work of the Master. They are doing what a Master cannot do. It would be an extreme waste of a fourth-degree initiate's time to ask him to do what a novice could do. There is no use asking the director of the company to teach the office boy how to make tea. It is a waste of his particular talents. Not that he is more important in the ultimate sense than the office boy, but he has different talents and different responsibilities.

This is a very important and difficult requirement for group initiation: the ability to work as a miniature Hierarchy and to function with unity in diversity. To realize — as a group, at different levels, performing different tasks, relating through inspiration, co-ordinating the approach to the public and so on — that all of this is an important part of the expansion of consciousness which leads to group initiation.

Occult silence

The fourth essential requirement towards group initiation is a very mysterious and difficult one to talk about and probably to understand: "cultivating the potency of occult silence".

People who study esoteric books learn that there is something called the "silence of the initiate". They learn that if you are approaching initiation you have to go through a period of silence. This is demonstrated, for example, in Mozart's opera *The Magic Flute*, which is about initiation.

I recommend those of you who do not know this opera to go and see it, because it demonstrates, in a very oversimplified way, of course, some of the requirements for initiation. Tamino, the hero, who has been given a magic flute which

616

protects him from all the terrors and evils of the astral plane as he goes through the fire of initiation, has to be silent. There is, by contrast, an ordinary man, Papageno, who cannot be silent for a moment. Every time he is called on to be silent, this very funny man chatters on. There is thus a play between the ordinary man and the initiated disciple which is played to the full by Mozart, who, some of you will know, was a third-degree initiate. He knew what he was talking about when he wrote that marvellous opera.

In the opera, Tamino has to refrain from speech. Every time he is spoken to by Papageno, even when Pamina, his betrothed, talks to him, he is not allowed to reply, and she thinks he does not love her any more. Occult silence has nothing to do with refraining from speech. It *might* entail refraining from speech, but just as likely it might entail speaking.

Occult silence is knowing *when* to speak, in what area to speak or not to speak. It is really to do with thought and not speech at all. Speech is the result of an overflow, a precipitation onto the physical plane, of a reservoir of thoughts and ideas, which overflow and come out as speech. You can either dam that up and they come out in a great explosion of speech sooner or later, or you can allow that to come out only as and when needed, in the required situation. If you are talking about the Reappearance of the Christ, you do not do that when shopping and buying groceries. Occult silence is knowing what to say when and what not to say when. It is really being able to categorize your thoughts and not allow one stream of thought to be spoken at times which are not correct for that line of thought to be used. It is a separating of thought, the withholding, if necessary, of speech about other areas of thought in a given situation.

It also includes refraining from certain *lines* of thought, for example reverie. Reverie, which is mistaken by very many people for meditation, is a wrong use of thought. That is the opposite of occult silence. The Master DK calls it "the unwholesome use of the creative imagination". The creative imagination, of course, is one of the means by which we build

617

the thoughtforms which colour the astral plane, enrich our astral life and confuse our mental life. If you use the forces of the creative imagination correctly, you will create ideas, paintings, political structures, whatever is your own line of creation. But the misuse of these forces, the unwholesome use of the creative imagination, creates unnecessary glamours and diverts attention from the real.

Speech is controlled at its source. The retention of speech, if you think it wrong, undesirable, or wasteful of energy, will simply increase an inner banking, and you will get an explosion later. What is to be cultivated is not the silence of speech, but the silence of thought and that is entirely different. This is done by a process of substitution. Instead of thinking along these wasteful, unhelpful ways of reverie, or of talking about ideas, group work, whatever, in the wrong place, in the wrong circumstances, you control it. Certain lines of thought are simply refused admission. You do not allow certain ideas to enter your mind. You do that by not following them. You do not repress them, or do anything violent to get rid of them. You simply do not give them headroom. You turn them away, withdraw your attention from them, because the energy follows your thought; where you place your attention your energy will flow. If you place it on these wrong lines of thought, you will stimulate these wrong lines of thought. If you withdraw your thought from them, if you see these as unhelpful and alien to your purposes, you simply withdraw your attention from them, and they die of lack of energy.

Certain habits of thinking are eradicated, and desirable thought processes result, when different areas of thought are kept separate. So that what pertains to the everyday work of going shopping, meeting people in the street, cleaning house, looking after the children, having friends in and so on, where the thought processes are on that, you can speak as openly and as freely as you like. Where it is to do with the work of the group, again you speak as freely as you like in that context. Were it to do with ashramic work, if a thought entered your mind about that and you were about to speak it aloud, you would drop dead. So very great care is taken that it does not even enter your mind. That is occult silence. It is keeping these various areas of thought, and the ideas associated with the different areas of work, in separate compartments which you can enter and leave at will. In each of these compartments you can be as vocal as you like. It is really a question of the right thought at the right time.

To end, let me reiterate two of the essentials for group initiation. They are not easy to achieve, but if they were not possible of achievement there would be no point even in talking about them. For the first time in history, the outer work of preparation for the Reappearance of the Christ is providing the magnetic, cohesive theme, idea, which is holding together groups of disparate individuals from all over the world in unity. The work of Transmission Meditation is providing the yoga, the technical stimulus and field of service which makes possible (as seen by Hierarchy and Maitreya Himself) group initiation for the first time. This group has that possibility. It is not a certainty. But it is a distinct possibility.

Maitreya's involvement

So much is it a possibility that Maitreya is now acting for this group in a certain way. This assures me that He believes that this achievement is not only possible but quite likely, that He believes that this group will create the inner and outer fusion, the group expansion of consciousness, which constitutes group initiation. That is one of the reasons why He overshadows me, and through me the groups which I have formed, or which have formed themselves in response to my information, in different parts of the world.

Until now, I have said that Maitreya is using this process of overshadowing to nourish spiritually the groups in the various countries to which I go, and, of course, this is correct, it is part of this work. But it is more than that. As He sees it, that spiritual stimulus has at its basis the stimulus of the group towards a group expansion of consciousness and group initiation. So from that point of view, Maitreya is Himself performing a work which otherwise would not be possible. One of the requirements for group initiation, as I have said, is the presence of a fourth-degree initiate in one or other of the groups. And one of the factors, when the group on the outer plane has set up a sufficiently potent vibratory, invocative demand, is that various fourth-degree initiates in the inner ashram respond to this invocation, and send their energy to stimulate the group along the right lines.

In our case, although long-since a Master, my Master has been doing this for a considerable length of time, because of the close overshadowing connection which exists between Him and myself. Maitreya has taken over this task from the Master and is doing for this group what, theoretically, is really the work of a fourth-degree initiate. In a very definite sense this group is the group of Maitreya. He has made it His own.

At one of our study groups in London in which we were studying the requirements for, and the laws governing, group initiation, Maitreya performed for the group in London (and as a ramification of that the other groups within the network) an act which my Master called the"gift of the Great Lord". He performed for the group what every group aiming at group initiation has to achieve for itself. He stepped in and, as it were, 'by-passed' in a certain respect, some of the requirements of group initiation. I have spelled them out. They are still requirements, it does not mean that they are not to be achieved. But by His work Maitreya is making it *possible* of achievement.

Maitreya is aiming for the very fast evolution of a group through whom He can work. He has chosen this group to be, as it were, the vanguard of this process. He aims to achieve group initiation quickly through this group, which will act as a model for groups of disciples in the future and so speed up their evolution. Every quickening of the evolutionary process by one individual speeds up the process for everyone. Where hundreds are involved, this speeds up the process immeasurably. Maitreya is stepping in and fulfilling for us some of the requirements which I have sought to explain. They still have to be met. There is still an enormous work to do, but we have the Christ acting for us.

Questions and Answers

Initiation Experience

It seems to me I've heard you say, and I've also read in the Alice Bailey books before, that initiation has been happening in groups. The difference between now and the past is that there are larger groups, is that it?

No. Until now, the initiatory experience has been an individual one. A man here, a woman there, has gone through this process at whatever stage they were. From the point of view of the Masters, they are still members of a group, individual representatives of an ashram. What is being attempted and has become possible for the first time is that an outer group has now the possibility of becoming fused and blended in its action in such a potent way that it can become fused with the original inner group in a Master's ashram.

That means group work in the world. This is really what the externalization of the Hierarchy is about. It is the externalization of the inner ashrams onto the outer plane. It is not simply the Masters coming out into the world, but the externalization of Their groups of disciples, working consciously in relation to the ashram on the inner plane.

That is why it is so important that these rules are seen for what they are and are built into the group consciousness. These are the essential requirements. The forces of destruction must be used so constructively that the obstacles to group fusion on the outer plane, corresponding to the inner fusion in the ashram, can take place. Normally, the forces of destruction are invoked in such a way that they cause great upheavals in the group life. The conscious intention must be to use these same forces constructively, to break down the obstacles, which are always personality differences, likings and dislikings and so on.

Are you saying that individual members of this group will be aware of initiation as a group experience?

621

It depends on the level they have attained at the time. A group is also a group of individuals. The expansion of consciousness in an individual sense is part of the expansion of consciousness in a group sense. But it is different in kind. You can have an individual expansion of consciousness but still not relate that in any meaningful way to other people in the group. What group initiation is about, or rather what it is the result of, and what group consciousness is the result of, is the overcoming of the sense of the separate individual.

Are you saying that people will be aware of it as not just their own experience, but part of a larger experience?
That is what it is about. As the group of individuals make group initiation possible, they individually become so fused and blended with the consciousness of the group that they do not see themselves as separate, they experience it only as a group expansion of consciousness. It is a very gradual process in which the consciousness is expanded little by little. If you read the rule correctly, you will see it is really the sum total of destructions. That is one of the things Picasso said about his painting which people do not like: "My painting is the result of its destructions." He utilized very much the 1st ray, which was strong in his makeup.

In terms of this group moving toward group initiation, you made the comment that many of us are between the first and second initiation. Are you saying that, in moving us towards group initiation, what Maitreya would attempt to do would be to take a big portion of all those people who are ready for, say, the second initiation, as many from the big overall group as possible, and then the next hunk of us, and the next hunk and so on?
Yes, that is precisely how it takes place. But what appears at present to be individual initiation — a disciple here, a disciple there — is essentially being done in group formation. The Masters see the groups, but the individual sees only himself. It does not mean that on 15 August 2005, say, this group is going to come before the Initiators, whether Maitreya or Sanat Kumara, and take the various initiations, those for which they

622

are ready. It means that as they are ready, the group itself is ready.

Individual initiation occurs in the sense of time to the individual, but outside the body there is no time, so from the point of view of the Christ the time factor does not enter into it. There is only the preparedness (or unpreparedness) of the group as a whole. So, although people would be going forward as a group, they would be doing so *in unison,* but not on the same day. Because there is not a day in which you take initiation. Initiation is a process, a result of a process — in this case, of the growth of group consciousness. What we are really seeking to achieve is the expanding of group consciousness, so that group initiation can take place — but not all on the same day.

How to Use the Forces of Destruction

You talked about the invocation of the spiritual will. Are you referring to some sort of conscious process whereby the group sits down and does a conscious invocation together, or are you speaking more in terms of the effects of the on-going group process to invoke the spiritual will?

It is the creating of an inner tension and total focus on the work. That focus can be brought to a point of such tension that it automatically invokes the energy of the will, which shatters the causal body in the individual initiate, and brings in the life aspect, the galvanizing will, to the outer work of the group.

That does not happen automatically — *it has to be achieved.* The group itself must recognize what is needed, and by united, focused action create the necessary spiritual tension. Everything that we are talking about could be said in two words: the creation, the maintenance, totally sustained, of *spiritual tension.* Spiritual tension is the invocative factor. This is generated by an impersonal focus on the work to be done. This can only be achieved, in its turn, by overcoming the obstacles brought about by wrong personality reactions. That is why these four points are so important, because the spiritual tension cannot be generated, the will cannot be invoked, while the personality reactions are clouding the issue all the time.

Regarding the uses of destruction, do you have any suggestions on what we can do in the group — some illustrations from things you know among other groups?

I was hoping you would see it as your role to find these answers. There are no simple answers to this. I cannot give you a formula by which you can reach that goal of expanded group consciousness. This is something which you can only do by living it, by actually going through the motions of destroying in yourself the obstacles to group consciousness. Group consciousness is *there*, as souls we already have it; this is the whole point. The soul only knows group consciousness. It does not have any sense of itself as a separate entity. It seeks nothing for itself, has no sense of separation whatsoever, no personal ambitions, personal goals, no need for personal recognition. None of these obstacles to group consciousness exist on the soul plane. This whole process is about demonstrating on the physical plane, through the personality, the qualities of the soul. So it is both an individual journey for the demonstration of his or her own soul quality and the fusing of that with the soul qualities of the other members of the group.

How do you do it? As a group, you have to recognize that you are souls. The first step is that everyone has to see everyone else as a soul, not as a personality with certain traits which you like or dislike, which you feel you must criticize, or would like to criticize but know you should not criticize. It is not to do with criticism or non-criticism, with liking or disliking. It is spiritual detachment which you have to cultivate. That is the primary quality.

Rule XI* really emphasizes what you should not be doing: you should not be motivated in terms of recognition or personal gain, and relationships should not be sentimentally-oriented. What is the positive side, what should your motivation be, what *should your relationships be? All this seems to be based on karmic bonds, ashramic necessity and soul direction. Can you explain this?*

These are the initial things that bring these disparate individuals together. Soul direction brings them into relation, they respond to certain ideas and so on. The karmic possibilities bring them together, perhaps from different parts of the world and into incarnation at the same time. And finally ashramic necessity — in this case the externalization of the Hierarchy. These three bring together a group on the physical plane. That is only the mechanism by which the group begins its work. What eventuates is that this group begins to respond to world need. And it is in response to world need that the soul qualities become evident. The positives are in the soul qualities, and these are: divine indifference, spiritual detachment, and an underlying love for the other members of the group.

This love does not demonstrate as liking or disliking. Love is totally impersonal. That is why it is called the 'Sword of Cleavage'. It divides by the fact that people respond to this impersonal energy in whatever way they are motivated. If they are motivated by good, desire for the best for all humanity, they will take that aspect and act on it. If their motive is 'evil', for want of a better word, if it is separative, non-inclusive, they will take that same energy of love and be galvanized in the opposite direction. So it stimulates everything, the good and the bad, the selfish and the altruistic. That is why Maitreya has to be very careful with it, very skilful, to make sure that the right reaction is uppermost.

We think of love as something completely personal; we love some people and we dislike other people. But love is nothing to do with that. It is an unbroken stream of God-given energy which magnetically ties together the tiny little blocks of matter which make the universe, and, at the same time, the individual blocks which make a group.

*The "Fourteen Rules for Group Initiation" are set out in *The Rays and the Initiations* by Alice A.Bailey.

In terms of personal relationships within group relationships, we seem to understand that we are having these personal relationships to process our own personal emotional problems — but it is hard to generate images of what true or correct inter-group relationships are like.

Well, you do not know until you can do it, that is the point. It unfolds by itself when you are so motivated by service to the world, so immersed in it, that you do not even notice group personality relations. You do not even think in those terms, but that the work is there, the need is there. You meet the need, and just by doing that there is an attrition of these polarizations. You become more and more impersonal in the correct sense, the spiritual sense. Then you are able to work with all sorts of people whom, otherwise, you would like or dislike. What we are now talking about goes beyond the life of the soul. We are not really talking about coming into contact with your soul and demonstrating soul quality. We are taking for granted, as it were, that this group of disciples have *already* made contact with the soul, are demonstrating soul qualities and are setting up a potent rhythm and note in the world which invokes the will. The destructive force of the will goes beyond the soul to the Monad, and is the energy which kills out personality desire of all kinds.

Taking a very simple example, is it the case that friendship, as we usually think about it, is replaced with a collegial or colleague type of relationship?

What you are trying to do, I think, is focus on a quality of relationship when it is not as simple as that. There can be friendship within the group. There can be love and demonstration of friendship in a group, and at the same time that has no place in the actual group work. It is a mistake, I would say, to try to formulate this in such a way that you rule out all affection between members of a group, all demonstrations of that affection. But where these hinder the purpose of the group, the group service to the world, then, of course, they have to be destroyed. It is where they present obstacles.

Where does the 7th ray fit into all this?
The force of destruction, the life aspect, is the first aspect. The 7th ray is related to this in the sense that the incoming 7th ray is the ray which anchors the spiritual idea on the physical plane. It is the relating ray. The incoming energies of Aquarius, which are fusing and blending, make it essential that this takes place in group formation. The creation of groups is the result of these energies. These energies cannot be utilized individually, only in group formation, because they are, by their nature, synthesizing forces.

Overcoming Personality Relationships

In developing the four essential points in group work, is there a danger of becoming authoritarian?
That depends on you, because that is another glamour. If you use a glamour to overcome a glamour, where are you? — at the same point. I personally do not see it, but tell me what is on your mind and maybe I can understand. Why does that thought occur to you?

I've seen other groups in which, in order to instil an ideal, it becomes a rigid sort of philosophy which people impose upon each other. And I can see how that might happen.
That is the very opposite of what we are talking about. That does not enter into it. A truly occult group, working in the way we are talking about, is a part of an inner ashram, not just doing Transmission Meditation or preparing the way for the Christ. These are the factors which have brought the group together and make group initiation possible.

You cannot impose that, it has to come about by itself. You cannot impose spiritual indifference. You can impose rules, that is something else. The individuals, as a group, must handle these group glamours, these problems of desire — for recognition, to be liked, applauded — all of these hinder the development of group consciousness. Group consciousness is only possible by overcoming the personality. Authoritarianism is a personality reaction, it has nothing to to with the will. In fact, to get rid of the personality demands which everyone makes on everyone else, you have to invoke the destructive forces of the will. You kill out that desire.

Many people mistake the will aspect for the authoritarian attitude. In our solar system the will aspect is love, but not only love. It is purpose motivated by love and working intelligently towards the fulfilment of the purpose. When the group sees the purpose and goes forward and totally absorbs itself in the purpose, then all these other things take care of themselves. You do not have to impose anything.

I wondered if there is a danger in trying to impose order on the group.
It is a danger if you make it so, but not if you understand what it is all about. If there is such a danger, then you are not doing what is necessary. You are simply bringing in another glamour, another personality reaction, because you are trying to achieve a certain result. You want to see order, to impose order. But imposition does not create order, it creates the problem. The order has to come out of the correct motive, followed intelligently with love.

People take the word for the object, the desire for the result. They say: "What we really need is correct group relationship. What are correct group relationships?" Then they enumerate the various things, which they formulate, and say: "That's correct group relationship, it is not that, it is this." They formulate it. And when they have these formulations, they imagine they have correct group relationships. You cannot formulate correct group relations. You might formulate desirable situations or desirable ways of relating and so on, but until you actually do it you do not have it. It is only an idea, only words.

Can you comment on a problem we are encountering in our group? There are a few people who think that a certain situation is an impediment to the group being more effective, and there are a number of people who don't. Because I've contacted both sides of the issue I get confused on whether it would be appropriate to bring it up, or for the group to discuss it. This is a particular personality conflict within the group that some people have difficulty with and some do not.

That is precisely what we are talking about — getting rid of these personality conflicts *by not even seeing them*, not giving them any kind of attention. You have to give no attention to the personality differences. If you do, you will either stimulate them or repress them. If you repress them, you will also stimulate them, so either way you will stimulate them. So you do not try to get rid of them. On the other hand you do not indulge them. You do not make them an issue. Ignore them. When you ignore something, you do not give it any energy. You work from a level above these differences. It can be formulated as: "How can a group work as souls rather than as personalities?" That is what this rule is about, the creation of non-sentimental group interrelation. What you are talking about is a sentimental group interrelation. In this case it is antagonism. But that is sentiment, an astral, emotional reaction. All emotional reactions, you will find, are obstacles to the correct working of group purpose. *All*, of any kind. As soon as you bring in these emotional factors, you can be sure they are from the personality, because the soul does not have any emotions.

What you said about ignoring personality reactions — it is not always entirely possible, such as if someone in the group has a personality problem but cannot bring it out. So how do you handle something like this?
Ignore it.

Just don't say anything?
Well, there are two things here. The trouble with putting things down in writing is that people take them as 'formulae'. They are not formulae. They are really lines of action to consider. These are the essential requirements. What is absolutely essential is a non-sentimental group interrelation. If people are creating circumstances in which that is not possible, then maybe they are not for that group. There are people who by dint of circumstances have found themselves attracted by an aspect of a certain group, but not the totality of the work of the

group. They themselves have to grapple with their problem. Perhaps their problem can be presented to them. But it must not become a group problem. Their problem is not a group problem. Individual personality problems, of glamour, of sentiment, have to be handled individually. As a group, the process is one of *not* reacting to that; it is the killing out of these personality reactions in the group interrelation. There are two things going on: one individual and one in group.

Ignoring it, or even if someone is not verbal about it, you just know that they have resentment toward someone and it is creating negative vibes.

Sometimes, in a group of this kind — in New Age groups of all kinds — there are unbalanced people who come into the group. Where that does not affect the group work, where their value to the group is sufficient to overcome that, to ignore it, then by all means go ahead. But where it begins to affect the intention of the group, takes up the time and energy of the group — which happens often enough, someone can be so unbalanced that the whole energy of individuals in the group is devoted to supporting and ameliorating the effects of that person's imbalance — that is destructive of the group work and they have to go.

The outer work of the group, the service to humanity, has to be the overriding factor. You cannot allow that kind of individual disruption to dominate and to draw all the attention of the group. You have to not allow it, because some unbalanced, neurotic people feed on this, that is what the neurosis is about. It is to gain attention, what they think is love, from all these dedicated people whom they admire. They draw away their time, their attention, their purpose, which should be focused outward to the world. They cannot be allowed to do that, and have to leave the group.

Particular Task of This Group

I believe that helping a child who is half-starving or badly treated next door is just the same as helping one who's in another country, do you know what I mean?

Yes, I know absolutely what you mean. World service is serving the world's needs, wherever you find the need. But this group has a special role to play, a special task — not helping the starving child next door, or even the starving child across the world, except as part of a general awakening of consciousness. This group is making the initial approach to the public about the externalization of the Hierarchy, which includes the Reappearance of the Christ in the world. That is quite a big task. That does not mean that you should not be involved in helping starving children either next door or around the world. Of course, you do whatever you can in terms of answering the need, but you organize your time and energy in such a way that you do what other groups, other individuals, do not do. How many groups or individuals are telling the world of Maitreya's presence? That is the task. If everyone were doing it, it would not become such a priority for this group.

It is precisely the uniqueness of, and also the pressures, the difficulties and the opportunities presented by, that idea, which is strong, magnetic enough, to draw together people from all over the world into making known the fact of the Christ's presence. This involves responding to His intentions for the world (which are to do with world service) and generating the conditions in which He can emerge into the world. That is a major task. So, inevitably, we must focus on that and not disperse our energies in different directions.

What kinds of people work best in this work of preparation for the Christ?
Those who are not complacent and can respond to world need. In the normal course of events I would be associating with painters, musicians, artists of various kinds. There are not too many of them in this work. They are usually too self-oriented, getting on with their careers, to bother to take this seriously. They tend to be intellectuals, and with intellectuals the lower mind tends to get in the way. My background is intellectual, the people I used to know are all intellectuals. But they are not in this work, not one of them.

Intellectuals usually get their pleasure and satisfaction from the discussion and interchange of ideas. This is not a bad thing, but it is limited, if you look at world need. We need people who, from the intuition, can go beyond the lower mind; whose minds are not simply focused on their careers, or academic or intellectual ideas. We need those who can respond to world need, and who can respond to the *idea* of the return of the Christ, however they see the Christ, and who can give of their time, energy and devotion.

My limited observation is that the greatest impediment to the group work in making known the fact of the Christ's presence in the world has not been the personality obstacles that these four requirements deal with, but more a lack of group purpose to motivate the groups to work more openly and effectively. Most of us still have very strong astral bodies, and while I realize that work on Rule XI is a necessity, I think it is relevant to any group work.

When you say purpose, you mean the will. The will aspect has to be invoked to galvanize the work. I think you are talking about two different things here. People have different degrees of conviction about the fact of the Christ's presence, which has therefore resulted in different degrees of absorption in and dedication to the work. That is inevitable. If you are not convinced about something, if it is not intuitively, inwardly, known to you, you are not going to put the time and energy into making it known, if that is what you are supposed to be doing.

If the intention of the group is to make known the fact of the Christ's presence and you do not really believe, or only half believe it, or sometimes believe and sometimes do not believe (which means it is an astral reaction and not an inner conviction at all), then of course you are going to vacillate in your dedication to the work. But where the soul experiences this reality, when your dedication is the result of intuition, there is no vacillation. There might be different degrees of commitment due to energy fluctuations, just sheer exhaustion, but not to fluctuations or vacillations of belief. (When I say 'belief', I mean inner awareness that such-and-such is so.)

You have to put yourself in the right attitude through 'acting as if', where you generate the energy which *proves* that it is so. You have to prove it to yourself.

Transmission Meditation

We have a situation where there are members of our Transmission group who feel it is not necessary to transmit regularly to still be a big part of the group. I don't know how to think of them as people who are 'fellow travellers', who are assisting the work; or can I just say: "Yes, you are a part of the Transmission group even though you don't meditate." What would you suggest about that?

There is such a thing as free will. In this work, as you will have noticed, I always leave everyone free to decide the amount of time they sit in Transmission. They then decide to take part or not take part, to sleep or not to sleep, or whatever. Free will is a very important factor. It should never be infringed. But group initiation has never yet taken place. It has always failed, for reasons of this sort. There has not been a powerful enough motivating theme, idea, or there has not been sufficient dedication to the work, which would have brought it about. A group is made up of people, some of whom will be totally effective, some quite effective, and some not effective at all.

If you study *Discipleship in the New Age,* by Alice Bailey, the Master DK is working with a group which, from the point of view of the individuals, has been a fantastic success. His work must have speeded the evolution of these individuals immeasurably. It must be one of the great Hierarchical achievements. But as a group experiment, it failed. Certain individuals actually failed to go forward in the group. By their own fault, their own decision, their own lack of ability to work in that way, they dropped out of the group. It seems extraordinary that any one would drop out, when they had a Master actually sending them letters, commenting on their meditational processes. However, some failed to respond to that opportunity. People have that right. This affects the group, but you cannot impose rules and regulations.

You have to make the work sufficiently magnetic to attract the right people. The work itself *is* magnetic, but after all, the bulk of people doing Transmission Meditation are between the first and second initiations, otherwise they would not be doing it. The soul impulse would not be strong enough below that level. There will be some who are coming up to the first initiation, on the threshhold (0.9, 0.8), where the soul is making some impact. Perhaps the people you are talking about are around that level, where the impulse to serve is there but is fluctuating, the personality is still too strong in relation to the soul purpose to become dedicated to such work.

The body, too, has its own glamours. These people falling asleep in the middle of the overshadowing by Maitreya — they would have done far better to be four hours totally awake, responsive to the energies, not interrupting the flow of the energies. Far better that than saying: "I'm going to be there until the end," but asleep for three-quarters of the time. That is not work, or service, or dedication. It is glamour.

You mentioned that powerful energies cause some people to go to sleep. Why?
Why do you go unconscious when you are hit on the head by a mallet? For a lot of people, this is like being hit on the head by a mallet. These are powerful, spiritual forces, cosmic forces, and they come down into the head chakra, which is etheric, so you do not even know, but it hammers you. And some people just go out. It is like a blow, they cannot stand the vibration, and the body just drops. It is a shock reaction, but they get used to it. Of course the more you do it, the more you get used to it, the higher power you will stand.

Inner and Outer Ashrams

About the inner ashram and the outer ashram, can you talk a little bit more about the relationship between those two, and how the fusion of the outer group affects the inner ashram. I'm not even clear what an inner ashram is.

An inner ashram is a group of disciples at the centre of which is a Master. The Master focuses and also stimulates the life of the ashram. His radiation embraces it, there is a 'ring-pass-not' which encloses the ashramic energy. It is always under a particular ray. There are 49 ashrams, seven of each ray. The inner ashram should be enriched by the life of the outer ashram.

This is not yet the case — there is only the experiment going on of creating the conditions on the outer plane in which a group, fused and united in their service and purpose on the outer plane, relates consciously in a fused and blended way with the inner ashram. The Master sees the inner ashram and the outer group. The group comes together from ashramic necessity, karmic opportunity, soul direction — for some specific outer work which the group itself initiates.

In this case the work was initiated by my Master through me. Through my work, groups have been drawn by the idea both of the Reappearance of the Christ and Transmission Meditation. They are all related to inner ashrams at the same time. Whoever has taken the first initiation is related to an ashram. In the centre is the Master, and His energy embraces the whole ashram. The ashram is fed, as it were, enriched, potentized, by the work of the group on the outer plane. That is the beauty. As group initiation becomes possible, the outer group is stimulated by and stimulates the work of the inner ashram, because of the now conscious connection between the two. It is really an attempt to demonstrate, on the outer plane, the inner ashram which is functioning perfectly well on the inner plane.

The inner ashram exists on the soul plane?
On the soul plane, yes. It is an attempt to bring that ashram on the soul plane into outer physical expression.

If it does exist on the soul plane, wouldn't it be perfectly manifested on that plane? Why would it need the energy from the outer plane?
It does not need it; it is an enrichening. Life does not stop. Where do you draw a line and say: "That is it." It is a creative

process, everything is creative, everything lives, creates a form, the form crystallizes and dies, the life creates new forms — it is a changing process. These ashrams are not the same as they were thousands of years ago. They will not be the same thousands of years from now. The work of the outer groups enriches and changes and potentizes the work of the inner ashram. The work of the inner ashram, from the soul level, works through the group, potentizing and enriching the work of the outer group. It is a two-way process.

When we die, do we go back to the inner ashram?
You do not have to die to go to the inner ashram. Every night you go to the inner ashram.

If the group is able to achieve this fusion, associated with a particular Master and a particular ashram, how does that affect the ashrams that individual disciples are already involved with?
In this case it is really to do with Maitreya. Maitreya is creating a group through which He can specifically work. This involves individuals who are not along the 2nd-ray line (which is Maitreya's ray), who are not necessarily 2nd-ray souls. The bulk of souls in incarnation are 2nd ray. So you always find in every group of this kind a large number of 2nd-ray souls. But in some countries you will find a preponderance of 3rd ray or 6th-ray souls. In Germany there are quite a lot of 4th-ray souls and some 1st-ray souls because it has a 1st-ray personality. In America and England, the bulk of the members of the groups are 2nd-ray souls. The groups create a group soul, and eventually the group soul itself is superseded. This is the result of bringing in the life aspect. The Monad is on only three rays: 1, 2 and 3. Maitreya can use souls of any ray; the fact that He is the Christ means He can utilize any energy.

What is being created in this case is a group which will relate to its inner ashram, but where, when you bring in the energy of the will, you have a correspondence in the group to the shattering of the causal body for the fourth-degree initiate, in which the soul itself is superseded. Likewise, through the outer work, a group soul is created by the interrelation of the

636

individuals and their own particular rays. The group soul is linked with the ashram and stimulates and potentizes the work of the ashram. But eventually the soul itself is superseded. The *soul* itself is not shattered, but the soul *body* is destroyed by the incoming life of the will aspect.

Could you enlarge on what you said about Maitreya stepping in in place of your Master?
Not very much more at the present moment. This concerns what I said about the "gift of the Great Lord", as my Master put it, in which Maitreya did something for the group which relates to the fact that the group has to bring in the energy of the will. The energy of will, the life aspect, is really only available when the intelligence and the love aspects are demonstrating. It is the last aspect of the Spiritual Triad to unfold, 'the jewel in the heart of the lotus'. Normally this role is played by fourth-degree initiates. That is why DK says that, in a group working towards group initiation, there has to be someone who can handle this energy, who has unfolded the will aspect in his makeup, or in whom the soul as an intermediary is no longer needed.

As you come to study the rule itself, you will find that this process of group initiation has its correspondence with the fourth, the initiation of Crucifixion or Renunciation. It is by a series of renunciations that the initiate takes the fourth initiation, where all ties which bind him to the phenomenal world have been overcome, until finally the vehicle of the soul itself, the causal body, is shattered. That is the experience of the fourth-degree initiate: the shattering of the soul body, the causal body, through which the life of the individual has progressed from the very beginning. It is the closest aspect of him, and once contact with the soul is made, it becomes the be-all and end-all of his aim. But once the soul is demonstrating fully through the personality, it is irrelevant, and its body is shattered.

A direct correspondence to that process is performed in group initiation. That is why the fourth-degree initiate is necessary in the group. The will, the life aspect, has to be invoked. The group by its own conscious effort has to invoke the energy of the will. Otherwise group initiation is impossible. Having fused and blended the individuals in a unified activity, having sounded out the word through its united intent and service, it has to go further and invoke the life which destroys — the destroyer aspect which has to be brought in to destroy all that hinders the expression of the soul life itself. That has been done by Maitreya for the group.

That is extraordinary. Maitreya has stepped in and taken over the evolution of this group in a very definite but very mysterious way which I really cannot go into. I cannot demonstrate to you what He has done. My Master has performed, up till now, the work which would normally be done by a group of fourth-degree initiates in the inner ashram. Maitreya has taken over that, and invoked the life aspect for the group. This is subtle but will demonstrate later and shift the focus of the group. It is something which we cannot realize at the moment because we are where we are and cannot see how we will be in five or 10 years' time.

Something totally changes when the life aspect is invoked. It takes time, of course, for that to demonstrate. It is as if the work shifts gear, and you go up in a spiral; you are working in the same work but at a different level, in a different gear. It is not just heightened activity, but heightened activity in the occult sense, a change in the quality of activity: not just demonstrating a quality, but evidencing a certain purpose.

The purpose of Maitreya is to create a group through which He can work in a very precise, potent way to carry out certain work which He has in mind for the world. And in a very definite sense this group has become, as I said, Maitreya's group. It is a vanguard for certain work which He sees in the future and as a model for that work for many such groups.

CHAPTER 20

THE CALL TO SERVICE

*This article is an edited version of a talk given during the 1991 Transmission Meditation/Tara Network conference held in San Francisco, USA. The section of Questions and Answers also includes material from the 1991 conference held in Veldhoven, the Netherlands. This talk was based on an article, 'The Call to Service', written for **Share International** (September 1991) by my Master.*

The Call to Service

by the Master —

When the call to service sounds, it behoves each earnest disciple to grasp the opportunity presented with both hands. Seldom is the call repeated, for the Masters have little time to waste. 'Many are called but few are chosen' should read: "Many are called but few respond."

Thus it is in the Great Service; only the elect realize the blessing conferred by the opportunity to serve the Plan. Service is the sacred duty which allows the disciple to shorten by many lives his sojourn on this Earth. Many know this but balk at the lightest task. Many forget the pledge they made long ago and shrug off the inner unease. Not for nothing do the Masters sadly shake Their heads and search once more among the waiting lights.

Not all who serve realize they do so. So instinctive is their response to the soul's or Master's call that they plunge in boldly without a second thought. So decentralized are they that the world's need is their only concern. They serve as they breathe, but in relation to the needs of the time they are few indeed. We on the inner side look for those who know, somewhat, the Plan, and whose priorities are sound. We search for those whose ardour is strong and whose hearts are aflame with love and sacrifice. We welcome such brave ones into Our midst and gladly present a field of service. Then We stand aside and watch. Over and again, their first glad steps slow and falter. Too often, their bright expectations turn to boredom and doubt, their lofty aspiration shrivels and dies.

The failure of faith looms large in these sad happenings. Without faith nothing lasting may be done, and for lack of this one quality many promising disciples have failed. Not for nothing, down the ages, have the teachings emphasized the need for faith, seeing it as the very heart of service.

Faith, to be sure, does not mean blind acceptance and belief. On the contrary, true faith rises only when the intuition, the voice of the soul, prompts an inner knowing, and, past all gainsaying, the heart tells you: this is true. When that moment comes, clasp firmly to you this new-found truth and "stay there". When the voices of envy and doubt assail you, keep serenely to your task. Remember that your mind belongs to you and no one has the right to tell you what to think.

Cultivate a wise rhythm which will allow your service to expand naturally. Eschew a service done in fits and starts for in this way is all momentum lost. Remember that you are here to serve the Plan. That, if you did but know it, is your soul's wish. As you make contact with the soul, the objectivization of experience begins to take place. The soul has no preference, no desire; it relates only to that which is consonant with its purpose, which is to serve the Plan of evolution to the greatest degree possible.

The time will come when the influence of the Masters will provide a field of study and experience by which those now standing on the threshold will enter into the realm of light and knowledge and know themselves for what they are. There are many awaiting the creation of a new age whose manifestation will profoundly affect the structures of their time. Serve and grow, serve and grow should be the keynote of your lives.

A few years ago I gave a talk both in San Francisco and Holland called 'The Role of Service in the Development of the Disciple' (published in *Maitreya's Mission, Volume One*) but, according to my Master, one cannot talk too often or too deeply about the idea of service. To the Masters, service is the be-all and end-all of existence, and Their role on this planet is serving the Plan of evolution. Based as it is on the Master's own words and ideas, I hope it will stimulate you, inspire you to put more time, more energy, more of yourself, into the very reason why you are in incarnation — to serve. That is your soul's purpose, first and foremost — to serve the Plan of evolution. For that the soul comes into incarnation.

I would like to remind you of the lines I wrote to begin that article: "The basic impulse behind all evolution is that activity of the soul which we call service. Service is nothing less than the demonstration in relationship of the Law of Love."

That is a very big statement indeed; I wonder how many people think of service in those terms. The basic impulse behind evolution is that activity of the soul which we call service. In other words, fundamental to the whole of evolution — and evolution, of course, not only on this planet, but on all planets; not only in this solar system, but in all solar systems — is service, the activity of the soul. It is the soul in all forms which serves just as it is the soul in all forms which incarnates. Incarnation itself is the result of the impulse of the soul to serve, in line with the Law of Love.

As you will know, we live in a 2nd-ray solar system. In this system God Itself is Love. The 2nd ray, Love-Wisdom, is the dominating ray of our system; therefore, for us God is Love. If service is nothing less than the demonstration in relationship of the Law of Love, that means God Itself is service. It could not be otherwise. If God is service, then service must be very important, basic, fundamental to everything we think of as life: the meaning, the purpose of life, the process of incarnation, that activity in which the soul comes into manifestation at this level. All of that is the impulse of love which is the same thing as the impulse of service. Service seen from that point of view must be the most important thing that we could think about, know about and demonstrate.

It is the love of God for Its creation, I went on to say, that impels the Logos Itself to take incarnation and to demonstrate through a planetary form. We are units of the Logos, therefore the same impulse governs our soul expression. As souls, we need to serve. It is the basic impulse of the soul, its fundamental purpose in coming into incarnation: to serve the Plan of the Logos, the evolutionary Plan about which we can never know all. As we grow in service, as we evolve along the evolutionary path, we become more and more aware of deeper aspects of the mind of the creating Logos of which we ourselves, of course, are the expression. We are thoughtforms in the mind of the Logos. Therefore, correctly to live, we must obey the laws governing the Logos' demonstration of love in the creation of this planetary form and to serve the Plan of evolution in so far as we can. That is what the soul seeks to do, why it takes incarnation.

Let us look at the words of my Master in His article. *"When the call to service sounds,"* (He is talking about the opportunity presented to groups by the Masters, not the call of the soul), *"it behoves each earnest disciple to grasp the opportunity presented with both hands. Seldom is the call repeated, for the Masters have little time to waste."*

As you approach the first initiation, your own soul brings you into meditation of some kind. This forms and strengthens the link between the soul and its vehicle, the man or woman in incarnation. Through meditation, the bridge, the antahkarana, a channel of light, is built downwards by the soul and upwards by the person meditating. Gradually a link is formed through which the soul can 'grasp' its vehicle and bend the personality to its will, its purpose — to serve the Plan of evolution under the Law of Love. The soul needs to serve. As soon as you come into contact with the soul, you desire to serve. You cannot help yourself because it is the soul's impulse to serve and it seeks to impress that on the mind of its reflection.

Of course, you can serve or not. No one makes you serve except the soul, but you can quite easily take no heed of the soul. The soul has endless aeons of time; it is in no hurry and will repeat the call again and again. Eventually, one day, you heed that call and start serving. In this way the soul is creating an instrument, a reflection of itself, through which its plans and purposes can be carried out. But it has no special time-frame in which to do it. A Master, on the other hand, may well have a very specific time-frame in which to carry out His work.

The Plan of evolution comes from Shamballa. It is in the mind of the Logos and therefore of Sanat Kumara, the Lord of the World. It is brought by the Buddha from Shamballa and revealed to the Three Great Lords of the Hierarchy: the Christ, the Manu and the Mahachohan, the Lord of Civilization. They take the Plan as presented by the Buddha and approximate it to what is possible in a given cycle — 1,000- or 2,000-year cycle — which is then broken down into shorter cycles of perhaps 100 years, sometimes 75 or 25 years. Particular aims are discussed and agreed on by the Masters by consensus and each Master then takes a portion of the presented Plan along His own ray line. He will determine how He would be useful along that line and then, through the various groups of disciples under His charge, seeks to put that part of the Plan into effect in the world. If the disciples respond — correctly, of course — the Master's work goes forward. If they do not, it does not. And if the Master's work goes forward in fits and starts, a little bit here and a little bit there, the Master may be sad about it but there is little He can do. He would not use force to produce a better rhythm.

If the disciples take that aspect of the Plan given to them and make a mess of it, then it is their responsibility, not the Master's. The Master is responsible only for the presentation of the opportunity of service, giving each disciple a role, a part of the Plan, a field of service which he or she may or may not take up.

The soul has endless time. It will repeat the call to service over and over again, life after life, if necessary. But the Master, working with the Plan as it is manifesting in the world, does not have that kind of time. He has a much more restricted time frame and will seek to manifest His part of the Plan in a given period of time — 25, 50, 75 or 100 years — whatever it happens to be. So the Master does not have time to waste. The

Master is so focused on all His manifold duties and works that He does not have the time to keep prodding someone who does not get on with the work. He presents the field of service, watches to see what happens, and if the person does not take it up, He may prod him once but usually not more. So it really does behoove each earnest disciple "to grasp the opportunity presented with both hands. Seldom is the call repeated, for the Masters have little time to waste".

"Many are called but few are chosen." The Master says: *"This should read: 'Many are called but few respond.' Thus it is in the Great Service."*

The Masters call Their work "The Great Service". They serve the Plan of evolution and that is Their total concern. That is why They are on this planet. As you may know, They are finished with this planet as a field of learning; it has nothing more to teach Them. The fact of Their being here is the result of Their desire, Their necessity, to serve.

"... only the elect realize the blessing conferred by the opportunity to serve the Plan."

It is a blessing, given to you. It is not something you even have to look for. Many people have said to me something like the following: "With all my varied talents, I really should be doing something of real importance in the world, real service, and I have very distinctly the impression, the intuition, that I have a real mission to perform in the world. But what is it, Mr Creme? What is it I have to do? I really want to serve, but I have never been able to find it."

I believe this shows a completely wrong approach to service — the idea that there is a mission waiting for this person suddenly to intuit and become aware of. Of course it never will dawn on him or her. Such a person has the glamour of service. There is no service without action. Service is not talking about service. It is not wanting to serve. It is actually serving. The act of service is action even if it is sitting at a desk, or sitting in a chair taking part in Transmission Meditation. You do not seem to be acting, but in fact that is action.

Imagine someone, looking at this vision of his or her great mission in the world. The glamour, of course, is in the fact that it has to be great, that it has to be "a mission".

The world is there to be served. The soul needs to serve, desires to serve. It is its very nature and being. But you do not have to have a great mission, you can serve from where you are. You can help the world in one way or another from where you are and from who you are. And, of course, depending on who you are will be the nature of your service. You alone can perform your service. Each one is unique and every act of unique service is valuable to the Masters and the Plan, because They have the task of presenting the Plan to the world, and presenting the mode of service to Their disciples as the lever of this evolutionary journey. It provides the method by which we can be who we are.

"Only the elect realize the blessing conferred by the opportunity to serve the Plan. Service is the sacred duty which allows the disciple to shorten by many lives his sojourn on this Earth."

I am sure many people like this Earth so much that they do not want to shorten their sojourn on it, but why stay on the Earth any longer than you need? You can always come back for a vacation, for a few generations, or a few incarnations. How much more interesting to have the freedom of the solar system, to go wherever your fancy takes you. That, to me, is a much more interesting and fascinating state than being chained to the Earth and its pollution.

"Many know this but balk at the lightest task."

It is quite extraordinary how 'light-minded' many people are. I say this as one who is 'light-minded' beyond measure; I include myself in this. It is extraordinary how 'light-mindedly' people take the Plan of evolution, the laws governing their own lives; who listen with half an ear to the words of great Masters; who put in half an hour of Transmission Meditation a week, out of which time perhaps they are actually aligned for three-quarters of a minute. That is hardly serving the world. That gives them the feeling, the satisfaction that they are actually engaged in service. Many know this, that if you take up the "sacred duty" of service you can speed up your evolution in the most extraordinary way and shorten, as the Master says, "your sojourn on this Earth".

"Many forget the pledge they made long ago and shrug off the inner unease."

Every disciple who becomes a pledged disciple has literally made the pledge to serve the Plan of evolution. That is what being a disciple is. Whether you know it or not, you have made a pledge to serve the Plan in so far as you can become aware of that Plan and to the extent of that awareness. Of course, when you think about it with the lower mind it is probable that you cannot think of the Plan at all. You do not know what it means, but in the interaction of life with other people, with groups, with whatever activities, your profession and so on — you are actually, moment to moment, taking part in the Plan of evolution. It is not something separate from your life. Your life is part of that Plan in so far as your actions go along with the intentions of the Plan, of the Master standing back of the group of which you are a part. Then of course you are acting altogether more consciously. What the Masters need are conscious and willing servers.

"Many forget the pledge they made long ago and shrug off the inner unease."

It is not possible to be a pledged disciple and to live a life not fulfilling your part in the Plan, taking on the service that is entailed as a "sacred duty" (as the Master calls it) without an inner sense of unease. You may never allow that unease to come up to the conscious level, but so long as you are pledged to serve and do not serve, or only half serve, then this inner unease will manifest and lead eventually to depression. The depression of disciples is, 99 times out of 100, the result of the non-response to the soul's impulse to serve. That energy, that impulse, niggles away and causes an inner malady, a sense of something not right with you and the world. That leads to depression, the inability to act, to love, the inability to share yourself and your being with others. Depression cuts you off from your group, from your inner Master, whether that is the Master of the group or your own soul, and eventually may drive the person to suicide. This is not, of course, always the case, and need not be the case. But unless you take up the service which, in His love, the Master presents to you, to the group for which He is responsible, then, inevitably, depression sooner or later sets in. It may well express itself as neurosis and physical illness.

"Not for nothing do the Masters sadly shake Their heads and search once more among the waiting lights."

The Masters look for those through whom They can work out the Plan. When They look into the world They see the disciples as lights. The light is the radiation from the chakras. There are bright lights and middling lights and not very bright lights. When They see bright lights or middling-to-bright lights, They may stimulate these lights by giving some field of service to the individual. This is a test to see how they respond to world need, not the Master's need. The Master does not need anything; the world, not the Master, needs the service of the individual. The Master does not even need your devotion, but He does need your devoted service to the Plan. That is all He calls for because that is what the world itself needs. The Master looks into the world and sees these shining lights, and where one maintains a steady glow, a steady radiance, He stimulates the person, sets a task. He may give a mental impression and the person is set on the road of service. They may or may not serve, and if they do not the Master sadly shakes His head and looks again into the world to pick another 'shining light', hoping that it will be more steady, more steadfast and of real use.

"Not all who serve realize they do so."

There are many people in the world who serve and never think of it as service. We can all think of people like that. They do not know they are disciples. They never think about being one. Do you think Mother Teresa thinks about being a disciple? The word would probably make her smile. She would probably say: "A disciple? Of whom? Jesus? All right, I am a disciple of Jesus." She might say that because she is a Christian. But a disciple in the esoteric meaning of the word — living the life of disciplined service, no. She would say: "I am just helping people who are dying, who are starving, who are ill. I just help them because they need it." People like that serve instinctively, straight from the heart. It is no burden to them. So instinctive is it, it is not a burden. If service is a burden, then, of course, it is not service. It means the heart is not involved. Service is the result of the outflow of the energy of love from the heart. It proceeds from the heart, informed by the intelligent mind. It is intelligent action motivated by love. Unless it is that, you cannot call it service at all.

"So instinctive is their response to the soul's or Master's call that they plunge in boldly without a second thought."

They do not even think about it. They do not even know they are being called. They just see the world's need and respond to that need. That is true service.

"So decentralized are they that the world's need is their only concern. They serve as they breathe, but in relation to the needs of the time they are few indeed."

If there were millions of such people, there would be no problem, but of course, there are very few Mother Teresas in relation to the needs of the world. With millions of people starving to death and hundreds of millions living in poverty, degradation, misery and want; with the world divided in such a way that nuclear war can explode at any moment; with pollution on a scale approaching destruction of the planet, then the world needs servers. It is a colossal problem. In relation to that need, the instinctive servers — the Mother Teresa type of server — are very few indeed.

"We on the inner side look for those who know, somewhat, the Plan, and whose priorities are sound."

If you know the Plan you can become a conscious server. In this way you are less likely to waste time going along blind alleys. There are many ways to serve the world but there are better ways than others. Everything is service if necessary, but you have to serve intelligently as well. That is, to serve not below, but slightly above, your capacity, to stretch yourself in service all the time. Not taking the line of least resistance but if necessary the line of major resistance. But to take the line of major resistance all the time can also be unintelligent. That way you go along blind alleys, you waste time and opportunities. The trick is to know when to take the line of least resistance and when to take the line of most resistance. That makes the intelligent server. You have to intuit which line to take — whether along the line of no resistance at all, the line of your own ray structure, the opportunities presented in your group activity, or to tackle something which somehow seems contrary to your nature — really very difficult for you — stretching you beyond your real desire. Of course, if you never stretch you never become flexible. You have to go beyond what you think you are capable of doing in order to grow. You will always become aware of being able to do more and more. Everyone in the groups with which I am associated, I think, has come to realize qualities, talents in performance in many different fields, which they never thought they had. People are talking publicly who never talked before; approaching media who were so timid about such a thing; talking on the media who would have balked at the idea at one time; organizing conferences like this. Complete amateurs. It is done by love, but it is done by amateurs using their intelligence and using the capacities which are innate in a great many people. The thing is to find these capacities by stretching yourself beyond the point that you would normally go. Serving beyond the needs of duty, as it is sometimes put.

The priorities have to be sound. The Masters look for people who know, somewhat, the Plan, who can work intelligently along the needs of the Plan, as they understand it, and whose priorities are sound. You have to have the right priorities: you have to put service first, the good of the group above your own personal good, the needs of the world before everything else.

If you are a disciple, you do not actually belong to yourself. You do not belong to your family, nor to the group of which you may be a part. You belong to the world. Of course you have a life function. You may be married, have children, a family duty that you must meet. You have to fulfil your family and life duties, but at the same time your primary duty and primary priority is the service of the world. That is the pledge which as disciples, knowingly or unknowingly, you have made.

It is a great problem for many people to decide which comes first, who has the greater need, how to arrive at a sound understanding of priorities. Very often you have to choose between two equal priorities. You have to put each action in a category of priorities and aim at the greatest. At the same time, perhaps two or three possible actions have equal priority in your consciousness. How do you choose? You have to come to a flexible, spontaneous, intuitive understanding of where your priorities must lie. This is an essential understanding for being a useful disciple: to know what to do when; to know what is more important, this or that. There may be many important things, but it is essential to learn to choose even between priorities. The number one priority, the number one testing ground of this choice, I would say, is an understanding of the need of the Plan of evolution, the need of the world. If you put that first, without fanaticism, you will be doing the right thing. If you do it with fanaticism, of course, you will not be making the right priority choices. You will choose to act because you believe the Plan is more important than anything else. Of course the Plan is more important than anything else, but the Plan takes place in time and perhaps it is more important on this day to serve your family or your friends, to serve your group, than to do a certain action which you see as altogether more in line with the Plan. The Plan cannot wait, but there is a time factor involved in the Plan too. You have to learn to work to the correct rhythm. None of this is easy. If it were easy, we would all be super disciples, which we are not.

"We search for those whose ardour is strong and whose hearts are aflame with love and sacrifice."

Ardour is another word for fire. The heart has to be aflame; if the service is proceeding from a heart filled with love, then the service will be done with ardour. Ardour is the fuel which drives the person forward. Very often, fanaticism takes the place of ardour and the result is always destructive, always ugly. There is a ray — the 6th — with a tendency to fanatical action which is often mistaken for ardour. There is all the difference in the world between desire and ardour.

Ardour is impersonal, fiery action. Desire is personal action which can be just as intense but if done with fanaticism will inevitably cause destruction because fanaticism separates. Anything which separates destroys the action of evolution which is always towards unity. You could say that synthesis is the fundamental quality governing the evolutionary process. That which we call God, of which we are a reflection, is aiming at synthesis. The purpose of God is to achieve unity by bringing together again all the diverse atoms which God has scattered in every direction. To bring it all together again unified by one purpose: the serving of the Plan of evolution itself; the understanding of how vast, how amazingly beautiful that Plan is in all its variety, its diversity, and bringing that into a unity. Anything that works against that, anything that from a fanatical, separatist attitude creates division, is destructive of evolution itself. That is why fanaticism is so destructive. It is actually against the Plan. *"We search for those whose ardour is strong and whose hearts are aflame with love and sacrifice."* The soul knows only sacrifice. It wishes to sacrifice its being for the Plan of evolution of which it is a part. It comes into incarnation as a sacrificial act to serve that Plan. The soul on its own plane is perfect. Why should it limit itself at this level? It does so as an act of sacrifice. It is a real limitation for the soul to tie itself up in matter in a long evolutionary process that takes hundreds of thousands of incarnations with all the inadequate reflections of itself which it sees, incarnation after incarnation, awaiting patiently a time when it can create a vehicle which will reflect its true nature: love and sacrifice. The Masters welcome those who can show that love and that sacrifice.

"We welcome such brave ones into Our midst and gladly present a field of service. Then We stand aside and watch."

The Masters are very patient. They stand aside and watch; They do not poke the fire. They see the fire, and They let it flame. They know that if They poke it They will break up the flame. Nice sparks come off when you do it, but They know it

651

is better to leave things alone and then, under test, the person goes forward and the Masters can judge the ardour, the ability to sacrifice, the ability to understand intelligently the Plan and the field of service presented by Them. They choose among those who correctly respond, those with whom They can work more closely, who can be trusted with certain tasks, knowing they will be carried out, who can be trusted to keep silent if necessary and to talk when required.

"And then we stand aside and watch. Over and again, their first glad steps slow and falter."

Sad, it is. It happens over and over again.

"Too often, their bright expectations turn to boredom and doubt."

How many times have you seen this in the groups connected with the Reappearance of the Christ? How many times have you seen people aflame with all the enthusiasm in the world, who cannot do enough, who are so devoted to the idea, who love Maitreya, and love everything about the service — for six months, or, perhaps, even a year. And then, bit by bit, they go down. They begin to wonder: "Is Maitreya really in the world?" It has nothing to do with whether Maitreya is in the world or not. It is to do with their inability to be steadfast in their service. It is simply a bubbling up of emotional response which has so little of the heart's love connected with it that inevitably they burn themselves out. Emotion always burns out. Love of the heart never burns out. It is inextinguishable because it has a huge reservoir — the whole of cosmos — from which the heart receives its energy. And if the gate from the reservoir through your heart is open, and the service is correctly motivated, it has an inexhaustible supply. You never lose faith. How could you? But if you are motivated, basically, by the emotions, the idea of service, the idea of the Plan, the idea of the return to the world of the Christ — if that is a thrilling emotion, but only an emotion, then very quickly in the hurly-burly, the disappointments, the waiting, the day-to-day niggly, boring work that grows humdrum, then, of course, many people burn out. They literally emotionally burn out. They think it is because they doubt that Maitreya is in the world but they do not doubt that at all. They see more and more evidence of it all the time. Every year that passes there is more evidence of the hand of Maitreya behind the events in the world. More and more evidence of Maitreya Himself: as hitchhiker, crosses of light, hands appearing on the crosses of light — all these manifestations which are evidence of His presence somehow, to these people, have less and less effect. They have emotionally burnt out.

You have to recognize that that is what it is. It is not a tragedy. Of course it feels, personally, like a tragedy. It is a stage in understanding what is glamour, and what is real service. Service and glamour are two opposites. You can serve even in a glamoured situation. If you could not, there would be no one serving because everyone is glamoured to some degree, from the lowliest disciple up to the fifth-degree initiate, that is, a Master. Only the fifth-degree initiate is completely clear of glamour. Theoretically, anyone who has taken the third initiation should be free of glamour. But if you examine the lives of the disciples of the third initiation, you find they were certainly glamoured. They may have been unimportant glamours and certainly did not too much interrupt their service, but they were glamours nevertheless.

It is easy to mistake this 'dark night of the soul' for the end of your belief in this work. Some people leave the work under this cloud of doubt, feeling that they chose the wrong group. Many think: "It would be easier if it were true." They imagine that the emergence of the Christ into the world should be easy. Maitreya does not consider it easy. He knows better than we do, how deep, how profound is superstition and therefore opposition to His presence. Humanity is deeply superstitious, ingrained with fear and doubt. Even many who would consider themselves able to believe such a manifestation, choose not to do so because they know it upsets the *status quo* and they do not want the *status quo* upset. So they choose to give it no energy even though they believe Maitreya is in the world.

"Too often their bright expectations turn to boredom and doubt, their lofty aspiration shrivels and dies. The failure of

653

faith looms large in these sad happenings. Without faith nothing lasting may be done and for lack of this one quality many promising disciples have failed."

That is a quotation from something the Master said when He first contacted me in the beginning of 1959. He gave me a long dissertation on faith and said at the end: *"For lack of this one quality, many promising disciples have failed. Have faith and affirm His coming."*

Many people do not like the idea of faith, thinking that faith is believing in something. Faith has nothing to do with belief at all. Faith is a state of being. Faith results when you are who you are. When you are demonstrating at this level as a soul and are in constant connection with your soul, you will have faith. You cannot help but have faith because faith is a quality of the soul.

The Master says: *"Not for nothing, down the ages, have the teachings emphasized the need for faith, seeing it as the very heart of service. Faith, to be sure, does not mean blind acceptance and belief."* That is the opposite of faith. *"On the contrary, true faith rises only when the intuition, the voice of the soul, prompts an inner knowing, and, past all gainsaying, the heart tells you: this is true."*

When intuitively you know that this is true, when it is not the outcome of a mental configuration of other people's minds, ideas and hopes, but of your own inner contact with your soul, and the soul tells you: This is true — then not only can you have faith, but you do have faith. It is not a choice. Faith is not the result of choice. If there is choice in it — you chose to believe that or that — there is no faith. Faith, true faith, only exists when you go beyond the necessity of choice, when there is no this or that. Then only, in a direct experience that this is true, can faith arise. While you hold to that contact with the soul, your faith will remain steady, strong and as true as it was the moment it arose. It is not something which goes away. What does go away is belief: your belief in the Reappearance, your non-belief in the Reappearance. This can come and go and has nothing to do with faith. Belief is a product of the mind, not of the soul. That which is a product of the soul's inner knowing and being cannot disappear. That is called faith.

"When that moment comes, clasp firmly to you this new-found truth and 'stay there'. When the voices of envy and doubt assail you, keep serenely to your task."

All of us know that many people, seeing the dedication, the joy that results from group work — and group work in particular associated with the Hierarchy, in this case the Reappearance of the Christ — begin to envy. Their dislike of this work, their slights, their anger, scepticism, hostility and so on — is the result of the fact that they see something that they do not understand, that grudgingly they admire, but which they do not have themselves. These are the "voices of envy and doubt". People love to bring you down, to create a situation in which you are brought down to their level. Everyone must have had this experience. And, of course, if you are exposed to the public eye in this work, you get a great deal of it. It is the result, not of scepticism at all, but of fear and envy. It is so much easier to disavow something than to avow it, to condemn than to acknowledge. Many people go in for these negatives because it is a very easy thing to do. It is always easier to deny than to affirm. So people go around denying what — if they thought for one second — they would see to be true. But to deny it absolves them from any responsibility *vis-à-vis* that event. If you deny that the Christ is in the world, you are absolved from the responsibility of doing anything about it. If you affirm that the Christ is in the world, of course, you take upon yourself the responsibility for that event. That is what is difficult in this work. That is why you have to "serenely keep to your task" despite "the voices of envy and doubt".

Sometimes these voices of envy and doubt come from the people who are nearest and dearest to you. That is a problem. The husbands of wives, the wives of husbands, connected with the work find, again and again, the inability of their spouses to understand what they are involved in. They see it often as some kind of cult which they do not even want to understand or have anything to do with. They really fear the extent to which their spouses are involved in the work. This, of course, will change as soon as they see Maitreya, but for the time being and over the years, it has been a real problem for many people. I have known people who have divorced because of it, or who have separated.

"Remember that your mind belongs to you and no one has the right to tell you what to think."

This is something you should always keep in mind. Your life as a disciple does not belong to you. As a disciple, your life belongs to the world. But your mind belongs to you and you should not allow anyone to tell you what to think. You should not be so impressionable as to concern yourself with what other people think about you: whether they think you are mad to be involved in this work.

Rhythm is all important. The Master says: *"Cultivate a wise rhythm which will allow your service to expand naturally. Eschew a service done in fits and starts for in this way is all momentum lost."*

Service which takes place in fits and starts is hardly worth doing at all. Of course, we all do it. The Master is talking about perfection. We all perform in fits and starts. But true service done with a correct rhythm will leave you time to breathe. You have to learn when to relax and when not to relax; to serve to the ultimate, the total extent of your power and strength, but in a relaxed way. As the Master DK puts it somewhere: "You must learn to sit lightly in the saddle."

We all know those beginning their service in this group — nothing can keep them from the work, they will take on every task: "I will do it! I will do it." They are doing everybody's work. They want to be indispensable so they take on everybody's work with the result that they do nothing because nobody can do everybody's work, it is just not possible. It leads to work going undone. Take on the task that you can do, and do it. When you take on small tasks and do them correctly, you find that you can take on bigger tasks. True world service is the result of being able to perform small services correctly. You grow into the sense that the bigger task is only a slight extension of that which you can do without too much trouble. You will find that the people who do most work in any group are the people who are already busiest. They are already so busy, in such a rhythm of work, of focus, that any new task they take on you can rely on them to do. The people who let you down are always the people who are doing pretty well nothing anyway. Always, the people who are "too busy" do nothing at all; therefore every task is a major task. Those who really are busy, all the time, in an actual rhythm of work — which does not mean they do not breathe, but have set up a rhythm which they can maintain — are always able to expand it a bit.

"Cultivate a wise rhythm which will allow your service to expand naturally. Eschew a service done in fits and starts for in this way is all momentum lost. Remember that you are here to serve the Plan. That, if you did but know it, is your soul's wish. As you make contact with the soul, the objectivization of experience begins to take place. The soul has no preference, no desire; it relates only to that which is consonant with its purpose, which is to serve the Plan of evolution to the greatest degree possible."

Remember, this is not your only life, but the present manifestation of a spiritual entity, your soul, which has seen hundreds of thousands of incarnations. All the experience of these incarnations is relayed to the soul in the causal body, which the soul uses on the causal plane, the highest of the four mental planes. All that you experience, everything that has gone into that life, is known to the soul through the memory bank, as you might call it, of the causal body. Not just of this life, but the memory of all incarnations. Nothing is lost. As soon as you make contact with the soul, the objectivization of that experience takes place. The soul brings down onto the objective world the experience which it has garnered over the ages in all these various incarnations.

This is why people can do things for the first time as if they had been trained. Everyone in these groups is an amateur. We are all amateurs. And yet some people in these groups are doing jobs that they would not — five or 10 years ago — have thought possible. It is because they are calling on the experience not only of this life, but of all the lives previous to

657

this. Of course, not all at once. The past achievements do not pour down through a chute; we would not know what to do with them all. But, as the need arises, as the opportunity is presented, as the soul's energy is felt, this bank of experience comes as necessary and shows itself as intuition, knowledge, capacity, as what we can only call experience, even though we may never have experienced this in the present incarnation. The soul objectifies that experience; this is one of the major factors behind correct service.

"The soul has no preference, no desire; it relates only to that which is consonant with its purpose, which is to serve the Plan of evolution to the greatest degree possible.

"The time will come when the influence of the Masters will provide a field of study and experience by which those now standing on the threshold will enter into the realm of light and knowledge and know themselves for what they are."

We know that the initiatory process constitutes the final phases of the evolutionary path. Initiation speeds up the evolutionary experience. Through it we become aware of the Plan in the mind of the Logos of our planet; aware, more and more, of His purpose, of why we are here, what is our individual task *vis-à-vis* the Plan of evolution. This is given through the initiatory experience. It may never become conscious until late in that process but the soul reveals that inspiration, knowledge and experience to its reflection, the man or woman. That becomes objectified in the service activity of the individual. In this way, the knowledge of the Plan works out.

Until a certain time, we cannot work consciously with the Plan but the Masters have given teachings which guide us along the way: the Theosophical, the Alice Bailey, the Agni Yoga teachings. These constitute a body of knowledge about the Plan which we can become aware of and find a niche for ourselves in the working out of the Plan. Service is the key to this process. As you serve, you grow in service. You become more and more able to grow. As you grow, more of the Plan is revealed to you, both intuitively and in fact. Until you can work, eventually, with a Master in a closer, conscious

658

THE CALL TO SERVICE

relationship, you have to go along in trust, with faith. The Master can guide you along certain lines not, as you might think, by teaching, but by presenting you with an ever-widening field of service. Through that widened service activity, you come to know more about the meaning behind the Plan. It is a world Plan; it is not to do with esotericism. Esotericism is the means by which the Plan is kept relatively intact and secret. But you become aware of it in its gradual working out in the world.

If you could see this world with the eyes of a person living 2,000 years ago, you would be astonished by radio and television, facilities for travel and so on. A completely different world pertains today from 2,000 years ago. If you had the vision to see ahead say, 1,000 years from now, you would be astonished by the world which would await your gaze at that time: modes of travel which today you cannot even imagine — thinking yourself to Australia if that is what you want to do. Can you imagine the world 1,000 years from now? A world in which unity is the keynote, in which synthesis actually prevails; in which there are no wars, no hunger, no great divisions; a world living in unity, in harmony; a world in which the cities are beautiful.

The world ahead has to be created and it is created under the Plan. The Plan is the creation of the world. The world is the Plan, the scene in which the Plan works out. If you could think of a man or woman of the seventh root race (we are the fifth root race), man in his perfection as envisioned by the Logos, you would see a God, a magnificent, Godlike being. The Plan is the future. The way to that future is to envision that Plan and make it your own, make it part of your life's work to further that Plan and to create in every respect that you can, that harmony, that beauty. It is to do with beauty. The 4th ray has to have its fling. The demonstration of the 4th ray is the revealing of the beauty of life, the beauty of the Lord. Where beauty demonstrates you have the Plan in its correct manifestation. There will not be beauty if the Plan is distorted, if there is separation or division. Beauty arises out of that perfect harmony which eventually will prevail throughout planet Earth. That is something which we all can aim at and work towards through service.

"There are many awaiting the creation of a new age whose manifestation will profoundly affect the structures of their time. Serve and grow, serve and grow should be the keynote of your lives." Thus spake the Master.

Questions and Answers

The Soul's Purpose

How can the disciple know the soul's purpose?
By meditation and intuition, and by getting involved in some service. The soul, which is the first Master, brings you to service, but if you do not serve it will wait for another incarnation. If you start serving, you will find that the capacity to serve will grow. The Masters watch this. They watch the 'waiting lights'. They test the person to see how well he does. If that does not work out they test another one. They are looking for those who can 'stay there', who can keep going and work with a degree of impersonality. Impersonality and objectivity are crucial in relation to service. That is what the Masters look for.

Is the soul's purpose a more general impulse which the personality then focuses and gives expression to?
It depends on the degree of evolution of the individual. In an advanced disciple, the soul's purpose and the personality's purpose would be one and the same because the personality, imbued with soul energy and consciousness, would know his or her purpose. But in a disciple of lesser degree, the purpose might be more vague in consciousness, and so the disciple enters into group work. That provides a field of service and it grows from there.

How is knowledge related to the awakening of the intuition?
The more you expand, vivify and nourish the mind, the more likely the intuition is to function. We generally think of knowledge as the activity of the lower mind but that is not

660

really what I mean. You do not have to know everything that exists in the world, but you have a brain and mind and you have the responsibility to enrich that as much as possible. That knowledge, when it reaches the higher levels of the mind, awakens the intuition. It is difficult for the intuition to work in a mind which is untutored, which has no data to work from.

Are there inner cues we can learn to recognize to help us discriminate between intuition and desires? If so, what are they?
When you work from the intuition this question does not arise. The intuition knows. It knows because it knows because it knows. There is no gainsaying anything that arises from intuition. Intuition is an inner, direct knowledge. You have a sense of it as a vivid enlightenment and knowledge that nothing can take from you because it comes from the soul. Your hopes and desires, on the other hand, bring in choice. You hope it is this or that. It would be nice if it were. But is it? These are personality questions. The cue is: what is the nature and intensity of this experience? Is it something I would like to be true or is it something I know to be true? If it is intuition, you will know. There is no question.

When we have a conflict between two services in our lives, is it possible that this is a conflict between the purpose of the soul and the purpose of the Master, or does the conflict simply come from the desires of the personality?
In every case, it is to do with the desires of the personality. Whenever there is conflict you have personality expression, because conflict is the result of the desire principle itself. Where you have desire, you will necessarily have conflict, because then you have a choice. Whenever you have a choice, you have conflict. Choice makes conflict.

The Master's purpose and the purpose of the soul are always identical. They are never in conflict. The Master works with the soul of the individual. He is very rarely interested in the personality expression. The soul is in the Master's group, not the personality. The Master is the centre of a group of souls. Necessarily, the soul's task in its expression as the man or woman is to carry out the Master's purpose which is, of course, the manifestation of His individual part of the Plan as it has been ascertained by Hierarchy.

Is there such a thing as action that is not the result of choice, of thought?
That is a Krishnamurti question if ever there was one. I believe there is, it is the thing we were talking about: action which is the result of a spontaneous awareness of the Self, of your own being manifesting. It is like when a painter creates a painting. On the physical plane he makes choices as to colour, thickness of paint and so on, but the creative act of painting, the concept, is choiceless. If it is not choiceless, it is not creative.

Most of our action is uncreative, reactive, the result of choice. We make choices to do this or that. Many people, caught up in the dilemma of choice, do nothing. I remember as a boy at school how night after night I would come home with hours of homework to do. But at the same time I longed to paint. I could not paint because I had all that homework. And I would not do the homework because I wanted to paint. I was caught in that dilemma; night after night I would stand in front of the fire doing absolutely nothing. True action, choiceless action, is when the soul acts from Itself, spontaneously and creatively, without any kind of thought. There is no need for thought when the soul's action takes place. When there is thought you have a dilemma, you have choice — and tension and conflict. The result is often inertia and stress.

How do the current structures of society inhibit the impulse to serve?
I do not think they do at all. The impulse to serve can find expression within the most unbeneficial structures. In fact, the impulse to serve is needed all the more where the structures themselves are unspiritual. The current structures are deeply unspiritual and this only makes the need to serve more pressing. Even in the coming cycle of Aquarius when things will change tremendously, when harmony and peace will generally prevail in the major sense throughout the world — service will be needed. Service is the mainspring of life. If

service is the impulse of God involving Itself in all that It creates, that which it creates needs to serve. It cannot be otherwise, because the impulse of Being is service. There is no level throughout cosmos where service is not the purpose of life. The greater always serves the lower. The Christ washing the feet of the disciples is a symbol for that fact of service. The greater in spiritual stature serves the lesser because it can serve the lesser.

I do not think, therefore, that the current structures inhibit the impulse. They might inhibit a good working out of that service. There is another point: how far should we look for results in our service activity? How should we measure the value of our service in relation to the results which it has? I would say not at all. Service is not true service if it is done with an end result in mind. That is motivated choice. In this whole question of service, motive is crucial.

How will the structures in the New Age be different in this regard?
It may be that the structures in the New Age will allow more people to serve in that they will enhance the ability of people to act as souls. What inhibits millions from living and acting as souls is that they are so taken up in the drudgery of finding the wherewithal to live, something to put in their family's mouths, that they have not the time or energy to turn their minds to the soul or its needs. It does not exist for them. What does exist is grinding poverty, the necessity to work constantly, to beat the body, to create or earn that little bit of sustenance which will keep their family alive. And they do not always succeed. So they go through the pain of children dying year after year. That is life for millions of people. That prevents them from engaging in a life of service. Their service is dedicated to their bodies, like animals, to feed them, and to their family, to feed it and keep it together.

As these realities are changed, service too will change. Service will be oriented, more and more, to the activity of the soul. Not in saving millions of people from starving who should not be starving at all. Nobody needs to starve; we know that, the food is there. But once the food is available, the service changes. It is the same service, but it changes to meet different priorities: number one priority, feeding the starving millions; number two priority, saving the planet from destruction. The focus of the service will change but service itself as a soul activity cannot change. It is always the same.

How to Recognize the Call to Service

How do we recognize the call?
You have to be aware. The call will come if it is coming. If you are aware, you will recognize it, but you will not necessarily recognize it as a call from your soul or, later, a Master. During sleep, a Master may give you a mental impression, and you may forget about it entirely. During the course of the next few days, weeks, months or years, you might think you would like to do something for the world, to serve in some way. You see that there is such anguish, such need in the world for your help that you cannot but respond. That may be all that you are doing in answering this call. You just feel that you have to do something. As soon as you do serve, the Master knows that you can be depended on to do it. If you do it rather well and objectively, impersonally, He will give you, perhaps, a stronger call, and again you will respond. You will be given more and more until you fulfil the life of service — as a way of life.

How do we find out which is one's own way of service?
People imagine that they have their own very special, distinguishable, way of serving. That is why they have not found it yet. They are still looking for that which does not exist. There is seldom one way of service for an individual. There is a world in travail needing to be served. There are different approaches and different departments in life and you can serve in any of them. It would have been rather a waste of Winston Churchill's talents to work in the Theosophical Society. On the other hand, one cannot imagine H.P.Blavatsky as the head of a government. There are obvious choices, depending on one's personality structure.

Find what attracts you in terms of a direction or department. Most people are not stupid. Normally they do not do things which are totally alien to them. They may do, but usually not for long. What attracts you and holds your attention — work to which you give time and energy for a long period — will probably be along your own natural line. A magnet attracts things to it because it is magnetic. Work, groups, activity, attract because they are magnets; you are attracted by the force of the magnet. If it is your magnet, you will work confidently within it. If it is not your magnet, you will know. It is self-regulating.

How do you choose intelligently between going the hard way or taking the line of least resistance?
Always choose the hard way. Then, if it is not too hard, it will become the line of least resistance. Always do what you do not like doing. I am exaggerating, of course. Everyone likes to do what they like to do but try doing what you do not like doing for a change. Then you are probably doing the right thing. Doing what you do not like doing is difficult, but that way you grow.

Masters search for the light of the disciples in the world. The Master tests the disciple and judges if he or she can receive a mental stimulus. How does a Master do that, personally or by telepathy?
It could be in sleep. During the course of sleep the Master might give a mental impression. This is the Science of Impression. You may think of telepathy as the sending and receiving of thoughts, ideas and so on from one mind to another. That is true. But the Science of Impression is a very big science and telepathy is just one aspect of it. The Masters put a thoughtform, energized by Their thought, into the mind of the disciple. This takes place on the higher mental planes. The mind works in the realm of ideas. The brain acts as a computer to rationalize and deal with them in a practical way.

There are many different ways in which the Masters work. They may simply galvanize the person by stimulating one of the chakras, the heart or throat chakra for instance. They may

665

give a more or less precise mental impression. They may do both of these things. It depends on the individual. If the person is evolved enough, and the time factor is right, They may call that person during sleep to Their office to suggest a certain action or activity. The person then wakes up forgetting it entirely. The impression acts as a suggestion, and the person begins to find an interest in that particular line of work.

Maintaining the Resolve to Serve

How can we best maintain and carry the intensity of our resolve into active service?

You know better than I how you personally can do this. It is a personal question; everyone has to answer it for him or herself. All I can say is: Have faith. Work from faith. Engender through faith the ardour and the sustained rhythm of work which makes service service. As the Master said, service is not service in fits and starts. It is sustained rhythm and steadfastness which creates the gravity and therefore the magnetism of the service.

There is a statement I found among some papers which was dictated to me by my Master in 1972 or 1973. It says: "Radiation: movement outwards, pulsation in form of wave or ray, light emitting. That quality of life which forms a bond between two forms. Magnetic service: that quality of life which is forever changing its attitude to itself, but not to others who may happen to come into focus of its scrutiny. Quality of service being such as to draw others to itself. A shining example. Service which leaves a stain or mark on reality, motivating works therefrom."

The aim should be so to intensify your service in that sustained ritual which we call rhythm that it becomes magnetic. It attracts others to it. It leaves a stain or mark on outer events and motivates others towards various work. Magnetic service is the result of a sustained rhythm and a service done with ardour. Then necessarily it radiates.

About magnetic personality the Master says: "That quality of life which exerts a pull on events and things as well as on others. That quality of personality which attracts the love and/or attention of others precisely through its radiating power."

This question of service is linked with the question of Being. You cannot ever get away from Being. Service, true service in the occult sense of the word, is the result of the expression of Being as the soul comes into manifestation. The person becomes more and more aware of the soul as his or her true nature. As you gain that sense (it is not an intellectual insight), that moment-to-moment awareness of yourself as a soul, the service naturally, without even thinking about it, becomes radiating, magnetic, attracts others to it, has an effect on other people's lives and even on events. It makes a stain or mark on reality which awakens others to do work stemming from that stimulus.

"How can we best maintain and carry the intensity of our resolve into active service?" By being who we are. By maintaining our sense of Beingness. By becoming less totally centralized. The beauty of service, as the key to the evolutionary process, is that it decentralizes. Almost everyone senses themselves as being at the centre of the universe but some rays have this glamour more than others. This is the result of the desire principle and shows how the personality experience differs from that of the soul. It is the personality which senses itself as the centre of the universe and demands that everything it desires should be fulfilled now. It feels that everyone else is there to serve its needs. It sounds extremely selfish and greedy and of course it is. The heresy is that we are separate. That sense of separateness is the big lie that everyone experiences. There is a ring around us: they out there and we here at the centre of the universe.

The beauty of service, when undertaken totally and seriously, is that it begins to break down that barrier; it begins to remove that sense of separateness because you identify with whatever it is you are serving. You identify with the needs of the world, the pain and suffering of the world. As you do that, you enlarge that identification until you are embracing the whole world.

667

That is the consciousness of the Master. He does not have any sense of being a separate personality. The Masters have unbelievably vivid and radiating personalities, but Their personality is totally God-infused. My Master always calls Himself "Master" to me, personally. I translate that as 'I', but He never says "I," because He has no sense of 'I'. It does not exist in His consciousness.

Our memory gives us the sense of separation. We carry the memory of everything that has happened to us, so far as we can remember. That gives us a sense of who we are. Of course, it is not who we are but our memory of what has happened to us. It is the memory of what we did, what we ate, who our children are.

All of that is memory. It is not who we are. It is a thoughtform which all of us carry around in our mind of who we are. That is false; it is all dead, past time. None of it is real at this particular moment.

The only thing which is real at this particular moment is who we are. When that is dwelt in, when that is the moment-to-moment experience, the person radiates, is magnetic; the person serves. How can we maintain it? Meditate more, transmit more, and with a better focus.

As the years go by with the Reappearance work, we tend to run out of steam. What must we do to build up steam again? What is involved in keeping our ardour functioning constantly at a high level and not becoming fanatical about it?
What must we do to build up steam again? Get together. Have a conference. Get a great inflow of the energy of Maitreya.

What is involved in keeping our ardour functioning constantly at a high level? Just hard work — keeping in touch with the Self as the soul and allowing that moment-to-moment Presence to dictate your life. If you do it, you will find that its energies will flow into you. If you do your meditation in a regular way and your Transmission Meditation in a focused way, you will not run out of steam so easily. Nobody goes in a constant, straight line, but you will find your dips will be less deep. Your heights may also be less high. You get a better, sustained rhythm of work. Sustained rhythm is better than high peaks and low nothings at all.

People are afraid of becoming fanatical. The danger really is not fanaticism but inertia. It is very difficult for groups who have not directly experienced Maitreya to go on year after year maintaining a high degree of activity around His appearance. It is true that Transmission Meditation and your personal meditation help to sustain a high level of commitment. But it does require faith. If you do not have faith, if it is simply hope and belief that Maitreya is here, against all the odds, then you are working against the grain. You have to know.

If you do not have a personal experience that Maitreya is real and is here, then it must be difficult. But, again, there is more and more evidence that He is here. The outer signs are growing every week so it becomes easier than it ever was before to accept this as a hypothesis and work as if it is true (which is all you can do in the first place). It is really a question of addressing yourself to your self and saying: "What do I really want to happen about this?" If this makes sense to you, if it has for you the ring of truth (even though you do not know with utter certainty) and you take it as a hypothesis and work on that hypothesis, the events themselves, the experience itself, proves to you that this is true. You find the energy of Maitreya flowing through you and there is no gainsaying that.

How does one deal with the conditioning of the mind from the cradle which inhibits the answer to the call for service?
That is another way of saying: "How do I become less lazy?" There is only one way of becoming less lazy. Stop being lazy! It is like sea bathing. No one hates bathing more than I do. You would never catch me in the water! But the odd time when I have gone in the water I do not plunge in. I put one foot in and test it. Then I find that the cold goes off a bit, it is not too bad. So I go in another inch and put two feet in, the water gradually getting up to about the knees. I stop there for a long, long time. I stand around looking interested. Gradually, I bend my knees in prayer and kneel down. That brings the water up to about the middle. It is appalling! Terrible! But I usually persevere. I

am not known often to have come out without getting wet all the way up. As you bend down and kneel, you find, willy-nilly, the water comes up high. You gasp and say: "Oh God, why am I doing this? I do not need to do it! It is only because I am on holiday! This is a holiday? Oh, God, give me work! Give me service! Do not give me holidays!" Then you do a quick plunge and say: "Good! Out!" A brisk rub down. I did it!

You can do it slowly or you can plunge in. You know those who just run in? In they go, just like that. You can choose your way to get round this inertia, this resistance, the conditioning of the mind. Just get in bit by bit until you forget that you are lazy. You actually begin to enjoy it. The worst thing is doing nothing. Standing at the edge does not work.

I know I can serve more. But how can I know when I am forcing it or when I am being lazy?
Serve more and find out. If you are being lazy, everyone around you will know. If you ask them, they will tell you. If you can do more, do more. You would be forcing it when you are becoming over-fatigued and when you are losing your interest in the work. When the work loses its appeal, it probably means you are forcing it or are working along the wrong lines — for emotional satisfaction rather than because it needs to be done.

These are the questions you have to ask yourself: do you feel emotion about it? If you are emotional about it, you become exhausted, burned out.

How can we overcome inertia in order to serve? How do you bring in the will to overcome inertia?
You overcome inertia by bringing in the will. The action of service breeds action, and brings in the energy to do it. It is a self-regulating process.

That is not to say you do not get tired. It is a question of regulation, of being able to relax, of 'sitting lightly in the saddle', not going to extremes.

Service is a function, an action, of the soul, but the soul has no desires of itself. It places its will, its purpose, in the hands of its reflection, the man or woman. It supplies the energy to do it. But if the person does not serve, there is inertia. How do you bring in the will? The will should be available if you are serving, which is the impulse of soul. You automatically bring in the will to do the service. If there is inertia, then it is not service but the desire principle at work.

If you are really serving, the will energizes the act of service in a dynamic way (we are talking about dynamic service, real help to the world, not half an hour of Transmission once a week). If there is inertia, it means that the impulse is a desire and not an intention. That which you intend automatically brings in the will. It is the intention of the will that invokes the energy to carry out the task. Keep at the task until it is completed. If your motive is wrong, you will feel inertia. If your action is unintelligent, you may overdo it to a point where inevitably you get inertia. Fatigue sets in, especially on the emotional plane.

If the desire principle is strong, the person may want to do everything. That kind of over-enthusiastic person, afire with what they feel is the ardour of service, which is really an emotional high, burns out. The result is inertia in which they can do nothing. This happens often with 6th-ray and 4th-ray types. The 4 and 6 tend to have a powerful, passionate desire to do the best, the ideal. They can always be fired for a time. The problem is keeping that fire going. If the fire is based only on emotion, inevitably it will burn out. If it is based on the will of the soul, it is inextinguishable because the soul itself is inexhaustible. You simply have to keep in touch with your soul to keep from suffering inertia.

People along the 1-3-5-7 line often lack easy contact with the soul. This can lead to inertia through lack of faith. The 2-4-6 types tend to suffer from inactivity. You have to solve the problem by bringing the two together — keeping in touch with the soul, and therefore with the energy of the soul, and actually working, in a self-regulatory way, with balance and a sense of proportion. I know people who take on everyone's work in order to be indispensable, but no one is indispensable. People want to be absolutely indispensable. That is a glamour and should be recognized as such. You do not have to kill yourself in working for Hierarchy and serving the world. Once you are dead, you are of no use to anyone.

Motive for Service

How important is motive in service?

It is tremendously important. Here is a quotation from Master DK: "Motive: all important. Obey the inward impulses of the soul." He goes on to say: "It is no easy or flattering task to find oneself out and to discover that perhaps even the service we have rendered and our longing to study and work has had a basically selfish origin, resting on a desire for liberation, or a distaste for the humdrum duties of every day. He who seeks to obey the impulses of the soul has to cultivate an accuracy of summation and a truthfulness with himself which is rare indeed these days."

Motive, then, is all important. If the desire is for a result, the motive is wrong, not impersonal. Impersonality is all-important in service. Of course, everyone's motive is mixed. Let us accept that. There is probably no one under the degree of a Master whose motive is 100 per cent impersonal and free from all selfish motive. There are degrees of impersonality; recognize the degree but do not let it inhibit your service.

I heard recently of a member of one of the groups who had suddenly realized that her motive in service was tarnished. For years she had worked, thinking that she was doing it from the highest possible motive: for the Reappearance work, spreading Transmission Meditation, for the externalization of the Hierarchy, working with the Masters and so on. Then she realized that part of it was personally motivated, to do with some ambition, or in competition with others in the group. That happens in every group. Everyone's motive will be more or less mixed. The thing is to recognize it, measure the degree and try to eradicate the selfish element in it. But to give up the work itself would not be intelligent. Hardly anyone in the world, I imagine, serves with totally impersonal motive.

Impersonality in group relations is absolutely essential. It is one of the qualities that must be built in before group initiation can take place. People seem not to understand about impersonality. Most people in most groups aim at creating loving relationships in the group but if they do that instead of aiming for impersonality, they will never create loving relationships, nor will they ever gain impersonality. They are putting it the wrong way around. They should be aiming at impersonality. When their aim and activity is impersonal, they open naturally the doors of love. Through these floodgates love can flow through the group. When everyone in the group is working impersonally, the love of the soul can manifest. When groups are working at creating loving relationship, it is only the personality desire principle which is being expressed. This principle creates the barriers in the group and makes it impossible for individuals on the different rays to work together. Aim first and foremost at impersonal work, impersonal group relations. The love that you think is love is personality desire. Become impersonal and love will constantly, and instinctively, flow. Then it can be expressed as it is, a soul quality, and not in a personality owning of another personality, or in the cliques which are formed in many groups. This is very important.

How can we distinguish where our motives come from — if it is a soul impulse or an astral desire?
What are you getting out of it? That is the question. Is this fulfilling your need for companionship or comradeship? You do not like to be alone so you work with other people. There are all sorts of motives for joining groups and carrying out group activity. You can call it service if that is what you are doing, but the motive of a lot of people is really for companionship. They like working with other people; most people do not like working alone. We say any task shared makes it lighter. They like to sit around a table and talk while they are doing their work. There is nothing wrong with that, of course, but that is what they enjoy. It is not the activity of service they enjoy. It is the companionship, the sense of shared activity. That is an emotional satisfaction which has nothing to do with the role of service, *per se*. I am not saying that if that is

673

what you get then you should not do it; that it is not service. It may well be service but not necessarily so. This is the way to recognize it: what gives you satisfaction? You will find that what gives you satisfaction is the satisfaction of your emotional desires. When you dislike it, when you really are rubbed the wrong way, when you would only be doing it because it is service and because you are an individual dedicated to service, then it is probably coming from the soul. If you do not like it, it is the soul.

What is the role of intention and motive in service?
The intention to serve is an action of the will. The will, properly understood, is a function of the soul. The question might arise: what is the difference between will and desire? There is all the difference in the world between will and desire. Will is intention, purpose. Desire is the satisfaction of an impulse, craving, or need.

DK says: "Out of duty, perfectly performed, will emerge those larger duties which we call world work. Out of the carrying of family responsibilities will come that strengthening of our shoulders which will enable us to carry out those of the larger group." This is to do with meeting the responsibilities of life and those of life in service.

Rhythm

How does one develop a wise rhythm of service with respect to the issues of ardour, fanaticism and inertia?
The thing to avoid is fanaticism. Fanaticism is ugly and destructive because it is against the Law of Life. The whole movement of life is towards synthesis, oneness and unity. Fanaticism, by its very nature, destroys that unity. It creates division and separations and is therefore against life. It is to be welcomed that people have different views of life. That gives variety. Life would be very boring if we all thought, felt and experienced in exactly the same way. We would be one person, clones. The fanatic wants everyone in the world to agree with him or her. The fanatic cannot accept the differences between people, the different ways of thinking, different types of mind,

approaches to reality. All of this is natural because we are individuals.

Individuality is a major fact in life; it is essential. It is what gives us our sparkle, the thing we enjoy about each other. But if you are fanatical, you cannot stand that difference, the fact that someone believes this, someone else thinks that, while someone else hopes for such and such. That makes the fanatic angry and fearful, because if other people have different views, perhaps his view is not the right one. Of course his view is the right one, the one and only view. He cannot accept that anyone could have any other view. That is the ugly and destructive nature of fanaticism. The thing to strive for is common sense. Have the enthusiasm and fiery ardour but not the fanaticism.

If you set yourself a rhythm, you can overcome inertia. Inertia is that state in which you have to make a major effort to start up cold every morning. If you are in a rhythm of work, there is nothing to start up, the engine is ticking over all the time. We all know that if you want a job done, give it to a busy person because that person is already involved in a hundred different ways in work. His or her engine is ticking over so fast that another bit of work is neither here nor there. But give it to the person whose "work" is the study of, for instance, the Alice Bailey teachings, or whatever, and the inertia is so total you will wait six months before you realize that they are not going to do anything about it because they are too busy studying the Alice Bailey teachings.

Inertia can be overcome by establishing a rhythm and keeping to it. Some rays find this more difficult than others. The 4th ray has what DK calls a balance of rajas and tamas — rajas being fiery and tamas inert. In the 4th-ray type these are "curiously balanced". The 4th-ray type tends to establish a rhythm, not so much day to day, but of cycles in which are smaller rhythms. There might be a cycle of intense activity followed by a period of lying fallow for a month or two, and then another phase of intense activity. In the period of activity there is a tremendously heightened, sustained action. It is as if the 4th-ray type needs a period to absorb, renew and charge up the batteries before it sets off again in this very intense period of work and activity. Others might have a more staccato type of rhythm.

Could you address the difference between rhythm that leads to expansion and service versus repetition which leads to crystallization and inertia? This seems to be an inherent problem in group work with rhythm.

The basis of all of this is common sense. Common sense is rather rare in individuals and groups. I am always amazed at the lack of common sense in the running of individual groups. It seems to me that to work correctly you need not only intelligence but common sense. Your intelligence must be correctly directed. You need to realize that you are working with people, not against people. You would think that would be easy to see, but obviously it is not. I meet with groups all the time who seem to find that a major problem. They cannot work together because they have little common sense. Their intelligence gets in the way of their common sense. Of course, it is not really intelligence in that case, but cleverness, bigotry or pigheadedness. It is the glamours of their rays rather than intelligence.

The intelligent way is to begin with the premise that everyone is right, is sharing a common purpose, and everyone involved in the work sincere. No one has the monopoly of intelligence and wisdom. Different rays bring different types of intelligence to bear on the group work. This, if understood, makes for correct group integration and mutual service. If that is not understood, you get the dominance of one or other individual over the rest of the group. That is the very antithesis of group work but I am afraid it is the kind of activity which goes under the heading of group work in many parts of the world. That group might be very effective on the physical plane — producing books, magazines, pamphlets, or whatever — but as a group they are in total disarray because they have no common sense, only what looks like intelligence.

Common sense leads to that expansion of group work which enhances service and induces a rhythm. Rhythm produces the consistency of work which is needed to do the task well. Otherwise it will be haphazard — sometimes good, sometimes mediocre, sometimes, perhaps, terrible. When this happens, you get a distaste for the work. That brings in inertia; inertia begins to crystallize the whole thing.

Inertia comes from a lack of the sense of hope, direction and purpose. Where that is missing, you get the malfunctioning of the group. I think it is too early in the lives of these groups to talk about crystallization, but inertia is a factor in a great many groups. Every group, to some extent, has that problem.

Do groups have soul cycles of inwardly- and outwardly-directed activity the way individuals do? If so, is it important for the group to recognize this rhythm and devote time to group study and contemplation as well as the outward tasks?
The answer to the first question is yes. Groups do have soul cycles of inwardly- and outwardly-directed activity as do individuals, but it is not, to my mind, important for the group to recognize this rhythm. It is important for the group to establish a rhythm of some kind. Most groups will give any amount of time to contemplation and study, but what they find difficult is to get on with the outward tasks. Most people in these groups are in good touch with their souls. What does not come so easily is relating that soul awareness to the task at hand, which in our case is the work for the Reappearance. So you will probably spend enough time doing nothing without deliberately doing nothing.

Awareness and Hope

To what degree is awareness important in service?
Awareness is crucial, not only in service but in every single action you take in life. In fact, in every moment, awareness is the be-all and end-all of your reason for being here. You are in incarnation to grow in conscious awareness. That is what evolution is about. You cannot separate awareness in service from awareness in general. If the reason for being in incarnation is to grow in conscious awareness, then conscious awareness should be the governing factor in every single thing you do.

Maitreya has said that the Self alone matters. "You are that Self, an immortal Being." Our pain, our problems, our suffering is due to the fact that we identify with everything and anything other than the Self. So if the Self alone matters, awareness of the Self must be the most important thing we can achieve. Awareness of the Self is not something that we sit down and do for five or 10 minutes and then leave alone for the rest of the day. Awareness of the Self is an ongoing process from moment to moment because it is only from moment to moment that we can become aware of who we are. We cannot leave aside for twenty-three-and-a-half hours who and what we are, and for a half-hour concentrate on that. It does not make sense.

Awareness is a moment-to-moment experiencing, directly, spontaneously, of what is, what actually exists in you and outside you. What is the difference, if there is one, between that which is in you and that which is outside you? You can only become aware of this in a generalized awareness of what is. That is something which you cannot take lessons in but which you have to learn to do. This is really a roundabout way of saying that you have to learn to Be. Most people do not know how to Be. They know how to become; the life of most people, as a personality, is a process of becoming. That is inevitable for it is the process which goes on in creation, in what you are as a vehicle, for who you are. It is a stage in evolution.

Service is the result of who you are, not what you are. It is who you are that needs to serve, what you are is the vehicle for the service. It provides the time frame, the area, for the activity we call service.

To serve correctly, you have to do it with awareness. I am saying all this so as not to limit awareness just to service. It is a moment-to-moment experience of what is, of who you are. The closer you come to that awareness and the longer that you can hold on to it, the better the service will be — the more focused, the more correct, the more in line with the Plan of evolution of the One of Whom you are a reflection, Whom we call God.

This question is important in allowing me not to separate awareness in service from awareness in general. You cannot serve properly in an unaware way. If you are unaware, you cannot be serving. If you are unaware, you cannot really be living. Living is awareness. It is the experience of Being, here and now — not yesterday, not tomorrow, but here, now. This moment is where you are and alone is important. The past is not important. It is over, finished, done with. Let it go. The future has not yet come. How can you be concerned with it if it has not yet come? What is important and what you can be concerned with, the only thing of which you can be aware, is this moment in what we call time. If you are truly aware of this moment, you will find that time, too, disappears. Your service goes on as a steady movement outside time.

Can you in an occult way differentiate between belief and hope and give a clearer meaning of the words?
Hope is different from belief. Belief is a function of the mind. It is something which, on the mental level, appears to you to be true, valuable, magnetic, attractive — a set of ideas which together make an ideology in which you can believe. It seems to answer the problems of life, to provide answers to various questions which arise about the meaning, the purpose, of life and so on. That is a very different thing from hope.

Hope, I would say, is of two kinds: there is the hope which is a wish-fulfilling fantasy and is astral in nature. It can go a long way in sustaining the person in difficult circumstances. It is the kind of hope of Mr Micawber, a famous Charles Dickens character. He was always in dire straits, impecunious, but always living in hope, waiting "for something to turn up". That kind of hope is astral desire, and will take you, as it took him, through a whole book, but will not of itself do other than sustain your ability to live life from day to day.

Hope, in the more occult sense, is very different indeed. Hope is the realization of the inner connectedness of all things; of your life and your daily activity with the cosmic scheme of things. The awareness of who you are, that you are the Self — that gives you faith or hope. Faith and hope stem from the same inner, intuitive realization of who you are, that you are here for a purpose and that nothing on Earth can shake that. Nothing can obliterate life. You can kill the body, do all sorts of things to the outer, physical-plane life, but you cannot get rid of Being. Hope arises from a sense of your own Beingness. That is the sustaining quality which we call faith, the inner connection with the soul, a soul quality. As Maitreya Himself has said: "I am your Hope." (Message No. 10) It is the Christ Principle within us, the energy of evolution itself, connecting us with the whole cosmic outflow that He means when He says: "I am your Hope." When what He is, the embodiment of the Christ Principle, is in your heart, you have hope.

To have hope is to have complete faith in life. It does not mean to say that everything is going to go smoothly. It does not mean that on the outer, physical plane you will have a life of ease, and that when you want to contact the media they will immediately respond, and when you are telephoning people they will always be there and you will never have to try again. Many people think that if everything works easily and smoothly they are somehow on the right track. Following the line of least resistance is not necessarily the right way to live one's life. It is the art of choosing the right action in relation to the line of least, or of most, resistance which brings about the tension we call service: the fire, the ardour which true service has.

Service and Daily Responsibilities

How do relationships to one's spouse and children relate to one's service?
The disciple has to satisfy the needs of life — to earn a living, to pay correct due to family duties — and also to serve as a disciple. That is the problem for the disciple: to be in the world totally, relating to, accepting the world, accepting one's responsibility as a human being among all human beings, no better and no worse; accepting the human karma that goes with that; accepting life as it happens day to day, with nothing getting you down, nothing taking you too high, but with a

steady, even response to life, with as great an equanimity as you can achieve without aloof coldness. The aloofness of the disciple is the aloofness of the individual who is isolated in the mainstream of life. He has to recognize that he does not belong to himself, nor to his family and friends. He does not belong to his group but to the world. Because he belongs to the world, he also has the duty to relate to the world, and not to see himself as an isolated and super-human figure, serving the world from a higher plane. The disciple is not on a higher plane; the Master is on the higher plane. The disciple is living and working in the world as one of us.

How does one balance being a disciple, engaged in service therefore, with fulfilling personal responsibilities?
This is a question which every individual must solve for him or herself. The problem for disciples is that you have to do both. It is not either/or but finding a balance. How do you find a balance? By finding a balance. I am sorry, but only you know how you can personally find a balance between your life responsibilities as a husband or wife, mother or father, your profession, earning a living and so on, and the service of a disciple. Every disciple is responsible for all of that. Being a disciple does not free you from those day-to-day responsibilities. One of the great glamours of discipleship is the belief that it does. It is a question of recognizing and choosing between priorities. That produces balance.

People enter into service quite often to get away from humdrum activity, and responsibility. That is why you see people with their eyes turned up to heaven all the time, and an Alice Bailey book under one arm. These people are obviously very 'spiritual'. We can see it. Their service consists in reading Alice Bailey. Of course, it is not service at all, but glamour. Service is getting down to it, doing the everyday jobs in a rhythm that you can sustain, which will engage your energy, strength and concentration, but not to the point of totally overtaxing it. That is finding the right rhythm — getting the maximum out of yourself with some conservation of energy.

To have a reasonable rhythm you have to recognize priorities and learn to choose between even major priorities. Nobody can do everything. You have to choose that which is the most valuable to the Plan, to the task at hand, and do that as the number one priority. At the same time you have the responsibilities of life. It is not in talking to the media or sitting in Transmission Meditation that you take initiation. It is in life, and only in life, that you undergo the transformations in character, the purification of both motive and bodies which allow you to take initiation. We are responsible for our duties — the human responsibilities of family life, professional life and so on. All of that has to be met as fully as we can. At the same time we have the duty of service.

The problem for the disciple is that he is in the world, and yet, in a sense, he is not of the world. He has to maintain this double relationship: both feet totally in life, relating with everything and everyone that comes his way, learning to cope with all of that and at the same time maintaining an isolation, an inner sense of himself as a disciple, in the midst of that maelstrom. For a disciple, life is more difficult than for everyone else.

Imagine a great river in flood. Where the water goes between the supports of a bridge, it is unhindered, meets no obstacle. When it hits the supports, these take the full weight of the flood. The disciple is the support of the bridge and necessarily takes the impact, the strains and stresses of life itself. It is not easy to be a disciple. You have to find a balance. Nobody can tell you. You have to do it in your own way, from your common sense.

How do I keep the balance between my daily activities and service?
Use your sense of proportion. Look objectively at the 24 hours of the day, and ask: "How much more time can I give to my family, my work, my service activity and so on? How do I divide my time?" You can do this in an organized way, like an office clerk. Write it down and say: "I have this and this to do, this is what I would like to do. But there are only 24 hours.

How can I find more time? Less sleep? Instead of eight hours, six, or five or four? Then, perhaps, less time over meals. No one has to spend an hour and a half or two hours to eat a meal, especially when they eat four times more than they need. You could cut it down. Then cut the talking time by half, the time spent chatting needlessly on the telephone. The amount of time that everyone wastes throughout the day can be given to service. You can do this; it is perfectly possible. You have to use your common sense.

How can you recognize the right priorities within your daily work?
It is a question, again, of common sense. What works for the greatest good, the greatest good for the greatest number.

What is the relation between everyday work and the Plan?
The Plan works out in everyday life. It is not separate from life. The Plan is the Plan of evolution of all the kingdoms on this planet. That is working out on all planes, including the physical. We are talking about your job, your life on the physical plane. You have to earn money to live. This is one of the realities of the present political economic situation in the world. Some people have to work too hard to earn enough to live. Other people do not work hard enough to earn their money. Some earn too much, more than they need, and should give the rest away, which, mostly, they do not. Others do not earn nearly enough for what they do. There are all sorts of inequalities and anomalies. But you have to work to earn the money to live, to contribute to your community, your nation and so on. You have to fulfil your duty as a citizen, father, mother, whatever. There is no way you can be a real human being and not be involved in the world.

You have to realize that you are no different from anyone else. Many people go around with the feeling that somehow they are different. They are either better than other people or less good than other people. This is a fantasy, a glamour. They do not experience people accurately. I do not mean only as equals, but as the same stuff, the same nature. Of course, there are differences. We recognize these differences, but the differences are really differences of personality, flavour, education and so on. They are not differences of kind.

The human being is one being, the human soul one soul. We are all reflections of that; we are really one. That is a very important experience and revelation. It is probably the most important one we can make. It is the beginning of the experience of God. I do not think you can experience God fully, in an immediate and true sense, if you experience yourself as a separated human being. The nature of God is unity, there is no separation in God. You can experience aspects of God — the divine energies — revelations, light, but you cannot experience what it is to be God unless you experience yourself as the same as everyone else.

That is quite difficult, probably the most difficult thing to do. Some people do it very easily, spontaneously. They are lucky. But for other, especially educated, people — esotericists, for example, people who are interested in some arcane philosophy, teachings, or religion — that very speciality of thought, the very nature of that interest, tends to make them feel different. Many people have an inferiority complex, they feel they are less good than others, that everyone is better than they are. Equally wrong is when you feel you are better than everyone else, because neither is true.

There is no group which is somehow better than anyone else. Leave aside all question of degrees of initiation. Some people are more evolved than others: Masters are more evolved than fourth-degree initiates, who are more evolved than thirds, seconds and so on. But as human beings, everyone will become a Master, will be perfect. Some sooner, some later, that is the only difference. It is only a question of time. Outside the physical brain, there is no time, so who really is any different?

Maitreya says: "Know who you are and be who you are." I think He is saying the same thing in another way: experience yourself as exactly the same as every other person and see the barriers drop away — the barriers that make it impossible to reach others, to love, to work with, others.

There are other kingdoms, of course, but you are part of the human kingdom. That is not a separate part of the world which pertains to something called the Plan. The Plan is not about esotericism. Esotericism works with the Plan, but is not the Plan. The Plan is the working out of the process of evolution in the world as a whole. Whatever you do can be along the line of the Plan or it can be contrary, depending on how destructive you are. If you are constructive, it will be along the line of the Plan. If you are destructive, separative, it is against the Plan.

Why are so many disciples leading lives of very little outward achievement?
It is not necessary that they should show great outward achievement. Most of the people in the groups that I am associated with around the world are somewhere between 0.9 and around 2.0. Few are 2.0, fewer even than think they are, and none of them are very great in outward achievement. But many of them are at least as evolved as people we know as household names in the world. Often, world leaders, scientists, writers, poets, artists, very well-known people who have made quite an impact in some area or other, are no more evolved than some people in these groups. Yet no one has heard of them; it is not necessary that they should. This is because, in the main, these people have focused their activity on that which concerns them most, their soul expression. That is why they are involved in the Reappearance work while the big names are not.

In the main, the people in these groups are rather introverted to the soul and therefore intuitive. It is your intuition which tells you that Maitreya is in the world and that Hierarchy is externalizing. Therefore you respond to this message. It is not I who is making you do this. Your own soul is making you respond. I bring it to the notice of your mind and your soul tells you: "This is right, this is the truth." You get involved because your soul wishes you to get involved. That is why you are in incarnation at this time. You hear it from somebody, who hears it from somebody, and you get involved. Your intuition is alive because you are introverted to the soul. It does not mean that you are completely introverted and unable to work on the outer plane. People vary in their ability to do both; the initiate can do both. That is what you should cultivate.

What is meant by a 'practical mystic'?
A practical mystic is someone who is aware of the soul and its purpose, aware of being a soul, and who also realizes the needs of the physical plane, that the plans and purposes of the soul need expression on the outer plane. They are practical. The mystic element is that which relates the person to the soul. The practical is that which relates the soul purpose to the outer work. That is what the Masters need.

For a long time They have been dealing mainly with 6th-ray souls, whose vision of the Plan is brilliant, whose awareness of the soul is probably second to none, but whose practicality is almost totally lacking. The 6th ray cannot bring the vision down to the physical plane. That has been the experience of the last 2,000 years, the noble ideals have remained vague promises: the brotherhood of man; peace on Earth; goodwill to all men. Everyone uses these phrases at least once a year. Yet there is no peace on Earth or real goodwill to men. They are only ideals. But the quality of the 6th ray (which has dominated over the last 2,000 years) leads people to believe that if the vision can be seen, if it can be conceived at all, it is already there; the thought of it is the deed of it. It is not so. As Maitreya says: "Nothing happens by itself. Man must act and implement his will." (Message No. 31) The 6th-ray person has the desire, enthusiasm, vision, ideas, concepts, and ideals, but no will at all to put them into effect on the physical plane. They feel that just to conceive it is enough. It remains astral, just a felt idea. It has to be made practical. That is the difference between the mystic and the practical mystic.

Can or should one's vocation be service?
Yes, indeed. One's vocation can be service. It would be an ideal situation if it were. But if it is your vocation, you might

get involved in the conflict of self-aggrandizement, ambition and so on, which could come into it. If you were a member of a large international aid agency and were fighting for position, it could lead to some degree of conflict. The ideal thing is for your service and vocation to be the same; if you are an artist of any kind, it is. Art is a means of serving the world, but not of course the only means. There are degrees of service, and degrees of usefulness of the service. If you are a Leonardo da Vinci, what better could you do than be what you are?

What is the correct relationship between the personality and soul? What is the purpose of the personality? How does the personality serve the soul?
I think people should read Alice Bailey books like *The Soul and Its Mechanism* for example. There are whole books devoted to the soul and its relation to the personality and vice versa.

Briefly, the personality is the reflection of the soul on the physical plane. The vehicles — physical, astral and mental — are the equipment of the personality which the soul uses to experience its becoming in time and space. The purpose of the personality is to provide a vehicle for the soul to do that, because the soul cannot live at this level at its own vibration. The soul is on the causal level, vibrating at a very high frequency. Its nature is fire. The fire of the soul should be lit as a fire in the spiritual heart centre in the physical body. When it is, you can act with the dynamic will of the soul. The purpose of the soul is to create a vehicle or a series of vehicles through which it can act without any kind of limitation, without blockages, without any diminution of its spiritual energies.

How can a disciple deal with the pain and sadness he/she feels due to the injustice, hatred and delusion in the world?
That is a hard one for some people. They need to become more detached, more able to see the ills, identify with them, but not to the point of total submersion of their energy, their sense of balance. You have to gain a sense of proportion. You have to know that these ills are there, identify with them, meet them as far as you can, to the best of your ability, but with detachment.

You have to be detached, not from the ills themselves but from your reaction to them. That sense of sadness and pain is real and shows that your heart is alive and well and responding to human need. Serve the need and you will find that the pain and the suffering will gradually recede. You will become more dispassionate as you become more effective. A great deal of pain and suffering is caused by the feeling that you are inadequate, helpless.

*In **Share International** there is much talk about service. But what is actually meant by that? In a sense, does not everyone serve? A farmer, for instance, provides raw material for our survival. His motivation may simply be to earn a living and provide a comfortable life for his family. He may not really care whether anyone else also lives well. But in spite of his selfish motives he is serving people by providing food.* (March 1987)
The question is — would he continue to provide food if it did not benefit himself and his family? In other words, is he serving himself or the world? Service is altruistic action carried out at the behest of the soul. In a sense, of course, the questioner is right, but motive is crucial. Service is done for the benefit of the not-self, just because it is needed, and for no personal reason at all.

You keep saying "we" must do so-and-so. Who's the "we"? (May 1991)
You and me.

Yes, but what's to do? (May 1991)
What's to do? There is a whole world out there in a mess, it is obvious. There are 450 million people hungry and millions of them literally starving to death. We have to feed them, that is what we have to do. There is 10 per cent surplus of food in the world per capita, so there is no need for anybody, not one person, to be hungry or to starve. Put these two together, the food with the people, the mouths with the food, that is what we have to do. There is a whole world out there needing educating. There are educational facilities throughout the

developed world — very little in the developing world. Go and teach. Join in. Spend your energy, your money, your time in serving these needs — and be alive and happy.

When Maitreya appears, what kind of service will we be assigned if we want to serve the world with Him? Perhaps it depends on one's point of evolution, rays and life interest. Could you give us some examples of that service? (January/February 1989)
I think it is a mistake to think that people will be assigned specific kinds of service by Maitreya (or the Masters). The needs of the world will be addressed by all who wish to serve, each one finding his or her best means through experience, specialized skills or trial and error. The Masters are not going to take over the world and tell us what to do. That would be infringement of our free will. Certainly, however, our point in evolution, rays and life interest will govern the particular department(s) in which we might serve.

How important is the organization of one's own life — job, shelter, love in relationships — to accomplishing the appropriate service intended for the current incarnation? (November 1988)
It depends how serious we are about service. The questioner seems to suggest that there is a given amount of service delegated to us for each incarnation — the least we can get away with! There is no limit to the service that anyone may feel called upon to give; it is simply a question of the degree of dedication. If service comes first, these other things necessarily take second place.

Is it more important to change the world or to change oneself? (April 1989)
Maitreya says: "Until you have helped yourself you cannot help others." By the same token, you cannot significantly change the world until you have changed yourself; the world is the sum total of people and a changed world must be the sum total of changed people. The question is really one of degree, and the acceptance of the duty of service to the world while

daily working for inner change and greater awareness. As that awareness grows, so, too, does the capacity to influence the world in the direction of change.

There are those who are sincerely motivated to serve but have little to offer because they lack the will-power, courage, steadfastness, skills — to what extent can they offer service? Is it possible that such a person who has good intentions but finds it very difficult to put them into practice could be at a turning point in his development? Would such a person need several lives before being able effectively to serve others? (April 1987)

No one who is not a disciple is called upon to serve. To be a disciple means to be responding to the soul's need to serve and to be 'disciplined'. A disciple needs — and the true disciple demonstrates — will-power, courage, steadfastness, skill in action. No amount of 'sincere motivation' means anything without the demonstration of the desire to serve. In service, only action counts.

For the Christ and the Masters, the major problem is not the opposition of the forces of materiality but the inertia of the disciples and aspirants of the world. Were they to act in accordance with their professed ideals and motivation the world would quickly be transformed.

Is guilt about not serving enough an astral reaction best ignored or a somewhat distorted reminder from the soul about what we should be doing?

Sometimes it is one and sometimes the other. Guilt can be the voice of conscience saying: "It is a long time since you did anything useful. A long time, ages and ages, since you did anything worthwhile." On the other hand it could be astral glamour about not doing enough, the glamour of spiritual ambition. Set yourself a rhythm, a reasonable, sustained rhythm of service, and then forget about it. Do not keep saying: "Am I doing enough?" Do not worry, you will have more than enough to do. If you are really serving, you will have more than you can possibly do.

If the Masters present an opportunity of service to a disciple, and the disciple does not fulfil the task, would the Masters present the same task to another or other disciples?

Yes, indeed. They look around and, if there is someone suitable to do the same job, they would pass it on to them. If a task is given to an individual or group (it is often given to a group), and they do not fulfil the task or go too much off the correct line, or get bogged down in organization — as has happened to many societies — or in personal quarrelling and bad group relations, or in too personal group relations, the Masters might withdraw the energy (and therefore the stimulus) behind the person or group, and pass it on to another. This happens all the time.

Groups are formed and given certain work to do. They may do it for a bit and then fail. People do not seem to realize this but a great many experiments by Hierarchy fail, come to very little or nothing. It is the nature of an experiment to be open to success or failure (because it is an experiment) and the Masters experiment all the time. You cannot know, precisely, in advance. A Master will know the probabilities, but even They do not know exactly how well a particular individual or group will carry out a task, what the benefit will be to the Hierarchical Plan, to the world. They cannot know totally until the task has been completed or has failed. Many experiments and trials have failed — not because the Masters set the wrong tasks or chose the wrong groups, or did not present it properly, or did not give enough energy; it is simply that the groups or individuals to whom the task was entrusted failed. They failed the test; usually, they were not able to work together.

One of the problems of all groups is how to work together. Many people can work for a group but cannot work with a group. It is a very different thing — to work for a group, in the group, with the group, and to work for a group while remaining psychologically separate, outside the group, never being able to sacrifice one's own little ideas for group consensus; always being the one who knows better than the rest of the group put together. There is someone like that in most groups. We all know who they are; the trouble is that they do not know who they are.

With respect to service, the Master says if there is a desire for a result, then the motive is wrong. I can understand this in certain circumstances. If you are trying to heal someone who is ill it may not actually be in their best interest to get well at that time. And if you give someone information they cannot accept, it does not matter; they must progress at their own pace. But surely if I were to give bread to a starving child it would be because I wanted the result of ending starvation and suffering. I must have misunderstood something. Could you clarify? (September 1992)

It is a question of acting with detachment, not of not acting at all. Of course, you feed the starving child because it is the right thing to do, not for any result that might accrue to you. It is a question not so much of desiring, or not desiring, a result, as of being detached from the result — doing what needs to be done because it needs to be done whether you succeed or fail.

I'm not Major, I'm not Bush, so how do we influence the Bushes and the Majors? (May 1991)

You do it through your vote, through your voice; you stand up and be counted and make a noise. You demonstrate. You say: "We need to help the others." Not "We want more of this," but "We need them to have more." At every election you say: "What is your attitude to the Third World — what are you going to do about it? If you want my vote you must do this and this and this." You have to participate, to see it as your responsibility, every one of us, because hunger will not go — these problems will never be addressed — unless each one sees it as his own individual responsibility, not someone else's. So long as we can see it as someone else's responsibility — the government's, or the international community's, or these rich people over there — nothing will be done. We are all part of humanity and all share the burden of responsibility. Who pulled down the Berlin Wall? Who overthrew Ceausescu? Not the Eastern Bushes and Majors but the ordinary people. Join with others and become strong and influential.

As soon as you see it as your responsibility you are galvanized, and when enough people are galvanized things happen. That is why the Berlin Wall came down, why suddenly *glasnost* became a possibility in the Soviet Union — it was not because one man, Mr Gorbachev, said: "Let there be *glasnost*." Not at all. He focused a demand which was rising up all the time.

Freedom is a natural state, but it has to be freedom for everyone. Millions of people in the world do not have freedom. Nearly one-fifth of the world's population, 900 million people, live in conditions of, officially, 'absolute poverty'. If we put up with that then we are simply being complacent and doing nothing at all. What can we do? We can refuse to put up with that. But I cannot tell you personally what you should do, that is up to you. Everyone, from their own background, their own nature, will find a whole big world out there waiting to be saved. If you take one step out into the arena you will find millions of people who think exactly like you, who have exactly your concerns. You are not alone. Millions of people in the world want to change the world. They have to get together.

Is it better to move around the world and live in another country or to live where you were born? (July/August 1991)
It depends on individual karma and destiny. Most advanced people today work in groups and very often these groups are formed of people from many parts of the world, coming together in one (new) place.

Transmission Meditation and Reappearance Work

Would you comment on the solutions to the following inertia: fear of ridicule regarding Reappearance work?
This fear is to do with sensing yourself to be at the centre of the universe. If you are at the centre of the universe, you will want to maintain that position. How can you maintain that position if you are ridiculed? Ridicule threatens your sense of yourself. But if you have no inflated sense of yourself there is nothing to ridicule. Nobody likes being ridiculed but who or what are they ridiculing? Only this personality expression,

nothing else. But that is a transitory and imperfect expression of a great spiritual truth, the Soul. If you know yourself as that, then what can ridicule do to you? Nothing. It cannot change you. It cannot hurt you because there is nothing to hurt. You are what is unhurtable, unchangeable by anything at all. Ask yourself: "Who is afraid of being ridiculed?" Cease to identify with the fear. Realize that you, the Soul, cannot be afraid. You are not that fear. Separate yourself from the fear and you will not fear ridicule or anything else for that matter. There is only one fear. It is just fear, whether of ridicule or anything else.

How does one deal with the resistance to service, selfishness which cannot be ignored?

Resistance to service is, usually, the dislike in certain types of the continuous activity, the chores, the humdrum, which constitutes much of service. Most people in the groups like the idea of service — especially for the Reappearance of the Christ because they think that it is important and would love to see the Christ. They want a better world; their aspiration, their hearts, their emotions, are activated by it. But when it comes down to it, they do not like the day-to-day, humdrum activity entailed: stuffing envelopes, licking stamps, taking parcels to the post, collating material. They like to talk, to be the representatives of the group, the ones who speak to the media about the Reappearance. Usually, the least fitted choose themselves for these categories: the least fitted to speak, the most opinionated, with their own, special, pet theories about it, think that they are peculiarly gifted to speak because they do a lot of talking. They are usually the very worst people to speak to the media. On the other hand, there are groups who think that only one or two key representatives should be allowed to speak to the media. This, of course, is nonsense. It is really an infringement of other people's free will and is a colossal arrogance.

For some of us, there is a process going on which diminishes the appeal of Transmission Meditation and the work for **Share International**. *There are individuals who appeal to their need, to them. This brings up questions like: Should I serve them (the* *people who are appealing) or the group? Are my priorities right? Am I not moving away from the group? This problem concerns people who have been practising Transmission Meditation for years.*

Transmission Meditation, being so scientific, is of more value to you and the world than any other thing you do. But if you are only aligned for three or four minutes out of an hour, I can understand if it seems limited. It is boring if you are not aligned. You have to be aligned, have to learn to keep your attention up. It can become the natural, continuous state of automatically holding your attention at the ajna centre. That is what you should be aiming for. Instead of whatever it is you are doing for the other 57 minutes of the hour, you should be focusing at the ajna centre. Doing it in a sharp, aware, intelligent way, not in a habitual way. That is why it loses its flavour.

Everyone, when they start something new, can stand 57 minutes of boredom, for the three minutes in which they feel this alignment. But to go on doing so is boring. You have to lengthen the time of alignment. It is better to transmit for one hour and be really aligned for that hour, than to sit for six hours in which you are aligned for only three minutes in each hour. You are transmitting for 60 minutes in the one case and 18 minutes in the other. Learn to keep the alignment — make that your purpose in doing the next Transmission Meditation. Resolve to use your will. Resolve that you will sit the whole time keeping your attention at the ajna centre. If you do this regularly and consistently, you will find that you can do it and your Transmission will improve enormously.

The questioner says: "There are individuals who appeal in their need to them. This brings up the question: Should I serve them or the group?" People come with needs and ask you to help them and you say: "Should I help them or should I serve the group?" That is, I think, a false choice, a glamour. I do not think that is actually the case. It may be in a particular instance, but it is not consistently the case.

This is self-deception. There is no group of people appealing to them so often, so consistently, that they cannot continue with their group work. I do not believe it for a minute. They are using that as an excuse to rationalize their growing distaste for the group work, for working for *Share International*, or for Transmission Meditation because they are becoming emotionally burnt out. This process of being burnt out is inevitable if your approach is based on desire. If, in the beginning, your desire is satisfied, you will go on working marvellously. But no one can go on with that kind of emotional high for ever. It burns out. You have to replace it with the will of the soul. That cannot burn out. If this question is actually true, what is happening is that these people are only emotionally focused on the work, and are beginning to burn out. It is a phase. Look once again at what is actually happening. Look at yourself and see if what I am saying is not true. If it is, relax and see it as a phase, and realize that it will change. As you become more focused you will certainly get more out of the Transmission and it will stop losing its appeal. If you regulate your time better you will find time for helping people and for the group. Who is to draw the line and say that that is service you may do and that is service you should not do? You have to use common sense and answer appeals as they come.

Won't people generally be sufficiently motivated in their own hearts to serve that they have relatively little need of divine energies made available through Transmission Meditation? (January/February 1988)
The energies which Transmission Meditation make available are for the benefit of the world as a whole and only incidentally for the practitioner of Transmission Meditation. It is a service for the world to help transform the present unspiritual structures into those conforming to the purpose of the Planetary Logos.

Lately I have a burning desire to clearly define my path. How can I speed this up and focus more? (November 1988)
The answer to such questions is always the same: meditation and service provide the surest path. Transmission Meditation combines both and is a 'forcing process', a 'hothouse'.

If the creation of a service group requires a considerable amount of finances, must they come by economic means, or donations, or also by winning the national lottery by spiritual intervention? (April 1989)

Groups must finance their activities themselves by activities (sales), donations, and/or lottery winnings (if they think that is possible!), but no 'spiritual intervention' would be given to help them win.

We are inundated with New Age teachings by means of books, tapes, workshops, etc. Some of these seem designed to increase our fear. I read that there is danger from "power socket radiation"; beware ley lines; if you haven't got a crystal you're missing something; don't drink the tap water; replace mercury fillings — the list seems endless. Now whilst some of this information might be true, it seems as though more and more 'dangers' are being discovered and one needs to be constantly protecting oneself by means of techniques, rituals, crystals, special diets, etc — all of which cost a considerable amount of time and money. One can get totally immersed in all this, thereby shutting oneself off from others' needs and serving humanity, especially those of the Third World.

How does one get the right balance between attending to one's own apparent needs and serving humanity, and how does one learn to discriminate between the true and the false? (July/August 1991)

I quite agree that too much focus is being placed on the negative aspects of contemporary life and technology. There are dangers, but most, I believe, are exaggerated. The answer, I think, is to use common sense and get on with answering needs without too much concern for the physical dangers, real or imaginary.

Use of Ray Structure in Service

In what way does a knowledge of our ray structure — in particular the soul focus and its vehicle — give an indication of the best area of service?

One of the points about knowing your ray structure is that it tells you your limitations. You know the areas in which you can function best. You will know that if you do not have particular rays then the qualities of these rays are unlikely to be present in your makeup. You would probably be unfitted for certain types of work if your ray structure is such as to not give you the qualities demanded by that work.

It also provides a sense of the bridges and the barriers — the bridges which can unite you with other people on different rays, and the barriers (because of these ray differences) which you and they automatically set up. If you know your rays, you know that you are likely to find difficulty in meeting, mind-to-mind, with people of certain other rays. The major thing to remember, and in my experience this is hardly ever remembered, is that there is no such thing as a good ray or a bad ray. They are all divine, all potentially perfect. It is up to us to give them perfect expression.

How does it indicate the best area of service?
If you are along the 2-4-6 line in the main, you will probably find that your quality of intuition is high, that your inner, instinctual knowledge of the Plan is pretty good, but that you might have difficulty in articulating that knowledge. It depends on the individual and on which body the rays are found. All the rays are divine, but have different qualities. A person along the 2-4-6 line will tend to be introverted to the soul and have very strong, clear contact with the soul. But they may, depending on the ray of the brain or mind, have difficulty in relating easily to other people, or performing well in outer physical-plane work and activity.

People on the 1-3-5-7 line, where these are the main rays, on the other hand, will have a limited contact with their own soul, but may be very efficient and active in the outer world, have little difficulty in contacting others and getting their ideas across. But the ideas themselves will be often rather more shallow than the 2-4-6 person and more limited in value as a demonstration of the Plan. The 1-3-5-7 line tends to deal with the outer physical form of a group, an institution, or society in general. Therefore, you get people who are good at dealing with the form: the political, economic and social life. Various scientists deal mainly with the form of life, but they do not really see, experience, the life which is within the form. The 2-4-6 exponent experiences this as a natural consequence of his or her alignment with the soul, and his ease of introversion to the soul and its purpose.

But hardly anyone is as clear-cut as that. Most people have a mixture of rays, and sub-rays which qualify the major rays. It is really rather unintelligent, in a group, to separate the 2-4-6 line from the 1-3-5-7 line and say the 2-4-6 line are good at doing this and the 1-3-5-7 line are good at doing that. Everyone has the potential. These rays are only for this life. The soul ray remains the same, but it is a good sound bet that the sub-rays in this life were the major rays of the previous life, more or less. Everyone, throughout their lives, has had the experience of all the rays. The soul brings in these rays again and again in different relationships and on different vehicles in order to round out the personality expression. To take anyone's rays in this life as the total expression of that person is stupid. It is lacking in understanding and can be very destructive in group work.

Since the modes of service of the 1-3-5-7 and the 2-4-6 are different, can the Master give some guidelines on how both can work together practically?
It is an illusion to imagine that the mode of service of the 1-3-5-7 line and the 2-4-6 line are so different. They are not so different as all that. There is nobody in this room who is exclusively on the 1-3-5-7 line or 2-4-6 line. Everyone is mixed, has the two lines in their make-up. It is a common mistake to imagine that someone is on the 1-3-5-7 line if they have a 3rd-ray mental or 1st-ray personality, but everything else 2-4-6. Or that if they have a 2nd-ray soul, a 4th-ray personality, a 3rd-ray mind and a 7th-ray brain that they are on the 2-4-6 line. Everyone is mixed, and everyone, therefore, has within themselves the capacity for a practical synthesis of these two modes.

The 2-4-6 way of service is the way of meditation and contemplation. These are the rays which give you an immediate, easy contact with the soul, which of course is what you want. The 1-3-5-7 line tends to be more extroverted to the outer world of form. They are the rays which organize, create, or build the form through which the life manifests. The 2-4-6 line is very aware of the life aspect, but may find it difficult to organize, construct, design, or build a form or forms through which that life can manifest.

The aim is to bring the two together: to have immediate, uninhibited, at-will, contact with the soul; being able spontaneously to go within, and, at will, to bring the life, knowledge, purpose of the soul into the outer world by constructing a form through which it can manifest. That is the ideal. It is that ability which characterizes the initiate. When I say the initiate, I mean someone who has taken the third initiation.

Can the Master give some guidelines on how both can work together practically?
There is really no difficulty in working along different lines. Everyone in every Transmission group in the world receives the energies of the line not specifically their own. No one receives just 2-4-6 or just 1-3-5-7. Everyone has the availability of all the rays if they would make use of them. Besides which, many of the rays, like the 1st and 2nd, are poured into the world in tremendous potency every day by Maitreya. They are there, in the world. Use them.

Everyone blames their rays for not being the person they want to be. If they do not have 1 or 7 in their makeup they are inclined to think there is no point in even trying to make a box, to organize a Transmission group, or a political party, or whatever. That is only an excuse. This is a misuse of the knowledge of the rays which is to give you a sense of your line of least resistance. But should you always work along the line of least resistance? Why not along the line of somewhat greater resistance? That is the way to grow.

You are who you are and this is not your only incarnation. People forget that they are who they are in this life as a result of untold incarnations. All of that is there. How many times have you been 1-3-5-7? How many times 2-4-6? How many times a mixture? And what about sub-rays? No one is isolated in one stream or the other. Bring them together. Utilize by doing, and find out whether you can do it. In most things, if you are reasonably intelligent and work at it, you can do it. It is not really a question of working on separate lines. You can bring both together without my Master, or any Master, giving you guidelines. There are no guidelines, except to do the thing.

Approach the task so impersonally that you forget whether you are 2-4-6 or 1-3-5-7. Take yourself as a whole — who you are. A knowledge of the rays will sharpen that knowledge, but the thing is to approach life spontaneously. Act in it. Do it. Whatever equipment you have, bring that to bear.

What is the value of knowing one's ray structure in determining one's path of service? (January/February 1990)
Knowing one's ray structure will show one where one's strengths and weaknesses lie and what will be the lines of least resistance (which should or should not be followed). It will also reveal one's limitations. But having said that, I am not convinced that ray knowledge is necessary or particularly helpful in determining a path of service. If the desire to serve and response to world need is strong enough and is followed by action, a path soon opens up to any sincere seeker.

If you make an obvious mistake in life — I did, I took the line of least resistance at work — would you have a chance to come back in the same situation again in the following life? I think I know where I went wrong — would I be able to come back in the same situation and react in a different way? (October 1992)
Unless it was something very important to the soul, which I doubt if that was, then no. What it would mean would be that the experience would have awakened your consciousness, made you more aware, and you would not repeat that mistake. You would be able to handle it in a completely different way

701

another time. You would not have to come back again to do that, you simply would not do it again in this life, let alone in another one.

APPENDIX

THE LIST OF INITIATES — PART II

Their Rays and Stage of Evolution

The figures in parenthesis immediately following the names refer to the initiate's exact point of development attained during that life. For example, if an initiate achieved a level halfway between the first and second initiation, it is indicated as 1.5. The initiatory degree has been omitted in the case of Avatars.

Nine figures, indicating the initiate's rays, follow the parenthesis; the rays relate to the soul, personality, mental apparatus, astral vehicle and physical body. The upper figures represent major rays; the lower figures represent sub-rays. The soul does not have a sub-ray. Also listed are the dates of birth and death, the country of origin, and the field of endeavour in which the initiate became known. Many of the people on the list were so versatile that it is virtually impossible to classify them in one category. However, the limits of space available left no option. In a few cases, unfortunately, it was impossible to find all relevant data; such omissions are noted by a question mark.

[*Note*: This list includes all the names of initiates published in *Share International* magazine from the publication of *Maitreya's Mission, Volume One* in 1986, to 1993.]

Aalto, Alvar (1.6)	2 4 7 6 3	(1898-1976)	Finland
	4 3 4 7	Architect	
Agrippa, H Cornelius (1.58)	3 4 6 6 7	(1486-1535)	Germany
	7 3 6 7	Theologian	
Aïvanhov, Mikhaèl (2.4)	3 6 6 2 7	(1900-1986)	Russia
	3 5 4 3	Founder of Fraternité Blanche	
Ananda Mayee Ma	2 2 6 4 3	(1896-1982)	India
	6 6 6 3	Avatar	

Armstrong, Louis (0.6)	4 4 7 6 3	(1899-1974)	USA
	4 6 2 3	Jazz musician	
Asimov, Isaac (1.6)	3 4 7 4 3	(1920-1992)	USA
	6 3 6 7	Writer	
Bach, Edward (1.6)	2 4 2 6 3	(1886-1936)	UK
	1 6 6 7	Naturopathic healer	
Bach, C P E (1.6)	4 4 5 6 3	(1714-1780)	Germany
	6 4 6 7	Composer	
Bacon, Francis (1.8)	3 4 3 4 7	(1909-1992)	UK
	4 3 6 3	Painter	
Bailey, Alice A (3.2)	2 1 1 2 3	(1880-1949)	UK
	6 4 6 7	Occultist	
Bailey, Foster (1.85)	2 2 6 6 3	(1887/8-1977)	USA
	6 4 2 7	Occultist	
Balaquer, Josemaria de (1.55)	6 6 6 2 7	(1902-1975)	Spain
	6 7 6 7	Writer	
Beauvoir, Simone de (1.6)	4 5 6 2 3	(1908-1986)	France
	6 2 4 7	Writer	
Beckett, Samuel (1.6)	2 6 1 4 7	(1906-1990)	Ireland
	6 6 4 7	Writer	
Beckmann, Max (1.6)	4 4 6 6 7	(1884-1950)	Germany
	6 3 6 3	Painter	
Beesley, Ronald (1.67)	2 6 3 4 7	(1903-1979)	UK
	7 4 2 3	Healer	
Berkeley, Lennox (1.55)	2 4 6 2 3	(1903-1989)	UK
	4 4 6 3	Composer	
Bernhardt, Oskar Ernst (2.0)	4 7 6 6 3	(1875-1941)	Germany
	5 2 4 7	Writer	
Bernstein, Leonard (1.6)	4 4 6 2 3	(1918-1990)	USA
	4 4 6 7	Conductor/composer	
Bettelheim, Bruno (1.5)	6 4 4 6 7	(1903-1990)	USA
	6 5 6 7	Psychologist	
Bhrikuti, the Green Tara (1.4)	2 4 2 4 3	(640-678)	Tibet
	6 6 6 3	Nepalese princess	
Biko, Steve (1.4)	2 4 6 4 3	(1946-1977)	South Africa
	6 6 6 7	Civil rights leader	
Bion, Wilfred (1.76)	2 7 7 6 7	(1897-1979)	UK
	4 4 3 3	Psychoanalyst	
Blavatsky, H P (4.0)	1 2 1 6 3	(1831-1891)	Russia
	7 4 6 7	Occultist	
Bloch, Ernest (1.7)	2 4 6 4 7	(1880-1959)	USA
	4 6 4 7	Composer	
Bloch, Ernst (1.5)	2 4 3 4 3	(1885-1977)	Germany
	6 6 6 7	Philosopher	
Bo, Yin Ra (1.55)	4 6 6 6 3	(1876-1943)	(?)
	6 6 2 7	Writer	

Boadicea (1.6)	4 1 1 6 3	(1st C. AD) England
	1 1 6 7	Warrior-queen
Bohm, David (1.6)	2 4 7 4 7	(1917-1992) USA
	6 3 6 3	Physicist
Booth, William (1.65)	2 6 6 2 7	(1829-1912) UK
	6 7 4 7	Founder of Salvation Army
Boulanger, Nadia (1.6)	4 4 7 6 7	(1887-1979) France
	6 6 6 7	Music instructor
Brancusi, Constantin (1.87)	4 6 7 6 4	(1876-1957) Romania
	6 4 6 7	Sculptor
Brandt, Willy (2.97)	2 1 5 2 1	(1913-1992) Germany
	4 7 4 3	Politician
Breton, André (1.7)	3 2 1 2 3	(1896-1966) France
	4 4 6 7	Poet
Brittain, Vera (1.5)	2 3 5 6 3	(1893-1970) UK
	4 6 6 7	Author/pacifist
Canaletto (1.6)	6 4 7 6 7	(1697-1768) Italy
	3 4 6 7	Painter
Carey, Howard Ray (1.5)	2 7 6 2 3	(1902-1989) USA
	2 7 6 7	Minister
Ceausescu, Nicolae (1.5)	7 6 7 6 7	(1918-1989) Romania
	6 4 6 3	Dictator
Cherenzi Lind, Om (2.4)	2 4 6 6 7	(d. mid-20th C.)
	2 4 6 7	Prince/disciple of K H
Chih-i (2.0)	6 6 7 4 3	(538-597) China
	7 4 6 2	Buddhism/T'ien't'ai sect
		founder
Chirico, Giorgio de (1.6)	4 4 1 6 7	(1888-1978) Italy
	4 6 6 7	Painter
Crosby, Bing (1.4)	2 4 6 6 7	(1904-1977) USA
	4 3 6 7	Singer/actor
cummings, e.e. (1.35)	6 4 4 6 7	(1894-1962) USA
	3 5 2 7	Poet
D'Aubuisson, Roberto (1.6)	1 1 6 6 7	(1944-1992) El Salvador
	6 4 6 3	Politician
Dali, Salvador (1.6)	6 4 6 4 7	(1904-1989) Spain
	4 6 4 7	Painter
Deguchi Na-o (1.7)	3 6 6 4 7	(1837-1918) Japan
	4 6 2 7	Omotokyo founder
Deguchi, Wanisaburo (1.7)	3 6 1 6 7	(1871-1948) Japan
	6 6 6 3	Omotokyo spiritual teacher
Dick, Philip K (1.6)	2 4 4 6 7	(1928-1982) USA
	6 7 6 4	Writer
Dogen (1.5)	6 1 6 4 7	(1200-1253) Japan
	7 3 2 4	Zen/Soto sect

Dolto, Françoise (1.58)	5 3 6 6 7	(1908-1988) France
	6 4 2 3	Psychoanalyst
Drees, Willem (1.6)	7 6 7 4 7	(1886-1988) Netherlands
	4 6 6 7	Politician
Dunnewolt, Hendrik W (1.6)	3 4 4 6 7	(1904-1968) Netherlands
	6 6 4 5	Author/theosophist
Ehret, Arnold (1.55)	2 6 2 4 7	(1856-1922) Germany
	7 6 6 3	Writer
Eisai (2.2)	7 4 6 6 7	(1141-1215) Japan
	7 4 6 3	Zen/Rinzai sect
Elgar, Edward (1.8)	2 4 4 4 3	(1857-1934) UK
	6 6 2 7	Composer
Ellington, Duke (0.6)	6 7 4 6 7	(1899-1974) USA
	4 6 4 7	Jazz musician
Faure, Gabriel (1.6)	4 4 3 4 7	(1845-1924) France
	6 6 4 3	Composer
Feynman, Richard (1.6)	6 7 4 6 7	(1918-1988) USA
	3 6 4 3	Physicist
Flagstad, Kirsten (1.4)	6 4 4 6 7	(1895-1962) Norway
	4 6 6 5	Opera singer
Fujii, Nittatsu (1.8)	2 4 6 6 7	(1885-1985) Japan
	6 6 2 3	Buddhism/Nichiren sect
Gandhi, Mahatma (2.0)	2 2 6 2 3	(1869-1948) India
	6 6 2 7	Nationalist leader
Garbo, Greta (1.65)	6 7 7 4 7	(1905-1990) Sweden
	4 2 6 3	Film actress
George, Henry (1.7)	3 7 4 2 1	(1839-1897) USA
	5 6 4 7	Political economist
Goi, Masahisa (2.1)	4 4 6 6 7	(1916-1980) Japan
	6 3 2 7	Spiritual teacher/Byakkokai
Gould, Glenn (1.6)	2 4 7 6 7	(1932-1982) Canada
	6 3 6 3	Pianist
Graham, Martha (1.47)	4 6 3 6 7	(1894-1991) USA
	4 7 6 7	Dancer
Greene, Graham (1.5)	3 4 7 6 3	(1904-1991) UK
	6 6 6 7	Writer
Gropius, Walter (1.68)	2 4 4 6 7	(1883-1969) Germany
	7 3 2 3	Architect
Hahn, Kurt (1.6)	4 6 4 6 3	(1886-1974) Germany
	3 6 6 7	Educator
Hahnemann, Samuel (1.75)	2 6 7 4 7	(1755-1843) Germany
	4 6 6 3	Founder of modern homoeopathy
Hall, Manley Palmer (1.6)	2 2 6 2 7	(1901-1990) USA
	6 6 6 7	Philosopher

Harrison, Rex (1.35)	2 4 4 6 7	(1908-1990) UK
	4 3 6 3	Actor
Heidegger, Martin (1.7)	4 3 4 6 7	(1889-1976) Germany
	7 6 2 3	Philosopher
Hess, Rudolf (1.35)	1 1 6 6 1	(1894-1987) Germany
	4 1 6 7	Nazi official
Hiawatha (0.9)	6 7 7 6 7	(ca. 1450) North America
	6 7 2 3	Native American leader
Hillesum, Etty (1.3)	3 7 6 6 7	(1914-1943) Netherlands
	6 5 6 7	Auschwitz victim/diarist
Hirohito (1.4)	7 6 6 6 7	(1901-1989) Japan
	2 4 2 3	Emperor
Hitler, Adolf (2.0)	2 4 1 4 3	(1889-1945) Germany
	1 6 6 7	Dictator
Honen (2.4)	6 4 6 2 7	(1133-1212) Japan
	6 7 4 7	Buddhism/Jodo sect founder
Hypatia (1.6)	2 4 3 4 7	(ca. 370-415) Egypt
	1 1 6 1	Philosopher
Jesus of Nazareth (4.0)	6 1 1 2 1	(24 BC-AD 9) Palestine
	6 7 2 3	Great Spiritual Teacher
John of the Cross (1.6)	6 6 6 4 7	(1542-1591) Spain
	6 4 6 7	Mystic
Jones, Marc Edmond (1.6)	4 6 4 6 7	(1888-1980) USA
	4 7 6 3	Astrologer
Joseph II (1.65)	4 6 1 4 7	(1741-1790) Austria
	6 5 4 1	Regent
Kalu Rinpoche (2.35)	6 6 3 2 1	(1905-1989) Tibet
	6 4 6 3	Buddhist teacher
Kasturi, N (1.55)	4 2 4 6 7	(1897-1987) India
	6 6 6 3	Sai Baba's interpreter
Kaye, Danny (1.55)	6 4 4 6 7	(1913-1987) USA
	4 6 4 3	Comic actor
Kazantzakis, Nikos (1.6)	3 4 4 6 3	(1883-1957) Greek
	6 7 6 3	Writer
Kelly, Petra (1.5)	2 4 3 4 7	(1947-1992) Germany
	6 7 6 3	Founder of Green Party
Kempis, Thomas à(1.5)	2 6 1 2 3	(1380-1471) Netherlands
	5 4 6 7	Religious writer
Kennedy, Robert (1.6)	2 6 7 6 7	(1925-1968) USA
	4 3 4 3	Politician
Kerouac, Jack (1.35)	6 6 7 6 7	(1922-1969) USA
	6 4 4 3	Writer
Khomeini, Ayatollah (1.6)	4 1 6 6 7	(1900-1989) Iran
	6 6 6 7	Islamic leader
Kon, Tokoh (1.7)	4 6 4 6 7	(1898-1977) Japan
	6 7 2 7	Writer/Buddhist priest

Kukai (2.0)	2 2 4 6 7	(774-835) Japan
	7 6 6 3	Esoteric Buddhism/Shingon
Laing, R D (1.3)	6 4 3 4 3	(1927-1989) UK
	3 6 4 3	Psychiatrist
Larkin, Philip (1.4)	2 4 6 4 7	(1922-1985) UK
	6 6 6 3	Poet
Lazarus (0.9)	4 6 6 6 7	(ca. AD 6) Palestine
	4 4 2 4	Biblical figure
Leo, Alan (1.6)	2 4 5 4 7	(1861-1917) UK
	6 6 6 3	Astrologer
Levi, Eliphas (1.8)	6 4 3 6 7	(1844-1911) USA
	7 5 2 3	Occultist
Lewis, Harvey Spencer (1.6)	4 5 5 6 7	(1883-1939) USA
	1 3 6 7	Founder of Rosicrucian Order
Lewis, Ralph M (1.7)	6 4 5 2 7	(1904-1987) USA
	6 6 4 3	Rosicrucian Order leader
Lind, Jenny (1.25)	4 4 6 6 7	(1820-1887) Sweden
	6 4 2 3	Opera singer
Lippi, Fra Filippo (2.0)	6 7 7 6 7	(1406-1469) Italy
	4 6 6 3	Painter
London, Jack (1.45)	4 4 4 4 7	(1876-1916) USA
	6 6 6 7	Writer
Lorber, Jacob (1.4)	3 2 5 6 7	(1800-1864) Germany
	6 4 6 3	Writer/astral sensitive
Lotto, Lorenzo (2.5)	4 4 6 2 7	(1480-1556) Italy
	4 1 4 3	Painter
Malcolm X (1.4)	4 6 7 6 7	(1925-1965) USA
	6 6 6 3	Civil rights leader
Maria Theresa (1.65)	4 6 1 6 7	(1717-1780) Austria
	6 6 4 7	Empress
Martha (1.6)	6 7 4 6 7	(1st C. AD) Palestine
	4 6 2 7	Biblical figure
Martinus (2.3)	2 4 1 6 7	(1890-1981) Denmark
	3 6 6 7	Writer
Mary Magdalene (0.9)	6 6 6 4 3	(1st C. AD) Palestine
	6 6 2 7	Biblical figure
Mary of Bethany (0.85)	4 6 6 6 7	(1st C. AD) Palestine
	2 2 4 3	Biblical figure
Maxwell, Robert (1.6)	2 4 1 2 3	(1923-1991) Czech Republic
	1 3 6 7	Publisher
Meiji (0.8)	3 4 4 6 7	(1852-1912) Japan
	6 7 6 3	Emperor
Messiaen, Oliver (1.76)	4 6 7 6 3	(1908-1992) France
	2 1 6 7	Composer
Miró, Joán (2.0)	2 2 6 6 3	(1893-1983) Spain
	4 4 2 7	Painter

Mirza Ghulam Ahmed, H (1.6)	4 6 7 6 3	(1835-1908) India
	4 7 6 7	Founder of Islamic sect
Misora, Hibari (1.35)	2 4 4 6 7	(1937-1989) Japan
	6 6 6 3	Singer
Miura, Sekizo (1.6)	3 3 2 4 7	(1883-1960) Japan
	7 6 2 3	Theosophist/yogi
Miyazawa, Kenji (2.0)	4 6 4 6 7	(1896-1933) Japan
	2 6 6 3	Writer/poet
Monet, Claude (1.9)	3 4 4 6 3	(1840-1927) France
	7 7 6 7	Painter
Monroe, Marilyn (0.9)	4 4 6 2 3	(1926-1962) USA
	2 4 4 3	Film actress
Montessori, Maria (1.65)	6 4 7 4 7	(1870-1952) Italy
	4 7 6 3	Educator
More, Thomas (1.5)	4 6 6 6 3	(1478-1535) UK
	4 4 6 3	Statesman/writer
Muhaiyaddeen, Bawa (3.0)	4 6 4 6 7	(d.1986) Sri Lanka
	6 6 6 7	Sufi teacher
Neal, Viola Petitt (1.5)	2 4 7 6 7	(1907-1981) USA
	6 3 6 3	Esoteric researcher/author
Nichiren (2.0)	3 6 6 2 7	(1222-1282) Japan
	6 1 2 7	Buddhism/Nichiren sect
		founder
Nityananda, Bhagavan (4.5)	2 6 4 2 7	(d.1961) India
	6 6 2 7	Spiritual teacher
Norman, Mildred (1.6)	6 6 6 2 7	(1908-1981) USA
	6 6 2 7	"Peace Pilgrim"
Oda, Nobunaga (0.7)	6 1 6 4 7	(1534-1582) Japan
	7 6 6 1	Feudal lord
Olivier, Laurence (1.6)	3 4 3 2 7	(1907-1989) UK
	6 1 4 3	Actor
Padmasambhava (3.0)	2 4 3 6 7	(8/9 C.) India
	6 7 6 3	Lama
Palmer, D D (1.6)	2 4 4 6 7	(1845-1913) USA
	6 2 2 3	Founder chiropractic
Panchen Lama (10th) (1.7)	6 4 4 6 7	(1938-1989) Tibet
	6 6 6 3	Religious leader
Parker, Charlie (0.6)	6 4 6 6 7	(1920-1955) USA
	2 6 2 7	Jazz musician
Pissarro, Camille (1.7)	6 4 6 4 7	(1830-1903) France
	6 2 4 3	Painter
Praag, Henri Van (2.0)	3 7 7 2 7	(1916-1988) Netherlands
	5 5 4 7	Parapsychologist
Pré, Jacqueline du (1.5)	2 4 4 6 2	(1945-1987) UK
	2 6 2 4	Cellist

Presley, Elvis (0.8)	4 4 1 1 7	(1935-1977) USA
	4 6 6 7	Rock-and-roll star
Purucker, G de (1.6)	6 4 6 6 3	(1874-1942) USA
	5 7 4 7	Theosophist
Rajneesh (2.3)	4 6 2 4 7	(1931-1990) India
	6 6 4 3	Spiritual teacher
Redon, Odilon (1.5)	4 5 2 4 3	(1840-1916) France
	6 6 4 7	Painter
Reinhardt, Django (0.6)	3 4 3 6 3	(1910-1953) USA
	2 7 6 7	Jazz musician
Rivière, Enrique Pichón (2.0)	6 4 7 4 7	(1907-1977) Argentina
	6 5 6 3	Psychoanalyst
Roberts, Estelle (1.2)	2 6 6 6 3	(1889-1970) UK
	4 4 2 3	Healer/medium
Robin, Marthe (1.8)	4 6 3 4 3	(1902-1981) France
	6 6 2 3	Mystic/stigmatist
Roerich, Helena (4.0)	1 2 1 6 3	(1879-1955) Russia
	6 2 4 7	Occultist
Rossini, Gioacchino (1.7)	4 4 6 2 3	(1792-1868) Italy
	4 6 4 3	Composer
Rubinstein, Arthur (1.75)	2 4 4 6 7	(1886-1982) Poland
	4 6 6 7	Pianist
Rudhyar, Dane (1.9)	2 4 4 6 3	(1895-1986) USA
	4 6 6 7	Astrologer/composer
Rulof, Joseph (1.5)	3 6 5 6 7	(1889-1952) Netherlands
	6 7 4 7	Parapsychologist
Russel, Walter (1.6)	4 4 7 6 7	(1871-1963) USA
	6 6 4 7	Sculptor
Sade, Marquis de (0.75)	3 6 6 1 3	(1740-1814) France
	6 4 1 7	Writer
Saicho (1.9)	6 7 4 6 3	(767-822) Japan
	6 6 4 7	Buddhism/Tendai sect founder
Saigo, Takamori (1.5)	6 7 1 6 7	(1827-1877) Japan
	7 7 4 7	Soldier/general
Sakharov, Andrei (2.0)	7 6 5 6 3	(1921-1989) Russia
	4 7 4 7	Physicist
Sanchez, Celia (1.5)	6 6 4 6 3	(d.1980) Cuba
	6 3 6 7	Fidel Castro's confidante
Sarkar, P R (2.5)	2 4 6 4 3	(1921-1990) India
(Sri Anandamurti)	6 2 4 3	Philosopher
Scott, Cyril (1.55)	2 4 3 6 3	(1879-1970) UK
	6 4 4 7	Composer
Segovia, Andres (1.7)	6 4 4 2 1	(1894-1987) Spain
	4 1 6 7	Guitarist
Selassie, Haile (1.6)	4 1 6 6 7	(1892-1975) Ethiopia
	6 1 6 7	Emperor

Sellers, Peter (1.4)	4 4 6 4 7	(1925-1980) UK
	6 6 4 7	Actor
Sen, Rikyu (0.8)	4 6 4 4 7	(1522-1591) Japan
	7 6 2 3	Tea ceremony teacher
Serkin, Rudolph (1.55)	4 4 7 4 3	(1903-1991) Germany
	6 3 6 7	Pianist
Shinran (1.8)	6 6 1 6 3	(1173-1262) Japan
	4 7 6 3	Buddhism/Jodo-shinshu
Shotoku-Taishi (2.0)	6 6 5 4 3	(574-622) Japan
	7 4 6 3	Prince/regent
Sibelius, Jean (1.8)	2 4 4 6 7	(1865-1958) Finland
	6 4 6 7	Composer
Sidis, William James (1.7)	4 7 4 6 3	(1898-1944) USA
	4 6 6 7	Scientist
Simenon, Georges (1.57)	3 6 4 2 7	(1903-1989) Belgium
	4 7 6 3	Writer
Smith, Samantha (1.5)	1 4 6 4 7	(1972-1985) USA
	6 6 2 3	Schoolgirl/diplomat
Srong-tsan-gam-po (2.0)	2 6 4 2 7	(623-689) Tibet
	6 6 2 3	King
Saint-Exupéry, Antoine de (1.5)	1 3 5 6 7	(1900-1944) France
	1 4 4 7	Writer
Stevenson, Adlai (1.6)	2 7 6 2 7	(1900-1965) USA
	4 6 4 7	Politician
Strauss, Franz Josef (1.65)	1 6 7 6 1	(1915-1988) Germany
	1 6 6 7	Politician
Suzuki, Daisetsu (1.7)	2 6 1 6 3	(1870-1966) Japan
		Zen scholar
Takahashi, Shinji (2.0)	6 6 7 4 7	(1927-1976) Japan
	6 3 6 7	Religious leader/GLA founder
Tati, Jacques (1.57)	4 4 2 4 7	(1907-1982) France
	4 2 6 7	Film maker/comedian
Taungpulu Sayadaw (1.7)	2 6 6 4 3	(1898-1986) Burma
	2 6 4 7	Buddhist teacher
Taylor, A J P (1.4)	2 4 4 6 3	(1906-1990) UK
	2 7 6 2	Historian
Telemann, Georg (1.9)	3 4 6 4 7	(1687-1767) Germany
	4 6 6 3	Composer
Tesla, Nikola (2.0)	2 3 1 6 5	(1856-1943) USA
	6 4 2 7	Inventor
Tezuka, Osamu (1.6)	6 4 4 6 7	(1926-1989) Japan
	4 7 4 3	Cartoonist
Tokugawa, Ieyasu (1.55)	2 1 3 6 7	(1542-1616) Japan
	4 7 6 1	Shogun
Tomonaga, Shin-ichiro (1.7)	4 6 4 6 7	(1906-1979) Japan
	7 3 6 5	Physicist

Tortelier, Paul (1.57)   2 4 1 6 7   (1914-1990) France
                                           4 7 6 7   Cellist/teacher
Uyl, Joop den (1.6)   3 6 6 6 7   (1919-1987) Netherlands
                                           4 1 4 3   Politician
van der Rohe, Ludwig Mies (1.6) 1 4 6 4 7   (1886-1969) Germany
                                           7 3 6 3   Architect
Vaughan Williams, Ralph (1.8)   4 4 4 6 7   (1872-1958) UK
                                           6 4 4 3   Composer
Wagner, Cosima (1.6)   4 6 1 2 7   (1837-1930) Germany
                                           6 6 2 3   Wife of Richard Wagner
Wen Ch'eng, White Tara (1.4)   2 2 3 4 3   (603-656)   Tibet
                                           4 7 6 7   Chinese princess
White, Patrick (1.55)   1 4 7 6 7   (1912-1990) Australia
                                           6 3 6 7   Writer
Wilson, Tom Two Bears (0.8)   4 6 4 6 7   (?-1980) USA
                                           6 4 6 7   Medicine man
Wood, Natalie (1.4)   2 6 4 4 7   (1938-1981) USA
                                           6 7 6 3   Actress
Woolf, Virginia (1.6)   4 4 7 6 7   (1882-1941) UK
                                           6 4 4 7   Writer
Wresinski, Joseph (1.6)   2 5 3 6 7   (1917-1988) France
                                           6 4 6 3   Humanist
Wright, Frank Lloyd (1.6)   2 4 7 4 7   (1869-1959) USA
                                           6 3 4 3   Architect
Yogi, Gururaj Ananda (1.75)   6 6 4 6 7   (1932-1988) India
                                           2 7 6 3   Spiritual teacher
Yoshida, Shigeru (1.55)   2 7 1 6 7   (1878-1967) Japan
                                           4 3 4 7   Statesman
Young, Lester (0.6)   2 4 4 2 3   (1909-1959) USA
                                           4 6 4 7   Jazz musician
Yukawa, Hideki (1.6)   7 4 6 6 3   (1907-1981) Japan
                                           7 5 2 3   Physicist

THE GREAT INVOCATION

From the point of Light within the Mind of God
Let light stream forth into the minds of men.
Let Light descend on Earth.

From the point of Love within the Heart of God
Let love stream forth into the hearts of men.
May Christ return to Earth.

From the centre where the Will of God is known
Let purpose guide the little wills of men —
The Purpose which the Masters know and serve.

From the centre which we call the race of men
Let the Plan of Love and Light work out
And may it seal the door where evil dwells.

Let Light and Love and Power restore the Plan on Earth.

The Great Invocation, used by the Christ for the first time in
June 1945, was released by Him to humanity to enable us to
invoke the energies which would change our world and make
possible the return of the Christ and Hierarchy. This World
Prayer, translated into many languages, is not sponsored by
any group or sect. It is used daily by men and women of
goodwill who wish to bring about right human relations among
all humanity.

THE PRAYER FOR THE NEW AGE

I am the creator of the universe.
I am the father and mother of the universe.
Everything came from me.
Everything shall return to me.
Mind, spirit and body are my temples,
For the Self to realize in them
My supreme Being and Becoming.

The Prayer for the New Age, given by Maitreya, the World Teacher, is a great mantram or affirmation with an invocative effect. It will be a powerful tool in the recognition by us that man and God are One, that there is no separation. The 'I' is the Divine Principle behind all creation. The Self emanates from, and is identical to, the Divine Principle.

The most effective way to use this mantram is to say or think the words with focused will, while holding the attention at the ajna centre between the eyebrows. When the mind grasps the meaning of the concepts, and simultaneously the will is brought to bear, those concepts will be activated and the mantram will work. If it is said seriously every day, there will grow inside you a realization of your true Self.

REFERENCES CITED BY THE AUTHOR

Alice A.Bailey, *Destiny of the Nations* (London: Lucis Press, 1949)

_____, *Discipleship in the New Age*, *Vols. I & II* (London: Lucis Press, 1944)

_____, *Education in the New Age* (London: Lucis Press, 1954)

_____, *Esoteric Healing* (London: Lucis Press, 1953)

_____, *Esoteric Psychology, Vol. I* (London: Lucis Press, 1936)

_____, *Esoteric Psychology, Vol. II* (London: Lucis Press, 1942)

_____, *Externalisation of the Hierarchy* (London: Lucis Press, 1955)

_____, *Initiation, Human and Solar* (London: Lucis Press, 1922)

_____, *Letters on Occult Meditation* (London: Lucis Press, 1922)

_____, *The Reappearance of the Christ* (London: Lucis Press, 1948)

H.P.Blavatsky, *The Secret Doctrine* (London: Theosophical Publishing House, 1888)

Brandt Commission, *North-South: A Programme for Survival* (Cambridge, MA: MIT Press, 1980)

Helena Roerich, *Leaves of Morya's Garden, Vol. I: The Call* (New York: Agni Yoga Society, 1924)

_____ , *Leaves of Morya's Garden, Vol. II: Illumination* (New York: Agni Yoga Society, 1925)

FURTHER READING

(Books listed in order of publication.)

The Reappearance of the Christ and the Masters of Wisdom
by Benjamin Creme

Creme's first book gives the background and pertinent information concerning the return of Maitreya, the Christ. A vast range of subjects is covered, including: the effect of the Reappearance on the world's institutions, the Antichrist and forces of evil, the soul and reincarnation, telepathy, nuclear energy, ancient civilizations, the problems of the developing world, and a new economic order.
ISBN 0-936604-00-X, 256 pages.

Messages from Maitreya the Christ

During the years of preparation for His emergence, Maitreya gave 140 Messages through Benjamin Creme during public lectures. The method used was mental overshadowing and the telepathic rapport thus set up. The Messages inspire readers to spread the news of His reappearance and to work urgently for the rescue of millions suffering from poverty and starvation in a world of plenty.
2nd Edition. ISBN 90-71484-22-X, 283 pages.

Transmission: A Meditation for the New Age
by Benjamin Creme

Describes a dynamic group process of stepping down powerful spiritual energies directed by the Masters of Wisdom. Introduced by Benjamin Creme, at the request of his own Master, this potent world service stimulates both planetary transformation and personal growth of the individuals participating.
4th Edition. ISBN 90-71484-17-3, 204 pages

A Master Speaks

Articles by Benjamin Creme's Master from the first 12 volumes of *Share International* magazine. The book includes such topics as: reason and intuition, health and healing, life in the New Age, glamour, human rights, Maitreya's mission, the role of man, sharing, the new education, co-operation and the end of hunger.
2nd Edition. ISBN 90-71484-10-6, 256 pages.

Maitreya's Mission, Volume One by Benjamin Creme

Presents further developments in the emergence of Maitreya and also covers a wide range of subjects, including the work and teachings of Maitreya, the externalization of the Masters, life ahead in the New Age, evolution and initiation, meditation and service, the Seven Rays.
ISBN 90-71484-08-4, 419 pages

The Ageless Wisdom Teaching by Benjamin Creme

This introduction to humanity's spiritual legacy covers the major principles: the Divine Plan, source of the teaching, evolution of human consciousness, the Spiritual Hierarchy, energies, the Seven Rays, karma, reincarnation, initiation and more. Includes a glossary of esoteric terms.
ISBN 90-71484-13-0, 62 pages.

Maitreya's Mission, Volume Three by Benjamin Creme

A chronicle of the next millennium. Political, economic and social structures that will guarantee the necessities of life for all people. New ways of thinking that will reveal the mysteries of the universe and release our divine potential — all guided and inspired by Maitreya and the Masters of Wisdom. Subjects include: Maitreya's priorities, world service, the Ageless Wisdom Teachings. Also includes a compilation of ray structures and points of evolution of all 950 initiates given in *Maitreya's Mission, Volumes I and II*, and in *Share International* magazine.
ISBN 90-71484-15-7, 704 pages.

The Great Approach by Benjamin Creme

In this prophetic book, Benjamin Creme addresses the problems of our chaotic world and its gradual change under the influence of a group of perfected men, the Masters of Wisdom, Who are returning openly to the world for the first time in 98,000 years. With Their leader, Maitreya, the World Teacher, They will guide humanity out of the present morass, and inspire the building of an entirely new kind of civilization where justice and freedom are the norm.
ISBN 90-71484-23-8, 336 pages.

The Art of Co-operation by Benjamin Creme

Emphasizes that co-operation among people and nations is *not optional* if we choose to survive, but is the very foundation upon which a brilliant new civilization can be built.

Creme traces the origins of the competitive spirit and shows its gradual replacement by co-operation as humanity advances; describes the illusions that hide our fundamental unity; and explains how ending our sense of separation will lead to a great leap forward in human evolution.
ISBN 90-71484-26-2, 256 pages.

These books have been translated and published in Dutch, French, German, Japanese and Spanish by groups responding to this message. Some have also been published in Chinese, Croatian, Finnish, Greek, Hebrew, Italian, Latvian, Portuguese, Romanian, Russian, Slovenian and Swedish. Further translations are planned. Books, as well as audio and video cassettes, are available from local booksellers.

Share International

Begun in 1982, this unique magazine features each month: up-to-date information about Maitreya, the World Teacher; an article from a Master of Wisdom; expansions of the esoteric teachings; articles by and interviews with people on the leading edge in every field of endeavour; news from UN agencies and reports of positive developments in the transformation of our world; Benjamin Creme's answers to a variety of topical questions submitted by subscribers and the public.

Share International brings together the two major directions of New Age thinking — the political and the spiritual. It shows the synthesis underlying the political, social, economic, and spiritual changes now occurring on a global scale, and seeks to stimulate practical action to rebuild our world along more just and compassionate lines.

Share International covers news, events, and comments bearing on Maitreya's priorities: an adequate supply of the right food, adequate housing and shelter for all, healthcare as a universal right, the maintenance of ecological balance in the world.

Versions of *Share International* are available in Dutch, French, German, Japanese, and Spanish. For subscription information, contact the appropriate office below. *ISSN 0169-1341.*

Excerpts from the magazine are published on the internet at: *http://www.share-international.org*

For North, Central and South America,
Australia, New Zealand and the Philippines
Share International
P.O. Box 971, North Hollywood, CA 91603, USA

For the UK
Share International
P.O. Box 3677, London NW5 1RU, UK

For the rest of the world
Share International

P.O. Box 41877, 1009 DB Amsterdam, Holland

INDEX

ABOUT THE AUTHOR

Scottish-born painter and esotericist Benjamin Creme has for the last 29 years been preparing the world for the most extraordinary event in humanity's history — the return of our spiritual mentors to the everyday world.

Creme has appeared on television, radio and documentary films worldwide and lectures throughout Western and Eastern Europe, the USA, Japan, Australia, New Zealand, Canada, and Mexico.

Trained and supervised over many years by his own Master, he began his public work in 1974. In 1982 he announced that the Lord Maitreya, the long-awaited World Teacher, was living in London, ready to present Himself openly when invited by the media to do so. This event is now imminent.

Benjamin Creme continues to carry out his task as messenger of this inspiring news. His books, ten at present, have been translated into many languages. He is also the editor of *Share International* magazine, which circulates in over 70 countries. He accepts no money for any of this work.

Benjamin Creme lives in London, is married, and has three children.

NOTES

NOTES

NOTES